Doing Gender Diversity

Doing Gender Diversity

READINGS IN THEORY AND REAL-WORLD EXPERIENCE

EDITED BY
Rebecca F. Plante AND Lis M. Maurer
Ithaca College

Westview Press
A Member of the Perseus Books Group

Published by Westview Press,
A Member of the Perseus Books Group

Find us on the World Wide Web at www.westviewpress.com.

Westview Press books are available at special discounts for bulk purchases in the United States by corporations, institutions, and other organizations. For more information, please contact the Special Markets Department at the Perseus Books Group, 2300 Chestnut Street, Suite 200, Philadelphia, PA 19103, or call (800) 810-4145, ext. 5000, or e-mail special.markets@perseusbooks.com.

Designed by Brent Wilcox

Library of Congress Cataloging-in-Publication Data
    Doing gender diversity : readings in theory and real-world experience / edited by
Rebecca F. Plante and Lis M. Maurer.
        p.   cm.
    Includes bibliographical references and index.
    ISBN 978-0-8133-4437-9 (pbk. : alk. paper)
    1. Sex role.   2. Sex differences.   3. Cultural pluralism.   4. Diversity in the workplace.
I. Plante, Rebecca F.   II. Maurer, Lis M.
HQ1075.D647 2010
305.48'8—dc22
                                                                                2009015537

10 9 8 7 6 5 4 3 2 1

CONTENTS

✳︎ Classic   ☐ Culture   @ Web   ⤴ POV   ⤴ Empirical   ~Theory

v

Section II The Microcosm of Gender: Individuals in Context

＊ Classic   ▢ Culture   @ Web   ⤵ POV   ⤵ Empirical   ~ Theory

CHAPTER 4 DOING "IT": SEXUALITIES

✱ Classic ☐ Culture @ Web ⤵ POV ⤶ Empirical ~ Theory

✳ Classic   ❒ Culture   @ Web   ⑤ POV   ⑤ Empirical   ~Theory

CHAPTER 6 THINKING CRITICALLY ABOUT STRUCTURES AND INSTITUTIONS IN OUR WORLD

CHAPTER 7 RATTLING THE CAGE: SOCIAL CHANGE

✳ Classic ❒ Culture @ Web ⇆ POV ↳ Empirical ~ Theory

✳ Classic ❑ Culture @ Web ⤴ POV ⤴ Empirical ∼ Theory

PREFACE

What is gender diversity? Doesn't "diversity" just mean that we focus on people who vary from (stereo)typically gendered people, such as intersex people, trans-folk, and drag queens? What would it mean to talk about gender diversities? What would it mean to argue that all forms of gender, from the usual to the un-usual, are socially constructed? How is gender developed, experienced, and pre-sented by all the people who "do gender" (in other words, each of us)? What does it mean to be conventionally gendered? How may conventional genders and alternate genders be described (and experienced) given dominant cultural scripts that presuppose two (and only two) diametrically opposed genders?

Let's start by defining diversity:

> The variety created in any society (and within any individual) by the presence of different points of view and ways of making meaning . . . flow[ing] from the in-fluence of different . . . heritages . . . , differences in how we socialize men and women, and from the differences that emerge from class, age, sexual orientation, sexual identity, ability, and other socially constructed characteristics. (Sue Rankin, National Consortium of LGBT Resources in Higher Education)

Following from this definition, the purpose of this reader is to make visible the multiple ways in which gender itself is diverse and socially, culturally, and historically constructed. Given that our gendered lives can be confusing, we need to explore these complexities more fully to reveal how the lived realities of gender and sexuality transcend our taken-for-granted, binary constructions.

How is this book different from every other academic gender anthology?

Most course anthologies are organized around gender as an aspect of broad so-cial institutions (e.g., gender and work, gender and family). Gender is a key variable, but the concept of gender itself is not necessarily questioned. This re-sults in texts that tend to balkanize both gender-diverse people and sexually diverse people, occasionally including a chapter or several readings that effectively set people apart in a "freaks on parade" fashion. Our book focuses on gender itself—how gender operates socioculturally, exists, functions, and is presented in micro and macro interactions. To avoid such balkanization, we seek to examine the various ways in which culture intersects with individuals to produce the range of presentations of self that we call "gender," from people born male who become adult men to lesbian women to people born female who become trans-men and everyone else on the diverse gender spectrum. We focus on hegemonic and transgressive gender development, roles, identities, and practices. In the language of sociologists Candace West and Don Zimmerman—this book is all about the diverse ways of doing, performing, or enacting gender.

In their now classic 1987 article, "Doing Gender," West and Zimmerman argue that we need to understand gender as "a routine, methodical, and recurring accomplishment. We contend that the 'doing' of gender is undertaken by women and men whose competence as members of society is hostage to its production. Doing gender involves a complex of socially guided perceptual, interactional, and micropolitical activities that cast particular pursuits as expressions of masculine and feminine 'natures'" (126). They clarify that, although their perspective seems more micro than macro, conceptualizing gender as a routine (and necessary) accomplishment enables us to see how gender is a "feature of social situations: both as an outcome of and a rationale for various social arrangements and as a means of legitimating one of the most fundamental divisions of society" (126). Thus this book uses gender as a micro and macro variable to illuminate its complexity and diversity.

Why this book at this time?

All over North America (globally, as well), college courses are increasingly exploring gender across a range of disciplines—anthropology, history, women's studies, cultural studies, and sociology, among others. Though intersectional readers merging race/class/gender have proliferated, gender remains a key, if not the key variable. (When we hear that a friend is pregnant, our first question is nearly always some variation of "Do you know the baby's sex?")

Students seem to have many questions about intersexuality, transgender issues, and other contemporary sex and gender topics. Narratives by trans and intersex people are easier to find than ever, in part because of the perceived "differentness" from those who are more conventionally gendered. This belief in difference tends to go largely unexamined, of course. Professors are often hampered by available materials that do not provide enough information on these topics, or the content simply reinscribes false divisions of "normals" versus "non-normals." This book enables professors to help students think critically about gender diversity by exploring gendered processes, interactions, and structures. Readers will understand how gender is "done" by all of us in ways that fully reveal our diversity and complexity.

How do we organize the book so that it offers a new perspective?

This text is not The Big Book of Gender Freaks or Freaks on Parade. We include readings from different perspectives, including websites, first-person narratives, and academic readings. Similarly, we wish to avoid the problem of balkanizing race, ethnicity, and multiple cultures. Thus the chapters are designed to incorporate intersectionality (race/class/gender) and sexualities as seamlessly as possible. To facilitate your work, each reading is tagged to highlight key aspects of the content; most will have more than one tag:

- culture (cross or multi)
- classic
- web
- P.O.V. (first person)
- empirical
- theory (or conceptual)

Many of the more recent empirical articles also represent attempts to build, expand, or develop theory or conceptual arguments. Because the primary audience for a book such as this is college or university students in the United States, the readings focus on the United States. Note therefore that we have applied the concept of "culture" somewhat broadly, to include work based on people living outside the United States. The text is organized into three sections with seven chapters:

Section One The Basics of Gender
   Chapter 1 Gender Diversity and the Binary
   Chapter 2 Learning How to "Do Gender"
Section Two The Microcosm of Gender: Individuals in Context
   Chapter 3 Constructing the Gendered Body
   Chapter 4 Doing "It": Sexualities
Section Three The Macrocosm of Gender: Institutions,
                Structures, and Politics
   Chapter 5 Doing Gender Diversity: At Home and at Work
   Chapter 6 Thinking Critically about Structures and Institutions in
                Our World
   Chapter 7 Rattling the Cage: Social Change

The initial chapters offer readings that clearly flesh out the book's key concepts and key arguments, helping instructors to capitalize on the initial lessons and to create/inform subsequent pedagogy. Our key concepts, questions, and arguments include:

- What are the signs and symbols of gender? How do we recognize gender, see it, and show it? How do we "do gender"?
- What are the multiple and broader implications of how gender is embodied?
- Who are our individual and collective audiences? Who are our generalized others?
- How do the intersections of genders, races, ethnicities, sexualities, and cultures operate?
- What is hegemonic or typical/conventional gender?
- What does it mean to argue that gender is a primary tool both for self-awareness *and* others' interactions with us or understandings of us?
- What does it mean to suggest that gender is a rationale for numerous social arrangements at the institutional or structural level (e.g., families, work, politics)?

Who is this book intended for? Why is it organized the way that it is?

We expect this book to be useful in a variety of disciplines, given that gender courses are taught in departments and programs including sociology, anthropology, women's studies, psychology, cultural studies, family studies/human development, and social work. As a text about gender diversity, it would also be suitable in primarily undergraduate courses that address gender alongside other issues, such as how the construction of race, ethnicity, and social inequality impact individuals.

Utilizing current, intriguing, and balanced selections, *Doing Gender Diversity* incorporates a microsociological, social psychological framework with a macrosociological analysis. This book also provides integrated coverage of trans and intersex people and sexuality.

Doing Gender Diversity has a provocative tone, but is designed to be easy to read and engaging for students at all levels. We start with the assertion that all people "do" gender—each and every one of us—and as such, gender is the key variable for understanding numerous aspects of stratification and inequalities. Key variables of social class, race, ethnicity, and culture are thus embedded within many of our selections, not arbitrarily separated into their own sections. The content includes multidisciplinary empirical and conceptual studies. Selections are intended to show how gender operates within multiple sociocultural structures that define, design, and delineate individuals' interactions and identities. Instructors should note that the selections are intended to lend themselves to a coherent narrative, so courses can be organized around some of our key questions in a logical and analytical manner.

So what's missing from this book?

We initially conceived of this book as a reader on gender diversity, across a wide range of intersections, perspectives, and possibilities. From our earliest discussions, we focused on designing the book to fill the gaps and address the areas in which students (and "society" generally) have lingering questions about often complicated themes. We wanted to provide content that we knew professors were actively seeking to incorporate in new and better ways than existing texts have allowed. Thus *Doing Gender Diversity* utilizes a multidisciplinary approach to examining the ways we all "do" gender, consciously or not. We also wanted to avoid simply replicating existing books and have worked deliberately to include as much novel content as possible, along with several more widely read and reprinted materials.

But the book is not and cannot be all that we, or you, may desire. It may not explore everything, including race, ethnicity, and some aspects of sexualities as fully as you (or we) may wish. The realities of getting permission to republish combined with the dynamics of the academic, scholarly universe present some challenges. The topics deemed worthy of academic study and the direction of emerging scholarship lead to a scarcity of available research on certain topics. Thus we searched to find undergraduate-friendly, readable material that fit the purpose of this book. We strove to include articles that present the everyday realities and implications of gender with complexity, nuance, and grace. Perhaps readers of *Doing Gender Diversity* will see the gaps in scholarly understanding and will be inspired to do undergraduate or graduate theses and research to address these omissions. Hopefully professors and students will also be inspired to find material to flesh out the perspectives offered here. Fill the gaps!

What will happen if you read and consider the articles in this book?

We hope that you will discover a new curiosity about things that are typically taken for granted. We hope you will look at the world with an enhanced point of view, one that enables you to see the diversity in everyday lives, like this blogger, Lesbiandad:

> Also, I was recently reminded of how very different I am, gender-wise, from my beloved, when I overheard her chirp on the phone to a chum: "Hey! Are you overdue for a manicure? Or a pedicure? Because some time just opened up for me and I thought I'd go freshen up my toes."
>
> For the record . . . I rarely freshen up my toes. . . . Help is on the way, though: a friend recently confessed that she gets what she calls a "butch pedicure" from someone who does not look askance at her when she says, No she does not want "color" on her toes, and neither does she want so much as a "shine." Also, the French-Algerian chap who gives me the smart short haircut I have sported for well over a decade gets himself a pedicure immediately upon arrival in Paris, on his annual visits to his pops. And he's even heterosexual, too. I don't know, though. I've still found that a gal such as myself can't pawn off cultured European

masculinity very well. It's too easily mistaken for Traditional Femininity. Or at least this is what I fear whenever I try on clogs. For those of you who don't know the inner angst of a soft butch/gentle-manly gal, this illustrates it as well as anything. A tragic kind of clog-philia/phobia. I know, I know: it could be worse. It also could be less confusing. (www.lesbiandad.net; used with permission)

It—gender diversity—could indeed all be less confusing, and we hope that this book contributes to dissolving some complexities while creating new ones.

SECTION I
The Basics of Gender

CHAPTER 1 Gender Diversity and the Binary

1 Candace West and Don H. Zimmerman

Doing Gender

In the beginning, there was sex and there was gender. Those of us who taught courses in the area in the late 1960s and early 1970s were careful to distinguish one from the other. Sex, we told students, was what was ascribed by biology: anatomy, hormones, and physiology. Gender, we said, was an achieved status: that which is constructed through psychological, cultural, and social means. To introduce the difference between the two, we drew on singular case studies of hermaphrodites (Money 1968, 1974; Money and Ehrhardt 1972) and anthropological investigations of "strange and exotic tribes" (Mead 1963, 1968).

Inevitably (and understandably), in the ensuing weeks of each term, our students became confused. Sex hardly seemed a "given" in the context of research that illustrated the sometimes ambiguous and often conflicting criteria for its ascription. And gender seemed much less an "achievement" in the context of the anthropological, psychological, and social imperatives we studied—the division of labor, the formation of gender identities, and the social subordination of women by men. Moreover, the received doctrine of gender socialization theories conveyed the strong message that while gender may be "achieved," by about

Excerpted from the original. Candace West and Don H. Zimmerman, "Doing Gender," *Gender & Society* 1, no. 2 (June 1987): 125–151. Copyright © 1987 Sociologists for Women in Society. Reprinted by permission of SAGE Publications.

AUTHOR'S NOTE: This article is based in part on a paper presented at the Annual Meeting of the American Sociological Association, Chicago, September 1977. For their helpful suggestions and encouragement, we thank Lynda Ames, Bettina Aptheker, Steven Clayman, Judith Gerson, the late Erving Goffman, Marilyn Lester, Judith Lorber, Robin Lloyd, Wayne Mellinger, Beth E. Schneider, Barrie Thorne, Thomas P. Wilson, and most especially, Sarah Fenstermaker Berk.

age five it was certainly fixed, unvarying, and static—much like sex.

Since about 1975, the confusion has intensified and spread far beyond our individual classrooms. For one thing, we learned that the relationship between biological and cultural processes was far more complex—and reflexive—than we previously had supposed (Rossi 1984, especially pp. 10–14). For another, we discovered that certain structural arrangements, for example, between work and family, actually produce or enable some capacities, such as to mother, that we formerly associated with biology (Chodorow 1978 versus Firestone 1970). In the midst of all this, the notion of gender as a recurring achievement somehow fell by the wayside.

Our purpose in this article is to propose an ethnomethodologically informed, and therefore distinctively sociological, understanding of gender as a routine, methodical, and recurring accomplishment. We contend that the "doing" of gender is undertaken by women and men whose competence as members of society is hostage to its production. Doing gender involves a complex of socially guided perceptual, interactional, and micropolitical activities that cast particular pursuits as expressions of masculine and feminine "natures."

When we view gender as an accomplishment, an achieved property of situated conduct, our attention shifts from matters internal to the individual and focuses on interactional and, ultimately, institutional arenas. In one sense, of course, it is individuals who "do" gender. But it is a situated doing, carried out in the virtual or real presence of others who are presumed to be oriented to its production. Rather than as a property of individuals, we conceive of gender as an emergent feature of social situations: both as an outcome of and a rationale for various social arrangements and as a means of legitimating one of the most fundamental divisions of society.

To advance our arrangement, we undertake a critical examination of what sociologists have meant by *gender*, including its treatment as a role enactment in the conventional sense and as a "display" in Goffman's (1976) terminology. Both *gender role* and *gender display* focus on behavioral aspects of being a woman or a man (as opposed, for example, to biological differences between the two). However, we contend that the notion of gender as a role obscures the work that is involved in producing gender in everyday activities, while the notion of gender as a display relegates it to the periphery of interaction. We argue instead that participants in interaction organize their various and manifold activities to reflect or express gender, and they are disposed to perceive the behavior of others in a similar light.

To elaborate our proposal, we suggest at the outset that important but often overlooked distinctions be observed among *sex*, *sex category*, and *gender*. *Sex* is a determination made through the application of socially agreed upon biological criteria for classifying persons as females or males. The criteria for classification can be genitalia at birth or chromosomal typing before birth, and they do not necessarily agree with one another. Placement in a *sex category* is achieved through application of the sex criteria, but in everyday life, categorization is established and sustained by the socially required identificatory displays that proclaim one's membership in one or the other category. In this sense, one's sex category presumes one's sex and stands as proxy for it in many situations, but sex and sex category can vary independently; that is, it is possible to claim membership in a sex category even when the sex criteria are lacking. *Gender*, in contrast, is the activity of managing situated conduct in light of normative conceptions of attitudes and activities appropriate for one's sex category. Gender activities emerge from and bolster claims to membership in a sex category.

We contend that recognition of the analytical independence of sex, sex category, and gender is essential for understanding the relationships among these elements and the interactional work involved in "being" a gendered person in society. While our primary aim is theoretical, there will be occasion to discuss fruitful directions for empirical research following from the formulation of gender that we propose.

We begin with an assessment of the received meaning of gender, particularly in relation to the roots of this notion in presumed biological differences between women and men.

Many roles are already gender marked, so that special qualifiers—such as "female doctor" or "male nurse"—must be added to exceptions to the rule. Thorne (1980) observes that conceptualizing gender as a role makes it difficult to assess its influence on other roles and reduces its explanatory usefulness in discussions of power and inequality. Drawing on Rubin (1975), Thorne calls for a reconceptualization of women and men as distinct social groups, constituted in "concrete, historically changing—and generally unequal—social relationships" (Thorne 1980, p. 11).

We argue that gender is not a set of traits, nor a variable, nor a role, but the product of social doings of some sort. What then is the social doing of gender? It is more than the continuous creation of the meaning of gender through human actions (Gerson and Peiss 1985). We claim that gender itself is constituted through interaction. To develop the implications of our claim, we turn to Goffman's (1976) account of "gender display." Our object here is to explore how gender might be exhibited or portrayed through interaction, and thus be seen as "natural," while it is being produced as a socially organized achievement.

Gender Display

Goffman contends that when human beings interact with others in their environment, they assume that each possesses an "essential nature"—a nature that can be discerned through the "natural signs given off or expressed by them" (1976, p. 75). Femininity and masculinity are regarded as "prototypes of essential expression—something that can be conveyed fleetingly in any social situation and yet something that strikes at the most basic characterization of the individual" (1976, p. 75). The means through which we provide such expressions are "perfunctory, conventionalized acts" (1976, p. 69), which convey to others our regard for them, indicate our alignment in an encounter, and tentatively establish the terms of contact for that social situation. But they are also regarded as expressive behavior, testimony to our "essential natures."

Goffman (1976, pp. 69–70) sees *displays* as highly conventionalized behaviors structured as two-part exchanges of the statement-reply type, in which the presence or absence of symmetry can establish deference or dominance. These rituals are viewed as distinct from but articulated with more consequential activities, such as performing tasks or engaging in discourse. Hence, we have what he terms the "scheduling" of displays at junctures in activities, such as the beginning or end, to avoid interfering with the activities themselves. Goffman (1976, p. 69) formulates *gender display* as follows:

> If gender be defined as the culturally established correlates of sex (whether in consequence of biology or learning), then gender display refers to conventionalized portrayals of these correlates.

These gendered expressions might reveal clues to the underlying, fundamental dimensions of the female and male, but they are, in Goffman's view, optional performances. Masculine courtesies may or may not be offered and, if offered, may or may not be declined (1976, p. 71). Moreover, human beings "themselves employ the term 'expression', and conduct themselves to fit their own notions of expressivity" (1976, p. 75). Gender depictions are less a consequence of our "essential sexual natures" than interactional portrayals of what we would like to convey about sexual natures, using conventionalized gestures. Our *human* nature gives us the ability to learn to produce and recognize masculine and feminine gender displays—"a capacity [we] have by virtue of being persons, not males and females" (1976, p. 76).

Upon first inspection, it would appear that Goffman's formulation offers an engaging sociological corrective to existing formulations of gender. In his view, gender is a socially scripted dramatization of the culture's *idealization* of feminine and masculine natures, played for an audience that is well schooled in the presentational idiom. To continue the metaphor, there are scheduled performances presented in special locations, and like plays, they constitute introductions to or time out from more serious activities.

There are fundamental equivocations in this perspective. By segregating gender display from the serious business of interaction, Goffman obscures the effects of gender on a wide range of human activities. Gender is not merely something that happens in the nooks and crannies of interaction, fitted in here and there and not interfering with the serious business of life. While it is plausible to contend that gender displays—construed as conventionalized expressions—are optional, it does not seem plausible to say that we have the option of being seen by others as female or male.

It is necessary to move beyond the notion of gender display to consider what is involved in doing gender as an ongoing activity embedded in everyday interaction.

And note, to "do" gender is not always to live up to normative conceptions of femininity or masculinity; it is to engage in behavior *at the risk of gender assessment*. While it is individuals who do gender, the enterprise is fundamentally interactional and institutional in character, for accountability is a feature of social relationships and its idiom is drawn from the institutional arena in which those relationships are enacted. If this be the case, can we ever *not* do gender? Insofar as a society is partitioned by "essential" differences between women and men and placement in a sex category is both relevant and enforced, doing gender is unavoidable.

Resources for Doing Gender

Doing gender means creating differences between girls and boys and women and men, differences that are not natural, essential, or biological. Once the differences have been constructed, they are used to reinforce the "essentialness" of gender. In a delightful account of the "arrangement between the sexes," Goffman (1977) observes the creation of a variety of institutionalized frameworks through which our "natural, normal sexedness" can be enacted. The physical features of social setting provide one obvious resource for the expression of our "essential" differences. For example, the sex segregation of North American public bathrooms distinguishes "ladies" from "gentlemen" in matters held to be fundamentally biological, even though both "are somewhat similar in the question of waste products and their elimination" (Goffman 1977, p. 315). These settings are furnished with dimorphic equipment (such as urinals for men or elaborate grooming facilities for women), even though both sexes may achieve the same ends through the same means (and apparently do so in the privacy of their own homes). To be stressed here is the fact that:

> The *functioning* of sex-differentiated organs is involved, but there is nothing in this functioning that biologically recommends segregation; *that* arrangement is a totally cultural matter . . . toilet segregation is presented as a natural consequence of the difference between the sex-classes when in fact it is a means of honoring, if not producing, this difference. (Goffman 1977, p. 316)

Standardized social occasions also provide stages for evocations of the "essential female and male natures." Goffman cites organized sports as one such institutionalized framework for the expression of manliness. There, those qualities that ought "properly" to be associated with masculinity, such as endurance, strength, and competitive spirit, are celebrated by all parties concerned—participants, who may be seen to demonstrate such traits, and spectators, who applaud their demonstrations from the safety of the sidelines (1977, p. 322).

Assortative mating practices among heterosexual couples afford still further means to create and maintain differences between women and men. For example, even though size, strength, and age tend to be normally distributed among females and males (with considerable overlap between them), selective pairing ensures couples in which boys and men are visibly bigger, stronger, and older (if not "wiser") than the girls and women with whom they are paired. So, should situations emerge in which greater size, strength, or experience is called for, boys and men will be ever ready to display it and girls and women, to appreciate its display (Goffman 1977, p. 321; West and Iritani 1985).

Gender may be routinely fashioned in a variety of situations that seem conventionally expressive to begin with, such as those that present "helpless" women next to heavy objects or flat tires. But, as Goffman notes, heavy, messy, and precarious concerns can be constructed from *any* social situation, "even though by standards set in other settings, this may involve something that is light, clean, and safe" (Goffman 1977, p. 324). Given these resources, it is clear that *any* interactional situation sets the stage for depictions of "essential" sexual natures. In sum, these situations "do not so much allow for the expression of natural differences as for the production of that difference itself" (Goffman 1977, p. 324).

Many situations are not clearly sex categorized to begin with, nor is what transpires within them obviously gender relevant. Yet any social encounter can be pressed into service in the interests of doing gender. Thus, Fishman's (1978) research on casual conversations found an asymmetrical "division of labor" in talk between heterosexual intimates. Women had to ask more questions, fill more silences, and use more attention-getting beginnings in order to be heard. Her conclusions are particularly pertinent here:

> Since interactional work is related to what constitutes being a woman, with what a woman *is*, the idea that it *is* work is obscured. The work is not seen as what women do, but as part of what they are. (Fishman 1978, p. 405)

We would argue that it is precisely such labor that helps to constitute the essential nature of women *as* women in interactional contexts (West and Zimmerman 1983, pp. 109–11; but see also Kollock, Blumstein, and Schwartz 1985).

Individuals have many social identities that may be donned or shed, muted or made more salient, depending on the situation. One may be a friend, spouse, professional, citizen, and many other things to many different people—or, to the same person at different times. But we are always women or men—unless we shift into another sex category. What this means is that our identificatory displays will provide an ever-available resource for doing gender under an infinitely diverse set of circumstances.

We have sought to show that sex category and gender are managed properties of conduct that are contrived with respect to the fact that others will judge and respond to us in particular ways. We have claimed that a person's gender is not simply an aspect of what one is, but, more fundamentally, it is something that one *does*, and does recurrently, in interaction with others.

What are the consequences of this theoretical formulation? If, for example, individuals strive to achieve gender in encounters with others, how does a culture instill the need to achieve it? What is the relationship between the production of gender at the level of interaction and such institutional arrangements as the division of labor in society? And, perhaps most important, how does doing gender contribute to the subordination of women by men?

Gender, Power, and Social Change

Let us return to the question: Can we avoid doing gender? Earlier, we proposed that insofar as sex category is used as a fundamental criterion for differentiation, doing gender is unavoidable. It is unavoidable because of the social consequences of sex-category membership: the allocation of power and resources not only in the domestic, economic, and political domains but also in the broad arena of interpersonal relations. In virtually any situation, one's sex category can be relevant, and one's performance as an incumbent of that category (i.e., gender) can be subjected to evaluation. Maintaining such pervasive and faithful assignment of lifetime status requires legitimation.

But doing gender also renders the social arrangements based on sex category accountable as normal and natural, that is, legitimate ways of organizing social life. Differences between women and men that are created by this process can then be portrayed as fundamental and enduring dispositions. In this light, the institutional arrangements of a society can be seen as responsive to the differences—the social order being merely an accommodation to the natural order. Thus if, in doing gender, men are also doing dominance and women are doing deference (cf. Goffman 1967, pp. 47–95), the resultant social order, which supposedly reflects "natural differences," is a powerful reinforcer and legitimator of hierarchical arrangements. Frye observes:

> For efficient subordination, what's wanted is that the structure not appear to be a cultural artifact kept in place by human decision or custom, but that it appear *natural*—that it appear to be quite a direct consequence of facts about the beast which are beyond the scope of human manipulation. . . . That we are trained to behave so differently as women and men, and to behave so differently toward women and men, itself contributes mightily to the appearance of extreme dimorphism, but also, the *ways* we act as women and men, and the *ways* we act toward women and men, mold our bodies and our minds to the shape of subordination and dominance. We do become what we practice being. (Frye 1983, p. 34)

If we do gender appropriately, we simultaneously sustain, reproduce, and render legitimate the institutional arrangements that are based on sex category. If we fail to do gender appropriately, we as individuals— not the institutional arrangements—may be called to account (for our character, motives, and predispositions).

Social movements such as feminism can provide the ideology and impetus to question existing arrangements, and the social support for individuals to explore alternatives to them. Legislative changes, such as that proposed by the Equal Rights Amendment, can also weaken the accountability of conduct to sex category, thereby affording the possibility of more widespread loosening of accountability in general. To be sure,

equality under the law does not guarantee equality in other arenas. As Lorber (1986, p. 577) points out, assurance of "scrupulous equality of categories of people considered essentially different needs constant monitoring." What such proposed changes *can* do is provide the warrant for asking why, if we wish to treat women and men as equals, there needs to be two sex categories at all (see Lorber 1986, p. 577).

The sex category/gender relationship links the institutional and interactional levels, a coupling that legitimates social arrangements based on sex category and reproduces their asymmetry in face-to-face interaction. Doing gender furnishes the interactional scaffolding of social structure, along with a built-in mechanism of social control. In appreciating the institutional forces that maintain distinctions between women and men, we must not lose sight of the interactional validation of those distinctions that confers upon them their sense of "naturalness" and "rightness."

Social change, then, must be pursued both at the institutional and cultural level of sex category and at the interactional level of gender. Such a conclusion is hardly novel. Nevertheless, we suggest that it is important to recognize that the analytical distinction between institutional and interactional spheres does not pose an either/or choice when it comes to the question of effecting social change. Reconceptualizing gender not as a simple property of individuals but as an integral dynamic of social orders implies a new perspective on the entire network of gender relations:

> [T]he social subordination of women, and the cultural practices which help sustain it; the politics of sexual object-choice, and particularly the oppression of homosexual

people; the sexual division of labor, the formation of character and motive, so far as they are organized as femininity and masculinity; the role of the body in social relations, especially the politics of child-birth; and the nature of strategies of sexual liberation movements. (Connell 1985, p. 261)

Gender is a powerful ideological device, which produces, reproduces, and legitimates the choices and limits that are predicated on sex category. An understanding of how gender is produced in social situations will afford clarification of the interactional scaffolding of social structure and the social control processes that sustain it.

References

Beer, William R. 1983. *Househusbands: Men and Housework in American Families*. New York: Praeger.

Bem, Sandra L. 1983. "Gender Schema Theory and Its Implications for Child Development: Raising Gender-Aschematic Children in a Gender-Schematic Society." *Signs: Journal of Women in Culture and Society* 8:598–616.

Berger, Joseph, Bernard P. Cohen, and Morris Zelditch, Jr. 1972. "Status Characteristics and Social Interaction." *American Sociological Review* 37:241–55.

Berger, Joseph, Thomas L. Conner, and M. Hamit Fisek, eds. 1974. *Expectation States Theory: A Theoretical Research Program*. Cambridge: Winthrop.

Berger, Joseph, M. Hamit Fisek, Robert Z. Norman, and Morris Zelditch, Jr. 1977. *Status Characteristics and Social Interaction: An Expectation States Approach*. New York: Elsevier.

Berk, Sarah F. 1985. *The Gender Factory: The Apportionment of Work in American Households*. New York: Plenum.

Bernstein, Richard. 1986. "France Jails 2 in Odd Case of Espionage." *New York Times* (May 11).

Blackwood, Evelyn. 1984. "Sexuality and Gender in Certain Native American Tribes: The Case of Cross-Gender Females." *Signs: Journal of Women in Culture and Society* 10:27–42.

Bourne, Patricia G., and Norma J. Wikler. 1978. "Commitment and the Cultural Mandate: Women in Medicine." *Social Problems* 25: 430–40.

Cahill, Spencer E. 1982. "Becoming Boys and Girls." Ph.D. dissertation, Department of Sociology, University of California, Santa Barbara.

———. 1986a. "Childhood Socialization as Recruitment Process: Some Lessons from the Study of Gender Development." Pp. 163–86 in *Sociological Studies of Child Development*, edited by P. Adler and P. Adler. Greenwich, CT: JAI Press.

———. 1986b. "Language Practices and Self-Definition: The Case of Gender Identity Acquisition." *The Sociological Quarterly* 27: 295–311.

Chodorow, Nancy. 1978. *The Reproduction of Mothering: Psychoanalysis and the Sociology of Gender*. Los Angeles: University of California Press.

Connell, R. W. 1983. *Which Way Is Up?* Sydney: Allen & Unwin.

———. 1985. "Theorizing Gender." *Sociology* 19:260–72.

Cucchiari, Salvatore. 1981. "The Gender Revolution and the Transition from Bisexual Horde to Patrilocal Band: The Origins of Gender Hierarchy." Pp. 31–79 in *Sexual Meanings: The Cultural Construction of Gender and Sexuality*, edited by S. B. Ortner and H. Whitehead. New York: Cambridge.

Firestone, Shulamith. 1970. *The Dialectic of Sex: The Case for Feminist Revolution*. New York: William Morrow.

Fishman, Pamela. 1978. "Interaction: The Work Women Do." *Social Problems* 25:397–406.

Frye, Marilyn. 1983. *The Politics of Reality: Essays in Feminist Theory*. Trumansburg, NY: The Crossing Press.

Garfinkel, Harold. 1967. *Studies in Ethnomethodology*. Englewood Cliffs, NJ: Prentice-Hall.

Gerson, Judith M., and Kathy Peiss. 1985. "Boundaries, Negotiation, Consciousness:

Reconceptualizing Gender Relations." *Social Problems* 32:317–31.

Goffman, Erving. 1967 (1956). "The Nature of Deference and Demeanor." Pp. 47–95 in *Interaction Ritual*. New York: Anchor/Doubleday.

———. 1976. "Gender Display." *Studies in the Anthropology of Visual Communication* 3:69–77.

———. 1977. "The Arrangement Between the Sexes." *Theory and Society* 4:301–31.

Henley, Nancy M. 1985. "Psychology and Gender." *Signs: Journal of Women in Culture and Society* 11:101–119.

Heritage, John. 1984. *Garfinkel and Ethnomethodology*. Cambridge, England: Polity Press.

Hill, W. W. 1935. "The Status of the Hermaphrodite and Transvestite in Navaho Culture." *American Anthropologist* 37:273–79.

Hochschild, Arlie R. 1973. "A Review of Sex Roles Research." *American Journal of Sociology* 78:1011–29.

———. 1983. *The Managed Heart: Commercialization of Human Feeling*. Berkeley: University of California Press.

Hughes, Everett C. 1945. "Dilemmas and Contradictions of Status." *American Journal of Sociology* 50:353–59.

Humphreys, Paul, and Joseph Berger. 1981. "Theoretical Consequences of the Status Characteristics Formulation." *American Journal of Sociology* 86:953–83.

Jaggar, Alison M. 1983. *Feminist Politics and Human Nature*. Totowa, NJ: Rowman & Allanheld.

Kessler, S., D. J. Ashendon, R. W. Connell, and G. W. Dowsett. 1985. "Gender Relations in Secondary Schooling." *Sociology of Education* 58:34–48.

Kessler, Suzanne J., and Wendy McKenna. 1978. *Gender: An Ethnomethodological Approach*. New York: Wiley.

Kollock, Peter, Philip Blumstein, and Pepper Schwartz. 1985. "Sex and Power in Interaction." *American Sociological Review* 50:34–46.

Komarovsky, Mirra. 1946. "Cultural Contradictions and Sex Roles." *American Journal of Sociology* 52:184–89.

———. 1950. "Functional Analysis of Sex Roles." *American Sociological Review* 15:508–16.

Linton, Ralph. 1936. *The Study of Man*. New York: Appleton-Century.

Lopata, Helen Z., and Barrie Thorne. 1978. "On the Term 'Sex Roles.'" *Signs: Journal of Women in Culture and Society* 3:718–21.

Lorber, Judith. 1984. *Women Physicians: Careers, Status and Power*. New York: Tavistock.

———. 1986. "Dismantling Noah's Ark." *Sex Roles* 14:567–80.

Martin, M. Kay, and Barbara Voorheis. 1975. *Female of the Species*. New York: Columbia University Press.

Mead, Margaret. 1963. *Sex and Temperament*. New York: Dell.

———. 1968. *Male and Female*. New York: Dell.

Mithers, Carol L. 1982. "My Life as a Man." *The Village Voice* 27 (October 5):1ff.

Money, John. 1968. *Sex Errors of the Body*. Baltimore: Johns Hopkins.

———. 1974. "Prenatal Hormones and Postnatal Sexualization in Gender Identity Differentiation." Pp. 221–95 in *Nebraska Symposium on Motivation*, Vol. 21, edited by J. K. Cole and R. Dienstbier. Lincoln: University of Nebraska Press.

——— and John G. Brennan. 1968. "Sexual Dimorphism in the Psychology of Female Transsexuals." *Journal of Nervous and Mental Disease* 147:487–99.

——— and Anke, A. Erhardt. 1972. *Man and Woman/Boy and Girl*. Baltimore: Johns Hopkins.

——— and Charles Ogunro. 1974. "Behavioral Sexology: Ten Cases of Genetic Male Intersexuality with Impaired Prenatal and Pubertal Androgenization," *Archives of Sexual Behavior* 3:181–206.

——— and Patricia Tucker. 1975. *Sexual Signatures*. Boston: Little, Brown.

Morris, Jan. 1974. *Conundrum*. New York: Harcourt Brace Jovanovich.

Parsons, Talcott. 1951. *The Social System*. New York: Free Press.

——— and Robert F. Bales. 1955. *Family, Socialization and Interaction Process*. New York: Free Press.

Raymond, Janice G. 1979. *The Transsexual Empire*. Boston: Beacon.

Rich, Adrienne. 1980. "Compulsory Heterosexuality and Lesbian Existence." *Signs: Journal of Women in Culture and Society* 5:631–60.

Richards, Renee (with John Ames). 1983. *Second Serve: The Renee Richards Story*. New York: Stein and Day.

Rossi, Alice. 1984. "Gender and Parenthood." *American Sociological Review* 49:1–19.

Rubin, Gayle, 1975. "The Traffic in Women: Notes on the 'Political Economy' of Sex." Pp. 157–210 in *Toward an Anthropology of Women*, edited by R. Reiter. New York: Monthly Review Press.

Sacks, Harvey. 1972. "On the Analyzability of Stories by Children." Pp. 325–45 in *Directions in Sociolinguistics*, edited by J. J. Gumperz and D. Hymes. New York: Holt, Rinehart & Winston.

Schutz, Alfred. 1943. "The Problem of Rationality in the Social World." *Economics* 10:130–49.

Stacey, Judith, and Barrie Thorne. 1985. "The Missing Feminist Revolution in Sociology." *Social Problems* 32:301–16.

Thorne, Barrie. 1980. "Gender . . . How Is It Best Conceptualized?" Unpublished manuscript.

———. 1986. "Girls and Boys Together . . . But Mostly Apart: Gender Arrangements in Elementary Schools." Pp. 167–82 in *Relationships and Development*, edited by W. Hartup and Z. Rubin. Hillsdale, NJ: Lawrence Erlbaum.

——— and Zella Luria. 1986. "Sexuality and Gender in Children's Daily World." *Social Problems* 33:176–90.

Tresemer, David. 1975. "Assumptions Made About Gender Roles." Pp. 308–39 in *Another Voice: Feminist Perspectives on Social Life and Social Science*, edited by M. Millman and R. M. Kanter. New York: Anchor/Doubleday.

West, Candace. 1984. "When the Doctor is a 'Lady': Power, Status and Gender in Physician-Patient Encounters." *Symbolic Interaction* 7:87–106.

——— and Bonita Iritani. 1985. "Gender Politics in Mate Selection: The Male-Older Norm." Paper presented at the Annual Meeting of the American Sociological Association, August, Washington, DC.

——— and Don H. Zimmerman. 1983. "Small Insults: A Study of Interruptions in Conversations Between Unacquainted Persons." Pp. 102–17 in *Language, Gender and Society*, edited by B. Thorne, C. Kramarae, and N. Henley. Rowley, MA: Newbury House.

Wieder, D. Lawrence. 1974. *Language and Social Reality: The Case of Telling the Convict Code*. The Hague: Mouton.

Williams, Walter L. 1986. *The Spirit and the Flesh: Sexual Diversity in American Indian Culture*. Boston: Beacon.

Wilson, Thomas P. 1970. "Conceptions of Interaction and Forms of Sociological Explanation." *American Sociological Review* 35: 697–710.

Zimmerman, Don H., and D. Lawrence Wieder. 1970. "Ethnomethodology and the Problem of Order: Comment on Denzin." Pp. 287–95 in *Understanding Everyday Life*, edited by J. Denzin. Chicago: Aldine.

Night to His Day
The Social Construction of Gender

Talking about gender for most people is the equivalent of fish talking about water. Gender is so much the routine ground of everyday activities that questioning its taken-for-granted assumptions and presuppositions is like thinking about whether the sun will come up.[1] Gender is so pervasive that in our society we assume it is bred into our genes. Most people find it hard to believe that gender is constantly created and re-created out of human interaction, out of social life, and is the texture and order of that social life. Yet gender, like culture, is a human production that depends on everyone constantly "doing gender" (West and Zimmerman 1987).

And everyone "does gender" without thinking about it. Today, on the subway, I saw a well-dressed man with a year-old child in a stroller. Yesterday, on a bus, I saw a man with a tiny baby in a carrier on his chest. Seeing men taking care of small children in public is increasingly common—at least in New York City. But both men were quite obviously stared at—and smiled at, approvingly. Everyone was doing gender—the men who were changing the role of fathers and the other passengers, who were applauding them silently. But there was more gendering going on that probably fewer people noticed. The baby was wearing a white crocheted cap and white clothes. You couldn't tell if it was a boy or a girl. The child in the stroller was wearing a dark blue T-shirt and dark print pants. As they started to leave the train, the father put a Yankee baseball cap on the child's head. Ah, a boy, I thought. Then I noticed the gleam of tiny earrings in the child's ears, and as they got off, I saw the little flowered sneakers and lace-trimmed socks. Not a boy after all. Gender done.

Gender is such a familiar part of daily life that it usually takes a deliberate disruption of our expectations of how women and men are supposed to act to pay attention to how it is produced. Gender signs and signals are so ubiquitous that we usually fail to note them—unless they are missing or ambiguous. Then we are uncomfortable until we have successfully placed the other person in a gender status; otherwise, we feel socially dislocated. In our society, in addition to man and woman, the status can be *transvestite* (a person who dresses in opposite-gender clothes) and *transsexual* (a person who has had sex-change surgery). Transvestites and transsexuals construct their gender status by dressing, speaking, walking, gesturing in the ways prescribed for women or men—whichever they want to be taken for—and so does any "normal" person.

For the individual, gender construction starts with assignment to a sex category on the basis of what the genitalia look like at birth.[2] Then babies are dressed or adorned in a way that displays the category because parents don't want to be constantly asked whether their baby is a girl or a boy. A sex category becomes a gender status through naming, dress, and the use of other gender markers. Once a child's gender is evident, others treat those in one gender differently from those in the other, and the children respond to the different treatment by feeling different and behaving differently. As soon as they can talk, they start to refer to themselves as members of their gender. Sex doesn't come into play again until puberty, but by that time, sexual feelings and desires and practices have been shaped by gendered norms and expectations. Adolescent boys and girls approach and avoid each other in an elaborately scripted and gendered mating dance. Parenting is gendered, with different expectations for mothers and for fathers, and people of different genders work at different kinds of jobs. The work adults do as mothers and fathers and as low-level workers and high-level bosses, shapes women's and men's life experiences, and these experiences produce different feelings, consciousness, relationships, skills—ways of being that we call feminine or masculine.[3] All of these processes constitute the social construction of gender.

Gendered roles change—today fathers are taking care of little children, girls and boys are wearing unisex clothing and getting the same education, women and men are working at the same jobs. Although many traditional social groups are quite strict about maintaining gender differences, in other social groups they seem to be blurring. Then why the one-year-old's earrings?

Why is it still so important to mark a child as a girl or a boy, to make sure she is not taken for a boy or he for a girl? What would happen if they were? They would, quite literally, have changed places in their social world.

To explain why gendering is done from birth, constantly and by everyone, we have to look not only at the way individuals experience gender but at gender as a social institution. As a social institution, gender is one of the major ways that human beings organize their lives. Human society depends on a predictable division of labor, a designated allocation of scarce goods, assigned responsibility for children and others who cannot care for themselves, common values and their systematic transmission to new members, legitimate leadership, music, art, stories, games, and other symbolic productions. One way of choosing people for the different tasks of society is on the basics of their talents, motivations, and competence—their demonstrated achievements. The other way is on the basis of gender, race, ethnicity—ascribed membership in a category of people. Although societies vary in the extent to which they use one or the other of these ways of allocating people to work and to carry out other responsibilities, every society uses gender and age grades. Every society classifies people as "girl and boy children," "girls and boys ready to be married," and "fully adult women and men," constructs similarities among them and differences between them, and assigns them to different roles and responsibilities. Personality characteristics, feelings, motivations, and ambitions flow from these different life experiences so that the members of these different groups become different kinds of people. The process of gendering and its outcome are legitimated by religion, law, science, and the society's entire set of values.

Gender as Process, Stratification, and Structure

As a social institution, gender is a process of creating distinguishable social statuses for the assignment of rights and responsibilities. As part of a stratification system that ranks these statuses unequally, gender is a major building block in the social structures built on these unequal statuses.

As a *process*, gender creates the social differences that define "woman" and "man." In social interaction throughout their lives, individuals learn what is expected, see what is expected, act and react in expected ways, and thus simultaneously construct and maintain the gender order: "The very injunction to be given gender takes place through discursive routes: to be a good mother, to be a heterosexually desirable object, to be a fit worker, in sum, to signify a multiplicity of guarantees in response to a variety of different demands all at once" (J. Butler 1990, 145). Members of a social group neither make up gender as they go along nor exactly replicate in rote fashion what was done before. In almost every encounter, human beings produce gender, behaving in the ways they learned were appropriate for their gender status, or resisting or rebelling against these norms. Resistance and rebellion have altered gender norms, but so far they have rarely eroded the statuses.

Gendered patterns of interaction acquire additional layers of gendered sexuality, parenting, and work behaviors in childhood, adolescence, and adulthood. Gendered norms and expectations are enforced through informal sanctions of gender-inappropriate behavior by peers and by formal punishment or threat of punishment by those in authority should behavior deviate too far from socially imposed standards for women and men.

Everyday gendered interactions build gender into the family, the work process, and other organizations and institutions, which in turn reinforce gender expectations for individuals.[4] Because gender is a process, there is room not only for modification and variation by individuals and small groups but also for institutionalized change (J. W. Scott 1988, 7).

As part of a *stratification* system, gender ranks men above women of the same race and class. Women and men could be different but equal. In practice, the process of creating difference depends to a great extent on differential evaluation. As Nancy Jay (1981) says: "That which is defined, separated out, isolated from all else is A and pure. Not-A is necessarily impure, a random catchall, to which nothing is external except A and the principle of order that separates it from Not-A" (45). From the individual's point of view, whichever gender is A, the other is Not-A; gender boundaries tell the individual who is like him or her, and all the rest are unlike. From society's point of view, however, one gender is usually the touchstone, the normal, the dominant, and the other is different, deviant, and subordinate. In Western society, "man" is A, "wo-man" is Not-A. (Consider what a society would be like where woman was A and man Not-A.)

The further dichotomization by race and class constructs the gradations of a heterogeneous society's stratification scheme. Thus, in the United States, white is A, African American is Not-A; middle class is A, working class is Not-A, and "African-American women occupy a position whereby the inferior half of a series of these dichotomies converge" (P. H. Collins 1990, 70). The dominant categories are the hegemonic ideals, taken so for granted as the way things should be that white is not ordinarily thought of as a race, middle class as a class, or men as a gender. The characteristics of these categories define the Other as that which lacks the valuable qualities the dominants exhibit.

In a gender-stratified society, what men do is usually valued more highly than what women do because men do it, even when their activities are very similar or the same. In different regions of southern India, for example, harvesting rice is men's work, shared work, or women's work: "Wherever a task is done by women it is considered easy, and where it is done by [men] it is considered difficult" (Mencher 1988, 104). A gathering and hunting society's survival usually depends on the nuts, grubs, and small animals brought in by the women's foraging trips, but when the men's hunt is successful, it is the occasion for a celebration. Conversely, because they are the superior group, white men do not have to do the "dirty work," such as housework; the most inferior group does it, usually poor women of color (Palmer 1989).

Freudian psychoanalytic theory claims that boys must reject their mothers and deny the feminine in themselves in order to become men: "For boys the major goal is the achievement of personal masculine identification with their father and sense of secure masculine self, achieved through superego formation and disparagement of women" (Chodorow 1978, 165). Masculinity may be the outcome of boys' intrapsychic struggles to separate their identity from that of their mothers, but the proofs of masculinity are culturally shaped and usually ritualistic and symbolic (Gilmore 1990).

The Marxist feminist explanation for gender inequality is that by demeaning women's abilities and keeping them from learning valuable technological skills, bosses preserve them as a cheap and exploitable reserve army of labor. Unionized men who could easily be replaced by women collude in this process because it allows them to monopolize the better-paid, more interesting, and more autonomous jobs: "Two factors emerge as helping men maintain their separation from women and their control of technological occupations. One is the active gendering of jobs and people. The second is the continual creation of sub-divisions in the work processes, and levels in work hierarchies, into which men can move in order to keep their distance from women" (Cockburn 1985, 13).

Societies vary in the extent of the inequality in social status of their women and men members, but where there is inequality, the status "woman" (and its attendant behavior and role allocations) is usually held in lesser esteem than the status "man." Since gender is also intertwined with a society's other constructed statuses of differential evaluation—race, religion, occupation, class, country of origin, and so on—men and women members of the favored groups command more power, more prestige, and more property than the members of the disfavored groups. Within many social groups, however, men are advantaged over women. The more economic resources, such as education and job opportunities, are available to a group, the more they tend to be monopolized by men. In poorer groups that have few resources (such as working-class African Americans in the United States), women and men are more nearly equal, and the women may even outstrip the men in education and occupational status (Almquist 1987).

As a *structure*, gender drives work in the home and in economic production, legitimates those in authority, and organizes sexuality and emotional life (Connell 1987, 91–142). As primary parents, women significantly influence children's psychological development and emotional attachments, in the process reproducing gender. Emergent sexuality is shaped by heterosexual, homosexual, bisexual, and sadomasochistic patterns that are gendered—different for girls and boys, and for women and men—so that sexual statuses reflect gender statuses.

When gender is a major component of structured inequality, the devalued genders have less power, prestige, and economic rewards than the valued genders. In countries that discourage gender discrimination, many major roles are still gendered; women still do most of the domestic labor and child rearing, even while doing full-time paid work; women and men are segregated on the job and each does work considered "appropriate"; women's work is usually paid less than men's work. Men dominate the positions of authority and leadership in government, the military, and the law; cultural productions, religions, and sports reflect men's interests.

In societies that create the greatest gender difference, such as Saudi Arabia, women are kept out of sight behind walls or veils, have no civil rights, and often create a cultural and emotional world of their own (Bernard 1981). But even in societies with less rigid gender boundaries, women and men spend much of their time with people of their own gender because of the way work and family are organized. This spatial separation of women and men reinforces gendered differ-

ences, identity, and ways of thinking and behaving (Coser 1986).

Gender inequality—the devaluation of "women" and the social domination of "men"—has social functions and social history. It is not the result of sex, procreation, physiology, anatomy, hormones, or genetic predispositions. It is produced and maintained by identifiable social processes and built into the general social structure and individual identities deliberately and purposefully. The social order as we know it in Western societies is organized around racial, ethnic, class, and gender inequality. I contend, therefore, that the continuing purpose of gender as a modern social institution is to construct women as a group to be the subordinates of men as a group.

The Paradox of Human Nature

To say that sex, sexuality, and gender are all socially constructed is not to minimize their social power. These categorical imperatives govern our lives in the most profound and pervasive ways, through the social experiences and social practices of what Dorothy Smith calls the "everyday/everynight world" (1990, 31–57). The paradox of human nature is that it is *always* a manifestation of cultural meanings, social relationships, and power politics; "not biology, but culture, becomes destiny" (J. Butler 1990, 8). Gendered people emerge not from physiology or sexual orientations but from the exigencies of the social order, mostly from the need for a reliable division of the work of food production and the social (not physical) reproduction of new members. The moral imperatives of religion and cultural representations guard the boundary lines among genders and ensure that what is demanded, what is permitted, and what is tabooed for the people in each gender is well known and followed by most (C. Davies 1982). Political power, control of scarce resources, and, if necessary, violence uphold the gendered social order in the face of resistance and rebellion. Most people, however, voluntarily go along with their society's prescriptions for those of their gender status, because the norms and expectations get built into their sense of worth and identity as [the way we] think, the way we see and hear and speak, the way we fantas[ize], and the way we feel.

There is no core or bedrock in human nature below these endlessly looping processes of the social production of sex and gender, self and other, identity and psyche, each of which is a "complex cultural construction" (J. Butler 1990, 36). *For humans, the social is the natural.* Therefore, "in its feminist senses, gender cannot mean simply the cultural appropriation of biological sexual difference. Sexual difference is itself a fundamental—and scientifically contested—construction. Both 'sex' and 'gender' are woven of multiple, asymmetrical strands of difference, charged with multifaceted dramatic narratives of domination and struggle" (Haraway 1990, 140).

Notes

1. Gender is, in Erving Goffman's words, an aspect of *Felicity's Condition*: "any arrangement which leads us to judge an individual's . . . acts not to be a manifestation of strangeness. Behind *Felicity's Condition* is our sense of what it is to be sane" (1983:27). Also see Bem 1993; Frye 1983, 17–40; Goffman 1977.

2. In cases of ambiguity in countries with modern medicine, surgery is usually performed to make the genitalia more clearly male or female.

3. See J. Butler 1990 for an analysis of how doing gender is gender identity.

4. On the "logic of practice," or how the experience of gender is embedded in the norms of everyday interaction and the structure of formal organizations, see Acker 1990; Bourdieu [1980] 1990; Connell 1987; Smith 1987.

References

Acker, Joan. 1990. "Hierarchies, jobs, and bodies: A theory of gendered organizations," *Gender & Society* 4:139–158.

Almquist, Elizabeth M. 1987. "Labor market gendered inequality in minority groups," *Gender & Society* 1:400–14.

Bem, Sandra Lipsitz. 1993. *The Lenses of Gender: Transforming the Debate on Sexual Inequality*. New Haven: Yale University Press.

Bernard, Jessie. 1981. *The Female World*. New York: Free Press.

Bourdieu, Pierre. [1980] 1990. *The Logic of Practice*. Stanford, Calif.: Stanford University Press.

Butler, Judith. 1990. *Gender Trouble: Feminism and the Subversion of Identity*. New York and London: Routledge.

Chodorow, Nancy, 1978. *The Reproduction of Mothering*. Berkeley: University of California Press.

Cockburn, Cynthia. 1985. *Machinery of Dominance: Women, Men and Technical Know-how*. London: Pluto Press.

Collins, Patricia Hill. 1989. "The social construction of black feminist thought," *Signs* 14:745–73.

Connell, R. [Robert] W. 1987. *Gender and Power: Society, the Person, and Sexual Politics*. Stanford, Calif.: Stanford University Press.

Coser, Rose Laub. 1986. "Cognitive structure and the use of social space," *Sociological Forum* 1:1–26.

Davies, Christie. 1982. "Sexual taboos and social boundaries," *American Journal of Sociology* 87:1032–63.

Dwyer, Daisy, and Judith Bruce (eds.). 1988. *A Home Divided: Women and Income in the Third World*. Palo Alto, Calif.: Stanford University Press.

Frye, Marilyn. 1983. *The Politics of Reality: Essays in Feminist Theory*. Trumansburg, N.Y.: Crossing Press.

Gilmore, David D. 1990. *Manhood in the Making: Cultural Concepts of Masculinity*. New Haven: Yale University Press.

Goffman, Erving. 1977. "The arrangement between the sexes," *Theory and Society* 4:301–33.

Haraway, Donna. 1990. "Investment strategies for the evolving portfolio of primate females," in *Jacobus, Keller, and Shuttleworth*.

Jacobus, Mary, Evelyn Fox Keller, and Sally Shuttleworth (eds.). (1990). *Body/politics: Women and the Discourse of Science*. New York and London: Routledge.

Jay, Nancy. 1981. "Gender and dichotomy," *Feminist Studies* 7:38–56.

Mencher, Joan. 1988. "Women's work and poverty: Women's contribution to household maintenance in South India," in *Dwyer and Bruce*.

Palmer, Phyllis. 1989. *Domesticity and Dirt: Housewives and Domestic Servants in the United States, 1920–1945*. Philadelphia: Temple University Press.

Scott, Joan Wallach. 1988. *Gender and the Politics of History*. New York: Columbia University Press.

Smith, Dorothy. 1987. *The Everyday World as Problematic: A Feminist Sociology*. Toronto: University of Toronto Press.

———. 1990. *The Conceptual Practices of Power: A Feminist Sociology of Knowledge*. Toronto: University of Toronto Press.

West, Candace, and Don Zimmerman. 1987. "Doing gender," *Gender & Society* 1:125–51.

3 Patricia Hill Collins

Toward a New Vision

Race, Class, and Gender as Categories of Analysis and Connection

The true focus of revolutionary change is never merely the oppressive situations which we seek to escape, but that piece of the oppressor which is planted deep within each of us.

—Audre Lorde, *Sister Outsider*, 123

Audre Lorde's statement raises a troublesome issue for scholars and activists working for social change. While many of us have little difficulty assessing our own victimization within some major system of oppression, whether it be by race, social class, religion, sexual orientation, ethnicity, age or gender, we typically fail to see how our thoughts and actions uphold someone else's subordination. Thus, white feminists routinely point with confidence to their oppression as women but resist seeing how much their white skin privileges them. African-Americans who possess eloquent analyses of racism often persist in viewing poor White women as symbols of white power. The radical left fares little better. "If only people of color and women could see their true class interests," they argue, "class solidarity would eliminate racism and sexism." In essence, each group identifies the type of oppression with which it feels most comfortable as being fundamental and classifies all other types as being of lesser importance.

Oppression is full of such contradictions. Errors in political judgment that we make concerning how we teach our courses, what we tell our children, and which organizations are worthy of our time, talents and financial support flow smoothly from errors in theoretical analysis about the nature of oppression and activism. Once we realize that there are few pure victims or oppressors, and that each one of us derives varying amounts of penalty and privilege from the multiple systems of oppression that frame our lives, then we will be in a position to see the need for new ways of thought and action.

To get at that "piece of the oppressor which is planted deep within each of us," we need at least two things. First, we need new visions of what oppression is, new categories of analysis that are inclusive of race, class, and gender as distinctive yet interlocking structures of oppression. Adhering to a stance of comparing and ranking oppressions—the proverbial, "I'm more oppressed than you"—locks us all into a dangerous

Patricia Hill Collins, "Toward a New Vision: Race, Class, and Gender as Categories of Analysis and Connection," *Race, Sex, and Class* 1, no. 1 (Fall 1993): 25–46. Reprinted by permission of the author.

dance of competing for attention, resources, and theoretical supremacy. Instead, I suggest that we examine our different experiences within the more fundamental relationship of damnation and subordination. To focus on the particular arrangements that race or class or gender takes in our time and place without seeing these structures as sometimes parallel and sometimes interlocking dimensions of the more fundamental relationship of domination and subordination may temporarily ease our consciences. But while such thinking may lead to short-term social reforms, it is simply inadequate for the task of bringing about long-term social transformation.

While race, class and gender as categories of analysis are essential in helping us understand the structural bases of domination and subordination, new ways of thinking that are not accompanied by new ways of acting offer incomplete prospects for change. To get at that "piece of the oppressor which is planted deep within each of us," we also need to change our daily behavior. Currently, we are all enmeshed in a complex web of problematic relationships that grant our mirror images full human subjectivity while stereotyping and objectifying those most different than ourselves. We often assume that the people we work with, teach, send our children to school with, and sit next to . . . will act and feel in prescribed ways because they belong to given race, social class or gender categories. These judgments by category must be replaced with fully human relationships that transcend the legitimate differences created by race, class and gender as categories of analysis. We require new categories of connection, new visions of what our relationships with one another can be. . . .

[This discussion] addresses this need for new patterns of thought and action. I focus on two basic questions. First, how can we reconceptualize race, class and gender as categories of analysis? Second, how can we transcend the barriers created by our experiences with race, class and gender oppression in order to build the types of coalitions essential for social exchange? To address these questions I contend that we must acquire both new theories of how race, class and gender have shaped the experiences not just of women of color, but of all groups. Moreover, we must see the connections between the categories of analysis and the personal issues in our everyday lives, particularly our scholarship, our teaching and our relationships with our colleagues and students. As Audre Lorde points out, change starts with self, and relationships that we have with those around us must always be the primary site for social change.

How Can We Reconceptualize Race, Class and Gender as Categories of *Analysis?*

To me, we must shift our discourse away from additive analyses of oppression (Spelman, 1982; Collins, 1989). Such approaches are typically based on two key premises. First, they depend on either/or, dichotomous thinking. Persons, things and ideas are conceptualized in terms of their opposites. For example, Black/White, man/woman, thought/feeling, and fact/opinion are defined in oppositional terms. Thought and feeling are not seen as two different and interconnected ways of approaching truth that can coexist in scholarship and teaching. Instead, feeling is defined as antithetical to reason, as its opposite. In spite of the fact that we all have "both/and" identities (I am both a college professor and a mother—I don't stop being a mother when I drop my child off at school, or forget everything I learned while scrubbing the toilet), we persist in trying to classify each other in either/or categories. I live each day as an African-American woman—a race/gender specific experience. And I am not alone. Everyone has a race/gender/class specific identity. Either/or, dichotomous thinking is especially troublesome when applied to theories of oppression because every individual must be classified as being either oppressed or not oppressed. The both/and position of simultaneously being oppressed and oppressor becomes conceptually impossible.

A second premise of additive analyses of oppression is that these dichotomous differences must be ranked. One side of the dichotomy is typically labeled dominant and the other subordinate. Thus, Whites rule Blacks, men are deemed superior to women, and reason is seen as being preferable to emotion. Applying this premise to discussions of oppression leads to the assumption that oppression can be quantified, and that some groups are oppressed more than others. I am frequently asked, "Which has been most oppressive to you, your status as a Black person or your status as a woman?" What I am really being asked to do is divide myself into little boxes and rank my various statuses. If I experience oppression as a both/and phenomenon, why should I analyze it any differently?

Additive analyses of oppression rest squarely on the twin pillars of either/or thinking and the necessity to quantify and rank all relationships in order to know where one stands. Such approaches typically see African-American women as being more oppressed than everyone else because the majority of Black women experience the negative effects of race, class and gender oppression simultaneously. In essence, if you add together separate oppressions, you are left with a grand oppression greater than the sum of its parts.

I am not denying that specific groups experience oppression more harshly than others—lynching is certainly objectively worse than being held up as a sex object. But we must be careful not to confuse this issue of the saliency of one type of oppression in people's lives with a theoretical stance positing the interlocking nature of oppression. Race, class and gender may all structure a situation but may not be equally visible and/or important in people's self-definitions. In certain contexts, such as the antebellum American South and contemporary South America, racial oppression is more visibly salient, while in other contexts, such as Haiti, El Salvador and Nicaragua, social class oppression may be more apparent. For middle-class White women, gender may assume experiential primacy unavailable to poor Hispanic women struggling with the ongoing issues of low-paid jobs and the frustrations of the welfare bureaucracy. This recognition that one category may have salience over another for a given time and place does not minimize the theoretical importance of assuming that race, class and gender as categories of analysis structure all relationships.

In order to move toward new visions of what oppression is, I think that we need to ask new questions. How are relationships of domination and subordination structured and maintained in the American political economy? How do race, class and gender function as parallel and interlocking systems that shape this basic relationship of domination and subordination? Questions such as these promise to move us away from futile theoretical struggles concerned with ranking oppressions and towards analyses that assume race, class and gender are all present in any given setting, even if one appears more visible and salient than the others. Our task becomes redefined as one of reconceptualizing oppression by uncovering the connections among race, class and gender as categories of analysis.

1. The Institutional Dimension of Oppression

Sandra Harding's contention that gender oppression is structured along three main dimensions—the institutional, the symbolic and the individual—offers a useful model for a more comprehensive analysis encompassing race, class and gender oppression (Harding 1989). Systemic relationships of domination and subordination structured through social institutions such as schools, businesses, hospitals, the workplace and government agencies represent the institutional dimension of oppression. Racism, sexism and elitism all have concrete institutional locations. Even though the workings of the institutional dimension of oppression are often obscured with ideologies claiming equality of opportunity, in actuality, race, class and gender place Asian-American women, Native American men, African-American women and other groups in distinct institutional niches with varying degrees of penalty and privilege.

Even though I realize that many . . . would not share this assumption, let us assume that the institutions of American society discriminate, whether by design or by accident. While many of us are familiar with how race, gender and class operate separately to structure inequality, I want to focus on how these three systems interlock in structuring the institutional dimension of oppression. To get at the interlocking nature of race, class and gender, I want you to think about the antebellum plantation as a guiding metaphor for a variety of American social institutions. Even though slavery is typically analyzed as a racist institution, and occasionally as a class institution, I suggest that slavery was a race, class, gender specific institution. Removing any one piece from our analysis diminishes our understanding of the true nature of relations of domination and subordination under slavery.

Slavery was a profoundly patriarchal institution. It rested on the dual tenets of White male authority and White male property, a joining of the political and the economic within the institution of the family. Heterosexism was assumed and all Whites were expected to marry. Control over affluent White women's sexuality remained key to slavery's survival because property was to be passed on to the legitimate heirs of the slave owner. Ensuring affluent White women's virginity and chastity was deeply intertwined with maintenance of property relations.

Under slavery, we see varying levels of institutional protection given to affluent White women, working class and poor White women and enslaved African women. Poor White women enjoyed few of the protections held out to their upper class sisters. Moreover, the devalued status of Black women was key in keeping all White women in their assigned places. Controlling Black women's fertility was also key to the continuation of slavery, for children born to slave mothers themselves were slaves.

African-American women shared the devalued status of chattel with their husbands, fathers and sons. Racism stripped Blacks as a group of legal rights, education and control over their own persons. African-Americans could be whipped, branded, sold, or killed, not because they were poor, or because they were women, but because they were Black. Racism ensured that Blacks would continue to serve Whites and suffer economic exploitation at the hands of all Whites.

So we have a very interesting chain of command on the plantation—the affluent White master as the reigning patriarch, his White wife helpmate to serve him, help him manage his property and bring up his heirs, his faithful servants whose production and reproduction were tied to the requirements of the capitalist political economy and largely propertyless, working class White men and women watching from afar. In essence, the foundations for the contemporary roles of elite White women, poor Black women, working class White men and a series of other groups can be seen in stark relief in this fundamental American social institution. While Blacks experienced the most harsh treatment under slavery, and thus made slavery clearly visible as a racist institution, race, class and gender interlocked in structuring slavery's systemic organization of domination and subordination.

Even today, the plantation remains a compelling metaphor for institutional oppression. Certainly the actual conditions of oppression are not as severe now as they were then. To argue, as some do, that things have not changed all that much denigrates the achievements of those who struggled for social change before us. But the basic relationships among Black men, Black women, elite White women, elite White men, working class White men and working class White women as groups remain essentially intact.

A brief analysis of key American social institutions most controlled by elite White men should convince us of the interlocking nature of race, class and gender in structuring the institutional dimension of oppression. For example, if you are from an American college or university, is your campus a modern plantation? Who controls your university's political economy? Are elite White men overrepresented among the upper administrators and trustees controlling your university's finances and policies? Are elite White men being joined by growing numbers of elite White women helpmates? What kinds of people are in your classrooms grooming the next generation who will occupy these and other decision-making positions? Who are the support staff that produce the mass mailings, order the supplies, fix the leaky pipes? Do African-Americans, Hispanics or other people of color form the majority of the invisible workers who feed you, wash your dishes, and clean up your offices and libraries after everyone else has gone home?

If your college is anything like mine, you know the answers to these questions. You may be affiliated with an institution that has Hispanic women as vice-presidents for finance, or substantial numbers of Black men among the faculty. If so, you are fortunate. Much more typical are colleges where a modified version of the plantation as a metaphor for the institutional dimension of oppression survives.

2. The Symbolic Dimension of Oppression

Widespread, societally sanctioned ideologies used to justify relations of domination and subordination comprise the symbolic dimension of oppression. Central to this process is the use of stereotypical or controlling images of diverse race, class and gender groups. In order to assess the power of this dimension of oppression, I want you to make a list, either on paper or in your head, of "masculine" and "feminine" characteristics. If your list is anything like that compiled by most people, it reflects some variation of the following:

Masculine	*Feminine*
aggressive	passive
leader	follower
rational	emotional
strong	weak
intellectual	physical

Not only does this list reflect either/or dichotomous thinking and the need to rank both sides of the dichotomy, but ask yourself exactly which men and women you had in mind when compiling these characteristics. This list applies almost exclusively to middle class White men and women. The allegedly "masculine" qualities that you probably listed are only acceptable when exhibited by elite White men, or when used by Black and Hispanic men against each other or against women of color. Aggressive Black and Hispanic men are seen as dangerous, not powerful, and are often penalized when they exhibit any of the allegedly "masculine" characteristics. Working class and poor White men fare slightly better and are also denied the allegedly "masculine" symbols of leadership, intellectual competence, and human rationality. Women of color and working class and poor White women are also not represented on this list, for they have never had the luxury of being "ladies." What appear to be universal categories representing all men and women instead are unmasked as being applicable to only a small group.

It is important to see how the symbolic images applied to different race, class and gender groups interact in maintaining systems of domination and subordination. If I were to ask you to repeat the same assignment, only this time, by making separate lists for Black men, Black women, Hispanic women and Hispanic men, I suspect that your gender symbolism would be quite different. In comparing all of the lists, you might begin to see the interdependence of symbols applied to all groups. For example, the elevated images of White womanhood need devalued images of Black womanhood in order to maintain credibility.

While the above exercise reveals the interlocking nature of race, class and gender in structuring the symbolic dimension of oppression, part of its importance lies in demonstrating how race, class and gender pervade a wide range of what appears to be universal language. Attending to diversity in our scholarship, in our teaching, and in our daily lives provides a new angle of vision on interpretations of reality thought to be natural, normal and "true." Moreover, viewing images of masculinity and femininity as universal gender symbolism, rather than as symbolic images that are race, class and gender specific, renders the experiences of people of color and of nonprivileged White women and men invisible. One way to dehumanize an individual or group is to deny the reality of their experiences. So when we refuse to deal with race or class because they do not appear to be directly relevant to gender, we are actually becoming part of someone else's problem.

Assuming that everyone is affected differently by the same interlocking set of symbolic images allows us to move forward toward new analyses. Women of color and White women have different relations to White male authority and this difference explains the distinct gender symbolism applied to both groups. Black women encounter controlling images such as the mammy, the matriarch, the mule and the whore, that encourage others to reject us as fully human people. Ironically, the negative nature of these images simultaneously encourages us to reject them. In contrast, White women are offered seductive images, those that promise to reward them for supporting the status quo. And yet seductive images can be equally controlling. Consider, for example, the views of Nancy White, a 73-year-old Black woman, concerning images of rejection and seduction:

> My mother used to say that the black woman is the white man's mule and the white woman is his dog. Now, she said that to say this: we do the heavy work and get beat whether we do it well or not. But the white woman is closer to the master and he pats them on the head and lets them sleep in the house, but he ain't gon' treat neither one like he was dealing with a person. (Gwaltney, 148)

Both sets of images stimulate particular political stances. By broadening the analysis beyond the confines of race, we can see the varying levels of rejection and seduction available to each of us due to our race, class and gender identity. Each of us lives with an allotted portion of institutional privilege and penalty, and with varying levels of rejection and seduction inherent in the symbolic images applied to us. This is the context in which we make our choices. Taken together, the institutional and symbolic dimensions of oppression create a structural backdrop against which all of us live our lives.

3. The Individual Dimension of Oppression

Whether we benefit or not, we all live within institutions that reproduce race, class and gender oppression. Even if we never have any contact with members of other race, class and gender groups, we all encounter images of these groups and are exposed to the symbolic meanings attached to those images. On this dimension of oppression, our individual biographies vary tremendously. As a result of our institutional and symbolic statuses, all of our choices become political acts.

Each of us must come to terms with the multiple ways in which race, class and gender as categories of analysis frame our individual biographies. I have lived my entire life as an African-American woman from a working class family and this basic fact has had a profound impact on my personal biography. Imagine how different your life might be if you had been born Black, or White, or poor, or of a different race/class/gender group than the one with which you are most familiar. The institutional treatment you would have received and the symbolic meanings attached to your very existence might differ dramatically from that you now consider to be natural, normal and part of everyday life. You might be the same, but your personal biography might have been quite different.

I believe that each of us carries around the cumulative effect of our lives within multiple structures of oppression. If you want to see how much you have been affected by this whole thing, I ask you one simple question—who are your close friends? Who are the people with whom you can share your hopes, dreams, vulnerabilities, fear and victories? Do they look like you? If they are all the same, circumstance may be the cause. For the first seven years of my life I saw only low income Black people. My friends from those years reflected the composition of my community. But now that I am an adult, can the defense of circumstance explain the patterns of people that I trust as my friends and colleagues? When given other alternatives, if my friends and colleagues reflect the homogeneity of one race, class and gender group, then these categories of analysis have indeed become barriers to connection.

I am not suggesting that people are doomed to follow the paths laid out for them by race, class and gender as categories of analysis. While these three structures certainly frame my opportunity structure, I as an individual always have the choice of accepting things as they are, or trying to change them. As Nikki Giovanni points out, "we've got to live in the real world. If we don't like the world we're living in, change it. And if we can't change it, we change ourselves. We can do something" (Tate 1983, 68). While a piece of the oppressor may be planted deep within each of us, we each have the choice of accepting that piece or challenging it as part of the "true focus of revolutionary change."

How Can We Transcend the Barriers Created by Our Experiences with Race, Class and Gender Oppression in Order to Build the Types of Coalitions Essential for Social Change?

Reconceptualizing oppression and seeing the barriers created by race, class and gender as interlocking categories of analysis is a vital first step. But we must transcend these barriers by moving toward race, class and gender as categories of connection, but building relationships and coalitions that will bring about social change. What are some of the issues involved in doing this?

1. Differences in Power and Privilege

First, we must recognize that our differing experiences with oppression create problems in the relationships among us. Each of us lives within a system that vests us with varying levels of power and privilege. These differences in power, whether structured along axes of race, class, gender, age or sexual orientation, frame our relationships. African-American writer June Jordan describes her discomfort on a Caribbean vacation with Olive, the Black woman who cleaned her room:

> . . . even though both "Olive" and "I" live inside a conflict neither one of us created, or even though both of us therefore hurt inside that conflict, I may be one of the monsters she needs to eliminate from her universe and, in a sense, she may be one of the monsters in mine (1985, 47).

Differences in power constrain our ability to connect with one another even when we think we are engaged in dialogue across differences. Let me give you an example. One year, the students in my course "Sociology of the Black Community" got into a heated discussion about the reasons for the upsurge of racial incidents on college campuses. Black students complained vehemently about the apathy and resistance they felt most White students expressed about examining their own racism. Mark, a White male student, found their comments particularly unsettling. After claiming that all the Black people he had ever known had expressed no such beliefs to him, he questioned how representative the viewpoints of his fellow students actually were. When pushed further, Mark revealed that he had participated in conversations over the years with the Black domestic worker employed by his family. Since she had never expressed such strong feelings about White racism, Mark was genuinely shocked by class discussions. Ask yourselves whether that domestic worker was in a position to speak freely. Would it have been wise for her to do so in a situation where the power between the two parties was so unequal?

In extreme cases, members of privileged groups can erase the very presence of the less privileged. When I first moved to Cincinnati, my family and I went on a picnic at a local park. Picnicking next to us was a family of White Appalachians. When I went to push my daughter on the swings, several of the children came over. They had missing, yellowed and broken teeth, they wore old clothing and their poverty was evident. I was shocked. Growing up in a large eastern city, I had never seen such awful poverty among Whites. The segregated neighborhoods in which I grew up made White poverty all but invisible. More importantly, the privileges attached to my newly acquired social class position allowed me to ignore and minimize the poverty among Whites that I did encounter. My reactions to those children made me realize how confining phrases such as "well, at least they're not Black," had become for me. In learning to grant human subjectivity to the Black victims of poverty, I had simultaneously learned to demand White victims of poverty. By applying categories of race to the objective conditions confronting me, I was quantifying and ranking oppressions and missing the very real suffering which, in fact, is the real issue.

One common pattern of relationships across differences in power is one that I label "voyeurism." From the perspective of the privileged, the lives of people of color,

of the poor, and of women are interesting for their entertainment value. The privileged become voyeurs, passive onlookers who do not relate to the less powerful, but who are interested in seeing how the "different" live. Over the years, I have heard numerous African-American students complain about professors who never call on them except when a so-called Black issue is being discussed. The students' interest in discussing race or qualifications for doing so appear unimportant to the professor's efforts to use Black students' experiences as stories to make the material come alive for the White student audience. Asking Black students to perform on cue and provide a Black experience for their White classmates can be seen as voyeurism at its worst.

Members of subordinate groups do not willingly participate in such exchanges but often do so because members of dominant groups control the institutional and symbolic apparatuses of oppression. Racial/ethnic groups, women, and the poor have never had the luxury of being voyeurs of the lives of the privileged. Our ability to survive in hostile settings has hinged on our ability to learn intricate details about the behavior and world view of the powerful and adjust our behavior accordingly. I need only point to the difference in perception of those men and women in abusive relationships. Where men can view their girlfriends and wives as sex objects, helpmates and a collection of stereotyped categories of voyeurism—women must be attuned to every nuance of their partners' behavior. Are women "naturally" better in relating to people with more power than themselves, or have circumstances mandated that men and women develop different skills? . . .

Coming from a tradition where most relationships across difference are squarely rooted in relations of domination and subordination, we have much less experience relating to people as different but equal. The classroom is potentially one powerful and safe space where dialogues among individuals of unequal power relationships can occur. The relationship between Mark, the student in my class, and the domestic workers is typical of a whole series of relationships that people have when they relate across differences in power and privilege. The relationship among Mark and his classmates represents the power of the classroom to minimize those differences so that people of different levels of power can use race, class and gender as categories of analysis in order to generate meaningful dialogues. In this case, the classroom equalized racial difference so that Black students who normally felt silenced spoke out. White students like Mark, generally unaware of how they had been privileged by their whiteness, lost that privilege in the classroom and thus became open to genuine dialogue. . . .

2. Coalitions around Common Causes

A second issue in building relationships and coalitions essential for social change concerns knowing the real reasons for coalition. Just what brings people together? One powerful catalyst fostering group solidarity is the presence of a common enemy. African-American, Hispanic, Asian-American, and women's studies all share the common intellectual heritage of challenging what passes for certified knowledge in the academy. But politically expedient relationships and coalitions like these are fragile because, as June Jordan points out:

It occurs to me that much organizational grief could be avoided if people understood that partnership in misery does not neces-

sarily provide for partnership for change. When we get the monsters off our backs all of us may want to run in very different directions (1985, 47).

Sharing a common cause assists individuals and groups in maintaining relationships that transcend their differences. Building effective coalitions involves struggling to hear one another and developing empathy for each other's points of view. The coalitions that I have been involved in that lasted and that worked have been those where commitment to a specific issue mandated collaboration as the best strategy for addressing the issue at hand.

Several years ago, master's degree in hand, I chose to teach in an inner-city parochial school in danger of closing. The money was awful, the conditions were poor, but the need was great. In my job, I had to work with a range of individuals who, on the surface, had very little in common. We had White nuns, Black middle class graduate students, Blacks from the "community," some of whom had been incarcerated and/or were affiliated with a range of federal anti-poverty programs. Parents formed another part of this community, Harvard faculty another, and a few well-meaning White liberals from Colorado were sprinkled in for good measure.

As you might imagine, tension was high. Initially, our differences seemed insurmountable. But as time passed, we found a common bond that we each brought to the school. In spite of profound differences in our personal biographies, differences that in other settings would have hampered our ability to relate to one another, we found that we were all deeply committed to the education of Black children. By learning to value each other's commitment and by recognizing that we each had different skills that were essential to actualizing that commitment, we built an effective coalition around a common cause. Our school was successful, and the children we taught benefited from the diversity we offered them.

. . . None of us alone has a comprehensive vision of how race, class and gender operate as categories of analysis or how they might be used as categories of connection. Our personal biographies offer us partial views. Few of us can manage to study race, class and gender simultaneously. Instead, we each know more about some dimensions of this larger story and less about others. . . . Just as the members of the school had special skills to offer to the task of building the school, we have areas of specialization and expertise, whether scholarly, theoretical, pedagogical or within areas of race, class or gender. We do not all have to do the same thing in the same way. Instead, we must support each other's efforts, realizing that they are all part of the larger enterprise of bringing about social change.

3. Building Empathy

A third issue involved in building the types of relationships and coalitions essential for social change concerns the issue of individual accountability. Race, class and gender oppression form the structural backdrop against which we frame our relationships— these are the forces that encourage us to substitute voyeurism . . . for fully human relationships. But while we may not have created this situation, we are each responsible for making individual, personal choices concerning which elements of race, class and gender oppression we will accept and which we will work to change.

One essential component of this accountability involves developing empathy for the experiences of individuals and groups different than ourselves. Empathy begins with taking an interest in the facts of other people's lives, both as individuals and as groups. If you care about me, you should want to know not only the details of my personal biography but a sense of how race, class and gender as categories of analysis created the institutional and symbolic backdrop for my personal biography. How can you hope to assess my character without knowing the details of the circumstances I face?

Moreover, by taking a theoretical stance that we have all been affected by race, class and gender as categories of analysis that have structured our treatment, we open up possibilities for using those same constructs as categories of connection in building empathy. For example, I have a good White woman friend with whom I share common interests and beliefs. But we know that our racial differences have provided us with different experiences. So we talk about them. We do not assume that because I am Black, race has only affected me and not her or that because I am a Black woman, race neutralizes the effect of gender in my life while accenting it in hers. We take those same categories of analysis that have created cleavages in our lives, in this case, categories of race and gender, and use them as categories of connection in building empathy for each other's experiences.

Finding common causes and building empathy is difficult, no matter which side of privilege we inhabit. Building empathy from the dominant side of privilege is difficult, simply because individuals from privileged backgrounds are not encouraged to do so. For example, in order for those of you who are White to develop empathy for the experiences of people of color, you must grapple with how your white skin has privileged you. This is difficult to do, because it not only entails the intellectual process of seeing how whiteness is elevated in institutions and symbols, but it also involves the often painful process of seeing how your whiteness has shaped your personal biography. Intellectual stances against the institutional and symbolic dimensions of racism are generally easier to maintain than sustained self-reflection about how racism has shaped all of our individual biographies. Were and are your fathers, uncles, and grandfathers really more capable than mine, or can their accomplishments be explained in part by the racism members of my family experienced? Did your mothers stand silently by and watch all this happen? More importantly, how have they passed on the benefits of their whiteness to you?

These are difficult questions, and I have tremendous respect for my colleagues and students who are trying to answer them. Since there is no compelling reason to examine the source and meaning of one's own privilege, I know that those who do so have freely chosen this stance. They are making conscious efforts to root out the piece of the oppressor planted within them. To me, they are entitled to the support of people of color in their efforts. Men who declare themselves feminists, members of the middle class who ally themselves with antipoverty struggles, heterosexuals who support gays and lesbians, are all trying to grow, and their efforts place them far ahead of the majority who never think of engaging in such important struggles.

Building empathy from the subordinate side of privilege is also difficult, but for different reasons. Members of subordinate groups are understandably reluctant to abandon a basic mistrust of members of powerful groups because this basic mistrust has traditionally been central to their survival. As a Black woman, it would be foolish for me to assume that White women, or Black men, or White men or any other group with a history of exploiting African-American women have my best interests at heart. These groups enjoy varying amounts of privilege over me and therefore I must carefully watch them and be prepared for a relation of domination and subordination.

Like the privileged, members of subordinate groups must also work toward replacing judgments by category with new ways of thinking and acting. Refusing to do so stifles prospects for effective coalition and social change. Let me use another example from my own experiences. When I was an undergraduate, I had little time or patience for the theorizing of the privileged. My initial years at a private, elite institution were difficult, not because the coursework was challenging (it was, but that wasn't what distracted me) or because I had to work while my classmates lived on family allowances (I was used to work). The adjustment was difficult because I was surrounded by so many people who took their privilege for granted. Most of them felt entitled to their wealth. That astounded me.

I remember one incident of watching a White woman down the hall in my dormitory try to pick out which sweater to wear. The sweaters were piled up on her bed in all the colors of the rainbow, sweater after sweater. She asked my advice in a way that let me know that choosing a sweater was one of the most important decisions she had to make on a daily basis. Standing knee-deep in her sweaters, I realized how different our lives were. She did not have to worry about maintaining a solid academic average so that she could receive financial aid. Because she was in the majority, she was not treated as a representative of her race. She did not have to consider how her classroom comments or basic existence on campus contributed to the treatment her group would receive. Her allowance protected her from having to work, so she was free to spend her time studying, partying, or in her case, worrying about which sweater to wear. The degree of inequality in our lives and her unquestioned sense of entitlement concerning that inequality offended me. For a while, I categorized all affluent White women as being superficial, arrogant, overly concerned with material possessions, and part of my problem. But had I continued to classify people in this way, I would have missed out on making some very good friends whose discomfort with their inherited or acquired social class privileges pushed them to examine their position.

Since I opened with the words of Audre Lorde, it seems appropriate to close with another of her ideas. . . .

Each of us is called upon to take a stand. So in these days ahead, as we examine ourselves and each other, our works, our fears, our differences, our sisterhood and survivals, I urge you to tackle what is most dif-ficult for us all, self-scrutiny of our complacencies, the idea that since each of us believes she is on the side of right, she need not examine her position (1985).

I urge you to examine your position.

References

Butler, Johnella. 1989. "Difficult Dialogues." *The Women's Review of Books* 6, no. 5.

Collins, Patricia Hill. 1989. "The Social Construction of Black Feminist Thought." *Signs*. Summer 1989.

Gwaltney, John Langston. 1980. *Drylongso: A Self-Portrait of Black America*. New York: Vintage.

Harding, Sandra. 1986. *The Science Question in Feminism*. Ithaca, New York: Cornell University Press.

Jordan, June. 1985. *On Call: Political Essays*. Boston: South End Press.

Lorde, Audre. 1984. *Sister Outsider*. Trumansberg, New York: The Crossing Press.

——. 1985. "Sisterhood and Survival." Keynote address, conference on the Black Woman Writer and the Diaspora, Michigan State University.

Spelman, Elizabeth. 1982. "Theories of Race and Gender: The Erasure of Black Women." *Quest* 5:36–32.

Tate, Claudia, ed. 1983. *Black Women Writers at Work*. New York: Continuum.

The Death of David Reimer

A Tale of Sex, Science, and Abuse

On May 4, 2004, David Reimer committed suicide in Winnipeg. Thirty-eight years old, he had been a slaughterhouse worker and an odd-job man. He had also been both a boy and a girl, thanks to one of the darker episodes in the history of pseudoscientific hubris.

Born Bruce Reimer in 1965, David suffered a botched circumcision when he was eight months old. Most of his penis was burned off, and reconstructive surgery was too primitive at the time to restore it. Dr. John Money, a sexologist at Johns Hopkins University, persuaded Reimer's parents to have their son completely castrated and raised as a girl.

This was not simply a matter of trying to make the best of a bad situation. Money had been a leading exponent of the theory that children were born psychosexually neutral and could be assigned to either gender in the first years of their life. He had retreated somewhat from the most radical statement of this thesis, but stood by the central contention that when it came to sexual identity, nurture trumped nature. Bruce—now named Brenda—was an ideal test case. Along with everything else, she was an identical twin; so as an object of study, she came bundled with a built-in control.

Money trumpeted the results in his 1972 book *Man & Woman, Boy & Girl*, written with the psychiatrist Anke A. Ehrhardt; a more popularized account appeared in *Sexual Signatures* (1976), written with the reporter Patricia Tucker. By Money's account, Bruce/Brenda moved easily into her new identity. She soon "was observed to have a clear preference for dresses over slacks and to take pride in her long hair," he wrote in *Man & Woman*. She "was much neater than her brother, and in contrast with him, disliked to be dirty." Though it "needed perhaps more training than usual," she usually urinated sitting down, and when she did attempt to stand she was simply "copying her brother." She took to housework and to helping her mother in the kitchen, while her brother "could not care less about it." Her taste in toys ran to dolls, and despite some "tomboyish traits" she clearly was adapting to life as a girl.

Scientists with a less enthusiastic view of infant sex reassignment, Money added, had been "instrumental in wrecking the lives of unknown numbers of hermaphroditic youngsters."

For two decades this remained the accepted view of what happened. It helped influence many parents—approximately one or two for every 1,000 births, according to

Jesse Walker, "The Death of David Reimer: A Tale of Sex, Science, and Abuse." Posted on reason.com, May 24, 2004. Reprinted by permission of *Reason Magazine*.

a 2000 paper in the *American Journal of Human Biology*—to opt for "corrective" sexual reassignment of their babies: not just hermaphrodites and victims of accidents like Reimer's, but boys born with abnormally small genitals. But then Dr. Milton Diamond, a longtime critic of Money's theories, reconstructed what had actually happened, co-authoring a paper on the case that was published in the March 1997 *Archives of Pediatrics and Adolescent Medicine*. Several follow-up stories appeared in the press, notably John Colapinto's excellent account in *Rolling Stone*; after Reimer agreed to make his identity public, Colapinto expanded the article into an engrossing book, *As Nature Made Him* (2000). Now that the patient was able to speak for himself, a very different story was on display:

- Brenda Reimer resisted being classified as a girl from the beginning. The first time she wore a dress, she tried to rip it off. She preferred her brother's toys to her own. (A toy sewing machine was untouched, Colapinto writes, "until the day when Brenda, who loved to take things apart to see how they worked, sneaked a screwdriver from her dad's tool kit and dismantled the toy.") She got into fights, insisted on peeing standing up, and ran into terrible problems at school, where the other kids quickly recognized her as someone who didn't fit the ordinary sexual categories. By the time she was 10, she was declaring that she wanted to grow up to marry a woman, not a man.

- Money's meetings with Brenda were a darkly comic study in how a scientist could refuse to see the evidence he didn't want to see, and how a subject can gradually learn to respond to his cues. Worse, his efforts to make her conform to his expectations were coercive and abusive. Her refusal to receive vaginal surgeries—her penis was gone, but her doctors had not yet put a vagina in its place—was met not with an effort to understand her stance but with a series of attempts to manipulate her into agreeing to the procedures. (She succeeded in avoiding the surgery but was compelled to take estrogen pills, though she flushed them when she could.) Also disturbing was Money's belief that Brenda, in Colapinto's words, "must understand at a very early age the differences between male and female sex organs." Not an objectionable idea in itself, except that Money accomplished it by showing Brenda and her brother pictures of adults having sex and by forcing them to disrobe and examine each other's genitals. Worst of all, he allegedly insisted, starting when the twins were six, that they "play at thrusting movements and copulation"—more bluntly, that they pretend to have sex in various positions while he watched. (This last detail has been disputed.)

- Finally, when Brenda Reimer learned the truth about herself, at age 14, she decided to start living her life as a boy. She had her estrogen-created breasts removed, took testosterone injections, changed her name to David, and eventually had surgery to create a penis. In 1990 David married. The allegedly successful transformation of a boy into a girl was in fact a complete failure.

For much of his career, Money's admirers saw him as a bold pioneer fighting puritanical reactionaries. This was his self-image as well. He touted himself as a defender of sexual liberation: for the rights of gays and other sexual minorities, for legalized pornography, for breaking down social taboos. But this seemingly libertarian attitude obscured an authoritarian core. When the truth about the Reimer case was exposed, the sexologist suddenly seemed much more repressive than the conservatives he hated.

Not that he acknowledged this. He told Colapinto that the press's embrace of Diamond's exposé was a product of right-wing media bias and "the antifeminist movement," insisting that "they say masculinity and femininity are built into the genes so women should get back to the mattress and the kitchen." By this time, though, his critics were emerging not just from the right but from the community of open intersexuals—people born with mixed or indeterminate gender. It turned out they don't like to be coerced by social engineers any more than they like to be coerced by the party of rigid sex roles.

It's the Intersex Society of North America that's leading the charge against the procedures Money championed, calling for "a model of care that is patient-centered, rather than concealment-centered." What this means in practice is summed up by a series of humane principles listed on the front page of the society's website, among them: "Intersexuality is basically a problem of stigma and trauma, not gender," "Parents' distress must not be treated by surgery on the child," and "Honest, complete disclosure is good medicine." It's significant that groups like the Intersex Society focus their attention not on the scientific debate over the roots of gender identification, but on the proper way to treat those people who have landed in their position. It's interesting to compare and contrast the battles they're fighting with the battles being fought by transsexuals. One group is often cited by those who favor the nature side of the nature/nurture debate, while the other is embraced by the nurturists; one group wants to stop involuntary surgeries, and the other wants fewer barriers to *voluntary* surgeries. But both are essentially asking that they be allowed to decide how to live their lives; both want final say on what is done to their own bodies. That basic respect for the individual is what's missing from people like Money, who preach liberation but practice something much less attractive.

And David Reimer? I of course don't know what went through his mind when he decided to end his life. He had just lost his job, a big investment had failed, his marriage had split up, and his twin brother had died not long before, depressing events all. But surely the "therapeutic" abuse he had suffered was a factor in his death. It figured heavily, after all, in almost everything else that happened in his life.

Whatever I Feel . . .

"Whatever I feel, that's the way I am. I was born a girl, and that girl died one day and a boy was born. And the boy was born from that girl in me. I am proud of who I am. A lot of people actually envy us." Chi-Chi, who lives in a village in the Dominican Republic, is speaking to filmmaker Rolando Sanchez for his 1997 documentary *Guevote*.

The film portrays the daily lives of Chi-Chi and Bonny, two "pseudo-hermaphrodites," and the way in which their families, partners and other villagers respond to them.

They are not alone. A rare form of pseudo-hermaphroditism was first found among a group of villagers in the Dominican Republic in the early 1970s. Thirty-eight people were traced with the condition, coming from 23 extended families and spanning four generations.

Chi-Chi's mother has ten children. Three of those ten are girls, three of them are boys "and four are of this special sort," she says. "I knew that this sort of thing existed before I had my own kids. But I never thought that it would happen to me . . . I told them to accept their destiny, because God knows what he's doing. And I said that real men often achieve less than those who were born as girls. And that's how it turned out. My sons who are real men haven't achieved as much as the others."

The medical explanation is that, while still in the womb, some male babies are unable to produce the testosterone which helps external male genitals to develop. They are born with a labia-like scrotum, a clitoris-like penis and undescended testes.

In the Dominican Republic many of these children were first assumed to be female and were brought up as such. But because they were genetically male, they began to develop male characteristics at puberty, including penis growth and descending testes. Villagers gave these children the local name guevedoche or "balls at twelve."

For some scientists the phenomenon presented an ideal "natural experiment" that would help them to prove once and for all that hormones are far more important than culture in the development of gender identity. A research team headed by Julliane Imperato-McGinley proposed that in a laissez-faire environment, with no medical or social intervention, the child would naturally develop a male gender identity at puberty, in spite of having been reared as female.

Not everyone agreed with this rather simplistic approach, however. Ethnographer Gilbert Herdt pointed out the guevedoche were different and they knew it as they had compared their genitals with those of girls during public bathing. Villagers,

Zachary I. Nataf, "Whatever I Feel . . ." Posted on newint.org, April 1, 1998. Reprinted by permission of *New Internationalist*.

who were familiar with the guevedoche over generations, accepted them as a "third sex" category, sometimes referring to them as machi-embra (male-female).

Furthermore, not all guevedoche wanted to adopt a male gender identity after puberty. In the documentary *Guevote*, Bonny relates the case of Lorenza. "She had more chances as a woman. Lots of men fell in love with her. She always wore women's clothes and had very long hair. She liked it when men fell in love with her. That's why she wanted to stay a woman and not become a man."

Here then is a community that recognizes the actual existence of "third sex" people as part of human nature and creates corresponding gender roles to accommodate them. It's an attitude that enables Bonny to say: "If I am like this, God will know why. . . . If I feel good, why should I change things? This is how I grew up, why look for something else?"

The Law and the Knife

Such an accepting approach to gender ambiguity has not been the pattern in most of the Western world. Far from it.

Since the routine practice of correcting the ambiguous genitalia of intersexed children began in the US and Europe in the late 1950s, debates have raged about whether gender identity and roles are biologically determined or culturally determined.

The work of John Money and colleagues at Johns Hopkins University and Hospital, Maryland, has had a major impact on the treatment of intersex children, transsexuals and other sex-variant people.

Money advised on the famous case of the identical twin boy who had been reassigned as a girl after he lost his penis in a circumcision accident at the age of seven months in 1963. The child underwent plastic surgery to make his genitals female-appearing and he was treated with female hormones at adolescence.

Between 1973 and 1975 Money reported a completely favorable outcome and this became the key case in the following 20 years. The case influenced the treatment of boys born with "too small" penises, and led to the recommendation that their penises and testes be removed and the boys be surgically reassigned as girls before the age of three "to grow up as complete a female as possible." In these cases quality of life was based on ideas of adequate heterosexual penetration. According to the Johns Hopkins team, the twin had subsequently been "lost to follow-up."

But this was not so. As it turned out, the twin did not feel or act like a girl and had discarded prescribed estrogen pills when aged 12. She had refused additional surgery to deepen the vagina that surgeons had constructed for her at 17 months, despite repeated attempts to convince her she would never find a partner unless she had surgery and lived as female. At the age of 14 the twin refused to return to Johns Hopkins and persuaded local physicians to provide a mastectomy, phalloplasty and male hormones. He now lives as an adult man.

Intersexuals, popularly referred to as "hermaphrodites," are usually born with genitals somewhere between male and female—rarely with two complete sets as in myth. The number of such births is more common than most people realize, with the highest estimates in the US as four percent of births.

According to the Intersex Society of North America one in every 2,000 infants is born with ambiguous genitalia from about two dozen causes. There are more than 2,000 surgeries performed in the US each year aimed at surgically assigning a sex to these intersex patients. The Intersex Society campaigns against what it sees as the unethical medical practice of performing cosmetic surgery on infants who cannot give consent.

Doctors believe that quality of life is only possible for individuals who conform to male or female sex and gender. But the founder of the Intersex Society, Cheryl Chase, believes that "most people would be better off with no surgery." Born with ambiguous genitalia herself she was raised as a boy until 18 months old when physicians told her family that she was really a girl and removed her enlarged clitoris. At the age of eight she underwent an operation to remove what she later learned was the testicular part of her ovo-testes. She currently lives as a woman and, like many intersex individuals, is lesbian. The surgical excision and scar tissue has left her without clitoral sensation or orgasmic response. Says Ms. Chase: "Genital mutilation" is a phrase that's easy for us to apply to somebody who belongs to a Third World culture, but any mutilating practice that's delivered by licensed medical practitioners in our world has an aura of scientific credibility."

Her experience is shared by many intersexuals who as children underwent repeated unexplained examinations, surgery, pain and infection. This has gone on for four decades and in most cases the children have been "lost to follow-up." This means there has been no reliable medical data to assess the effects of surgery or to provide guidance for future practice.

Cosmetic genital surgery is used to "normalize" the appearance of ambiguous genitalia. It is admitted by surgeons to be an attempt to alleviate a "psychosocial emergency" rather than a medical one. Instead of offering intersex children and their families or friends counseling to support them in accepting difference, doctors whip up a crisis which they can then fix with available medical technology. Ambiguous genitals are referred to as "deformed" before surgery and "corrected" after. But the reported experience of intersexuals who went through this in childhood is a sense of having been "intact" before surgery and mutilated after it.

And children were often lied to. A typical example is recounted by a woman who, when her body began to change at the age of 12, was told that she needed surgery to remove her ovaries because she had cancer. What actually happened during the operation was her clitoris and newly descended testes were removed.

The adage that "it is easier to dig a hole than build a pole" accounts for why most intersex individuals are made into girls. The standards which mark maleness allow penises as short as 2.5 cm and femaleness allow clitorises only as large as 0.9 cm. Infants with appendages between 0.9 cm and 2.5 cm are, according to Suzanne Kessler, considered unacceptable and require surgical intervention. In some cases where parents haven't even noticed a problem doctors still insist on surgery. Baby girls as young as six weeks may be operated upon to deepen their vaginas, even though the surgery is not always successful and has to be repeated at various stages as they grow up.

Some experts have their doubts. Dr. Reiner, Assistant Professor of child and adolescent psychiatry at Johns Hopkins University warns against placing too great an emphasis on the genitals, pointing out that "the brain is the most important sex organ in the body."

Telling the Difference

So how do we determine someone's sex? It's actually far more complex than most people imagine. There are no absolutes in nature, only statistical probabilities. We all begin life with a common anatomy which then differentiates if there is a Y chromosome present. This activates the production of testosterone, appropriate receptors in the brain and the formation of testes. The other features which do not develop remain in the body in vestigial form.

Several factors can be taken into account in determining a person's biological sex. They include chromosomal sex (X and Y, for example); hormonal sex (estrogen and testosterone); gonadal sex (ovaries and testes); genital sex (vagina and penis, for example); reproductive sex (sperm-carrying and inseminating; gestating and lactating); and other associated internal organs (like the uterus or the prostate).

These factors are not always consistent with each other. In fact science admits everyone falls somewhere along a continuum. But few people would know if they were 100-percent male or 100-percent female, chromosomally or hormonally, as there are not many cases in everyday practice in which this would be tested. Unless you want to take part in the Olympic Games, that is, in which case you would have to undergo a chromosome sex test, although this has been abandoned as unfair and unreliable by other sports bodies. The *British Journal of Sports Medicine* claims that one in 500 female athletes and about one in 500 male athletes would fail the chromosome gender test. This is because chromosome variations do not necessarily affect physical appearance. A test might determine an athlete is not a woman for the sake of competition, but that certainly does not make her a man in her everyday life. Other indicators of sex are subject to similar variations. Even the capacity to reproduce is not a clear indicator: some intersex people have had children. The so-called biological line between male and female is frankly quite fuzzy.

So much for sex. But sex is not gender. Sex is biological. Gender is social, cultural, psychological and historical. It is used to describe people and their roles in society, the jobs they do and the way they dress, how they are meant to behave.

A person's gender is usually assigned at birth, with a cursory look at the genitals. The "boy" or "girl" which is documented on the birth certificate affects almost everything else that happens to that child socially for the rest of his or her life.

The Third Gender

Responses to ambiguous genitals vary from culture to culture. But in some societies that do not have access to surgery or whose world view is not mediated by biological "facts" of science, there is more space for those who don't fit the norm. These children are accepted as a "third sex" within the social order.

One of the most humane and enlightened approaches was observed in the 1930s among the Native American Navajo people. The Navajo recognized three physical categories: male, female and hermaphrodite or nadle. Nadles had a special status, specific tasks and clothing styles, and were often consulted for their wisdom and skills.

In India the hijra have a 2,500-year-old history. Known contemporarily as a "third gender" caste, hijra translates as hermaphrodite or eunuch or "sacred erotic female-man." They include intersex people, assigned both as male or female, but also attract to their community a wide range of transvestites, homosexual prostitutes and religious devotees of the Mother Goddess Bahuchara Mata.

Elsewhere, in the Eastern highlands of Papua New Guinea, third-sex people are known as kwolu-aatmwol or "female thing transforming into male thing." Medically they are like the guevedoche in the Dominican Republic. Although in some instances they may be killed at birth, most kwolu-aatmwol are accepted as such and are partially raised in the direction of masculinity. They retain some female elements to their unique identity but this does not prevent them from becoming respected shamans or war leaders.

In most parts of the world, however, powerful taboos operate, underpinning fear and discrimination. Sexually ambiguous bodies are threatening. Perhaps they elicit desire, possessing it might seem an erotic potential beyond those with ordinary genitals. Maybe the notion of sex or gender mutability provokes a kind of terror or gender vertigo.

Whatever the cause, medical professionals and others end up favoring drastic surgical remedies for minor conditions that present no medical or functional dangers.

But what about compassion and faith in the ability of the parents to cope with their own emotional pain and distress about their child's "imperfection" and to nurture that child despite their difference? What about the rights of the child, especially the right of the child to decide their gender identity, if different from what the experts have designated it to be?

Challenging such rigidity is the Transgender Movement. This is a broad alliance of people who are inclined to cross the gender line. It includes cross-dressers and transvestites as well as intersex people and transsexuals—both those who have and have not had "gender realignment" surgery.

Transsexuals whose gender identity is in conflict with their birth gender usually want to achieve a congruence of identity, role and anatomy by having sex-reassignment surgery. But increasingly transsexuals are taking the option to be "out" as transsexual and are deciding against surgery, without compromising their core gender identity. It's simple. Some men don't have penises and have vaginas, some women have penises and don't have vaginas.

The trend toward gender non-conformity is growing and has come about partly as a result of anger at discrimination, stigmatization, lack of civil rights and a reluctance on the part of the authorities to pursue those who commit hate crimes against nonconformists.

As a transgendered man (female to male transsexual) I do not "pass" as simply male but am "out" in order to campaign for nondiscrimination and Transgender Pride. I did not choose to be transsexual, nor did I change gender roles in protest against society's oppressive gender system. I did it to achieve an authenticity and outward expression of a deeply abiding sense of myself as a gendered being. During transition I became more fully and truly myself, suspending the symbolic hold society's rules had over my body in order to achieve it. The rigidity of the rules is what is not natural.

There are specific struggles, such as trying to get legal recognition and legal rights in societies where one has to be either male or female. Attitudes are very fixed. In Britain, for example, even post-operative transsexuals are legally padlocked forever to the gender written on their birth certificates, even though this contravenes the European Charter on Human Rights. While in the US, gender non-conformists are still listed in the American Psychiatric Association's Diagnostic and Statistical Manual of Mental Disorders.

But those who don't fit the rules are drawing encouragement from information about third-gender identities in other cultures. As this space expands, more transgender and intersex people are opting to live bi-gendered or hybrid gendered lives, choosing hermaphroditic bodies, through surgery, to match their core sense of who they are.

This expansion is not only an issue for intersex or transgender people. It liberates everyone from rigid and stereotypic ways of being masculine and feminine, mixing the best of all for everyone.

Perhaps it will help pave the way to greater gender equality—or better still, irrelevance.

Defining and Producing Genitals

Obstetricians do not stand at the delivery table with ruler in hand, comparing the genitals they see with a table of values. They seem to know ambiguity when they see it. In the medical literature on intersexuality, where physicians communicate their findings and their assumptions, the phrase "ambiguous genitals" is used freely with no apparent need to define what "ambiguous" means in this context. One could say that ambiguous genitals are described ambiguously. It is not uncommon to read statements like, "Their [intersexed] external genitals look much more like a clitoris and labia than a penis or scrotum." One surgeon writes, without further specification, that the tip of the phallus should be the "expected size for the patient's age." Another states that the need for surgery "must be judged on the basis of the size of the shaft and glans of the clitoris in relation to the size of the patient and the interrelationship of the labia, mons veneris, and pubis.

One way to interpret this vagueness is that the ambiguity is so obvious that a physician who has seen scores of genitals has no need to validate the obvious. But the nonmedical reader is left wondering to what extent genitals must be ambiguous before they are seen to be in need of "correction."

There are, of course, normative data on genital size, shape, and location, but I will delay a discussion of specifications in order to consider the meaning of genital variations for physicians, as projected through their justifications for surgery and their descriptions of aberrant genitals.

Genital Intolerance

Physicians describe all genital surgery on intersexed infants as necessary. Yet there are at least three categories of distinguishable genital surgery:

1. that which is *lifesaving*—for example, a urethra is rerouted so that the infant can pass urine out of his or her body;
2. that which *improves the quality of life*—for example, the urethral opening is redesigned so that a child can eventually urinate without spraying urine on the toilet seat; and
3. that which is *aesthetic*—for example, the small penis is augmented so that the (eventual) man will feel that he looks more manly.

Nowhere in the medical literature on intersexuality are these different motivations alluded to. In fact, although variant genitals rarely pose a threat to the child's life, the postdelivery situation is referred to as a "neonatal psychosexual emergency," seeming to require life-saving intervention.

Few arguments are put forth in defense of performing a surgery on intersexed infants. When pressed for a reason, physicians assert that "normal" genitals will maximize the child's social adjustment and acceptance by the families. Physicians claim they are acting in the interest of parents, who are motivated by a desire to protect their child from teasing.

Teasing is not an insignificant construct in theories about gender. Philosopher Ellen Feder exposes the way psychiatry uses testimony about teasing not only to justify treatment of Gender Identity Disorder in children but also to define it. Feder notes that what alarms teachers and parents about a child's cross-gender behavior is not the behavior per se but the other children's reactions to it. Teasing and name-calling are one of the manifest symptoms of a child gender disturbance. Children on the playground are treated "as a kind of natural tribunal," and the medical profession imbues this with authority, rather than treating the teasing and the institutions that tolerate it as in need of correction. Obviously, the same could be said of the management of intersex. Much is made of the possibility of teasing, but documentation is not provided for how teasing has negatively impacted those rare people whose intersexed genitals were not "surgicalized." Nor is there a discussion in the medical literature about procedures for counteracting (or curing) the teasing.

One endocrinologist and intersex specialist, in defending current practices, says that not doing surgery would be unacceptable to parents because "some of the prejudices run very deep." Implicit in this defense is that the genitals themselves carry the burden of evoking acceptance. There is no sense that the burden is or ought to be on people to learn to accept the genitals. As one intersexual said, "It's difficult to be Black in this culture, too, but we don't bleach the skin of Black babies."

An argument for surgery that is grounded in prejudice overlooks the fact that many bodily related prejudices have been moderated. More people than ever before discuss their cancer histories in public, are open about their AIDS status, and admit to having had an abortion. These changes have required a different way of talking, and it can be argued that the mere fact of talking differently has helped create changes in the way people think about cancer, AIDS, and abortion. Rather than assuming that physicians (like anyone else) are primarily motivated by greed and the power to impose their definitions on the ignorant, we could be more generous and assume that they (like anyone else) find it difficult to imagine new ways of talking in familiar situations. . . . I propose some new ways for physicians to talk differently about intersexuality, predicated on more comfortable attitudes about variant genitals.

Current attitudes about variant genitals are embedded (not too deeply) in medical reports and offer insight into the late-twentieth-century medical management of intersexuality. Feelings about larger-than-typical clitorises are illustrated by these representative quotations (my emphasis):

The excision of a hypertrophied clitoris is to be preferred over allowing a *dis-*

figuring and embarrassing phallic structure to remain.

The anatomic *derangements* [were] surgically corrected. . . . Surgical techniques . . . remedy the *deformed* external genitals. . . . [E]ven patients who suffered from major clitoral *overgrowth* have responded well. . . . [P]atients born with *obtrusive* clitoromegaly have been encountered. . . . [N]ine females had persistent phallic enlargement that was *embarrassing* or *offensive* and incompatible with satisfactory feminine presentation or adjustment. [After] surgery no prepubertal girl . . . described *troublesome* or painful erections.

Female babies born with an *ungainly* masculine enlargement of the clitoris evoke grave concern in their parents. . . . [The new clitoroplasty technique] allow[s] erection without cosmetic *offense*.

Failure to [reduce the glans and shaft] will leave a button of *unsightly tissue*.

[Another surgeon] has suggested . . . total elimination of the *offending* shaft of the clitoris.

[A particular surgical technique] can be included as part of the procedure when the size of the glans is *challenging* to a feminine cosmetic result.

These descriptions suggest not only that there is a size and malformation problem but that there is an aesthetic and moral violation. The language is emotional. Researchers seem disgusted. The early items on the list suggest that the large clitoris is imperfect and ugly. The later items suggest more of a personal affront. Perhaps the last item says it most transparently: the clitoris is "challenging."

A social psychologist should ask: How were embarrassment and offense displayed? If the clitoris is troubling, offending, and embarrassing, who exactly is troubled, offended, and embarrassed and why? Not only are these questions not answered by intersex specialists, they are not even asked. A comment from an intersexed adult woman about her childhood is a relevant counterpoint: "I experienced the behavior of virtually everyone towards me as absolutely dishonest, embarrassing." Her comment reminds us that objects in the world (even non-normative organs) are not embarrassing; rather, people's reactions to them are. Another intersexual woman's "uncorrected" clitoris was described by her sexual partner as "easy to find." Whether a clitoris is easy to find is arguably of some importance in sexual interactions, but it is not a criterion that physicians use for determining the suitable size for a clitoris.

An unexceptional quotation about the clitoris further substantiates the physicians' attitude:

> The clitoris is not essential for *adequate* sexual function and sexual *gratification* . . . but its preservation would seem to be *desirable* if achieved while maintaining *satisfactory* appearance and function. . . . Yet the clitoris clearly has a relation to erotic stimulation and to sexual gratification and its presence is desirable, even in patients with intersexed anomalies if that presence does not interfere with *cosmetic, psychological, social and sexual* adjustment. (my emphases)

Using my emphases as a guide, the alert reader should have some questions about the above quotation: Is "adequate sexual function" the same as "gratification"? If not, then which refers to the ability to orgasm?

Why is the presence of the clitoris only desirable if it maintains a satisfactory appearance (whatever that is) and does not interfere? Lastly, how are the four different adjustments assessed and ranked, and is the order accidental?

Compared to language describing the larger-than-average clitoris, the language describing the small penis is less emotional but no less laden with value judgments. Common descriptors for the small penis are "short, buried, and anomalous." Sometimes there is a discussion about whether the microphallus is normally proportioned or whether it has a "*feminine stigmata* typical of intersexuality" indicative of "*arrested (feminine) development*" (my emphases).

The emotionality in the case of the small penis is reserved for the child "who cannot be a boy with this insignificant organ. . . . They *must* be raised as females. . . . They are *doomed* to life as a male without a penis." This last quotation suggests . . . that if the penis is small enough, some physicians treat it as though it does not actually exist. Given its size, it does not qualify as a penis, and therefore the child does not qualify as a boy. "Experience has shown that the most *heartbreaking* maladjustment attends those patients who have been raised as males in the vain hope that the penis will grow to a more masculine appearance and size 'at a later date'" (my emphases).

Physicians do not question whether a large clitoris ill prepares a girl for the female role. The emphasis is more on its ugliness. In contrast, physicians' descriptions of the micropenis are tied quite explicitly to gender role (my emphases): "Is the size of the phallus . . . *adequate* to support a male sex assignment? [If not], those patients [regardless of genotype] are *unsuited* for the mascu-

line role." A ten-year-old boy (with a microphallus) considering sex change was given testosterone ointment, after which he "*reaffirmed his allegiance to things masculine.*" "The sexual identification of the patients by their parents seemed less ambiguous following [testosterone] treatment, and the parents encouraged *more appropriate male behavior* in the patients following treatment." After Barbara's sixteenth birthday, her penis developed erections, she produced ejaculations, and she found herself feeling a *sexual interest in girls.*"

The penis needs to be large enough to support masculinity (in the eyes of the parents and the child). If it is really a penis, it will push the child toward the "male" gender role, even, as the last example shows, if the child is a girl.

Given the pejorative language used to portray the large clitoris, and the pitying language applied to the child with the small penis, it is not surprising that genital surgery in these cases is described as necessary. It is affirmed as necessary, though, not because anyone (or any one profession) has deemed it so but because the genital, itself, required the improvement. The quotations below (my emphases) establish that the organ carries the message itself; there is no messenger:

Given that the clitoris *must* be reduced, what is the best way to do it?

When the female sex is assigned, an operation on the clitoris together with other *necessary* procedures to modify the genitalia becomes *necessary* for the establishment of proper psychological and social adjustment.

The size of an enlarged clitoris *demanding* clitorectomy cannot be stated in exact measurements.

The child with hypertrophy of the clitoris will *require* corrective surgery to achieve an acceptable functional and cosmetic result.

Where does the clitoris get its right to demand reduction? Presumably from nature. If it is an affront to nature, it is understandable why the language used to describe it is so emotional. Unlike the large clitoris, which is too big for its own good, the micropenis is too small for its own good and "demands" to be made into a clitoris. However, although it is widely assumed that men with micropenises are unhappy—and should these men be lucky enough to have female partners, they, too, will be unhappy—there is evidence to the contrary. The physicians' assertion that penises of insufficient length are "inadequate" implies that penises that fall within the measurement range are adequate. Adequacy as a physical measurement rather than an interpersonal negotiation is a neat way of side-stepping a difficult social-psychological determination. (It is probably not irrelevant that the vast majority of genital surgeons are male.)

To summarize, the medical point of view is that large clitorises and small penises are wrong and need to be, in the words of medical management, "corrected." The term "correction" not only has a surgical connotation but a disciplinary one as well. In this, as in all important enterprises, words matter. An intersexed woman chastised me for the title of a paper I wrote, "Creating Good Looking Genitals in the Service of Gender." "Fact is," she said, "they don't create, they destroy."

Who has the power to name? Physicians talk about "medical advancements in surgical correction," but some people subjected to such surgeries refer to them as "genital mutilations." Those opposed to male circumcision contribute to the argument about the power to name genital interventions. They refer to the penis with a foreskin as the penis in its natural, *intact* state and write about circumcision as *amputation*. In their graphic descriptions, they refer to the *"stripping* of the glans" and even *"skinning* the infant penis alive" (my emphases), instead of the benign "snipping" of the foreskin. If, as happens on rare occasion, a male is born without a foreskin, it is noted in his records as a birth defect called aposthia, suggesting that the foreskin should have been there all along. It is a peculiar body part that should have been there only to be removed. Why, too, does the medical profession refer to the natural bonds between the foreskin and the glans of the newborn as "adhesions," since the ordinary meaning of adhesions is "unwanted and unhealthy attachments which often form during the healing process after surgery or injury"? Why do physicians write about "a more natural appearance of a penis without the foreskin," when what they really mean is "nicer looking"?

"Mutilation," a word we usually apply to other cultures, signals a distancing from and denigration of those cultures, and reinforces a sense of cultural superiority. One culture's mutilation is another's ritual. The manner in which intersex management is medically ritualized protects it from claims of mutilation until one moves outside the medical culture and takes a different perspective.

7 Catherine Lord

Subject

Her Baldness Meets Beth and Gets High on Gender

Wednesday/September 27, 2000

In a message dated 9/27/00 CBLORD@UCI.EDU writes to FOCL'SRB:

Subject: Her Baldness Meets Beth and Gets High on Gender

American Airlines, flight 19, JFK to LAX, last Sunday

10:30 a.m., Eastern Standard Time. Her Baldness, upgraded by her gracious and generous and very GIRL (that particular morning) friend from coach to business class and loving her wide window seat with her own blanket and her own pillow says Perrier please while giving the flight attendant her black leather jacket and spilling the Sunday *New York Times*, the real one, the big one, out of a plastic bag, not to mention two thick unillustrated academic books on the history of food, which will of course go unread during the flight, and the latest issue of *Vanity Fair*, which will not.

10:45 a.m. Flight 19 takes off, on time.

11:00 a.m. The flight attendant distributes menus. Pasta involving cream sauce and a lot of cheese, chicken involving a lot of butter, and salad involving a lot of cold beef.

11:15 a.m. The flight attendant, the same flight attendant, a thin white woman in her forties, offers her a choice of drinks. Kim takes club soda with ice and lime. What would you like, sir? the flight attendant inquires of Her Baldness. As Her Baldness has previously encountered gender misidentification, she adopts the pedagogical strategy of nonconfrontation. She manifests enormous indecisiveness about goodies, wavering between mixed nuts and oyster crackers, or both, or neither, or lemon or lime, or ice or not, or flat or sparkling. She settles on club soda, ice, no lime. She is so anxious to give the flight attendant an opportunity to reflect on gender possibilities that she asks for tomato juice in addition to club soda. The flight attendant is amicable, cooperative and patient. Her Baldness congratulates herself on her maturity in using details such as the temperature of a warmed cashew to give the flight attendant an opportunity to reconsider the social construction of gender

Catherine Lord, "Subject: Her Baldness Meets Beth and Gets High on Gender," from *The Summer of Her Baldness: A Cancer Improvisation* (Austin: University of Texas, 2004), 117–123. Copyright © 2004. By permission of the University of Texas Press.

NOTE: In this excerpt from Catherine Lord's photo memoir on cancer, she refers to herself as "Her Baldness."

without provocation or direct criticism. Perhaps, after all, cancer has been a transformative experience for Her Baldness. When the cart rolls off, Her Baldness and the girlfriend agree that the real question is how long it took the flight attendant to change her mind.

11:39 a.m. The flight attendant inquires as to our lunch preferences. As before, she approaches Kim first. Kim votes chicken. The flight attendant turns to Her Baldness. Sir, what will you have this morning? So. Her Baldness has passed from the category of sick female (or possibly, recovering Buddhist nun) into the category of white male. The problem of female baldness has found a solution: disappear female. If bald isn't female, bald is fine. If bald isn't female, bald isn't grotesque. Out there among the clueless heteros, it's easier to see a straight couple than a queer one. The luscious lipstick lesbian, blonde, good haircut, loaded with the signifiers of femme (an identity Kim emphatically rejects) is disappeared into straight woman. The skinny tortured pale butch (an identity to which I, on the other hand, aspire) is disappeared into straight man.

Her Baldness chooses the gourmet salad with slow roasted tomatoes, please hold the chateaubriand and substitute smoked salmon if there is any left after the appetizer course, a long conversation designed to give the flight attendant another opportunity to reflect upon the nuances of gender. Why not try the chicken, CATHERINE? Kim asks. Oh, I forgot, CATHERINE, you're not eating chicken these days.

11:41 a.m. Her Baldness observes, silently, to herself, that in addition to her black cap, she is wearing a wrinkled white man's shirt from the thrift store, black jeans, and Prada shoes that could go either way. She does sport, however, three bead bracelets on the wrist nearest the flight attendant as well as an earring in the ear nearest the flight attendant. Presumably the flight attendant would rather serve a guy who wears bracelets than Her Baldness. Her Baldness decides she is flattered to be called sir.

11:43 a.m. Has Her Baldness unwittingly been sir in New York for the entire week of her cancer vacation? Her Baldness acknowledges that this may well have been the case, with the exception of her friends, who say they find her more fashionable than she used to be, and for Sadie Gund-Hope who said, Catherine, Catherine, stop, Catherine, I want to see your head. Her Baldness felt unbearably shy at this moment. She wanted to run. She was terrified, which made her feel like a freak, as Sadie is only three years old. She showed Sadie the front of her head, but she wasn't brave enough to take off the entire cap. It was hardly one of Her Baldness's finest moments.

12:01 p.m. The flight attendant comes down the aisle with the navy blue polyester tablecloths. Her Baldness is buried in the *New York Times*, reading about how late night talk shows have replaced the news as a source of reliable political commentary. Her Baldness apologizes for the delay in extricating her little plastic food tray from underneath her right armpit. "There's no rush, sir," says the flight attendant. "We've got all the time in the world. The flight is five hours and twenty minutes." Her hair is dyed brown, and she is very thin. Her Baldness tries to make out the flight attendant's name tag but it is obscured by her apron. There are no other same sex couples in business class. Her Baldness wonders who the flight attendant thinks brings home the most bacon in this straight couple—the femme who is used to ordering club soda and lime or the guy in bracelets.

12:03 p.m. Reality check. Ever since Her Baldness handed over her leather jacket on Flight 19, she has been a sir. But isn't Her Baldness a VERY smooth shaven guy? Or does the flight attendant think she's a depilatory minded fag? Or an F2M?

12:12 p.m. The flight attendant rolls the cart to the front of the cabin. Time for wine and the tossed green salad with smoked salmon. The flight attendant puts on her glasses so that she can read the labels.

12:14 p.m. Kim observes that flight attendants live in a bubble. They are totally out of touch with the sort of popular culture of which bald people in black knit caps are an example.

12:35 p.m. Kim's chicken arrives, along with Her Baldness's two slow roasted tomatoes, four pieces of asparagus, and half a piece of smoked salmon, the exact provenance of which Her Baldness, who still has an iffy sort of immune system, prefers not to consider. The flight attendant, who is no longer wearing her glasses, turns to Kim first. Ma'am, would you like anything else? Excuse me, please, says Her Baldness, could I possibly have a bit more club soda? Her Baldness thinks she's getting positively girlish about the way she strings words into sentences and, in her head, tries to rehearse a more manly way to get the club soda off the cart. More club soda please. That would have sufficed. Her Baldness puts on her own glasses. BETH. That's what the name

tag says. Her Baldness takes hummus and crackers out of her backpack.

12:38 p.m. Of course, I am not wearing lipstick today.

12:39 p.m. I have worn lipstick perhaps twice in the last five years.

12:41 p.m. Her Baldness wonders whether BETH's patience with her many requests is in fact an effect of being a guy. Perhaps Her Baldness is sufficiently manly, in her quiet and understated way, to obviate the need for anyone actually to utter the word sir. Her Baldness conceives of this as the deployment of male privilege. She rather likes feeling the ripple effect, which she visualizes as the way the muscles of the abdomen roll when those who have them use them.

12:46 p.m. Today's movie is *Here on Earth*. Gorgeous working-class babe falls while running. There's something I've been meaning to tell you, she confesses to rich boyfriend. Oops. Cancer.

12:52 p.m. While she was in New York, Her Baldness checked out Nancy Burson's "Race Machine" at Exit Art. You sit in a little booth. You line the corners of your eyes up against two cross hairs. You are scanned. Afterwards you get a choice of five menu items: White, Black, Asian, Hispanic, and Indian. Nancy Burson is not particularly critical of the social construction of race or gender. Nancy Burson has worked for the FBI to help them figure out how what certain of their Most Wanted would look like if they changed sex. When Her Baldness pushes White she looks unrecognizably femme. When she pushes

Black she looks recognizably male. She likes the idea that the Race Machine, by showing white as something foreign to white people, might get them to denaturalize their racial category. Her Baldness realizes that BETH is unaware she lives in a Gender Machine.

1:06 p.m. BETH removes the tray. She asks whether she should leave the navy blue polyester tablecloths for dessert. Yes, says Kim and YES, says Her Baldness, who immediately regrets her enthusiasm. Her craving for sugar might dissolve the shiny patina of male privilege. Her Baldness wants those abs. She may have blown her cover. Or perhaps Her Baldness's interest in whether BETH reads her as male or female is in itself a feminizing sort of hormone.

1:08 p.m. It is true that Her Baldness is in business class and that she is wearing a black hooded sweatshirt on top of the big man's shirt. She doesn't look like a suit. However it is Sunday and though everyone is white, no one is wearing a suit. Her Baldness wonders whether the bulk of the Sunday *New York Times* obscured Beth's view of the breast signifier from the outset.

1:11 p.m. BETH needs glasses to see the labels on the wine.

1:21 p.m. BETH comes by to offer macadamia nut ice cream and pie of some sort, as well as coffee, tea and after dinner drinks. Her Baldness refuses everything, but Her Baldness is too fucking accommodating. No, thank you very much, instead of no thanks. The girlfriend is an emphatic ma'am. Her Baldness doesn't rate a sir. Her Baldness is a gender nothing.

1:23 p.m. On the David Letterman show, a cross between a golden retriever and a dalmation catches balls in a baseball glove.

1:31 p.m. Her Baldness heads for the bathroom, minus her black sweatshirt. She does a few yoga stretches and sticks her chest out. Her Baldness has two fair-sized knockers. BETH is very helpful in explaining the exact location of the bathroom.

2:15 p.m. BETH comes by again. Would you like anything more to drink, sir? Perhaps Her Baldness is an academic male, the vegan sort, of minor fame. Her Baldness asks for club soda. You must have drunk a whole bottle of club soda already, CATHERINE, says Kim, who is completely exasperated with BETH and therefore has a fit of protectiveness. She has been trying to shield Her Baldness from gender insult for almost four hours. I don't want you to correct her, says Her Baldness when BETH goes off. I WANT to be sir for five hours and twenty minutes. I'd rather be a bald white guy with bracelets than a sick white woman.

2:17 p.m. What is it that BETH can't spell? L.E.S.B.I.A.N. or C.H.E.M.O.?

Thursday/September 28, 2000
In a message dated 9/28/00 WHYRAIN writes:
BETH is totally unfamiliar with both L.E.S.B.I.A.N. and C.H.E.M.O. As your femmie partner said, she lives in a bubble of misrecognition. Interesting that you were able to get some satisfaction out of passing. I never do, maybe because I've never allowed myself to let the instrument of such passing get away with it for very

long. I always disabuse the erring flight attendant (who, by the way, is usually female; if it's a male, and he is in doubt, he will omit any gendered address). Something puritan in me feels guilty in the face of deception. Also, telling them before they "find me out" on their own is important to my sense of retaining the upper hand.

Forget Her Hirsuteness. Her Baldness is morphing into His Baldness.

Exhaustion by 1:30 p.m. I am only on my third radiation. This cannot be.

Friday/September 29, 2000
In a message dated 9/29/00 VOLT writes: ca m'a bien fait rigolé, sir.

In a message dated 9/20/00 SEC writes: The gay men are all shaving their heads to mystify their baldness/aging effects, so you were probably passing as a gay man, who was trying to pass as a young man. Just think, as you try to look more and more indecisive and "girlish"—BUTCH BOTTOM!

Saturday/September 30, 2000
Borders? Nuances? What's the difference between bald and short hair, between sick and Marine, between Marine and gym teacher, between gym teacher and dyke?

Hoowahyoo?

"Who are you," asks the third blue-haired lady, peering up at me through the thick lenses of her rhinestone cat glasses. Only it comes out in one word, like "Hoowahyoo?" I'm wearing black, we all are. It's my mother's funeral service after all, and the little old ladies are taking inventory of the mourners. Me, I have to take inventory of my own identities whenever someone asks me who I am, and the answer that tumbles out of my mouth is rarely predictable. But this is my mother's funeral, and I am devastated, and to honor the memory of my mom, I'm telling each of them the who of me I know they can deal with.

"I'm Kate Bornstein," I answer her in this quiet-quiet voice of mine, "Mildred's daughter."

"Daughter?!" She shoots back incredulously the same question each of her predecessors had asked, because everyone knew my mother had two sons. That was her claim to fame and prestige amongst this crowd. No do-nothing daughters in my mother's family, no sir. Two sons. That was her worth as a woman.

"Mildred never mentioned she had a daughter." The eyes behind those glasses are dissecting my face, looking for family resemblances. When I was a boy, I looked exactly like my father. Everyone used to say

so. Then, when I went through my gender change, those same people would say, "Y'-know, you look just like your mother." Except I'm tall.

Nearly six feet of me in mourning for the passing of my mother, and I'm confronting this brigade of matrons whose job it seems to be to protect my mother from unwanted visitors on this morning of her memorial service down the Jersey shore.

"You're her daughter? So who's your father? It's not Paul, am I right?"

Now there would be a piece of gossip these women could gnaw on over their next mahjongg game. "Mildred had another child," they'd say after calling two bams, "a daughter no less! And Paul, God rest his soul, he never knew."

My mother had told only a tight circle of friends about my gender change. She knew that spreading the word meant she'd be torn to shreds by the long pink fingernails so favored by the arbiters of propriety of the small town she lived in. She was raised in a nearly-orthodox household, my mother was. As a young girl, she would wake up every morning just in time to hear the men and boys wake up and utter the phrase, "Thank God I was not born a woman." She lived her life placing her self-worth on the presence of the men in her

Kate Bornstein, "Hoowahyoo?" Originally posted at www.tootallblondes.com. Reprinted by permission of the author.

life. Her father, a successful merchant, died a year before I was born. Her husband, a successful doctor, died a year before I told her that one of her two sons was about to become a dyke. She preferred the word "lesbian." "My son, the lesbian," she would tell her close friends with a deep sigh and a smile on her lips.

My mother was there the night the rabbi asked me who I was. I was a senior in college, a real hippie: beard, beads, and suede knee-high moccasins with fringe hanging down past my calves.

I was home for some holiday or other, and my parents thought it would be nice if I came to synagogue with them. They wanted to show off their son who was going to Brown. I'd always enjoyed Friday night services. There's something lullingly familiar about the chanting, something comforting in the old melodies and the Hebrew, which I never ever understood but had down phonetically.

But when the rabbi gave her sermon, I was incensed. To this day, I don't remember what I was so outraged by, any sense of my anger having been eclipsed by the events that followed. But there I was, jumping to my feet in the middle of the rabbi's sermon, arguing some point of social justice.

My father was grinning. He'd never been bar mitzvah'ed, having kicked his rabbi in the shins the first day of Hebrew school. My mother had her hand over her mouth to keep from laughing. She was never very fond of our rabbi, not since the time he refused to make a house call to console my father the night my grandfather died. So there we were, the rabbi and the hippie, arguing rabbinical law and social responsibility. We both knew it was going nowhere. He dismissed me with a nod. I dismissed him with a

chuckle, and the service continued. On the way out of the synagogue, we had to file by the rabbi, who was shaking everyone's hand.

"Albert," he said to me, peering up through what would later be known as John Lennon glasses, "Hoowahyoo? You've got the beard, so now you're Jesus Christ?"

I've done my time as an evangelist. Twelve years in the Church of Scientology, and later, when I'd escaped Hubbard's minions, four or five years as a reluctant spokesperson for the world's fledgling transgender movement. But somewhere in between Scientology and postmodern political activism, I found time to do phone sex work. My mother never knew about that part. It was one of the who's I'd become I knew she couldn't deal with. So I never told her of the day I was standing in line in the corner store in West Philly, chatting with the woman behind the counter. From behind me, a deep male voice says, "Excuse me, who are you?" And I turn to see this middle-aged yuppie peering up at me through tortoise-rimmed glasses.

"Stormy?" he asks me. Stormy was the name I'd chosen for the smoky-voiced phone sex grrrl who did erotic dancing on the side and had a tattoo on her thigh. "Stay on the line with me a little longer, sugar," I'd purr into the phone, "and I'll tell you what it is."

So this young urban professional is standing behind me looking like he'd died and was meeting the Virgin Mary. I'm trying to figure out what fantasy of his we'd played out. But I'm scared. Way scared. If word got out that Stormy is a tranny, I'd lose my job for sure. I fix this guy with the same icy stare I'd learned from my mother, and he eventually slinks away to inspect the Pringles.

My mother died before she could hear the blue-haired ladies ask "Hoowahyoo" of the tall-tall woman with mascara running down her cheeks. She never heard the producer from the Riki Lake Show ask me, "Who are you?" when I told her I wasn't a man or a woman. My mother never heard the Philadelphia society matron ask me the same question when I attempted to attend her private women-only AA group.

My mother only once asked me, "Who are you?" It was about a week before she died. "Hoowahyoo, Albert?" she asked anxiously, mixing up names and pronouns in the huge dose of morphine, "Who are you?"

I told her the truth: I was her baby, I always would be. I told her I was her little boy, and the daughter she never had. I told her I loved her.

"Ha!" she'd exclaimed, satisfied with my proffered selection of who's, "That's good. I didn't want to lose any of you, ever."

CHAPTER I STUDY QUESTIONS

1. What is gender and why is it important? What is the difference between "sex" and "gender"?

2. What do Candace West and Don H. Zimmerman (Reading 1) mean by "doing gender"? Is it something that only occurs on the individual level or is it also structural, institutional, or societal?

3. West and Zimmerman (Reading 1) observe that "any social encounter can be pressed into service in the interests of doing gender." Describe some examples of "social encounters."

4. What purposes does gender serve in various capacities—as a structure, as a process, as an institution?

5. What brings people together for social change? Is it possible to (as Patricia Hill Collins describes in Reading 3) "transcend barriers created by our . . . experience"? In what ways do our similarities and differences inform our ability to make social change? How do power and privilege frame our relationships?

6. Author and activist Pat Califia has said, "To be differently gendered is to live within a discourse where other people are always investigating you, describing you, and speaking for you." In what ways might this affect us as individuals? As learners? As a culture?

CHAPTER 2 Learning How to "Do Gender"

9 Abigail A. Fuller

What Difference Does Difference Make?
Women, Race-Ethnicity, Social Class, and Social Change

Try this exercise: make a list of traditional "masculine" traits and "feminine" traits. Now, assess the list (Collins, 1993). Did you write words like "strong" or "aggressive" on the masculine list? And "emotional" and "passive" on the feminine list? Most people do. Now think about *which* men and women these terms are meant to describe. In reality, these ideals apply to white, middle-class men and women. For example, it is not acceptable for Black men to be aggressive: that makes people afraid, because of the stereotype of Black men as violent. And, historically working-class or poor women and women of color have not been passive, because they could not afford to be in the face of poverty and racial discrimination. (In one experiment, white students who were asked about their perceptions of "women in general" chose different traits than when asked about African-American women in particular. And, the traits they chose for African-American women were substantially more negative: while women in general were thought to be "sensitive," Black women were characterized as "loud" and "stubborn" [Weitz & Gordon, 1993].)

The point of this exercise is to illustrate the tendency to universalize the experiences and characteristics of *some* women to *all* women. On the one hand, women do share many common experiences. For example, they have been subject to similar legal constraints: before 1924, no woman in the United States could vote. On the other hand, within the category of "woman," people's experiences are remarkably different. Take a woman faced with an abusive husband: if she is from a wealthy family

Abigail A. Fuller, "What Difference Does Difference Make? Women, Race-Ethnicity, Social Class, and Social Change," *Race, Gender & Class* 11, no. 4 (2004): 8–29. Reprinted by permission of *Race, Gender & Class*.

and has a college degree from a prestigious university, her options are likely to be much greater than for a working-class woman who did not graduate from high school. A working-class woman may not have the money to make a deposit on an apartment, buy her own car, and find a job that can support her (and her children). [It is important to note that men's experiences also differ based on things like economic resources. This chapter focuses primarily on women, however.]

Why is it important to analyze differences among women? First, it creates a more complete and accurate picture of the situation of women in our society. The history of feminist activism and scholarly work on women is a history of women who are relatively privileged universalizing their experiences and concerns to all women. It is a history of women who are less privileged—who are poor, or Hispanic, or lesbian, or older—making their voices heard to expand and correct that limited view of what it means to be a woman. But white, middle/upper-class, heterosexual women who have analyzed and written and marched for gender equality have not intentionally, in most cases, excluded the concerns of other women. Privileged people are no more evil or stupid than anyone else. But their view of social reality is typically limited by two things. The first is the *dominant ideology*, a picture of social life, perpetuated by the news media, entertainment industry, schools, and public leaders, that either ignores the existence of poor/working-class people, people of color, and others, or paints them as deviant/bad/immoral/inferior by asserting that we live in a meritocracy—everyone has a chance to succeed, so if you don't, it's your own fault. Second, this is exacerbated by the lack of contact that privileged people typically have

with disadvantaged people in our society, so that this distorted view doesn't get corrected by actual experience. It is possible, through conscious effort, to learn the truth about society—and many privileged people have. Nevertheless, the default situation is that their view of social reality is limited. (People from disadvantaged groups are also influenced by the dominant ideology, but tend to have an easier time developing a more accurate view of social reality because their experiences contradict it.) The ultimate importance of understanding the experiences and perspectives of diverse women lies in the effect it has on our efforts to create a more just society. I will discuss this further at the end of the chapter, but briefly, if we ignore racial-ethnic and social class differences among women, we cannot be effective in helping women better their lives.

What Is Gender, Race, and Class?

The origins of women's diverse experiences in our culture are many; they include religious background, sexual preference, age, physical ability, and the like. However, at this point in history the most salient factors influencing a person's life chances—the factors that most strongly confer privilege or disadvantage on people—are gender, race-ethnicity. (Other important sources of differences are sexual preference, age, physical ability or disability.) *Gender* refers to the expected ways of behaving and relating that a society attaches to a person's biological sex. So, for example, most people expect females to smile a lot, wear jewelry, and take care of others, while males are supposed to be in charge, not wear dresses, and not cry.

A *race* is a group of people who are categorized as similar based on some physical attributes, like skin color or facial features.[1]

An *ethnic group* shares a common culture and sense of shared history. Race and ethnicity are distinct concepts, so everyone has both a race and an ethnicity. For example, I am racially white, and ethnically from an Irish, Scottish, English, and Dutch background. (The U.S. Census, which distributes lots of information about the American population, typically reports data for the major racial groups—white, Black, Asian, and Native American—plus one major ethnic group, Hispanics [or, as the latest census says, Spanish/Hispanic/Latino—people who trace their ancestry to Mexico, Puerto Rico, Cuba, or Central or South America.] About 5 percent of Blacks, 15 percent of American Indians, and 6 percent of Asians report Hispanic ethnicity.) Since there is substantial overlap between racial and ethnic categories, the terms may be combined into *race-ethnicity*. The term *people of color* is often used in the U.S. to refer to those whose background is Native American, Asian, African, or Hispanic.

Finally, a person's *social class* is their position within the economy, identified by their wealth and income, occupation, level of education, and cultural capital (attitudes, beliefs, and behaviors that are distinctive to a particular social class). While there are different ways to categorize people by class, and different labels for those categories, for the purpose of this essay I will discuss difference between less privileged (poor and working-class women), and more privileged (middle- and upper-class) women.

It is important to recognize gender, class, and race-ethnicity as systems of domination or oppression. That is, not only are some people disadvantaged by these systems, but others are privileged, at their expense. These systems of domination grant power and authority to some people *over* others.

So, for example, it is tempting for middle/upper-class people to believe that poor people just need some help to succeed financially. But in fact the wealth of some in our society actually depends on others working for low wages so businesses can make huge profits. Gender, class, and race-ethnicity do not just identify differences; they are patterns built into our social structure that give some people advantages at the expense of others.

The Gendering of Ethnicity

Stereotypes are used to justify relations of domination and subordination. (A stereotype is the belief that some attitude, behavior, or trait characterizes all members of some social group.) In American society, people of color are stereotyped not only on the basis of their race-ethnicity, but by gender as well. Espiritu refers to this as "the gendering of ethnicity" (Espiritu, 1992). Its primary function is to promote the image of white, middle-class Americans as "normal" in their gender and sexuality, and others as deviant. So, women of color are typically stereotyped as being either hyperfeminine or hypersexual, or hypofeminine or hyposexual (the prefix "hyper-" means too much; "hypo-" means too little).[2]

The predominant stereotype of Asian women in popular culture is the exotic sex object who is submissive to men—"concubine, geisha girl, mail-order bride; dragon lady, lotus blossom, precious pearl" (Lu, 1997). This has resulted in a market for pornographic films and images of Asian women being sexually dominated, and for Asian "mail-order brides"—women who correspond with, and eventually marry, American men (Halualani, 1995). Latino women (Latinas) are also stereotyped as sexually "hot," as are Latino men (Cofer, 1998). (Do a web search for mail-order brides. Notice the preponderance of women from Asian and Latin countries and what is said about them: that in comparison to U.S. women, they are more "traditional," dedicated to pleasing their husbands, and the like—in other words, hyperfeminine). As with many stereotypes, this stereotype of Latin women as hypersexual may be understood in the context of its origin: as one Puerto Rican woman notes, in Latin American countries women often "felt freer to dress and move provocatively" because they are protected both by Catholic morality and by the tradition of men protecting their women relatives against sexual exploitation (Cofer, 1998). Stereotypes can be contradictory, too. Another stereotype of Latinas in popular culture is the domestic, like the maid, Rosario, on the popular television program "Will and Grace." This stereotype also has a basis in reality: the difficulty for poor/working-class Latinas, especially those with limited knowledge of English, of finding anything but low-wage domestic work.

Black women are also stereotyped as hypersexual. In pornography, they are shown as "wild animals who are ready for any kind of sex, any time, with anybody"—an image that is promoted by city zoning practices that often locate strip clubs and massage parlors in Black neighborhoods (Nelson, 1993). Since the colonization of Africa, Black women, like Black men, have been stereotyped as animal-like as a way of justifying white domination of them (Collins, 1991). The hypersexual stereotype is also found in the image of the "welfare queen" with numerous children, and the drug addict trading sex for drugs. On the other hand, Black women have also been stereotyped as hyposexual: in the post slavery era,

the mammy image of the large, unattractive, nurturing woman who takes care of white people's homes and children was prominent in films and advertisements. (The movie "Ethnic Notions" depicts this.) More recently, Black women are often stereotyped as hypofeminine: loud, aggressive, violent. For example, a study of the top Hollywood films of 1996 found that 89 percent of Black female movie characters were shown using vulgar profanity, while only 17 percent of white female movie characters were, and 56 percent of Black female movie characters were shown being physically violent, compared with 11 percent of white female characters (Entman et al., 1998).

"JAP baiting" is a result of the interaction of sexism and anti-Semitism (prejudice against Jewish people) [Pogrebin, 2000]. It refers to the practice of denigrating Jewish women (JAP stands for Jewish American Princess) for their supposed pushiness, wealth and materialism, concern for appearance, and the like. If you live in an area with a relatively small Jewish population, you might not be aware that there exists an entire genre of JAP jokes. (One I remember from my college years is, "What does a JAP make for dinner? Reservations.") Jews have long been the targets of discrimination and violence, both before the Holocaust and since. Why, in this case, are the targets specifically women? Probably because since women are considered inferior to men, attacking them is okay—it is not considered anti-Semitic (Pogrebin, 2000). Part of the insidiousness of stereotypes is the extent to which they may be internalized by the very people they hurt. JAP baiting encourages Jewish men to avoid dating and marrying Jewish women, and has prompted Jewish women to try to distance themselves from Jewish culture.[3]

Notice who is neither too feminine nor not feminine enough, neither too sexual nor not sexual enough: white women. The main function of gendered and sexualized images of people of color is to reinforce the image of white men and women as "normal"—and so to justify the economic exploitation and other forms of harm done to people of color. This is an important point: these stereotypes of people of color do not exist in isolation from how white people see themselves. Instead, they are the necessary contrast that enables whites to label themselves "normal."

Women, Work, and Income

Stereotypes are not just ideas. They have an important material function: they support and justify the mistreatment of people from particular social groups—in particular, economic mistreatment. One of the most important ways that women's experiences differ is whether they work in the paid labor force or not; the kinds of jobs they have; and how much they earn. These are profoundly influenced by both a woman's social class and her racial-ethnic background. First, middle/upper-class women can choose whether or not to work outside the home, whereas poor/working-class women—who are disproportionately women of color—typically must work to support themselves and their families. Notice how misleading are statistics that do not identify these differences: of all married women with children under 6, 61.8 percent are in the paid labor force—but for white women the figure is 60.6 percent, and for Black women, 80 percent (Statistical Abstract of the United States, 2000). Second, the types of jobs in which women work differ depending on their background. Women from

poorer backgrounds are much more likely to end up in lower-paying, clerical or menial jobs, while those from wealthier backgrounds pursue well-paid careers in business or professions like medicine or law. And, occupations are segregated by race-ethnicity (as well as by gender) as shown in Table 9.1.

Even within an occupation, race-ethnicity can make a difference. For example, Black women professionals remain, like white women, clustered in female-dominated fields (social worker, teacher, librarian). But, they are more likely to hold these jobs in the public sector than are white women (working for government at the local, county, state, or federal level), and public sector jobs are generally less secure and do not pay as well as jobs with private companies (Higginbotham, 1997). The result of job segregation is clear. They are in part responsible for the fact that while the median weekly income for full-time white male workers in 2001 was $638, the comparable figure for white females was $483; for black females, $409; and for Hispanic females, $348.

Working-class women have pointed out that middle/upper-class women are sometimes blind to the fact that their ability to have a career depends on the exploitation of poor women.

After the birth of my second child, I was working two part-time jobs—one loading trucks at night—and going to school during the days. While I was quite privileged because I could take my colicky infant with me to classes and the daytime job, I was in a state of continuous semi-consciousness. I had to work to support my family; the only choice I had was between school or sleep: Sleep became a privilege. A white, middle-class instructor at the university suggested

TABLE 9.1 Occupations with the Highest Concentration by Race/Gender, 1995

Hispanic men	surveyor's helpers, plasterers, farm workers, agricultural nursery workers
Hispanic women	graders and agricultural workers, housekeepers, inspectors of agricultural products, child care workers (private households)
African-American men	longshore equipment operators, inspectors of agricultural products, baggage porters and bellhops, garbage collectors, barbers
African-American women	cooks (private households), housekeepers, winding and twisting machine operators, nursing aids
White men	mining engineers, agricultural engineers, supervisors of carpenters and related workers, supervisors of plumbers, pipe and steam fitters
White women	dental hygienists, stenographers, secretaries, dental assistants, speech therapists

Source: Eitzen and Zinn, 2000:358

to me, all sympathetically, that I ought to hire someone to clean my house and watch the baby. Her suggestion was totally out of my reality, both economically and socially. I'd worked for years cleaning other people's houses. Hiring a working-class woman to do the shit work is a middle-class woman's solution to any dilemma which her privileges, such as a career, may present to her. (Langston, 1991)

Notice, in Table 9.1, that women of color are especially apt to work taking care of the homes and children of wealthier (usually white) families. The availability of cheap, mostly minority labor has made it more attractive for wealthy women to work in the paid labor force (Cohen, 1998).

Occupational and income differences between categories of women are partly due to discrimination: though it is illegal to do so, it is not uncommon for employers to make hiring decisions based on a woman's race-ethnicity. They are also partly due to education. Children from wealthier families are more likely to attend college than children from poorer families, and increased educational attainment correlates with increased income. In 1999, 49.4 per-

TABLE 9.2 Percentage of 25–29-Year-Olds with a Bachelor's Degree or Higher, by Race/Ethnicity, 2000

White women	Black women	Hispanic women
37.6	20.2	16.6

Source: Wirt et al., 2001

cent of people completing high school that year who were from low-income families were enrolled in college that fall, while the figure for people from high-income families was 76 percent (Wirt et al., 2001). There are racial-ethnic differences, too, as can be seen in Table 9.2.

What explains the differences? Black and Hispanic women are more likely to come from poor/working-class families, and so are (1) more likely to attend inferior public schools, which prepare them less well for college (the book *Savage Inequalities* by Jonathan Kozol is a moving account of inequities in public schools in this country); (2) less able to afford college; and (3) more likely to drop out—again, largely for financial reasons. What does this mean for people's earnings? In 1999, women with a bachelor's degree earned an average $17.50 an hour, while women with a high school degree earned $10.17 per hour, and women who did not complete high school earned $7.39 an hour (Mishel et al., 2001).

As I note above, people of color are more likely to come from poor/working-class families (another way of saying this is that they are *disproportionately* poor and working class) because of the historical and current discrimination they face in the labor force. Most poor people in the U.S. are white (68 percent). However, people of color have a much greater chance of being poor than do whites: while 7.7 percent of white, non-Hispanic people are poor, 10.7 percent of Asian and Pacific Islanders are poor, as are 23.6 percent of Black non-Hispanics, 22.8 percent of Hispanics, and 25.9 percent of Native Americans (Statistical Abstract of the United States, 2000).

So, it is important to remember that when a difference is identified between racial-ethnic groups, it may actually be due to social class differences, rather than group differences in customs, beliefs, attitudes, and the like. (In fact, social scientists spend a lot of time trying to sort out whether race-ethnicity or class is responsible for various differences in the life chances of whites and people of color.)

Women in Families

Another way that race-ethnicity and social class influences women's lives is through their relationships with their families. White, middle/upper-class feminists have tended to see marriage and the family as oppressive, a place where women are isolated with their children, under the authority of a husband. Feminist scholars agree that the family has been one of the primary institutions that shape gender inequality in U.S. society. However, many women from poor/working-class families and families of color argue that in some ways, this picture of family life is too simplistic. They are more apt to be part of extended families, where multiple generations live near or with each other, provide social and economic support for each other, and share household and child care responsibilities (see, for example, Glenn, 1987; Stack, 1974; Griswold de Castillo, 1984). In contrast, middle/upper-class and white families are more often nuclear families—comprised of husband, wife, and children—which are relatively isolated from kin networks, both economically and socially.

What is the origin of these differences in families? One is economic realities: an important way that poor/working-class families cope with the lack of money and jobs is to pool resources with others in their extended families and neighborhoods—such as by sharing babysitting or lending money. Where middle/upper-class families can buy the services they need, families with less money must help each other out instead. Another is the reality of racial-ethnic oppression: families provide a safe haven from mistreatment by others. bell hooks paints a moving portrait of the historical importance to African-Americans of creating a safe, nurturing home space in the midst of the violence and repression of a white-dominated society (hooks, 1990). Finally, in some cases, such as for Native American women, the origin may also be cultural: people of color are more likely than white people to retain at least some aspects of pre-industrial family formations that were characterized by extended kin networks and an emphasis on responsibility to one's family—as compared to modern, capitalist society's emphasis on the individual.

Of course, there is great diversity among families even within a particular racial-ethnic group. Families vary by degree of acculturation (the extent to which they have adopted "western" or American culture). For example, recent Asian and Latino immigrant families are likely to be more traditional than Asian-American and Latino families that have lived in the U.S. for several generations. Families also vary by social class. Willie (1991) found that in middle/upper-class Black families, both parents typically must work to achieve a middle/upper-class income (as compared to white families, who can more easily attain the same class standing with one income), and couples tend to depend on their marriages for psychological well-being. Black working-class families are held together more by cooperating in the struggle to survive, with the husband often working two jobs.

These differences between families have several consequences. Women in poor/working-class families and families of color may experience more bonding and camaraderie with other women, because there is more interaction and cooperation between women in their families and communities (Stack, 1974). So, for white, middle/upper-class feminist women, creating communities of women (women's groups, households, etc.) may feel novel and necessary; women of color already know such communities. As bell hooks remembers taking her first women's studies class at Stanford University in the 1970s:

> white women were reveling in the joy of being together—to them it was an important, momentous occasion. I had not known a life where women had not been together, where women had not helped, protected, and loved one another deeply. (hooks, 1984)

The extended family form bears on older women's status, too. In such families, older women have more integral roles in caring for young grandchildren, giving advice, and such, and so are more respected (Hyde, 2000). In Native American families in particular, grandmothers and grandfathers are often the primary caretakers of children.

Another consequence of the extended family is that women of color and working-class women may feel more loyalty and indebtedness to their relatives. Unlike middle/upper-class women:

> We are not allowed to simply go out on our own, ignoring family responsibilities, focusing only on what we need to do to accomplish upward mobility and success in our career . . . [W]orking-class women are expected to provide support for both their family of origin and their current family, while middle-class women are allowed to distance themselves from their family of origin. In other words, middle-class women are expected to be good mothers and wives, while working-class women are expected to be good mothers, wives, daughters, sisters, cousins, etc. I have noticed this pattern in the lives of some of my women students (white, African-American, and Latina) from working-class families. They seem to leave town at least once a semester to go home and help with a family emergency, while their working-class brothers are left to focus exclusively on their college life. (Barker, 1995)

One study found that Black women, from both working-class and middle-class backgrounds, feel a greater sense of debt to their families and communities when they experience financial success than do white women, reflecting the greater degree of encouragement and aid they receive (Higginbotham & Weber, 2000).[4]

While the traditional extended family form has many strengths, it is important not to romanticize it. In many traditional cultures, families are (or were) patriarchal. (*Patriarchy* refers to a social system in which men have power and authority over women.) This is true in Mexican culture, for example, where the concept of machismo emphasizes the male as provider and protector, holding authority in the family. At the same time, gender roles should be examined in their cultural contexts. For example, while the primary role of women in traditional Mexican culture is wife and mother, that role carries much respect. Marianismo, the female counterpart to machismo, promotes the ideal of women's self-sacrifice for their families—but also the highest respect for this devotion. And, research has shown that external circumstances can change gender roles: women's power and autonomy in Mexican families increases when males leave for the U.S. in search of work (Hondagneu-Sotelo, 2000). In any case, as one observer has suggested, sexism may just be more visible in Latino culture—Anglo (white) culture is more sexually repressed, so sexism is expressed less blatantly, but it's still there.

Asian cultures traditionally value family loyalty, group harmony, respect for elders, and stoicism—expectations that can be at odds with women's quest for equality (Hyde, 1995). In Asian cultures, women are taught to be modest and passive—but these qualities are not necessarily seen as signs of weakness, as they are in white, middle/upper-class culture. And, men may have greater power than women in the public sphere, but this power does not fully extend into the home, where women traditionally have a say in family matters (Lavender, 1986).

A notable exception to the patriarchal tradition is Native American cultures, many of which are traditionally egalitarian—while men and women typically performed different tasks, they had relatively equal power. Oftentimes, women were—and still are—perceived as spiritually powerful because of their childbearing capacities.

The tribes see women variously, but they do not question the power of femininity. Sometimes they see women as fearful, sometimes peaceful, sometimes omnipotent and omniscient, but they never portray women as mindless, helpless, simple, or oppressed. . . . My ideals of womanhood, passed on largely by my mother and grandmothers, Laguna Pueblo women, are about practicality, strength, reasonableness, intelligence, wit, and competence (Allen, 2000).

Numerous white women have written about sexism as the fundamental oppression, which predates and has served as the model for other types of oppression. But women of color are less likely than white women to see men as "the enemy," because they observe firsthand the devastating effects of white racism on the men in their families and communities. Men of color are seen more as allies in the struggle against racism than enemies in the struggle against sexism. In fact, the very notion of equality with men is problematic for women whose brothers, fathers, and husbands face prejudice and discrimination that saps their dignity and consigns them to low-level jobs (hooks, 1984). At the same time, communities of color are by no means exempt from male domination and violence against women. Women of color have often written about the dilemma of criticizing men of color for sexist behavior, which risks reinforcing negative stereotypes of their racial-ethnic group, versus keeping silent but betraying the cause of justice for women. (See especially the work of bell hooks.)

Reproductive Rights

A woman's race-ethnicity and social class affect her access to reproductive rights. Let's look at abortion. While abortion remains legal in the U.S., poor women have more difficulty obtaining abortions than non-poor women. First, abortions are expensive—typically $200–$400 for first-trimester abortions, a lot of money for a woman who is struggling to pay the rent. Most private insurance plans cover abortion, but one-third of working women do not have employer-provided health insurance coverage (Mueller & Dudley, 1997). Medicaid is the federal- and state-funded program providing medical coverage for many poor Americans, but federal law prohibits using federal funds for abortion under most circumstances, and many states have passed similar laws. (There are private organizations and abortion facilities that help women pay for abortions—the National Network of Abortion Funds maintains a list of them.) Second, many women must travel hours to obtain an abortion, because 84 percent of all counties in the U.S. have no abortion provider (and the number increases to 94 percent for all rural counties, populated disproportionately by poor women) (Mueller & Dudley, 1997). Finally, combine all this with the fact that fifteen states require a mandatory delay (typically 24 hours) following state-directed counseling before a woman may obtain an abortion. This means, then, that many women seeking abortions must find the money to pay for it, drive long distances to a clinic or doctor, receive counseling, then receive an abortion the next day—adding the expenses of overnight accommodations, childcare while she is gone from home, and lost income due to absence from work. But pro-choice organizations may not always serve the needs of poor women, as reproductive rights activist Marlene Gerber Fried relates:

> "Mary" calls me from South Dakota, asking if we can help. "Susan," her seventeen-year-old daughter, is pregnant. The man involved is the father of Susan's two-year-old child, but Susan has a restraining order against him. She is in her second trimester, and the only clinic in their state doesn't do abortions past fourteen weeks, so she will have to go to Kansas to have the abortion. Susan and her mother have tried, but they can't raise all the money needed for the trip and the procedure. The man's mother could contribute, but she is pressuring Susan to have the baby and give it to her to raise. Mary is worried and scared. She is also angry, after calling all the pro-choice groups she knows and finding no resources for women in her daughters' situation. (Fried, 1990)

Poor/working-class women and women of color have also redefined the very definition and scope of reproductive rights. In addition to the right to have an abortion, it means the freedom *to* have children when and if one wants them, and access to the resources necessary to raise them adequately. The histories of forced or coerced sterilization of Native American women and Puerto Rican women are blatant examples of the violation of this right (England, 1999; Bauza, 1994). By 1982, 42 percent of Native American women and 35 percent of Puerto Rican women had been sterilized, as had 24 percent of African-American women—compared to 15 percent of white women (Feminist Women's Health Center, 2001). Poor and disabled women have also been subject to higher rates of sterilization than non-poor women (DeFine, 1997).

How did this happen? Doctors have sterilized women without their consent, or badgered or coerced them into signing consent forms (such as by threatening to take away their children), or had illiterate women sign consent forms that they couldn't read. Yet women who are more privileged have a very different view of sterilization, as pointed out by reproductive rights activist Dorothy Roberts.

In the seventies . . . women of color said, "Let's put limits on sterilization because doctors are guilty of abuse." But this just didn't register with some of the mainstream reproductive rights groups that had been pushing for greater access to sterilization for white, middle-class women. While poor black women were, in some cases, forcibly sterilized, sometimes without their knowledge, let alone consent, white women had a hard time getting sterilized. There were all sorts of formulas to figure out if you should allow a white woman to be sterilized. This exemplifies how diametrically opposed the experience of the struggle for reproductive rights has been for these two groups. (Brennan, 2001)

In addition, some feminists have pointed out that poor women are denied the financial means to raise children in a healthy environment. For example, there is a severe shortage in the U.S. of high-quality, low-cost childcare. Wealthier women can afford to buy good care for their children, but poor/working-class women cannot. They can afford to take unpaid parental leave to care for a new baby or a sick child, but poor/working-class women cannot. Accordingly, groups like the National Black Women's Health Project have expanded discussions of reproductive rights by advocating for universal health care, effective and affordable contraceptives, paid parental leave, and higher wages (Brenner, 2000). All this has important strategic implications for pro-choice feminists: namely, that working only to keep abortion legal does not fully address the reproductive needs of all women. Instead, if the movement is to be one that truly represents the interests of women, it must address the issues like women's wages, child care, health care, and the like.

Violence

White and middle/upper-class women are safer in our society than women of color and poor/working-class women. Women living in urban areas (who are disproportionately women of color) are more likely than suburban or rural women to be violently attacked by a stranger (Bachman & Saltzman, 1995). Among racial-ethnic groups, Native American women are significantly more likely than other women to be raped and/or sexually assaulted (at a rate of 64.8 per 1,000, as compared with rates of 54.5 for white women, 55.1 for Black women, and 51.9 for Asian/Pacific Islander women) (Tjaden & Thoennes, 1998).

For women (and children, too) the family is perhaps the most violent social institution in our culture. Most of the violence that women experience is at the hands of an intimate partner: 76 percent of women who are raped and/or physically assaulted since age 18 are assaulted by a current or former spouse, cohabiting partner, or date (compared with 18 percent of men who are raped and/or physically assaulted) [Tjaden & Thoennes, 1998]. About 30 percent of women who are murdered are killed by an intimate, while the rate for men is 4 percent (Rennison & Welchans, 2000). Again, the incidence varies by social class and race-ethnicity. The rate of victimization by intimate partners of women living in households with the lowest annual household income was nearly 7 times that of women living in households with the highest annual household income (20 versus 3 per 1,000) [Rennison & Welchans, 2000]. Black women are victimized by intimate partners at a rate 35 times that of white women, though the difference disappears when social class is taken into account (Hampton & Gelles, 1994). For Hispanic women, the statistics vary by country of origin. The percentage of Puerto Rican women assaulted by intimates is 20.4, compared with 2.5 percent for Cuban women, for example. No definitive national studies have been done of domestic abuse in Asian-American or Native American families, but discussions with women and community leaders suggest that it is a significant problem in both communities, but particularly for Native Americans (Huisman, 1996; Bachman, 1992).

In general, the higher rates for women of color are probably due to the fact that they are more likely to be poor. Poverty and unemployment contribute to male abuse of their partners, because they cause stress. (Educational materials often report that domestic violence cuts across all social classes and racial-ethnic groups. On the one hand, this helps combat stereotypes of poor people and people of color as prone to violence—but it has also been criticized by some as a way to gain support for domestic violence programs by playing up white, middle/upper-class victims and downplaying other victims.)

Why are these differences important? If efforts to reduce violence against women are to be effective, they must take into account the circumstances that make poor/working-class women and women of color especially vulnerable to violence. For example, staff at shelters for battered women (most women who use shelters are poor) report spending large amounts of time on tasks like finding affordable housing and helping women apply for food stamps—in short, dealing not simply with the violence itself, but with the lack of resources that created a situation in which a woman had few or no other options than to stay with an abusive partner (Crenshaw, 1994). Yet this oftentimes places shelters at odds with funding agencies that expect the staff to spend the money delivering the kinds of services that meet the needs of white, middle-class women, like medical care, psychological counseling, and accompanying women to court (white women are more likely to have their cases pursued by the criminal justice system) (Crenshaw, 1994).

It is interesting that an important way to prevent violence against women may be not only to insure their economic self-sufficiency, but to make sure men get good jobs. A research study found that when a male partner is employed, then women's labor force participation lowers the risks of spousal abuse, because it increases her power and independence relative to her partner. But when he is not employed, then a woman's employment actually raises the risk of violence—because then he experiences a decline in status compared with hers, which he perceives as a threat to his authority (MacMillan & Gartner, 1999).

As in the case of reproductive rights, some feel that the very definition of "violence against women" should be expanded beyond domestic abuse or sexual assault: "Many women of color argue that violence against women must also be understood as part of labor exploitation, government land-grabs, attacks on immigrants, militarism, and racist violence" (Yeung, 2000–2001).

Some groups of women may be less likely than others to report violent victimization or to seek help from established organizations. Immigrant women who are not fluent in English are unlikely to utilize the services without staff or volunteers who can translate for them. Additional problems confront women who are in this country illegally—problems that organizations serving women don't always address.

[M]any state coalitions on domestic/sexual violence have refused to take stands against the anti-immigration backlash, arguing that this is not a sexual/domestic violence issue. However, as the anti-immigration backlash intensifies, many immigrant women do not report abuse—from the INS, police, employers, or family members—for fear of deportation. (Smith, 2000–2001)

Women of color and poor/working-class women who experience violence may be reluctant to report it or seek help, due to a history of being ignored or mistreated by the criminal justice system and social service organizations. As one woman said, "Because I am a Black woman, I thought no one would believe me" (Nelville, 2001). An anti-violence activist reports:

A young Native woman was once gang raped by prominent members of an urban Indian community I lived in. When she sought justice, the community instead blamed her—she was dividing the community by airing its "dirty laundry." At the same time, she had difficulty getting help from the mainstream anti-violence movement. In fact, the year before I began working in sexual assault services in that city, only one Native woman had received services at a rape crisis center. The primary reason Native women gave for not going outside the community for help was that it was like appealing to a "foreign government" for assistance. (Smith, 2000–2001)

In Asian communities, women may feel reluctant to report domestic violence because of the shame associated with marital problems and the stigmatization of divorce. Organizations need to make extra efforts, then, to address these various concerns so that they can help more women.

Conclusion: The Necessity of Understanding Differences

There are several reasons why it is important to avoid universalizing the experiences of some women. The fundamental reason is, I think, a moral one. Basic respect for people dictates that we acknowledge who they are (not just individually, but as part of a particular community and/or culture) and what they have gone through, especially those whom our society disadvantages. In a society that ignores or erases the experiences and perspectives of people with less power, we owe it to such people to hear their voices.

A second reason is self-interest: racial-ethnic, social class, and other types of domination hurt us all. (An excellent example is found in an article by Tim Wise on the school shootings in Santee, California, that circulated widely on the Internet. Wise argued that as long as white Americans stereotype people of color as violent, they will be blind to the warning signs of violence in their own communities [Wise, 2001].) In addition, you grow by learning more about people who are different from you. I have become much more comfortable with differences, less frightened of them, less apt to avoid people who are different from me—and the world looks much more interesting.

The third reason is that taking account of differences is necessary to make social change efforts more effective. As some of the examples above show, if you are working with a group promoting women's rights, and you don't talk about racial-ethnic, social class, and other differences, then you probably will fail to do all you can to promote the rights of women of color and poor/working-class women. And, you risk reinforcing racial-ethnic and social class domination. For one thing, people will simply avoid joining your cause if their needs are not represented. The feminist movement is rife with examples of women feeling that white, middle-class organizations that purport to represent "women" do not represent them.[5] And fewer supporters means less power to change things. What this means in practice is that groups that have focused on what are largely white, middle/upper-class concerns must expand their agendas.[6] As noted above, working for reproductive rights means not just keeping abortion legal, but also making sure women have the money to pay for an abortion and for contraceptives and to raise their kids. Working to eradicate violence against women means not just focusing on the ideology of male privilege that normalizes abuse of women, but also working to insure that women have the resources to leave relationships when they have to.

Working to combat dehumanizing stereotypes of women in the entertainment industry means looking at how particular groups of women are depicted based on their race-ethnicity. These are just some examples.

Understanding differences is also vital to creating an organizational climate that welcomes people from diverse backgrounds. Again and again, women of color tell painful stories of joining, then quitting, groups because they felt looked down upon or ignored or accepted only as a token to make white women feel like they are not racist.

Last year in Los Angeles, after volunteering to work for a local white feminist magazine, repeatedly offering my services and having my ideas and poems rejected, I was finally asked to be one of the few token black wimmin at a reception for Ntozake Shange. And the beat, like the song says, goes on (davenport, 1983).

But we can change. The first step is to listen to, and learn from, people who are different from us.

Notes

1. Today, scientists agree that race is a social construction: that is, the racial categories that societies create have no clear biological basis. And, physical attributes like skin color have no direct biological relationship to a person's beliefs, behaviors, or mental capacities.

2. Black men are stereotyped in our culture as hypersexual: a persistent theme in U.S. history is the supposed threat that they pose to white women. From the end of slavery through the 1930s, the most common justification for the thousands of lynchings that were carried out by whites during that time was that the man had allegedly made sexual advances toward a white woman. (A more recent example is the scene in the movie *Traffic*, in which a black drug dealer is

shown having intercourse with the white daughter of the film's main character, the nation's newly appointed drug czar. Critics point out that this plays on white Americans' age-old fear of—and fascination with—Black males' supposed sexual desire of white women.) The current stereotype of the violent Black male is a manifestation of this hypermasculinization as well. Images of Asian men in popular culture often show them as hypomasculine, such as the "sexless Asian sidekick" exemplified in the characters of Charlie Chan; the Asian servant in *Falcon Crest* during the 1980s or *Bonanza* during the 1970s; or more currently the "model minority" who obediently follows society's rules. But contradictory stereotypes often exist in our culture. The "Yellow Peril" stereotype that shows Asians as a threat to American society has taken different forms, but included from 1940 to 1950 the hypermasculine image of Asian men lusting after white women.

3. Similarly, stereotypes of Asian men as hypomasculine may influence Asian women to marry out of their racial-ethnic group (Espiritu, 1992).

4. A note about making generalizations: as an astute student, you might be thinking, Wait a minute: the point of this chapter is that we shouldn't universalize the experiences of some women to all women—but isn't the author still making generalizations, albeit about sub-groups of women? (For example, Asian-American women aren't all alike; and even Asian-American women who are recent immigrants and living in poor families aren't all alike.) The answer is, yes: it's important to remember that within any group defined by common characteristics, there are always individual variations. Humans are not robots! At the same time, generalizing—based on sound evidence—is useful. Social scientists do it because, despite it's drawbacks, it helps us to capture important similarities between people that result from the fact that they "share the same rung" on some social hierarchy (Shah, 1997). In other words, social hierarchies (ranking groups of people based on some characteristic, like race/ethnicity or gender or class) *do* result in shared experiences—even though diversity within groups exists as well.

5. The classic *This Bridge Called My Back: Writings by Radical Women of Color*, edited by Cherrie Moraga and Gloria Anzaldúa, has an entire chapter of pieces titled "And When You Leave Take Your Pictures With You: Racism in the Women's Movement."

6. You might be thinking, Okay, since women of color (and, less often, poor/working-class women) often create groups to specifically address their own concerns—the Asian Task Force Against Domestic Violence, for example—then what's wrong with white, middle/upper-class women forming their own organizations? One problem is that the latter often have more resources to affect change—time, money, education—so one could argue that they have an obligation to use those resources on behalf of others as well as themselves. The other problem is that unlike groups like the Asian Task Force Against Domestic Violence, white, middle/upper-class organizations have frequently claimed to represent *all* women, rather than admitting that they do not.

Bibliography

Allen, P.G. (2000). Where I come from is like this. In V. Cyrus (ed.), *Experiencing race, class, and gender in the United States*, pp. 78–81. Mountain View, CA: Mayfield.

Bachman, R. (1992). *Death and violence on the reservation: Homicide, family violence, and suicide in American Indian populations.* Westport, CT: Auburn House.

Bachman, R., Saltzman, L.E. (1995). *Violence against women: estimates from the redesigned survey.* U.S. Department of Justice, Office of Justice Programs, Bureau of Justice Statistics, NCJ-154348 (August).

Barker, J. (1995). White working-class men and women in academia. *Race, Gender, and Class* 3(1):65–77.

Bauza, V. (1994). Puerto Rico: The covert campaign to sterilize women. *MS*, p. 5.

Brennan, M. (2001, April/May). Dorothy Roberts: What we talk about when we talk about reproductive rights. *MS*, pp. 77–79.

Brenner, J. (2000). *Women and the politics of class.* New York: Monthly Review Press.

Cohen, P. (1998). Replacing domestic labor in the service economy: Gender, class, and racial-ethnicity in household service spending. *Gender and Society*, 12:219–31.

Cofer, J.O. (1998). The myth of the Latin woman: I just met a girl named Maria. In P.S. Rothenberg (ed.), *Race, class, and gender in the United States: An integrated study*, 4th edition, pp. 292–296. New York: St. Martin's Press.

Collins, P.H. (1993). Race, class, and gender as categories of analysis. *Race, Sex, and Class*, 1(1):25–45.

———. (1991). *Black feminist thought: Knowledge, consciousness, and the politics of empowerment*. New York: Routledge Crenshaw.

davenport, d. (1983). The pathology of racism: A conversation with third world wimmin. In C. Moraga & G. Anzaldua (eds.), *This bridge called my back: Writings by radical women of color*, pp. 85–90. New York: Kitchen Table: Women of Color Press.

DeFine, M.S. (1997). A history of governmentally coerced sterilization: The plight of the Native American woman. *Native American Political Issues*, May 1. http://www.geocities.com/CapitolHill/9118/mike2.html.

England, C.R. (1999). A look at the Indian health service policy of sterilization, 1972–1976. http://www.dickshovel.com/IHSSterPol.html.

Entman, R., Boayue, S., Groce, C.K., Raman, A., Kenner, B., & Merritt, C. (1998, February 26). "Race and ethnicity in the top Hollywood films, 1996," ch. 4 in *Media and Reconciliation, Report to the Advisory Board of President Clinton's Initiative on Race*. http://www.raceandmedia.com/chp4.asp.

Espiritu, Y.L. (2000). Americans have a different attitude: Family, sexuality, and gender in Filipina American lives. In M.B. Zinn, P. Hondagneu-Sotelo & M.A. Messner (eds.), *Gender through the prism of difference*, pp. 222–231. Boston: Allyn and Bacon.

———. (1992). *Asian American panethnicity: Bridging institutions and identities*. Temple University Press.

Feminist Women's Health Center. (2001). *Tubal Ligation–Female Sterilization*. http://www.fwhc.org/tubalig.htm.

Fried, M.G. (1990). *From abortion wars: A half-century of struggle, 1950–2000*. Boston, MA: South End Press.

Glenn, E.N. (1987). Racial ethnic women's labor: The intersection of race, gender, and class oppression. In C. Bose, R. Feldberg, & N. Sokoloff (eds.), *Hidden aspects of women's work*, pp. 46–73. New York: Praeger.

Griswold del Catillo, R. (1984). *La familia*. Notre Dame, IN: University of Notre Dame Press.

Halualani, R.T. (1995). The intersecting hegemonic discourses of an Asian mail-order bride catalog: Philipina "oriental butterfly" dolls for sale.

Hampton, R.L. & Gelles, R.J. (1994). Violence toward Black women in a nationally representative sample of Black families. *Journal of Comparative Family Studies*, 25(1):105–119.

Higginbotham, E. (1997). Black professional women: Job ceilings and employment sectors. In D. Kendall (ed.), *Race, Class, and Gender in a Diverse Society*, pp. 405–418. Boston: Allyn and Bacon.

Higginbotham, E. & Weber, L. (2000). Moving up with kin and community: upward social mobility for Black and White women. In M.B. Zinn, P., Hondagneu-Sotelo, & M.A. Messner (eds.), *Gender through the prism of difference*, chap. 37. Boston: Allyn and Bacon.

Hondagneu-Sotelo, P. (2000). Overcoming patriarchal constraints: The reconstruction of gender relations among Mexican immigrant women and men. In M.B. Zinn, P. Hondagneu-Sotelo, & M.A. Messner (eds.), *Gender Through the Prism of Difference*, pp. 184–205. Boston: Allyn and Bacon.

hooks, b. (1990). Homeplace: A site of resistance. In *Yearning: Race, Gender, and Politics*, pp. 41–49. Boston: South End Press.

———. (1984). Black women shaping feminist thought. In *Feminist Theory: From Margin to Center*, pp. 1–16. Boston: South End Press.

Huisman, K.A. (1996). Wife battering in Asian American communities. *Violence Against Women*, 2(3):260–283.

Hyde, J.S. (2000). Gender roles and ethnicity. In V. Cyrus (ed.), *Experiencing race, class, and gender in the United States*, pp. 75–78. Mountain View, CA: Mayfield.

Kimberle, W. (1994). Mapping the margins: Intersectionality, identity politics, and violence against women of color. In M.A. Fineman, R.

Mykitiuk (eds.), *The public nature of private violence*, pp. 93–118. New York: Routledge.

Langston, D. (1991). Tired of playing monopoly? In J. Whitehorse Cochran, D. Langston, & C. Woodward (eds.), *Changing our power: An introduction to women's studies*. Dubuque, Iowa: Kendall/Hunt Publishing.

Laurence, J. (2000). The Indian health service and the sterilization of Native American women. *American Indian Quarterly*, 24(3):400–419.

Lavender, A.D. (1986). *Ethnic women and feminist values: Toward a "new" value system*. Lanham, MD: University Press of America.

Lu, L. (1997). Critical visions: The representation and resistance of Asian women. In S. Shah (ed.), *Dragon ladies: Asian American feminists breathe fire*. Boston: South End Press.

MacMillan, R. & Gartner, R. (1999). When she brings home the bacon: Labor-force participation and the risk of spousal violence against women. *Journal of Marriage & the Family*, 61(4, November).

Mishel, L., Bernstein, J., & Schmitt, J. (2001). *The state of working America 2000–2001*. Ithaca, NY: Cornell University Press.

Mueller, S. & Dudley, S. (1997). *Access to abortion: Fact sheet*. National Abortion Federation.

Nelson, V. (1993). Prostitution: Where racism and sexism intersect. *Michigan Journal of Gender & Law*, 1:81–89. http://www.prostitutionresearch.com/nelson.html.

Neville, H. (2001, June 12). The real deal about sexual assaults of Black women. *BRC News*.

Pogrebin, L.C. (2000). The Jewish American princess. pp. 208–209. In V. Cyrus, (ed.), *Experiencing race, class, and gender in the United States*. Mountain View, Calif.: Mayfield.

Rennison, C.M. & Welchans, S. (2000, May). Intimate partner violence. U.S. Department of Justice, Office of Justice Programs, Bureau of Justice Statistics, NCJ 178247.

Shah, S. (1997). Slaying the dragon lady: Toward an Asian-American feminism, in S. Shah (ed.), *Dragon ladies: Asian American feminists breathe fire*, pp. xxi–xxi. Boston: South End Press.

Smith, A. (2000–01). Colors of violence. *ColorLines*, 3(4, Winter).

Stack, C. (1974). *All our kin*. New York: Harper and Row.

Tjaden, P. & Thoennes, N. (1998). Prevalence, incidence, and consequences of violence against women: Findings from the national violence against women survey. U.S. Department of Justice, Office of Justice Programs, National Institute of Justice and Centers for Disease Control and Prevention.

Weitz, R. & Gordon, L. (1993). Images of Black women among Anglo college students. *Sex Roles*, 28:19–34.

Willie, C. (1991). *A new look at Black families*. Dix Hills, NY: General Hall.

Wirt, J., Choy, S., Gerald, D., Provasnik, P., Rooney, P., Watanabe S., Tobin, R., & Glander, M. (2001). The condition of education 2001. National Center for Education Statistics, U.S. Department of Education, NCES 2001-072.

Wise, T. (2001, March 6). School shootings and White denial. *AlterNet*. http://www.alternet.org/story.html?StoryID=10560.

Yeung, B. (2000–01). Fighting the many faces of violence. *ColorLines*, 3(4, Winter).

10 Natalie Adams and Pamela Bettis

Commanding the Room in Short Skirts
Cheering as the Embodiment of Ideal Girlhood

In the United States, the cheerleader is a cultural icon, on one hand, symbolizing "youthful prestige, wholesome attractiveness, peer leadership and popularity," while simultaneously representing "mindless enthusiasm, shallow boosterism, objectified sexuality, and promiscuous availability" (Hanson 1995, 2). A staple of American life and popular culture, the cheerleader has received little scholarly attention. When discussed at all in academic research, as illustrated in the following quote, cheerleading is typically presented as an activity that exploits and demeans girls: "The function of the cheerleader is to encourage the worship of the men—the prettiest, nicest and most lively are selected to show and encourage adoration" (Weis 1997, 83).

In this article, we challenge such trivialization of cheerleading in academic research and argue that a feminist poststructuralist reading of cheerleading offers a unique opportunity to theorize this role in ways that honor the concrete realities of girls' lives. We follow Walkerdine's (1993, 15) suggestion to problematize traditional approaches to studying girls, as found in developmental psychology and socialization theories, by carrying out research that understand[s] the social world as constituted materially and discursively and replete with fantasies and fictions which shore up power in all its many guises. To understand the constitution of girls within this means that we understand girlhood as constituted in and through the discursive practices that make up the social world.

Drawing on an ethnographic study of a Midwestern middle school, we discuss cheerleading as one such discursive practice that operates as a socially sanctioned space for a few girls to create multiple gendered subject positions that accommodate the shifting and often contradictory meanings of normative adolescent femininity. Our intent is to offer an examination of cheerleading that acknowledges the multiple meanings embedded in this cultural institution. We argue that cheerleading represents a liberating shift in normative femininity while simultaneously perpetuating a norm that does not threaten dominant social values and expectations about the role of girls and women. In doing so, we draw from Fraser's (1992, 80) work in asking, "What are the processes by which definitions and interpretations inimical to women's interests [i.e., cheerleading] acquire cultural authority? What are the prospects for mobilizing counterhegemonic feminist definitions and interpretations to create oppositional groups and alliances?"

Girl Power: Adolescent Femininity in the New Millennium

As numerous scholars of girlhood have documented (Adams 1999; Inness 1998; Mitchell 1995; Nelson and Vallone 1994), normative adolescent femininity is constantly being rewritten. McRobbie (1993) and Budgeon (1998) have argued that new subject positions are being made available to girls that provide a counterdiscourse to the girl as victim. This is most notable in the shift of discourse on adolescent femininity away from romance to a new theme of independence and assertiveness. Passivity, quietness, acquiescence, and docility no longer represent the primary markers for signifying normative girlhood. Budgeon pointed out that girls are being taught that self-determination, individualism, self-efficacy, independence, sexual subjectivity, and assertiveness are all desirable traits of the new ideal girl. Similarly, Lemish (1998) reported that the middle-class Jewish Israeli girls in her study thought the ideal girl of today was one who embodied strength, independence, and success. Solomon (1999) argued that participation in sports, athleticism, and a fit body have become normalized as essential components of girl culture today.

However, Budgeon (1998), Lemish (1998), and others (Adams and Bettis in press; Currie 1997; Oliver 1999) have also pointed out that the shifting landscape of ideal girlhood still mandates an adherence to certain nonnegotiable markers of ideal femininity. One such marker is that of at-

tractiveness. As one of the girls in Lemish's (1998, 155) study stated, "A girl could be anyone—as long as she was pretty." Another marker is that of heterosexuality. Normative femininity continues to be defined against the expectation that women eventually marry and have children (Inness 1998). Douglas (1997, 21) described the tenuous landscape of contemporary girlhood in this way: "Girls today are being urged, simultaneously, to be independent, assertive, and achievement oriented, yet also demure, attractive, soft-spoken, fifteen pounds underweight, and deferential to men."

Feminist Poststructuralism and the Study of Girlhood

Following Davies (1989, 1993), Walkerdine (1990), and Kenway and Willis (1998), we employ feminist poststructuralism as a theoretical tool for examining how ideal girlhood is being produced, circulated, and consumed within the context of real girls' lives. Kenway et al. (1994, 201) argued that

> poststructuralism offers an understanding of girls which is able to accommodate the complex qualities of girlhood. Rather than insisting that girls are one thing or another, it recognizes that they are all the above at different moments and in different circumstances. It recognizes girls as subjects who are variously "rational" and "irrational" and acknowledges their commonalities and their many differences. It indicates that girls are productions and producers of themselves and their times.

One of the primary contributions of feminist poststructuralists has been to demonstrate how certain social material practices are deeply imbued with a set of cultural and symbolic meanings and how girls and women create gendered subjectivities "both in concert with and in opposition to the ways in which others choose to position them" (Davies 1989, xi). In this article, we focus on a particular gendered social practice, cheerleading, and how its discursive practices have changed to accommodate the shifting notions of ideal girlhood and how girls themselves play an active role in producing their own version of the ideal girl.

Another major contribution of feminist poststructuralists has been to point out that discourses of femininity and masculinity are fluid, are temporal, and change with historical conditions. Consequently, there is no fixed meaning of the ideal girl; rather, the meaning of ideal girlhood is always in flux and constantly subject to dispersal. Although it acts as a symbolic form, the ideal girl becomes situated as a truth about what constitutes normative adolescent girlhood. As Weedon (1987) has argued, even though meaning (e.g., the meaning of the ideal girl of the new millennium) is only fixed temporarily and bears little resemblance to the realities of most girls' lives, this temporary fixing has important social implications for all girls. Similarly, Foucault (1979) stated that one of the primary functions of any discourse is to normalize and regulate what is considered appropriate or normal behavior. Thus, the discourse of ideal girlhood operates to normalize and regulate the behaviors of all girls, even those girls who consciously choose to resist or reject dominant ideology of normative girlhood.

Because cheerleading is an indigenous cultural practice and its long history has reflected American society's shifting understandings of ideal and normative gender, it provides a rich opportunity to explore how the discourse of ideal girlhood plays out in the daily lives of adolescent girls. Although derided by feminists, popular culture icons, and many involved in the sports world as a demeaning activity for girls in the post–title IX era, it is practiced by 3.3 million people every year, 97 percent of whom are girls and women. In this article, we examine how girls position themselves in multiple and complex ways within the discursive practices of cheerleading while simultaneously being subjected to material practices and understandings of ideal girlhood that restrict their positionings as gendered beings.

From the late 1800s to the 1930s, cheerleading squads comprised primarily men, and cheerleading signified ideal masculinity. However, by the mid-1950s, cheerleading had changed significantly from an activity representing normative masculinity to one representing ideal femininity. In discussing the shift from a masculine activity to a naturalized feminine activity during this time period, Davis (1990, 155) pointed out that cheerleaders came to symbolize "dominant ideology about how females should look and act in our society." That is, women/cheerleaders were to be pretty, were to possess appealing figures, were to play a secondary role to males, and were not to be taken too seriously. In the aftermath of title IX and the second wave of women's rights, notions of the appropriate role and behavior of women in society began to shift; thus, cheerleading had to change to reflect new ideals about normative femininity and ideal girlhood. This study illuminates those changes.

Data Collection

In August 1998, along with two other researchers, we began a study focusing on girls and leadership at Powhaton Middle School, a sixth- and seventh-grade school located in a Midwestern town of 26,000. The racial composition of the student body was 75 percent white, 14 percent Native American, 8.3 percent Hispanic, 4.5 percent African American, and 0.8 percent Asian. During the initial interviews with 61 seventh-grade girls, and throughout our field notes, cheerleaders were frequently mentioned as leaders in the school. Therefore, beginning in January 1999, we began five months of weekly observations of two cheerleading classes the school had instituted to prepare girls for the March cheerleading tryouts.

The two cheer prep classes were scheduled back to back to meet the schedule of the part-time instructor who was the cheerleader sponsor for the junior varsity cheerleading squad at the local high school. Typically, we situated ourselves along the gym wall and took copious field notes while the girls participated in the various activities Louise Stone, the teacher, planned for helping them prepare for tryouts. We conducted initial interviews before the tryouts with 22 of the 64 girls enrolled in the class. A second round of interviews with 18 of the 22 was conducted following tryouts.

Of the 20 girls ultimately chosen for the squad, 19 were white, and 1 was Native American. The racial composition of the girls we initially interviewed consisted of 14 whites, 5 Native Americans, and 3 African Americans: 13 of the 20 girls chosen for the squad were among those we interviewed. In addition, 9 other girls who did not make the squad or who decided not to try out, but who were in the cheer preparation class, were interviewed. The two formal interviews were semistructured and conducted in a variety of locations during the cheer preparation class while informal interviews took place at lunch and before and after classes. The cheer preparation teacher, Ms. Stone, was also interviewed. Documents pertinent to the study, including handouts disseminated to students and parents about tryouts, local newspaper articles featuring the cheerleaders, and Powhaton School Board minutes, were also studied.

We analyzed our field notes, interviews, and documents based on data reduction and interpretation (Berg 2001; Coffey and Atkinson 1996; Marshall and Rossman 1995). Each of us separately read the transcriptions and field notes carefully several times. After becoming familiar with the data, we each created a list of initial codes and separately coded the data, and then we met once a week for four weeks to discuss these initial codes and collapsed and refined the list. We each returned to the data and coded specifically for these final codes. From that process, along with more discussion and debate, we generated the following categories: discipline, the body, networking, masculinity, femininity, sexuality, race, social class, and preparation for adulthood.

Data: Cheerleading and the Ideal Girl

I am not arrogant.
I am confident.
I am not a daredevil.
I am daring.
I am not a beauty queen.
I am an athlete.

I am not a stereotype.
I am my own person.
I am not interested in the past.
I am living for the future.
I am not afraid of success.
I am afraid of nothing.
I am not another face in the crowd.
I am the one others wish they could be.
I am not just any cheerleader.
I am the one in the Varsity uniform.
　　　—Varsity Spirit Corporation (1999, 1)

As is evident in the above poem from the 1999 Varsity Cheerleading catalog, the cheerleader has been reconstructed to represent new ideals of normative femininity, which include confidence, rationality, risk taking, athleticism, independence, and fearlessness. In this section, we demonstrate how the girls in our study take up these signifiers of ideal girlhood to create their own version of femininity, one that allows them to dabble with the traditional markers of masculinity without having to give up those feminine characteristics they deem enjoyable and desirable. We argue that while they are playing an active role in constituting their own gendered identity within the discursive practice of cheerleading, they are also "constrained by larger material practices, structures and discourses that shape and coerce as well as potentiate individual action" (Davies 1989, xi). By doing so, we hope to demonstrate how girls are both productions of and producers of their own gendered subjectivities.

Masculinity and the Cheerleader Athlete: Discipline, Risk Taking, and Power in the Physical

In the cheerleading preparation classes we observed at Powhaton Middle School, cheerleading as an athletic endeavor was emphasized repeatedly. In preparation for trying out in front of three judges, the cheerleader sponsor continuously instructed the girls to show off their muscular bodies: "All right, girls, make your muscles tight so the judges can see them. Tight across the shoulders. Tomorrow you should hurt. Legs are tight. This is a great time to show off your muscles." In addition to having a muscular, fit body, the ability to tumble and maintain tight motion technique—rigid body movements that some would characterize as almost militaristic in style—were also critical to making the squad. Lisa, a petite blonde who scored the highest number of points at tryouts, explained the importance of being tight:

> Like when you cheer, your arms have to be tight, and your emotions are like aggressive, not like to where you're going to punch someone, just like when they're tight. Like when I get up there, I'm like [hard snapping noise] push my arms down and slap them.

This aggressive attitude was encouraged by Ms. Stone, whose language during practices was replete with militaristic jargon. "Command the room" was a phrase she frequently used to motivate the girls into maintaining an aggressive attitude toward the judges and audience. In teaching proper motion techniques, she would instruct them, "Punch forward—don't swing your arms. Keep everything close to your body. Think close. Tight, tight, tight." Much like a drill sergeant, while working with the girls on motion technique, Ms. Stone would yell,

> Chins up, shoulders back, smiles. Hit the motion. Hit. Hit. Hit. 1, 2, 3, hit, 1, 2, 3,

hit. When I say, Hit, do a V. When I say, Hit, do a down V. Hit L; Hit V; Hit Down V.

At one point, she advised the girls, "Don't be afraid to push through the floor. Smash—power off your toes." At another time, she told the girls, "Attack those jumps even if you don't like the side you're doing." In addition to the girls' using robotic, tight motions, cheers were to be yelled in a deep, masculine voice.

Disciplining the body is an integral part of cheerleading. Preparation for cheerleading at Powhaton means that one must work long hours to master the movements, techniques, and tumbling required to be a serious contender for the cheerleading squad. Two of the criteria judges use at Powhaton to select the girls for the junior high squad are jumps (e.g., herkies, toe touches) and tumbling (back handsprings, back tucks), both of which require practice, perseverance, and athletic prowess. Every girl we interviewed who eventually was selected cheerleader either participated in tumbling classes at one of the local gyms or paid money to individuals to help them in mastering the requisite cheerleading skills. Although Ms. Stone would often tell the girls that tumbling was not an absolute requirement for making the squad, the reality was, as Patti, eventually selected co-captain of the squad, noted, "all of us can do a back handspring."

Part of disciplining the cheerleader body entailed assuming a stance of invulnerability to pain. Embodying the image of the fierce athlete who is able to overcome pain to emerge the triumphant victor, Lisa recounted the harrowing events of tryouts, which eventually led to her obtaining the number 1 spot on the cheerleading squad:

On the day of tryouts, I had 104 degrees fever; I had pneumonia. I had been sick for days and lost six pounds before tryouts. At tryouts, I fell on my head during my back handspring. It was like my wrists just collapsed. But I scored number 1. I couldn't even come to school the next day because I was so sick. My dad said he was proud of me because I showed determination.

During the cheer prep class, Leslie tore a ligament and had to be sent to the emergency room. Michelle suffered a severe sprain and was on crutches for two weeks. Neither saw these injuries as a deterrent to their trying out.

In describing the typical cheerleader, Julie, who was selected to be an eighth-grade cheerleader, said, "They are really peppy and hyper and just jump all over the place all the time." Sharon, also selected cheerleader, stated that she wanted to be a cheerleader because she was "always hyper." The reality is that cheering is not a spontaneous emotional activity. Rather, cheerleaders are to practice rationality and discipline. Indeed, unbridled emotion and spontaneity is appropriate only on the sidelines of sports events and only in certain contexts (e.g., a football player intercepts the ball and runs for a 60-yard touchdown). At all other times, cheerleading is a very controlled, organized, and disciplined activity. Cheers are orchestrated with complex tumbling moves, pyramid building, and partner stunts; dances are choreographed with precision; and chants often sound like military yells. There is little room for individual creativity in cheerleading at Powhatan.

Part of controlling one's emotion means the girls were to act in a way that on the surface seemed inauthentic. As preparation for tryouts, Ms. Stone repeatedly told the girls, "Pretend that you are having the time of your life. Show it in your faces, in your smiles." The ability to assume an inauthentic stance was most readily visible in the edicts to the girls to always have a smile on their face. More than any other quality, the ability to smile at all times seemed to be the most prized cheerleading attribute. Yet smiling in this context is not a spontaneous emotional response; rather, the ability to plaster a smile on one's face at a moment's notice was a very disciplined activity requiring a particular mind-set and lots of practice, as illustrated in the following comments:

> You have to have a cheerleading personality, you know, smile all the time. Like Ms. Stone told me, "I don't care if it's a fake smile or not, just smile." (Terry, selected cheerleader)
> You have to smile to look good, so everyone will think you're having a wonderful time. (Allison, selected cheerleader)
> When you see a cheerleader, she's always smiling. But I can't smile if I don't feel like smiling. (Tamara, member of the cheer prep class, did not try out)
> You've got to have fake smiles all the time. You know, cheesey. It takes practice to smile without it looking fake. I practice all the time in front of my mirror. It's hard work. (Lisa, selected cheerleader)
> You have to be a prep to become a cheerleader because they got that fake happy look about them. I can't get that. I have to really be happy to look happy. (Daneka, member of cheer prep class, did not try out)

The ability to execute tight movements and complicated jumps and tumbling feats was a source of confidence for the girls selected cheerleader, as explained by Lisa— "It just gives you confidence, makes you feel good when you know you can make your body do these really hard things"— and Allison—"the prep girls will make it because they have confidence; they can jump, tumble, and do tight motions. They have it all." Karla, who tried out but was not selected, probably because of her lack of tumbling ability, noted,

> When you can tumble, the judges think of you as more flexible. Like you can do things better than everybody else. It gives them confidence. If they mess up, they don't just sit there. They get back up and do it again.

Clearly, for some girls, cheerleading offers a space for them to gain confidence in their bodies and themselves.

The desired female body is continuously rethought and reshaped through disciplining and normalizing practices that reflect both contemporary and historical understandings of what constitutes ideal femininity. Unlike the ideal female body of yesteryear that was prized because of its inertness, delicacy, and helplessness, the revered female body today is that of the hard-muscled, sleek athlete, and girls today are being taught that it is not only appropriate but desirable to run, jump, tumble, act boldly, and move daringly (Bordo 1993). Cheerleading offers a safe space for girls to do just this, that is, to revel and delight in the physicality of their bodies. This is one of the main reasons why cheerleading, despite feminist critiques, continues to grow and attract large numbers of girls. With the assumption of many of the discursive practices once associated primarily with men and sports (e.g., musculature, strength, athletic prowess, fear of danger, and risk taking), cheerleading offers a space for some girls to embody the masculine look of the athlete and the concomitant values of self-discipline, aggressiveness, and self-mastery, thus entering a sphere once relegated to only boys and men.

Femininity and Girlie Girls Diverting the Gaze: Pleasure and Sexualized Subjectivity in Cheerleading

Most of us want to be cheerleaders because we are more into being a girlie girl. (Lisa)

The girls selected cheerleader at Powhaton embraced the public nature of cheerleading, which allowed them to demonstrate to the world that they were confident, assertive, competitive, and athletic. However, the appeal of cheerleading went beyond simply the opportunity to prove they were athletes. In fact, the majority of the girls selected cheerleader were already known at their school as accomplished athletes; many of them had to juggle track and basketball practice with the mandatory cheerleading preparation clinic. This number is in line with recent data from a poll of 2,500 cheerleaders conducted by the Universal Cheerleaders Association, which found that more than 50 percent of girls who cheer also participate in other athletic activities at this school (Roenigk 2002). Cheerleading was appealing to these girls because it also offered them a space to revel in what they called being a girlie girl. Unlike other athletes, these girls are participating in an activity that remains firmly entrenched within a feminine discourse; thus, they do not have to veil their masculinity nor worry, like other athletes, about being stigmatized as too masculine or as lesbians. These girls embrace cheerleading as a way to have it

all—to flirt with the masculine without ever questioning or having someone else question their femininity or their sexual identity.

Traditionally, cheerleading has been constructed as an activity that valorizes stereotypical feminine virtues such as nurturance, selflessness, subservience, and loyalty. Cheerleading as a stereotypical feminine discourse was certainly evident at Powhaton, particularly as enacted in the values and beliefs of Ms. Stone, who explains the purpose of cheerleading as follows:

My school spirit comes from the heart, and these young women need to learn how to be loyal. They need to learn how to take the eyes off of themselves. We're there for other people; we're not there for ourselves. . . . If it weren't for the athletes in the building, there would be no reason for us; we're to give of ourselves; we are serving our athletes.

For the girls in this study, one of the primary joys of being a cheerleader derived from the knowledge that cheerleaders are the object of everyone's gaze—not just males. Most of the girls who were selected cheerleader told stories of how they, as early as four years old, envied and wanted to emulate the cheerleaders they saw from their view in the stands. Lisa explained,

There are so many people who aren't into basketball or football and all they do is watch the cheerleaders and say, "Wow! I want to do that!" And they think of them as a role model, like, Yeah, mom there's a cheerleader. I want to be that when I grow up. That's what I did.

Being the center of attention, being the one "others wish they could be," offered these girls a form of power and pleasure not experienced in other activities, such as playing basketball or being in the school orchestra. Milea, the only Native American chosen for the squad, explained the difference between cheerleading and other sports: "Cheerleading is a sport you can have fun at. Sports were invented so that people could have fun, but most sports have turned into work not fun. But not cheerleading. It's just fun!" The cheerleaders in this study saw themselves as central to the sporting event being observed and believed they had the power to control how the crowd and the players respond to the game on the field or the court.

In conveying her implicit understanding of the ideal woman as one who is heterosexual, a wife, and a mother, Ms. Stone explicated how cheerleading prepares girls for adult womanhood:

> Cheerleaders are still very feminine, and we work on those characteristics. We have rules, no burping, no farting. You are young ladies. But we build, we jump, we try to get a balance because cheerleading does prepare them for later on in life. They've got to be strong. They've got to bear pain to have children. . . . They've got to be able to stand on their feet and make decisions when it may be mom, or dad, or husband, who's laid out there and you've got to do what is the right thing to do. You've got to support. You've got to lift up. That's the whole role of being an adult woman.

Undoubtedly, cheerleading can still be read as a discourse that affirms heterosexualized femininity in which a woman's most basic desire is to be affiliated with a man. Although none of the girls expressed the sentiment that cheerleading was excellent preparation for being a wife and mother, many of the girls trying out for cheerleader at Powhaton expressed the belief that cheerleading made one more popular, thus increasing one's likelihood of gaining a boyfriend, a high-status marker for adolescent girls at this school. For example, Milea pointed out, "Boys like cheerleaders so that makes you popular. I want more boys to like me." Shanna, who was in the cheer prep class but did not try out, explained, "Some girls think the boys will like you if you're a cheerleader 'cause boys like the cheeriest people." Daneka, who did not try out for cheerleader although she participated in the cheer prep class, stated that "girls want to be cheerleaders because they believe that guys will like them more—they will see them as cute women in short skirts."

Daneka's use of "girls" and "women" in the same sentence reflects a primary attraction of cheerleading for many girls: It allows girls to try on a womanly (i.e., sexualized) identity in a school-sanctioned space. Walkerdine (1993) argued that in most accounts about girls' experiences in schools, the schoolgirl typified is the one who follows rules and is deferential, is loyal, is quiet, and works hard. This image of the schoolgirl, Walkerdine (1993, 20) asserted, has been constructed as a "defence against being the object of male fantasies. The erotic is displaced [in school accounts] as too dangerous. But it re-enters, it enters in the spaces that are outlawed in the primary school: popular culture." Cheerleading does allow the erotic to enter into school spaces; in fact, cheerleading at Powhaton Middle School offered the only school-sanctioned space for girls simultaneously to play with or to try on the identity of the all-

American nice girl next door and the sexually provocative woman. Cheerleaders are allowed to wear short skirts and tight-fitting vests, which violate school dress codes, while performing sexually provocative dance moves (e.g., pelvic thrusts) on the school stage to popular music typically not allowed elsewhere in school. For many of the girls, such as Julie, this opportunity to play with a sexualized identity was a primary reason cheerleading was so appealing. She explained, "I'm in it for the short skirts, the guys, getting in front of everybody, and making a total fool of myself."

Undeniably, the sexualized nature of cheerleading, which situates girls as objects of desire—clad in short skirts and tight-fitting vests—was part of the discourse of cheerleading at Powhaton. While performing tight, militaristic movements and using a deep voice, the girls were also instructed to look at the judges in a sexy way. "When you make that turn," instructed Ms. Stone, "give the judges a sexy look." She further instructed them, "You should be oozing out cheerleading stuff. Dazzle me, smile, give me goosebumps. I want to be dazzled." The last advice Ms. Stone gave the girls before the day of tryouts was to "put Vaseline on your teeth and put on a little extra makeup, but not too much. Don't come looking like someone who could stand on the street."

Conclusion

Operating at the juncture of all-American good looks, traditional femininity, and sports-like athleticism, contemporary cheerleading provides a culturally sanctioned space for performing the requisite traits of the ideal girl in the new millennium. Quite literally, cheerleading is a performative act—one that has been traditionally understood as

girls performing for the pleasure of others, particularly men. Many would argue, as in the film *American Beauty*, that this performance situates the girl body as the object of the masculine gaze and male fantasy. As Kurman (1986, 58) noted, "the cheerleader is a disturbing erotic icon. . . . She incarnates, in a word, a basic male-voyeuristic fantasy." Yet Kenway et al. (1994, 205), in discussing their work with adolescent girls and gender reform in Australia, offered a different reading of the performance metaphor:

> The performance metaphor allows the girls to feel a sense of control over different performance genres, to pick up, discard, play and take risks within them, and even to go beyond them through improvisation, collage, and carnival. Femininity can then become a source of power and pleasure rather than a source of control.

We found ample evidence in our study to suggest that cheerleading offers a critical space for certain girls to take risks, to try on different personas, to delight in the physicality of their bodies, and to control and revel in their own power and desire. In other words, cheerleading offers some girls the opportunity to perform ideal girlhood without being located in a disabling discourse of femininity that equates femininity with exploitation and oppression. In many ways, these girls have embraced cheerleading as a way of accommodating the contradictions of constructing oneself as a feminine subject. Thus, any reading of cheerleading and the new girl order must acknowledge that girls themselves play an active role in reconstituting ideal femininity as they resist, rethink, and re-envision for themselves who they want to be as gendered individuals.

Although the girls in this study took up multiple gendered subjectivities within the discursive practices of cheerleading, they are not free to construct any gender identity they desire. As feminist poststructuralists (Davies 1989; Walkerdine 1993; Weedon 1987) have pointed out, constructing a gendered identity is always constrained by larger material practices, structures, and discourses. This study shows how these shape and influence the ways in which girls negotiate a gendered identity within a patriarchal society that continues to define ideal girlhood very narrowly. Hence, we are reminded how powerful certain discourses are despite the changing landscape for normative masculinity and femininity. As several researchers of girl culture have pointed out (Brumberg 1997; Inness 1998; Johnson, Roberts, and Worrell 1999), growing up female is not an easy task, particularly in a time when the signifiers of masculinity and femininity seem to be always in flux. As ideal femininity has shifted, girls in the twenty-first century are faced with the problem of how far they can go in displaying femininity and masculinity, in what contexts such displays are appropriate, and to what degree. This study reveals how these contradictions play out in the discursive practices associated with contemporary cheerleading and sports. For example, cheerleaders dressed in short skirts and tight vests often cheer for female basketball players dressed in baggy shorts and shirts. Through their uniforms, the cheerleaders accentuate their femininity while the basketball players hide theirs. The cheerleaders try to play up their masculinity, not through their clothing but through their stunts and tumbling, while the female basketball players often play up their femi-

ninity off court to become the "heterosexy" athlete (Griffin 1992), thus gaining acceptance and avoiding the lesbian label.

Obviously, cheerleading is but one avenue for girls to contest stereotypical images of the docile, unathletic female body. Girls now have opportunities, although much more limited, to engage in ice hockey, football, boxing, and bodybuilding. However, as Inness (1999) and Lowe (1998) pointed out, despite the gains women have made in many areas once relegated solely for men, in the twenty-first century, we still do not exactly know what to do with women who box, women bodybuilders, and women who want to play professional football and ice hockey. When women enter a masculine discourse and assume masculine signifiers, mainstream society is threatened, and when a woman steps over the boundaries of acceptable feminine behavior, she is typically viewed as gender deviant (Adams 1999; Inness 1999). Similar to the All-American Girls Baseball League begun in the 1940s and disbanded in the 1950s, cheerleaders, as personification of the ideal girl, merely flirt with the masculine. As Candice Berry, coach of the Greenup County High cheerleading squad in Kentucky, one of the top cheerleading squads in the country, stated, "cheerleading offers budding young women something that girls' basketball, track, soccer, softball can't offer: lessons in how to be a *lady*, how to be tough without imitating men" (McElroy 1999, 199). Cheerleaders, for all their athleticism, toughness, and risk taking, do not disrupt twenty-first century, taken-for-granted notions of normative femininity and masculinity. In other words, they ultimately do not challenge the status quo by transgressing gendered boundaries.

References

Adams, Natalie. 1999. Fighting to be somebody: The discursive practices of adolescent girls fighting. *Educational Studies* 30:115–39.

Adams, Natalie, and Pamela Bettis. In press. *Spirit! Let's hear it! The making and remaking of the American cheerleader*. New York: Palgrave Press.

Argetsinger, Amy. 1999. When cheerleaders are the main event: For private teams, victory is their own. *Washington Post*, 10 July, A1.

Berg, Bruce. 2001. *Qualitative research methods for the social sciences*. Boston: Allyn & Bacon.

Bordo, Susan. 1993. *Unbearable weight: Feminism, Western culture, and the body*. Berkeley: University of California Press.

Brenner, Elsa. 1999. Cheerleading changes as boys join sidelines: Stereotypes slip away, attitudes shift and a sport calls for more acrobatics. *New York Times*, 2 May, Section 14, 1, 4–5.

Brumberg, Joan. 1997. *The body project: An intimate history of American girls*. New York: Random House.

Budgeon, Shelley. 1998. "I'll tell you what I really, really want": Girl power and self-identity in Britain. In *Millennium girls: Today's girls around the world*, edited by Sherrie Inness. Lanham, MD: Rowman & Littlefield.

Coffey, Amanda, and Paul Atkinson. 1996. *Making sense of qualitative data*. Thousand Oaks, CA: Sage.

Currie, Dawn. 1997. Decoding femininity: Advertisements and their teenage readers. *Gender & Society* 11:453–77.

Davies, Bronwyn. 1989. *Frogs and snails and feminist tales*. Sydney, Australia: Allen and Unwin.

———. 1993. *Shards of glass: Children reading and writing beyond gendered identity*. Cresskill, NJ: Hampton Press.

Davis, L. 1990. Male cheerleaders and the naturalization of gender. In *Sports, men and the gender order*, edited by Michael Messner and Don Sabo. Champaign, IL: Human Kinetics Books.

Deardorff, Julie. 1999. Cheerleaders want R-E-S-P-E-C-T: Competitions take pep squads beyond old sis-boom bah. *Chicago Tribune*, 30 May, 1, 3.

Douglas, Susan. 1997. Girls 'n' spice: All things nice? *Nation*, 25 August, 21. Retrieved 16 October 2000 from wysiwygillbodyframe.5/http://ehostgw13…=39&booleanTerm=Girl%20Powre&fuzzyTerm=.

Eckert, Penelope. 1989. *Jocks and burnouts*. New York: Teachers College Press.

Foucault, Michael. 1979. *Discipline and punish*. New York: Vintage.

Fraser, Nancy. 1992. The uses and abuses of French discourse theories/or feminist politics. In *Revaluing French feminism: Critical essays on difference, agency, and culture*, edited by Nancy Fraser and Susan Bartkey. Bloomington: Indiana University Press.

Gonzales, Arturo. 1956. The first college cheer. *American Mercury* 83:100–104.

Griffin, Pat. 1992. Changing the game: Homophobia, sexism, and lesbians in sport. *Quest* 44:251–65.

Hanson, Mary Ellen. 1995. *Go! Fight! Win! Cheerleading in American culture*. Bowling Green, OH: Bowling Green University Press.

Inness, Sherrie. 1998. *Millennium girls: Today's girls around the world*. Lanham, MD: Rowman & Littlefield.

———. 1999. *Tough girls: Women warriors and wonder women in popular culture*. Philadelphia: University of Pennsylvania Press.

Johnson, Norine, Michael Roberts, and Judith Worell. 1999. *Beyond appearance: A new look at adolescent girls*. Washington, DC: American Psychological Association.

Kenway, Jane, and Sue Willis. 1998. *Answering back: Girls, boys and feminism in schools*. London: Routledge.

Kenway, Jane, Sue Willis, Jill Blackmore, and Leonia Rennie. 1994. Making "hope practical" rather than "despair convincing": Feminist poststructuralism, gender reform and educational change. *British Journal of Sociology of Education* 15:187–210.

Kurman, George. 1986. What does girls' cheerleading communicate? *Journal of Popular Culture* 20:57–64.

Kutz, F. B. 1955. Cheerleading rules, desirable traits and qualifications. *School Activities* 26:310.

Lemish, Dafna. 1998. Spice Girls' talk: A case study in the development of gendered identity. In *Millennium girls: Today's girls around the world*, edited by Sherrie Inness. Lanham, MD: Rowman & Littlefield.

Lowe, Maria. 1998. *Women of steel: Female body builders and the struggle for self-definition.* New York: New York University Press.

Marshall, Catherine, and Sharon Rossman. 1995. *Designing qualitative research.* Thousand Oaks, CA: Sage.

McElroy, James. 1999. *We've got spirit: The life and times of America's greatest cheerleading team.* New York: Simon & Schuster.

McRobbie, Angela. 1993. Shut up and dance: Youth culture and changing modes of femininity. *Cultural Studies* 7:406–26.

Mitchell, Sally. 1995. *The new girl: Girls' culture in England 1880–1915.* New York: Columbia University Press.

Nelson, Claudia, and Lynne Vallone. 1994. *The girl's own: Cultural histories of the Anglo-American girl, 1830–1915.* Athens: University of Georgia Press.

Oliver, Kimberly. 1999. Adolescent girls' body-narratives: Learning to desire and create a "fashionable" image. *Teachers College Record* 101:220–46.

Organized cheering. 1911. *Nation* 92:5–6.

Roenigk, Alyssa. 2002. Cheer safety: Setting the record straight. *American Cheerleader* 8:46–48.

Solomon, Alisa. 1999. Girlpower? *Village Voice*, 27 April, 59–63. Retrieved 13 October 2000 from http://proquest.umi.com/pqdweb?TS=97144...mt=4&Sid=1&Idx=196&Deli=1&RQT=309&Dtp=1.

Varsity Spirit Corporation. 1999. *Varsity.* Memphis, TN: Varsity Spirit Corporation.

Walkerdine, Valerie. 1990. *Schoolgirl fictions.* London: Verso.

———. 1993. Girlhood through the looking glass. In *Girls, girlhood and girls' studies in transition*, edited by Marion de Ras and Mieke Lunenberg. Amsterdam: Het Spinhuis.

Weedon, Chris. 1987. *Feminist practice and poststructuralist theory.* Oxford, UK: Basil Books.

Weis, Lois. 1997. Gender and the reports: The case of the missing piece. In *Feminist critical policy analysis: A perspective from primary and secondary schooling*, edited by Catherine Marshall. London: Falmer.

Woodmansee, Ken. 1993. Cheers! Jeff Webb's multicolored world wide spirit machine. *Memphis Business* 3:14–19.

11 C. J. Pascoe

"Dude, You're a Fag"
Adolescent Masculinity and the Fag Discourse

"There's a faggot over there! There's a faggot over there! Come look!" yelled Brian, a senior at River High School, to a group of 10-year-old boys. Following Brian, the 10 year olds dashed down a hallway. At the end of the hallway Brian's friend, Dan, pursed his lips and began sashaying towards the 10-year-olds. He minced towards them, swinging his hips exaggeratedly and wildly waving his arms. To the boys Brian yelled, "Look at the faggot! Watch out! He'll get you!" In response the 10-year-olds raced back down the hallway screaming in terror. (From author's fieldnotes)

The relationship between adolescent masculinity and sexuality is embedded in the specter of the faggot. Faggots represent a penetrated masculinity in which "to be penetrated is to abdicate power" (Bersani, 1987: 212). Penetrated men symbolize a masculinity devoid of power, which, in its contradiction, threatens both psychic and social chaos. It is precisely this specter of penetrated masculinity that functions as a regulatory mechanism of gender for contemporary American adolescent boys.

Feminist scholars of masculinity have documented the centrality of homophobic insults to masculinity (Lehne, 1998; Kim-

mel, 2001) especially in school settings (Wood, 1984; Smith, 1998; Burn, 2000; Plummer, 2001; Kimmel, 2003). They argue that homophobic teasing often characterizes masculinity in adolescence and early adulthood, and that anti-gay slurs tend to primarily be directed at other gay boys.

This article both expands on and challenges these accounts of relationships between homophobia and masculinity. Homophobia is indeed a central mechanism in the making of contemporary American adolescent masculinity. This article both critiques and builds on this finding by (1) pointing to the limits of an argument that focuses centrally on homophobia, (2) demonstrating that the fag is not only an identity linked to homosexual boys[1] but an identity that can temporarily adhere to heterosexual boys as well and (3) highlighting the racialized nature of the fag as a disciplinary mechanism.

"Homophobia" is too facile a term with which to describe the deployment of "fag" as an epithet. By calling the use of the word "fag" homophobia—and letting the argument stop with that point—previous research obscures the gendered nature of sexualized insults (Plummer, 2001). Invoking homophobia to describe the ways in which boys aggressively tease each other overlooks the powerful relationship between masculinity and this sort of insult. Instead, it seems incidental in this conventional line of argument that girls do not harass each other and are not harassed in this same manner.[2] This framing naturalizes the relationship between masculinity and homophobia, thus obscuring the centrality of such harassment in the formation of a gendered identity for boys in a way that it is not for girls.

"Fag" is not necessarily a static identity attached to a particular (homosexual) boy. Fag talk and fag imitations serve as a discourse with which boys discipline themselves and each other through joking relationships.[3] Any boy can temporarily become a fag in a given social space or interaction. This does not mean that those boys who identify as or are perceived to be homosexual are not subject to intense harassment. But becoming a fag has as much to do with failing at the masculine tasks of competence, heterosexual prowess and strength or in any way revealing weakness or femininity, as it does with a sexual identity. This fluidity of the fag identity is what makes the specter of the fag such a powerful disciplinary mechanism. It is fluid enough that boys police most of their behaviors out of fear of having the fag identity permanently adhere and definitive enough so that boys recognize a fag behavior and strive to avoid it.

The fag discourse is racialized. It is invoked differently by and in relation to white boys' bodies than it is by and in relation to African-American boys' bodies. While certain behaviors put all boys at risk for becoming temporarily a fag, some behaviors can be enacted by African-American boys without putting them at risk of receiving the label. The racialized meanings of the fag discourse suggest that something more than simple homophobia is involved in these sorts of interactions. An analysis of boys' deployments of the specter of the fag should also extend to the ways in which gendered power works through racialized selves. It is not that this gendered homophobia does not exist in African-American communities. Indeed, making fun of "Negro faggotry seems to be a rite of passage among contemporary black male rappers and filmmakers" (Riggs, 1991: 253). However, the fact that "white women and men, gay and straight, have more or less colonized cultural debates about sexual representation" (Julien and Mercer, 1991: 167) obscures varied systems of sexualized meanings among different racialized ethnic groups (Almaguer, 1991; King, 2004).

Theoretical Framing

The sociology of masculinity entails a "critical study of men, their behaviors, practices, values and perspectives" (Whitehead and Barrett, 2001: 14). Recent studies of men emphasize the multiplicity of masculinity (Connell, 1995) detailing the ways in which different configurations of gender practice are promoted, challenged or reinforced in given social situations. This research on how men do masculinities has explored gendered practices in a wide range of social institutions, such as families (Coltrane, 2001) schools (Skelton, 1996; Parker, 1996; Mac an Ghaill, 1996; Francis and Skelton, 2001), workplaces (Cooper, 2000), media (Craig, 1992), and sports (Messner, 1989; Edly and Wetherel, 1997; Curry, 2004). Many of these studies have developed specific typologies of masculinities: gay, Black, Chicano, working class, middle class, Asian, gay Black, gay Chicano, white working class, militarized, transnational business, New Man, negotiated, versatile, healthy, toxic, counter, and cool masculinities, to name a few (Messner, 2004). In this sort of model the fag could be (and often has been) framed as a type of subordinated masculinity attached to homosexual adolescent boys' bodies.

Heeding Timothy Carrigan's admonition that an "analysis of masculinity needs to be related as well to other currents in feminism" (Carrigan et al., 1987: 64), in this article I integrate queer theory's insights about the relationships between gender, sexuality, identities and power with the attention to men found in the literature on masculinities. Like the sociology of gender, queer theory destabilizes the assumed naturalness of the social order (Lemert, 1996). Queer theory is a "conceptualization which sees sexual power as embedded in different levels of social life" and interrogates areas of the social world not usually seen as sexuality (Stein and Plummer, 1994). In this sense queer theory calls for sexuality to be looked at not only as a discrete arena of sexual practices and identities, but also as a constitutive element of social life (Warner, 1993; Epstein, 1996).

While the masculinities' literature rightly highlights very real inequalities between gay and straight men (see for instance Connell, 1995), this emphasis on sexuality as inhered in static identities attached to male bodies, rather than major organizing principles of social life (Sedgwick, 1990), limits scholars' ability to analyze the myriad ways in which sexuality, in part, constitutes gender. This article does not seek to establish that there are homosexual boys and heterosexual boys and the homosexual ones are marginalized. Rather this article explores what happens to theories of gender if we look at a *discourse* of sexualized identities in addition to focusing on seemingly static identity categories inhabited by men. This is not to say that gender is reduced only to sexuality, indeed feminist scholars have demonstrated that gender is embedded in and constitutive of a multitude of social structures—the economy, places of work, families and schools. In the tradition of post-structural feminist theorists of race and gender who look at "border cases" that explode taken-for-granted binaries of race and gender (Smith, 1994), queer theory is another tool which enables an integrated analysis of sexuality, gender and race.

As scholars of gender have demonstrated, gender is accomplished through day-to-day interactions (Fine, 1987; Hochschild, 1989; West and Zimmerman, 1991; Thorne, 1993). In this sense gender is the "activity of managing situated conduct in light of normative conceptions of attitudes and activities appropriate for one's sex category" (West and Zimmerman, 1991: 127). Similarly, queer theorist Judith Butler argues that gender is accomplished interactionally through "a set of repeated acts within a highly rigid regulatory frame that congeal over time to produce the appearance of substance, of a natural sort of being" (Butler, 1999: 43). Specifically she argues that gendered beings are created through processes of citation and repudiation of a "constitutive outside" (Butler, 1993: 3) in which is contained all that is cast out of a socially recognizable gender category. The "constitutive outside" is inhabited by abject identities, unrecognizably and unacceptably gendered selves. The interactional accomplishment of gender in a Butlerian model consists, in part, of the continual iteration and repudiation of this abject identity. Gender, in this sense, is "constituted through the force of exclusion and abjection, on which produces a constitutive outside to the subject, an abjected outside, which is, after all, 'inside' the subject as its own founding repudiation" (Butler, 1993: 3). This repudiation creates and reaffirms a "threatening specter" (Butler, 1993: 3) of failed, unrecognizable gender, the existence of which must be continually repudiated through interactional processes.

I argue that the "fag" position is an "abject" position and, as such, is a "threatening specter" constituting contemporary American adolescent masculinity. The fag discourse is the interactional process through which boys name and repudiate this abjected identity. Rather than analyzing the fag as an identity for homosexual boys, I examine uses of the discourse that imply that any boy can become a fag, regardless of his actual desire or self-perceived sexual orientation. The threat of the abject position infuses the faggot with regulatory power. This article provides empirical data to illustrate Butler's approach to gender and indicates that it might be a useful addition to the sociological literature on masculinities through highlighting one of the ways in which a masculine gender identity is accomplished through interaction.

Method

Research Site

I conducted fieldwork at a suburban high school in north-central California which I call River High.[4] River High is a working class, suburban 50-year-old high school located in a town called Riverton. With the exception of the median household income and racial diversity (both of which are elevated due to Riverton's location in California), the town mirrors national averages in the percentages of white collar workers, rates of college attendance, and marriages, and age composition (according to the 2000 census). It is a politically moderate to conservative, religious community. Most of the students' parents commute to surrounding cities for work.

On average Riverton is a middle-class community. However, students at River are likely to refer to the town as two communities: "Old Riverton" and "New Riverton." A busy highway and railroad tracks bisect the town into these two sections. River High is literally on the "wrong side of the tracks," in Old Riverton. Exiting the freeway, heading north to Old Riverton, one sees a mix of 1950s-era ranch-style homes, some with neatly trimmed lawns and tidy gardens, others with yards strewn with various car parts, lawn chairs and appliances. Old Riverton is visually bounded by smoke-puffing factories. On the other side of the freeway New Riverton is characterized by wide sidewalk-lined streets and new walled-in home developments. Instead of smokestacks, a forested mountain, home to a state park, rises majestically in the background. The teens from these homes attend Hillside High, River's rival.

River High is attended by 2000 students. River High's racial/ethnic breakdown roughly represents California at large: 50 percent white, 9 percent African-American, 28 percent Latino and 6 percent Asian (as compared to California's 46, 6, 32, and 11 percent respectively, according to census data and school records). The students at River High are primarily working class.

Research

I gathered data using the qualitative method of ethnographic research. I spent a year and a half conducting observations, formally interviewing 49 students at River High (36 boys and 13 girls), one male student from

Hillside High, and conducting countless informal interviews with students, faculty and administrators. I concentrated on one school because I explore the richness rather than the breadth of data (for other examples of this method see Willis, 1981; MacLeod, 1987; Eder et al., 1995; Ferguson, 2000).

I recruited students for interviews by conducting presentations in a range of classes and hanging around at lunch, before school, after school and at various events talking to different groups of students about my research, which I presented as "writing a book about guys." The interviews usually took place at school, unless the student had a car, in which case he or she met me at one of the local fast food restaurants where I treated them to a meal. Interviews lasted anywhere from half an hour to two hours.

The initial interviews I conducted helped me to map a gendered and sexualized geography of the school, from which I chose my observation sites. I observed a "neutral" site—a senior government classroom, where sexualized meanings were subdued. I observed three sites that students marked as "fag" sites—two drama classes and the Gay/Straight Alliance. I also observed two normatively "masculine" sites—auto-shop and weightlifting.[5] I took daily field notes focusing on how students, faculty and administrators negotiated, regulated and resisted particular meanings of gender and sexuality. I attended major school rituals such as Winter Ball, school rallies, plays, dances and lunches. I would also occasionally "ride along" with Mr. Johnson (Mr. J), the school's security guard, on his battery-powered golf cart to watch which, how and when students were disciplined. Observational data provided me with more

insight to the interactional processes of masculinity than simple interviews yielded. If I had relied only on interview data I would have missed the interactional processes of masculinity which are central to the fag discourse.

Given the importance of appearance in high school, I gave some thought as to how I would present myself, deciding to both blend in and set myself apart from the students. In order to blend in I wore my standard graduate student gear—comfortable, baggy cargo pants, a black t-shirt or sweater and tennis shoes. To set myself apart I carried a messenger bag instead of a backpack, didn't wear makeup, and spoke slightly differently than the students by using some slang, but refraining from uttering the ubiquitous "hecka" and "hella."

The boys were fascinated by the fact that a 30-something white "girl" (their words) was interested in studying them. While at first many would make sexualized comments asking me about my dating life or saying that they were going to "hit on" me, it seemed eventually they began to forget about me as a potential sexual/romantic partner. Part of this, I think, was related to my knowledge about "guy" things. For instance, I lift weights on a regular basis and as a result the weightlifting coach introduced me as a "weight-lifter from U.C. Berkeley" telling the students they should ask me for weightlifting advice. Additionally, my taste in movies and television shows often coincided with theirs. I am an avid fan of the movies "Jackass" and "Fight Club," both of which contain high levels of violence and "bathroom" humor. Finally, I garnered a lot of points among boys because I live off a dangerous street in a nearby city famous for drug deals, gang fights and frequent gun shots.

What Is a Fag?

"Since you were little boys you've been told, 'hey, don't be a little faggot,'" explained Darnell, an African-American football player, as we sat on a bench next to the athletic field. Indeed, both the boys and girls I interviewed told me that "fag" was the worst epithet one guy could direct at another. Jeff, a slight white sophomore, explained to me that boys call each other fag because "gay people aren't really liked over here and stuff." Jeremy, a Latino Junior, told me that this insult literally reduced a boy to nothing, "To call someone gay or fag is like the lowest thing you can call someone. Because that's like saying that you're nothing."

Most guys explained their or other's dislike of fags by claiming that homophobia is just part of what it means to be a guy. For instance Keith, a white soccer-playing senior, explained, "I think guys are just homophobic." However, it is not just homophobia, it is a *gendered* homophobia. Several students told me that these homophobic insults only applied to boys and not girls. For example, while Jake, a handsome white senior, told me that he didn't like gay people, he quickly added, "Lesbians, okay that's *good*." Similarly Cathy, a popular white cheerleader, told me "Being a lesbian is accepted because guys think 'oh that's cool.'" Darnell, after telling me that boys were told not to be faggots, said of lesbians, "They're [guys are] fine with girls. I think it's the guy part that they're like ewwww!" In this sense it is not strictly homophobia, but a gendered homophobia that constitutes adolescent masculinity in the culture of this school. However, it is clear, according to these comments, that lesbians are "good" because of their place in heterosexual male fantasy not necessarily because of

some enlightened approach to same-sex relationships. It does however, indicate that using only the term homophobia to describe boys' repeated use of the word "fag" might be a bit simplistic and misleading.

Additionally, girls at River High rarely deployed the word "fag" and were never called "fags." I recorded girls uttering "fag" only three times during my research. In one instance, Angela, a Latina cheerleader, teased Jeremy, a well-liked white senior involved in student government, for not ditching school with her, "You wouldn't 'cause you're a faggot." However, girls did not use this word as part of their regular lexicon. The sort of gendered homophobia that constitutes adolescent masculinity does not constitute adolescent femininity. Girls were not called dykes or lesbians in any sort of regular or systematic way. Students did tell me that "slut" was the worst thing a girl could be called. However, my field notes indicate that the word "slut" (or its synonym "ho") appears one time for every eight times the word "fag" appears. Even when it does occur, "slut" is rarely deployed as a direct insult against another girl.

Highlighting the difference between the deployment of "gay" and "fag" as insults brings the gendered nature of this homophobia into focus. For boys and girls at River High "gay" is a fairly common synonym for "stupid." While this word shares the sexual origins of "fag," it does not *consistently* have the skew of gender-loaded meaning. Girls and boys often used "gay" as an adjective referring to inanimate objects and male or female people, whereas they used "fag" as a noun that denotes only unmasculine males. Students used "gay" to describe anything from someone's clothes to a new school rule that the students did not like, as in the following encounter:

In auto-shop Arnie pulled out a large older version black laptop computer and placed it on his desk. Behind him Nick said "That's a gay laptop! It's five inches thick!"

A laptop can be gay, a movie can be gay or a group of people can be gay. Boys used "gay" and "fag" interchangeably when they refer to other boys, but "fag" does not have the non-gendered attributes that "gay" sometimes invokes.

While its meanings are not the same as "gay," "fag" does have multiple meanings which do not necessarily replace its connotations as a homophobic slur, but rather exist alongside. Some boys took pains to say that "fag" is not about sexuality. Darnell told me "It doesn't even have anything to do with being gay." J.L., a white sophomore at Hillside High (River High's cross-town rival) asserted "Fag, seriously, it has nothing to do with sexual preference at all. You could just be calling somebody an idiot you know?" I asked Ben, a quiet, white sophomore who wore heavy metal t-shirts to auto-shop each day, "What kind of things do guys get called a fag for?" Ben answered "Anything . . . literally, anything. Like you were trying to turn a wrench the wrong way, 'dude, you're a fag.' Even if a piece of meat drops out of your sandwich, 'you fag!'" Each time Ben said "you fag" his voice deepened as if he were imitating a more masculine boy. While Ben might rightly *feel* like a guy could be called a fag for "anything . . . literally, anything," there are actually specific behaviors which, when enacted by most boys, can render him more vulnerable to a fag epithet. In this instance Ben's comment highlights the use of "fag" as a generic insult for incompetence, which in the world of River High, is central to a masculine identity. A boy could get called a fag for exhibiting any

sort of behavior defined as non-masculine (although not necessarily behaviors aligned with femininity) in the world of River High: being stupid, incompetent, dancing, caring too much about clothing, being too emotional or expressing interest (sexual or platonic) in other guys. However, given the extent of its deployment and the laundry list of behaviors that could get a boy in trouble it is no wonder that Ben felt like a boy could be called "fag" for "anything."

One-third (13) of the boys I interviewed told me that, while they may liberally insult each other with the term, they would not actually direct it at a homosexual peer. Jabes, a Filipino senior, told me

I actually say it [fag] quite a lot, except for when I'm in the company of an actual homosexual person. Then I try not to say it at all. But when I'm just hanging out with my friends I'll be like, "shut up, I don't want to hear you any more, you stupid fag."

Similarly, J.L. compared homosexuality to a disability, saying there is "no way" he'd call an actual gay guy a fag because

There's people who are the retarded people who nobody wants to associate with. I'll be so nice to those guys and I hate it when people make fun of them. It's like, "bro do you realize that they can't help that?" And then there's gay people. They were born that way.

According to this group of boys, gay is a legitimate, if marginalized, social identity. If a man is gay, there may be a chance he could be considered masculine by other men (Connell, 1995). David, a handsome white senior dressed smartly in khaki pants and a white button-down shirt said, "Being gay is just a lifestyle. It's someone you choose to sleep with. You can still throw around a football and be gay." In other words there is a possibility, however slight, that a boy can be gay and masculine. To be a fag is, by definition, the opposite of masculine, whether or not the word is deployed with sexualized or non-sexualized meanings. In explaining this to me, Jamaal, an African-American junior, cited the explanation of popular rap artist, Eminem,

> Although I don't like Eminem, he had a good definition of it. It's like taking away your title. In an interview they were like, "you're always capping on gays, but then you sing with Elton John." He was like "I don't mean gay as in gay."

This is what Riki Wilchins calls the "Eminem Exception. Eminem explains that he doesn't call people 'faggot' because of their sexual orientation but because they're weak and unmanly" (Wilchins, 2003). This is precisely the way in which this group of boys at River High uses the term "faggot." While it is not necessarily acceptable to be gay, at least a man who is gay can do other things that render him acceptably masculine. A fag, by the very definition of the word, indicated by students' usages at River High, cannot be masculine. This distinction between "fag" as an un-masculine and problematic identity and "gay" as a possibly masculine, although marginalized, sexual identity is not limited to a teenage lexicon, but is reflected in both psychological discourses (Sedgwick, 1995) and gay and lesbian activism.

Becoming a Fag

"The ubiquity of the word faggot speaks to the reach of its discrediting capacity" (Corbett, 2001: 4). It is almost as if boys cannot help but shout it out on a regular basis—in the hallway, in class, across campus as a greeting, or as a joke. In my fieldwork I was amazed by the way in which the word seemed to pop uncontrollably out of boys' mouths in all kinds of situations. To quote just one of many instances from my fieldnotes:

> Two boys walked out of the P.E. locker room and one yelled "fucking faggot!" at no one in particular.

This spontaneous yelling out of a variation of fag seemingly apropos of nothing happened repeatedly among boys throughout the school.

The fag discourse is central to boys' joking relationships. Joking cements relationships between boys (Kehily and Nayak, 1997; Lyman, 1998) and helps to manage anxiety and discomfort (Freud, 1905). Boys invoked the specter of the fag in two ways: through humorous imitation and through lobbing the epithet at one another. Boys at River High imitated the fag by acting out an exaggerated "femininity," and/or by pretending to sexually desire other boys. As indicated by the introductory vignette in which a predatory "fag" threatens the little boys, boys at River High link these performative scenarios with a fag identity. They lobbed the fag epithet at each other in a verbal game of hot potato, each careful to deflect the insult quickly by hurling it toward someone else. These games and imitations make up a fag discourse which highlights the fag not as a static but rather as a fluid identity which boys constantly struggle to avoid.

In imitative performances the fag discourse functions as a constant reiteration of the fag's existence, affirming that the fag is out there; at any moment a boy can become a fag. At the same time these performances demonstrate that the boy who is invoking the fag is *not* a fag. By invoking it so often, boys remind themselves and each other that at any point they can become fags if they are not sufficiently masculine.

> Mr. McNally, disturbed by the noise outside of the classroom, turned to the open door saying "We'll shut this unless anyone really wants to watch sweaty boys playing basketball." Emir, a tall skinny boy, lisped "I wanna watch the boys play!" The rest of the class cracked up at his imitation.

Through imitating a fag, boys assure others that they are not a fag by immediately becoming masculine again after the performance. They mock their own performed femininity and/or same-sex desire, assuring themselves and others that such an identity is one deserving of derisive laughter. The fag identity in this instance is fluid, detached from Emir's body. He can move in and out of this "abject domain" while simultaneously affirming his position as a subject.

Boys also consistently tried to put another in the fag position by lobbing the fag epithet at one another.

> Going through the junk-filled car in the auto-shop parking lot, Jay poked his head out and asked "Where are Craig and Brian?" Neil, responded with "I think they're over there," pointing, then thrusting his hips and pulling his arms back and forth to indicate that Craig and Brian might be having sex. The boys in auto-shop laughed.

This sort of joke temporarily labels both Craig and Brian as faggots. Because the fag discourse is so familiar, the other boys immediately understand that Neil is indicating that Craig and Brian are having sex. However these are not necessarily identities that stick. Nobody actually thinks Craig and Brian are homosexuals. Rather the fag identity is a fluid one, certainly an identity that no boy wants, but one that a boy can escape, usually by engaging in some sort of discursive contest to turn another boy into a fag. However, fag becomes a hot potato that no boy wants to be left holding. In the following example, which occurred soon after the "sex" joke, Brian lobs the fag epithet at someone else, deflecting it from himself:

> Brian initiated a round of a favorite game in auto-shop, the "cock game." Brian quietly, looking at Josh, said, "Josh loves the cock," then slightly louder, "Josh loves the cock." He continued saying this until he was yelling "JOSH LOVES THE COCK!" The rest of the boys laughed hysterically as Josh slinked away saying "I have a bigger dick than all you mother fuckers!"

These two instances show how the fag can be mapped, momentarily, on to one boy's body and how he, in turn, can attach it to another boy, thus deflecting it from himself. In the first instance Neil makes fun of Craig and Brian for simply hanging out together. In the second instance Brian goes from being a fag to making Josh into a fag, through the "cock game." The "fag" is transferable. Boys move in and out of it by discursively creating another as a fag through joking interactions. They, somewhat ironically, can move in and out of the fag position by transforming themselves, temporarily, into a fag, but this has the effect of reaffirming their masculinity when they return to a heterosexual position after imitating the fag.

These examples demonstrate boys invoking the trope of the fag in a discursive struggle in which the boys indicate that they know what a fag is—and that they are not fags. This joking cements bonds between boys as they assure themselves and each other of their masculinity through repeated repudiations of a non-masculine position of the abject.

Racing the Fag

The fag trope is not deployed consistently or identically across social groups at River High. Differences between white boys' and African-American boys' meaning making around clothes and dancing reveal ways in which the fag as the abject position is racialized.

Clean, oversized, carefully put together clothing is central to a hip-hop identity for African-American boys who identify with hip-hop culture.[6] Richard Majors calls this presentation of self a "cool pose" consisting of "unique, expressive and conspicuous styles of demeanor, speech, gesture, clothing, hairstyle, walk, stance and handshake," developed by African-American men as a symbolic response to institutionalized racism (Majors, 2001: 211). Pants are usually several sizes too big, hanging low on a boy's waist, usually revealing a pair of boxers beneath. Shirts and sweaters are similarly oversized, often hanging down to a boy's knees. Tags are frequently left on baseball hats worn slightly askew and sit perched high on the head. Meticulously clean, unlaced athletic shoes with rolled up socks under the tongue complete a typical hip-hop outfit.

This amount of attention and care given to clothing for white boys not identified with hip-hop culture (that is, most of the white boys at River High) would certainly cast them into an abject, fag position. White boys are not supposed to appear to care about their clothes or appearance, because only fags care about how they look. Ben illustrates this:

Ben walked in to the auto-shop classroom from the parking lot where he had been working on a particularly oily engine. Grease stains covered his jeans. He looked down at them, made a face and walked toward me with limp wrists, laughing and lisping in a high pitch sing-song voice "I got my good panths all dirty!"

Ben draws on indicators of a fag identity, such as limp wrists, as do the boys in the introductory vignette to illustrate that a masculine person certainly would not care about having dirty clothes. In this sense, masculinity, for white boys, becomes the carefully crafted appearance of not caring about appearance, especially in terms of cleanliness.

However, African-American boys involved in hip-hop culture talk frequently about whether or not their clothes, specifically their shoes, are dirty:

In drama class both Darnell and Marc compared their white Adidas basketball shoes. Darnell mocked Marc because black scuff marks covered his shoes, [say]ing incredulously "Yours are a week old and they're dirty—I've had mine for a month and they're not dirty!" Both laughed.

Monte, River High's star football player echoed this concern about dirty shoes when looking at the fancy red shoes he had lent to his cousin the week before, told me he was frustrated because after his cousin used them, the "shoes are hella scuffed up." Clothing, for these boys, does not indicate a fag position, but rather defines membership in a certain cultural and racial group (Perry, 2002).

Dancing is another arena that carries distinctly fag associated meanings for white boys and masculine meanings for African-American boys who participate in hip-hop culture. White boys often associate dancing with "fags." J.L. told me that guys think "'nSync's gay" because they can dance. 'nSync is an all white male singing group known for their dance moves. At dances white boys frequently held their female dates tightly, locking their hips together. The boys never danced with one another, unless engaged in a round of "hot potato." White boys often jokingly danced together in order to embarrass each other by making someone else into a fag:

> Lindy danced behind her date, Chris. Chris's friend, Matt, walked up and nudged Lindy aside, imitating her dance moves behind Chris. As Matt rubbed his hands up and down Chris's back, Chris turned around and jumped back startled to see Matt there instead of Lindy. Matt cracked up as Chris turned red.

However dancing does not carry this sort of sexualized gender meaning for all boys at River High. For African-American boys dancing demonstrates membership in a cultural community (Best, 2000). African-American boys frequently danced together in single sex groups, teaching each other the latest dance moves, showing off a particularly difficult move or making each other laugh with humorous dance moves. Students recognized K.J. as the most talented dancer at the school. K.J. is a sophomore of African-American and Filipino descent who participated in the hip-hop culture of River High. He continually wore the latest hip-hop fashions. K.J. was extremely popular. Girls hollered his name as they walked down the hall and thrust urgently written love notes folded in complicated designs into his hands as he sauntered to class. For the past two years K.J. won first place in the talent show for dancing. When he danced at assemblies the room reverberated with screamed chants of "Go K.J.! Go K.J.! Go K.J.!" Because dancing for African-American boys places them within a tradition of masculinity, they are not at risk of becoming a fag for this particular gendered practice. Nobody called K.J. a fag. In fact in several of my interviews boys of multiple racial/ethnic backgrounds spoke admiringly of K.J.'s dancing abilities.

Implications

These findings confirm previous studies of masculinity and sexuality that position homophobia as central to contemporary definitions of adolescent masculinity. These data extend previous research by unpacking multi-layered meanings that boys deploy through their uses of homophobic language and joking rituals. By attending to these meanings I reframe the discussion as one of a fag discourse, rather than simply labeling this sort of behavior as homophobia. The fag is an "abject" position, a position outside of masculinity that actually constitutes masculinity. Thus, masculinity in part becomes the daily interactional work of repudiating the "threatening specter" of the fag.

The fag extends beyond a static sexual identity attached to a gay boy. Few boys are permanently identified as fags; most move in and out of fag positions. Looking at "fag" as a discourse rather than a static identity reveals that the term can be invested with different meanings in different social spaces. "Fag" may be used as a weapon with which to temporarily assert one's masculinity by denying it to others. Thus "fag" becomes a symbol around which contests of masculinity take place.

The fag epithet, when hurled at other boys, may or may not have explicit sexual meanings, but it always has gendered meanings. When a boy calls another boy a fag, it means he is not a man, not necessarily that he is a homosexual. The boys in this study know that they are not supposed to call homosexual boys "fags" because that is mean. This, then, has been the limited success of the mainstream gay rights movement. The message absorbed by some of these teenage boys is that "gay men can be masculine, just like you." Instead of challenging gender inequality, this particular discourse of gay rights has reinscribed it. Thus we need to begin to think about how gay men may be in a unique position to challenge gendered as well as sexual norms.

This study indicates that researchers who look at the intersection of sexuality and masculinity need to attend to the ways in which racialized identities may affect how "fag" is deployed and what it means in various social situations. While researchers have addressed the ways in which masculine identities are racialized (Connell, 1995; Ross, 1998; Bucholtz, 1999; Davis, 1999; Price, 1999; Ferguson, 2000; Majors, 2001) they have not paid equal attention to the ways in which "fag" might be a racialized epithet. It is important to look at when, where and with what meaning "the fag" is deployed in order to get at how masculinity is defined, contested, and invested in among adolescent boys.

Research shows that sexualized teasing often leads to deadly results, as evidenced by the spate of school shootings in the 1990s (Kimmel, 2003). Clearly the fag discourse affects not just homosexual teens, but all boys, gay and straight. Further re-

search could investigate these processes in a variety of contexts: varied geographic locations, sexualized groups, classed groups, religious groups and age groups.

Notes

1. While the term "homosexual" is laden with medicalized and normalizing meanings, I use it instead of "gay" because "gay" in the world of River High has multiple meanings apart from sexual practices or identities.

2. Girls do insult one another based on sexualized meanings. But in my own research I found that girls and boys did not harass girls in this manner with the same frequency that boys harassed each other through engaging in joking about the fag.

3. I use discourse in the Foucauldian sense, to describe truth producing practices, not just text or speech (Foucault, 1978).

4. The names of places and respondents have been changed.

5. Auto-shop was a class in which students learned how to build and repair cars. Many of the students in this course were looking into careers as mechanics.

6. While there are several white and Latino boys at River High who identify with hip-hop culture, hip-hop is identified by the majority of students as an African-American cultural style.

References

Almaguer, Tomas (1991) "Chicago Men: A Cartography of Homosexual Identity and Behavior," *Differences* 3:75–100.

Bersani, Leo (1987) "Is the Rectum a Grave?" *October* 43:197–222.

Best, Amy (2000) *Prom Night: Youth, Schools and Popular Culture*. New York: Routledge.

Bucholtz, Mary (1999) "'You Da Man': Narrating the Racial Other in the Production of White Masculinity," *Journal of Sociolinguistics* 3/4:443–60.

Burn, Shawn M. (2000) "Heterosexuals' Use of 'Fag' and 'Queer' to Deride One Another: A

Contributor to Heterosexism and Stigma," *Journal of Homosexuality* 40:1–11.

Butler, Judith (1993) *Bodies that Matter.* Routledge: New York.

Butler, Judith (1999) *Gender Trouble.* New York: Routledge.

Carrigan, Tim, Connell, Bob and Lee, John (1987) "Toward a New Sociology of Masculinity," in Harry Brod (ed.) *The Making of Masculinities: The New Men's Studies*, pp. 188–202. Boston, MA: Allen & Unwin.

Coltrane, Scott (2001) "Selling the Indispensable Father," paper presented at *Pushing the Boundaries Conference: New Conceptualizations of Childhood and Motherhood*, Philadelphia.

Connell, R.W. (1995) *Masculinities.* Berkeley: University of California Press.

Cooper, Marianne (2000) "Being the 'Go-To Guy': Fatherhood, Masculinity and the Organization of Work in Silicon Valley," *Qualitative Sociology* 23:379–405.

Corbett, Ken (2001) "Faggot=Loser," *Studies in Gender and Sexuality* 2:3–28.

Craig, Steve (1992) *Men, Masculinity and the Media.* Newbury Park: Sage.

Curry, Timothy J. (2004) "Fraternal Bonding in the Locker Room: A Profeminist Analysis of Talk About Competition and Women," in Michael Messner and Michael Kimmel (eds.) *Men's Lives.* Boston: Pearson.

Davis, James E. (1999) "Forbidden Fruit: Black Males' Constructions of Transgressive Sexualities in Middle School," in William J. Letts IV and James T. Sears (eds.) *Queering Elementary Education: Advancing the Dialogue about Sexualities and Schooling*, pp. 49 ff. Lanham, MD: Rowman & Littlefield.

Eder, Donna, Evans, Catherine and Parker, Stephen (1995) *School Talk: Gender and Adolescent Culture.* New Brunswick, NJ: Rutgers University Press.

Edly, Nigel and Wetherell, Margaret (1997) "Jockeying for Position: The Construction of Masculine Identities," *Discourse and Society* 8:203–17.

Epstein, Steven (1996) "A Queer Encounter," in Steven Seidman (ed.) *Queer Theory/Sociology*, pp. 188–202. Cambridge, MA: Blackwell.

Ferguson, Ann (2000) *Bad Boys: Public Schools in the Making of Black Masculinity.* Ann Arbor: University of Michigan Press.

Fine, Gary (1987) *With the Boys: Little League Baseball and Preadolescent Culture.* Chicago, IL: University of Chicago Press.

Foucault, Michel (1978) *The History of Sexuality, Volume I.* New York: Vintage Books.

Francis, Becky and Skelton, Christine (2001) "Men Teachers and the Construction of Heterosexual Masculinity in the Classroom," *Sex Education* 1:9–21.

Freud, Sigmund (1905) *The Basic Writings of Sigmund Freud* (translated and edited by A.A. Brill). New York: The Modern Library.

Hochschild, Arlie (1989) *The Second Shift.* New York: Avon.

Julien, Isaac and Mercer, Kobena (1991) "True Confessions: A Discourse on Images of Black Male Sexuality," in Essex Hemphill (ed.) *Brother to Brother: New Writings by Black Gay Men*, pp. 167–73. Boston, MA: Alyson Publications.

Kehily, Mary Jane and Nayak, Anoop (1997) "Lads and Laughter: Humour and the Production of Heterosexual Masculinities," *Gender and Education* 9:69–87.

Kimmel, Michael (2001) "Masculinity as Homophobia: Fear, Shame, and Silence in the Construction of Gender Identity," in Stephen Whitehead and Frank Barrett (eds.) *The Masculinities Reader*, pp. 266–187. Cambridge: Polity.

Kimmel, Michael (2003) "Adolescent Masculinity, Homophobia, and Violence: Random School Shootings, 1982–2001," *American Behavioral Scientist* 46:1439–58.

King, D.L. (2004) *Double Lives on the Down Low.* New York: Broadway Books.

Lehne, Gregory (1998) "Homophobia among Men: Supporting and Defining the Male Role," in Michael Kimmel and Michael Messner (eds.) *Men's Lives*, pp. 237–149. Boston, MA: Allyn and Bacon.

Lemert, Charles (1996) "Series Editor's Preface," in Steven Seidman (ed.) *Queer Theory/Sociology.* Cambridge, MA: Blackwell.

Lyman, Peter (1998) "The Fraternal Bond as a Joking Relationship: A Case Study of the Role of Sexist Jokes in Male Group Bonding," in Michael Kimmel and Michael Messner (eds.) *Men's Lives*, pp. 171–93. Boston, MA: Allyn and Bacon.

Mac an Ghaill, Mairtin (1996) "What about the Boys—School, Class and Crisis Masculinity," *Sociological Review* 44:381–97.

MacLeod, Jay (1987) *Ain't No Makin It: Aspirations and Attainment in a Low Income Neighborhood*. Boulder, CO: Westview Press.

Majors, Richard (2001) "Cool Pose: Black Masculinity and Sports," in Stephen Whitehead and Frank Barrett (eds.) *The Masculinities Reader*, pp. 208–17. Cambridge: Polity.

Messner, Michael (1989) "Sports and the Politics of Inequality," in Michael Kimmel and Michael Messner (eds.) *Men's Lives*. Boston, MA: Allyn and Bacon.

Messner, Michael (2004) "On Patriarchs and Losers: Rethinking Men's Interests," paper presented at Berkeley *Journal of Sociology* Conference, Berkeley.

Parker, Andrew (1996) "The Construction of Masculinity within Boys' Physical Education," *Gender and Education* 8:141–57.

Perry, Pamela (2002) *Shades of White: White Kids and Racial Identities in High School*. Durham, NC: Duke University Press.

Plummer, David C. (2001) "The Quest for Modern Manhood: Masculine Stereotypes, Peer Culture and the Social Significance of Homophobia," *Journal of Adolescence* 24:15–23.

Price, Jeremy (1999) "Schooling and Racialized Masculinities: The Diploma, Teachers and Peers in the Lives of Young, African-American Men," *Youth and Society* 31:224–63.

Riggs, Marlon (1991) "Black Macho Revisited: Reflections of a SNAP! Queen," in Essex Hemphill (ed.) *Brother to Brother: New Writings by Black Gay Men*, pp. 153–260. Boston, MA: Alyson Publications.

Ross, Marlon B. (1998) "In Search of Black Men's Masculinities," *Feminist Studies* 24:599–626.

Sedgwick, Eve K. (1990) *Epistemology of the Closet*. Berkeley: University of California Press.

Sedgwick, Eve K. (1995) "Gosh, Boy George, You Must be Awfully Secure in Your Masculinity!" in Maurice Berger, Brian Wallis and Simon Watson (eds.) *Constructing Masculinity*, pp. 11–20. New York: Routledge.

Skelton, Christine (1996) "Learning to be Tough: The Fostering of Maleness in One Primary School," *Gender and Education* 8:185–97.

Smith, George W. (1998) "The Ideology of 'Fag': The School Experience of Gay Students," *The Sociological Quarterly* 39:309–35.

Smith, Valerie (1994) "Split Affinities: The Case of Interracial Rape," in Anne Herrmann and Abigail Stewart (eds.) *Theorizing Feminism*, pp. 155–70. Boulder, CO: Westview Press.

Stein, Arlene and Plummer, Ken (1994) "'I Can't Even Think Straight': 'Queer' Theory and the Missing Sexual Revolution in Sociology," *Sociological Theory* 12:178 ff.

Thorne, Barrie (1993) *Gender Play: Boys and Girls in School*. New Brunswick, NJ: Rutgers University Press.

Warner, Michael (1993) "Introduction," in Michael Warner (ed.) *Fear of a Queer Planet: Queer Politics and Social Theory*, pp. vii–xxxi. Minneapolis: University of Minnesota Press.

West, Candace and Zimmerman, Don (1991) "Doing Gender," in Judith Lorber (ed.) *The Social Construction of Gender*, pp. 102–21. Newbury Park: Sage.

Whitehead, Stephen and Barrett, Frank (2001) "The Sociology of Masculinity," in Stephen Whitehead and Frank Barrett (eds.) *The Masculinities Reader*, pp. 472–6. Cambridge: Polity.

Wilchins, Riki (2002) "Do You Believe in Fairies?" *The Advocate*, 4 February.

Willis, Paul (1981) *Learning to Labor: How Working Class Kids Get Working Class Jobs*. New York: Columbia University Press.

Wood, Julian (1984) "Groping Toward Sexism: Boy's Sex Talk," in Angela McRobbie and Mica Nava (eds.) *Gender and Generation*. London: Macmillan Publishers.

12 Robert Jensen

Masculine, Feminine or Human?

In a guest lecture about masculinity to a college class, I ask the students to generate two lists that might help clarify the concept.

For the first, I tell them to imagine themselves as parents whose 12-year-old son asks, "Mommy/daddy, what does it mean to be a man?" The list I write on the board as they respond is not hard to predict: To be a man is to be strong, responsible, loving. Men provide for those around them and care for others. A man weathers tough times and doesn't give up.

When that list is complete, I ask the women to observe while the men answer a second question: When you are in all-male spaces, such as the locker room or a night out with the guys, what do you say to each other about what it means to be a man? How do you define masculinity when there are no women present?

The students, both men and women, laugh nervously, knowing the second list will be different from the first. The men fumble a bit at first, as it becomes clear that one common way men define masculinity in practice is not through affirmative statements but negative ones—it's about what a man isn't, and what a real man isn't is a woman or gay. In the vernacular: Don't be a girl, a sissy, a fag. To be a man is to not be too much like a woman or to be gay, which is in large part about being too much like a woman.

From there, the second list expands to other descriptions: To be a man is to be a player, a guy who can attract women and get sex; someone who doesn't take shit from people, who can stand down another guy if challenged, who doesn't let anyone else get in his face. Some of the men say they have other ideas about masculinity but acknowledge that in most all-male spaces it's difficult to discuss them.

When that process is over, I step back and ask the class to consider the meaning of the two lists. On the first list of the culturally endorsed definitions of masculinity, how many of those traits are unique to men? Are women ever strong? Should women be strong? Can women be just as responsible as men? Should women provide and care for others? I ask the students if anyone wants to make the argument that women are incapable of these things, or less capable than men. There are no takers.

I point to the obvious: The list of traits that we claim to associate with being a man—the things we would feel comfortable telling a child to strive for—are in fact not distinctive characteristics of men but traits of human beings that we value, what we want all people to be. The list of understandings

Robert Jensen, "Masculine, Feminine or Human?" Posted on www.slepton.com, June 2, 2008. Reprinted by permission of the author.

of masculinity that men routinely impose on each other is quite different. Here, being a man means not being a woman or gay, seeing relationships as fundamentally a contest for control, and viewing sex as the acquisition of pleasure from a woman. Of course that's not all men are, but it sums up the dominant, and very toxic, conception of masculinity with which most men are raised in the contemporary United States. It's not an assertion about all men or all possible ideas about masculinity, but a description of a pattern.

I ask the class: If the positive definitions of masculinity are not really about being a man but simply about being a person, and if the definitions of masculinity within which men routinely operate are negative, why are we holding onto the concept so tightly? Why are we so committed to the notion that there are intellectual, emotional, and moral differences that are inherent, that come as a result of biological sex differences?

From there, I ask them also to think about what a similar exercise around femininity might reveal? How might the patterns be similar or different? If masculinity is a suspect category, it would seem so is femininity.

I have repeated this discussion in several classes over the past year, each time with the same result: Students are uncomfortable. That's not surprising, given the reflexive way the culture accepts the idea that masculinity and femininity are crucial and coherent categories. People may define the ideal characteristics of masculinity and femininity differently, but most people accept the categories. What if that's misguided? What if the positive attributes ascribed to

"men" are simply positive human characteristics distributed without regard to gender, and the negative ones are the product of toxic patriarchal socialization?

Because the questions flow from their own observations and were not imposed by me, the discomfort is intensified. It's difficult to shrug this off as just one more irrelevant exercise in abstract theory by a pontificating professor. Whatever the conclusion the students reach, the question is on the table in a way that's difficult to dismiss.

It's obvious that there are differences in the male and female human body, most obviously in reproductive organs and hormones. It is possible those differences are significant outside of reproduction, in terms of broader patterns concerning intellectual, emotional, and moral development. But given our limited knowledge about such complex questions, there isn't much we can say about those differences. In the absence of definitive answers, I prefer to be cautious. After thousands of years of patriarchy in which men have defined themselves as superior to women in most aspects of life, leading to a claim that male dominance is natural and inevitable, we should be skeptical about claims about these allegedly inherent differences between men and women.

Human biology is pretty clear: People are born male or female, with a small percentage born intersexed. But how we should make sense of those differences outside reproduction is not clear. And if we are to make sense of it in a fashion that is consistent with justice—that is, in a feminist context—then we would benefit from a critical evaluation of the categories themselves, no matter how uncomfortable that may be.

13 Aída Hurtado and Mrinal Sinha

More than Men

Latino Feminist Masculinities and Intersectionality

Introduction

During this historical moment, hegemonic masculinity is embodied at the specific intersections of race, class, and sexuality (Collins 2004). It is currently defined as white, rich, and heterosexual. Because these social identities are privileged ones, they interact in ways that exclude specific groups of men from systems of privilege on the basis of their devalued group memberships. In other words, being a man of Color, gay, and working class or poor creates various obstacles to accessing the full range of male privilege. Hegemonic masculinity not only excludes certain groups of men from accessing aspects of male privilege in this way, it is an impossible ideal that many men are socialized to strive to attain, but cannot (Connell 1995; Pleck 1981). According to Connell (1995) hegemonic masculinity "can be defined as the configuration of gender practices which embodies the currently accepted answer to the problem of the legitimacy of patriarchy which guarantees (or is taken to guarantee) the dominant position of men and the subordination of women" (p. 77). Hegemonic masculinity not only oppresses women, it also restricts men from engaging in certain behaviors, particularly those that would undermine the dominant position of men as a group.

Adhering to hegemonic conceptions of masculinity is associated with negative social and psychological consequences at the same time that it provides material privileges (hooks 1991; Hurtado and Sinha 2005; Messner 1997). A large body of literature has documented the negative consequences of adhering to masculine gender roles on men's mental health (see Pleck 1981 for a review). These consequences include alcoholism (Lemle and Mishkind 1989), depression (Good and Wood 1995; Good et al. 2004; Mahalik and Rochlen 2006), restriction on expressions of emotion generally (O'Neil 1981, 1998), and within familial relationships specifically (DeFranc and Mahalik, 2002; Mahalik and Morrison 2006). Given the negative consequences associated with adherence to hegemonic masculinity, feminist engagement on the part of men can be a more constructive (and social justice oriented) response to the oppressive restrictiveness of masculinity as a social construct.

The present study explores the definitions of manhood provided by a sample of feminist identified, working class Latino

Aída Hurtado and Mrinal Sinha, "More than Men: Latino Feminist Masculinities and Intersectionality," *Sex Roles* 59, nos. 5/6 (September 2008): 337–349. Copyright © 2008 Springer Science + Business Media. Reprinted by permission of Springer Science + Business Media.

men. Prior qualitative studies have examined perceptions of manhood with African-American men (Diemer 2002; Hammond and Mattis 2005; Hunter and Davis 1992, 1994), Latino men (Mirande 1997), and young white men (Messner 1989; Pascoe 2003) of varying social classes, however, few have utilized samples that are composed entirely of feminist identified men of Color (see White 2008, for an exception). One of the insights that can be gleaned from these previous examinations is the idea that, while there are certain commonalities across different groups of men, masculinity is defined in racially, culturally, and class specific ways. In other words, the fact that participants belong to different social groups (as organized around their common membership to the category of "man") has implications for how they define manhood, and fundamentally produces commonalities and differences in the way that this social construct is perceived. For example, young boys raised in immigrant families in the US (or those who themselves immigrated) many times must contend with competing (and in some cases contradicting) discourses as they are socialized into masculinity (España-Maram 2006). The content of these competing discourses is dependent on the cultural background of individuals, which, along with the value attached to the specific culture in the host society, can function to create differences in the way that manhood is viewed. This socialization process is further complicated by the racial and class based oppression experienced by many young men of Color (Ferguson 2000), particularly when considered in conjunction with the male privilege bestowed on them within families (Hurtado and Sinha 2005). For young men experiencing privilege in the home, the harsh re-

ality of material deprivation, growing up in dangerous neighborhoods, and witnessing violence against women (especially female family members) can create commonalities in experience (Collins 2000), which can potentially facilitate similarities in the way that manhood is perceived. In this way, race, class, and ethnicity can interact to produce complicated, group specific experiences of the social world. Such experiences can contribute to complex perceptions of what it means to be a man in contemporary US society. These perceptions become even more complex when considered in light of feminist consciousness and highlights the importance of intersectionality for the present project—it allows for an exploration of participants' views towards manhood at the intersections of feminist consciousness, race, class, and ethnicity. More specifically, the present study uses an intersectional framework in examining the role of Latino culture and its effects on the complex perceptions of manhood with an educated sample of working class Latino men who identify as feminist.

The few qualitative studies with feminist identified men have focused predominantly on the experiences of working class and middle class white men. Findings from these projects have indicated four major dimensions associated with feminist masculinities—these include emphases on being an ethical human being, having emotionally healthy relationships with others (both women and men), being involved in activism and social justice oriented activities, and rejecting aspects of hegemonic masculinity. The aspects of hegemonic masculinity that participants rejected included male bonding around the objectification of women (Christian 1994; Vicario 2003), physical and sexual domination of women

(Vicario 2003; White 2008), and homophobia (White 2008). For many participants, the rejection of hegemonic masculinity was linked to their own experiences of class- and sexuality-based oppression. This is relevant to the present study in that we attempt to document the effects of racial and class based oppression, in conjunction with feminist consciousness, on views towards masculinity. Further, the dimensions identified in these empirical examinations are used as a framework informing analysis of participants' definitions of manhood in the present study.

The dimensions outlined above are also partially consistent with research conducted with samples of African-American men, both feminist identified (White 2008) and not (Hammond and Mattis 2005; Hunter and Davis 1992). Hammond and Mattis (2005) and Hunter and Davis (1992) found that African-American men of varying social classes defined manhood in ethical and relational ways. Being responsible and accountable for one's actions was the most frequently endorsed category—almost half of their sample defined manhood in this way (Hammond and Mattis 2005). Findings also indicated that all participants constructed the meaning of manhood in relationship to self, family, and others. In doing so, they stressed the importance of emotional connections with family and emphasized that the construction of masculinity was an interdependent process (Hammond and Mattis 2005). The importance placed on interdependence in the construction of masculine identity could be a result of the material deprivation historically experienced by African-American communities, where interdependence is more than just a tool used to carve out identities, but is a class-specific survival tactic (Fine and Weis 1998). In many ways, the definitions of

manhood provided by the feminist and African-American men described above run counter to dominant conceptions of what it means to be a man in the USA insofar as they stress characteristics that are in opposition to traditional, negative attributes of hegemonic masculinity. Levant (1992) has described some of the negative attributes associated with hegemonic masculinities based on his assessment of the empirical literature regarding the gender role strain paradigm. These attributes include emotional restrictiveness and isolation from others (e.g., family, intimate partners), nonrelational attitudes and behavior towards heterosexuality, and inflicting violence upon others. Further, Kimmel (2000) has conceptualized homophobia as a core characteristic of hegemonic masculinity. Masculinity defined as such contrasts in important ways with the responses provided by the feminist and African-American men described in the studies above in that homophobia, violence, physical domination, and emotional isolation were not present in their definitions of manhood.

Levant (1992) has also identified aspects of hegemonic masculinity worth rescuing in reconstructing manhood. Among the positive attributes described are self sacrifice for the family, ability to withstand hardship and pain to protect others, loyalty, dedication, and commitment. It is interesting to note here that Levant's (1992) formulation corresponds with two of the overarching themes associated with feminist and African-American participants' definitions of masculinity—ethical and relational definitions (Christian 1994; Hammond and Mattis 2005; Hunter and Davis 1992; Vicario 2003; White 2008).

The present study attempts to contribute to this body of literature by utilizing the concept of intersectionality, as postulated by feminists of Color (Crenshaw 1995; Collins 2000; Hurtado 1996), in exploring the varied definitions of masculinity provided by feminist, working class, educated Latino men. To date, only one qualitative study has examined the experiences of feminist men of Color using an intersectional perspective (White 2008), and none have done so with Latinos, feminist or otherwise. As such, this research seeks not only to address a deficiency in the literature regarding Latino men generally, but seeks to provide insights as to the way that *feminist* Latino men define masculinity. How do feminist, working class Latino men view manhood as a social construct? Do these views differ from their African-American and white counterparts? What discourses do they draw from in defining manhood? Further, we attempt to explicate the role that participants' multiple and intersecting social identities have in shaping definitions of masculinity. Intersectionality allows for such an analysis with men of Color in that it provides the opportunity to explore contradictory experiences of power (and disadvantage). This has been one of the major limitations in prior studies of masculinity with men of Color—analyses have focused on experiences of powerlessness (Majors and Billson 1992) *or* privilege (Wallace, as cited in Franklin 1998), without explicit attention to the space "in-between." In other words, little social scientific knowledge has been generated as to the ways in which these experiences interact to ultimately affect views towards gender, generally, and masculinity specifically.

Social Identities and Intersectionality

There is a theoretical distinction in the way that identity is conceptualized. This distinction, as held by most social psychologists, is between *personal* and *social identity*, which together form a person's total sense of self (Baumeister 1998). Tajfel (1981) posits that personal identity is that aspect of self composed of psychological traits and dispositions that give rise to personal uniqueness. Personal identity is derived from intrapsychic influences, many of which are socialized within family units (however these units are defined; Hurtado 1997). From this perspective, human beings have a great deal in common precisely because their personal identities are comprised of universal processes, such as loving, mating, doing productive work—activities that are considered universal components of self. Personal identity is much more stable and coherent over time than social identity. Most individuals do not have multiple personal identities, nor do their personal identities change dramatically from one social context to another (Hurtado and Gurin 2004).

On the other hand, *social identity* is that aspect of self derived from the knowledge of being part of social categories and groups, together with the value and emotional significance attached to those group formations (Hurtado 1997). Tajfel (1981) argues that the formation of social identities is the consequence of three social psychological processes. The first is *social categorization*. Nationality, language, race and ethnicity, skin color, or other social or physical characteristics that are meaningful in particular social contexts can be the basis for social categorization and thus the foundation for the creation of social identities. For example, Latinos immigrating to the USA are surprised to be categorized as "ethnic minorities" when in their individual countries of origin, they enjoyed full citizenship and membership within a national culture, a notably different social category (Solis 2006).

Another process underlying the construction of social identities is *social comparison*. In this process, a group's status, degree of affluence, or other characteristic achieves significance *in relation to* perceived differences, and their value connotations, from other social formations. For example, Latino/a students may see themselves as "middle class" when they are in their predominantly working class communities; upon entering institutions of higher education attended largely by upper middle class white students, they shift the comparison from neighborhood to college peers and reassess their class identification, most often from middle class to poor (Hurtado 2003).

The third process involves psychological work, both cognitive and emotional, that is prompted by what Tajfel assumes is a universal motive—the achievement of a positive sense of self. The social groups that present the greatest obstacles to a positive sense of self are those that are devalued, whose memberships have to be negotiated frequently because of their visibility, that have become politicized by social movements, and so on. They are the most likely to become problematic social identities for individuals. Moreover, these social identities become especially powerful psychologically; they are easily accessible and dwelt upon, apt to be salient across situations, and likely to function as schema, frameworks, or social scripts (Gurin et al. 1994; Hurtado and Gurin 2004). For example, a poor African-American woman with a physical disability is more likely to reflect on her social identities than is a wealthy white heterosexual male with no physical impediments. Unproblematic group memberships—ones that

are socially valued or accorded privilege and are not obvious to others—may not even become social identities. Until very recently, being white was not the subject of inquiry and it is still not widely thought of as a social identity (Fine et al. 2004; Hurtado and Stewart 2004; Phinney 1996). Thus, people belonging to social categories that are problematic and devalued in various contexts are more likely to engage in psychological work aimed at revaluing their group memberships in order to preserve a positive sense of self (Hurtado 1997).

Individuals belong to multiple groups and therefore possess multiple social identities. Social identities gain particular significance in relationship to "master statuses" and when they are stigmatized. Race, social class, gender, ethnicity, physical challenges, and sexuality are the social identities assigned master statuses, because individuals must psychologically negotiate their potentially stigmatizing effects—this is particularly the case when individuals do not belong to dominant groups in society. In the USA, as in many other countries, master statuses are used to make value judgments about group memberships. Tajfel's theory of social identity provides a sophisticated framework for understanding how individuals make sense of their group memberships—both unproblematic and stigmatized memberships.

Thus social identity, which consists of an individual's group affiliations and emotional attachments to those group memberships, is largely derived through social comparison. The meaning of an individual's group affiliation—its value and significance—is largely based on the presence and significance of other social formations in the environment. When different values are attached to different group affiliations, individuals have to do psychological work to come to terms with their social identities. As Tajfel posits, individuals strive not only to be different from other groups, the difference has to be positive.

The Significance of Social Identities for Intersectionality

The concept of *intersectionality* was developed by feminist scholars and has facilitated an understanding of the social and economic conditions of women of Color (traditionally considered problematic social categories; Anzaldúa 1987; Collins 2000; Hurtado 1996, 2003; Sandoval 2000). Sociologist Patricia Hill Collins (2000) broadly describes several components of intersectionality:

> The very notion of the intersections of race, class, and gender as an area worthy of study emerged from the recognition of practitioners of each distinctive theoretical tradition that inequality could not be explained, let alone challenged, via a race-only, or gender-only framework. No one had all of the answers and no one was going to get all of the answers without attention to two things. First, the notion of interlocking oppressions refers to the macro-level connections linking systems of oppression such as race, class, and gender. This is a model describing the social structures that create social positions. Second, the notion of intersectionality describes micro-level processes—namely, how each individual and group occupies a social position within interlocking structures of oppression described by the metaphor of intersectionality. Together they shape oppression. (p. 82)

More concretely, theories of intersectionality developed as a reaction to primarily white feminist analyses that privileged gender as the cornerstone of oppression that united women worldwide (Nesiah 2000). Intersectionality theorists like Patricia Hill Collins argue that "gender-only" or "race-only" analyses do not lead to an understanding of the position of all women or to a dismantling of the structures that oppress them. Intersectionality theorists also refuse to "rank the oppressions" (Moraga 1981, p. 29) and instead argue that membership in oppressed social formations, such as being poor, of color, or lesbian, intersect in significant ways that affect women's experience of oppression.

While some social scientists have challenged the intersectionality framework as too abstract and not addressing the concreteness of social interaction (Fenstermaker and West 2002), nonetheless it has had an enormous influence in the fields of political science (Kosambi 1995), sociology (Browne and Misra 2003), psychology (Stewart and McDermott 2004), and humanities (Saldívar-Hull 2000). Hurtado (1996, 1997, 2003) links the theories of social identity, as first proposed by Henri Tajfel, to the theoretical framework of intersectionality and contends that from a social psychological point of view, intersectionality refers to the particular constellation of social identities that are the primary basis for stigmatization: class, race, sexuality, gender, ethnicity, and physical ableness.

The framework of intersectionality provides the impetus for uniting the various themes outlined above, namely, hegemonic masculinity, feminist and marginalized masculinities, and social identity. It does so by considering within group variation. By providing an analytical tool that explicates difference within the social category "man," intersectionality allows us to examine the ways that other disparaged social identities can influence experiences of gender in the USA. Exploring such variation in men's experiences contributes to more nuanced understandings of how different groups of men view and respond to hegemonic conceptions of masculinity at the same time that it provides insight as to how they resist such notions of gender. In other words, experiences of male privilege in conjunction with race-, class-, and in some cases, sexuality-based disadvantage, can potentially influence the way that manhood is defined.

In this article we address several research questions based on a study of educated, young Latinos who identify as feminists and come from poor and working class backgrounds. In order to apply the theoretical framework of intersectionality to these participants' narratives, the first research question asks: To what extent did the participants in this study identify with their gender, race, ethnicity, sexuality, and class background? Second, how do participants apply their consciousness as feminists and working class men in subjectively defining what it means to be a man? Third, if participants include broader definitions of being men, what are they?

Method

Participants

The data for this project come from a larger study of interviews conducted with 105 Latino men (Hurtado and Sinha 2006). The larger study (Hurtado and Sinha 2006) addressed a wide range of topics with a nationally non-representative sample of Latinos with some experience of higher education and is a mirror study to research conducted by Hurtado (2003) with a sample of 101 Mexican descent women. The topics ad-

dressed in both studies included issues related to early adolescence and dating, sexuality, gender, relationships with parents, political participation, and educational achievement. In this study, we examine only the gender issues portion of the interview. The interviews were semi-structured, utilizing open and closed ended questions, however, participants were encouraged to share experiences that they deemed relevant to the topics addressed.

Latino was defined as participants who had at least one parent of Latino ancestry. The majority of the participants (72%) were of Mexican descent, 4% were of Puerto Rican descent, 2% were of Central American descent, 7% were of South American descent, and 15% were of mixed ancestry. The participants were between the ages of 19 and 33, the average age was 24, and all were attending or had attended an institution of higher education. They were interviewed in five southwestern states— California, Colorado, New Mexico, Texas, and Arizona—as well as in Illinois, Massachusetts, Michigan, New York, and Washington, DC.

Of the 105 participants, 36 considered themselves feminist and identified their class background as poor or working class. Because one of the goals of the larger study was to explore definitions of feminism (Hurtado and Sinha 2006; Sinha 2007), participants were allowed to identify as feminist according to their subjective understanding of the term. Further, participants were asked to identify the economic background of their family while they were growing up—for those that identified as working class or poor, this was verified utilizing questionnaire data that was also a part of the larger study from which this data set is derived. The present study explores the responses given by this subset of the larger sample. We chose to examine the responses exclusively from working class, feminist identified participants in order to explore the way that race, class, and gender interacted to influence their subjective definitions of masculinity. The age range for the sub-sample of 36 participants was between 19 and 33 years and the average age was 25 years. Thirty of the participants were born in the USA and six were born in Latin American countries (Colombia, El Salvador, and Mexico) and came to this country before they were 11 years old. Seven of the 36 participants had graduated with a bachelor's degree, 1 had earned a master's degree, 4 were enrolled in a master's program, 6 were doctoral students, 1 was a medical student and 16 were undergraduates. One participant had attended some community college, but was not enrolled in school at the time of the interview. Participants attended 20 different institutions of higher education across the USA. These institutions ranged from community college (e.g., La Guardia Community College), state colleges (e.g., California State University, Monterey Bay), to large scale universities (e.g., University of Michigan). Thirty-three of the participants identified as heterosexual and three identified as gay. Most participants were single (*n*=34), one was married without children, and one was married and had a child.

Design and Procedure

Participants were contacted using the social networks of counselors, professors, student organizations, and personnel of student affairs offices on various college campuses. Specifically, an electronic message was sent describing the study and outlined the age and ethnic requirements for potential par-

ticipants. The study was advertised as a follow up study to Hurtado (2003) that wished to explore the experiences and stories of Latino men involved in higher education in a number of different domains. In addition, a brief description of Hurtado's (2003) study was included in the advertisement. All people responding to the advertisement were interviewed if they met the study's criteria, were available within the interviewer's schedule, and arrived at the set interview location. Participants were not compensated for participation in the study.

Six of the interviews were conducted in focus groups (two were in a group of three, the others in groups of two) and the remaining participants were interviewed individually. Because some participants were interviewed individually and some in focus groups, this may have affected the nature of responses. However, we found little variation in terms of the number of mentions each participant provided in response to the question "what does the word 'manhood' mean to you?" across the different interview formats. The interviews took between 2 and 3 hours, were audio- and videotaped, and took place in a variety of locations including hotel rooms, participants' homes, and private rooms in ethnic resource centers and libraries. The audiotapes were transcribed by bilingual, bicultural research assistants and crosschecked with the videotapes. Although all participants were English dominant speakers, and all but one was a US citizen (this participant was scheduled to be naturalized a few weeks after the date of the interview) they occasionally spoke in Spanish when referring to specific cultural practices and their ethnic heritage. As such, we used bilingual and bicultural research assistants to transcribe and crosscheck interviews in order to ensure that we captured the nuances and complexities of participants' responses in a comprehensive manner.

All interviews were conducted in English by the second author of this article (a 30-year-old man of East-Indian descent). Because the interviewer shared certain social identities with participants, but not others, there were distinct advantages and disadvantages. In terms of advantages, the interviewer was male—this could have implications in that it may have potentially reduced the likelihood of social desirability being a factor affecting participants' responses. Past research indicates that social desirability biases may vary according to the demand characteristics associated with the research context (Hebert et al. 1997). The present study examines manhood as a social construct, and because domination and objectification of women are core components of hegemonic masculinity (Connell 1995; Kimmel 2000), being interviewed by a woman could potentially have affected participants responses.

In terms of other commonalities, the interviewer was a graduate student and in the same age range as participants. Because many of the participants were also graduate students, and in the same age group, this could have created a sense of comfort in facilitating participants sharing information. In terms of differences, the interviewer was not of Latin American ancestry, thereby limiting his ability to probe at opportune moments due to a lack of "insider" cultural knowledge. However, in terms of participants' willingness to speak candidly, the differences in ethnicity may have been ameliorated by the dark phenotype of the interviewer, which is often associated with Latino ancestry. Five participants were of mixed ethnic heritage as well, which may have made them more understanding of difference. Further, participants were highly educated

and had traveled and lived in very culturally and racially diverse cities. Many of them mentioned having dated inter-ethnically and inter-racially, and mentioned having friendships and other social relationships across ethnic and racial differences. We therefore concluded that the interviewer's social identities did not systematically alter the findings reported here.

The transcripts from the interviews conducted with the 36 participants were coded and data analyses were conducted on the participants' responses to the question "What does the word 'manhood' mean to you?" Thematic qualitative analysis was performed on the participants' answers to identify the core characteristics of their definitions of manhood. A theme was defined as a common thread that continually emerges in the data, although the form of the theme is not always identical (Morse and Richards 2002). In conducting the thematic analysis, we used a combination of inductive and deductive coding techniques (Fink 2003; Fereday and Muir-Cochrane 2006). The overarching themes used in coding responses were developed using prior qualitative studies of feminist masculinities (Christian 1994; Cornish 1999; Vicario 2003; White 2008) and the writings of feminists of Color, particularly as they pertained to multiple group memberships (Collins 1998, 2000, 2004; Hurtado 1997, 2003). The specific subcategories were inductively derived in that they were grounded in participants' responses and developed upon a preliminary examination of the data by both authors of this article.

In conducting the qualitative analysis outlined above, the first three responses mentioned by each participant in response to the question "What does the word 'manhood' mean to you?" were coded. Because few participants discussed more than three things in their responses, coding the first three mentions allowed us to account for the full range of responses in the sample. The second author of this article coded the 36 interviews. Next, a graduate student was trained in the coding protocol and coded the interviews independently a second time to determine inter-coder reliability. The second coder was not aware of the research questions being addressed in this study. Overall inter-coder reliability was 79%. All disagreements were reconciled by a third coder, also a graduate student who was trained in the coding protocol (and who was also unaware of the research questions being addressed). Participants were given the option of using their real names or pseudonyms. The majority chose to use their real names, others elected to use only their first names, while some chose to use a first name pseudonym or a first and last name pseudonym. We obtained written permission from participants to use their names in publishing findings. In direct quotations, (. . .) indicates that a part of the participants' narrative was omitted because it was repetitive and did not add to the main point of the quote.

Results

Participants' Social Identifications— Embodying Intersectionality

Consistent with the definition of identification provided by Tajfel and colleagues and with the concept of intersectionality proposed in this article, participants provided identifications with their various significant social groups to varying degrees. All 36 participants identified as men and Latino as a prerequisite to be a part of the study. Further, all of the 36 participants considered in this study also identified the economic background of their family as working class or poor. In order to further explore the ways in which participants embodied intersectionality via identifications with their multiple social groups, we conducted a content analysis of the entire gender issues section of the interviews, providing a count of each time they referenced their race, ethnicity, class, and sexuality. The gender issues portion of the interview contained a total of 11 open and closed ended questions. The questions asked about participants' views on feminism and manhood, whether they felt anyone in their family was feminist, if there were strong women and men in their family, if they could provide examples of people they admired as men (as well as the reasons for admiring them), their views towards male privilege, and whether they considered themselves to be "men of Color." The frequencies presented below are in relationship to the interview questions outlined above.

Table 13.1 presents the results from the content analysis exploring participants' identifications with their significant social groups. All 36 participants referenced their race in their narratives. The number of mentions for participants referencing this social identity ranged from 1 to 14 mentions (median number of responses was 4). They talked extensively about being racialized by their families, communities, and society in general based on their phenotype—that is, whether they were light- or dark-skinned and whether they looked "indigenous" or "European" to others. If participants were fair skinned, they were aware how they were often confused as not being Latino both by other Latinos and non-Latinos. Further, a few participants discussed the ways in which their face had affected their experiences of

TABLE 13.1 **Participants' Identifications with Significant Social Groups**

Social Group	Number of participants	Number of mentions	
		Range	Median
Race	36	1–14	4
Ethnicity	32	1–15	6
Social Class	22	1–11	2
Sexuality	8	1–9	2

higher education. This was particularly salient for participants who had attended private institutions, as they were many times one of the few working class students of Color in their classes and at graduation ceremonies. In some cases, participants wove references to race throughout their discussions of male privilege. These responses illustrated the way that their race interacted with their gender to complicate their experience of male privilege. Some felt as though their race kept them from being able to access patriarchal privilege in the same way that white men could. Albert Dominguez III, who was 27 years old and working as a program coordinator at George Washington University, provides an illustrative example:

> Let's not forget we're Latinos. I am not a white male . . . if I was a white man I could say "Hey, I have certain privileges" in terms of societies I could get into or a certain door you can open a little bit easier . . . I am a Latino male . . . let me give you a better example of what I am trying to say. It's as if you are Black, you're Jewish and you're gay . . . that's the ultimate minority right there, right? So I feel like to a certain extent I am a male but I am a Latino male so if I was just a male . . . being of a different ethnicity or a different nationality there may be a little bit of extra perks.

Albert's narrative illustrates an awareness of the stigma attached to his racial identity and an understanding of how this stigma intersects with and limits his access to male privilege. He repeatedly brings up the fact that he is "a Latino male" in his discussion of male privilege. In other words, in talking about his gender identity, he also mentions his racial identity, and does so repeatedly in the same passage. Albert also demonstrates an understanding of the way that various disparaged social identities (e.g., being Black, Jewish, and gay) can act in combination to limit people's opportunities. His narrative is illustrative of the way many participants felt about their race as an important (stigmatized) social identity influencing their views of gender. Overall, participants were aware of their subordinate status in society based on their racial categorization, and viewed this as influencing their experience of being men.

Thirty-two participants mentioned their ethnicity in their narratives. The number of mentions for participants referencing this social identity ranged from 1 to 15 mentions (median number of responses was 6). Participants discussing their ethnicity talked about speaking Spanish in the home, cultural practices, and their parents' immigration experiences. Jorge Morales, a 27-year-old doctoral student in comparative literature at the University of California, Berkeley emphasized the role of culture in the way that masculinity was constructed by saying:

> I guess it depends on what kind of manhood you're talking about, whether it's manhood as constructed in American culture or as it's constructed in Mexican culture. I think they're very different constructions.

Twenty-two participants referenced their class in their narratives. The number of mentions for participants referencing this social identity ranged from 1 to 11 mentions (median number of responses was 2). These participants discussed their parents' education levels, occupations and the economic hardships their families experienced while growing up. Jose "Nike" Martinez, who was 22 years old and had graduated from California State University, Monterey Bay, with a degree in Computer Science, was unemployed and looking for work at the time of the interview. He described the struggles his father went through while raising their family:

He went to like the second or third grade and then he had to drop out of school to support his family. Once he gained his own family, which is us, he immigrated to the United States in search of work . . . back in Mexico, we had it really hard . . . it's just hard to make a living over there . . . he's pretty much worked all his life, he's worked in the fields, like lettuce and strawberries . . . and I've seen him get up everyday at like three or four in the morning and come back at like five or six in the evening and everyday doing this backbreaking job all sunburned . . . that's all he's done all his life, is work in the fields . . . he's done that for us.

Jose's narrative describes the reasons that he admired his father *as a man*, alluding to the way that ethnicity and class have interacted in his life to influence his views of what it means to be a good father (and ultimately what it means to be a man). It is interesting to note the way that class and ethnicity, via discussions of the physical hardships his father endured for the sake of the family, are interwoven throughout his response. As is seen in the above quotation, Jose references his class (via his father's educational level, occupation, and long work hours) and ethnicity multiple times in talking about why he admires his father as a man. In other words, Jose's narrative, like many of the other participants in the sample, illustrates the way that his Mexican immigrant background (his ethnicity) is inextricably tied to his class background to shape his views towards gender.

Finally, only eight participants referenced their sexuality in their narratives. The number of mentions for participants referencing this social identity ranged from 1 to 9 mentions (median number of responses was 2). Two participants discussed the fact that they were gay, some talked about their heterosexuality in unproblematic ways (e.g., their relationships with girlfriends or partners), while others discussed how their heterosexuality complicated their notions of masculinity. This was particularly the case in terms of how heterosexuality bestowed them with unearned structural privilege and was stigmatized in racially specific ways. Issaac, a 25-year-old elementary school teacher who obtained a master's degree from Colombia University, in discussing his sexuality, said that he had to "fight more stereotypes because" he was not a "macho male of color." He thought that "in people's minds" the prototypical "Latino male is Ricky Martin" or "Antonio Banderas," both of whom were represented in the media as that "suave model." Issaac felt as though this way of thinking was a "paradigm" that "still exists" and one that his version of heterosexuality did not "fit into." Issaac's response illustrates intersectionality in that his discussion of heterosexuality is intimately tied to his membership in a disparaged racial category—his experience of being heterosexual (a dominant social identity) cannot be separated from his experience of being a racialized man of Color (a stigmatized social identity).

These results suggest that participants were aware that they belonged to various social categories, and further, that some of these categories were disparaged and problematic. In Tajfel (1981) and Hurtado's (1997) terms, the way that they identified with these categories was indicative that their social identities were linked to their views towards gender. Participants illustrated this link by including discussions of their devalued social identities in their narratives addressing gender. This was particularly the case when considered in light of the way that ethnicity, race, social class, and to a lesser degree, sexuality, interacted in their views of the way that masculinity was constructed in culturally specific ways, experiences of male privilege, and reasons for admiring men *as men*. An important finding here was that the social identities that participants discussed most (e.g., race, ethnicity, and class) were ones that were disparaged in certain contexts. This is consistent with the principles of social identity theory (Tajfel 1981) and intersectionality (Anzaldúa 1987; Collins 2000; Hurtado 1997, 2003) outlined above in that problematic social identities are reflected on more often than dominant social identities and require constant negotiation. It is suggestive that the majority of the sample was heterosexual (i.e., this was a dominant social category) and that this group membership was mentioned the fewest times.

Participants' Definitions of Manhood

Table 13.2 presents the results from the participants' answers to the open-ended question "What does the word 'manhood' mean to you?" The thematic coding scheme used in analyzing this interview question was developed using prior studies addressing feminist men's views of masculinity (Christian 1994; Cornish 1999; Vicario 2003; White 2008). The coding scheme was organized around four overarching themes that were derived from the studies outlined above: relational definitions, positive ethical positionings, definitions based in political action, and rejection of hegemonic masculinity. *Relational definitions* included themes that emphasized relationships with family, community, and other groups of people as part of the definition of manhood. *Positive ethical positionings* included themes that emphasized individuals taking an ethical stand in life and exhibiting values such as respect, being truthful, respecting oneself enough to have confidence in one's own decisions and identity as a man, and pursuing education to become a better person. The theme *definitions based in political action* was not endorsed by any participants, and as such was dropped from the coding scheme and will not be discussed here. *Rejecting hegemonic masculinity* included themes that explicitly critiqued dominant definitions of manhood, including equating

TABLE 13.2 Themes Mentioned by Participants in Their Definitions of Manhood (Multiple Mentions)

Theme	Number of participants (N=36)	Number of mentions	
		Range	Mode
Relational Definitions	18	1–22	1
Positive Ethical Positioning	22	1–35	1
Rejection of Hegemonic Masculinity	14	1–20	1

manhood with biological sex and instead valuing an individual's personhood regardless of gender, rejecting dominance and patriarchy, and openly emphasizing positive characteristics to counteract the negative aspects of masculinity. In the majority of these themes, the participants mentioned their significant social identities such as ethnicity, race, class, and sexuality as influencing their definitions of manhood.

Mean number of mentions per participant was 2.13. Using an intersectional theoretical framework that takes other significant social identities into account (in addition to gender), we conducted a thematic analysis allowing for multiple mentions. Below we present the results.

Definitions of Manhood: Relational

Eighteen participants mentioned relational definitions of manhood in their responses. The number of mentions for participants referencing this theme ranged from 1 to 22 mentions (modal number of responses was 1). The participants who emphasized this theme gave long elaborate explanations of manhood being a developmental process that unfolded as individuals matured. The end point of the process was when an individual got married and raised children. As Andrés Elenes, a 26-year-old senior at MIT majoring in managerial science indicated:

> The word manhood, it's when . . . our mind matures enough that you start thinking as a grown adult. . . . It's a person who from now on instead of thinking about himself is someone who starts thinking about repercussions about his actions for his family and for [his] community.

Andrés's emphasis on manhood being a developmental process that culminates in a commitment to the family and community with which one lives is consistent with the way that manhood has been defined with middle and working class African-American men (Hammond and Mattis 2005).

A second component of this theme was the notion that manhood can only be understood in relationship to cultural and community practices within families and groups of individuals. As Alberto Barragan, a 27-year-old medical student at the University of Michigan stated:

> Manhood to me is a culture . . . the ring of men at our family functions—manhood is being able to stand in that ring. And when you stand in that ring that means that you have a job . . . adolescents are able to stand in the ring even though they are low ranking members. You're a full member of that ring when you're married and have children. . . . Like I said, the men [in his family] tend to be quiet and passive. You don't brag about things. Manhood means being able to stand in that ring and talk and be respected, have an opinion . . . my father having all of his children in college is an incredible booster in the manhood ring.

Alberto's response demonstrates the way that ethnicity interacts with gender to influence his definition of masculinity. In particular, the fact that he emphasizes manhood as being constructed in the context of "a culture" and among "the ring of men" at family functions highlights the relational and culturally specific nature of such definitions, and echoes the words of Jorge Morales quoted above (that constructions of manhood vary from one cultural context to another). The emphasis on manhood being constructed in the context of relationships with family, culture, and community is also consistent with the findings of studies conducted with African-American men (Hammond and Mattis 2005; Hunter and Davis 1992).

Definitions of Manhood: Positive Ethical Positionings

Twenty-two participants mentioned definitions of manhood based in positive ethical positions in their responses. The number of mentions for participants referencing this theme ranged from 1 to 35 (modal number of responses was 1). This theme was mentioned the most times across all three themes addressing participants' definitions of manhood. These participants felt that manhood entailed being ethical and standing behind one's word and not cheating or being untruthful, being a good human being, and respecting others. For example, Hugo Hernandez, a 21-year-old junior at the University of Arizona, said "manhood would be to work hard to respect people." Furthermore manhood was a commitment to viewing everyone as equals and honoring people as people and emphasizing their "humanhood." Issaac, the 25-year-old elementary school teacher quoted above discussing his sexuality, eloquently stated his views on the definition of "manhood":

It's coming into one's own about being open to change and to new ideas but also staying strong to principles or values that you have out for yourself . . . like Gandhi says, "being the peace that you wish to see"; it's like being the man that you wish to see in others . . . walking through the world in a way that is open but strong. In that sense, it's not only men; all people should be [that way]; kind of like a peoplehood, where we all learn to be strong but also collaborative and open to

help and conversation, being open to dialogue about those things but also holding strong to whatever it is you bring to the table in whatever conversations you engage in; knowing who you are. . . . To me that's coming into one's own about being a man or womanhood or peoplehood or personhood, I guess that's how I define it.

Issaac's views towards manhood highlight the influence of his feminist orientation insofar as the ethical characteristics he highlights directly contradict aspects of hegemonic masculinity. Specifically, he emphasizes "being open to change and new ideas" and equates this openness not only as a positive quality that men should strive for, but that all people, regardless of gender, should try and attain. Issaac's response resonates with prior work with feminist men (Christian 1994; Vicario 2003; White 2008) in that he emphasizes a version of masculinity predicated on a version of selfhood that stresses the importance of connections (as opposed to isolation), particularly in terms of being collaborative and receiving help from others.

Participants also felt that part of being a good and ethical person entailed being comfortable with one's self, being independent, and approaching things more confidently. Jesse Obas, who was 30 years old and working for the Educational Partnership Center at the University of California, Santa Cruz, said:

Manhood is when you are comfortable with your identity. I'm not saying complacent or that's all you want to achieve, I'm not saying it's the pinnacle of your manliness, but . . . for the longest time I was uncomfortable with who I was as a man and who I was as a person . . . I feel like right now I'm probably the closest I've ever been to the man, the person, the Chicano, the Filipino, that I've ever been . . . encompassing all those identities . . . I think that's what manhood is.

Jesse's response directly connects his views of manhood with his other, disparaged social identities. In particular, he defines manhood as something that is achieved when one is comfortable with their memberships in various social categories—in his case, this amounts to becoming comfortable with his (bi)racial identity as a Chicano, a Filipino, and ultimately as a person of Color. By defining manhood in this way (as intimately connected to his race based social identity), Jesse embodies intersectionality as postulated by Hurtado (1997, 2003) and other feminists of Color (Anzaldúa 1987; Collins 2000, 2004).

Definitions of Manhood: Rejection of Hegemonic Masculinity

Fourteen participants provided definitions of manhood that rejected aspects of hegemonic masculinity in their responses. The number of mentions for participants referencing this theme ranged from 1 to 20 (modal number of responses was 1). These participants felt that definitions of manhood are in flux because of the intense questioning of gender and sexual roles and, as a result, definitions need to go beyond biology and the objectification of women as the basis for manhood. In particular, participants were concerned that hegemonic definitions excluded others from the rubric of manhood if they did not meet the "physical" requisites. Some were especially worried about excluding women who had the responsibilities usually assigned to men, such as being the main breadwinners in

their families, and gay men because of their sexuality. Jesse Obas, the participant quoted above, also indicated that "manhood to me doesn't mean heterosexual, educated man . . . it could also mean gay, white or whatever." Other participants rejected particular behaviors associated with hegemonic masculinity. Ryan Ramírez, a 20-year-old sophomore majoring in philosophy at the University of Colorado, Boulder, provides an illustrative example:

> There's always that whole thing when you are younger . . . the whole virginity thing, you know, if you don't sleep with someone by the time you're this age, then you're not a man and I'm like, well whatever . . . I consider myself a man because I've done things.

Ryan explicitly rejects the notion that in order to achieve manhood, one has had to have engaged in sexual intercourse with a woman—an indication of heterosexuality. Instead, he considers himself a man because he has "done things." In so doing, he refers specifically to the fact that he has overcome economic obstacles in order to attain an education. Ryan traveled from Denver to Boulder, Colorado, by himself, enrolled in courses, and was working his way through school independent of any financial support from his mother because she was the single head of household and had to take care of his sisters. His narrative is illustrative of the ways that participants refused to objectify women in defining masculinity, instead celebrating their educational accomplishments in light of their working class social identities. Ryan's rejection of the gender-specific, developmental ritual of sex with a woman fundamentally runs counter to one of the core behaviors associated with hegemonic masculinity (Collins 2004).

Furthermore, participants were concerned that hegemonic and normative definitions of manhood reinforced the negative aspects of masculinity. In particular they were concerned about personal negative characteristics of manhood that entailed harshness and domination of others. Among the dispositional characteristics enumerated were such things as being rude, aggressive, insulting others' beliefs, and not listening. Instead of including the negative characteristics as part of their definitions of manhood, participants enumerated the desirable ones that men should ascribe to, for example, being supportive, being less selfish and expressing emotions.

The last theme mentioned by participants was the rejection of manhood because it is a social construction that has no value—a construction that participants were openly rebelling against by deconstructing its meaning. As Jonathan Rosa, a 23-year-old doctoral student in anthropology at the University of Chicago stated:

> [Manhood] means a constructed image of masculinity . . . it means an idea that I am trying to fight against; something that I am trying to unsettle personally, and in the world individually, and among the social networks where I occupy different positions . . . manhood is bullshit, basically.

From Jonathan's perspective, as well as from the perspectives of other participants, manhood was equated with patriarchy and undeserved male privileges. Patriarchy hurts everyone and therefore manhood is a false ideology that should be questioned and eventually obliterated and replaced with more equitable arrangements between people. Jonathan's views towards manhood, in addition to the other participants endorsing

this theme, echo the words of other feminist men (Vicario 2003; White 2008) in that he is not only advocating for a fundamental restructuring and transformation of social relationships, he provides an outright rejection of masculinity as a social construct. This point is made most poignantly in his summation that "manhood is bullshit, basically."

Discussion

In considering findings in light of the research questions posed above, we see that participants identified with their significant social identities in various ways, thereby providing an illustration of how individuals embodied intersectionality via their lived experience. In doing so, they referenced those social identities that were devalued in society more often than those that were unproblematic (e.g., heterosexuality), implying that they reflected on and negotiated these identities in numerous social contexts. Further, participants implicated their various social identities as influencing their views of gender and masculinity, thereby indicating an intimate connection between their disparaged group memberships and their dominant ones. Participants illustrated this in the content analysis by weaving references to their race, ethnicity, social class, and to a lesser degree, sexuality throughout their narratives. These findings are consistent with past qualitative research utilizing an intersectional framework with Mexican descent women (Hurtado 2003), African-American women (Collins 2000, 2004), and feminist African-American men (White 2008).

In defining what manhood meant to them, participants applied their feminist and class consciousness in complex ways.

They wove in and out of definitions that were relational, ethical, and that rejected aspects of hegemonic masculinity. For example, some participants would discuss relational and ethical definitions of masculinity, while rejecting aspects of hegemonic masculinity *in the same narrative*. In doing so, they provided definitions of manhood that ran counter to mainstream ideas of what it means to be a man in the USA, while simultaneously drawing on positive aspects of hegemonic masculinity (Levant 1992). This was particularly the case in terms of the relational and ethical definitions of manhood provided by some participants. Aspects of each of these themes (e.g., sacrificing and being committed to the welfare of the family, being respectful and standing up for one's word), have been conceptualized as positive components of hegemonic masculinity worth rescuing in the reconstruction of masculinity (Levant 1992), and reinforce previous research examining manhood meaning with African-American men (Hammond and Mattis 2005; Hunter and Davis 1992, 1994). Further, participants rejecting aspects of hegemonic masculinity demonstrated the impact of ascribing to feminist ideology by positioning themselves in direct opposition to dominant conceptions of manhood. These definitions resonate with findings of past studies with feminist men (Vicario 2003; White 2008), particularly in terms of advocating for a complete restructuring of social relations and rejecting manhood as a social construct.

Participants provided definitions of manhood that were also influenced by their membership in various social groups. This was especially salient in relationship to their race, ethnicity, social class, and sexuality (although sexuality played a lesser role in the context of this sample). They defined manhood in ways that integrated their cultural background, racial categorizations, social class, and in some cases, the questioning of their heterosexual, male privilege. These findings are consistent with past research conducted with feminist identified African-American men (White 2008) that utilized an intersectional analysis.

Finally, it is important to stress the fact that the definitions of manhood endorsed by this sample of educated, feminist identified, working class Latinos expands masculine identity as currently conceptualized in the literature (Connell 1995; Pleck 1981). Participants in this sample defined manhood in ways that emphasized emotional connections with others, being open to change and help from others, being collaborative, and being comfortable with one's multiple (and in some cases, derogated) social identities. In other words, participants redefined masculinity in ways that allow men to experience the full range of the human experience (e.g., emotional expression, meaningful relationships with family, community, and others) unencumbered by the restrictions imposed by traditional masculine gender roles (Pleck 1981). They defined manhood in ways that let men be *more than men*.

The findings described above may not be surprising, given the fact that all participants in this sample were educated and feminist identified. What is surprising is the dearth in the literature on this topic—few studies have incorporated an intersectional analysis in exploring the experiences of men of Color generally (see White 2008 for an exception), and Latinos specifically. Further, the findings discussed here suggest a number of future directions for research. Gay men were underrepresented in this sample. The fact that the majority of participants were heterosexual inevitably affected the way that manhood was defined. Further, it is important to note here that all three gay men in this sample provided definitions that rejected aspects of hegemonic masculinity. Future studies utilizing intersectional analyses with working class, gay men of Color could yield fruitful results, thereby lending to a more comprehensive understanding of the way that multiple subordinated group memberships interact to produce group specific conceptions of what it means to be a man.

References

Anzaldúa, G. (1987). *Borderlands—La frontera: The new mestiza.* San Francisco: Spinsters/ Aunt Lute.

Baumeister, R. F. (1998). The self. In D. T. Gilbert, S. T. Fiske, & G. Lindzey (Eds.) *The handbook of social psychology, vol. one* (pp. 680–740). New York: Oxford University Press.

Brown, I., & Misra, J. (2003). The intersection of gender and race in the labor market. *Annual Review of Sociology, 29,* 487–513.

Christian, H. (1994). *The Making of anti-sexist men.* London: Routledge.

Collins, P. H. (1998). *Fighting words: Black women and the search for justice.* Minneapolis, MN: University of Minnesota Press.

Collins, P. H. (2000). *Black feminist thought.* New York: Routledge.

Collins, P. H. (2004). *Black sexual politics: African-Americans, gender, and the new racism.* New York: Routledge.

Connell, R. W. (1995). *Masculinities.* Oxford: Polity Press.

Cornish, P. A. (1999). Men engaging feminism: A model of personal change and social transformation. *Journal of Men's Studies, 7,* 173–190.

Crenshaw, K. W. (1995). Mapping the margins: Intersectionality, identity politics, and violence against women of color. In K. W. Crenshaw, N. Gotanda, G. Peller, & K. Thomas (Eds.) *Critical race theory: The key writings that formed the movement* (pp. 357–383). New York: The New Press.

DeFranc, W., & Mahalik, J. R. (2002). Masculine gender role conflict and stress in relation to parental attachment and separation. *Psychology of Men & Masculinity, 3,* 51–60.

Diemer, M. A. (2002). Constructions of provider role identity among African-American men: An exploratory study. *Cultural Diversity & Ethnic Minority Psychology, 8,* 30–40.

España-Maram, L. (2006). *Creating masculinity in Los Angeles's Little Manila: Working-class Filipinos and popular culture, 1920s–1950s.* New York: Columbia University Press.

Fenstermaker, S., & West, C. (Eds.) (2002). *Doing gender, doing difference: Inequality, power, and institutional change.* New York: Routledge.

Fereday, J., & Muir-Cochrane, E. (2006). Demonstrating rigor using thematic analysis: A hybrid approach of inductive and deductive coding and theme development. *International Journal of Qualitative Methods, 5,* Article 7. Retrieved 05/09/07 from http://www.ualberta.ca/~iiqm/ backissues/5_1/html/fereday.htm

Ferguson, A. A. (2000). *Bad boys: Public schools in the making of Black masculinity.* Ann Arbor, MI, USA: University of Michigan Press.

Fine, M., & Weis, L. (1998). *The unknown city: The lives of poor and working class adults.* Boston, MA, USA: Beacon Press.

Fine, M., Weis, L., Powell Pruitt, L., & Burns, A. (Eds.) (2004). *Off white: Readings on power, privilege, and resistance.* New York: Routledge.

Fink, A. (2003). *How to manage, analyze, and interpret survey data* (2nd ed.). Thousand Oaks, CA, USA: Sage Publications.

Franklin II., C. W. (1998). Black male–Blake female conflict: Individually caused and culturally nurtured. In M. S. Kimmel & M. A. Messner (Eds.) *Men's Lives* (pp. 415–422). Boston, MA, USA: Allyn & Bacon.

Good, G. E., Heppner, P. P., DeBord, K. A., & Fischer, A. R. (2004). Understanding men's psychological distress: Contributions of problem-solving appraisal and masculine role conflict. *Psychology of Men & Masculinity, 5,* 168–177.

Good, G. E., & Wood, P. K. (1995). Male gender role conflict, depression, and help seeking: Do college men face double jeopardy? *Journal of Counseling & Development, 74,* 70–75.

Gurin, P., Hurtado, A., & Peng, T. (1994). Group contacts and ethnicity in the social identities of Mexicanos and Chicanos. *Personality and Social Psychology Bulletin, 20,* 521–532.

Hammond, W. P., & Mattis, J. S. (2005). Being a man about it: Manhood meaning among African-American men. *Psychology of Men & Masculinity, 6,* 114–126.

Hebert, J. R., Ma, Y., Clemow, L., Ockene, I. S., Saperia, G., Stanek, E. J., et al. (1997). Gender differences in social desirability and social approval bias in dietary self-report. *American Journal of Epidemiology, 146,* 1046–1055.

hooks, b. (1992). *Black looks: Race and representation.* Boston, MA, USA: South End Press.

Hunter, A. G., & Davis, J. E. (1992). Constructing gender: An exploration of Afro-American men's conceptualization of manhood. *Gender & Society, 6,* 464–479.

Hunter, A. G., & Davis, J. E. (1994). Hidden voices of Black men: The meaning, structure, and complexity of manhood. *Journal of Black Studies, 25,* 20–40.

Hurtado, A. (1996). Strategic suspensions: Feminists of color theorize the production of knowledge. In N. Goldberger, J. Tarule, B. Clinchy, & M. Belenky (Eds.) *Knowledge, difference and power: Essays inspired by women's ways of knowing* (pp. 372–392). New York: Basic Books.

Hurtado, A. (1997). Understanding multiple group identities: Inserting women into cultural transformations. *Journal of Social Issues, 53,* 299–328.

Hurtado, A. (2003). *Voicing Chicana feminisms: Young women speak out on sexuality and identity.* New York: New York University Press.

Hurtado, A., & Gurin, P. (2004). *¿Quién soy? ¿Quienes somos? (Who am I? Who are we?): Chicana/o identity in a changing U.S. society.* Tucson: University of Arizona Press.

Hurtado, A., & Sinha, M. (2005). Restriction and freedom in the construction of sexuality: Young Chicanas and Chicanos speak out. *Feminism & Psychology, 15,* 33–38.

Hurtado, A., & Sinha, M. (2006). Social identity and gender consciousness with Latinos. Paper presented at the meeting of the National Association for Chicana and Chicano Studies, Guadalajara, Jalisco, Mexico, June–July.

Hurtado, A., & Stewart, A. J. (2004). Through the looking glass: Implications of studying whiteness for feminist methods. In M. Fine, L. Weis, L. Powell Pruitt, & A. Burns (Eds.) *Off White: Readings on power, privilege, and resistance* (pp. 315–330). New York: Routledge.

Kimmel, M. S. (2000). Masculinity as homophobia. In E. Disch (Ed.) *Reconstructing gender: a multicultural anthology* (pp. 132–139). Boston, MA, USA: McGraw-Hill.

Kosambi, M. (1995). An uneasy intersection: Gender, ethnicity, and crosscutting identities in India. *Social Politics, 2,* 181–194.

Lemle, R., & Mishkind, M. E. (1989). Alcohol and masculinity. *Journal of Substance Abuse Treatment, 6,* 213–222.

Levant, R. (1992). Toward the reconstruction of masculinity. *Journal of Family Psychology, 5,* 379–402.

Mahalik, J. R., & Morrison, J. A. (2006). A cognitive therapy approach to increasing father involvement by changing restrictive masculine schemas. *Cognitive and Behavioral Practice, 13,* 62–70.

Mahalik, J. R., & Rochlen, A. B. (2006). Men's likely responses to clinical depression: What are they and do masculinity norms predict them? *Sex Roles, 55,* 659–667.

Majors, R., & Billson, J. M. (1992). *Cool pose: The dilemmas of Black manhood in America.* New York, NY, USA: Lexington Books.

Messner, M. A. (1989). Masculinities and athletic careers. *Gender & Society, 3,* 71–88.

Messner, M. A. (1997). *Politics of masculinity: Men in movements.* Thousand Oaks, CA, USA: Sage Publications.

Mirandé, A. (1997). *Hombres y machos: Masculinity and Latino culture.* Boulder, CO, USA: Westview.

Moraga, C. (1981). La güera. In C. Moraga, & G. Anzaldúa (Eds.) *This bridge called my back: Writings by radical women of color* (pp. 27–34). Watertown, MA, USA: Persephone.

Morse, J. M., & Richards, L. (2002). *Read me first for a users guide to qualitative methods.* Thousand Oaks, CA, USA: Sage.

Nesiah, V. (2000). Toward a feminist internationality: A critique of U.S. feminist legal scholarship. In A. K. Wing (Ed.) *Global critical race feminism: An international reader* (pp. 42–52). New York: New York University Press.

O'Neil, J. M. (1981). Male sex role conflicts, sexism, and masculinity: Psychological implications for men, women, and the counseling psychologist. *Counseling Psychologist, 9,* 61–80.

O'Neil, J. M. (1998). Wade and Gelso's contribution to the new psychology of men: Male reference group identity dependence theory. *Counseling Psychologist, 26,* 413–421.

Pascoe, C. J. (2003). Multiple masculinities? Teenage boys talk about jocks and gender. *American Behavioral Scientist, 46,* 1423–1438.

Phinney, J. S. (1996). When we talk about American ethnic groups, what do we mean? *American Psychologist, 51,* 918–927.

Pleck, J. (1981). *The myth of masculinity.* Cambridge, MA, USA: MIT Press.

Saldívar-Hull, S. (2000). *Feminism on the border. Chicana gender politics and literature.* Berkeley: University of California Press.

Sandoval, C. (2000). *Methodology of the oppressed.* Minneapolis: University of Minnesota Press.

Sinha, M. (2007). *Intersecting social identities: The (feminist) standpoint(s) of Latino men.* Doctoral Dissertation. University of California, Santa Cruz.

Solis, J. (2006). Transborder violence and undocumented youth: Extending cultural-historical analysis to transnational immigration studies. In C. Daiute, Z. Beykont, C. Higson-Smith, & L. Nucci (Eds.) *International perspectives on youth conflict and development* (pp. 305–319). New York: Oxford University Press.

Stewart, A., & McDermott, C. (2004). Gender in psychology. *Annual Review of Psychology, 55,* 519–544.

Tajfel, H. (1981). *Human groups and social categories: Studies in social psychology.* London: Cambridge University Press.

Vicario, B. A. (2003). *A qualitative study of profeminist men.* Doctoral Dissertation. Auburn University.

White, A. (2008). *Ain't I a feminist: African-American men speak out on fatherhood, friendship, forgiveness, and freedom.* Albany, NY: SUNY Press.

14 Tracey Lee

Trans(re)lations
Lesbian and Female to Male Transsexual Accounts of Identity

Introduction

A recent academic exchange on butch/ FTM borders that concerns issues of similarity and difference between butch lesbians and female-to-male transsexuals (FTMs) has been sustained primarily through a discussion of the tenability of maintaining categorical boundaries between each identity category.[1] Through queer theoretical and/or political approaches, some have suggested that the categorical boundaries are blurred, permeable and fluid (Halberstam, 1994, 1996, 1998; Hale, 1998; Rubin, 1992). Others, holding the view that queer perspectives are inappropriate lenses through which to view transsexuals, have argued that such categorizations should be seen as discrete and specific, relating to individuals with particular and distinctive histories (Prosser, 1996, 1998, 1999). However, to date, the arguments put forward have been founded upon observation and personal experience (Rubin, 1992) and media/literary representations and autobiographical accounts (Halberstam, 1994, 1996, 1998; Hale, 1998; Prosser, 1998). Empirical social research has not been utilized within the debate, and no attention has been given to systematically comparing the experiential accounts given by butch lesbians and FTMs to explain their coming to awareness of their particular sexual and gender identities and/or to the ways in which members of each group differentiate themselves from the other.

The aim of this article, based in primary social research, is to bridge this gap and begin to extend and develop the debate by offering such a comparative analysis, with the purpose of illuminating the processes and articulations of identification and differentiation within and between each group. The accounts of experiences and interpretations of identity referred to and analyzed in the article are drawn from semistructured interviews that I conducted with 6 lesbians and 12 FTMs.[2] Beginning by indicating the relevance of issues of similarity and difference to lesbians and FTMs and moving through the comparative analysis of the experiences of childhood, adolescence, and adulthood recounted during the interviews, the article concludes by showing how, through processes of "othering," the lesbians and FTMs distinguished themselves from one another *even though* their experiences were shown to be more similar than different.

Tracey Lee, "Trans(re)lations: Lesbian and Female to Male Transsexual Accounts of Identity," *Women's Studies International Forum* 24, nos. 3/4 (May–August 2001): 347–357. Reprinted by permission of Elsevier.

Similarity, Difference, and the Problem of "Masculinity"

Holly Devor (1997) suggests that lesbian feminist conceptions of lesbianism as a form of woman identification, together with the increasing visibility of transsexuality, have constituted social ideas through which many FTMs have come to reject lesbian identities. From her research with FTMs in the USA, Devor found that:

> Participants who lived part of their lives as lesbian women were thus often in the position of having been drawn to lesbian identities on the basis of older definitions of lesbians as women who wanted to be men. . . . When participants tried to measure themselves against the more woman-centered images promulgated by lesbian-feminists they found themselves lacking . . . when [they] compared themselves to both generalized and specific lesbian others, they were struck more by the contrasts than by the similarities. It therefore became apparent to these participants that they had more in common with straight men than with lesbian women. (Devor, 1997, p. 99)

However, lesbian authors concerned with lesbian masculinities have criticized this definition, suggesting that butch lesbians have, both historically and contemporarily, pushed the category "lesbian" beyond the interpretation of the "woman-identified-woman" (see Burana & Due, 1994; Halberstam, 1994, 1996, 1998; Pratt, 1995; Rubin, 1992). "Butch" is defined by Gayle Rubin (1992) as encompassing " . . . individuals with a broad range of investments in 'masculinity'" (p. 467), and, in view of this term, both she and others have called for the recognition that

there are in fact many points of overlap in respect of the "masculinities" of those who identify themselves as lesbian or FTM (see also Halberstam, 1994, 1996, 1998). Such overlaps are evidenced in the broadest sense through FTMs' and lesbians' simultaneous recuperation of the same historical and contemporary masculine, female embodied figures. For example, Radclyffe Hall (1880–1943), Billy Tipton (c. 1915–1989), and Brandon Teena, tragically murdered in the United States in 1993, have each been claimed by both lesbians and FTMs as belonging to their histories and cultures (Cromwell, 1999; Hale, 1998; Newton, 1984; Prosser, 1998). In the present postmodernist and poststructuralist milieu such competing claims suggest a certain fuzziness and "queerness" of the boundaries between lesbian and FTM masculinities, which has resulted in issues of difference and similarity within and between the two categories becoming the subject of the recent academic exchange on the butch/FTM border.

However, in general, lesbians and FTMs have each tended to hold quite clear and "non-fuzzy" views about each others' identities. For example, FTMs have been portrayed by lesbians as misguided, unenlightened "women" who probably are "really" lesbians (Jeffreys, 1994; Raymond, 1979). Conversely, FTMs have depicted lesbians as essentially content with their birth gender, and have described them as primarily woman-identified women who celebrate their femaleness and womanhood in both themselves and other women. In such accounts, lesbians are not perceived to experience a disjunction between sex, gender, and sexuality, and the "gender dysphoria," which is seen to be specific to the transsexual "condition" (see Hewitt & Warren, 1995; Rees, 1996;

Thompson & Sewell, 1995).[3] But how accurately does each group represent the other? And what purposes can these representations be said to serve? These are questions that the following analysis seeks to address.

The Research Background

Although none of the lesbian participants self-identified as butch, all could be accommodated into the broad definition of the term as outlined by Rubin (1992), that is, from mildly to strongly masculine in feeling and/or presentation. The FTM participants spanned the various stages of gender reassignment, although none had had phalloplasty to make a surgically constructed penis. They reflected the general FTM population, most of whom do not have phalloplasty due to high costs and the lack of satisfactory surgical techniques available (Nataf, 1996). All of the FTMs had either previously self-identified as a lesbian, or through their sexual relationships with women, had at one time been considered to be so by others. Through the interviews I invited the participants to recount their experiences from childhood through to adulthood, and their understandings of these experiences in relation to their identification as either lesbian or FTM. The material that follows is presented chronologically in order to facilitate comparative description and analysis. Quotations from the accounts of the participants are shown in italics.

Experiences of Childhood Gender Identities: The Significance of "Tomboyhood"

The Lesbians

The most commonly reported feature of the lesbian participants' childhood was their tomboy identity. This was described as not being "girl-like," and thus not fitting into society's expectations/demands of how a girl should be. As an experience it involved "being one of the boys," doing what was/is considered to be "boys' activities," desiring what was/is considered to be "boys' things," and resisting pressures to act and present themselves as girls. This is exemplified in Ruth's account:

> I was totally a tom-boy . . . my mother had a major struggle getting me to wear skirts and dresses, I spent my whole life in jeans and trousers. I spent most of my time sort of playing in the back alleys with the boys, playing things like conkers and chasing around on my bike with the lads and I kind of loved it. I thought of myself as one of the lads . . .

For all of the lesbians, social and/or parental pressures to conform to "girlness" had been experienced throughout their childhood. The most common pressure concerned the wearing of dresses and skirts, which none had wanted to wear, but which they had been required to wear for school and at times of family celebration. Wearing such clothes had generated feelings of awkwardness, powerlessness, embarrassment, and a general sense of false self-presentation. As described by Anne:

> I felt stupid in a dress . . . it stopped me from being who I was whereas when I wore trousers I felt like I could be me. People treated me like a girl when I wore a dress and I hated it . . .

Whilst being required to conform to the norms of female dress and behavior caused a sense of erasure of self identity and undesired responses in others, those lesbians who reported that they were regularly perceived as boys found this to be equally disconcerting. Susan and Anne recalled a conscious desire to be boys and, although they found some pleasure in being perceived as such, they also experienced feelings of *shame* and *embarrassment*. Anne, for example, recounted her experience at the age of 10 of going shopping for her mother and the shop keeper addressing her as "*son*." At first his mistake generated a feeling in her of intense excitement and pleasure, although this quickly turned into shame as she began to feel uncomfortable in her feeling that "*his mistake was something that should not happen.*" In not being seen as the girl she knew she was, but as something she was not, and could not be, she became aware and ashamed of her failure to fulfill either gender role:

> . . . *he had seen me as someone I wanted to be rather than who I really was and I felt a sense of a dark feeling, a feeling that I was wrong . . . I felt ashamed that I hadn't been seen as a girl as I knew I was one . . . it was my fault, I couldn't be a girl or a boy . . .*

Similar feelings were recalled by Susan, who remembered that she had not been too distraught when, after falling off her bike during her paper round, a passer-by asked "*Are you all right, lad?,*" but that she had been after a particular incident at school. Susan had been chased around the playground by a girl who, having caught her and kissed her on the cheek, then ran away shouting "*Susan is a boy! Susan is a boy!*" For Susan, this was a sharp reminder of her outsiderness and generated feelings of embarrassment and shame as though she wanted to be a boy she knew that she was not one. Natalie and Lynn had both wanted to do

"boys' things" but did not feel a similar desire to be boys. For them, being perceived as a boy produced not so much a sense of shame but of confusion. Natalie and Lynn were regularly told by family and friends that they looked like and should have been boys and both had felt confused by the disjuncture between their own inner sense of "self" and how they were perceived and seen by others. As a result, like Anne and Susan, they too had felt themselves to occupy a place of "outsiderness" to both genders. As Natalie commented: *I actually found it really hard. In a sense, I wasn't a boy but I wasn't a girl, so what was I?*

For the lesbians, being a tom-boy was an emotional, presentational, and behavioral expression of being unable, and/or unwilling, to fit into the category of either "girl" or "boy." Each could not/would not, in the words of Judith Butler (1993) " . . . inhabit the ideal [they were] compelled to approximate" (p. 231), experiencing therefore, a disjuncture between sex and gender. This disjuncture was interpreted by all of them as evidence of their lesbianism.[4]

The FTMs

Each of the FTM participants also reported that they had been tom-boys during their childhood and, as with the lesbians, all considered themselves as having been, or as having wanted to be, one of the boys. Each held the view that they had neither been nor felt "girl-like" and considered that "tom-boyness" constituted the expression of the way they did not fit into society's expectations of what a girl should be. However, despite the equivalence of their experiences to those of the lesbians, the meaning of "tom-boyness" was differently interpreted. For all of the FTMs, having been a tom-boy was judged to be an early indicator of their transsexualism, as exemplified in the following extracts from the conversations with Carl and Nigel. Carl remarked:

I played with GI Joes and dressed in uniforms for play from when I was about seven. It was bloody screaming fights to get me into a dress, because I couldn't stand wearing them. I don't think that I thought about it much that it was odd to play with Tonka trucks and popguns. My folks were not apparently into hard stereotyping on the toy front, and I never had a reason to think that other folks might not find this usual.

For Carl, the childhood experience of not fitting into or wanting to fit into the conventional expectations of "girlness" is considered with hindsight to have been an oddity. He later perceived his desire for "boys' things" to indicate his inherent "boyness" because had he been really a girl, he would have wanted "girls' things." For Carl, there is assumed to be an inherent gender difference that should, in childhood, manifest itself through conformity to conventional gendered expectations. Based in similar experiences to those of both Carl and the lesbians, Nigel made an explicit connection between his tomboyhood and his embodiment:

At that age I did not know what was wrong. I just knew things were not right. I later realized that I was in the wrong body for everything I felt, enjoyed and thought.

Although it has been suggested that this is an oversimplistic description of the experiences of most transsexuals (Nataf, 1996), Nigel and 10 of the other respondents were insistent that this was indeed how they ex-perienced themselves, particularly at the onset of puberty. Out of all the FTM participants, it was only Simon who considered that the phrase did not reflect his experience:

I did not feel "trapped" within my body so much as I felt trapped by the expectations that accompany the body which I occupied.

Adolescence and Puberty: Gender Identities and the Body

The Lesbians

Simon's feeling of being "*trapped by the expectations that accompany the body [being] occupied*" was similarly echoed by the lesbian participants. The beginning of menstruation and other bodily changes, such as the growth of breasts and pubic hair, had been recognized as confirmation that they were growing into "women," and these changes had negative impacts upon their sense of self. For the most part, puberty had been experienced as unwanted and traumatic. "Becoming women" had generated feelings of horror, resentment, and fear and they had been embarrassed by, and ashamed of, those bodily changes which did not fit the sense of who they felt themselves to be. Natalie found that she had *got this body that people were sexualizing that didn't feel like that to me*, and she *couldn't cope with the attentions that [the changes in her body] brought from men*. Similarly, Susan had felt uncomfortable with, and ashamed of, this *new woman's body*, which had become *somehow sexualized*. She felt that she had to hide her breasts and thus avoided any activity such as swimming, which meant that her body would be re-vealed, continuing in this way until she en-tered her late 20s. For both Natalie and Susan, puberty meant a loss of freedom and self-confidence: their changing bodies sug-gested to them that they could no longer be active tomboys, and they could not identify themselves within, or accept, the social meanings and expectations inscribed upon their "woman's body."

Anne had been horrified at the changes she observed in her body at the onset of pu-berty, knowing that this meant a transfor-mation into "womanhood," a state that she consciously did not want to attain. She re-called associating "womanhood" with *weakness, dependency, passivity* and the ex-tremes of conventional femininity in her childhood, and that she could not identify herself within this characterization. In re-jecting this model of "woman," she rejected her changing body. For example, the growth of her breasts had been particularly disturbing, but, rather than simply covering them as Susan did, she consciously "*flat-tened*" them by wearing a child's "*petticoat*," which was too small for her, beneath her clothes. For Anne:

> The whole experience of puberty was horri-ble . . . I hated having to be a girl and I cer-tainly didn't want to be a woman. I remember laying in bed looking down at my body and I could see my breasts growing and pubic hair and I just cried . . . this wasn't me. I didn't think that I should have a penis or anything, just that I shouldn't have this new woman's body. I realized that they [boys] were kind of seeing me as a woman and so I couldn't be with them any more . . . but I couldn't be with the girls either. I remember thinking where can I go now? I had to fit in somewhere . . .

For Anne, changes in her body, and the ac-companying changes in others' reactions to her, had brought to her attention not only that her body was being sexualized but that she was being seen as a "woman." She did not want to lose her "tom-boyhood," and felt that "woman-hood" was robbing her of her identity. Anne considered that such an expe-rience exemplified her difference as a lesbian from heterosexual women, whom she imag-ined would not share her experiences. For Anne, that she *didn't think [she] should have a penis or anything* exemplified to her that her horror at her changing body was a specifically lesbian response, rather than an indication of a desire to be a man.

All the lesbians shared the view that dur-ing puberty, "womanhood" did not fully encompass their self-identities. They all considered that they had felt a sense of dif-ference from their female peers, during adolescence as well as in childhood, and considered this in retrospect to be further indicative of their later lesbian identifica-tion. As Ruth remarked:

> The thing [about becoming a woman] was that I never did want to wear dresses or skirts and that just carried on. I never particularly wanted to look feminine and I was very con-scious of that, very conscious of being different to other girls, they seemed quite happy wearing flowery dresses and so on and I never wanted to do that.

For the lesbians, puberty was experienced as traumatic, involving complex and reflexive relationships between changing embodiment and social responses to it. Retrospectively, this aversion to their sexualized bodies and their rejection of conventional heterosexual womanhood was universally identified as signifying their lesbian identities. Lesbian identification, then, represented a "third option"—a space between womanhood and manhood.

The FTMs

Although none of the FTM participants considered that they had been conventional girls in their childhood, it was not until puberty that most began to be more conscious of their feelings of gender difference. Each of the FTMs reported identical responses to the lesbians with regard to the physical changes in their bodies, seeing these as unwanted, embarrassing and disturbing. As described by Lee:

> The entire experience of puberty was extremely traumatic. I hated the body. Breast development was horrific, embarrassing, humiliating and uncomfortable. I was quite large, 36C, but would not wear a suitable, supporting bra . . . but instead wore one . . . that had a "flattening" effect. Attention to my figure was feared, avoided, I was painfully self-conscious, and felt like I was in drag when persuaded/obliged to dress in female clothes . . .

Seeking to mask the developing/developed breasts and to avoid others' recognition of the female body echoes Anne's and Susan's behavior. Russell too showed a similarity to the lesbians when he recalled his reaction to the start of menstruation and the recognition of his new and "alien" womanhood:

> when I started by first period my mum told my dad and my dad bought me a bunch of roses the next day and congratulated me on becoming a woman. I was very upset by it, I was really rude to him . . .

Such similarities in experience suggest, then, that alienation from the developing female body, seen by these FTMs and others as a signifier of their "gender dysphoria," is not wholly specific to those individuals who come to identify themselves as transsexual. Indeed, for 9 out of the 12 FTMs, the feeling of "not fitting" the conventional model of womanhood during puberty and adolescence was understood by them in the first instance to be explainable in terms of lesbian identity. As Russell remarked:

> When I came out and started going out with women, I thought, you know, this is it, so there was the euphoria of coming out to yourself and like, you know, finally sorting it . . . I wasn't mature enough to figure [being a transsexual] out and I wasn't sure at first because I didn't really see myself as wanting a dick, I just wanted to grow up to be a man, if you know what I mean.

That he didn't really see himself as *wanting a dick* suggested to Russell, as it had to Anne, that he must be a lesbian. Of the FTMs, only Martin, Ian and Lee had not considered their gender confusion during puberty to be an indicator of lesbianism. However, Martin had self-identified for a short period as bisexual, and Ian and Lee had experienced relationships with girls through which they had been considered by others to be lesbian. Thus, for all the FTMs, the rejection of conventional womanhood and aversion to female embodiment led to the ownership or attribution of a lesbian identity, which then became significant in the further development of their transsexual identity.

Adulthood: Experience, Identity and Interpretation

The FTMs: Masculinity and Lesbian Experiences

Most of the FTMs considered that the period during which they had experienced sexual relationships with lesbian women had been crucial to their later identification as FTM. Simon, Russell and Carl reported that, initially, being a lesbian was felt to be *"the answer"* to their emotional and social experiences of being unable to fit into the conventional woman's role, and that it seemed for them at the time, to be an identity through which they could express their masculinities. For Simon, the lesbian "community" appeared to offer him the opportunity to be himself and constituted a space through which, in the guise of a butch lesbian, his masculinity could be accepted. Russell expressed a similar experience:

> . . . it gave me a legitimate excuse for being butch, you know, 'cos people expect dykes, like sort of dungarees and really heavy boots and funny hair and I fitted that so I thought, this is me, this is my little niche in a way.

Although Martin's experience was somewhat different, as he had identified as bisexual rather than lesbian and had later come to identify himself as a gay man, he also found that lesbian relationships allowed him to more completely realize his masculinity:

> . . . when I was dating women, I felt free to finally express my masculinity for the first time after so many years of subconsciously toning it down for the benefit of straight male partners.

Martin considered that the short period during which he had had relationships with women was critical to his recognition of himself as transsexual.

As in Devor's study (1997), common to most of the FTMs' experiences of these relationships was a developing perception of themselves as misfits in a lesbian category/context. However, such perceptions cut across a variety of lesbian lifestyles and subcultures, including social circles of lesbian feminists, non-feminist lesbians, drag-kings, and S/M leather dykes, showing that the reasons for this were more diverse than simply a rejection of the woman-centeredness characterized by Devor as specific to lesbian feminism. Nigel hated his female body and could not bear for it to be touched. Carl felt himself within a group of lesbians to be: *some kind of trusted foreigner who was socially mannered to fit the situation without causing too much distress around [him].* He had been involved in the *"dyke leather community"* and along with others, had *"played in the scene as a 'boy.'"* However, he had recognized his difference from the other lesbian "boys" through his awareness that for him *"it wasn't just play,"* and that unlike the others, he really desired to have male genitalia. Lee, who had not self-identified as lesbian, had felt uncomfortable with the sexual and social dynamics of his relationships with women. Whilst he had been expected to take the masculine role within his relationships, he felt that his masculine behaviors were *compromised so as to fit the expectations of a butch.* Unlike Simon and Russell, he had not felt at any time that he could express himself within a lesbian role, feeling it to be *as alien to his self-perception as a female role would have been.*

Both Simon and Russell, however, reported that eventually their masculinities could not be expressed or contained in a butch identity. Both had felt that there was a basic "woman centeredness" underneath the masculinities of most butch lesbians that they could not relate to. Ray initially thought that, as he was a "woman" and desired women, then "*logically*" he should be a lesbian. However, once he became involved in lesbian relationships he began to recognize that his *psyche was more male than other lesbians*, and that their *woman centeredness* was something that he *could not share*. Each of the participants had concluded that as they did not feel themselves to be either a heterosexual or lesbian woman, then they must be a man.

For all apart from Ian, who reported that all of his partners had accepted him as male, it was during their relationships and/or friendships with lesbians that they had begun to fully recognize their transsexuality. Whilst initially, for most a lesbian identity/position had provided a place through which their "difference" in sexuality from heterosexual women could be articulated, it also recontextualized their experiences, allowing a process of further differentiation between themselves and lesbians through the issue of "womanhood." For the most part, the FTMs' recognition of their "difference" was not so much based within a certain and preexisting knowledge that they were really male, but rather, through their awareness of what they were not: women. Seen against their own complex gendered positioning, apart from being attracted to other women, lesbians were seen to be unproblematically "women" and were thus reinscribed by the FTMs under the terms of essentialism and con-

ventional heterosexualized gender. As Nigel's remark demonstrates:

FTMs and lesbians are as different as men and women. As an FTM I know that my thought processes have been and are different from most women. I approach things differently. I am not as emotional about things, I am more logical. Lesbians are women, the only difference is that they enjoy the company of other women. They enjoy the softness, closeness that one woman can bring to another.

The Lesbians: Masculinity and Sexual Practices

As we have seen, in childhood and adolescence the lesbians had, in fact, been problematically "women" in that they did not fit into the category "woman" as understood within the terms of heterosexualized gender. For all, this disjuncture had continued into their adulthood, and as the FTMs had once considered, being a lesbian constituted an identity through which they could articulate their "difference" in sexuality from heterosexual women and express their masculinities. Each of the lesbians considered that their masculinity cut across all areas of their lives, and was expressed primarily through forms of dress, demeanor, and in their sexual relationships. However, none of the lesbians considered that through their masculinities they were emulating men, nor that their masculinity indicated that they should be a man. Whilst in their adulthood, Lynn, Natalie, Anne, and Ruth had often been mistaken for men or young boys in public places. This was seen to be a result of other people's *rigid gender values* rather than suggestive of anything "wrong" with them, as they had felt in their childhood. As Natalie explained: *Because they associate masculine things with men, then they think I'm a man and I just sort of think, well, you've got to fit into discrete categories, there's no shades of grey. . . .* For them, the unrealistic *discrete categories* had obscured the *shades of grey*, the "third option," in which they considered themselves to be located.

Further *discrete categories* through which the lesbians negotiated their masculinities and lesbian identities were "heterosexual" and "lesbian" sexual practices. All were familiar with the ways in which some sexual practices between lesbians, such as the use of dildos, had been interpreted by some lesbian feminists as imitating heterosexual sex (see, e.g., Jeffreys, 1994). However, none agreed with this interpretation. Four lesbians stated that they regularly used dildos in their sexual activities with their partners. Two reported that they did not use them out of personal preference, but did not consider themselves to be against their use. For a long time, Susan and Carol had shied away from using dildos as they had at one time associated them with *wanting to be a man*, although at the time of the interview both had ceased to make this association and had begun to integrate them into their sexual activities. Their change in attitude was primarily due to their increasing visibility and acceptability within lesbian "culture," evidenced in lesbian magazines and other media. Neither Carol or Susan used them with a harness that straps the dildo to the body, although this was not a matter of choice but of circumstance: Susan could not afford one, and Carol could not find one to fit. Both considered that by not wearing a harness they were, in fact, unable

to mirror heterosexual penetrative sex, regarding the use of dildos as a specifically lesbian sexual activity and experiencing their use as somehow expressive of their "masculinity." As Susan stated:

I didn't want to be a man but I did have a sort of sexual appetite, a sexual aggression and wanting to, you know, express myself in that way. I've accepted that aspect of myself as a woman, my masculinity, you know.

Anne and Ruth, however, considered their use of dildos to be a conscious act through which they could play with a male gender role. Both used a dildo with a harness, and although they did not feel themselves to be men, they reported that they did experience pleasure from being like men. Ruth, for example, stated that being *like a man* in her sexual practice was accompanied by the fantasy of being one because:

. . . it's really odd using a dildo because you can't feel it and sometimes . . . I do sort of acknowledge that I'd quite like to have a penis just for twenty four hours to see what it was like . . . I'd quite like to do it, go out and shag lots of women.

Anne had similar fantasies and, like Ruth, she bemoaned the lack of physical sensation. For Anne, sexual pleasure in wearing the dildo was derived from within the sexual dynamic created with her partner, from the pleasure she gave to her partner and the way in which this enhanced Anne's feeling of masculinity:

When I wear my dildo and harness, I feel like it is part of me, it belongs on my body, if you know what I mean. Wearing it makes me feel different from usual, but not really different from myself . . . when I fuck my girlfriend I can really feel my masculinity, I feel sort of male, but not like a man, more like a boy, maybe that's because as the dildo isn't really part of my body it can feel awkward, you can't feel it so you don't know what you're doing and it gives you a feeling of being novice-like . . .

For Anne, feeling *sort of male, but not like a man, more like a boy* and *novice-like* was not, however, about wanting to be a man as for her *having sex with a woman with a dildo [was] a totally different experience.* For Anne and Ruth, the impermanence of the dildo and the absence of "real" sensation whilst wearing it constituted a significant difference between themselves and men: whereas they could be *like* men they could not *be* men. The dildo symbolized the *lack* of being a man and concomitantly the failure of heterosexual sex, rather than enabling their signification. Thus, they were able to enact a form of masculinity within their sexual practices whilst simultaneously retaining a sense of female identification. Like Carol and Susan, Anne and Ruth considered their sexual activities as specifically lesbian, involving their specifically lesbian form of masculinity. As in the case of the FTMs the lesbians similarly employed the terms of conventional heterosexualized gender to assert their difference. Through this "being a man" was seen against their own complex gendered location as unproblematic, insofar as in order to be a man one must have a penis. It is this, I suggest, which facilitates the process of differentiation from lesbians by FTMs, in that "woman identification" can be inferred

from the lesbian rejection of an association with maleness.

The FTMs: Sexual Practices and Being a Man

The idea that "being a man" required having a penis was, however, strongly contested by the FTMs. None had undergone surgery to acquire a penis and, although all reported that they would undergo this surgery if the cost was reduced and the techniques were improved, none considered that being without a penis made them "any less of a man." For the most part, being without a penis was experienced as generally unproblematic, as most social circumstances did not require the exposure of the genitals. Thus, in their presentation as men, having a penis was assumed rather than questioned.[5] However, this was not the case within their sexual relationships, which constituted contexts wherein the absence of a penis could not be disguised.

Out of the 12 FTMs, 6 volunteered information about their personal, sexual activities and how these had affected their own and others' perceptions of them as men. All reported that the lack of a penis did not make them feel, or appear to their sexual partners, as any less male than genetic males and that during their sexual practices, their genitalia did not present a problem to either their partners or themselves. All six had experienced sexual relationships with women prior to deciding on transition, and four stated that they continued to engage in the same sexual activities as previously although now, as men, these activities were *experienced differently.* This difference was attributed to the fact that, as heterosexual men, they appropriated a dildo as an extension of their *own penis.* As Richard, who always wore a dildo during his sexual activities with his partner explained:

> . . . *the dildo is merely an extension of my own penis and by focusing my energy on that area of my body I am able to feel what it feels during intercourse. I also translate what my hands and fingers have felt to my penis and that heightens the experience. I am quite orgasmic using dildos—both for oral sex (blow jobs) and intercourse.*

In contrast to the lesbians Ruth and Anne, Richard was able to experience physical sensation through his dildo, and considered the dildo as necessary for both his own and his partner's perception of him *as a man*. He considered his sexual activities to be nothing other than *heterosexual sex.*

However, Pete, on the other hand, reported that he had experienced a change in both his use of, and feelings about, dildos. Prior to deciding on transition he had often used one, but since then he had always found that, far from enhancing his sense of being a man, it had increasingly made him aware of the penis that he lacks. Unlike Richard, but similar to Ruth and Anne, he experiences no physical sensation whilst wearing it, which for him raised many unwanted emotions. He felt that as man he should experience fully the sensation that is inherent in penetrative sex and, in his failure to do so, he experienced *an unwanted reminder that I'm not the kind of guy I long to be sexually.* Apart from these emotions, Pete also found a dildo clumsy to use, and felt that it reduced intimacy by creating a *barrier* between himself and his sexual partner. Pete had subsequently gone on to identify as a gay man and reported that his partners

had no difficulty in desiring and responding to him as a man and that in his sexual activities he was able not only to use his own genitalia but, through so doing, more fully express his maleness as being *of [him]self.* Similarly, Martin recounted how, as a gay man, the act of vaginal penetration had acquired new meaning for him:

> *Before my first encounter with a man as a man I was worried that being penetrated might make me feel feminized or remind me of my old life, but it did not, I felt completely male and was related to as a male.*

In presenting as a man and attracting male sexual partners, Pete and Martin had redefined their sexual role and gendered status. Vaginal penetration and the incorporation of their own genitalia within this sexual context did not in any way generate a feeling or perception of femininity, demonstrating the ways in which the physical body need not always be of significance. As has been suggested by Judith Halberstam (1994), contexts " . . . and readers of gender fiction, as much as bodies, create sexuality and gender and their transitivities. In many situations gender or gendering takes at least two" (p. 220).[6]

The FTMs' narratives of experience explicitly contradict the view of the lesbians: that to be a man you have to have a penis. For one FTM the use of a dildo enabled heterosexual sex, whilst for the lesbians it signified its impossibility. For yet another FTM, a dildo highlighted his difference from genetic men, though the lack of male genitalia was experienced by two FTMs as unproblematic in the context of homosexual sexual activity. For all of the FTMs, sexual activity was not experienced as a context through which their "being men" would be likely to be called into question, providing that there was a correlation between their sense of self, self presentation and others' perceptions.

Conclusion

A comparative analysis of these lesbians' and FTMs' accounts of their experiences of their bodies, gender identifications and sexualities over their life courses show that there were more similarities than differences in their experiences. During childhood, adolescence and puberty every participant understood themselves as failing to fit the conventional expectations of girlhood and early womanhood, which their female bodies both signified and were signifiers of. It was in retrospect, from their current positions of identification, that both the lesbians and FTMs interpreted and claimed this shared past as specifically "lesbian" and specifically "transsexual." Whilst the sexual practices of both the lesbians and the heterosexual FTMs were also more similar than they were different, the accounts showed how through the particular identifications of lesbian "women" and transsexual "men" their experiences are always and already interpreted as specific to the identities claimed.

In the context of the analysis the similarities across the experiences can thus be seen to bring each categorical definition of identity into a visible crisis, supporting the "queer" view that the categorical boundaries between "butch lesbian" and "FTM" identities are blurred, permeable, and fluid (Halberstam 1994, 1996, 1998; Hale, 1998; Rubin, 1992). However, this is not the way in which the participants *understood* their identities. Each group, locating

itself within the category of "lesbian" (female) or "FTM" (male), understood the categories as impervious and their occupation of them as extending or reinforcing the categorical boundaries rather than blurring or negating them. The issue of "specificity" thus arises through this contradiction, but does this necessarily point to the inappropriateness or inadequacy of a "queer" view and, therefore, that discrete and distinctive identities of "butch lesbian" and "FTM" necessarily remain (Prosser, 1996, 1998, 1999)?

I suggest, from the analysis I have presented, that the answer is no. Specificity can be seen as a product, not of experience, but of *narrative construction*. Each participant's account of their life experience and their understandings of their gender and sexual identity formation relied upon the continuous reinscription of categorical boundaries. The juxtaposition of the lesbian and FTM accounts reveals, therefore, not only clear similarity of experience but an indication of the *processes* involved in this narrative construction of categorical boundaries.

To differentiate themselves and mark the borders of their self-identified categorical location, participants engaged in processes of "othering," accomplished through recourses to essentialism and notions of heterosexualized gender attributed to the "other." Crucially, the "other" invoked was not simply *one another* as is suggested by the discussions concerning a "butch/FTM border" (Halberstam 1994, 1996, 1998; Hale, 1998; Prosser, 1996, 1998, 1999), but other "others" against whom, in different contexts, "difference" and therefore specificity, could be claimed. For the lesbians, the social "other" was heterosexual women and the sexual "other" was heterosexual men, whilst for the FTMs the social and sexual "other" was both heterosexual women and lesbians-as-women. In each case, "specificity" of identity was achieved in relation to an "other" who was seen as unproblematic against their own complex selfhood and identity. Both the lesbian and FTM participants illustrated through their accounts, as Gayatri Chakravorty Spivak (1990) puts it, that: "The person who *knows* has all the problems of self-hood. The person who is *known* somehow seems not to have a problematic self . . . the self of the other is authentic without a problem" (p. 66: emphasis in original).

Notes

1. For the discussion on the butch/FTM border see Judith Halberstam (1994, 1996, 1998); Jay Prosser (1996, 1998, 1999); and C. Jacob Hale (1998).

2. My intention is to indicate the potential for further research in this field and, therefore, no claims are being made here regarding generalizability from this small sample.

3. For diagnostic criteria that identify "transsexuality" see the *Diagnostic and Statistical Manual IV* (American Psychiatric Association, 1994).

4. The popularity of the idea of tom-boyhood as an early expression of lesbian identity is exemplified in the collection by Yamaguchi and Barber (1995), who write: "As tomboys, we were 'other' then; as lesbians, we are 'other' now. Though we were defined as tomboys by what we did, for many of us, what we did turned out to be who we were and who we became, the behavior an expression of identity" (p. 13).

5. Kessler and McKenna (1978) use the term "cultural genitalia" to explain this assumption: "The cultural genital is the one which is assumed to exist and which, it be believed, should be there. . . . Even if the genital is not present in a physical sense, it exists in a cultural sense if the person feels entitled to it and/or is assumed to have it" (p. 154).

6. For a broader discussion on gay FTM experience see Holly Devor (1997) *FTM: Female-to-Male Transsexuals in Society.*

References

American Psychiatric Association. (1994). *Diagnostic and statistical manual of mental disorders* (4th ed.). Washington, DC: American Psychiatric Association.

Burana, Lily Roxxie, & Due, Linnea (Eds.). (1994). *Dagger: On butch women.* Pittsburgh: Cleis Press.

Butler, Judith. (1993). *Bodies that matter.* New York: Routledge.

Cromwell, Jason. (1999). Passing women and female-bodied men: (Re)claiming FTM history. In Kate More & Stephen Whittle (Eds.), *Reclaiming genders: Transsexual grammars at the fin de siecle* (pp. 34–61). London: Cassell.

Devor, Holly. (1997). More than manly women: How female transsexuals reject lesbian identities. In Bonnie Bullough, Vern Vern, & James Elias (Eds.), *Gender blending* (pp. 87–102). New York: Prometheus Books.

Halberstam, Judith. (1994). F2M: The making of female masculinity. In Laura Doan (Ed.), *The lesbian postmodern* (pp. 210–228). New York: Columbia University Press.

Halberstam, Judith. (1996). Lesbian masculinity or even stone butches get the blues. *Women & Performance: A Journal of Feminist Theory, 8*(2), 61–73.

Halberstam, Judith. (1998). Transgender butch: Butch/FTM border wars and the masculine continuum. *GLQ: A Journal of Lesbian and Gay Studies, 4*(2), 287–310.

Hale, C. Jacob. (1998). Consuming the living, dis(re)membering the dead in the butch/FTM borderlands. *GLQ: A Journal of Lesbian and Gay Studies, 4*(2), 311–348.

Hewitt, Paul, & Warren, Jane. (1995). *A self-made man.* London: Headline.

Jeffreys, Sheila. (1994). *The lesbian heresy.* London: Women's Press Ltd.

Kessler, Suzanne, & McKenna, Wendy. (1978). *Gender: An ethnomethodological approach.* Chicago: The University of Chicago Press.

Nataf, Zachary. (1996). *Lesbians talk transgender*. London: Scarlet Press.

Newton, Esther. (1984). The mythic mannish lesbian: Radclyffe Hall and the New Woman. *Signs, 9*(4), 557–575.

Pratt, Minnie Bruce. (1995). *S/he*. New York: Firebrand Books.

Prosser, Jay. (1996). No place like home: The transgendered narrative of Leslie Feinberg's stone butch blues. *Modern Fiction Studies, 41*(3–4), 483–514.

Prosser, Jay. (1998). *Second skins: The body narratives of transsexuality*. New York: Columbia University Press.

Prosser, Jay. (1999). Exceptional locations: Transsexual travelogues. In Kate More & Stephen Whittle (Eds.), *Reclaiming genders: Transsexual grammars at the fin de siecle* (pp. 83–114). London: Cassell.

Raymond, Janice. (1979). *The transsexual empire: The making of the she-male*. London: The Women's Press.

Rees, Mark. (1996). *Dear sir or madam*. London: Cassell.

Rubin, Gayle. (1992). Of catamites and kings: Reflections on butch, gender, and boundaries. In Joan Nestle (Ed.), *The persistent desire: A femme-butch reader* (pp. 466–482). Boston: Alyson Publications, Inc.

Spivak, Gayatri. (1990). *The post-colonial critic: Interviews, strategies, dialogues*. Sarah Harasym (Ed.). London: Routledge.

Thompson, Raymond, & Sewell, Kitty. (1995). *What took you so long? A girl's journey to manhood*. London: Penguin.

Yamaguchi, Lynne, & Barber, Karen. (Eds.). (1995). *Tom-boys!: Tales of dyke derring-do*. Boston: Alyson Publications, Inc.

15 Karen D. Pyke and Denise L. Johnson

Asian American Women and Racialized Femininities
"Doing" Gender across Cultural Worlds

The study of gender in recent years has been largely guided by two orienting approaches: (1) a social constructionist emphasis on the day-to-day production or doing of gender (Coltrane 1989; West and Zimmerman 1987), and (2) attention to the interlocking systems of race, class, and gender (Espiritu 1997; Hill Collins 2000). Despite the prominence of these approaches, little empirical work has been done that integrates the doing of gender with the study of race. A contributing factor is the more expansive incorporation of social constructionism in the study of gender than in race scholarship where biological markers are still given importance despite widespread acknowledgment that racial oppression is rooted in social arrangements and not biology (Glenn 1999). In addition, attempts to theoretically integrate the doing of gender, race, and class around the concept of "doing difference" (West and Fenstermaker 1995) tended to downplay historical macro-structures of power and domination and to privilege gender over race and class (Hill Collins et al. 1995). Work is still needed that integrates systems of oppression in a social constructionist framework without granting primacy to any one form of inequality of ignoring larger structures of domination.

The integration of gender and race within a social constructionist approach directs attention to issues that have been overlooked. Little research has examined how racially and ethnically subordinated women, especially Asian American women, mediate cross-pressures in the production of femininity as they move between mainstream and ethnic arenas, such as family, work, and school, and whether distinct and even contradictory gender displays and strategies are enacted across different arenas. Many, if not most, individuals move in social worlds that do not require dramatic inversions of their gender performances, thereby enabling them to maintain stable and seemingly unified gender strategies. However, members of communities that are racially and ethnically marginalized and who regularly traverse interactional arenas with conflicting gender expectations might engage different gender performances depending on the local context in which they are interacting. Examining the ways that such individuals mediate conflicting expectations would address several unanswered questions. Do marginalized women shift

Excerpted from the original. Karen D. Pyke and Denise L. Johnson, "Asian American Women and Racialized Femininities: 'Doing' Gender across Cultural Worlds," *Gender & Society* 17, no. 1 (February 2003): 33–53. Copyright © 2003 Sociologists for Women in Society. Reprinted by permission of SAGE Publications.

their gender performances across mainstream and subcultural settings in response to different gender norms? If so, how do they experience and negotiate such transitions? What meaning do they assign to the different forms of femininities that they engage across settings? Do racially subordinated women experience their production of femininity as inferior to those forms engaged by privileged white women and glorified in the dominant culture?

We address these issues by examining how second-generation Asian American women experience and think about the shifting dynamics involved in the doing of femininity in Asian ethnic and mainstream cultural worlds. We look specifically at their assumptions about gender dynamics in the Euro-centric mainstream and Asian ethnic social settings, the way they think about their gendered selves, and their strategies in doing gender. Our analysis draws on and elaborates the theoretical literature concerning the construction of femininities across race, paying particular attention to how controlling images and ideologies shape the subjective experiences of women of color. This is the first study to our knowledge that examines how intersecting racial and gender hierarchies affect the everyday construction of gender among Asian American women.

The work concerning the effects of controlling images and the relational construction of subordinated and hegemonic femininities has mostly been theoretical. The little research that has examined how Asian American women do gender in the context of racialized images and ideologies that construct their gender as "naturally" inferior to white femininity provides only a brief look at these issues (Chen 1998; Lee 1996). Many of the Asian American women whom we study here do not construct their gender in one cultural field but are constantly moving between sites that are guided by ethnic immigrant cultural norms and those of the Euro-centric mainstream. A comparison of how gender is enacted and understood across such sites brings the construction of racialized gender and the dynamics of hegemonic and subordinated femininities into bold relief. We examine how respondents employ cultural symbols, controlling images, and gender and racial ideologies in giving meanings to their experiences.

Gender in Ethnic and Mainstream Cultural Worlds

We study Korean and Vietnamese Americans, who form two of the largest Asian ethnic groups in southern California, the site of this research. We focus on the daughters of immigrants as they are more involved in both ethnic and mainstream cultures than are members of the first generation. Koreans and Vietnamese did not immigrate to the United States in substantial numbers prior to 1965 and 1975, respectively (Zhou 1999). Fully 80 percent of Korean Americans (Chang 1999) and 82 percent of Vietnamese Americans are foreign born (Zhou and Bankston 1998). The second generation, who are still mostly children and young adults, must juggle the cross-pressures of ethnic and mainstream cultures without the groundwork that a long-standing ethnic enclave might provide. This is not easy. Disparities between ethnic and mainstream worlds can generate substantial conflict for children of immigrants, including conflict around issues of gender (Kibria 1993; Zhou and Bankston 1998).

Method

Our sample (*N*=100) consists of 48 daughters of Korean immigrants and 52 daughters of Vietnamese immigrants. Respondents ranged in age from 18 to 34 and averaged 22 years of age. Respondents either were U.S. born (*n*=25) or immigrated prior to the age of 16 (*n*=74), with 1 respondent having arrived at 18. Both parents of respondents were born in Korea or Vietnam. The data consist of 81 individual interviews and seven group interviews with 26 women—7 of whom were also individually interviewed. Data were collected in California between 1996 and 1999 using a convenience sample located through interviewers' networks and announcements posted at a university campus. We tried to diversify the sample by recruiting community college students and those who had terminated their education prior to receiving a college degree. College graduates or currently enrolled university and community college students compose 81 percent of the sample, and 19 percent are college dropouts or women who never attended college.

The data are part of a larger study of adaptation among second-generation Korean and Vietnamese Americans. These two groups were selected for study to enable a comparison of how their ethnic and socioeconomic distinctions affect different adaptation pathways. Vietnamese arrived as poorer, less-educated refugees than Koreans, who voluntarily immigrated. Among first-generation heads of households, only 19 percent of Vietnamese hold a college degree compared to 45 percent of Koreans (Oropesa and Landale 1995). However, analyses of these data have not produced the expected ethnic or class distinctions (Pyke 2000; Pyke and Dang in press). As the sample is mostly college educated, our data may not capture the economic distinctions of these two groups.

As this is an interpretive study that emphasizes the meanings and understandings of respondents, we used a grounded theory method (Glaser and Straus 1967). This approach assumes that researchers should not define the areas of research interest and theoretical importance prior to data collection but rather should follow the issues and themes that respondents suggest are important, allowing theoretical explanation to emerge from the data. The emphasis is on the understandings of those being studied rather than the a priori assumptions of researchers.

During the initial stage of data collection, we asked 47 women and 26 men questions related to ethnic identity as well as about their experiences growing up in an immigrant family, relations with parents, reactions to parents' discipline, and desires for change within their families (Pyke 2000). Gender loomed large in the accounts of female respondents, who commonly complained about parents' gender attitudes, especially the stricter rules for girls than for boys. We noted that women tended to denigrate Asian ethnic realms and glorify mainstream arenas. They did so in ways both subtle and overt and typically focused on gender behavior, although not always. Some respondents described different behavior and treatment in settings with coethnics compared to those dominated by whites and other non–Asian Americans. We began asking about gender in ethnic and mainstream settings in later interviews. In addition to earlier questions about family dynamics and ethnic identity, we asked if respondents ever alter their behavior around people of different ethnicities, whether people of different ethnicities treat them differently, and if being American and Vietnamese or Korean were ever in opposition. When necessary to prompt a discussion of gender, we also asked respondents to describe any time someone had certain stereotypical expectations of them, although their responses often focused on gender-neutral racial stereotypes of Asians as good at math, bad drivers, or unable to speak English. A few were asked if others ever expected them to be passive or quiet, which several women had described as a common expectation they encountered. When respondents failed to provide examples of gender behavior, the topic was usually dropped and the interview moved to other areas of study not part of this analysis. We interviewed an additional 53 women for a total sample of 100. Trained assistants, most of whom are daughters of Asian immigrants, and the first author collected the data. Tape-recorded interviews and video-taped group interviews lasted from one to three hours.

The transcribed interviews were read closely, and recurring themes concerning gender dynamics and beliefs as well as changes in behavior across cultural settings were extracted for analysis. The sorted data were analyzed for underlying meanings and reread in the context of our emerging findings to ensure their validity (Glaser and Straus 1967). The analysis focused on two themes. The first concerned racialized beliefs about gender, which came in a variety of forms and recurred throughout the interviews. We use these data to describe the ways that respondents think about Asian and "American" (meaning white) femininity. The second theme concerns changes in gender behavior or treatment in ethnic and mainstream settings, with 44 of the 100 respondents (20 Korean Americans and 24 Vietnamese Americans) having provided clear examples.

That nearly half of the sample provided descriptions of gender switching across settings indicates it is prominent enough to warrant our investigation. However, we cannot ascertain from our convenience sample how prominent this issue is for Asian American women in general, which is beyond the aim of our study. Our purpose is to describe these emergent themes and what they suggest about how racialized notions of gender are embedded in the construction of identity for second-generation Asian American women.

In presenting the data, we provide the respondent's age and ethnicity, using the abbreviations VA for Vietnamese American and KA for Korean American. Respondents used the term "American" to refer to non–Asian Americans, particularly whites. The use of "American" as a code for "white" is a common practice (Espiritu 2001; Pyke and Dang in press). This usage reflects the racialized bias of the dominant society, which constructs Asian Americans as perpetual foreigners and whites as the only true Americans. We stay close to this language so as to underscore our respondents' racialized assumptions.

Gender across Cultural Terrains: "I'm Like a Chameleon. I Change My Personality"

The 44 respondents who were aware of modifying their gender displays or being treated differently across cultural settings framed their accounts in terms of an oppressive ethnic world and an egalitarian mainstream. They reaffirmed the ideological constructions of the white-dominated society by casting ethnic and mainstream worlds as monolithic opposites, with internal variations largely ignored. Controlling images that denigrate Asian femininity and glorify white femininity were reiterated in many of the narratives. Women's behavior in ethnic realms was described as submissive and controlled, and that in white-dominated settings as freer and more self-expressive.

Some respondents suggested they made complete personality reversals as they moved across realms. They used the behavior of the mainstream as the standard by which they judged their behavior in ethnic settings. As Elizabeth (19, VA) said,

> I feel like when I'm amongst other Asians . . . I'm much more reserved and I hold back what I think. . . . But when I'm among other people like at school, I'm much more outspoken. I'll say whatever's on my mind. It's like a diametric character altogether. . . . I feel like when I'm with other Asians that I'm the *typical* passive [Asian] person and I feel like that's what's expected of me and if I do say something and if I'm the *normal* person that I am, I'd stick out like a sore thumb. So I just blend in with the situation. (emphasis added)

Elizabeth juxtaposes the "typical passive [Asian] person" and the "normal," outspoken person of the mainstream culture, whom she claims to be. In so doing, she reaffirms the stereotypical image of Asians as passive while glorifying Americanized behavior, such as verbal expressiveness, as "normal." This implies that Asian ethnic behavior is aberrant and inferior compared to white behavior, which is rendered normal. This juxtaposition was a recurring theme in these data (Pyke 2000). It contributed to respondents' at-tempts to distance themselves from racialized notions of the typical Asian woman who is hyperfeminine and submissive by claiming to possess those traits associated with white femininity, such as assertiveness, self-possession, confidence, and independence. Respondents often described a pressure to blend in and conform with the form of gender that they felt was expected in ethnic settings and that conflicted with the white standard of femininity. Thus, they often described such behavior with disgust and self-loathing. For example, Min-Jung (24, KA) said she feels "like an idiot" when talking with Korean adults:

> With Korean adults, I act more shy and more timid. I don't talk until spoken to and just act shy. I kind of speak in a higher tone of voice than I usually do. But then when I'm with white people and white adults, I joke around, I laugh, I talk, and I communicate about how I feel. And then my voice gets stronger. But then when I'm with Korean adults, my voice gets really high. . . . I just sound like an idiot and sometimes when I catch myself I'm like, "Why can't you just make conversation like you normally do?"

Many respondents distanced themselves from the compliant femininity associated with their Asianness by casting their behavior in ethnic realms as a mere act not reflective of their true nature. Repeatedly, they said they cannot be who they really are in ethnic settings and the enactment of an authentic self takes place only in mainstream settings. Teresa (23, KA) provides an example. She said,

> I feel like I can be myself when I'm around white people or mixed people. The Korean

role is forced on me; it doesn't feel natural. I always feel like I have to put on this act so that I can be accepted by Korean people. I think whites are more accepting of other people. Maybe that's why I feel more comfortable with them.

Similarly, Wilma (21, VA) states, "Like some Asian guys expect me to be passive and let them decide on everything. Non-Asians don't expect anything from me. They just expect me *to be me*" (emphasis added). Gendered behavior engaged in Asian ethnic settings was largely described as performative, fake, and unnatural, while that in white-dominated settings was cast as a reflection of one's true self. The femininity of the white mainstream is glorified as authentic, natural, and normal, and Asian ethnic femininity is denigrated as coerced, contrived, and artificial. The "white is right" mantra is reiterated in this view of white femininity as the right way of doing gender.

The glorification of white femininity and controlling images of Asian women can lead Asian American women to believe that freedom and equity can be acquired only in the white-dominated world. For not only is white behavior glorified as superior and more authentic, but gender relations among whites are constructed as more egalitarian. Katie (21, KA) explained,

Like when I'm with my family and stuff, I'm treated like my ideas or feelings of things really don't make a difference. I have to be more submissive and quiet. I really can't say how I feel about things with guys if it goes against them in public because that is like disrespectful. With Caucasians, I don't quite feel that way. I feel my opinion counts more, like I have some pull. I think society as a whole—America—still

treats me like I'm inferior as a girl but I definitely feel more powerful with other races than I do with my own culture because I think at least with Americans it's like [politically correct] to be equal between men and women.

Controlling images of Asian men as hypermasculine further feed presumptions that whites are more egalitarian. Asian males were often cast as uniformly domineering in these accounts. Racialized images and the construction of hegemonic (white) and subordinated (Asian) forms of gender set up a situation where Asian American women feel they must choose between white worlds of gender equity and Asian worlds of gender oppression. Such images encourage them to reject their ethnic culture and Asian men and embrace the white world and white men so as to enhance their power (Espiritu 1997). This was the basis on which some respondents expressed a preference for interacting with whites. As Ha (19, VA) remarked,

Asians would expect me to be more quiet, shy. . . . But with white friends, I can act like who I am. . . . With Asians, I don't like it at all because they don't take me for who I am. They treat me differently just because I'm a girl. And whites . . . I like the way they treat me because it doesn't matter what you do.

In these accounts, we can see the construction of ethnic and mainstream cultural worlds—and Asians and whites—as diametrically opposed. The perception that whites are more egalitarian than Asian-origin individuals and thus preferred partners in social interaction further reinforces anti-Asian racism and white superiority. The cultural dominance of whiteness is reaffirmed through the co-construction of race and gender in these narratives. The perception that the production of gender in the mainstream is more authentic and superior to that in Asian ethnic arenas further reinforces the racialized categories of gender that define white forms of femininity as ascendant. In the next section, we describe variations in gender performances within ethnic and mainstream settings that respondents typically overlooked or discounted as atypical.

Gender Variations within Cultural Worlds

Several respondents described variations in gender dynamics within mainstream and ethnic settings that challenge notions of Asian and American worlds as monolithic opposites. Some talked of mothers who make all the decisions or fathers who do the cooking. These accounts were framed as exceptions to Asian male dominance. For example, after Vietnamese women were described in a group interview as confined to domesticity, Ngâ (22, VA), who immigrated at 14 and spoke in Vietnamese-accented English, defined her family as gender egalitarian. She related,

> I guess I grow up in a *different* family. All my sisters doesn't have to cook, her husbands cooking all the time. Even my oldest sister. Even my mom—my dad is cooking. . . . My sisters and brothers are all very strong. (emphasis added)

Ngâ does not try to challenge stereotypical notions of Vietnamese families but rather reinforces such notions by suggesting that her family is different. Similarly, Heidi (21, KA) said, "Our family was kind of *different*

because . . . my dad cooks and cleans and does dishes. He cleans house" (emphasis added). Respondents often framed accounts of gender egalitarianism in their families by stating they do not belong to the typical Asian family, with "typical" understood to mean male dominated. This variation in gender dynamics within the ethnic community was largely unconsidered in these accounts.

Other respondents described how they enacted widely disparate forms of gender across sites within ethnic realms, suggesting that gender behavior is more variable than generally framed. Take, for example, the case of Gin (29, KA), a law student married to a Korean American from a more traditional family than her own. When she is with her husband's kin, Gin assumes the traditional obligations of a daughter-in-law and does all the cooking, cleaning, and serving. The role exhausts her and she resents having to perform it. When Gin and her husband return home, the gender hierarchy is reversed. She said,

> When I come home, I take it all out on him. "Your parents are so traditional, look what they are putting me through . . . ?" That's when I say, "You vacuum. [Laughing] You deserve it." And sometimes when I'm really mean, "Take me out to dinner. I don't want to cook for a while and clean for a while." So he tries to accommodate that. . . . Just to be mean I will say I want this, he will buy me something, but I will return it. I want him to do what I want, like I want to be served because I serve when I'm with them. . . . [It's] kind of like pay back time. It's [a] strategy, it works.

Gin trades on the subservience and labor she performs among her in-laws to boost her marital power. She trades on her subservience to her in-laws to acquire more power in her marriage than she might otherwise have. Similar dynamics were described by Andrea (23, VA). She remarked,

> When I'm with my boyfriend and we're over at his family's house or at a church function, I tend to find myself being a little submissive, kind of like yielding or letting him make the decisions. But we know that at home it ain't gonna happen. . . . I tend to be a strong individual. I don't like to conform myself to certain rules even though I know sometimes in public I have to conform . . . like being feminine and being submissive. But I know that when I get home, he and I have that understanding that I'm not a submissive person. I speak my own mind and he likes the fact that I'm strong.

Controlling images of Asian men as hyperdomineering in their relations with women obscures how they can be called on to compensate for the subservience exacted from their female partners in some settings. Although respondents typically offered such stories as evidence of the patriarchy of ethnic arenas, these examples reveal that ethnic worlds are far more variable than generally described. Viewing Asian ethnic worlds through a lens of racialized gender stereotypes renders such variation invisible or, when acknowledged, atypical.

Gender expectations in the white-dominated mainstream also varied, with respondents sometimes expected to assume a subservient stance as Asian women. These examples reveal that the mainstream is not a site of unwavering gender equality as often depicted in these accounts and made less so for Asian American women by racial images that construct them as compliant.

Many respondents described encounters with non-Asians, usually whites, who expected them to be passive, quiet, and yielding. Several described non-Asian (mostly white) men who brought such expectations to their dating relationships. Indeed, the servile Lotus Blossom image bolsters white men's preference for Asian women (Espiritu 1997). As Thanh (22, VA) recounted,

> Like the white guy that I dated, he expected me to be the submissive one—the one that was dependent on the guy. Kind of like the "Asian persuasion," that's what he'd call it when he was dating me. And when he found out that I had a spirit, kind of a wild side to me, he didn't like it at all. Period. And when I spoke up—my opinions—he got kind of scared.

So racialized images can cause Asian American women to believe they will find greater gender equality with white men and can cause white men to believe they will find greater subservience with Asian women. This dynamic promotes Asian American women's availability to white men and makes them particularly vulnerable to mistreatment.

There were other sites in the mainstream, besides dating relationships, where Asian American women encountered racialized gender expectations. Several described white employers and coworkers who expected them to be more passive and deferential than other employees and were surprised when they spoke up and resisted unfair treatment. Some described similar assumptions among non-Asian teachers and professors. Diane (26, KA) related,

> At first one of my teachers told me it was okay if I didn't want to talk in front of the

class. I think she thought I was quiet or shy because I'm Asian. . . . [Laughing.] I am very outspoken, but that semester I just kept my mouth shut. I figured she won't make me talk anyway, so why try. I kind of went along with her.

Diane's example illustrates how racialized expectations can exert a pressure to display stereotyped behavior in mainstream inter-actions. Such expectations can subtly co-erce behavioral displays that confirm the stereotypes, suggesting a kind of self-fulfill-ing prophecy. Furthermore, as submissive-ness and passivity are denigrated traits in the mainstream, and often judged to be in-dicators of incompetence, compliance with such expectations can deny Asian American women personal opportunities and success. Not only is passivity unrewarded in the mainstream; it is also subordinated. The as-sociation of extreme passivity with Asian women serves to emphasize their otherness. Some respondents resist this subordination by enacting a more assertive femininity as-sociated with whiteness. Lisa (18, KA) de-scribed being quiet with her relatives out of respect, but in mainstream scenes, she con-sciously resists the stereotype of Asian women as passive by adjusting her behav-ior. She explained,

I feel like I have to prove myself to every-body and maybe that's why I'm always vocal. I'm quite aware of that stereotype of Asian women all being taught to be submis-sive. Maybe I'm always trying to affirm that I'm not like that. Yeah, I'm trying to say that if anything, I don't fit into that image and I don't want that to be labeled on me.

Several respondents were aware that they are presumed to be "typical" Asian women,

and thus compliant and quiet, in main-stream settings. They describe extra efforts they enlisted to disprove such assumptions. Katie, who said that she feels like her opin-ion counts more in mainstream settings, described a pressure from white peers to be more outspoken so as to demonstrate that she is not "really" Asian and is thus worthy of their company. She stated,

When I'm with non-Asians and stuff, I feel as though I need to prove myself like they expect me to prove I'm worthy to be with them, and that even though I look Asian, I really am not. . . . Like I have to act like them—kind of loud, good at partying and stuff, just more outgoing . . . like if I stand out in a negative way, then I'm not cool to be with or something.

To act Asian by being reserved and quiet would be to "stand out in a negative way" and to be regarded as "not cool." It means one will be denigrated and cast aside. Katie consciously engages loud and gregarious behavior to prove she is not the typical Asian and to be welcomed by white friends. Whereas many respondents describe their behavior in mainstream settings as an au-thentic reflection of their personality, these examples suggest otherwise. Racial expecta-tions exert pressure on these women's gen-der performances among whites. Some go to great lengths to defy racial assumptions and be accepted into white-dominated so-cial groups by engaging a white standard of femininity. As they are forced to work against racial stereotypes, they must exert extra effort at being outspoken and socially gregarious. Contrary to the claim of re-spondents, gender production in the main-stream is also coerced and contrived. The failure of some respondents to recognize variations in gender behavior within mainstream and ethnic settings probably has much to do with the essentialization of gender and race. That is, as we discuss next, the racialization of gender renders variations in behavior within racial groups invisible.

The Racialization of Gender: Believing Is Seeing

White femininity, which was glorified in accounts of gender behavior across cultural settings, was also accorded superiority in the more general discussion of gender.

Respondents' narratives were structured by assumptions about Asian women as submissive, quiet, and diffident and of American women as independent, self-assured, outspoken, and powerful. That is, specific behaviors and traits were racialized. As Ha (19, VA) explained, "sometimes I'm quiet and passive and shy. That's a Vietnamese part of me." Similarly, domesticity was linked with Asian femininity and domestic incompetence or disinterest, along with success in the work world, with American femininity. Several women framed their internal struggles between career and domesticity in racialized terms. Min-Jung said,

> I kind of think my Korean side wants to stay home and do the cooking and cleaning and take care of the kids whereas my American side would want to go out and make a difference and become a strong woman and become head of companies and stuff like that.

This racialized dichotomy was central to respondents' self-identities. Amy (21, VA) said, "I'm not Vietnamese in the way I act. I'm American because I'm not a good cook

and I'm not totally ladylike." In fact, one's ethnic identity could be challenged if one did not comply with notions of racialized gender. In a group interview, Kimberly (21, VA) described "joking around" with coethnic dates who asked if she cooked by responding that she did not. She explained,

> They're like, "You're Vietnamese and you're a girl and you don't know how to cook?" I'm like, "No, why? What's wrong with that?" [Another respondent is laughing.] And they go, "Oh, you're not a Vietnamese girl."

Similarly, coethnic friends tell Hien (21, VA), "You should be able to cook, you are Vietnamese, you are a girl." To be submissive and oriented toward family and domesticity marks Asian ethnicity. Conformity to stereotypes of Asian femininity serves to symbolically construct and affirm an Asian ethnic identity. Herein lies the pressure that some respondents feel to comply with racialized expectations in ethnic settings, as Lisa (18, KA) illustrates in explaining why she would feel uncomfortable speaking up in a class that has a lot of Asians:

> I think they would think that I'm not really Asian. Like I'm whitewashed . . . like I'm forgetting my race. I'm going against my roots and adapting to the American way. And I'm just neglecting my race.

American (white) women and Asian American women are constructed as diametric opposites. Although many respondents were aware that they contradicted racialized notions of gender in their day-to-day lives, they nonetheless view gender as an essential component of race. Variation is ignored or recategorized so that an Asian American woman who does not comply is no longer Asian. This was also evident among respondents who regard themselves as egalitarian or engage the behavioral traits associated with white femininity. There was the presumption that one cannot be Asian and have gender-egalitarian attitudes. Asian American women can engage those traits associated with ascendant femininity to enhance their status in the mainstream, but this requires a rejection of their racial/ethnic identity. This is evident by the use of words such as "American," "whitewashed," or "white"—but not Asian—to describe such women. Star (22, KA) explained, "I look Korean but I don't act Korean. I'm whitewashed. [Interviewer asks, 'How do you mean you don't act Korean?'] I'm loud. I'm not quiet and reserved."

Discussion and Summary

Our analysis reveals dynamics of internalized oppression and the reproduction of inequality that revolve around the relational construction of hegemonic and subordinated femininities. Respondents' descriptions of gender performances in ethnic settings were marked by self-disgust and referred to as a mere act not reflective of one's true gendered nature. In mainstream settings, on the other hand, respondents often felt a pressure to comply with caricatured notions of Asian femininity or, conversely, to distance one's self from derogatory images of Asian femininity to be accepted. In both cases, the subordination of Asian femininity is reproduced.

In general, respondents depicted women of Asian descent as uniformly engaged in subordinated femininity marked by submissiveness and white women as universally assertive and gender egalitarian. Race, rather than culture, situational dynamics, or individual personalities, emerged as the primary basis by which respondents gave meaning to variations in femininity. That is, despite their own situational variation in doing gender, they treat gender as a racialized feature of bodies rather than a sociocultural product. Specific gender displays, such as a submissive demeanor, are required to confirm an Asian identity. Several respondents face challenges to their ethnic identity when they behave in ways that do not conform with racialized images. Indeed, some claimed that because they are assertive or career oriented, they are not really Asian. That is, because they do not conform to the racialized stereotypes of Asian women but identify with a hegemonic femininity that is the white standard, they are different from other women of Asian origin. In this way, they manipulate the racialized categories of gender in attempting to craft identities that are empowering. However, this is accomplished by denying their ethnicity and connections to other Asian American women and through the adoption and replication of controlling images of Asian women.

Our findings illustrate the powerful interplay of controlling images and hegemonic femininity in promoting internalized oppression. Respondents draw on racial images and assumptions in their narrative construction of Asian cultures as innately oppressive of women and fully resistant to change against which the white-dominated mainstream is framed as a paradigm of gender equality. This serves a proassimilation function by suggesting that Asian American women will find gender equality in exchange for rejecting their ethnicity and adopting white standards of gender. The construction of a hegemonic femininity not only (re)creates a hierarchy that privileges white women over Asian American women but also makes Asian American women available for white men. In this way, hegemonic femininity serves as a handmaiden to hegemonic masculinity.

Our study attempts to bring a racialized examination of gender to a constuctionist framework without decentering either race or gender. By examining the racialized meaning systems that inform the construction of gender, our findings illustrate how the resistance of gender oppression among our respondents draws ideologically on the denigration and rejection of ethnic Asian culture, thereby reinforcing white dominance. Conversely, we found that mechanisms used to construct ethnic identity in resistance to the proassimilation forces of the white-dominated mainstream rest on narrow definitions of Asian women that emphasize gender subordination. These findings underscore the crosscutting ways that gender and racial oppression operates such that strategies and ideologies focused on the resistance of one form of domination can reproduce another form. A social constructionist approach that examines the simultaneous production of gender and race within the matrix of oppression, and considers the relational construction of hegemonic and subordinated femininities, holds much promise in uncovering the micro-level structures and complicated features of oppression, including the processes by which oppression infiltrates the meanings individuals give to their experiences.

References

Baker, Donald G. 1983. *Race, ethnicity and power*. Boston: Routledge Kegan Paul.

Chang, Edward T. 1999. The post–Los Angeles riot Korean American community: Challenges and prospects. *Korean American Studies Bulletin* 10:6–26.

Chen, Anthony S. 1999. Lives at the center of the periphery, lives at the periphery of the center: Chinese American masculinities and bargaining with hegemony. *Gender & Society* 13:584–607.

Chen, Edith Wen-Chu. 1998. The continuing significance of race: A case study of Asian American women in white, Asian American, and African American sororities. Ph.D.diss., University of California, Los Angeles.

Coltrane, Scott. 1989. Household labor and the routine production of gender. *Social Problems* 36:473–90.

———. 1994. Theorizing masculinities in contemporary social science. In *Theorizing masculinities*, edited by Harry Brod and Michael Kaufman. Thousand Oaks, CA: Sage.

Connell, R. W. 1987. *Gender and power*. Stanford, CA: Stanford University Press.

———. 1995. *Masculinities*. Los Angeles: University of California Press.

Espiritu, Yen L. 1997. *Asian American women and men*. Thousand Oaks, CA: Sage.

———. 2001. "We don't sleep around like white girls do": Family, culture, and gender in Filipina American life. *Signs: Journal of Women in Culture and Society* 26:415–40.

Glaser, Barney G., and Anselm L. Straus. 1967. *The discovery of grounded theory*. New York: Aldine.

Glenn, Evelyn Nakano. 1999. The social construction and institutionalization of gender and race. In *Revisioning gender*, edited by Myra Marx Ferree, Judith Lorber, and Beth B. Hess. Thousand Oaks, CA: Sage.

Gramsci, Antonio. 1971. *Selections from the prison notebooks of Antonio Gramsci*, edited and translated by Quintin Hoare and Geoffrey Nowell Smith. New York: International.

Hill Collins, Patricia. 2000. *Black feminist thought*. New York: Routledge.

Hill Collins, Patricia, Lionel A. Maldonado, Dana Y. Takagi, Barrie Thorne, Lynn Weber, and Howard Winant. 1995. Symposium: On West and Fenstermaker's "Doing difference." *Gender & Society* 9:491–513.

Ishii-Kuntz, Masako. 2000. Diversity within Asian American families. In *Handbook of family diversity*, edited by David H. Demo, Katherine Allen, and Mark A. Fine. New York: Oxford University Press.

Kendall, Lori. 2000. "Oh no! I'm a nerd!" Hegemonic masculinity on an online forum. *Gender & Society* 14:256–74.

Kessler, Suzanne, and Wendy McKenna. 1978. *Gender: An ethnomethodological approach.* Chicago: University of Chicago Press.

Kibria, Nazli. 1990. Power, patriarchy, and gender conflict in the Vietnamese immigrant community. *Gender & Society* 4:9–24.

———. 1993. *Family tightrope: The changing lives of Vietnamese Americans.* Princeton, NJ: Princeton University Press.

———. 1997. The construction of "Asian American": Reflections on intermarriage and ethnic identity among second generation Chinese and Korean Americans. *Ethnic and Racial Studies* 20:523–44.

Kim, Byong-suh. 1994. Value orientations and sex-gender role attitudes on the comparability of Koreans and Americans. In *Gender division of labor in Korea*, edited by Hyong Cho and Oil-wha Chang. Seoul, Korea: Ewha Women's University Press.

Lee, Jee Yeun. 1996. Why Suzie Wong is not a lesbian: Asian and Asian American lesbian and bisexual women and femme/butch/gender identities. In *Queer studies*, edited by Brett Beemyn and Mickey Eliason. New York: New York University Press.

Lim, In-Sook. 1997. Korean immigrant women's challenge to gender inequality at home: The interplay of economic resources, gender, and family. *Gender & Society* 11:31–51.

Lorber, Judith. 1994. *Paradoxes of gender.* New Haven, CT: Yale University Press.

Lorde, Audre. 1984. *Sister outsider.* Trumansberg, NY: Crossing Press.

Lowe, Lisa. 1991. Heterogeneity, hybridity, multiplicity: Marking Asian American differences. *Diaspora* 1:24–44.

Lucal, Betsy. 1999. What it means to be gendered me: Life on the boundaries of a dichotomous gender system. *Gender & Society* 13:781–97.

Min, Pyong Gap. 1998. *Changes and conflicts.* Boston: Allyn & Bacon.

Oropesa, R. S., and Nancy Landale. 1995. *Immigrant legacies: The socioeconomic circumstances of children by ethnicity and generation in the United States.* Working paper 95-01R. State College: Population Research Institute, Pennsylvania State University.

Osajima, Keith. 1993. The hidden injuries of race. In *Bearing dreams, shaping visions: Asian Pacific American perspectives*, edited by Linda Revilla, Gail Nomura, Shawn Wong, and Shirley Hune. Pullman: Washington State University Press.

Palley, Marian Lief. 1994. Feminism in a Confucian society: The women's movement in Korea. In *Women of Japan and Korea*, edited by Joyce Gelb and Marian Lieff. Philadelphia: Temple University Press.

Pyke, Karen. 1996. Class-based masculinities: The interdependence of gender, class, and interpersonal power. *Gender & Society* 10: 527–49.

———. 2000. "The normal American family" as an interpretive structure of family life among grown children of Korean and Vietnamese immigrants. *Journal of Marriage and the Family* 62:240–55.

Pyke, Karen, and Tran Dang. In press. "FOB" and "whitewashed": Intra-ethnic identities and internalized oppression among second generation Asian Americans. *Qualitative Sociology.*

St. Jean, Yanick, and Joe R. Feagin. 1998. *Double burden: Black women and everyday racism.* Armonk, NY: M. E. Sharpe.

Schwalbe, Michael, Sandra Godwin, Daphne Holden, Douglas Schrock, Shealy Thompson, and Michele Wolkomir. 2000. Generic processes in the reproduction of inequality: An interactionist analysis. *Social Forces* 79: 419–52.

Tajima, Renee E. 1989. Lotus blossoms don't bleed: Images of Asian women. In *Making waves*, edited by Asian Women United of California. Boston: Beacon.

West, Candace, and Don H. Zimmerman. 1987. Doing gender. *Gender & Society* 1:125–51.

West, Candace, and Sarah Fenstermaker. 1995. Doing difference. *Gender & Society* 9:8–37.

Zhou, Min. 1999. Coming of age: The current situation of Asian American children. *Amerasia Journal* 25:1–27.

Zhou, Min, and Carl L. Bankston III. 1998. *Growing up American*. New York: Russell Sage.

CHAPTER 2 STUDY QUESTIONS

1. How do young women and men develop gender roles? What messages do they receive about gender and from what sources?

2. What is ideal girlhood/womanhood? What is ideal boyhood/manhood?

3. How do contemporary constructions of sex, race, class, sexual orientation, gender identity, age, and (dis)ability intersect with the construction of gender?

4. Do you agree with the arguments C. J. Pascoe (Reading 11) makes about language and the symbolic value of the word "fag"? Why or why not? What implications might this have for men and masculinity?

5. What overlaps, similarities, and differences exist between the people in Tracey Lee's account of identities and gender (Reading 14)?

SECTION II
The Microcosm of Gender: Individuals in Context

CHAPTER 3 Constructing the Gendered Body

16 Dionne P. Stephens and April L. Few

The Effects of Images of African American Women in Hip Hop on Early Adolescents' Attitudes Toward Physical Attractiveness and Interpersonal Relationships

Although researchers have greatly benefited from understanding how sexual images affect heterosexual European American adolescents (e.g., Alksnis, Desmarais, & Wood, 1996; Rose & Frieze, 1989, 1993) and gay men and lesbians (e.g., Klinkenberg & Rose, 1994) the research on African Americans' sexual images and their relationship to physical attractiveness and relationship patterns is limited. Psychologists and family scientists have traditionally examined African American female adolescents' sexual outcome behaviors, such as unplanned pregnancy, early sexual onset, or sexually transmitted disease acquisition, rather than the meanings of sexuality that guide these behaviors (East, 1998; Gibbs, 1998; McLoyd, 1998; Rome, Rybicki, & Durant, 1998; Smith, 1997). Thus, negative developmental outcomes have been the dominant foci of studies of African Americans (McLoyd, 1998). Further, researchers commonly have (mis)represented the experiences of African American families and women through comparative quantitative data (Jones, 1991) collected from high-risk and convenience samples (Staples, 1994).

Research on images of African American womanhood by women's studies and African American studies scholars has informed our understandings of the ways in which we give meaning to visual cues

Dionne P. Stephens and April L. Few, "The Effects of Images of African American Women in Hip Hop on Early Adolescents' Attitudes Toward Physical Attractiveness and Interpersonal Relationships," *Sex Roles* 56 (2007): 251–264. Copyright © Springer Science + Business Media, LLC. Reprinted with kind permission of Springer Science + Business Media.

through theoretical frameworks such as Black feminism, womanism, and racial identity development. Both disciplines have produced iconographic data that have led to the identification of the promiscuous Jezebel, the asexual Mammy, the emasculating Matriarch, the disagreeable Sapphire, and the breeding Welfare Mother as the foundational images of African American womanhood (see Collins, 1991; Morton, 1991). The addition of a psychological lens to the analysis of this developmental process can increase our explanatory power for outcomes of African American female adolescents' sexuality. For instance, Erikson's theory of identity development provides an appropriate framework for how environmental factors (e.g., family, peers, community, media) influence the evolution of adolescents' sexual identity and their exploration and adoption of specific sexual images. The integration of ecological frameworks and iconographic data has created a qualitative body of work that has become a starting point from which to explore African American women's sexuality within the context of African American youth culture (Stephens & Phillips, 2005).

Eight Women: Sexual Images of African American Women's Sexuality

The details that qualitative data impart about African American women's sexuality not only provide descriptions of images, but also give clues into the meanings of sexuality for this population. Further, the socio-historical frameworks of race, class, sexual orientation, and gender embedded within sexual images highlight the distinctive identity processes unique to African American women. Remnants of the Jezebel, Mammy, Welfare Mother, and Matriarch

images remain, as exemplified by the similar, yet more sexually explicit images of the Diva, the Gold Digger, the Freak, the Dyke, the Gangster Bitch, the Sister Savior, the Earth Mother, and the Baby Mama sexual images (Stephens & Phillips, 2003). These eight images were found to be widely accepted frameworks used to illustrate beliefs about African American women's sexuality in the heterosexual, male-dominated, African American–based, youth culture known as Hip Hop.

The Diva image projects a woman who has sex to enhance her social status, even though she may already be financially independent and middle class or above. The Gold Digger image, particularly when cues of economic disadvantage are included, illustrates a woman who intentionally has sex for money or material goods. When an African American woman is portrayed as desiring and engaging in "wild and kinky" sex with a multitude of partners for her own gratification, the Freak image is being enacted. The Dyke image projects a self-sufficient and "hard" woman who has rejected sex with men and may have adopted masculine postures. The image of the Gangster Bitch shows a "street tough" woman who has sex to demonstrate solidarity with or to help her man; she may also be involved in gangs or gang culture. The Sister Savior image is that of a pious woman who rejects all but marital, procreative sex for religious reasons. In contrast, the Earth Mother image portrays a woman who has sex for spiritual or nationalistic reasons to show her support for "the race" or "the nation." Finally, a woman who has had a child by a man but is no longer his partner is projected as the Baby Mama image; she has sex to maintain a financial or emotional connection with the man through the child.

The everyday consumption of cultural and interpersonal messages regarding sexual images has a direct impact on young African Americans' sexual self-identity, behaviors, and experiences. In an earlier study of African American adolescents' responses to these sexual images, we (Stephens & Few, 2007) found that the descriptive titles and associated behaviors were universally identifiable and understood. This negotiation of these eight cultural images and interpersonal level messages relies on individuals' understanding of their own identity's relationship to the sexual images and the internalization messages (Stephens & Phillips, 2005). This is because the construction of an identity not only shapes individuals' sexual identity, but also informs their decision-making and behavior outcomes.

Identity Development among African American Early Adolescents

Identity development has been argued to be a pivotal crisis in the transition from childhood to adulthood (Worrell, 2000). "Who Am I?" and "Who do others think I am?" are the key identity development questions that Erikson (1968) argued are important to answer during this phase of the lifespan. Erikson (1968) believed that peer relationships were particularly influential in this phase of self-definition. To achieve peer approval, adolescents may adopt or strive for an admired trait or behavior elicited by the group (Zimmerman, Copeland, Shope, & Dielman, 1997). The desire to conform to behaviors viewed as acceptable by peers is common during adolescence (Clasen & Brown, 1985). Adolescents develop perceptions of their sexuality and beliefs that address desired sexual needs by using self-comparison and relying on messages

about appropriate or desirable sexual and physical traits from peers, family members, and other cultural influences (Buzwell & Rosenthal, 1996).

African American adolescents must recognize their value and worth not only in terms of their gender, but also their race, if they want to develop healthy identities. African American adolescents' ideas about the self as a racial minority are developed through the understanding of symbols and meanings of their position within their family, community, or society. For example, prior research has shown that parents are the primary socialization forces for developing African American adolescents' positive attitudes toward physical attractiveness and cultural beliefs or norms (see Stephens & Phillips, 2003, 2005; Stephens & Few, 2007). Peers are also important for shaping ideas about racial and cultural norms. African American adolescents are not only inclined to have peers of the same race, but also tend to compare themselves to those who are most like them rather than to the majority culture (Botta, 2000). Similarly, studies on racial identity development indicate that self-awareness as a member of a racial minority is based on self-evaluations and group comparison in terms of others' perceptions of one's racial group (see Cross, 1995; Helms & Parham, 1990). Thus, we argue that it is important to examine both gender and racial identity factors that moderate African American adolescents' use of sexual images to give meaning to physical attractiveness and interpersonal relationships.

Physical Attractiveness

Skin tone as beauty. Colorism, or discrimination based on skin tone within a racial group, is one of many legacies from American slavery (Lake, 2003; Russell, Wilson, & Hall, 1992). African American children learn about the significance of skin tone when and if they see people treated better or worse based upon having lighter or darker skin (Celious & Oyserman, 2001). Although lighter skin has been highly valued (Hudson, 1995), people whose skin tone is "too light" or "too close to White" have been stigmatized by some within African American communities (Pinderhughes, 1995). A lighter skin tone may be seen as a lack of racial purity or solidarity, whereas a dark skin tone may be viewed as more beautiful or "real" (Hall, 1992, 1995; Keenan, 1996; Wade, 1996). A medium skin tone has been seen as the ideal within some African American communities (Hall, 1992).

Body image. Women are socialized to be interested in maintaining an attractive physical appearance for potential mates. In contemporary Western societies, to be considered physically attractive is to have a thin body (Seid, 1994). The research on African American women's body image and self-esteem indicates that this is not true for all African American women; class may be an important mediating factor in determining within group differences of body ideals. High- and middle-income African American women appear to be more susceptible to unhealthy views of thinness and more likely to suffer from eating disorders than are African American women from low-income backgrounds (Lott, 1994; Root, 1990). Working class and low-income African American women seem to be less influenced by European American cultural standards of beauty. In fact, among these women, a full-figured body is more acceptable or desirable than a slim body (Thomas, 1989; Thomas & James, 1988). African American girls and women tend to be more

satisfied with their body size, weight, and overall appearance than European American women are, despite the fact that they are, on average, heavier (Akan & Grilo, 1995; Parker et al., 1995; Story, French, Resnick, & Blum, 1995). However, one cannot extrapolate from these findings that working and low-income African American women do not experience high body dissatisfaction and low self-esteem.

Interpersonal Relationships

The relationship between dating preferences and physical attractiveness in the African American community should not be ignored. Distinctions made about skin tone and what is considered beautiful or physically attractive is a gendered experience that has implications for the dating context among African Americans (Baynes, 1997). Researchers have proposed that successful African American men, regardless of their skin tone, can "exchange" their wealth for a woman of lighter skin tone (Hall, 1995; Okazawa-Rey, Robinson, & Ward, 1987). Hall (1995) has described this exchange as evidence of a kind of pathological self-loathing rooted in colorism. Hall (1995) and Okazawa-Rey et al. (1987) have used phrases such as "color struck" and "bleaching syndrome" to indicate a preference among some African Americans for lighter skinned mates as a means to "lighten up" the family and achieve social status. However, in a study by Wade (1996), dark-skinned men rated themselves as more attractive than lighter skinned men did. In this sense, skin tone may be more valuable for light-skinned women and dark-skinned men because men are able to exchange their wealth for marriage partners, and men are judged less by their physical appearance than are women (Celious & Oyserman, 2001). If individuals believe that they have an attractive partner, their self-esteem may be raised because they may believe that they must have desirable qualities to attain such an attractive mate (Murstein, Merighi, & Malloy, 1989).

The meanings of racialized and gendered messages about physical attractiveness have been found to affect women's self-esteem directly. For example, Frederickson and Roberts (1997) found that women who were high in appearance orientation were more likely than women who were low in appearance orientation to internalize harmful cultural standards of beauty and attractiveness. Women high in appearance orientation tended to be very self-conscious about how their body appeared to others, in particular, to men. Men's attention, especially their sexual attention, was the gauge of women's self-esteem and self-perceptions of attractiveness or desirability. This type of behavior, known as self-objectification, indicates low levels of self-esteem or self-worth.

Research indicates that adolescent girls and adult women carry their evaluations of self-esteem and body image into their dating relationships. Self-esteem and body image are molded by both internal and external sources of validation. In adolescence, external validation (e.g., peer response) is particularly important in shaping girls' self-evaluations (Zimmerman et al., 1997). Thus, among sources that guide girls' and women's perceptions of self (i.e., identity) and competence at being herself (i.e., self-esteem) are the positive, negative, and inconsistent feedback received from boyfriends or potential mates.

The goal of the present study was to identify African American early adolescents' subjective meanings of African American women's sexuality and how their experiences

as members of marginalized groups may influence their understandings. Culturally-based sexual images are projected in African American Hip Hop youth culture, and variations have been identified by Stephens and Phillips (2003). As visual cues used to categorize norms regarding appropriate sexual beliefs and behaviors, these sexual images are useful for identifying the meanings and values African American youth give to race, ethnicity, gender, sexual orientation, beauty, and interpersonal relationships in the context of sexuality (Stephens & Few, 2007; Stephens & Phillips, 2003). For instance, the internalization of racialized sexual images may influence ideas about the physical attractiveness of potential mates and how individuals should interact in intimate interpersonal relationships.

To explore these phenomena, we examined the following research questions about African American adolescent girls' sexuality:

1. In what ways do the eight sexual images reflect attitudes and beliefs about African American women's physical attractiveness and subsequent assumptions about sexuality?
2. How do these beliefs about physical attractiveness inform attitudes toward and beliefs about interpersonal relationships?

Method

We employed qualitative data collection techniques in the present study. Qualitative research is rooted in a phenomenological paradigm, which holds that reality is socially constructed through individual or collective definition of the situation (Firestone, 1987), and it requires an examination of the processes by which individuals and groups construct meaning and a description of what those meanings are (Bogdan & Biklen, 1998). The use of qualitative methods, particularly interviews or narrative documents, has been instrumental in informing researchers of the various dynamics that shape sexuality, race, and gender interactions (Bell-Scott, 1998; Few, Stephens, & Rouse-Arnette, 2003). For example, Brooks-Gunn and Paikoff (1997) suggested that interviews with youth provide the most direct window into adolescents' sexual experiences through rich descriptions that can detail facts that are not easily quantified.

Participants

We employed purposeful sampling, which involved identifying participants who might give the most comprehensive and knowledgeable information about sexual images in African American youth culture. Fifteen African American early adolescents aged 11–13 participated in the study (seven boys and eight girls). Data were gathered from both boys and girls as the frameworks for African American adolescents' sexual images are informed through heterosexual relationship expectations. Further, collecting data at this phase of the lifespan highlights the changing meanings given to men's and women's roles and interactions, as prior to this point African American children experience unisex socialization. Black family scholars have found that African American children have been socialized with fewer gender role constraints until pubertal onset, as reflected by family structure (McAdoo & McAdoo, 1985; Staples, 1994; Weddle-West, 2000).

Participants were recruited from a federally funded after-school program designed for low income families. All attended public middle schools and had resided in the large southeastern college town all their lives. None of the participants were currently involved in a romantic or sexual relationship. The majority had never experienced any form of sexual activity; all reported that they had not experienced sexual onset, specifically sexual intercourse. Only four boys and two girls indicated that they had ever kissed or "made out" with a member of the other sex. No participant reported currently being involved in an intimate relationship with a person of the other sex, although several discussed having had "boyfriends" or "girlfriends." The participants described themselves as "brown" or "dark-skinned;" none viewed themselves as "light-skinned."

Procedure

Three data collection techniques were used: (1) semi-structured focus group interviews, (2) written feedback documentation, and (3) the researchers' notes. These multiple sources of data were collected in order to triangulate the data and to confirm emergent themes and inconsistencies in the data. The focus groups coincided with the open period of the after-school programming schedule. Participants were brought to a private classroom in the academic area of the facility. Boys and girls were interviewed on separate days. After some initial discussion, the questioning process focused on sexuality. A questioning route provided a framework for developing and sequencing a series of focused, yet flexible questions (Rubin & Rubin, 1995). Some questions included: What kind of messages have you received about African American women's sexuality? What kind of messages in the media, particularly videos, are being shown about African American women? Are African American women portrayed in the same way as other racial groups when it comes to sexuality? Probes were prepared for each question to elicit further information from the participants if the responses given were not comprehensive or failed to provide understandable information.

In addition, each participant was given a handout with an image of a female Hip Hop artist who personified the image being discussed. The purpose of the handout was for participants to list beliefs about these images as they related to sexual behaviors and attitudes from the perspective of (a) themselves, (b) their female cohort, and (c) their male cohort. The images were introduced individually, so that participants were not made aware in advance of what images were to be discussed.

Finally, throughout this process, the researchers made notes about participant-researcher interactions and salient issues that emerged through the focus group discussions. Participant-researcher interactions, body language, subsequent interview questions, and outlines of possible categories, themes, and patterns were also included in the researchers' notes. Pseudonyms are used to identify the participants' voices.

Data Analysis

Principles of the constant-comparative method (Lincoln & Guba, 1985) were used to guide data analysis. An integration of Simon and Gagnon's (1984, 1986, 1987) sexual scripting levels and symbolic interaction theory were used to develop the coding schemes. Reissman's (1993) levels of representation model guided our continuing attempts to represent and interpret the data. Before coding, transcripts were read three times by the researchers. The analysis process began with open coding to develop categories of concepts and themes that emerged from the data. Selective coding, where first level codes were condensed and recategorized, followed. Prior research and the body of literature on African Americans' sexuality were integrated into this process, during which core categories about the phenomena being studied were devised. Once these coding techniques were completed, the transcripts were further triangulated with the researchers' notes and participants' written documentations.

Results

Two significant themes that emerged from the data analysis are presented here. The data from three sources (focus group transcripts, participants' notes written on the handouts, and the researchers' notes) were integrated into this overview of two questions that served to guide the present study:

1. In what ways do the eight sexual images reflect attitudes and beliefs about African American women's physical attractiveness and subsequent assumptions about sexuality?
2. How do beliefs about physical attractiveness inform attitudes toward and beliefs about interpersonal relationships?

Physical Attractiveness

The eight sexual images provided cues regarding values given to African American female physical attractiveness. Hair texture, skin color, and body image were central to participants' descriptions of appropriate sexual image characteristics. However, dominant culture ideals about physical attractiveness were not expressed. These young women gave less value to Westernized standards of beauty than expected.

Crystal: No, I think Mary J [dark-skinned artist] is a Diva. You can be darker skin and be beautiful. Like all light-skinned girls are not pretty. People think they are. But not all are. A Diva is about how you carry yourself.

It is important to note that the girls often referred to what men found physically attractive in conjunction with what they themselves considered attractive. This was a pattern that did not emerge among the boys' responses. For example, although some of the girls expressed how beautiful they thought representations of the Earth Mother image were, they also acknowledged that men may not perceive that image as attractive for a potential partner. The girls themselves did not like the idea of shaving their hair short or putting in dreadlocks for fear of how unattractive and unfeminine they would be perceived by others, namely boys and men.

Tracy: I think [Lauryn Hill] is beautiful. Even with her dreads. Yeah, she is. I like her hair. Yeah, [Lauryn Hill] is beautiful. But I wouldn't put in dreads. I don't want it for me.

Researcher: What about shaving your hair off short?

Tracy: No, oh no, no. No, Erykah [Badu] looks good. But no. My dad wouldn't like it.

However, this awareness did not undermine their beliefs about their own physical attractiveness. All of the girls in our study were comfortable with their appearance, and none expressed any dissatisfaction. They all expressed happiness with their overall appearance.

Leesa: I'm not super pretty but I'm not ugly. I'm happy, and I think my body is nice.

Crystal: I'm happy. Even if you don't like something . . . you can get your hair done up nice if you don't like it and feel good.

The girls' comments regarding men's beliefs about attractive physical traits were accurate. Five of the boys mentioned that they liked women with long hair and shapely bodies; the Diva was viewed by seven of the boys as the most beautiful and desirable image. Traditionally, this image is projected as having Westernized features: long, straight hair, slim nose, slender body, and lighter skin (Stephens & Phillips, 2003). These features were all cited by the boys as attractive, and they also influenced boys' beliefs about the Diva's sexual health. On their handouts boys wrote that the Diva is sexually "clean," meaning that they assumed she did not have sexually transmitted diseases. Four noted that "no condoms" were necessary for engaging in sexual relations with Divas. In contrast, the Afrocentric Earth Mother was not labeled as attractive or seen as desirable by the boys in the present study. For example, although they did not make specific comments about the value of skin color, six boys wrote that Earth Mothers are dark-skinned. Some boys harshly viewed hairstyles and textures typical of women projecting this image.

Tyrone: [The Earth Mother] is bald headed or has braids. I don't like girls like that. She's got to have a fat booty and nicely kept hair.

Shawn: Those Erykah [Badu] girls are all right. I would get with them—they're alright. Just their hair . . .

Anthony: Like Lauryn Hill looks good. But Erykah Badu—they is all bald and looks crazy. India [Arie] look too rough.

Curtis: If she has nice skin . . . that's important. Smooth and clean. You want her to look clean before you get with her. Then you want to touch her . . . all over (laughter).

Wayne: Especially if she's shaped nice-round.

This discussion about the physical development of girls and women continued for approximately 30 minutes after the time originally allotted for the focus groups. This participant-driven divergence from the main discussion reinforced the value and importance given to physical appearance by boys, even among those of the age of the study's participants.

Interpersonal Relationships

It was clear that ideals about potential partners drew on traditional ideas about African American women's sexuality as it relates to the physical attractiveness beliefs, gender expectations, and sexual permissiveness discussed in previous sections. All eight girls acknowledged that women's appearance is what initially attracts men and is used by men to determine who they choose to pursue. Similarly, six of the seven boys listed physical traits before personality traits to describe ideal sexual partners. They noted that women's physical attributes were key components in their mate selection decision-making processes:

David: You want to be with a girl that looks good . . . because then you'll like to see her and be around her with your friends.

Michael: What you see is what you get, so you pick the prettiest girl.

Both male and female participants tended to view men as "sexually-driven" and knowledgeable about sexuality. It was conveyed that men would experience sexual activity with a variety of women before marriage. However, all seven of the boys planned to marry a "good" woman. A good woman was perceived as highly feminine and physically attractive. The specific images that boys described as "good woman" were the Diva and the Sister Savior. Three boys noted that they would never have casual sex with a Sister Savior but would be willing to have a long term relationship with one in the future. As one boy wrote, a Sister Savior is "not a good person to have sex with" but he would marry her.

Shawn: You want a girl who is really nice and would be good to you.

Researcher: Which of these women would be like that?

David: [points to Diva and Sister Savior] They don't want trouble and go to church.

These two sexual images were also selected to identify other women whom the boys held in esteem. When asked which of the eight images they would expect to be associated with their sisters or mothers, all of the boys selected the Diva, and Sister Savior images. These two images were acceptable due to their apparent lack of sexual aggressiveness and their attractive appearance. It is interesting to note, however, that boys also liked the Gangster Bitch image.

Michael: I like girls like that. They are fun to be around and just hang out with.

However, the Gangster Bitch was only liked in the context of a platonic relationship, not as an image for a sister or mother. The boys wrote that Gangster Bitches were "cool," "funny," "nice," and "just like another boy." Only one girl acknowledged that she saw similarities between herself and this image, although she rejected the usage of the term "Bitch." Instead, she thought that her desire to hang around and play with boys was because she preferred their forms of play (namely basketball) and the boys lived in her area. She was not interested in a sexual relationship with them. It is interesting that the boys did not have the same reaction to the Dyke image, which also does not project a highly feminine sexualized persona. Instead, the boys viewed the Dyke as unattractive, or useful if she were engaging in same-sex interactions that they could watch or join in (see Stephens & Phillips, 2003; Stephens & Few, 2007). The acceptability of the Gangster Bitch image for boys and the one girl was due to its asexual persona grounded in a specific heterosexual context.

The ideology of heterosexuality or *heteronormativity* (Oswald, Blume, & Marks, 2005)—within the context of men's desires—guided these girls' understandings of appropriate sexual behaviors. As was found among the boys, seven of the eight girls stated that their fathers, brothers, or uncles would want them to be a Diva or a Sister Savior. Again, the lack of an overtly sexual persona appeared to influence this attitude. These girls stated that their male relatives would accept their utilization of these images because they represented what is "good" and "nice" in terms of sexual behaviors and general decorum. All of the girls rejected the possibility of using the Dyke or Freak images around their male relatives

due to these images' projection of sexual deviance. Girls were particularly negative in their assessment of the Dyke's sexual behaviors, and referred to them as "nasty" in their written feedback comments.

Despite the positive and high status given to these "good girl" sexual images, girls thought that men could potentially cheat with women who would entice them sexually. The girls unanimously agreed that the boys' favorite images for non-monogamous intimate relationships would be the Freak and the Diva.

Keisha: They want the girl who will give them sex and looks good, too. Boys like girls like these and want us to be like them.

Nicole: I really don't like being friends with [Freaks] because they give you a bad reputation. If they're your friend and they do something nasty [others] might think that you do that. It just gets all out of hand and people get to asking you to do stuff . . . they'll think you are like her when you not. But like her more than you still.

Pam: To me, it might matter, if I have a friend that is a Freak and we go shopping and stuff or to the club. The way she dress or the way she acts when she sees a fine boy that might make me dislike her because maybe he wanted to talk to me.

Leesa: If she is going around boys and being nasty anywhere . . . disturbed me because there she is trying to go and be with the boy that I may like.

Clearly the majority of these eight images do not promote positive woman–woman platonic relationships. Only the Sister Savior was noted by one girl as "easy to make friends with." It is interesting that boys were aware of the tensions these images could create among girls. Boys thought that their female cohort used these sexual images to accept or reject peers. They indicated that girls would be jealous of other girls who enacted highly sexualized or physically attractive images (e.g., Diva, Freak).

> *Wayne:* I think they really want to be like Diva and hate the girls that do dress like that.
> *Anthony:* Girls get jealous of other girls just because we're not paying attention to them, but another girl instead.

Discussion

The results of the present study in regard to perceptions of physical attractiveness and interpersonal relationships provide evidence that identity development does not occur in a vacuum. In this study, a space was observed where social constructions of race and gender intersected to create, maintain, and reproduce sexual identities. Erikson (1968) believed that peer relationships were particularly influential during adolescence. Although for some adolescents, peer influences may override the influence of parental and community processes (Blanton, Gibbons, Gerrard, Conger, & Smith, 1997; Patterson, Reid, & Dishion, 1992), the preadolescent girls in our study were additionally influenced by perceptions of their fathers' approval in regard to physical attractiveness and attributes (e.g., hair, body type, skin tone), women's platonic relationships, and nonparticipation in certain sexual behaviors. These adolescents used self-comparison and relied on messages about appropriate or desirable sexual and physical traits from peers, media, and parents to develop perceptions of their sexual-

ity and beliefs about their own sexual needs (Buzwell & Rosenthal, 1996).

In addition, the comments of both girls and boys reflected how the developmental processes of racial identity influenced African American adolescents' beliefs about and attitudes toward physical attractiveness and interpersonal relationships. Wheeler, Jarvis, and Petty (2001) argued that individuals who have a positive racial and self identity are successful in overriding the effects of external stereotyped messages about their own racial group. The degree to which an individual uses social comparison processes depends upon how secure that person is with her or his racial identity. Although the preadolescent girls and boys in our study displayed an African American orientation in terms of self-identity, their perceptions of sexual images revealed a conflicted internalization of Eurocentric standards of beauty. This discussion of the influence of sexual images on perceptions of physical attractiveness and mate selection in interpersonal relationships provides a framework for understanding "the marriage" of African American and Eurocentric values and its influence on African American women's sexuality.

Physical Attractiveness

In the present study, physical attractiveness was central to how the images were given values. Physical traits associated with African Americans and cultural attitudes expressed within the Hip Hop culture together informed how physical appearance was validated across the sexual images. In particular, hair texture and skin tone were two phenotypic traits central to participants' descriptions of appropriate sexual image characteristics. This is not surprising as these two characteristics have historically been used as measures of social, political, and economic worth for African Americans (Collins, 1991; Hooks, 1992, 1995). Traditionally, those who possess hair or skin color that more closely resembles that of European Americans have been given higher status in American society. This attitude trickled down into the psyche of African Americans and created a system of beliefs and values that informed social hierarchies and interpersonal relationships (Herring, Keith, & Horton, 2003; Hill, 2002; Morton, 1991). This reality continues to shape the beliefs and attitudes of individuals today, as was made evident through the results of our study and in prior research (e.g., Banks, 2000; Coard, Breland, & Raskin, 2001; Herring et al., 2003; Jones, 1994; Makkar & Strube, 1995).

In both the boys' and the girls' groups, it was found that lighter skin was viewed as more attractive in this southeastern African American community. As has been found in prior research, this skin tone differentiation was thought to be externally imposed as well as an internally driven process aided and abetted by African Americans themselves (Herring et al., 2003). This reality is grounded in the historical value given to Whiteness in American society. The lighter people's kin, the more likely they were to receive privileges afforded European Americans (Herring et al., 2003; Hill, 2002; Morton, 1991). Although the girls in our study acknowledged that men often view lighter skin as more attractive in general, they thought that darker skin was just as beautiful. African American girls may attain additional messages about beauty that simultaneously reaffirm a positive racialized and gendered identity from familial sources, particularly mothers (Stephens & Few, 2007; Stephens & Phillips, 2005).

These informal cultural "interventions" that resist and deconstruct exclusive Westernized notions of beauty are conveyed by African American mothers, female role models, and female significant others. This informal intervention, in the form of conversations or consumption of select media, validates African American physical attributes over European American attributes and teaches that European American beauty is neither an attainable nor desirable goal. For example, successful female rap artists who are not light-skinned provide African American girls with a standard to emulate and to contribute to their own definitions of what is beautiful.

In contrast, the comments of boys in the present study about what they found attractive indicated their preference for lighter skin. However, it is important to note that the boys considered skin tone as just another commodity that could be disembodied or partitioned from the whole, as were breasts, buttocks, and hair. In these preferences, the legacy of sexual hierarchies maintained by the ecopolitical institution of American slavery to the psyche of contemporary youth is made evident. Skin tone is still a social commodity with privileges that can be attained by courtship or marriage and passed on to one's progeny/children. Sexual hierarchies or preferences from the American slavery era are also replicated by representations of women (e.g., background dancers, sexual partners for male performers) in Hip Hop music and videos for male preadolescents to internalize as a "golden standard" of beauty. The Hip Hop music industry and the cultural niche it reproduces is predominantly an extension of European American patriarchy within a racialized context of racial identity (Henderson, 1996; Wahl, 1999). Thus, African

American boys internalize cultural messages of what constitutes beauty in a different way than African American girls do.

Body size and shape also emerged as important aspects of physical attractiveness. The boys in our study spent a considerable amount of time discussing the shapes and sizes of African American women's bodies. It was clear that traditional European American body shapes were not considered the most attractive. Rather, these boys preferred the more curvaceous body types typically associated with African American women (Arogundade, 2000; Willis & Williams, 2002). Buttocks that were "large and round," "big breasts," and "thick thighs" were listed as ideal in the comments written by the boys. Within the African American community and other communities of color, this attitude is common among men (Becker, Yanek, Koffman, & Bronner, 1999; Fraser, 2003; Jackson & McGill, 1996; Nasser, 1988; Simeon et al., 2003).

However, in the context of our study, the boys further partitioned the female body, such that it was discussed in terms of individual parts. They could be attracted to a woman's large breasts, for example, but have no interest in her flat buttocks. As one boy explained, "If her [buttocks] is nice and round, who cares about the rest—you don't have to look at it." Thus, her body was viewed in pieces, not as a whole person. As has been found in research on pornography (e.g., Cameron & Frazer, 1996; Dworkin, 1996; Jackson, 1996; Walkowitz, 1996), this objectification of specific female body parts has been normalized in Hip Hop culture's projections of female imagery. This male-directed focus on parts of women's bodies, rather than the whole, disregards a woman's identity as a person. This process makes it easier for men to sexualize and objectify women without consideration of their feelings or desires.

The discussion of body type ideals was not as extensive or as detailed among the girls. This may be because, unlike European American women, African American women often report that "looking good" is related more to public image and personality than to weight (Demarest & Allen, 2000; Wade & DiMaria, 2003), a belief that was articulated by two participants in the present study. This may explain why African American women are more positive and flexible in their ideal body than European American women are (Henriques, Calhoun, & Cann, 1996; Parker et al., 1995; Rand & Kuldau, 1992). Still, one cannot ignore the importance given to body type among African American women. Parker et al. (1995) noted that African American women did not evaluate their bodies in relation to the European American ideal in the media, but rather in comparison to other African American women. Furthermore, Frisby (2004) found that, even though they were not affected by images of European American women, African American women reported lower levels of body satisfaction after they viewed media images of other African American women. Thus, the continued consumption of these sexual images may affect girls as they move into adolescence and start giving even more value to appearance.

African American body types, skin color, and hair texture clearly served as an identifying racial marker about beauty. Overall, it was found here that the boys gave more value to Westernized standards of beauty than the girls did by selecting those sexual images that embodied such traits as long hair and lighter skin as more attractive. The girls indicated that all skin shades and textures of hair can be attractive; the personality of the individual is what is most important.

Thus, when not directly questioned, the traditional value given to more European American phenotypic features appeared to dominate the thoughts of the girls in our study. Previous researchers have found similar patterns with African American young adults whereby men were more likely than women to view lighter-skinned potential mates as more attractive (Bond & Cash, 1992; Breland, Coleman, Coard, & Steward, 2002; Coard et al., 2001; Hill, 2002; Hughes & Bradley, 1990; Ward & Robinson, 1995). However, these young men's beliefs affected the women's views of themselves. This may explain why girls in the present study often referenced what boys liked in conjunction with what they liked, a pattern that did not emerge among the boys' responses. This phenomenon may occur because of the added value men give to physical traits over psychological traits when considering dating processes, findings that have been consistently found in mate selection research (e.g., Feingold, 1990; Perlini, Marcello, Hansen, & Pudney, 2001; Regan & Joshi, 2003). Studies of African American populations have shown that men's interpretations of women's physical appearance, including body shape and dress, are an important part of mate selection and relationship quality (Landolt, Lalumiere, & Quinsey, 1995; Lundy, Tan, & Cunningham, 1998). Thus, to remain competitive in the dating market, women must try to meet men's standards of beauty. Although the girls in our study were not as yet dating, it was evident that they were knowledgeable about and gave value to boys' opinions. Future researchers should examine the degree to which men's values

regarding physical attractiveness increase or decrease in importance as girls age.

Overall, it is clear that traditional Western standards of beauty continue to be normalized and valued among these participants despite changing role models of attractiveness in general society. Those sexual images that embody these traits (e.g., long hair, shapely yet slender build, lighter skin) were generally viewed as the most attractive. The ways in which Hip Hop culture specifically promotes these ideals must be explored further in future research. This is particularly important given the centrality of and value given to women's physical appearance in music videos and other Hip Hop culture expressions.

Interpersonal Relationships

Sexual images not only provide individuals with appropriate frameworks for their own behavior, but also inform them about others' behaviors and how to respond to them. African American cultural critic bell hooks has pointed out that the messages of the Hip Hop culture do not promote healthy intimate interactions: "As much as I enjoy hip-hop, I feel there is not enough rap out there embracing and affirming love that is about communication and accountability" (Jones, 1995, p. 190). Similarly, Hip Hop feminist Tara Roberts explains, "If you are a woman in Hip Hop, you are either a hard bitch who will kill for her man, or you're a fly birth who can sex up her man, or you're a *****d-up lesbian" (Roberts & Ulen, 2000, p. 70). The implications of these scholars' assertion are clear: These current culture frameworks of African American women's sexuality do not project women as empowered beings with identities outside of male-defined desires. Instead, there is a focus on utilizing interpersonal relationships for achieving material gain and social success (Stephens & Few, 2007; Stephens & Phillips, 2003).

The limited research on values given to personal and material factors in adolescents' dating has garnered mixed results (e.g., Buss, 1984; Goodwin, 1990). However, it appears that the degree to which adolescents focus on personality traits versus status markers is affected by the stage of the relationship. In long term relationships, personality traits are rated higher in importance for both men and women (e.g., Bolig, Stein, & McKenry, 1984; Hansen & Hicks, 1980; Smith, 1996). However, the limited research on African Americans' dating patterns during early stages of dating does not support this. For example, Herold (1974) found that, although African American college students ranked personality characteristics high in dating relationships, prestige factors—namely charm and good looks—had more influence at the initial dating stage. Also, Hansen (1977) found that African American high school students ranked materialistic factors more highly than personality factors, whereas European American students ranked personality traits higher than materialistic factors. This trend among African Americans may be due to the various barriers and limited access to material resources. In the present study, the boys tended to focus on factors clearly associated with the sexual images' physical appearance and allusions to sexuality when they identified which factors would initially attract them to a woman they want to "be with." As this was a study of women's sexual images within a heterosexual context, girls' assessments of how these images would affect their dating choices were not addressed.

It is important to consider these initial dating-stage values in an examination of early adolescents' dating values. Both the girls and the boys in our study made comments that they were not ready to be in a stable, long-term relationship. Rather, they understood that who they "liked" today might not be the same person to whom they would be attracted next month. A sense of fluidity in relationships is common at this age, when adolescents are beginning to seek out non-platonic relationships with the other sex (Miller, Notaro, & Zimmerman, 2002).

Even beyond the realm of potential intimate partners, beliefs of their male family members influenced the ways in which the girls in our study perceived the sexual images and their own attitudes toward sexuality. Several girls stated that their fathers' disapproval of certain sexual behaviors, dress, or physical traits (particularly hairstyles) was extremely influential. This observation fits with prior research findings in the area of African American fathers' influence on adolescents' sexuality whereby their opinions have a more direct impact and immediate impact than maternal communications regarding sexual risk taking (Jaccard & Dittus, 1997; Nolin & Petersen, 1992; Noller & Callan, 1990). Jemmott and Jemmott (1992) found that African American adolescents who perceived their fathers as strict reported using condoms more consistently than did those whose fathers were lenient. In light of the importance that the preadolescent girls gave to their fathers' opinions about these sexual images, there is a need for future research to move beyond focusing on the mother-child dyad; fathers need to be more directly targeted in sexual imagery research before findings regarding the importance of parental relationships with their adolescents can be definitively stated (Miller, Forehand, & Kotchick, 2000).

Although the girls in our study did not comment on how these images would affect their dating choices, the influence of their male peers' and family members' attitudes cannot be ignored. As was found in prior research, boys' opinions regarding girls' appearance directly impact the quality and stability of the relationship when determining the value given to a partner (Landolt et al., 1995; Lundy et al., 1998; Schooler & Wieling, 2000). This means that the boys' interpretations and acceptances of sexual images illustrate their beliefs about the women with whom they will enter intimate relationships. For girls transitioning into adolescence and learning to negotiate what it means to be a sexual being, the influence of self-approval versus men's desires and expectations could potentially be important in determining which sexual images they choose to follow or reject (Washington, 1995). Thus it is imperative that researchers identify ways in which African American preadolescent girls are able to ensure that they are empowered in their relationships to debunk the myth of self-fulfillment through relationships with men. Future researchers can build on our findings to focus on positive adolescent dating processes in the African American community in order to move away from the current deficit approach that focuses on partner violence and abuse (e.g., Gorman-Smith, Tolan, Sheidow, & Henry, 2001; Weisz & Black, 2001; West & Rose, 2000).

However, these eight sexual images do not promote or illustrate healthy female-female relationships, either platonic or sexual. The girls did believe the sexual images were applicable to their own friends or other girls they interacted with. However, excluding the Sister Savior image, these girls thought that these images illustrated the ways in which their interactions with other women were negative. The most disapproved of image was the Freak. These girls thought that peers enacting the Freak image would damage their own reputations through association, and they feared the possibility of losing a man's attention. In both cases, the potential of friendship was measured against the sexuality risks associated with these images.

It is interesting that the boys commented on how these images would influence girls' relationships with one another. They noted that girls could potentially be jealous of those who enact sexual images viewed as attractive to boys. Similarly, girls' statements illustrated their potential resentment toward other girls who might use the sexual images to gain attention from men. There is a need to explore how sexual images affect girls' relationships with one another. Future researchers will need to identify how sexual images can help girls or hinder them from building strong, healthy relationships with one another as a means to buffer the effects of negative sexual image associations.

Research Implications

There are some limitations to the present study. Generalization of the results from our study to a different population should be done with careful consideration of the contextual and socio-demographic factors involved. The African American preadolescents in our study were all young (ages 11–13) and living in a large college town in the southern part of the United States. Clearly, issues of age, geographic norms and beliefs—particularly as they relate to music preferences, race, sexuality, and gender—are important to consider. Whether African American preadolescents in another part of the country that is more or less urbanized would assign the same meanings and values to the sexual images reviewed by our participants is an important research question that should be addressed in future studies. Further, only 15 respondents participated in this study; a larger sample would provide even more detailed information about these phenomena that could be generalized to the broader population.

Despite these limitations, findings from this study contribute to the existing body of literature on African Americans' sexuality. They provide new evidence of the importance of sexual imagery in the understanding of the role of physical attractiveness and interpersonal relationships and provide valuable insights into African American adolescents' sexuality beliefs that have not been fully explored in previous research.

Critical analysis of qualitative data collected during adolescence is of great importance due to the psychological and physiological changes taking place in this population, including the onset of pubertal development, first sexual initiation, and changes in self-concepts, particularly concerning sexual and racial identity (e.g., Debold, 1995; McCluskey, Krohn, Lizotte, & Rodriguez, 2002; Phinney, 1990; Phinney & Alipuria, 1996; Wade & Olayiwola, 2002). Further, only a few studies of African American adolescents' understandings of sexuality do not involve high risk populations (e.g., Brody et al., 2001; Xiaojia, Conger, Simons, Brody, & Murry, 2002).

Although exploratory, information gleaned from our study of early adolescents is valuable to those seeking to improve the quality of African American adolescents' sexual health. Intervention programs and projects about sexuality must acknowledge and integrate discussions about sexual images. Programs that seek to achieve changes

in the attitudes toward and beliefs about African American sexuality but fail to recognize the unique cultural messages that influence these processes are likely to fail (Whatley, 1994). Including discussions of sexual images can increase individuals' comfort with sexual topics and their sense of general empowerment. Furthermore, discussions of sexual images provide a safe area to engage in explicit talk, which can commonly keep women from being as open as they truly want to be. Early adolescent African American girls require tools, such as these sexual images, to help them to visualize and identify sexual behaviors within a specific gender and racial context.

Conclusion

The African American female body has been a site of beauty and malicious contention. It continues to be so in the cultural context of Hip Hop. In the present study, the ways in which working class African American preadolescents relate to African American women's sexual images and negotiate constructions of race, gender, class, age, and sexuality within the framework of interpersonal relationships were examined. Although the girls and boys in our study displayed an African American orientation in terms of self-identity, the perceptions of sexual images revealed a conflicted internalization of Eurocentric standards of beauty. In other words, boys and girls placed different values on skin tone, hair, and body type in their perceptions of women's physical attractiveness. The responses of female participants indicated that African American women may receive a unique cultural intervention from their mothers, female role models, and female significant others that bolsters a positive racialized and gendered identity. This informal intervention, in the form of conversations or female Hip Hop role models, emphasizes and validates African American physical attributes over European American attributes and that European American beauty is neither an attainable or desirable goal. This racialized and gendered consciousness may also develop in such a way as to protect some African American girls from unhealthy body image issues. Although boys combined both Eurocentric and Afrocentric physical attributes to define physical beauty, European American standards for skin tone and hair texture were preferred most often. However, it is important to note that skin tone and hair texture were just as likely to be compartmentalized as separate commodities as to consider the female body as a whole. Thus, an extension of European American men's sexual preferences emulated to an extent by African American male preadolescents is made evident. African American men's sexual images would need to be studied and identified to explore further these choices.

In summary, racial and sexual identities bidirectionally influence the development of one another and are indeed a gendered process that has complex implications for intervention strategies. The use of sexual images may be a novel approach to research the quality of African American adolescents' sexual health. We suggest that, through the use of sexual images, creative programming that taps into culturally relevant imagery of this Hip Hop generation may produce effective intervention tools. Early adolescent African Americans need such tools to help them to identify healthy and unhealthy sexual behaviors within a specific gender and racial context. Otherwise, we will continue to see traditional programs that do not address unique cultural nuances fail to achieve desired behavioral outcomes.

References

Akan, G., & Grilo, C. (1995). Sociocultural influences on eating attitudes and behaviors, body image, and psychological functioning: A comparison of African-American, Asian-American, and Caucasian college women. *International Journal of Eating Disorders, 18*, 181–187.

Alksnis, C., Desmarais, S., & Wood, E. (1996). Gender difference in scripts for different types of dates. *Sex Roles, 34*, 499–509.

Arogundade, B. (2000). *Black beauty: A history and celebration.* New York: Thunder's Mouth.

Banks, I. (2000). *Hair matters: Beauty, power, and Black women's consciousness.* New York: New York University Press.

Baynes, L. (1997). If it's not just Black and White anymore, why does darkness cast a longer discriminatory shadow than lightness? An investigation and analysis of the color hierarchy. *Denver University Law Review, 75*, 131–185.

Becker, D. M., Yanek, L. R., Koffman, D. M., & Bronner, Y. C. (1999). Body image preferences among urban African Americans and whites from low income communities. *Ethnicity and Disease, 9*, 377–386.

Bell-Scott, P. (1998). *Flat footed truths: Telling Black women's lives.* New York: Henry Holt.

Blanton, H., Gibbons, F. X., Gerrard, M., Conger, K. J., & Smith, G. E. (1997). Role of family and peers in the development of prototypes associated with substance use. *Journal of Family Psychology, 11*, 271–288.

Bogdan, R. C., & Biklen, S. K. (1998). *Qualitative research for education: An introduction to theory and methods* (3rd ed.). Boston: Allyn & Bacon.

Bolig, R., Stein, P. J., & McKenry, P. C. (1984). The self-advertisement approach to dating: Male-female differences. *Family Relations, 33*, 587–592.

Bond, S., & Cash, T. F. (1992). Black beauty: Skin color and body images among African-

American college women. *Journal of Applied Social Psychology, 22,* 874–888.

Botta, R. A. (2000). The mirror of television: A comparison of Black and White adolescents' body image. *Journal of Communication, 50,* 144–162.

Breland, A., Coleman, H., Coard, S., & Steward, R. (2002). Differences among African American junior high students: The effects of skin tone on ethnic identity, self-esteem, and cross-cultural behavior. *Dimensions of Counseling: Research, Theory, and Practice, 30,* 15–21.

Brody, G., Ge, X., Conger, R., Gibbons, F. X., Murry, V. M., & Gerrard, M. (2001). The influence of neighborhood disadvantage, collective socialization, and parenting on African American children's affiliation with deviant peers. *Child Development, 72,* 1231–1246.

Brooks-Gunn, J., & Paikoff, R. (1997). Sexuality and development transitions during adolescence. In J. Schulenburg, J. L. Maggs, & K. Hurrelmann (Eds.), *Health risks and developmental transitions during adolescence* (pp. 190–219). Boston: Cambridge University Press.

Buss, D. M. (1984). Martial assortment for personality dispositions: Assessment with three different data sources. *Behavior Genetics, 14,* 111–123.

Buzwell, S., & Rosenthal, D. (1996). Constructing a sexual self: Adolescents' sexual self-perceptions and sexual risk taking. *Journal of Research on Adolescence, 6,* 489–513.

Cameron, D., & Frazer, E. (1996). On the question of pornography and sexual violence: Moving beyond the cause and effect. In S. Jackson & S. Scott (Eds.), *Feminism and sexuality: A reader* (pp. 62–73). New York: Columbia University Press.

Celious, A., & Oyserman, D. (2001). Race from the inside: An emerging heterogeneous race model. *Journal of Social Issues, 57,* 149–165.

Clasen, D. R., & Brown, B. B. (1985). The multidimensionality of peer pressure in adolescence. *Journal of Youth and Adolescence, 14,* 451–468.

Coard, S., Breland, A., & Raskin, R. (2001). Perceptions of and preferences for skin color, Black racial identity, and self esteem among

African Americans. *Journal of Applied Social Psychology, 31,* 2256–2275.

Collins, P. H. (2000). *Black feminist thought: Knowledge, consciousness, and the politics of empowerment* (2nd ed.). New York: Routledge.

Cross, W. E. (1995). The psychology of Nigrescence: Revising the Cross Model. In J. G. Ponterotto, J. M. Casas, L. A. Suzuki, & C. M. Alexander (Eds.), *Handbook of multicultural counseling* (pp. 93–144). Thousand Oaks, CA: Sage.

Debold, E. (1995). Helping girls survive the middle grades. *Principal, 74,* 22–24.

Demarest, J., & Allen, R. (2000). Body image: Gender, ethnic, and age differences. *Journal of Personality and Social Psychology, 65,* 293–307.

Dworkin, A. (1996). Pornography. In S. Jackson & S. Scott (Eds.), *Feminism and sexuality: A reader* (pp. 62–73). New York: Columbia University Press.

East, P. L. (1998). Racial and ethnic differences in girls' sexual, marital and birth expectations. *Journal of Marriage and the Family, 60,* 150–162.

Erikson, E. H. (1968). *Identity: Youth and crisis.* New York: Norton.

Feingold, A. (1990). Gender difference in the effects of physical attractiveness on romantic attraction: A comparison across five research paradigms. *Journal of Personality and Social Psychology, 59,* 981–993.

Few, A., Stephens, D., & Rouse-Arnette, M. (2003). Sister-to-sister talk: Transcending boundaries in qualitative research with Black women. *Family Relations, 52,* 205–215.

Firestone, W. (1987). Meaning in method: The rhetoric of quantitative and qualitative research. *Educational Researcher, 16,* 16–21.

Fraser, H. S. (2003). Obesity: Diagnosis and prescription for action in the English-speaking Caribbean. *Revista Panamericana de Salud Pública, 13,* 336–340.

Frederickson, B., & Roberts, T. A. (1997). Objectification theory: Toward understanding women's lived experiences and mental health risks. *Psychology of Women Quarterly, 21,* 173–206.

Frisby, C. (2004). Does race matter?: Effects of idealized images on African American women's perceptions of body esteem. *Journal of Black Studies, 34*, 323–347.

Gibbs, J. T. (1998). High-risk behaviors in African American youth: Conceptual and methodological issues in research. In V. C. McLoyd & L. Steinberg (Eds.), *Studying minority adolescents: Conceptual, methodological, and theoretical issues* (pp. 55–86). Mahwah, NJ: Erlbaum.

Goodwin, R. (1990). Sex differences among partner preferences: Are the sexes really very similar? *Sex Roles, 23*, 501–513.

Gorman-Smith, D., Tolan, P. H., Sheidow, A. J., & Henry, D. B. (2001). Partner violence and street violence among urban adolescents: Do the same family factors relate? *Journal of Research on Adolescence, 11*, 273–300.

Hall, R. (1992). Bias among African-Americans regarding skin color: Implications for social work practice. *Research on Social Work Practice, 2*, 479–486.

Hall, R. (1995). The bleaching syndrome: African Americans' response to cultural domination vis-à-vis skin color. *Journal of Black Studies, 26*, 172–184.

Hansen, S. L. (1977). Dating choices of high school students. *Family Coordinator, 26*, 133–138.

Hansen, S. L., & Hicks, M. W. (1980). Sex-role attitudes and perceived dating-mating choices of youth. *Adolescence, 15*, 83–90.

Helms, J. E., & Parham, T. A. (1990). Black racial identity attitudes scale. In J. E. Helms (Ed.), *Black and White racial identity: Theory, research, and practice* (pp. 245–248). Westport, CT: Praeger.

Henderson, E. L. (1996). Black nationalism and rap music. *Journal of Black Studies, 26*, 308–340.

Henriques, G., Calhoun, L. G., & Cann, A. (1996). Ethnic differences in women's body satisfaction: An experimental investigation. *Journal of Social Psychology, 136*, 689–698.

Herold, E. S. (1974). Stages of date selection: A reconciliation of divergent findings on campus values in dating. *Adolescence, 9*, 113–120.

Herring, C., Keith, V., & Horton, H. (2003). *Skin deep: How race and color matter in the color blind era*. Chicago: University of Illinois Press.

Hill, M. (2002). Skin color and the perceptions of attractive among African Americans: Does gender make a difference? *Social Psychology Quarterly, 65*(1), 77–93.

hooks, b. (1992). *Black looks: Race and representations*. Toronto: Between the Lines.

hooks, b. (1995). *Killing rage: Ending racism*. New York: Owl Books.

Hudson, B. (1995). Images used by African Americans to combat negative stereotypes. In H. Harris, H. Blue, & E. Griffith (Eds.), *Racial and ethnic identity* (pp. 135–172). New York: Routledge.

Hughes, M., & Bradley, R. (1990). The significance of color remains: A study of life chances, mate selection, and ethnic consciousness among Black Americans. *Social Forces, 68*, 1105–1120.

Jaccard, J., & Dittus, P. (1997). The impact of African American fathers on adolescent sexual behavior. *Journal of Youth and Adolescence, 26*, 445–465.

Jackson, L. A., & McGill, O. D. (1996). Body type preferences and body characteristics associated with attractive and unattractive bodies by African Americans and Anglo Americans. *Sex Roles, 35*, 295–307.

Jackson, S. (1996). The social construction of female sexuality. In S. Jackson & S. Scott (Eds.), *Feminism and sexuality: A reader* (pp. 62–73). New York: Columbia University Press.

Jemmott, L. S., & Jemmott, J. B. (1992). Family structure, parental strictness, and sexual behavior among inner city Black male adolescents. *Journal of Adolescent Research, 7*, 192–197.

Jones, J. M. (1991). Psychological models of race: What have they been and what should they be? In J. D. Goodchilds (Ed.), *Psychological perspectives on human diversity in America* (pp. 7–46). Washington, DC: American Psychological Association.

Jones, L. (1994). *Bullet proof diva: Tales of race, sex, and hair*. New York: Doubleday.

Jones, L. (1995, May). Sister knowledge: Interview with bell hooks. *Essence, 26*, 187–188.

Keenan, K. (1996). Skin tones and physical features of Blacks in magazine advertisements. *Journalism and Mass Communication Quarterly, 73*, 905–912.

Klinkenberg, D., & Rose, S. (1994). Dating scripts of gay men and lesbians. *Journal of Heterosexuality, 26*, 23–35.

Lake, O. (2003). *Blue veins and kinky hair: Naming and color consciousness in African America.* Westport, CT: Praeger.

Landolt, M. A., Lalumiere, M. L., & Quinsey, V. L. (1995). Sex differences in intra-sex variations in human mating tactics: An evolutionary approach. *Etiology and Sociobiology, 16*, 3–23.

Lincoln, Y. S., & Guba, E. G. (1985). *Naturalistic inquiry.* Beverly Hills, CA: Sage.

Lott, B. (1994). *Women's lives: Themes and variations in gender learning* (2nd ed.). Pacific Grove, CA: Brooks/Cole.

Lundy, D. W., Tan, J., & Cunningham, M. R. (1998). Heterosexual romantic preferences: The importance of humor and physical attractiveness for different types of relationships. *Personal Relationships, 5*, 311–325.

Makkar, J. K., & Strube, M. J. (1995). Black women's self-perceptions of attractiveness following exposure to White versus Black beauty standards: Moderating role of racial identity and self-esteem. *Journal of Applied Social Psychology, 25*, 1547–1566.

McAdoo, H. P., & McAdoo, J. (1985). *Black children.* Newbury Park, CA: Sage.

McCluskey, C. P., Krohn, M. D., Lizotte, A. J., & Rodriguez, M. L. (2002). Early substance use and school achievement: An examination of Latino, White, and African American youth. *Journal of Drug Issues, 32*, 921–944.

McLoyd, V. C. (1998). Changing demographics in the American population: Implications for research on minority children and adolescents. In V. C. McLoyd & L. Steinberg (Eds.), *Studying minority adolescents: Conceptual, methodological, and theoretical issues* (pp. 167–182). Mahwah, NJ: Erlbaum.

Miller, A. L., Notaro, P. C., & Zimmerman, M. A. (2002). Stability and change in internal working models of friendship: Associations with multiple domains of urban adolescent functioning. *Journal of Social and Personal Relationships, 19*, 233–260.

Miller, K. S., Forehand, R., & Kotchick, B. A. (2000). Adolescent sexual behavior in two ethnic minority groups: A multi-system perspective. *Adolescence, 35*, 313–333.

Morton, P. (1991). *Disfigured images: The historical assault on Afro-American women.* New York: Praeger.

Murstein, B. I., Merighi, J. R., & Malloy, T. E. (1989). Physical attractiveness and exchange theory in interracial dating. *Journal of Social Psychology, 129*, 325–334.

Nasser, M. (1988). Culture and weight consciousness. *Journal of Psychosomatic Research, 322*, 573–577.

Nolin, P., & Petersen, K. (1992). Gender differences in parent-child communication about sexuality: An exploratory study. *Journal of Adolescent Research, 7*, 59–79.

Noller, P., & Callan, V. J. (1990). Adolescents' perception of the nature of their communication with parents. *Journal of Youth and Adolescence, 19*, 349–362.

Okazawa-Rey, M., Robinson, T., & Ward, J. (1987). Black women and the politics of skin color and hair. *Women & Therapy, 6*(1/2), 89–102.

Oswald, R., Blume, L. B., & Marks, S. (2005). Decentering heteronormativity: A model for family studies. In V. L. Bengtson, A. C. Acock, K. R. Allen, P. Dilworth-Anderson, & D. M. Klein (Eds.), *Sourcebook of family theory & research* (pp. 143–165). Thousand Oaks, CA: Sage.

Parker, S., Nichter, M., Nichter, M., Vuckovic, N., Sims, C., & Rittenbaugh, C. (1995). Body image and weight concerns among African-American and White adolescent females: Differences that make a difference. *Human Organization, 54*, 103–113.

Patterson, G. R., Reid, J. B., & Dishion, T. J. (1992). *Antisocial boys.* Eugene, OR: Castalia.

Perlini, A. H., Marcello, A., Hansen, S. D., & Pudney, W. (2001), The Effects of Male Age and Physical Appearance on Evaluations of Attractiveness, Social Desirability and Resourcefulness. *Social Behavior and Personality, 29*, 277–287.

Phinney, J. S. (1990). Ethnic identity in adolescents and adults: Review of research. *Psychological Bulletin, 108*, 499–514.

Phinney, J., & Alipuria, L. L. (1996). At the interface of cultures: Multiethnic/multiracial high school and college students. *Journal of Social Psychology, 2*, 139–159.

Pinderhughes, E. (1995). Biracial identity—asset or handicap? In H. Harris, H. Blue, & E. Griffith (Eds.), *Racial and ethnic identity* (pp. 73–94). New York: Routledge.

Rand, C. S., & Kuldau, J. M. (1992). Epidemiology of bulimia and symptoms in a general population: Sex, age, race, and socioeconomic status. *International Journal of Eating Disorders, 11*, 37–44.

Regan, P. C., & Joshi, A. (2003). Ideal partner preferences among adolescents. *Social Behavior and Personality, 31*, 13–20.

Reissman, C. K. (1993). *Narrative analysis qualitative research methods.* Newbury Park, CA: Sage.

Roberts, T., & Ulen, E. N. (2000). Sisters spin talk on hip hop: Can the music be saved? *Ms. Magazine, 10*, 69–74.

Rome, E., Rybicki, L. A., & Durant, R. H. (1998). Pregnancy and other risk behaviors among adolescent girls in Ohio. *Journal of Adolescent Health, 22*, 50–55.

Root, M. (1990). Disordered eating in women of color. *Sex Roles, 22*, 525–536.

Rose, S., & Frieze, I. H. (1989). Young singles' scripts for a first date. *Gender & Society, 3*, 258–268.

Rose, S., & Frieze, I. H. (1993). Young singles' contemporary dating scripts. *Sex Roles, 28*, 1–11.

Rubin, H. J., & Rubin, I. S. (1995). *Qualitative interviewing.* Newbury Park, CA: Sage.

Russell, K., Wilson, M., & Hall, R. (1992). *The color complex: The politics of skin color among African Americans.* New York: Harcourt Brace Jovanovich.

Schooler, D., & Wieling, E. (2000). *Effects of heterosexual African American males' perception of ideal female body image on their partners.* Unpublished manuscript, Texas Tech University.

Seid, R. (1994). Too "close to the bone": A historical context for women's obsession with slenderness. In P. Fallon, M. Katzman, & S. Wooley (Eds.), *Feminist perspectives on eating disorders* (pp. 3–16). New York: Guilford.

Simeon, D. T., Rattan, R. D., Panchoo, K., Kungeesingh, K. V., Ali, A. C., & Abdool, P. S. (2003). Body image of adolescents in a multiethnic Caribbean population. *European Journal of Clinical Nutrition, 57*, 157–162.

Simon, W., & Gagnon, J. H. (1984). Sexual scripts. *Society, 22*, 52–60.

Simon, W., & Gagnon, J. H. (1986). Sexual scripts: Permanence and change. *Archives of Sexual Behavior, 15*, 97–120.

Simon, W., & Gagnon, J. H. (1987). A sexual scripts approach. In J. H. Greer & W. T. O'Donohue (Eds.), *Theories of human sexuality* (pp. 363–383). New York: Plenum.

Smith, C. (1997). Factors associated with early sexual activity among urban adolescents. *Social Work, 42*, 334–345.

Smith, S. P. (1996). Dating-partner preferences among a group of inner-city African-American high school students. *Adolescence, 31*, 79–91.

Staples, R. (Ed.) (1994). *The Black family: Essays and studies.* Belmont, CA: Wadsworth.

Stephens, D. P. & Few, A. L. (2007). *African American preadolescents' understanding of female sexual scripts in Hip Hop culture.* Manuscript submitted for publication (copy on file with author).

Stephens, D. P., & Phillips, L. D. (2003). Freaks, gold diggers, divas, and dykes: The sociohistorical development of African American female adolescent scripts. *Sexuality and Culture, 7*, 3–47.

Stephens, D. P., & Phillips, L. D. (2005). Integrating Black feminist thought into conceptual frameworks of African American adolescent women's sexual scripting processes. *Sexualities, Evolution, and Gender, 7*, 37–55.

Story, M., French, S. A., Resnick, M. D., & Blum, R. W. (1995). Ethnic/racial and socioeconomic differences in dieting behaviors and body image perceptions in adolescents. *International Journal of Eating Disorders, 18*, 173–179.

Thomas, V. (1989). Body image satisfaction among Black women. *Journal of Social Psychology, 129*, 107–112.

Thomas, V., & James, M. (1988). Body image, dieting tendencies, and sex-role traits in urban Black women. *Sex Roles, 18*, 523–529.

Wade, T. J. (1996). The relationship between skin color and self-perceived global, physical, and sexual attractiveness, and self-esteem for African Americans. *Journal of Black Psychology, 22*, 358–373.

Wade, T., & DiMaria, C. (2003). Weight halo effects: Individual differences in perceived life success as a function of women's race and weight. *Sex Roles, 48*, 461–465.

Wade, J. C., & Olayiwola, O. (2002). Racial peer group selection in African American high school students. *Journal of Multicultural Counseling and Development, 30*, 96–109.

Wahl, G. (1999). I fought the law, and the cold won: Hip hop in mainstream. *College Literature, 26*, 98–113.

Walkowitz, J. (1996). The politics of prostitution. In S. Jackson & S. Scott (Eds.), *Feminism and sexuality: A reader* (pp. 62–73). New York: Columbia University Press.

Ward, J. V., & Robinson, T. L. (1995). African American adolescents and skin color. *Journal of Black Psychology, 21*, 256–274.

Washington, P. (1995). Positive sexuality: Does it begin at home? *Womanist, 1*(2), 5–7.

Weddle-West, K. (2000). African American families: Trends and issues over the life course. In S. Price, P. McKenry, & M. Murphy (Eds.), *Families across time: A life course perspective* (pp. 64–76). Los Angeles: Roxbury.

Weisz, A. N., & Black, B. M. (2001). Evaluating a sexual assault and dating violence prevention program for urban youths. *Social Work Research, 25*, 89–111.

West, C. M., & Rose, S. (2000). Dating aggression among low income African American youth: An examination of gender differences and antagonistic beliefs. *Violence Against Women, 6*, 470–495.

Whatley, M. H. (1994). Keeping adolescents in the picture: Construction of adolescent sexuality in textbook images and popular films. In J. Irvine (Ed.), *Sexual cultures and the construction of adolescent identities* (pp. 187–188). Philadelphia, PA: Temple University Press.

Wheeler, S. C., Jarvis, W. B. G., & Petty, R. E. (2001). Think unto others: The self-destructive impact of negative stereotypes. *Journal of Experimental Social Psychology, 37*, 173–180.

Willis, D., & Williams, C. (2002). *The Black female body*. Philadelphia: Temple University Press.

Worrell, F. (2000). A validity study of scores on the multigroup ethnic identity measure based on a sample of academically talented adolescents. *Educational and Psychological Measurement, 3*, 439–448.

Xiaojia, G., Conger, R. D., Simons, R. L., Brody, G. H., & Murry, V. M. (2002). Contextual amplification of pubertal transition on deviant peer affiliation and externalizing behavior. *Developmental Psychology, 38*, 42–55.

Zimmerman, M., Copeland, L., Shope, J., & Dielman, T. (1997). A longitudinal study of self-esteem: Implications for adolescent development. *Journal of Youth and Adolescence, 26*, 117–141.

17 Virginia Braun

In Search of (Better) Sexual Pleasure

Female Genital "Cosmetic" Surgery

Like cosmetic surgery generally, FGCS can be seen as both *surgical* practice and *cultural* product (see Adams, 1997; Fraser, 2003b) and practice (Haiken, 2000). Dubbed the "designer vagina," FGCS has received considerable media attention in recent years. Headlines range from the sensational— "I've saved my sex life" (M30)[1]—to the serious—"Designer vagina service a first for NZ" (N10). There is an apparent increase in the popularity of FGCS. One magazine reported that "the operation is not new, he's been doing it for 20 years, but back then he was getting a couple of requests a year. Now he performs the operations once or twice a month" (M23), while another clinic performs "40 operations each month" (M23). Apparently, "there is no question there's a big trend, . . . it's sort of coming out of the closet. It's basically where breast augmentation was 30 years ago" (M24). By some accounts, this increasing popularity is due, at least in part, to media coverage.

The material practice of FGCS, and women's participation in it, are enabled within particular sociocultural (and technological) contexts which render certain choices possible, and locate cosmetic surgery as a solution (K. Davis, 2003). The contexts of women's ongoing, widespread, and increasingly specific, body dissatisfactions (Bordo, 1997; Sullivan, 2001), ongoing negative meanings around women's genitalia (Braun and Wilkinson, 2001, 2003), and women's engagement in a wide range of body modification practices—such as hair removal (Toerien and Wilkinson, 2004)—cohere to render women's genitalia a viable site for surgical enhancement. FGCS can thus be theorized as an extension of other currently more culturally normative bodily subjectivities, desires and practices, for women:

> Logically, [labioplasty] operations are merely an extension of other procedures designed either to draw attention to female genitals . . . or to render invisible signs of secondary sexual development. . . . In this context, the "trimming" of visible labia minora . . . is part of a continuum. While labia reduction is not a well-known procedure, hair removal products and procedures are common. (Allotey et al., 2001: 197)

In this article, I focus specifically on the issue of (female) sexual pleasure in accounts of FGCS. Female sexual pleasure appears as a central concern, mirroring a broader sociocultural shift towards the "eroticization of female sexuality" (Seidman, 1991: 124) with women's sexual pleasure located as central in (hetero)sex (e.g., Braun et al., 2003; Gordon, 1971) and beyond. A 1996 article in *Flare* magazine ("The Sex Files") identified that "female pleasure is officially a trend" (M27). More generally, for men *and* women, sex has become highly important (Weeks, 1985: 7), with "frequent, pleasurable, varied, and ecstatically satisfying sex . . . a preeminent sign of personal happiness" (D'Emilio and Freedman, 1997: 340; Weeks, 1985), and even identity (Heath, 1982). This increased attention to pleasure has also resulted in an increased attention to the body and sexual technique (Seidman, 1991), with possible concurrent increases in feelings of sexual inadequacy (Hart and Wellings, 2002). I will show that the story of FGCS is, at least in part, a story of the (legitimate) search for (better) female sexual pleasure, and argue that this functions not only to legitimate, and promote, FGCS, but also to reaffirm particular models of desirable sexual bodies and practices.

Theorizing and Researching FGCS

This article is part of a broader project on FGCS which analyses data drawn from two datasets: media accounts and surgeon interviews.[2] The research is situated within a (feminist) social constructionist framework (Burr, 1995; Tiefer, 1995, 2000; White et al., 2000), which theorizes language and social representations as an integral part of the production of social (and material) realities for individuals, as well as producing possibilities for individual practices. Sexuality is thus a material, but always social, practice (Connell, 1997; Jackson and Scott, 2001).

Media data consist of 106 English-language items from print (newspaper, maga-

zine) and electronic (television, radio, Internet) mass-media sources. My convenience sample was located primarily through Google searches using terms like "designer vagina" and "labiaplasty," and through surgeon websites. The sample comprises: 31 print magazine items; 24 Internet-based magazine items; 23 other Internet items; 13 news media items; and 15 other related items. My analysis in this article focuses on the print magazine data.

While the media have various potential uses for consumers at an individual level (Berger, 1998), my primary interest is in the media's roles in contributing to the social construction of FGCS. The media have a range of influences on health (Brown and Wash-Childers, 2002), and are significant contributors to the social construction of ideas about appearance, health, illness, and sexuality (Carpiano, 2001; Sullivan, 2001). They have been theorized as influential in women's decisions and "choices" about cosmetic surgery (Blum, 2003; Gagne and Mc-Gaughey, 2002; Goodman, 1996), their feelings about the appearance of their vulva (Bramwell, 2002; see also Reinholtz and Muehlenhard, 1995), and their "body image" more generally (Bordo, 1993; Grogan, 1999). Women's magazines, in particular, have been identified as "a significant cultural source of ideas about appearance as a medical problem" (Sullivan, 2001: 159), and are seen to work "in tandem with surgeons to promote cosmetic surgery" (Fraser, 2003b: 125). Surgeons consider them to be one of the most important sources of public ideas about cosmetic surgery (Sullivan, 2001).

Surgeons were primarily located via the media (except two, who were located via word of mouth). In total, 24 surgeons were contacted and invited to take part in semi-structured interviews, with 15 agreeing. The sample of surgeons varied in terms of the following.

A. Geographical location: surgeons were practicing in the USA (5), UK (4), Canada (2), Australia (2) and New Zealand (2).
B. Surgical specialty: nine were plastic surgeons (one was also a urologist), six were gynaecologists.
C. Type of practice: all but three surgeons who worked on the UK's National Health Service did these surgeries privately, at direct cost to the patient.
D. Experience: the average time of doing "cosmetic" genital procedures was more than 11 years (range 25 to 2 years). The estimated *total* number of FGCS procedures performed ranged from over 1,000 to fewer than 50.
E. Sex: twelve were male, three female.
F. Ethnicity: one identified as black, one as Jewish, and 11 as white/Caucasian/Anglo-Saxon (two provided no ethnicity information).

Fourteen of the interviews, which lasted between 15 and 70 minutes, were conducted in person (one was via telephone), and all except one were tape recorded. Participants were told that "the research focuses on ideas about female genital cosmetic surgery, and on the reasons for such procedures" and that I was "interested in how ideas about women, women's bodies, and women's sexuality relate to these procedures."

FGCS and Female Sexual Pleasure

Women's sex lives or their sexuality was often reported to be impeded in some way, with pre-operative genitalia:

Extract 1: Woman's Day Magazine, *NZ, 2004*
Amanda was utterly miserable. She no longer enjoyed sex with Russell, the husband she adored, and on those rare occasions when they made love, Amanda would insist they switch off the lights. (M30)

In this and other extracts, general pre-surgical sexual "impediments" were noted. In addition, specific causes of such sexual impediments were identified in many accounts:

Extract 2: male plastic surgeon, UK
S1: what comes in more and in my practice it is not—quite often it's not purely cosmetic but there are functional complaints with the labia the size of the labia too (Int: mhm) for example . . . it can be painful during intercourse because the labium keeps going in and out with every thrust.

Although physical pain was often discussed, the *psychological* response to genital morphology was frequently highlighted as the crux of the problem which "hampered" or "ruined" their sex life:

Extract 3: male plastic surgeon, NZ
SA: I think most w— of the women that I've dealt with have thought that this was a real impediment to sexual enjoyment (Int: mhm) not so much from *their* point of view but from their partner's point of view (Int: oh okay) if they were worried about their *partner* not liking whatever they could see or or touch or whatever then they felt tense themselves (Int: mhm) and so the enjoyment of everything goes (spiraling) (Int: mnn) down.

Int: Yeah so sort of sex was an area of difficulty (S6: yeah) for most of them (S6: yeah) or for (S6: yeah) all of them.

S6: Abso— oh absolutely.

Extract 4: Cosmopolitan Magazine, *AUS/NZ, 1998*

Sarah, a 27-year-old secretary, is a case in point. Throughout puberty, she thought her vaginal lips were too long and was embarrassed by one that hung lower than the other.

"They ruined my sex life," she recalls. "I never felt confident during sex—I felt like a freak. I'd never let anyone see me naked." (M1)

Extract 5: New Woman Magazine, *AUS, 2003*

. . . the biggest problem was sex. I've been with my boyfriend since I was 15 but I always felt self-conscious when we made love. I'd engineer positions so that he'd always be behind me and couldn't see my vagina, and I'd never have oral sex because I couldn't bear him seeing me up close. (M20)

The psychological problems invoked to explain a (pre-surgery) sexual impediment included embarrassment, self-consciousness, lack of confidence, and shame. The inclusion of such concepts fits with Frank's (2003) observation of an "inflation of the language of pain" around medicine to include such psychological concepts.[3] In my data, this negative psychological response to *appearance* often resulted, via other psychological responses like anxiety or self-consciousness, in an inability to "receive" oral sex from a male partner, an account which fits with women's reports of various genital anxieties, particularly around oral sex (Braun and Wilkinson, 2003; Reinholtz and Muehlenhard, 1995; Roberts et al., 1996). Women's reports of genital anxiety reflect a range of negative sociocultural representations of women's genitalia (Braun

and Wilkinson, 2001), and it seems some women "live these [negative] cultural meanings in their embodiment" (Roberts et al., 1996: 119). However, my concern is not just about women's embodiment, as psychology here provides the "moral justification" (Frank, 2003) for cosmetic surgery to alleviate this distress.

While *impeded* sexual possibilities and pleasures were central in media and surgeon accounts of why women might choose to have FGCS, *increased* sexual pleasure as an outcome of surgery was the main area in which sexual pleasure was discussed. FGCS, in a variety of forms, was represented as increasing sexual pleasure. The *aim* of sexual enhancement was often explicitly stated in the titles of magazine articles about FGCS—"THE G-SHOT . . . plastic surgery for your orgasm" (M22)— and in the setting up of media stories:

Extract 6: New Woman Magazine, *UK, date unknown*

Would you go under the knife to improve your sex life? These four women did. (M29)

Extract 7: Marie Claire Magazine, *UK, 2000*

What are the reasons for surgery? Firstly, to improve their sex lives. (M4)

Extract 8: Marie Claire Magazine, *US, 2000*

Some women are going under the knife to change the appearance of their genitals, while others are having surgery in the hopes of better orgasms. (M3)

In some, the possibility of increased sexual pleasure was initially framed with mild skepticism:

Extract 9: Cosmopolitan Magazine, *AUS/NZ, 1998*

Doctors [in the US] claim to be able to boost women's sexual pleasure, taking them to previously uncharted erotic heights. And their secret weapon in the quest for sexual ecstasy? The scalpel. (M1)

Extract 10: Marie Claire Magazine, *UK, 2000*

The sales pitch being that sexual gratification of the female is diminished if friction is lost because of a slack vagina, so this procedure tightens up your bits and helps you reach orgasm. (M4)

Extract 11: FQ Magazine, *NZ, 2004*

Will sex be mind-blowing once you've been trimmed or tightened? Well, the jury is still out. (M31)

Any initial skepticism in reporting the doctors' "claim" that the operations "supposedly increase sexual pleasure" (M3) was typically not reiterated in most media accounts of surgical results and patient experiences, or in surgeon accounts. Instead, overwhelmingly, increased pleasure was noted:

Extract 12: Cleo Magazine, *NZ, 2001*

Feedback from patients suggests their sex lives have improved enormously. (M7)

Extract 13: male urologist, AUS

S7: I've known women who are mono-orgasmic to become multiply orgasmic as a result.

All procedures, even ostensibly cosmetic ones such as labiaplasty, were frequently framed as being "successful" in terms of increased sexual pleasure:

Extract 14: Cosmopolitan Magazine, *AUS/NZ, 2004*

I am no longer embarrassed to be naked and my sex life has improved because I'm more confident. (M23)

Extract 15: Company Magazine, UK, 2003

I was so thrilled with my new vagina, Dan and I "tried it out" after just four weeks. What a difference—it was like my whole sex life was beginning again. Suddenly I discovered how amazing oral sex could be, because I could finally relax and be myself during sex. I didn't have to worry about my boyfriend seeing me naked. (M18)

In these extracts, improved sexual function was identified as a key outcome of "cosmetic" procedures. In Extract 15, psychological changes post-surgery allowed the woman to experience cunnilingus. Surgery reportedly expanded women's sexual repertoires. However, such reports continue to situate heterosex within the bounds of normative heterosexuality, through the suggestion that certain sexual acts (cunnilingus) can only be engaged in, and enjoyed, by either or both partners, within a very limited range of female genital aesthetics. This aesthetic is one where the labia minora do not protrude beyond the labia majora—a youthful, almost pre-pubescent aesthetic, and one often associated with, and derived from, the "unreal" vulvas displayed in heterosexual male-oriented pornography (see Adams, 1997; S. W. Davis, 2002). This was explicitly noted:

Extract 16: Shine Magazine, *AUS/NZ, 2001*

A lot of women bring in *Playboy*, show me pictures of vaginas and say, "I want to look like this." (M5)

The genital produced is one in which diversity is replaced with conformity to this particular aesthetic, a "cookie cutter" (I25) genital. FGCS becomes a practice of changing women's diverse bodies to fit a certain (male-oriented) aesthetic of what women's genitals *should look like*, if they are to engage in cunnilingus (or other sexual activities). With male (hetero)sexuality continuing to be constructed as *visual* (e.g., Moghaddam and Braun, 2004), with desire based on the aesthetic, such accounts reinforce a traditional model of male sexuality, and female sexuality alongside it. FGCS effectively becomes surgery to change bodies to fit, and to enable certain sexual practices, through psychological/emotional changes enabled by bodily transformation. A pathologization of "large" labia minora has a long history, and a long association with perceived sexual "deviance" (S. Gilman, 1985; Terry, 1995). FGCS appears to offer a surgical process for subsequently passing—to oneself, as well as others—as "sexy" or just as "normal" (see K. Davis, 2003).

In these accounts, sexual pleasure occupies a status of almost unquestioned good, which mirrors liberal sexual rhetoric, arguably the dominant form of sexual discourse currently available in western countries. With sex constructed as a "domain of pleasure" (Seidman, 1991: 124), the pursuit of (more and better) sexual pleasure is situated as a legitimate, or even obligatory (Hawkes, 1996; Heath, 1982), pursuit for the "liberated" (sexual) subject. There are "cultural expectations that each individual has a right and a duty to achieve and give maximum satisfaction in their sexual relationships" (Nicolson, 1993: 56). FGCS is framed as a viable means to achieve this. A key question to consider, however, is what (female) sexual pleasure is being offered:

Extract 17: Cosmopolitan Magazine, *AUS/NZ, 1998*

Four months after the operation, Kate claims to be enjoying the best sex of her life . . . "removing the excess fat has made me much more easily aroused. Now I achieve orgasm easily and often." (M1)

Extract 18: New Woman Magazine, *AUS, 2003*

"The G-Shot procedure is all about maximizing sexual pleasure for women. By injecting a fluid made up partly of collagen we can increase the G spot to three or four times its normal size, so it's easier to stimulate.

"The effects last about four months and my patients tell me how even something as gentle as yoga is giving them orgasms!" (M20)

Extract 19: New Woman Magazine, *UK, date unknown*

What a result though! All I have to do is think about sex and I can feel my G spot react. Even during my spinning class I can feel the bike seat pressing on it—and I have to pretend I'm just enjoying the workout! I've also had my first ever multiple orgasm and it was great. (M29)

The conception of "sexual pleasure" for women was typically synonymous with orgasm—or multiple-orgasm. By prioritizing orgasm over other forms of sexual pleasure, such accounts work to reaffirm an orgasm imperative (Heath, 1982; Potts, 2000). Orgasm was framed, a-contextually, as positive—the possibility of orgasm in non-sexual situations was identified not negatively (as, for instance, impeding the woman's ability to partake in exercise without fear of orgasm), but rather positively.

Typically, orgasm was framed in unequivocally positive ways:

Extract 20: Cleo Magazine, *NZ, 2003*
Rosemary is promised about four months of orgasmic delights . . . having heard about the G-Shot through a friend who raved about her endless climaxes, Rosemary had no hesitation in handing over US$1850 [NZ$3000] for a dose of heightened pleasure. (M22)

Therefore, the accounts of pleasure in heterosex—and it typically *was* heterosex—presented in the data failed to offer any radical questioning of orgasm as the pinnacle of sexual pleasure and achievement (Jackson and Scott, 2001; Potts, 2000). "Better" sex typically meant orgasmic sex (or, sometimes, simply more sex), and more (and better) sex was inherently framed as good. By locating orgasm as so central to women's sexual pleasure, other ways in which sex could be more pleasurable—e.g., more fun, more intense, more relaxed, more intimate—were relegated to second place, if any, behind orgasm. This affirms what Seidman (1992: 7) has identified as a "new tyranny of orgasmic pleasure."

Although physical changes, such as an enlarged G-spot or tighter vagina, were often identified as resulting in increased pleasure, *psychological* elements were also highlighted as key in explanations for increased sexual pleasure, post-surgery:

Extract 21: male plastic surgeon, UK
S1: when you feel better about what you look like down there if you feel happier with the cosmetic aspect of (Int: mhm) yourself of your genitalia then you are more relaxed in the bedroom (Int: mhm) and a lot of patients report back to

me that they *do* feel better and therefore have better sex because (Int: mhm) they're less embarrassed.
Int: 'cos they're more relaxed.
S1: yeah.

Extract 22: Flare Magazine, *CA, 1998*
What does work, according to Angela, is the boost in self-esteem that stems from feeling sexually confident. "I spent years not feeling good about myself and my sexuality," she says. "I started to retreat from my husband. I tried to avoid him sexually because every time we tried, it was disastrous."
It all gets back to the psychosexual response, says Dr. Stubbs. (M26)

Extract 23: Shine Magazine, *AUS/NZ, 2001*
My sex life has improved so much since the operation—we have more sex now than we've ever had. I'm much more into my boyfriend and now that I'm tighter, I'm much more confident about initiating sex. Even better, my boyfriend is enjoying sex with me more, as there's much more stimulation for him, too. (M5)

In these extracts, the psychological was invoked as an essential ingredient in the production of female pleasure, and, indeed, situated as a primary reason this surgery was effective in producing increased sexual pleasure for women. The account was one of (psychological) transformation, from a state of impeded sexuality, to one of liberated, (multi) orgasmic sexuality (transformation is a key theme in accounts of cosmetic surgery, see Blum, 2003; K. Davis, 1995, 2003; Frank, 2003; Gagne and McGaughey, 2002; Gimlin, 2002; Haiken, 1997; Sullivan, 2001). In such accounts, the psychological was framed as a reason why surgery was necessary, and, in the form of psychological *change*, an explanation of why the surgery was successful. The mind was implicitly constructed as impervious to change *without* surgery, but then as changing once surgical alteration was completed. Cosmetic surgery is thus about changing the body to change the mind (Blum, 2003), and becomes the "best or most effective means of attaining satisfaction" about bodily distress (Fraser, 2003a: 39).[4] Thus, the body is situated as ontologically prior to the mind, but the mind is located as the crucial variable, in sexual pleasure terms. The idea of cosmetic surgery as "psychotherapy" can be found in Gilman's (1998; 1999) analyses (see also Fraser, 2003a, 2003b).[5]

Extract 23 is relatively unusual in that increased male sexual pleasure was noted. Women were the primary focus in accounts of sexual pleasure, with comparatively little discussion of male sexual pleasure. This is not surprising, as cosmetic surgery is necessarily often framed as "for oneself" rather than for others (see Fraser, 2003b). Where male sexual pleasure was referred to, it was often positioned as secondary to, or less important than, female sexual pleasure. For instance, Extract 23 situates her boyfriend's increased sexual pleasure as secondary to her pleasure, as an added bonus, something that makes it "even better." The prioritizing of *female* sexual pleasure in accounts of FGCS can be seen in Extract 24:

Extract 24: male gynaecological surgeon, USA

Int: [Vaginal tightening] . . . is talked about as being for sexual gratification um is that um for female sexual gratification or is that um for if they're in a relationship with a male for male sexual gratification or some combination of both um.

S5: The purpose is for the female (Int: mhm) my objective is for the female I'm a gynaecologist my ah ah I've dedicated my career my life to the healthcare of women and treating women (Int: mhm) damn the man (pause) there's plenty of things (if) I had a problem (clicks fingers) plenty of things (but we're) (Int: mhm) involved with women (Int: mhm) we're involved with women so *my* philosophy there's plenty of things out there *this* is for her I'm happy to say that women come in on their own volition and want to have these procedures *I find* women want to enjoy sex, women want to have the best sexual experience possible that's it (pause) men have got everything okay but women want to have the best sexual experience possible.

Int: And vaginal tightening's important to that I'm just thinking about how . . .

S5: Important to (unclear)

Int: how a tightened vagina *is* necessarily more . . .

S5: Ah it's important to them.

Int: sexually preferable for women.

S5: It's important to them it's important now I've treated patients from all 50 states (Int: mhm) and it's over 30 (unclear) countries it's important to the people (Int: mhm) it's important to the people to the women (pause) *obviously* if I'm enhancing sexual gratification for a female I can enhance sexual gratification for the male (Int: mhm) yeah (Int: mn) but again if a man is *pushing* her I won't do it.

While this extract could be extensively analysed, for the purposes of this article, it is important to note how hard S5 has to work to undermine the suggestion (implicit in my question) that the surgery might "really" be about male sexual pleasure. Instead he situates male sexual pleasure as a peripheral concern. Such accounts exist in contrast to reports of other genital procedures, such as the "husband stitch" (Kitzinger, 1994) after childbirth/episiotomy, which tightens a woman's vagina, where *male* sexual pleasure has been emphasized (e.g., Jahoda, 1995).

Overall, the prioritizing of female sexual pleasure and general lack of discussion of male sexual pleasure, work to construct FGCS as something that is in the (sexual) interests of women, rather than in the sexual interests of (heterosexual) men. Through current accounts, FGCS is effectively constructed as a liberatory action for women—it produces sexual pleasure, which is, socioculturally, almost mandatory for women—rather than a capitulation to unreasonable patriarchal demands on women's bodies. However, while FGCS offers (apparent) empowerment to individuals who have it, albeit within a limited range of options, it simultaneously reinforces oppressive social norms for women (see Gagne and McGaughey, 2002; Gillespie, 1996; Negrin, 2002).

FGCS: Normative Heterosexuality, Generic Bodies, and Generic Pleasures

The central role that (female) pleasure plays in accounts of FGCS is revealing in terms of contemporary discourses of (hetero)sexuality and what it could/should mean to be a woman in the West today. Women's sexual pleasure—or ability to orgasm—appears as a central concern for women, and indeed for society. The account is almost exclusively one where, sexually, women should be comfortable in their bodies and should be able to enjoy sex—and the more sex, and sexual pleasure, the better. Women are represented as (inherently) entitled to sexual pleasure, and indeed, inherently

(hetero)sexual. That *these* women are not sexually "liberated," sexually "satisfied," or, even, as sexually satisfied as other people appear to be, is, at least in part, what is "wrong" with their preoperative genitalia. In this sense, accounts of FGCS and women's sexual pleasure fit squarely within a discourse of liberal sexuality (Hollway, 1989), and even, within some feminist discourse around the importance of equality in sex (see Braun et al., 2003). It also affirms an imperative for "more and better sexual gratification" (Hart and Wellings, 2002: 899), by whatever means possible.

However, the construction of female sexual pleasure in relation to this surgery fails to challenge the bounds of normative heterosexuality. First, sexual pleasure was often (although not exclusively) framed as being derived through coitus, particularly in the case of vaginal tightening, and the sexual pleasure that is derived was typically orgasmic. In this sense, it can be seen to be (at least in part) a practice of designing bodies to fit certain sexual practices, rather than designing sexual practices to fit bodies. We then have to ask whether it is so different from the "love surgery" of the now disgraced Dr. James Burt, who surgically altered women's genitalia to make them more amenable to stimulation during coitus (Adams, 1997). As Adams (1997: 64) noted, such surgeries "make women conform to traditional heterosexual values." The same criticism applies to FGCS: the sexual "freedom" that is being produced is a freedom to enjoy sex within a very limited frame of reference.

Moreover, at the same time as it constructs the legitimate female body as an orgasmic one, it reinforces this "ideal" as something not all women necessarily (easily) achieve (without surgery). So sexual pleasure, through orgasm, is simultaneously situated both as what most women can/should do and as a current impossibility for some women. The very construction of FGCS as surgery to enhance or enable orgasm fits with an ongoing construction of a woman's orgasm as difficult to achieve, in contrast to a man's inevitable one (Jackson and Scott, 2001; Moghaddam and Braun, 2004). Moreover, although couched in terms of liberation of women (to a "full" enjoyment of sex), rather than pathology, the framing of FGCS as a solution to "sub-par" sexual pleasure on the woman's part decontextualizes sex, locating any deficiency in the woman's body/mind, and offering an individualized solution. In this way, FGCS fits within a broadening medicalization of sexual behavior (Hart and Wellings, 2002; Tiefer, 1997), which, Tiefer (1997: 112) has argued, has "only reinforced a limited script for heterosexual sexual life."

These points raise the question of the generic versus the particular. The idea of a surgical "fix" or enhancement of (lack of) sexual pleasure locates sexual pleasure at the level of the *individual* body, rather than in relation to a "fit" between bodies/people and the practices they are engaged in. In this sense, the sexual enhancement of the body is framed as generic sexual enhancement, regardless of with whom, and how, one might be having sex. This framing disregards the particularities of sex, with different partners, with different practices, for different purposes, and, indeed, in different moods, modes, and venues. Sex, sexual pleasure, and even sexual desires vary hugely according to this range of contextualizing variables. Accounts of FGCS not only fail to account for this, but actually work to promote the idea of generic sexual pleasure as possible.

The context of consumer culture provides another angle from which to examine public discourse around FGCS. Bordo's (1997: 42) analysis identifies that a consumer system "depends on our perceiving ourselves as defective and that will continually find new ways to do this." Media accounts that demonstrate a "cure" to some problem for women can be seen to also contribute to the creation of that problem in the first place. FGCS, and media coverage of it, have the potential to produce consumer anxiety (S. W. Davis, 2002). One item commented that media coverage had "taken a very unusual phenomena and concocted a new 'embarrassing problem' that could get readers squinting nervously at the privates" (M28). In the case of labiaplasty, then, there is the potential that "a brand-new worry is being created" (S. W. Davis, 2002: 8). In these accounts, the appearance and sexual function of women's genitalia are rendered *legitimately* problematic and sub-optimal; this part of the body is legitimately commodified, and positioned as "upgradeable" (see Negrin, 2002). More than this, these media have the potential to construct the very nature of problems and their *solutions*, simultaneously. Both the problem of aesthetically "unappealing" genitalia and the desire for better sex have a ready worked-up solution—surgery.

While FGCS might seem relatively arcane, a form of cosmetic surgery very few women would access, and one that is unlikely to become popular, the surgeons I interviewed indicated that media coverage seems to increase demand for their services. This fits with Kathy Davis's (2003: 134) observation that media coverage of new surgical interventions "seduc[es] more individuals to place their bodies under the surgeon's knife" (see also Wolf, 1990). The history of other cosmetic procedures does nothing to dispute this concern. Indeed, as Haiken has commented in her history of cosmetic surgery, individual change can often be "easier" than social change.

> Americans, most of them women, found it easier to alter their own faces than to alter the cultural norms and expectations about aging that confronted them. Together, surgeons and their patients forged a new image of the face-lift as a sensible, practical and relatively simple solution to the social problem of aging. In doing so, they both became producers and products of the modern "culture of narcissism" and created powerful incentives toward cosmetic surgery that are still in place today. (Haiken, 1997: 135–6)

The appearance of FGCS raises important questions about the alteration of the body in the pursuit of pleasure, which I have only started to address. If media coverage can contribute to the nature of, and legitimate, a "new" problem for women, with a ready-made surgical solution, we need to continue to act as "cultural critics" (Bordo, 1993), and question the assumptions on which such surgery rests, and the models of sexuality, bodies, and practices it promotes.

Notes

1. Quotations from data are coded by letter and number: S=surgeon; M=magazine; N=news media; I=Internet material other than "Internet magazines." Numbers were applied sequentially across each data source, starting from 1. In the surgeon extracts, material in parentheses (like this) indicates a best guess as to what was said at that point on the tape.

2. Although there are differences between the datasets (e.g., see K. Davis' [1998] comments about media accounts of cosmetic surgery), my analysis treats all data in the same way—as cultural texts.

3. This point is demonstrated by Blum's (2003: 287) observation that "the surgical patient's shame is intolerable."

4. Breast surgery has been identified as "a means of establishing congruency between the body and mind, or developing an embodied self that was comfortable" (Gagne and McGaughey, 2002: 822).

5. This dualistic construction of mind and body is questioned in Budgeon's (2003) work on young women talking about the possibilities of bodies, identity and practice around cosmetic surgery.

References

Adams, A. (1997) "Moulding Women's Bodies: The Surgeon as Sculptor," in D. S. Wilson and C. M. Laennec (eds.) *Bodily Discursions: Gender, Representations, Technologies,* pp. 59–80. New York: State University of New York Press.

Allotey, P., Manderson, L. and Grover, S. (2001) "The Politics of Female Genital Surgery in Displaced Communities," *Critical Public Health* 11: 189–201.

Berger, A. A. (1998) *Media Analysis Techniques* (2nd edn). Thousand Oaks, CA: Sage.

Blum, V. L. (2003) *Flesh Wounds: The Culture of Cosmetic Surgery.* Berkeley: University of California Press.

Bordo, S. (1993) *Unbearable Weight: Feminism, Western Culture, and the Body.* Berkeley: University of California Press.

Bordo, S. (1997) *Twilight Zones: The Hidden Life of Cultural Images from Plato to O.J.* Berkeley: University of California Press.

Bramwell, R. (2002) "Invisible Labia: The Representation of Female External Genitals in Women's Magazines," *Journal of Sexual and Relationship Therapy* 17: 187–90.

Braun, V., Gavey, N. and McPhillips, K. (2003) "The 'Fair Deal'? Unpacking Accounts of Reciprocity in Heterosex," *Sexualities* 6(2): 237–61.

Braun, V. and Wilkinson, S. (2001) "Socio-cultural Representations of the Vagina," *Journal of Reproductive and Infant Psychology* 19: 17–32.

Braun, V. and Wilkinson, S. (2003) "Liability or Asset? Women Talk about the Vagina," *Psychology of Women Section Review* 5(2): 28–42.

Brown, J. D. and Walsh-Childers, K. (2002) "Effects of Media on Personal and Public Health," in J. Bryant and D. Zillmann (eds.) *Media Effects: Advances in Theory and Research*, 2nd edn, pp. 453–88. Mahwah, NJ: Lawrence Erlbaum Associates.

Budgeon, S. (2003) "Identity as Embodied Event," *Body and Society* 9: 35–55.

Burr, V. (1995) *An Introduction to Social Constructionism.* London: Routledge.

Carpiano, R. M. (2001) "Passive Medicalization: The Case of Viagra and Erectile Dysfunction," *Sociological Spectrum* 21: 441–50.

Connell, R. W. (1997) "Sexual Revolution," in L. Segal (ed.) *New Sexual Agendas*, pp. 60–76. New York: New York University Press.

Davis, K. (1995) *Reshaping the Female Body: The Dilemma of Cosmetic Surgery.* New York: Routledge.

Davis, K. (1998) "Facing the Dilemma," in P. D. Hopkins (ed.) *Sex/Machine: Readings in Culture, Gender and Technology*, pp. 286–305. Bloomington: Indiana University Press.

Davis, K. (2003) *Dubious Equalities and Embodied Differences: Cultural Studies on Cosmetic Surgery.* Lanham, MD: Rowman and Littlefield.

Davis, S. W. (2002) "Loose Lips Sink Ships," *Feminist Studies* 28: 7–35.

D'Emilio, J. and Freedman, E. B. (1997) *Intimate Matters: A History of Sexuality in America*, 2nd edn. Chicago, IL: The University of Chicago Press.

Essen, B. and Johnsdotter, S. (2004) "Female Genital Mutilation in the West: Traditional Circumcision versus Genital Cosmetic Surgery," *Acta Obstetricia et Gynecologica Scandinavica* 83: 611–13.

Frank, A. W. (2003) "Connecting Body Parts: Technoluxe, Surgical Shapings, and Bioethics." Paper presented at the *Vital Politics* Conference, London.

Fraser, S. (2003a) "The Agent Within: Agency Repertoires in Medical Discourse on Cosmetic Surgery," *Australian Feminist Studies* 18: 27–44.

Fraser, S. (2003b) *Cosmetic Surgery, Gender and Culture.* Houndmills: Palgrave Macmillan.

Gagne, P. and McGaughey, D. (2002) "Designing Women—Cultural Hegemony and the Exercise of Power Among Women Who Have Undergone Elective Mammoplasty," *Gender and Society* 16: 814–38.

Gillespie, R. (1996) "Women, the Body and Brand Extension in Medicine: Cosmetic Surgery and the Paradox of Choice," *Women and Health* 24(4): 69–85.

Gilman, S. (1985) *Difference and Pathology: Stereotypes of Sexuality, Race and Madness.* Ithaca, NY: Cornell University Press.

Gilman, S. L. (1998) *Creating Beauty to Cure the Soul.* Durham, NC: Duke University Press.

Gilman, S. L. (1999) *Making the Body Beautiful: A Cultural History of Aesthetic Surgery.* Princeton, NJ: Princeton University Press.

Gimlin, D. L. (2002) *Body Work: Beauty and Self-Image in American Culture.* Berkeley, CA: University of California Press.

Goodman, M. (1996) "Culture, Cohort, and Cosmetic Surgery," *Journal of Women and Aging* 8(2): 55–73.

Gordon, M. (1971) "From an Unfortunate Necessity to a Cult of Mutual Orgasm: Sex in American Marital Education Literature 1830–1940," in J. M. Henslin (eds.) *Studies in the Sociology of Sex*, pp. 53–77. New York: Appleton-Century-Crofts.

Grogan, S. (1999) *Body Image: Understanding Body Dissatisfaction in Men, Women and Children.* London: Routledge.

Haiken, E. (1997) *Venus Envy: A History of Cosmetic Surgery.* Baltimore, MD: The Johns Hopkins University Press.

Haiken, E. (2000) "The Making of the Modern Face: Cosmetic Surgery," *Social Research* 67: 81–93.

Hart, G. and Wellings, K. (2002) "Sexual Behaviour and its Medicalisation: In Sickness and Health," *British Medical Journal* 324: 896–900.

Hawkes, G. (1996) *The Sociology of Sex and Sexuality.* Buckingham: Open University Press.

Heath, S. (1982) *The Sexual Fix.* New York: Schocken Books.

Hollway, W. (1989) *Subjectivity and Method in Psychology: Gender, Meaning and Science*. London: Sage.

Jackson, S. and Scott, S. (2001) "Embodying Orgasm: Gendered Power Relations and Sexual Pleasure," in E. Kaschak and L. Tiefer (eds.) *A New View of Women's Sexual Problems*, pp. 99–110. New York: The Haworth Press.

Jahoda, S. (1995) "Theatres of Madness," in J. Terry and J. Urla (eds.) *Deviant Bodies: Critical Perspectives on Difference in Science and Popular Culture*, pp. 251–76. Bloomington: Indiana University Press.

Kitzinger, S. (1994) *The Year after Childbirth: Surviving and Enjoying the First Year of Motherhood*. Toronto: HarperCollins Publishers.

Manderson, L. (1999) "Local Rites and the Body Politic: Tensions Between Cultural Diversity and Universal Rites," paper presented at the *Sexual Diversity and Human Rights: Beyond Boundaries* conference, Manchester, July.

Moghaddam, P. and Braun, V. (2004) "'Most of us Guys are Raring to go Anytime, Anyplace, Anywhere': Male (and Female) Sexuality in *Cosmopolitan* and *Cleo*," Manuscript under submission.

Negrin, L. (2002) "Cosmetic Surgery and the Eclipse of Identity," *Body and Society* 8: 21–42.

Nicolson, P. (1993) "Public Values and Private Beliefs: Why do some Women Refer Themselves for Sex Therapy?" in J. M. Ussher and C. D. Baker (eds.) *Psychological Perspectives on Sexual Problems: New Directions in Theory and Practice*, pp. 56–76. London: Routledge.

Potts, A. (2000) "Coming, Coming, Gone: A Feminist Deconstruction of Heterosexual Orgasm," *Sexualities* 3: 55–76.

Reinholtz, R. K. and Muehlenhard, C. L. (1995) "Genital Perceptions and Sexual Activity in a College Population," *Journal of Sex Research* 32: 155–65.

Roberts, C., Kippax, S., Spongberg, M. and Crawford, J. (1996) "'Going Down': Oral Sex, Imaginary Bodies and HIV," *Body and Society* 2(3): 107–24.

Seidman, S. (1991) *Romantic Longings: Love in America, 1830–1980*. New York: Routledge.

Seidman, S. (1992) *Embattled Eros: Sexual Politics and Ethics in Contemporary America*. New York: Routledge.

Sheldon, S. and Wilkinson, S. (1998) "Female Genital Mutilation and Cosmetic Surgery: Regulating Non-therapeutic Body Modification," *Bioethics* 12: 263–85.

Sullivan, D. A. (2001) *Cosmetic Surgery: The Cutting Edge of Commercial Medicine in America*. New Brunswick, NJ: Rutgers University Press.

Terry, J. (1995) "Anxious Slippages Between 'Us' and 'Them': A Brief History of the Scientific Search for Homosexual Bodies," in J. Terry and J. Urla (eds.) *Deviant Bodies: Critical Perspectives on Difference in Science and Popular Culture*, pp. 129–69. Bloomington: Indiana University Press.

Tiefer, L. (1995) *Sex Is Not a Natural Act and Other Essays*. Boulder, CO: Westview Press.

Tiefer, L. (1997) "Medicine, Morality, and the Public Management of Sexual Matters," in L. Segal (ed.) *New Sexual Agendas*, pp. 103–12. New York: New York University Press.

Tiefer, L. (2000) "The Social Construction and Social Effects of Sex Research: The Sexological Model of Sexuality," in C. B. Travis and J. W. White (eds.) *Sexuality, Society, and Feminism*, pp. 79–107. Washington, DC: American Psychological Association.

Toerien, M. and Wilkinson, S. (2004) "Exploring the Depilation Norm: A Qualitative Questionnaire Study of Women's Body Hair Removal," *Qualitative Research in Psychology* 1: 69–92.

Weeks, J. (1985) *Sexuality and Its Discontents: Meanings, Myths and Modern Sexualities*. London: Routledge & Kegan Paul.

White, J. W., Bondurant, B. and Travis, C. B. (2000) "Social Constructions of Sexuality: Unpacking Hidden Meanings," in C. B. Travis and J. W. White (eds.) *Sexuality, Society, and Feminism*, pp. 11–33. Washington, DC: American Psychological Association.

Wolf, N. (1990) *The Beauty Myth*. London: Vintage.

18 Max Beck

My Life as an Intersexual

When I was born, the doctors couldn't tell my parents what I was: They couldn't tell if I was a boy or a girl. Between my legs they found "a rudimentary phallus" and "fused labio-scrotal folds." They ran their tests, they poked and prodded, and they cut open my belly, removed my gonads, and sent them off to Pathology. My parents sat in the hospital cafeteria, numb, their hearts as cold as the Manhattan February outside.

All they had wanted was a healthy baby. That's all anybody who is pregnant or trying to get pregnant wants, right?

"Are you hoping for a boy or a girl?"
"It doesn't matter, so long as it's healthy."

My parents had struggled for years to have children—my mother had suffered through three miscarriages and a still-birth—and all that time, through all those tears, they prayed and prayed for a healthy baby. Too late, they realized they'd meant normal.

I *was* healthy. Medical records from that grim period describe me as "a well-developed, well-nourished infant in no acute distress." Every mother's dream.

After five weeks of study and surgery, they weren't any closer to the truth; mine was a fuzzy picture. Not even the almighty gene provided any clear answers, since it was discovered that I was a mosaic, with some cells in my body having the XY genotype and others having XO. The decision was made to raise me female.

Could my parents do that? Could they ever hope, after all they had been through, to "raise me female"? What sort of instruction is that anyway?

"Feed the baby every two hours, burp well after feeding, and raise it female."

Who gives a thought to such things? You have a son, you have a daughter, you take him or her home, and you get on with your life, period. Consciously, deliberately "raising me female"—it's like consciously, deliberately breathing.

So they took me home, named me Judy, and did whatever it was they did, whatever it was they knew how. I grew into a rough-and-tumble tomboy, a precocious, insecure, tree-climbing, dress-hating show-off with a Prince Valiant haircut and razor-sharp wit who was constantly being called "little boy" and "young man."

I never gave a thought to what went through my mother's heart and mind every

Max Beck, "My Life as an Intersexual." Posted at www.pbs.org, 2001. Reprinted by kind permission of Tamara Beck, on behalf of the estate of Max Beck.

time this happened, this common misperception-that-wasn't. What did she see every time she looked at me? Did she watch my entire childhood, every developmental milestone, every triumph, every tear, through a darkening lens of gender? I imagine memories of me, all those special Kodak moments, all captured in my mother's mind in eerie photonegative. I don't know how my father felt or feels about it; he has never spoken about it except to reinterpret my mother's feelings.

I quickly came to understand that that tomboy—the gender identity with which I had escaped childhood—was less acceptable in adolescence. Yearly visits to endocrinologists and pediatric urologists, lots of genital poking and prodding, and my mother's unspoken guilt and shame had all served to distance me considerably from my body: I was a walking head. In retrospect, it seems odd that a tomboy should have been so removed from her body. But instead of a daily, muddy, physical celebration of life, my tomboyhood was marked by a reckless disregard for the body and a strong desire to be annihilated. So I reached adolescence with no physical sense of self, and no desire to make that connection. All around me, my peers and former playmates were dating, fooling around, giving and getting hickeys, while I, whose puberty came in pill form, watched aghast from the sidelines.

What *was* I? The doctors and surgeons assured me I was a girl, that I just wasn't yet "finished." I don't think they gave a thought to what that statement would mean to me and my developing gender identity, my developing sense of self. The doctors who told me I was an "unfinished girl" were so focused on the lie—so invested in selling me "girl"—that I doubt

they ever considered the effect a word like "unfinished" would have on me.

I knew I was incomplete. I could see that compared to—well, compared to everyone!—I was numb from the neck down. When would I be finished?

The "finishing" the doctors talked about occurred during my teen years—hormone replacement therapy and a vaginoplasty. Still, the only thing that felt complete was my isolation. Now the numbness below my neck was real—a maze of unfeeling scar tissue.

I wandered through that labyrinth for another ten years, with a gender identity and desires born of those medical procedures. I began to experience myself as a sort of sexual Frankenstein's monster.

Not that I was having much sex. I was incredibly inhibited about my body, the scars, the mysterious medical condition and history that I—the patient!—knew next to nothing about. Sexual experiences were few and far between. At 21 I found myself, a college dropout and a runaway, in bed with an older woman, my second sexual partner and the first naked woman I had ever seen or touched. The differences between our bodies were staggering. Too numb and shaken to even be embarrassed or shy, I showed her what worked, how much pressure to use, what to touch, what not to touch. She listened and learned, and gave me similar lessons in her anatomy. And then, one night in bed, she whispered playfully in my ear: "Boy, Jude, you sure are weird."

Exactly.

When I boarded the plane that would take me back to the East Coast, back to the angry family and the patient university I had fled via Greyhound bus weeks earlier, I carried the knowledge that I was a lesbian. No single thing I had ever learned about myself could feel as important, carry such weight, or offer such healing. Everything that didn't make sense in my tortured world—even the scars—blossomed into perfect clarity when viewed through that lens: I am a lesbian! My nerves sang.

But I also carried another truth, a terrible corollary to the first secret: I cannot be with women. For being with a woman revealed that I wasn't—"finished," a girl, normal—and (so much worse) revealed what I was—a freak, a monster, an anomaly.

While my single male partner had been relatively nonplussed about my manmade parts, my single female partner couldn't help but notice and comment on the fact that I was different. I used these ridiculously inadequate sample sizes to draw the painfully obvious, jaded, bitter conclusion: Men wouldn't care or comment on my scars; focused only on having someplace to "stick it," they would barely notice any difference between me and other women they might have had sex with, since they simply wouldn't be paying that kind of attention. Women, on the other hand, would notice immediately the dreadful gulf between normal and me and run the other way.

Not surprisingly, I tried to kill myself.

In the days before Prozac and HMOs, recovery from a suicide attempt meant three months in a community mental health center, time I used to resign myself to a meaningless life with a man I couldn't love. Once released, I continued to take my self-loathing to therapy, bedding down with (and eventually marrying) the next guy to come along.

At this time, during a routine check of my immunization records for a job I was applying for at a hospital, I obtained some old medical records and learned things my parents and doctors had never intended me

to know. Desperately confused, my therapist and I had sent for and received the neonatal surgical records that outlined the medical history described above. What had been an embarrassingly large clitoris was suddenly revealed to have been a hideously deformed penis, and the possibility of ever being with a woman became even more remote; the wondrous, wonderful identity that had lasted all of a plane flight from LAX to JFK—lesbian—was robbed again, seemingly forever.

Now fully convinced I was a monster, I stayed with my husband, certain no one else could ever love or want me. Until, thankfully, I met Tamara. With all the force and subtlety of a tsunami, she flooded my senses, roared through my heart and my bed. I found myself swept into divorce, scandal, debt, and—such unimagined bliss—her.

Coming out as a lesbian was the single most powerful act I had ever undertaken. Despite social and family pressures, despite a mountain of shame surrounding my queered genitals, I did it, and my liberation—I thought—was complete. I wasn't an "unfinished girl"—I was butch!

But a proud butch identity and a powerful femme at my side weren't enough; Frankenstein's monster would not be propitiated. After the "honeymoon" period of our relationship, the old self-loathing returned, self-loathing and self-destructiveness. How could I be a butch if I was "really" a man? How could I call myself "lesbian" when I wasn't even a woman? I felt like an imposter, a fraud, and now more than ever, a freak.

Another hospitalization for depression—a shorter stay this time, thanks to the advent of antidepressants and HMOs. A dark chrysalis period, focused on another, deeper coming out: coming out as intersexed.

Tomboy, unfinished girl, walking head, Frankenstein, butch—these were all just so many wonderful/terrible, sharp/ill-fitting suits; the body wearing them was and is transgendered, hermaphroditic, queer. And an important, even essential element of that queerness was the trauma that accompanied it, the medicalization, the scars, the secrecy, the shame. I was born a tiny, helpless almost-boy, but the way my world responded to me is what made and makes me intersexed.

In March of 1998, after over a decade of therapy, I decided to switch to testosterone and transition to male. Since 1996, I had been an active part of the intersex community, and by deciding to transition, I thought I was copping out. I felt like a deserter, a coward, fleeing the frontlines of the gender war. As a politically aware intersexual, I felt it was my duty to be as brazenly androgynous, as visibly hermaphroditic as possible. But to return to the body/suit metaphor, I was starting to feel very naked and very cold. My "naked" body was scaring little old ladies out of public restrooms, making seemingly simple tasks, such as shopping, surprisingly difficult.

"Is this your mother's credit card, young man?"

So I've found a new suit—a different name, the "other" hormone, a different letter on my driver's license—that fits better, that's tailored to me.

Tamara and I have been together for seven years now, despite my—now "our"—continued struggle with my issues of shame and anger, my muddled, muddied, fuzzy gender. We married in February 2000 and now have a baby girl, Alder, whom we conceived using Tamara's egg and a donor's sperm. We both still identify as lesbians, so "becoming" heterosexual is not without its challenges. Tamara constantly feels she is masquerading and must explain and challenge those assumptions. In fact, my change of clothes has forced her to reexamine her entire wardrobe—both literally and figuratively.

Looking in the mirror every morning, I am reminded of just how outward outward appearances are. Moving through the world, I'm just a guy: a husband, a father, a computer geek, a manager, looking forward to becoming a grandfather and a sage. Does the Y chromosome in (only) some of my cells and the facial hair I'm growing make me any less a girl, a tomboy, a lesbian, a butch, a woman? I have worn all of these identities, so surely they are mine, even if they no longer fit, even if they were never my birthright, never mine to wear. I cannot undo my history, and I am sick to death of regretting it, so those hard-won honorifics will have to stand. When I look in a mirror, I see all of them.

19 Jamison Green

Part of the Package
Ideas of Masculinity among Male-Identified Transpeople

Female-to-male (FTM) transsexual people are the least studied group of all when it comes to masculinity. While many writers mention transsexualism (albeit superficially) in their analyses of gender, my research shows that so far, only Holly Devor, Henry Rubin, and Salvador Vidal-Ortiz, all sociologists, have (separately) designed, conducted, analyzed, and published studies focusing on transsexual men. Devor's 1989 book *Gender Blending: Confronting the Limits of Duality* studied "females who, although they thought of themselves as women, didn't always successfully communicate that fact to others" (Devor 1997, xv). That study attempted to make sense of that phenomenon, and the framework for Devor's analysis was the dominant gender schema as informed by a feminist interpretation of gender reformative ideology, concluding that

> were people to become no longer distinguishable on the basis of sex, were all gender choices open to all people, were there to cease to be a cognitive system which measured the world in gendered units, the material basis for sexism would cease to exist. (P. 154)

Years later, in her work on transsexual men (1997), Devor expressed a slightly different view of gender:

> Many people who live their daily lives as men carry with them wombs, ovaries, and breasts. Some people live as men without the aid of virilizing hormones. Nonetheless, they live as men. The possession of gender confirming sex characteristics enlarges the sphere in which such persons may move uncontested as men, but the lack of them does not eliminate such persons from the ranks of men. . . . What my contact with transsexual people has taught me is that the time is upon us to reevaluate how we think about gender, sex, and sexuality. It now seems perfectly clear to me that we live in a world which is far more diverse than any number of simplistic dichotomies can describe. . . . It is time that we begin to recognize that there are far more "mistakes of society" than there are "mistakes of nature." (Pp. 607–8)

The difference between these two observations is rooted in Devor's understanding and acceptance of the validity of the masculinity expressed by the transmen she

Excerpted from the original. Jamison Green, "Part of the Package: Ideas of Masculinity among Male-Identified Transpeople," *Men and Masculinities* 7, no. 3 (January 2005): 291–299. Copyright © 2005 SAGE Publications. Reprinted with permission of SAGE Publications.

studied. She is pointing out that social validation of gender identity is important for people who may have been gender blending at some time in their lives but who found that landing firmly on one side of the fence rather than the other (in this case, the masculine side), at least in most social contexts, is important and meaningful for some people and that the task of doing so is neither trivial nor disordered nor unnatural, and it is a mistake of society not to recognize this.

Vidal-Ortiz's research with transmen is reflected in his 2002 chapter "Queering Sexuality and Doing Gender: Transgender Men's Identification with Gender and Sexuality" in *Gendered Sexualities*. Rubin's work is contained in his 2003 book *Self-Made Men: Identity and Embodiment among Transsexual Men*. Both these studies, along with Devor's work, crack open the heretofore hidden world of men who were born with female bodies. Rather than comment on that work here, I encourage readers to engage this material directly. Also, watch for the ongoing work of Aaron H. Devor, now that Holly has undertaken the transition to male himself. I'm sure he will have further insights on masculinity as time goes on.

Two other books are important to mention here because of the originality of the authors' stances with respect to the existing body of literature. First, Judith Halberstam's *Female Masculinity* (1998). Halberstam approaches the topic from the perspective of literary analysis and social commentary ("cultural studies") based on the author's experience of butch lesbians, drag kings, FTM transgendered and transsexual people, and a close reading of film and literature presentations of women with masculine characteristics or identities. Full of interesting and important observations, Halberstam's book is also focused on the interpretations

of male presentation from within female bodies and the sometimes subtle, sometimes brutal judgments different communities of people can make about gender expression. For example, in lesbian space, drag king performance often satirizes masculinity, particularly white, middle-class masculinity, replayed in hyperbolic satire and parody, exposing the vulnerability of male midlife crisis (pp. 259–60) or poking fun at male homosexual panic (pp. 265). Black and Latino drag kings have other cultural stereotypes to play off of in addition to these, such as gangsta, stud, or macho lover, and Halberstam notes that most white drag kings (though not all, to be sure!), when not playing cultural icons like Elvis or John Travolta, seem to have trouble making theater out of their presentations (pp. 248). The net effect of Halberstam's observations are, to me, that there are legitimate taxonomies for representing and interpreting female masculinities, and there is still a struggle playing out between ideas of legitimacy of masculinity represented by female bodies and the very real analyses of masculine supremacy, masculine normalcy, and/or masculine dominance that are made possible by examining masculinity as experienced from within a female body. She also rightly notes that "there are transsexuals, and we are not all transsexuals; gender is not fluid, and gender variance is not the same wherever we may find it. Specificity is all. . . . Who . . . can afford transition? . . . Who can afford metaphors? I suggest we think carefully, butches and FTMs alike, about the kinds of men or masculine beings that we become and lay claim to: alternative masculinities, ultimately, will fail to change existing gender hierarchies to the extent to which they fail to be feminist, antiracist, and queer" (p. 173). These are ideas that I have written about repeatedly in the pages of the *FTM Newsletter* since 1991 in an effort to encourage an analysis of masculinity within the burgeoning FTM community. That effort has not yet come to fruition.

Jason Cromwell's *Transmen & FTMs* (1999) is an insider's view with an anthropological perspective. Cromwell immersed himself in the west coast FTM world in the 1990s (though he transitioned much earlier) and records his observations and analysis. His anger at being marginalized his entire life, even while functioning as a white, middle-class male, comes through strongly. He analyzes the dominant medical discourse about FTM transsexualism and deftly displays its biases and shortcomings. He gives an idea of the diversity and variety of interpretations that are possible for all facets of life through FTM experience. Hegemonic masculinity is not a universal goal for transmen, contrary to the opinion of several medical professionals and Janice Raymond. While Cromwell does not directly discuss the concept or meaning of *masculinity* or the nature of assumptions of masculinity among FTM-identified people, he does present the first insider's attempt at a comprehensive view of FTM experience within the context of North American culture, and he frequently refers to masculinity and maleness as markers of that experience.

One of the greatest challenges in discussing masculinity is the contemporary preoccupation with gender as a system of power. As I have written previously,

> If we agree that man and woman are words that signify male-bodied or female-bodied people (respectively), or at least people whose clothed bodies appear to be male or female, then we may also agree that the terms man and male and woman and female refer to specific types of bodies (or representations of those bodies) in a way that connotes a social role, such as the wearing of certain clothing that indicates the body. But through our agreements we are not creating a capacity to observe the gender of the people to whom we are referring. It is a logical leap to suppose that the man who is male is also masculine, or the woman who is female is also feminine, regardless of the clothing he or she is wearing. If gender distinguishes the "nonbiological features resulting from a person's ascribed status of either female or male" (Doyle and Paludi, 1998, p. 6), then gender studies are focused on the social differences between persons with (presumably) male and female bodies. This is not really talking about gender, but about sociology and politics, which are fine, important topics, but they still are not gender. Like the notion that "femininity unfolds naturally, whereas masculinity must be achieved" (Herdt, G., quoted in Gilmore, 1990, p. 146), our biases about gender are rooted in biological theory, sociobiological functions, and the extent of our resistance to these positions.

We find it easy to trivialize gender expression. The very term "gender role" connotes its pliability, its lack of serious reality for students of social science and others concerned with definitions and the social processes. At the same time, the baseline values of Western culture have encouraged us to trivialize gender diversity as a means of retaining social order, particularly with respect to sexual behavior, as reflected in the widespread assumptions that men with feminine characteristics are homosexual, women with masculine characteristics are lesbians (and all lesbians want to be men!),

men who cross-dress are homosexual (that is, they want to be women), and female cross-dressers simply do not exist. Here, the conflation of assumed meanings for bodies and derived signals for gender becomes the basis for misinformation because for someone who does not understand gender diversity there is supposed to be a correlation between a body and its gender and all that gender is "supposed" to stand for: sexual orientation, sexual behavior, physical appearance, social role.

When it comes to gender, if we are invested in the dichotomy between masculine and feminine as a system of socially constructed power distribution, we will never be able to value the naturalness or artfulness of an individual's gender expression because we will always suspect the individual's motives: anything out of the ordinary must be a quest for power, and is therefore victimizing someone. But gender, like race, is not a power system in itself; gender, like race or like language, is a physical trait that some people use to gain or distribute power. Like language, our gender is both natural and artificial; the ability to have gender and language both reside in the natural or native beingness of individuals, whether their expressed gender reinforces, contradicts, or is randomly confused by an observer's cultural concepts of their body, or whether their ability to speak is compromised by physical deformity, or they happen to speak a different language than their listener can comprehend. (Green 2001, 61–65)

I do not believe that it is gender that gives certain individuals certain types of power in society but that actual bodies in concert with other arbitrary factors like heritage, wealth, and particular skills and abilities do so. When we focus on the proposition that dichotomous gender is the bellwether of social privilege, and when we view transsexual people as social constructions of social constructions in an attempt to understand how gender conventions are learned or manipulated, we actually deny the incredible potential of gender variance and its natural diversity, and we categorically deny both transindividuals and non-transindividuals agency in experiencing or freely expressing their own genders. We also set up the paradigm that women are good and men are bad; hence, the constant refrain of apology from within the ranks of profeminist men, and the teasing, goading, and baiting that women engage in when criticizing men who are perceived as SNAGs, or sensitive, new-age guys. Making everyone else wrong is easy; understanding difference as complementary rather than oppositional seems to be a much more difficult project.

In the summer of 2002, I asked a group of eight transmen at an FTM International meeting a series of six questions about their notions of masculinity, and I also had similar dialog with four other individual transmen, privately, outside of the group context. In addition, I asked the same questions of four non-transmen, and I was intrigued by the similarities in the responses. I would not claim this investigation was scientific in any way, so the results remain anecdotal; I offer them to further the discussion.

First, I asked whether maleness and masculinity are the same thing. The universal response was "no." I would suggest, then, that the majority of the literature about masculinity (at least, that which I have reviewed) is not sufficiently subtle or specific in its use of terminology. In other words, I think most of the literature makes an assumption that only male bodies express masculinity.

Second, I asked whether masculinity depends on having a male body or on having a penis. Again, the universal response was "no." I must admit my sample was somewhat skewed since I expected the transmen to resist this type of essentialism, and the non-transmen that I asked about this are sufficiently exposed to transgender culture and sensibilities (though none of them is transgendered or transsexual himself) to possess a level of sophistication that I would not expect to see in the mainstream culture. Because of the kind of questions I am asked in university and college human sexuality courses (I lecture to roughly thirty classes every year), I think that most people still believe that the body is the marker of gender and that gender and sexuality are dictated by the genitalia; thus, I believe most non-transmen or nonqueer people who have not had to analyze some aspect of gender variance in making sense of their relationship to society would indicate that a male body was a prerequisite for masculinity, in spite of a more common recognition that women are more capable today of cultivating masculine qualities without becoming male or even butch. I suspect that the "normative" quality of masculine subjectivity (as critiqued in Whitehead [2002], May [1998], and Bourdieu [1998/2001]) is informing these assumptions, and it requires either a marginalized or specifically reeducated point of view to observe or perceive things differently. Vidal-Ortiz's (2002) work explores this much more deeply.

Third, I asked, "How did you, as a transman or FTM (or man—if the subject was nontrans), come to understand your masculinity?" Here, there were two different classes of response: the first was external—that is "people told me"; and the second was internal—that is "I felt different from girls or women." It was interesting to me that all of the non-transmen noted that the internal understanding was primary for them and only three of the twelve transmen felt this way. The rest of the transmen (numbering nine) stated that they knew they were masculine because other people told them so. Of these nine, five further stated that they also felt different from girls or women. For the non-transmen, when I prodded them about being told they were masculine, they said, "Well, sure, of course I got told that," but this event was minimized because of their assumption that it was because of their male body that the masculine label was placed on them. In their minds, they had either had not earned that label yet or it was a "natural given," which indicated to me either that even well-educated non-transmen could fall back on normative presumptions or essentialist positions in moments of unconsciousness or that they were aware of the normative presumptions on the part of others and expected that essentialist prescriptions would be projected onto them because of these presumptions.

Fourth, I asked, "Where does masculinity come from?" Most of the responses indicated that since masculinity is determined by behaviors or actions—that is, by extroverted expressions of qualities that are ascribed to males—and that these qualities and associated roles are based on the expectations placed on people with male bodies in a given culture, that masculinity comes from a person's ability to correlate his or her behaviors and/or actions with those expected from people with male bodies. I thought this was interesting considering the fact that everyone had also said masculinity was not contingent on possession of a male body; therefore, I caution readers against leaping to the conclusion that these respondents believe a male body is required for masculine expression in spite of their declaration that it is not. I want to emphasize that the respondents seemed very clear that masculinity is judged based on cultural understandings of maleness ascribed to male bodies, but the expression of masculinity is not solely the province of male bodies. There was also no indication among the respondents that there was any negative association with respect to female bodies that expressed masculine qualities or behaviors, and that applies equally to the responses of non-transmen. This group seemed to be particularly neutral with respect to sexist attitudes about masculinity.

Fifth, I asked, "How is masculinity expressed?" It was interesting to me that the respondents here resorted to stereotypical divisions, noting that masculinity is expressed in body language, behavior, occupation, speech, vocalization, inflection, content, and cultural stereotypes of appropriate actions for people with male bodies. The understanding seems to be that if one is to be properly interpreted by others as male, then one must know the language of masculinity. Transmen, on the whole, did not seem particularly concerned about being perceived as insufficiently masculine, but they did worry about being perceived as male. Early transition transmen (those with one to five years living as men) indicated that they were more likely to deliberately exhibit behaviors designed to communicate masculinity when they were worried about being perceived as not male in male-dominated spaces, potentially in the workplace or in superficial social exchanges such as at a gasoline service station or a hardware store. Transmen who had been living as men for more than five years did not have the same anxiety. Transmen who had very male appearances commented on the necessity for self-confidence as a factor in one's expressed masculinity quotient: an appearance of maleness did not always correlate to a strong sense of masculinity within a subject, nor did a subject's masculinity as perceived by others (in the group setting) necessarily correlate to the person's sense of his own masculinity, which is separate from his sense of himself as male.

Finally, I asked, "What does it mean to be masculine or to have masculinity?" Here is where the greatest divergence between transmen and non-transmen appeared. Transmen reflected on the changes in their experience since acquiring a socially readable masculinity, and they were quite conscious of the ways in which masculinity is interpreted as power, of the ways it confers privilege, but also of the ways masculinity placed them at risk. Part of that risk is the violence that men visit on other men, but part of it is the fear of being persecuted as transmen, too. For the non-transmen, having greater continuity in their male bodies, and possibly less fully developed feminist consciousness compared to transmen, having masculinity meant a particular psychic destiny that is opposite and complementary to that of femininity. To them, masculinity meant a trajectory of unity, separation, and reunion, a journey or a quest, not a state or quality, but something lived. These men expected to live lives marked by separations from other people, particularly women, culminating (if they are lucky) in a reunion, symbolized by a relationship with the right partner (male or female). They viewed the feminine as the maintenance of unity, integration, relationship, and communion. These are very Jungian concepts, heroic in the Joseph Campbell sense of mythological underpinnings to social organization, even in today's society, and they show a different kind of mental organization with respect to the men's reflections on the meaning of their own masculinity as compared with that of transmen.

All this leads me to theorize that masculinity is a socially negotiable quality that is understood through agreed-on symbols (such as the body and its secondary sex characteristics) and signals (such as clothing, behaviors, occupations, speech patterns, etc., understood within a given cultural context) that together inform other people in that context concerning the individual person's status in a given group. However, I think this is not a simple equation. High masculinity does not always equate to high status in every social situation. And high masculinity does not necessarily equate to elevated social power, or dominance, either. Furthermore, there are multiple taxonomies of masculinity, as Halberstam (1998) and Whitehead (2002) explicate, within given cultures. The idea that high masculinity is equivalent to high testosterone, and therefore may be toxic, is reductive and unnecessarily divisive. From my personal transmale perspective, I believe masculinity is a collaborative project that starts with innate characteristics and behaviors (whether the expressor has a female body or a male body), and these are emphasized or deemphasized by social interactions (both sexual and nonsexual) in such a way that the innate characteristics and behaviors are magnified, elaborated on, or suppressed, and ultimately the individual internalizes these characteristics and behaviors, incorporating them into her or his personality. The measure of social adaptability,

acceptability, and success that an individual experiences with this constellation of characteristics and behaviors is dependent on multiple factors, particularly the extent to which the individual is capable of empathy and consciousness in the application of his or her own values and beliefs to the social relationships in which one engages. Masculinity by itself is not the problem for feminism; maleness is not the problem for women. The problem is the paradigm that frames females as inferior and encourages men (and women) to see maleness and masculinity as "not feminine."

In the August 24, 1995, issue of the *San Francisco Bay Times*, reporter Jack Fertig wrote an article titled "The World's First FTM Conference Held in SF" in which he noted that

> FTMs [are] some of the sexiest men on the planet. In a way, they are real men as no other men are. For the most part, straight men take their masculinity for granted, acting out scripts without questioning. Gay men have had to struggle with sexual issues and have a certain amount of freedom and insight. FTMs have had to construct their masculinity from the ground up, to overcome everything around them just to be men. Our mythos of masculinity tells us that this is what a "real man" is— self-creative, independent, willing to stand up to convention to be himself, to live a life of honest responsibility.

The reason Fertig (1995) found FTMs to be "some of the sexiest men on the planet" is that they are men who have the capacity to fully integrate feminine experience, qualities, and behaviors (however limited or unexpressed in their masculine psyches) without feeling threatened. They have a very real sense of the compatibility of the two extremes of gender because they have brought them together in dynamic combination, and they have found a home in their bodies for the conscious balance they have found in their psyches. For transmen, it is the bodily confirmation of the male identity that matters. Once that has been achieved to a transman's satisfaction, he can start to integrate his personality in the same ways that non-transpeople do. Trans or non-trans, when individuals realize that they can give up the struggle of trying to prove who they are, or how butch they are, or how male, or how masculine, they can realize that whatever qualities of character they have, they are all part of the package.

References

Bourdieu, Pierre. 1998 [2001]. *Masculine domination.* Stanford, CA: Stanford University Press.

Cromwell, Jason. 1999. *Transmen & FTMs: Identities, bodies, genders, & sexualities.* Urbana: University of Illinois Press.

Devor, Holly. 1989. *Gender blending: Confronting the limits of duality.* Bloomington: Indiana University Press.

———. 1997. *FTM: Female-to-male transsexuals in society.* Bloomington: Indiana University Press.

Doyle, James A., and Michele A. Paludi. 1998. *Sex & gender: The human experience.* 4th ed. New York: McGraw-Hill.

Gilmore, David D. 1990. *Manhood in the making: Cultural concepts of masculinity.* New Haven, CT: Yale University Press.

Green, Jamison. 2001. The art and nature of gender. In *Unseen genders: Beyond the binaries,* edited by F. Haynes and T. McKenna, 59–70. New York: Peter Lang.

Halberstam, Judith. 1998. *Female masculinity.* Durham, NC: Duke University Press.

Haynes, F., and T. McKenna, eds. 2001. *Unseen genders: Beyond the binaries.* New York: Peter Lang.

May, Larry. 1998. *Masculinity & morality.* New York: Cornell University Press.

Rubin, Henry. 2003. *Self-made men: Identity and embodiment among transsexual men.* Nashville, TN: Vanderbilt University Press.

Vidal-Ortiz, Salvador. 2002. Queering sexuality and doing gender: Transgender men's identification with gender and sexuality. In *Gendered sexualities,* edited by Patricia Gagne and Richard Tewksbury, vol. 6, 181–233. San Diego, CA: Elsevier.

Whitehead, Stephen M. 2002. *Men and masculinities.* Cambridge, UK: Polity.

20 Sean

Diary of an Anorexic

It is simple. It is complicated. "It" is my ethnic heritage. Many have written about their own experiences of being mixed, but my own experience is one that I have never seen addressed, nor has anyone I've met ever shared.

It is a specific disease associated with many insecurities and it remains an enigma to those who cannot understand it. This disease is anorexia nervosa. Many will wonder, well, what does anorexia have anything to do with one's ethnicity? In my case, it had plenty. It became the solution to many of my insecurities about being part Filipino and all that it entailed. At its onset I was barely aware of its source, but as the years progressed, the disease advancing to frightening lows, I began to seek answers to this problem. I came to the sad conclusion that it stemmed from my feelings of inferiority about the part of me that is not white.

It is true that there have been many teens and young women who came out of those years relatively unscathed and unaffected by the media, literature and music geared towards filling their young heads with messages to be thin, desired, accepted and successful. But there are those of us who did not escape unharmed, and this is about one young woman who failed miserably in shutting out these messages.

I was further burdened by having to prove to the world that she was strong and completely unlike the stereotypes of Filipino women often seen on TV or in the movies. What are these stereotypes? That Filipino women are poor, uneducated, work abroad as domestics, prostitutes, are treated as slaves and are physically abused. And on the other end of the spectrum, there are the rich socialites who are vacuous, spoiled and intellectually lazy. One who stands out as an example lived in Malacanang Palace owning thousands of pairs of shoes. Where was the middle ground?

One can imagine my frustration in trying to find positive stereotypes when on a popular sitcom, a character made a rather racist comment about Pinays being domestics as if this were a norm for that group of people. I now realize that I only need to look around me and there are many positive role models, but at the time I was merely a child who had a very limited imagination. Admittedly, I was and still am rather sensitive. I would like to think that Rosa Parks was sensitive in the same way. Allow me this delusion for I would like to think that I am raising some important points regarding the women from my Asian side. And that one of the small steps to providing young women like me more positive media images is to object to what is being played as reality.

I saw myself not as white, not fully Filipino but a mix of these two seemingly

---

Sean, "Diary of an Anorexic." Originally posted at www.eurasiannation.com, December 2003–January 2004.

different disparate colors and cultures. I have always known that I was not white enough to be white and not Filipino enough to be Filipino. Someone who is of mixed ethnicity can appreciate this assessment. But I did relate culturally to the Filipino side because by nature, I have always been for the underdog. I am not going to get into a historical diatribe but what is worth mentioning is that Filipinos have been the underdog for literally thousands of years.

So, here I was, a pre-teen, virtually a tabula rasa when it came to ideas about the world. And still as a teen, I was just as if not more susceptible to media messages. I remember seeing for the first time the movie, *Full Metal Jacket*. I still remember the prostitute begging for the Black man not to have sex with her because he was "beaucoup big." Even though she portrayed a Vietnamese woman, she still resembled someone Filipino. I was not equipped with the sophistication of an adult. In my mind, they were inextricably the same. And so, shame was insidiously hatching subconsciously which will come to full fruition later in the form of the disease.

Thereafter, I picked up on little things like reading somewhere that the *Oxford English Dictionary*'s definition for Filipina is one who is a domestic; that mail order brides existed; that there have been horror stories arising from this sort of marriage arrangement; that other Filipinos deemed native features to be inferior; that Filipinas who work in the Middle East are abused and sometimes murdered; that Filipinos in the Philippines are very poor and are seen by the rest of Southeast Asia as the relative to be ashamed of; that there are so many indignities suffered by many Pinays because they are poor and uneducated.

Coincidentally, this was when I started college when I had often been asked "what are you?" At this point, I had started to diet more vigorously "just to lose a few pounds on my waist." This was what I told friends and family. Then, not being aware of the relationship of the rising shame and my desire to lose weight, I kept on losing more, which made me feel powerful and ironically, invincible. How can one be invincible and powerful while being rail-thin and looking as weak as a hungry third world child? The reason lay in having control over something which at the time was my weight. And that there were not many Filipina-Americans who have achieved this (in my mind, this was something to be proud of).

I have read many articles and books about this illness, and they have often indicated that anorexia is a middle-class white woman's disease. Well, there you go! I had a white woman's disease! I was that much farther from being and looking Filipino! This was great. Everything was wonderful until I realized I had dropped to a weight so low that people suspected that I was fatally ill with some incurable disease. Of course, this was not too far from the truth: anorexia is a disease and many of those who suffer from it never recover to a normal and healthy life.

What does being asked "what are you?" have anything to do with anorexia? To begin with, I had no real identity I could claim. I was neither and both. In junior high, I was like a freak—an unidentifiable person who happened to be a rather masculine girl. I did not care about make-up, fashion nor did I engage in girly activities. I was too busy playing with the guys and getting mud all over me. Still, there was a kernel of desire to be "pretty" and to be talked about by some of the boys in their secret chats about the pretty girls in school. I then equated this lack of appeal to my being mixed, having gone to an almost all white school. I am listing my train of thought here. The part of me which was unattractive must have been the Filipino part. In that case, that Filipino part had to go. So, by the end of high school when I did finally have the courage to want to be attractive and smart and desirable, I experimented with my weight for what seemed to be an inexplicable reason back then. I found that by losing weight on a body that was not fat to begin with, I was on my way to achieving that waspy waist which to me was literally what it was, WASPy: White Anglo Saxon Protestant-y. Considering that I was and am Catholic, this was, as you can imagine, a real stretch.

College was an eye opener and dare I say, a liberating period in my life. Not only was I in a diverse environment but I was away from the protective enclave of my family. I was able to lose all the weight I wanted. I was able to re-invent myself. But was I able to, really? In my mind, I was doing just that: re-inventing myself. But to others, I was an anorexic Eurasian young woman who was neither white nor Asian. I can see that now but not then. In college it seemed that all the women dieted: Caucasians, Asians, African-Americans, Latinas. So, it made it that much easier to justify this obsession. And by golly, I was going to be thinner than all of them. By being thinner, I made myself feel superior, a feeling that had been alien and elusive to me since I can't remember when. Losing weight became an addiction because who would not want to feel superior and better than everyone else? Except I was not—I was just pathetically thin and I hungry. I was hungry for a legitimate way to be proud of myself. I was hungry for self-acceptance. Mostly, I was hungry to be accepted for who I was: Part Flip and White, a woman who was flawed but demanded and deserved respect.

Now, I know and am actually glad that I cannot change my mixed ethnicity. Besides, not accepting this is not an option. Anyone who tries to deny a big part of them, I guarantee, will always feel something is amiss. It was a long road to recovery and to this realization. It was, at times, horrible because my health was in danger. Most importantly, I now know that that part of me which I was ashamed of and the shame to which my own culture's self-hatred had contributed, is something that I have to convey. I have become a writer and in my first yet unpublished novel, I discuss this shame and this affliction called anorexia as well as other demons that have plagued my ego about being mixed. I can claim to be special or just ordinary. But what I like to claim these days is that I am a woman, a mother, a wife and yes, I am proud to be part Filipino.

21 Kathleen F. Slevin

Disciplining Bodies
The Aging Experiences of Older Heterosexual and Gay Men

This article explores ways that men in later life may attempt to retain or regain notions of youthful manhood—in particular, by disciplining their bodies through exercise or dieting. Sexual orientation is also a focus because it shapes experiences with manhood and with aging. Because heterosexuality is venerated and homosexuality stigmatized, gay men may experience old age differently compared to heterosexual men. Throughout the paper, I draw on unpublished empirical data collected through intensive interviews with a group of fifty-two heterosexual and homosexual men who are in their 60s, 70s, and 80s. Interestingly, at least for this small, nonrandom sample of older, mostly privileged men, exercise and diet, the health behaviors I explore in this paper, evidence no discernable differences between gay and heterosexual respondents. Both groups of respondents attempt to deal with the stigma of aging bodies by engaging in fitness activities and body maintenance techniques that emphasize youthful appearances.

Of course, relations of power shape relations between gender, age, race, sexuality, and the body; variability in aging experiences is the norm, not the exception.

Bodies, Aging, and Ageism

While the ways that people experience their bodies have garnered significant attention in recent decades, until recently, scholarship has largely ignored aging bodies (Calasanti and Slevin, 2001; Faircloth, 2003; Katz, 2005; Slevin, 2006). Cruikshank (2003) also reminds us that despite the body's critical role as a marker of age, even social gerontologists have given it scant attention in understanding how we experience the aging of the body, except in cases of disease and illness (Cruikshank, 2003). The researchers who have focused on the bodies of people in later and even mid life have primarily emphasized loss of function; the emphasis has been on a "narrative of decline" (Gullette, 1997). Indeed, because commonplace physical experiences with aging bodies are ignored, older people experience their bodies in an environment of "profound cultural silence" (Twigg, 2000, p. 115).

Yet, the story of aging is intimately connected with the meanings we ascribe to our aging bodies. Indeed, these meanings are critical to making sense of age and aging (Laz, 2003). Laz (1998) also reminds us that age is an accomplishment, that it is more social than chronological.

Kathleen F. Slevin, "Disciplining Bodies: The Aging Experiences of Older Heterosexual and Gay Men," *Generations* 32, no. 1 (Spring 2008): 36–42. Copyright © 2008 American Society on Aging. Reprinted by permission of the American Society on Aging.

At the same time, the body has definite biological and physiological characteristics—bodies are more than social constructions—they do age and we do eventually die (Turner, 1996). Within literature on the body, scholars have given little attention to empirically exploring the accuracy of their broad and often sweeping theoretical claims (Williams and Bendelow, 1998). There has been little attention to "the voices that emanate from the bodies themselves" (Nettleton and Watson, 1998, p. 2). With the exception of a sizable volume of empirical literature on chronic illness and disability, the embodied experience of people in their everyday worlds is absent.

In our culture, growing old and being old are constructed as a problem, and we are now led to believe that not only can we chart the paths of how we grow old, we can go farther and decide whether we do it at all. Apparently, technology has trumped biology; growing old has become the new century's solvable problem (Cruikshank, 2003). Accordingly, the widely preached exhortation to accept old age with grace is, in fact, no longer supported by practice (Gilleard and Higgs, 2000). Indeed, nowadays—at least in many Western societies—old age is seen as a pathology and stigmatized; more and more, it is viewed as a personal failure—one that especially affects those who lack the requisite economic resources or physical abilities to partake of the consumerism that surrounds aging (Katz, 2005). Consumerism touts desirable bodies as those that are young, toned, and thin; the media convey to us that to be young and beautiful is to possess the most desirable form of cultural capital. Indeed, Bordo (1993) reminds us that taking care of one's physical appearance has long been a moral impera-

tive in Western societies: self-control and will power are symbolized in muscular, trim, fit bodies, and overweight bodies are symbols of laziness and lack of control. Furthermore, we have witnessed an accelerated breakdown in the demarcation between mature and youthful bodies; increasingly, consumer messages suggest an ageless obligation to discipline bodies through diet and exercise throughout the life course. Consequently, the body has become central in the framing of age-resisting cultural practices and in defining individuality; exercising, dieting, cosmetics, and cosmetic surgeries are pushed as strategies to resist growing old (Gilleard and Higgs, 2000). All of these strategies emphasize being fit, staying young, looking young, or at least not looking old. These strategies are the linchpins of "successful aging"; they allow those who engage in these activities to be judged "productive" in old age (Faircloth, 2003; Oberg and Tornstam, 2001). Indeed, current standards of successful aging " . . . stretch the anxieties of middle age across the life course" (Marshall and Katz, 2006, p. 77).

To what extent do the cultural messages described above influence how older people experience their aging bodies? Empirical knowledge on the topic is quite sparse, especially for men over the age of 50; it is even more scarce for older gay men. Yet, we know that cultural domination is never complete and that older people may elect in various ways to resist ageist messages that emphasize youthful bodies. That said, we need to acknowledge that even resistance strategies are determined by the hegemonic cultural norms of youthfulness. Hegemony is insidious because it is internalized (Gagne and McGaughey, 2002). Perhaps this mechanism helps explain the findings of two studies that are important for our focus: First, Grogan's (1999) empirical data found that respondents thought they would look younger if they were thinner. Second, Oberg and Tornstam (2001, p. 21) found that, for their respondents, "keeping a youthful look becomes more important with age."

Masculinity and Old Age

Normative notions of masculinity are strongly tied to youth and to heterosexuality, to physical and sexual prowess, to economic production. Standards of manhood typically presume young men or men not beyond middle age (Calasanti and King, 2005), ignoring older men. The growing literature on "masculinities," which criticizes stereotypical views of manhood, reminds us that multiple forms of masculinity exist—that there are many different ways to be a man based on the various intersections of class, race/ethnicity, and sexuality. Such recognition does not imply similar status for all, however.

Connell (1995) reminds us that at any one time it is likely that one form of masculinity is culturally exalted. But even given its preferential status, scholars caution that " . . . hegemonic masculinity may not be the lived form of masculinity at all" despite the fact that it is a powerful, even dominant script, against which men judge themselves and others (Thompson and Whearty, 2004, p. 6). Beneath the preferred ideal lie other, subaltern masculine forms (e.g., nonwhite, working class, old, gay). These subaltern, or subordinate, variants of masculinity are defined as inferior and inadequate (Spector-Mersel, 2006). For instance, men who reveal their homosexuality frequently find that their masculinity is assumed to be

questionable; homosexuality is routinely associated with gender inversion (Rosenfeld, 2003). Gay men are frequently "demasculinized," or feminized—and the arbiters of this feminizing are often gay men themselves (Slevin and Linneman, 2007).

Talk about hegemonic notions of manhood leads us to explore how as men, both heterosexual and gay, age, they negotiate these standards—especially in light of the fact that increasingly they become consumers rather than producers and come to occupy feminized spaces (the home) rather than the workplace (Meadows and Davidson, 2006). Scholars who have studied aging men in these regards provide varying responses to how men deal with growing old and being men. It is critical, however, to emphasize that much of the scholarship is theoretical in nature and lacks empirical verification. Some scholars argue that men are emasculated by old age: "To many people, aging is a negation of masculinity, and thus older men become effeminate over time" (Thompson, 1994, p. 13). Others suggest that as they age, men adapt, they renegotiate, they create alternative images and definitions of masculinity (Meadows and Davidson, 2006; Slevin and Linneman, 2007; Thompson, 1994). Still others suggest that hegemonic masculinity scripts conclude in middle age (Calasanti, 2004), and that old age is understood as contradicting masculinity. Older men are "an invisible, paradoxical and unmasculine social category" (Spector-Mersel, 2006, p. 68; Thompson, 1994). Thus, scripts for masculinity in old age are uncertain and ambiguously perceived, if not ill-formed; older men not only constitute an ambiguous social category, they "live in a hybrid state" (Spector-Mersel, 2006).

What do we know of gay men as they age? Again, while literature is sparse, a common theme throughout suggests that gay men experience "accelerated aging" (Wahler and Gabbay, 1997). Gay male culture is highly commodified (that is, treated as a marketable commodity)—even more than heterosexual culture—and reveres a masculine ideal that is young, muscular, and beautiful. One consequence of this is that homosexual men consider themselves and other men to be "middle-aged and elderly . . . at an earlier age than heterosexual men" do (Bennett and Thompson, 1991, p. 66). Again, empirical data that examine how gay men actually experience this phenomenon are both scarce and contradictory (Jones and Pugh, 2005).

Strategies for Aging: Men's Health Behaviors

One way to manage one's aging body, to adhere to hegemonic ideals, is to attain or maintain a youthful appearance by engaging in fitness activities and other body maintenance techniques (Oberg and Tornstam, 2001). Accordingly, we might expect that those older men who decide to engage in fitness and exercise regimes, whatever their sexual orientation, will share some of the same gendered and ageist notions of ideal masculinity that are touted by the culture at large. The data in my own study described above shed some light on the topic, but in doing so they also illuminate the need for additional data on how older men manage their aging bodies within an ageist and homophobic culture.

Reducing stigma. One strategy that men sometimes use in the face of the ambiguity that they face as older men in our culture is to resist such ambiguity by denying that they fit the category "old" (Gilleard and Higgs, 2000; Meadows and Davidson, 2006; Minichiello, Browne, and Kendig, 2000). Indeed, they may actively attempt to avoid or deny the stigma of old age. For instance, they may adopt a strategy of engaging in physical activities that deny or minimize the realities of their aging bodies. Sometimes the consequences can be deadly, as conveyed by Donald (age 70) when he told of his same-aged friend's tragedy: "I had a good friend . . . whom I biked with, who was determined to do 100 miles one day, and he had a heart attack and died beside the road." Trying to hold onto a bygone image of himself as an athlete who pushes his body may also signify lack of acceptance of aging. We see some of this behavior in the exercise regimes established by one of my respondents, Mark (age 64), who exercises at the gym for at least an hour almost every day and also runs six days a week for a total of 35–40 miles per week. A fanatic about his weight and diet (147 pounds, 6'1" tall, and 7 percent overall body fat), Mark called on a classic masculine metaphor of the body as a machine to be controlled in order to justify his behaviors: "[The body] is much like a car. If you don't oil it and grease it and gas it and maintain it, it's going to fall apart."

This statement illustrates another theme of modern aging, that living a healthy life is more than a choice—it is now a duty, it is a responsibility that we take charge of our bodies by practicing healthy lifestyles (Marshall and Katz, 2006). This idea is also implicit in my interview with Thad (age 80), who tells me that he continues a three-day-a-week walking regime despite the fact that "—it's a little more difficult to do that now. But, I just push myself."

Controlling weight. Not all health behaviors associated with trying to maintain standards of hegemonic masculinity are negative in their consequences. Certainly, one can argue that adopting a lifestyle that involves regular exercise and weight control illustrates positive self-care at any age. No doubt reflective not only of constant anti-aging media messages but also of their relative class privilege and high levels of education, the majority of the men I talked with were very tuned-in to health and fitness issues; they were attuned also to concerns about controlling their weight. Like other older people (Hurd, 2000), they generally emphasized health, not looking youthful, as a motivator for staying active. Most described themselves as being in decent health, even when suffering from chronic conditions such as diabetes, high blood pressure, and heart disease.

It was striking that only seven of the twenty-six men in my study judged themselves to be at their ideal weight. The remaining nineteen men defined themselves as overweight. The overweight range given by these men was from 2 to 80 pounds: seven men were 10 pounds or under, five were between 11 and 25 pounds overweight, and seven were between 26 and 80 pounds overweight. All were concerned to varying degrees about their weight. Whether they were heterosexual or gay appeared to make no discernible difference.

Interestingly, even the men who considered themselves at their ideal weight were also quite concerned that they stay at that weight. Several mentioned that they monitor their food intake. For instance, Daniel (age 68) talked about his motivation to stay at his ideal weight and how it was shaped by his desire to "look good, look trim—without wearing a girdle." For the over-weight men (nineteen), the majority (eleven) claimed to diet (formal dieting as opposed to "watching caloric intake") on a fairly regular basis. For example, Thad (age 80) was only 2 pounds overweight at the time of the interview and talked about how he will have returned to his ideal weight by the end of the week: "Anytime I start to put on weight, then I diet. Every morning I drink a can of Slimfast and then for lunch I'll eat a Slimfast bar, bananas and fruits."

At age 82, John, 9 pounds over his ideal weight, was one of the oldest interviewees. When asked if he ever dieted, he quickly replied, "I sure do," and went on to talk about how he restricted his intake of desserts and sweets and told his wife not to buy his favorite cookies. Others talked at some length about their dieting challenges.

For example, Jake (age 78), 45 pounds overweight, struck a common cord when he admitted, "Yes, I've been to Weight Watchers and I know the right things to do, but I don't always do them." Interestingly, Jake also demonstrated how contradictory and paradoxical issues of weight often are—both in relation to self and in relation to others. While quite content with his own overweight body, he exhibited and reinforced a common prejudice against others who are overweight. He admitted that while he preferred to spend time with gay men his own age, he preferred them to be "slender."

Exercising

In addition to dieting, many of the men interviewed also engaged in some form of physical activity or exercise in order to remain healthy. A subtext in their narratives reinforces the theme of desire to keep their bodies as trim and fit as possible so that they avoid the stigma of looking like old men. For those who exercised regularly (fifteen men, out of the total of twenty-six), typical exercise took the form of running, walking, swimming, and workouts in the gym. For a few, golf and sailing were also mentioned as forms of exercise—illustrating the importance of financial means to keeping active. Running, by contrast, requires no specific financial capital. Thus, at age 69, Alex, who still worked part-time as a maintenance man, ran 2 miles each day, and Mark (age 64) ran 35–40 miles a week. For those who exercised regularly, there was often a sense that it was not enough; that they had not met their obligation to suitably discipline their older bodies. Hence, Bart (age 67) expressed a common sentiment: "I don't exercise as much as I should." Even those who do not exercise were at pains to tell me that they remained active in their daily lives. For instance, as Wayne (age 80) was keen to point out, "I don't exercise but I stay busy." Jacob (age 73) was 30 pounds overweight and did not exercise. However, he anticipated that when the new YMCA opened in his town he would take up swimming again (he was on the swim team in college) because "I've got to get back in the pool. I've got to cut my weight down." Indeed, he was optimistic that in the future his body would look better than it did.

Conversations with the men who were not regular exercisers revealed that they were also quite aware of the healthful benefits of exercise—especially if they were overweight. While they claimed to be unwilling to do the body work necessary to gain or regain a more youthful body image, their indifference or resistance was tinged with a certain amount of ambivalence:

Yeah, I could be better. I could tone up, I could lose weight, I could do a lot of things. But, I am not willing to go through

what you have to go through to do it. (Victor, age 71)

Actually, this is terribly vain, but for my age I think I look pretty good. I could lose ten pounds and be happy but I am not going to obsess about it. (Peter, age 62)

Even for the two men who considered themselves the most overweight (75 and 80 pounds, respectively) and who claimed to be quite indifferent to their appearance, evidence contradicted their expressed lack of concern. Landon (age 71) loudly and cavalierly proclaimed at one point in our interview, "Look at my belly and say 'That's a beauty!'" but he later admitted that he did not like his big belly, that it was what he liked least about his aging body. Indeed, he talked several times about the fact that he was regularly defeated in his attempts to control his weight; he spoke of how he tried, unsuccessfully, to "watch what I eat" every day of his life.

Looking Youthful

Whether or not they exercised or dieted, the narrative themes of the interviews I conducted with the older men underscored the appeal of looking youthful or at least not looking old. Keeping healthy was one motivation in their daily lives, but not looking old was another. Social locations, including age cohort, appeared to make little difference in this regard. Overall, the interviewees were keenly aware of all of the positive cultural capital that accompanies youthful images. Tom (age 61) captured a sentiment that the men in this study would all likely agree when he stated, "Everyone wants to be young. Young is always 'in,' [it is] always cool to be young, it's fashionable." Such sentiments also seemed to shape

Alan's approach to aging. At age 75, he talked about how important it was for him to appear youthful, and he confessed that he had just devoted considerable time to figuring out how best to whiten his teeth in order to make his smile more youthful. Also, he had this to say about what guided him as he picked his clothes: "I want to appear as if I'm energetic and not a has-been, that I am current and with-it." Others were even more explicit about avoiding looking old. William (age 75) was adamant in this regard: "I don't go around wearing old folks' clothes." At age 80, Wayne also appeared to have such concerns on his mind: "I don't dress like an old man."

Conclusions

While the literature provides us with few direct cues about how men experience and negotiate their aging bodies, my limited data suggest some interesting observations—ones that bear exploration in additional studies. This article has briefly explored the experiences of aging men in general, and a sample of gay and heterosexual men specifically. The article has touched on some of the issues they face as they age in a society where hegemonic notions of manhood revere youthfulness. Specifically, I have examined some of the health behaviors my respondents engage in as they negotiate growing old. Throughout, I reveal the age relations that render the body a site of struggle and ambivalence as people age. It is important to emphasize, however, that the ways that aging gay men in my limited sample share common ground with their heterosexual counterparts do not negate the complicated ways body image and related behaviors as men age are shaped by sexual

orientation (Rosenfeld, 2003; Slevin, 2006; Thompson and Whearty, 2004; Wahler and Gabbay, 1997).

Overall, the narratives of the older men in my study reveal how coercive are the norms of youthfulness and the accompanying emphasis on actively fighting aging bodies. Through the voices of these men, we learn how deeply age matters and how ageist notions of aging prevail. As well, because most of these older men are privileged by being financially comfortable and retired, we come to appreciate that they have the time and resources to devote to fighting aging. For the most part, their bodies still function well enough to allow them to engage in activities that illuminate and reinforce the "cultural imperialism of youthfulness" that increasingly dominates our society (Laws, 1995) and notions of masculinity (Connell, 1995).

While there is no one universal experience with aging and with aging bodies, my exploration of how the men in my sample discipline their bodies through exercise and diet reveals some strategies common to these older men, whatever their sexual orientation. In some interesting ways, we see evidence that supports the notion of an ageless obligation to discipline bodies through exercise and diet throughout the life course. This evidence reinforces the claims of Oberg and Tornstam (2001, p. 26) that the "behaviors for people in different age categories are becoming blurred," and that " . . . people are becoming more alike in different periods of life." Thus, hegemonic standards of youthfulness and masculinity, which stigmatize old age and old men and highlight the desirability of being slim, trim, and active, increasingly apply to people whatever their social locations.

References

Bennett, K. C., and Thompson, N. L. 1991. "Accelerated Aging and Male Homosexuality: Australian Evidence in a Continuing Debate." *Journal of Homosexuality* 20(3/4): 65–75.

Bordo, S. 1993. *Unbearable Weight: Feminism, Western Culture, and the Body.* Berkeley: University of California Press.

Calasanti, T. 2004. "Feminist Gerontology and Old Men." *Journal of Gerontology* 59B: S305–14.

Calasanti, T., and King, N. 2005. "Firming the Floppy Penis." *Men and Masculinities* 8: 3–23.

Calasanti, T., and Slevin, K. F. 2001. *Gender, Social Inequalities, and Aging.* Walnut Creek, Calif.: Alta Mira Press.

Connell, R. W. 1995. *Masculinities.* Berkeley: University of California Press.

Cruikshank, M. 2003. *Learning to Be Old: Gender, Culture, and Aging.* Lanham, Md.: Rowman and Littlefield.

Faircloth, C. A. 2003. *Aging Bodies: Images and Everyday Experience.* Walnut Creek, Calif.: Alta Mira Press.

Gagne, P., and McGaughey, D. 2002. "Designing Women: Cultural Hegemony and the Exercise of Power Among Women Who Have Undergone Elective Mammoplasty." *Gender and Society* 16: 814–38.

Gilleard, C., and Higgs, P. 2000. *Cultures of Ageing: Self, Citizen, and the Body.* Harlow, England: Prentice Hall.

Grogan, S. 1999. *Body Image.* London: Routledge.

Gullette, M. M. 1997. *Declining to Decline: Cultural Combat and the Politics of the Midlife.* Charlottesville: University Press of Virginia.

Hegelson, V. S. 1995. "Masculinity, Men's Roles, and Coronary Heart Disease." In D. Sabo and D. F. Gordon, eds., *Men's Health and Illness: Gender, Power, and the Body.* Thousand Oaks, Calif.: Sage.

Hurd, L. C. 2000. "Older Women's Body Image and Embodied Experience: An Exploration." *Journal of Women and Aging* 12(3/4): 77–97.

Jones, J., and Pugh, S. 2005. "Aging Gay Men." *Men and Masculinities* 7: 248–60.

Katz, S. 2005. *Cultural Aging: Life Course, Lifestyle, and Senior Worlds.* Ontario, Canada: Broadview Press.

Laws, G. 1995. "Understanding Ageism: Lessons from Feminism and Postmodernism." *The Gerontologist* 35: 112–8.

Laz, C. 1998. "Act Your Age." *Sociological Forum* 13: 85–113.

Laz, C. 2003. "Age Embodied." *Journal of Aging Studies* 1: 503–19.

Marshall, B. L., and Katz, S. 2006. "From Androgyny to Androgens: Resexing the Aging Body." In T. M. Calasanti and K. F. Slevin, eds., *Age Matters: Realigning Feminist Thinking,* pp. 75–98. New York: Routledge.

Meadows, R., and Davidson, K. 2006. "Maintaining Manliness in Later Life: Hegemonic Masculinities and Emphasized Femininities." In T. M. Calasanti and K. F. Slevin, eds., *Age Matters: Realigning Feminist Thinking,* pp. 295–312. New York: Routledge.

Minichiello, V., Browne, J., and Kendig, H. 2000. "Perceptions and Consequences of Ageism: Views of Older People." *Ageing and Society* 20: 253–78.

Nettleton, S., and Watson, J. 1998. *The Body in Everyday Life.* London and New York: Routledge.

Oberg, P., and Tornstam, L. 2001. "Youthfulness and Fitness—Identity Ideals for All Ages?" *Journal of Aging and Identity* 6: 15–29.

Rosenfeld, D. 2003. "The Homosexual Body in Lesbian and Gay Elders' Narratives." In C. A. Faircloth, ed., *Aging Bodies: Images and Everyday Experience,* pp. 171–203. Walnut Creek, Calif.: Alta Mira Press.

Spector-Mersel, G. 2006. "Never-Aging Stories: Western Hegemonic Masculinity Scripts." *Journal of Gender Studies* 15: 67–82.

Slevin, K. F., and Linneman, T. J. 2007. Unpublished Manuscript.

Slevin, K. F. 2006. "The Embodied Experiences of Old Lesbians." In T. M. Calasanti and K. F. Slevin, eds., *Age Matters: Realigning Feminist Thinking,* pp. 247–268. New York: Routledge.

Thompson, E. H. 1994. "Older Men as Invisible in Contemporary Society." In E. Thompson, ed., *Older Men's Lives*, pp. 1–21. Thousand Oaks, Calif.: Sage.

Thompson, E. H., and Whearty, P. M. 2004. "Older Men's Social Participation: The Importance of Masculinity Ideology." *The Journal of Men's Studies* 13: 5–24.

Turner, B. S. 1996. *The Body and Society*. Thousand Oaks, Calif.: Sage.

Twigg, J. 2000. *Bathing: The Body and Community Care*. London and New York: Routledge.

Wahler, J., and Gabbay, S. G. 1997. "Gay Male Aging: A Review of the Literature." *Journal of Gay and Lesbian Social Services* 6(3): 1–20.

Williams, S. J., and Bendelow, G. 1998. *The Lived Body: Sociological Themes, Embodied Issues*. London: Routledge.

CHAPTER 3 STUDY QUESTIONS

1. Describe some idealized versions of how women are and have been defined. How has this changed historically? How do these idealizations differ depending on race, class, sexuality, and ethnicity?

2. Are there cultural parallels between female genital cutting and the trend for designer cosmetic surgery? If so, is there a difference between those procedures in which one is free to choose versus compelled to submit?

3. What connections can you make between Suzanne Kessler's account (in Chapter 1; Reading 6) of genital surgeries for intersex people and Max Beck's account of his life (Reading 18)?

4. How do race, age, and trans status intersect with socially constructed bodily concerns?

5. In what ways does sexual orientation shape experiences with manhood and aging?

CHAPTER 4 Doing "It": Sexualities

22 Jenny A. Higgins and Irene Browne

Sexual Needs, Control, and Refusal
How "Doing" Class and Gender Influences Sexual Risk Taking

Introduction

Understanding the social dynamics of sexual risk taking—particularly among socially disenfranchised women—remains central to public health research and policy. In the United States, almost one out of every two pregnancies (48%–49%) is unintended (Henshaw, 1998), and this rate has worsened among the most economically disadvantaged women in the last decade (Finer & Henshaw, 2006). Women also face an increasing risk of contracting HIV through heterosexual transmission, with poor women of color disproportionately affected (Centers for Disease Control and Prevention [CDC], 2002). While researchers have established that poorer Americans are more "at risk" for negative sexual health out-

comes, the *sexual processes* through which these classed and gendered disparities come about are not fully understood. How do socially disadvantaged women and men *do*—that is, socially enact—their class, gender, or both, and how does this affect their sexual behaviors?

What does it mean to "socially enact"—or "do"—class and gender? Sociologists maintain that individuals actively construct their social reality through ongoing social interaction (Goffman, 1959). Much of this social interaction involves the negotiation of taken-for-granted understandings about the desired or appropriate behavior within a social situation (Fenstermaker & West, 2002). What is considered desirable or appropriate behavior depends on salient

Excerpted from the original. Jenny A. Higgins and Irene Browne, "Sexual Needs, Control, and Refusal: How 'Doing' Class and Gender Influences Sexual Risk Taking," *Journal of Sex Research* 45, no. 3 (August 2008): 233–245. Reprinted by permission of Taylor & Francis Group, http://www.informaworld.com.

aspects of an individual's social environment and identity, including gender and social class.

Social class often has been oversimplified in public health research on sexuality. Most studies rely on education level (Laumann, 1994; Laumann & Michael, 2001) or percentage of the poverty level (Henshaw, 1998) as a proxy for social class. Socioeconomic status, or SES, usually is described in public health research as a static independent variable that consists of one's education level, income, occupation, or all of these (Mosher, Chandra, & Jones, 2004). One of the problems with this approach is that class and race/ethnicity are treated as static and preexisting categorical variables, as opposed to dynamically created variables or social processes unto themselves (Bettie, 2003). Others have taken a neighborhood approach to class, exploring sexual health outcomes by the economic constitution of geographic community and not by individual alone (Krieger, Waterman, Chen, Soobader, & Subramanian, 2003). This research, however, does not articulate the psychosocial processes involved in creating and enacting class and gender in those settings. A few researchers use *intersectional* approaches to examine social class in conjunction with the effects of gender and race inequality (Krieger, 2005; Schulz & Mullings, 2006), but with notable exceptions (Berge, 2004; Skeggs, 1997), few have applied this framework to a study of sexual behaviors.

In contrast, a large body of public health research suggests that women and men's social enactment of their gender can influence their sexual health. For example, gendered cultural meanings value women's virginity and devalue their promiscuity; fearing to appear sexual, many girls report that (first) intercourse "just happened" and they thus failed to prepare for sex with condoms or hormonal contraception (Carpenter, 2005; Tolman, 2002). In contrast, social encouragement of men's virility and sexual conquest means that men are more likely to have sex earlier and with a larger number of lifetime sexual partners, including sex workers, extra-marital partners, or both (Mosher et al., 2004; Santelli, Brener, Lowry, Bhatt, & Zabin, 1998). Here, men's enactment of masculinity may increase their susceptibility to STIs and unintended pregnancy, as well as the way they place their partners at risk.

Gendered power asymmetry also sometimes places women in positions that make pressing for contraception—especially condoms—difficult if not impossible (Amaro, Raj, & Reed, 2001; Exner, Dworkin, Hoffman, & Ehrhardt, 2003; Worth, 1989). Women are much more likely than men to experience forced or coerced sex, as well as nonsexual violence at a partner's hands, compromising women's ability to protect themselves from unwanted pregnancy and disease (Farmer, Connors, & Simmons, 1996). Due to men's relative access to greater economic security, as well as widespread cultural constructions that denigrate women with multiple sex partners and assume women are supposed to be sexually available but not sexually active (Aggleton, Rivers, & Scott, 1999), a nearly universal sexual double standard affords men more access to sexual self-determination, autonomy, and pleasure than women (Blanc, 2001).

Furthermore, due to gendered socialization and women's reliance on love and romantic relationships with men (Cancian, 1986), women may deliberately abandon pregnancy or disease prophylaxis, even when a baby is not consciously desired. For example, even when women *are* able to negotiate for condom use, they may not *want* to because condoms seem antithetical to sex that feels intimate, loving, and trusting (Hirsch, Higgins, Nathanson, & Bentley, 2002; Sobo, 1993, 1995). Women's emotional dependence on love, relationships, and intimacy may make them less inclined to protect themselves against unintended pregnancy, STIs, and HIV.

Thus, scholarship demonstrates how gender shapes sexual attitudes and behaviors. Comparatively unexplored are the ways in which people *"do" social class and sex.* That is, while poverty has been established as a sexual risk factor, we still know little about how living in poverty shapes sexual attitudes and behaviors, particularly in comparison to the experience of economic security.

Present Research

As part of a larger project on sexual pleasure and contraceptive use, we collected qualitative data on some of the ways in which social class and gender shaped women's and men's sexual experiences. The original aim of the project was to examine attitudes toward and experiences of sexual pleasure, sexual risk taking, and contraceptive use; we also wanted to explore how gender and social class shaped those phenomena. During the study, we found that striking themes and patterns emerged related to *intersections* of gender and social class. The current article focuses on two themes that provide particularly clear illustrations of these intersections: the connected issues of *sexual needs and controllability* and *sexual refusal.* These themes not only strongly exemplify intersectionality, but they also provide a potential link to class differences in contraceptive use, which we review in the discussion section. Here, then, we describe how respondents enacted their class and gender through sexual needs, controllability, and refusal, and we conclude the article by outlining some of the ways in which these sexual processes may affect sexual risk taking, unintended pregnancy, and STI and HIV transmission. Along the way, we share our process of operationalizing social class.

Method

Sample Strategy and Construction

We explored our research questions by using theoretical sampling to recruit 36 respondents (24 women, 12 men) from metropolitan Atlanta. Similar to purposive or quota-driven sampling, theoretical sampling (Hirsch, 2002; Hirsch & Nathanson, 2001) and systematic ethnographic sampling (Hirsch et al., 2007) select participants based on the variables most likely to affect the outcomes of interest, based on the literature and on any previous experience with the population. The variables are used to create cells within a sampling frame that must be filled as recruitment ensues. In this case, *gender* and *social class* served as the primary sample stratifiers. As the focus of this project, women composed the majority of the sample (*N*=24). Men were included for comparative purposes to explore how gender shapes relationships between pleasure and contraception (*N*=12). Similarly, as we discussed above, given the strong and persistent social class differences in reproductive health outcomes in the United States, we sought a mixed-class sample in order to explore whether class-based differences existed in women's experiences of sexual pleasure and, if so, if these differences might help explain disparities in unintended pregnancy, STIs, and HIV.

In keeping with theoretical sampling, we also selected participants to represent a range of other variables theorized to influence contraceptive use and unintended pregnancy: race/ethnicity, age, marital status, and parity (Abma, 1997; Malat, 2000; Morgan, 1996; Mosher & Bachrach, 1996). Thus, within each of the four main cells of the sample (middle-class women, poor and working-class women, middle-class men, poor and working-class men), we deliberately tried to capture both Whites and African Americans[1] and a range of ages.[2]

Operationalization of class. We sought to analyze the processes underlying class differences in sexual behavior. To do this, we combined the indicators of social class used most often in public health research (education level and income) with those included in alternative models. Krieger and colleagues (1997) have suggested collecting data at the individual, household, and neighborhood levels, characterizing both childhood and adult socioeconomic status, as well as changes in financial situation over the life course. Further, extensive literature from sociology and anthropology indicates that social class also encompasses nontangible resources, such as social and cultural capital and distinctive worldviews. In other words, social class represents one's ability to draw on and enact both *financial* resources and opportunities and *cultural* resources such as knowledge, skills, tastes, and preferences (Bourdieu, 1984; Bourdieu & Passeron, 1990). Individuals usually develop the tastes and preferences that are associated with a particular class through socialization processes when they are children (Bourdieu, 1984; Lamont & Lareau, 1988). We and others (Skeggs, 1997) argue that these latter cultural and psychological

dimensions of social class may be equally if not more important in shaping sexual behavior than income and education.[3]

Thus, our final social class variable was operationalized using four categories, which reflect both financial and cultural capital: (1) level of education; (2) occupation or, in some cases, homemaker or unemployment status; (3) current financial situation, needs, or both (if any) for housing, food, clothing, or other essentials; and (4) social class of origin, including parents' education, occupation, and income; early home environment; and cultural resources. During the initial screening call, we asked participants about their education level (any college or no college); their occupation status (white-collar, blue-collar, or unemployed and homeless); and their neighborhood, based on census data characteristics. We assigned the most prevalent class of the three markers (at least two out of three), using labels of either *middle class* or *poor and working class*. During the interviews, we collected information on the remaining social class criteria. If the first interview revealed information that contradicted our original assignment, particularly on the fourth factor (e.g., family upbringing or social class of origin), we reassigned the class label accordingly. Reassignment occurred in only two cases. These were women whose current circumstances corresponded to the working-class category (e.g., working in retail with poverty-level income), but whose family of origin and cultural capital (e.g., reading *The New Yorker*, attending a private elite university) placed them in the middle-class category. Ultimately, we sought 24 women and 12 men who were strategically divided into these two class categories.

Recruitment. Participants were recruited through several mechanisms: notices sent through Internet listservs, flyers dispensed in numerous Atlanta neighborhoods that captured the social-class distributions of interest, and referrals from other participants. Interested respondents called a telephone number associated with the study and were informed by the first author of the inclusion criteria: participants had to be 18 years old or older and must have used some type of pregnancy prophylaxis in the past 12 months. Individuals also provided information on the sampling variables of interest, such as gender, social class, race/ethnicity, age, and parity. We filled in the sampling frame's cells as recruitment ensued.

Interview Protocol

Respondents read and signed a consent form at the first meeting. The study protocol and instruments were reviewed and approved by the Institutional Review Board at Emory University, the home institution for the authors at the time of data collection. At the completion of the entire interview, which usually took place over two or sometimes three separate sessions, participants were paid $40.

Interviews were conducted in participants' homes or in public places near their residences or workplaces. This allowed not only for greater rapport but also for observation in people's homes and neighborhoods, which provided contextual information on class differences in housing, neighborhoods, and community geographies. Each interview took approximately 3 hours to complete. A total of 104 hours of interviews were recorded digitally and transcribed.

The semistructured sexual life history interview guide contained sections on health care history, reproductive and contraceptive histories, current and previous romantic and sexual relationships, where and from whom the participant learned about sex, sexual stereotypes, and participants' sexual preferences and positive and negative sexual experiences. The guide was designed so that topics moved from less to more sensitive, as a way to enhance rapport and data validity. We also administered close-ended questionnaires that collected information on income level, public assistance, and highest level of education completed.

Qualitative Analysis

The first author read, reread, and summarized the transcripts and her fieldnotes based on each participant. We employed an ethnographic, grounded theory approach in analyzing the data: we used both preexisting codes derived from the literature and research questions as well as codes that arose from the data themselves. Examples of preestablished codes included "current sexual relationship," "contraceptive use," and "preferred sexual activities." Examples of codes established during analyses included "perceptions of men's and women's sex drives" and "consequences of sexual refusal." We then used the codes to compare and contrast phenomena and individuals. *Coding sorts* involved the collection of coded blocks of text and the creation of new thematic data files capturing various dimensions of the key themes, such as frequency, duration, size, specific vocabulary, and differences in intensity and emphasis (Ulin, Robinson, Tolley, & McNeill, 2002). We also analyzed topics using *conceptually clustered matrices* (Miles & Huberman, 1994), which are concise row-by-column summaries that allow identification of both preestablished and emergent themes (Abrams, 2003). The matrices also allowed us to conduct *descriptive cross-case analysis* and *analytic cross-case analysis* (Miles &

Huberman, 1994), in which we compared and contrasted gender and class subgroups across themes such as sex drives, intracouple libido (a)symmetry, and perceptions and experiences of sexual refusal.

Results

Before turning to the issues of sexual needs, control, and refusal, we first present data on sexual health outcomes. Doing so provides a benchmark comparison with the public health literature, as well as a context for the sexual attitudes that we discuss in the next section. As expected, the middle class profited from more consistent contraceptive use and thus fewer unintended pregnancies and STIs.[4] Poor and working-class respondents reported lower rates of contraceptive use both at last sexual encounter and first sexual encounter. Eighteen respondents (50%) reported experiencing at least one unintended pregnancy during their lives, but this figure hides a major class discrepancy. While 83% of the poor and working-class women experienced at least one unintended pregnancy, the same was true for only 42% of the middle-class women. Among the men, 25% *confirmed* their involvement in an unintended pregnancy, but their reports suggested that upward of 50% were likely to have been involved in at least one. For example, both Joseph and Shawn had partners who indicated they were pregnant, but paternity remained unconfirmed when the women had an abortion or a miscarriage, respectively. Only one middle-class man in the sample had been involved in a suspected or confirmed unintended pregnancy.

The class differences in terms of lifetime STI prevalence[5] were pronounced among men but not among women. Exactly one

in four women from both class categories reported ever having had an STI. None of the middle-class men reported a lifetime STI, however, whereas exactly half of the poor and working-class men reported at least one.

Now we turn to two prevalent interview themes that illustrate some of the ways in which people "do" class and gender in the bedroom, perhaps shedding light on the sexual pathways through which these outcomes come about: perceptions of men's sexual controllability and the phenomenon of refusing sex. These were not the only classed and gendered pathways to sexual health outcomes that we encountered in the study. Other examples included the following: (1) disparate motivation to avoid unintended pregnancy between those who were college bound and those who had few educational and professional opportunities; (2) the ability to sexually "let go" either with or without contraception (i.e., the eroticization of safety versus the eroticization of risk); (3) the physical geography of advantaged versus disadvantaged neighborhoods, especially in an urban setting, and its effects on the supervision of young people, sexual experimentation, and sexual pairings; (4) classed differences in age gaps between sexual partners at sexual initiation; and (5) reproductive health services for advantaged versus disadvantaged women, and the matching and mismatching of bodies with contraceptive methods (Higgins, 2005). Here, however, we focus on the issues of sexual needs, controllability, and refusal, not only because they are so strongly illustrative of the intersections between class and gender, but also because they have been less documented in the literature as related to sexual health and contraception.

Perceptions of Sexual Needs and Sexual Controllability

The overwhelming majority of respondents indicated that, on average, men's sex drives are greater than women's. In other words, one of the ways that men were expected to enact their masculinity in the sexual realm was to demonstrate sexual appetite. Sometimes respondents invoked stereotypes or social origins, as in, "There's this idea that men need it more than women" (middle-class woman) or "The stereotype is that men are insatiable sexually" (middle-class woman). Sometimes gender asymmetry was expressed as a biological given, as in, "Men need more sex than women" (poor/working-class man), or, "Men, you know, need to spread their seed" (poor/working-class woman). Class influenced whether social or physiological explanations were used to describe gender asymmetries in libido. Middle-class respondents commonly embraced a sexual discourse of social influence and thus sexual controllability. In contrast, poor and working-class respondents were more likely to portray men's stronger sex drives as rooted in biology and thus uncontainable and potentially destructive.

"Men have no control": Poor and working-class respondents discuss men's sexual needs. Poor and working-class women were critical of men's sexual appetites but often presented them as an unfortunate given. They suggested that, for better or worse, men enacted masculinity by acting on irrepressible sexual urges. In a typical response, Sally (all names are pseudonyms) reported, "Men need sex all the time. It's terrible. Men just want somebody for a piece of ass. It's just, 'Wham, bam, thank you ma'am.'" Similarly, Frances said, "Men

overdo it with sex. They have no control. Women can control it more, especially independent women." Despite these women's criticism of men's sexual lawlessness, they were aware of the power men have when "out of control." Both women had been sexually assaulted by strangers, one in an alley while prostituting and one at gunpoint on the side of the road. Woven into their class consciousness was the social expectation of male sexual aggression and, sometimes, violence.

More than half of the poor and working-class men reported that their sexual needs must be met in order to maintain proper mental and physical functioning. Jay reported that, barring illness, he "required" sex (his word) at least every other day. If his girlfriend were out of town or out of the mood, secretly he would either call one of his regular lovers or hit a club and find a new one. Along similar lines, Jo Jo thought that men's well-being could deteriorate quickly without regular sex. "If a man goes without [sex], his attitude changes, his mood changes," he said. "Going for 20 or 30 days without sex for a man is like going without water. A woman's got more strength and she can hide it." To maintain his sexual needs, Jo Jo tried to maintain sexual relationships with at least two women at all times so he could have sex as often as he wanted. "If one [partner] won't give it," he said, "the other will." And Eric said that it was nearly impossible to imagine *not* being in the mood for sex. "It's something a man needs," he said.

When these and other poor and working-class men suggested that sex is about meeting bodily demands, they enacted a sexual paradigm based on physiological *needs* versus social influences and sexual *wants*. Their enactment of sexual virility seems more understandable when considered in the context of their social disenfranchisement. That is, these men described extremely limited employment opportunities, substance abuse, bouts of homelessness, harassment by the police, or all of these; sexuality seemed to be one of the few ways that they could express their power and autonomy. (See Anderson, 1999 for similar arguments in reference to poor, urban African American men.)

"The Darwinian argument is kind of flimsy": Middle-class respondents stress nurture over nature. Middle-class women and men were more likely to enact their class by emphasizing the social influences on sex drive. A number of middle-class women suggested that men's social privilege allowed them to use sexual needs as an excuse for inappropriate behavior. Adair, for example, challenged "the idea that men need it more than women," and criticized it as a justification for infidelity. "Men use it as an excuse," she said, "you know, like, 'We just have different needs, baby, so it's okay if I sleep with other women.'" Several of her peers also were reluctant to cite physiological origins of gender differences in libido, or even to acknowledge those differences at all. Alexandra said, "My partners' drives are often lower than mine, but there's no way for me to say if that's because of how we're *wired*, you know, or how society tells us we should be." Clara refused to agree that men are more libidinous than women. "I think it's completely individual," she said. "Some women want [sex] all the time, some want it every 3 months. Men usually want it more as young men, but this evens out over time." Elizabeth said that her family had raised her to believe that "Only men want sex. It took me a long time," she reported, "to re-

alize that it's healthy and normal for women to want it, too."

A number of middle-class men also resisted a biological imperative. Benjamin suggested that men's supposedly higher libido may be a self-fulfilling prophecy: "I think it's social rather than biological." He continued, "The Darwinian argument is kind of flimsy. Men have just been portrayed as more sexually active for so long. I think people internalize this and then make it true." Matthew reported a gendered asymmetry in libido, but attached sexual expression to emotional expression: "There's a stereotype about sexual interest or libido," he said, "[that] men in general may be hornier than women. But men may want to express things sexually instead of emotionally. Demonstrating their feelings sexually is more appealing to men. Women have other outlets for emotion than men." These and other middle-class men enacted their sexual perceptions in a way that challenged men's greater need for sex and possibly opened the door to shared sexual power and responsibility.

The Politics of Sexual Refusal

Ideas about men's sexual controllability informed respondents' notions of under what circumstances women and men reasonably could refuse sex from their partners.

"Men get so messed up that they'll wreck somebody": Poor and working class women and men and the risks of sexual refusal. Poor and working-class women, like the vast majority of respondents, said that women have the right to refuse sex. However, a number of poor or working-class women, and at least a few socially disadvantaged men, indicated that exercising this right can come with costs, including infidelity, conflict, or even violence. For exam-

ple, several said that if a man's partner refused sex, he could not be blamed for looking for sex with other women. "[Refusing] would make a man go elsewhere for sex," said Susan. (Above, we described how several poor and working-class men upheld this social construction by seeking sex with other women if and when their main partner failed to meet their sexual needs, thereby putting their primary partners at greater risk for STIs.) Frances reported that women "shouldn't be forced" to have sex. Later, however, she described men's sexual impulses and their sometimes violent consequences:

Nothing happens to a woman if she doesn't have sex. But men get so messed up with sex that they'll wreck somebody. This can lead to rape sometimes. We can't avoid rape. It isn't right. But sometimes men get all pent up and they can't help it.

In Frances's depiction, men's lack of control was unfortunate but unavoidable. Similarly, Rose reported that "women can refuse sex, yeah. You ain't gotta have sex with him unless you want to." She also spoke, however, of how men can get "a little violent" if too much time passes without sex. Whereas women may get "kind of agitated" during a long period of abstinence, "you know, like a kind of chip on your shoulder," men could become dangerously enraged. "Once they have sex with a woman, they cool down. Sex calms men down." She, too, believed that women could refuse sex, but she was aware of the tangible dangers involved in doing so.

Thus, for some poor and working-class women, the benefits of acquiescing to unwanted sex outweighed the threats of conflict, infidelity, or emotional discord that

could occur if sex were refused. When speaking about her passionate but tumultuous partnership with an ex, Destiny said:

I would have sex with him sometimes just because I was too tired to resist. The sex was good, but my libido was down because of all I had to do. The kids were still young. He would get angry with me if I didn't want it; he'd think I was cheating on him. Most of the time, I would just give in.

Here, sex serves as a way to maintain relationship harmony, not necessarily in terms of building intimacy or affection, but primarily in terms of soothing a partner's agitation and averting conflict. Class informed the sexual perceptions and realities of poor and working-class women in a way that resulted in tangible consequences such as infidelity, volatility, or even violence for exercising sexual autonomy (i.e., not having sex when not in the mood).[6]

Poor and working-class men never mentioned situations in which they wanted to refuse sex. Turning down sexual advances seemed exterior to the social construction of socially disadvantaged masculinity; these men were more interested in upholding constructions of consistent sexual appetite. In a typical example, Eric said, "You're asking if I'm ever not in the mood if a woman wants to have sex with me? Unless I don't find her attractive, no, never. And with my girlfriend . . . no, I can't think of a time when she approached me and I said no. Why would I do that unless I was sick or something?" In regards to how these men dealt with their partners' refusals, as expected, few men spoke directly about coercing or assaulting their partners, although some did mention participation in "train rides" or gang bangs. A few, however, hinted at women's sexual duties. Martin, for example, suggested that "part of a woman's obligation in a relationship is to have sex" with her partner. Also, as described above, some men reported feeling justified in their infidelity if a girlfriend refused sex.

Middle-class women, sexual affirmation, and the gendered politics of refusal. In comparison to poor and working-class women, middle-class women were more likely to express concern with their feminine attractiveness and desirability than they were to report using sex to avert infidelity or conflict. Despite their resistance to biological justifications for men's higher libido, many middle-class women still wanted and expected men to be readily interested in and prepared for sex. Thus, when their male partners refused sex, they could feel rejected, sad, and even angry. While the socially disadvantaged women discussed *men's* anger in relation to refusing sex, the middle-class women more often reversed the scenario and spoke about *their own* anger, feelings of rejection, or both when their partners were sexually uninterested. Ironically, even with this alternate construction among the middle-class women, the balance of power still seemed to tilt toward their male partners.

As reported above, most respondents suggested that men's sex drives are more powerful than women's. Exceptions to this "rule" led to insecurity and emotional vulnerability in some middle-class women. Rashani, whose sex drive was often greater than her partners', said, "It can be very hard to want it more. My current partner—he's very, very busy. I understand that, but there are moments when . . . I feel like if he were more attracted to me, he would *make* time [for sex]." Rashani interpreted her partner's weaker sex drive as an indication of his weaker sexual attraction to her. Abby also felt personally rejected when her partner refused sex: "Like, what's *wrong* with me?" she bemoaned. And Maya said, "I can probably refuse sex more in my relationship, because I want it less than he does. When he refuses, it's weird." Her use of "weird" here conveys an uncharacteristic and potentially problematic sentiment: "I worry that he may be mad at me or upset about something else." Like Rashani and Abby, Maya indicated that she felt rejected in these circumstances, even though she did not think her boyfriend would suffer from the same feelings of rejection on the frequent occasions that she turned *him* down.

Notably, although middle-class women felt rejected when their partner expressed disinterest in sex, they rarely feared their partners' feelings of rejection on the frequent occasions that they turned *them* down. Alex described a situation in which her partner refused sex:

I wanted to have sex and he said he just didn't feel like it. I was totally shocked, especially when he stood his ground. I tried kissing him, sitting on his lap, you know, and he *still* wasn't in the mood. I was like, "Are you kidding me??" After a while, I thought he was refusing just to make a point—to show me what it was like to be turned down. I was definitely pissy about it for a while.

Alex had become so accustomed to her partner's sexual responsiveness that his refusal was baffling and upsetting. She recognized her double standard: there were times when she turned her partner down, but "not because I want to punish him or because he isn't attractive to me. Sometimes

I'm just not in the mood." Because Alex and other middle-class women had come to *expect* men to want sex more ("Most men will rise to the occasion, you know?" Alex said), they often interpreted men's rejection as deeply personal.

Middle-class men confront "the headache phenomenon". Middle-class men also expressed frustration when their own desire for sex was unmatched by their partners'. Middle-class women were more likely to blame themselves and their lack of desirability for the refusal, however, whereas men were more likely to invoke the cultural notion that women's libido is weaker than men's and assume their partner simply wasn't in the mood. In a typical statement in this regard, Zack said, "Yeah, it definitely happens that my girlfriend doesn't want sex all the times that I do. I don't take it personally—it's just part of what it means to be a guy." Miles said, "As you'd expect, she declines my advances much more often than I decline hers. It's just part of our natural system." Men generally were protected from personal rejection by cultural constructions of gender and sexuality.

A few middle-class men problematized the refusal issue, however, and alluded to their own vulnerabilities in these situations. When asked if both women and men can refuse sex, Matthew responded, "Of course. [Pause.] But then there's that whole 'headache phenomenon.'" He explained that while it is socially acceptable for women to reject men's sexual advances, a man risks inflicting emotional injury or harm to his partner when he does the same. He recounted saying no to a sexual partner on one memorable occasion: "She was hurt. She asked, 'Are you not attracted to me?' It wasn't good. It affected sex and the dynamic between us." In order to have his

partner feel good about herself and to keep her invested in their sex life, Matthew felt he had to fulfill the cultural expectation that he always wanted sex. He showed sensitivity to women's gendered needs around affirmation, but he also was critical of the double standard, suggesting that men cannot access the same kind of distancing mechanisms from sex lest they offend their women partners.

Here, another respondent (Max) described the politics of refusal with his current long-term partner:

> Women have more power in those situations. There's a certain expectation that women's sex drive will be lower. The stage is already set for her refusal.
>
> It's harder for men to turn sex down—it makes women doubt their attractiveness, as if it's personal, whereas men are not supposed to take it personally if women turn down sex. There's some dynamic in my relationship that makes it difficult for me to refuse sex from her.

Max said that he, too, felt rejected when his partner turned him down. He highlighted the cultural pressures placed on men to be the ones who ask for sex, and to accept women's refusal without comment or injury.[7] Even as middle-class men problematized women's easier access to sexual refusal, however, none of them mentioned that women's lower interest in sex gave men the "right" to seek sex elsewhere.

Discussion

Summary

This article has explored *sexual needs and controllability* and *sexual refusal* to illustrate some of the ways in which women and men "do" class and gender in the bedroom. In terms of *sex drive and sexual control*, men were widely perceived to have greater libido than women, although respondents differed by class in their use of biological or social explanations for this disparity. Middle-class respondents tended to problematize the idea that men must have more sex than women, instead invoking discourses of control and mind over matter. Middle-class women criticized the way in which the stereotype of men's sexual cravings has been used to justify inappropriate behaviors such as infidelity or unprotected sex. In turn, middle-class men seemed invested in appearing as if they were above this sexual compulsion and, in contrast, that they were sensitive, respectful, and in control of their sexual appetites.[8] These respondents' accounts evoke the Schneiders' *Festival of the Poor*, in which wealthier Sicilians adopted withdrawal as a contraceptive before the peasant classes, causing a decline in fertility rates (Schneider & Schneider, 1996). In this setting, controlling one's body in the form of sexual restraint in the heat of the sexual moment became a desirable trapping of modernity and affluence.

In contrast, poor and working-class respondents in our study were more likely to present men's sexual needs as biological. Poorer women reported that the thwarting of men's pursuit of sexual gratification and release could lead to aggression, poor health, or physical volatility. Thus, men could not necessarily be blamed if infidelity or encroachment occurred when their sexual needs were unmet, even though these outcomes were unfortunate. For their part, poor and working-class men tended to uphold these notions of their uncontainable sexual desires. Echoing work on masculine virility and power (Bourgois, 2001, 2003;

Collins, 2004; hooks, 2004), poor and working-class men were invested in presenting themselves as potently and even uncontrollably sexual, which could lead them to carry out multiple sexual relationships at once or, sometimes (as seen with Martin), to suggest that women were obligated to have sex with their partners. Sex provided an arena for these men to enact power in a social system that devalues and disenfranchises them.

Along these lines, we believe our findings on libido or sexual control contribute to the literature on the social constructedness of sexuality, particularly how those constructions may both reflect and perpetuate social inequality along the lines of gender, social class, and race. For example, work on the history of sexuality has challenged the notion that men's great libido is a static, biological given (Laqueur, 1990; Tolman & Diamond, 2001). In certain historical moments and cultural settings, *women* have been perceived as possessing uncontrollable sexual appetites. Women of color, historically and currently, have been portrayed as more "animalistic" than White women (Collins, 1990/2000; hooks, 1992), and therefore have been particularly affected by this perception.[9] Such scholarship reminds us that what seems like second nature—in this case, men's (especially socially disadvantaged men's) greater libido—also can be *social* nature (Bourdieu & Passeron, 1990).[10] In the process, these enactments of sexuality actually may uphold social inequality, the same way, for example, that fear of Black sexuality can uphold White racism (Collins, 2004; West, 2001).

Respondents' perceptions of sexual control shaped the contexts of their sexual encounters and, thus, the consequences of *sexual refusal*. Although poor and working-class women certainly described sexual situations that were desirable, consensual, and satisfying, they also spoke of using sex not to seek pleasure but to "cool men down" and to avert infidelity, conflict, and even violence.[11] In other words, the potential consequences of refusal could be grave, which sometimes led these women to have sex even when they were not experiencing sexual desire. Notably, no poor or working-class men spoke of not wanting sex when a partner did. Turning down sexual advances seemed exterior to the social construction of socially disadvantaged masculinity; these men were more interested in upholding constructions of consistent sexual appetite. These men spoke about sexual experiences that were less *enjoyable* than others, but not about unwelcome sexual advances from their partners.

In contrast to poor and working-class women, middle-class women discussed their own anger and sense of rejection when their partners were sexually uninterested. When middle-class men were not in the mood, they worried that their partners would not feel loved or affirmed. Despite middle-class women's criticism of men's alleged sexual "needs," they nonetheless expected men to respond to their sexual advances without fail. If their partners turned down their sexual advances, women felt personally rejected, despite their own occasional or even frequent sexual refusals. Contributing to this double standard is women's heavy social reliance on serving as sexually desirable objects of male attention (Schwartz & Rutter, 1998). Given the social importance placed on women's attractiveness to men, the gendered refusal dynamics we observed with middle-class respondents is not surprising. This finding contributes to the literature on *doing hetero-*

sexuality (Dworkin & O'Sullivan, 2005; Johnson, 2002, 2005; Schwartz & Rutter, 1998), which indicates that the gendered scripts around the "who" and "how" of sexual dynamics may be in flux.[12] Our results also dovetail with Tolman and colleagues' (2003) concept of "gender complementarity," which suggests that the roles and behaviors of both women and men need to be enacted to uphold the current system of heteronormativity.

Implications for Sexual Health Outcomes

Finally, we discuss how the classed and gendered enactments, or *doing*, of sexuality may have shaped the sexual situations in which women and men use—or do not use—contraception. Instead of merely reporting disparities in unintended pregnancy and STI rates among middle-class and poor and working-class individuals, we have tried to describe at least some of the sexual processes that influence those outcomes. For example, we suggest that middle-class respondents' discourse of sexual control contributed to greater efficacy over contraceptive use. That is, pregnancy and disease prevention became an enactment of a kind of sexual discipline and independence. As we describe elsewhere (Higgins & Hirsch, in press), middle-class respondents were more able to "let go" sexually when protected against unwanted pregnancy and disease. (In a typical example of this phenomenon, one middle-class woman said she was "horrified" of getting pregnant. "For me," she said, "sex equals pregnancy. I am always linking the two in my mind." Intercourse was not enjoyable unless she felt fully protected, which helped explain her use of both oral contraceptives and male condoms with her long-term partner. "Sex is just downright unsexy without a condom," she said.) A middle-class social milieu advocated sexual control and discipline, which could be bolstered by effective contraceptive use, and *not* by coercing partners, or by taking certain compensatory measures such as reacting angrily or looking for outside partners when sex was refused, or both of these techniques. In this way, classed cultural capital and worldview helped protect the middle class from poorer sexual health outcomes such as unintended pregnancy.

In comparison, socially disadvantaged respondents adhered to models of sexual uncontrollability, at least in regards to masculine sexuality, that were harder to rein in with contraception. We argued above that enacting a sexual bravado may have given poorer men an opportunity to feel powerful in the face of social disenfranchisement. *Doing* sexuality in this way distanced men from the responsibilities of pregnancy and disease prevention, however, since alleged sexual uncontrollability often contraindicated condom use. It also constrained socially disadvantaged women's ability to refuse sex, to prevent pregnancy or disease, or both. Particularly at sexual onset, a period when many poorer respondents experienced unintended pregnancies, the age gap between sexual partners tended to be much larger than in middle-class settings. Girls are even less likely to meet their contraceptive needs when their partners are 5, 10, or even 15 years older (Liebmann-Smith, 2001).

Thus, the social construction of sexual uncontrollability among poor and working-class respondents contributed to an environment in which sex was a more volatile, less alterable force than in the middle-class respondents' frameworks. As such, we argue that individual-level interventions that try to "empower" poor women to use condoms will do little to address or understand the larger social processes that shape women's and men's sexual encounters, goals, and enactments. Our results reveal that the socially disadvantaged are not merely "at risk" for worse sexual health outcomes; rather, sexual situations are classed and gendered in a way in which contraception is not as salient a concern as, say, maintaining harmonious relationships with men, or upholding notions about sexual needs, control, and responsibility. We encourage public health practitioners to take up the vital challenge of using more multifaceted approaches to social class and gender as a way of better understanding and addressing health disparities. Our results suggest that more public health programs should be developed for social class groups and not merely for women only, men only, or groups based on race or ethnicity. Programs that target socially disadvantaged youth in particular should address taken-for-granted ideologies regarding the "uncontrollability" of men's sexual desire and the politics of refusal. Teaching boys and young men to respect their partner's wishes should be further incorporated into programs intended to reduce the risk of unintended pregnancy, STIs, and HIV.

Indeed, we believe that some of the limiting perceptions of sexual control and refusal held by our respondents are shared by the greater public health community. For example, we suspect that the social acceptance and enactment of men's greater sexual "needs" also contributes to the following widely held notion in public health: Because of their greater sexual control, women must assume responsibility for both pregnancy *and* disease prevention, even though women are not the ones who wear male condoms (Exner et al., 2003). That is, masculinity dictates that men cannot or will not take responsibility for these pursuits in the same way women can.[13] A recent editorial on microbicides in *The Globe and Mail*, which ran during the 2006 International AIDS Conference in Toronto, read, "Changing the behavior of men is probably hopeless. But giving women education and a reliable microbicide might be something we can do" to curb the spread of HIV (Wente, 2006). Such assumptions benefit neither men nor women, nor are they fully effective in promoting condom and contraceptive use given their reliance on a single model of gendered sexuality. The public health field has the opportunity to embrace the path-breaking possibility that all people can and should take responsibility for averting disease and unwanted pregnancy. Of course, we recognize this is a tall order, given the brawn of sexism, classism, and heteronormativity at the structural level.

In closing, we want to acknowledge that this article has narrowed its focus on sexual controllability and sexual refusal, which are only two examples of the classed and gendered aspects of sexuality and which can hardly explain all of the variance in sexual risk taking. For the purposes of this article, however, instead of providing an exhaustive list of the ways in which class seemed to affect sexuality and sexual health outcomes in the data, we instead wanted to look more closely at narrower sexual pathways and to operationalize and define our use of social class in the process. In other words, we set out not to explain everything about the ways that class affects sexual processes, but rather to use two case studies to understand how class and gender are enacted in a way that affects contraception use—and not simply because of lack of contraceptive knowledge or access. We hope future research in this area will deepen our understandings of the ways in which class, gender, and other forms of social inequality shape sexual practices and, in turn, sexual risk taking.

Notes

1. The racial makeup of urban Atlanta made it difficult to recruit lower-class Whites, most of whom live in Georgia's rural areas. Thus, the poor and working-class group was composed mainly of African Americans. We found repeatedly, however, that class seemed to "trump" race in terms of contraceptive use patterns, sexual experiences, and sexual health outcomes, which were more similar across class groups than racial groups. Thus, we focus on class and gender comparisons in this article. This was not a study intended to look primarily at the relationship between race and pleasure—that is, given our interest in social inequality and the specific landscape of urban Atlanta, it was inevitable that more of the poor respondents would be African American. Future studies should examine the associations between race/ethnicity and pleasure in greater depth.

2. The original sample was designed to capture two main social class groups: "middle-class" and "lower-class" respondents. The "lower-class" category included both poor and working-class respondents. When we analyzed the data, we did not find any differences between the poor and working-class respondents in the variables of interest. Therefore, we kept them in a single category. We use the poor/working-class terminology, however, due to its precision as well as its less pejorative connotation.

3. Abby (pseudonym), one of the study participants, illustrates the role of both financial and cultural capital in shaping class. This 25-year-old woman worked behind the counter at a coffee shop. Her poverty-level income would designate her to a "low SES" category in most public health research. She had grown up in a professional, white collar family, however, attended an elite

private college, and ostensibly could have called on the resources of her parents if she were to fall into debt. Furthermore, her education level could have garnered a better-paying job had she sought one. She demonstrated a middle-upper-class cultural capital through her style and worldview, including her vernacular and manner of speaking, the books and media sources she referenced (feminist academic publications, *The Nation*, and *The New Yorker*), and her recreational activities (radio documentary). Her sexual development had occurred during chats with her mother over a copy of *Our Bodies, Ourselves*, extensive sex education in school, and first vaginal intercourse as an older teenager who had already started taking oral contraceptives. We classified Abby as middle class even though her salary and occupation were working class in nature.

4. No respondents reported HIV infection.

5. Because we collected more in-depth data on pregnancy than on STIs, our reported findings for the latter are less detailed.

6. It is possible that poor and working-class women felt more open to talk about the presence of these things in their relationships than middle-class women. This possible disparity in acceptable topics to share with the interviewer could also expose differences in how class is enacted in relation to sexuality.

7. Like Matthew, Max perceived refusal as a power that women have more access to than men. As such, he did not seem to consider women's sexual subordination and the ways in which women are pressured to seek different things in sex than men. That is, because of their sexual and social reliance on men's attention and affection, women would be in particular need of sexual affirmation from men. In other words, Max and other men exhibited some myopia about their own gender privilege.

8. This finding echoes masculinity scholarship that describes how White men sometimes construct themselves as more moral and less sexually excessive than "other" men (Messner, 1997).

9. A number of critical race scholars have written about the racist linking of underprivileged racial ethnic groups with certain animalistic or essentialist characteristics; when people of color are portrayed as closer to "nature," maltreatment and discrimination can be more easily justified (hooks, 1992; Nederveen Pieterse, 1992).

10. The question of who has more desire, men or women, has long been central to sexuality research. However, as Tolman and Diamond (2001) suggest, perhaps of greater interest is not who has *more* desire but rather the *quality* and *characteristics* of those desires, as well as how physiological processes interact with social and relational ones to shape sexual desire in various contexts.

11. Poor and working-class women were more exposed than middle-class women to violence of all kinds, including sexual violence. Due to the physical and cultural geographies of poor neighborhoods, these communities often were burdened by chemical addiction, higher crime, and less police protection, as well as less adult supervision of children, all of which may facilitate sexual abuse, assault, and coercion.

12. Future research could explore further how the tensions of enacting heterosexuality affect contraceptive use (Schultz & Hedges, 1996). How, for example, does the feminine quest for attractiveness and sexual desirability affect contraceptive patterns? Middle-class women in this study complained frequently about hormonal methods' side effects such as weight gain and a reduction in libido. Contraceptive discontinuation in these circumstances could be at least partly caused by women's gendered experience of their bodies in the bedroom.

13. These assumptions also have shaped the long-delayed development of hormone-based contraception for men. Researchers have exhibited far greater concern about potentially diminishing men's sex drive than they have in the development of methods for women (Oudshoorn, 2003; Sanders, Graham, Bass, & Bancroft, 2001).

References

Abma, J. C. (1997). *Fertility, family planning, and women's health: New data from the 1995 National Survey of Family Growth* (vol. 19). Hyattsville, MD: U.S. Dept. of Health and

Human Services Centers for Disease Control and Prevention National Center for Health Statistics.

Abrams, L. S. (2003). Contextual variations in young women's gender identity negotiations. *Psychology of Women Quarterly, 27*(1), 64–74.

Aggleton, P., Rivers, K., & Scott, S. (1999). Use of the female condom: Gender relations and sexual negotiations. In *Sex and youth: Contextual factors affecting risk for HIV/AIDS. A comparative analysis of multi-site studies in developing countries* (pp. 104–145). Geneva: UNAIDS.

Amaro, H., Raj, A., & Reed, E. (2001). Women's sexual health: The need for feminist analyses in public health in the decade of behavior. *Psychology of Women Quarterly, 25*, 324–334.

Anderson, E. (1999). *Code of the street: Decency, violence, and the moral life of the inner city* (1st ed.). New York: W.W. Norton.

Berger, M. T. (2004). *Workable sisterhood: The political journey of stigmatized women with HIV/AIDS*. Princeton, NJ: Princeton University Press.

Bettie, J. (2003). *Women without class: Girls, race, and identity*. Berkeley: University of California Press.

Blanc, A. (2001). The effect of power in sexual relationships on sexual and reproductive health: An examination of the evidence. *Studies in Family Planning, 32*, 189–213.

Bourdieu, P. (1984). *Distinction: A social critique of the judgment of taste*. Cambridge, MA: Harvard University Press.

Bourdieu, P. & Passeron, J. C. (1990). *Reproduction in education, society and culture* (R. Nice, Trans. 1990 ed.). Newbury Park, CA: Sage Publications.

Bourgois, P. I. (2001). In search of masculinity: Violence, respect, and sexuality among Puerto Rican crack dealers in East Harlem. In M. S. Kimmel & M. A. Messner (Eds.), *Men's lives* (5th ed., pp. 42–55). Boston: Allyn and Bacon.

Bourgois, P. I. (2003). *In search of respect: Selling crack in El Barrio* (2nd ed.). Cambridge: Cambridge University Press.

Cancian, F. M. (1986). The feminization of love. *Signs: Journal of Women in Culture and Society, 11*(4), 692–709.

Carpenter, L. M. (2005). *Virginity lost: An intimate portrait of first sexual experiences*. New York: New York University Press.

Centers for Disease Control and Prevention. (2002). *HIV/AIDS Surveillance Report*. Washington, D.C.: Author.

Collins, P. H. (1990/2000). *Black feminist thought: Knowledge, consciousness, and the politics of empowerment* (2nd, Rev. tenth anniversary ed.). New York: Routledge.

Collins, P. H. (2004). *Black sexual politics: African Americans, gender, and the new racism*. New York: Routledge.

Dworkin, S. L. & O'Sullivan, L. (2005). Actual versus desired initiation patterns among a sample of college men: Tapping disjunctures within traditional male sexual scripts. *J Sex Res, 42*(2), 150–158.

Exner, T. M., Dworkin, T., Hoffman, S., & Ehrhardt, A. A. (2003). Beyond the male condom: The evolution of gender-specific HIV interventions for women. *Annual Review of Sex Research, 14*, 114–136.

Farmer, P., Connors, M., & Simmons, J. (1996). *Women, poverty, and AIDS: Sex, drugs, and structural violence*. Monroe, ME: Common Courage Press.

Fenstermaker, S. & West, C. (2002). *Doing gender, doing difference: Inequality, power, and institutional change*. New York: Routledge.

Finer, L. B., & Henshaw, S. K. (2006). Disparities in rates of unintended pregnancy in the United States, 1994 and 2001. *Perspectives on Sexual and Reproductive Health, 38*(2), 90–96.

Goffman, E. (1959). *The presentation of self in everyday life*. Garden City, NY: Doubleday.

Henshaw, S. K. (1998). Unintended pregnancy in the United States. *Family Planning Perspectives, 30*(1), 24–29, 46.

Higgins, J. A. (2005). *The pleasure deficit: The role of desire in contraceptive use*, doctoral dissertation, Emory University, Atlanta.

Higgins, J. A. & Hirsch, J. S. (in press). Pleasure and power: Incorporating sexuality, agency, and inequality into research on contraceptive use and unintended pregnancy. *American Journal of Public Health*.

Hirsch, J. S. (2002). *"A courtship after marriage": Gender, sexuality and love in a Mexican migrant community.* Berkeley, CA: University of California Press.

Hirsch, J. S., Higgins, J., Nathanson, C. A., & Bentley, P. (2002). Social constructions of sexuality: The meanings of marital infidelity and STD/HIV risk in a Mexican migrant community. *American Journal of Public Health, 92*(8), 1227–1237.

Hirsch, J. S., Meneses, S., Thompson, B., Negroni, M., Pelcastre, B., & del Rio, C. (2007). The inevitability of infidelity: Sexual reputation, social geographies, and marital HIV risk in rural Mexico. *American J. Public Health, 97*(6), 986–996.

Hirsch, J. S. & Nathanson, C. A. (2001). Some traditional methods are more modern than others: Rhythm, withdrawal, and the changing meanings of gender and sexual intimacy in the Mexican companionate marriage. *Culture, Health and Sexuality, 3*(4), 413–428.

hooks, b. (1992). *Black looks: Race and representation.* Boston: South End Press.

hooks, b. (2004). *We real cool: Black men and masculinity.* New York: Sage.

Johnson, M. L. (2002). Wanting him anyhow: Third wave feminism and the problem of romance. In M. L. Johnson (Ed.), *Jane sexes it up: True confessions of feminist desire.* New York: Four Walls Eight Windows.

Johnson, P. (2005). *Love, heterosexuality, and society.* London; New York: Routledge.

Krieger, N. (Ed.). (2005). *Embodying inequality: Epidemiologic perspectives.* Amityville, NY: Baywood Publishers.

Krieger, N., Waterman, P., Chen, J., Soobader, M.-J., & Subramanian, S. (2003). Monitoring socioeconomic inequalities in sexually transmitted infections, tuberculosis, and violence: Geocoding and choice of area-based socioeconomic measures—The Public Health Disparities Geocoding Project (US). *Public Health Reports, 118*, 240–260.

Krieger, N., Williams, D. R., & Moss, N. E. (1997). Measuring social class in US public health research: Concepts, methodologies, and guidelines. *Annual Review of Public Health, 18*, 341–378.

Lamont, M. & Lareau, A. (1988). Cultural capital: Allusions, gaps and glissandos in recent theoretical developments. *Sociological Theory, 6*(2), 153–168.

Laqueur, T. W. (1990). *Making sex: Body and gender from the Greeks to Freud.* Cambridge, MA: Harvard University Press.

Laumann, E. O. (1994). *The social organization of sexuality: Sexual practices in the United States.* Chicago: University of Chicago Press.

Laumann, E. O. & Michael, R. T. (2001). *Sex, love, and health in America: Private choices and public policies.* Chicago: University of Chicago Press.

Liebmann-Smith, J. (2001). Preteenage relationship with an older partner may lead to early first sex. *Family Planning Perspectives, 33*(3), 134.

Malat, J. (2000, May). Racial differences in Norplant use in the United States. *Social Science & Medicine, 50*(9), 1297–1308.

Messner, M. A. (1997). *Politics of masculinities: Men in movements.* Thousand Oaks, CA: Sage Publications.

Miles, M. B. & Huberman, A. M. (1994). *Qualitative data analysis: An expanded sourcebook* (2nd ed.). Thousand Oaks, CA: Sage Publications.

Morgan, S. P. (1996). Characteristics of modern American fertility. *Population and Development Review, 22*(Suppl.), 19–63.

Mosher, W. D. & Bachrach, C. A. (1996). Understanding U.S. fertility: Continuity and change in the National Survey of Family Growth, 1988–1995. *Family Planning Perspectives, 28*(1), 4–12.

Mosher, W. D., Chandra, A., & Jones, J. (2004). Sexual behavior and selected health measures: Men and women ages 15–44 years of age. *Advanced Data* (362), 1–56.

Nederveen Pieterse, J. (1992). *White on black: Images of African and Blacks in Western popular culture.* New Haven, CT: Yale University Press.

Oudshoorn, N. (2003). *The male pill: A biography of a technology in the making.* Durham, NC: Duke University Press.

Sanders, S. A., Graham, C. A., Bass, J. L., & Bancroft, J. (2001). A prospective study of the effects of oral contraceptives on sexuality and well-being and their relationship to discontinuation. *Contraception, 64*(1), 51–58.

Santelli, J. S., Brener, N. D., Lowry, R., Bhatt, A., & Zabin, L. S. (1998). Multiple sexual partners among U.S. adolescents and young adults. *Family Planning Perspectives, 30*(6), 271–275.

Schneider, J. & Schneider, P. T. (1996). *Festival of the poor: Fertility decline & the ideology of class in Sicily, 1860–1980*. Tucson: University of Arizona Press.

Schultz, J. & Hedges, W. (1996). Hearing ourselves talk: Links between male sexuality and reproductive responsibilities. In S. Zeidenstein & K. Moore (Eds.), *Learning about sexuality: A practical beginning* (pp. 45–70). New York: The Population Council.

Schulz, A. J. & Mullings, L. (Eds.). (2006). *Gender, race, class & health*. San Francisco: Jossey-Bass.

Schwartz, P. & Rutter, V. (1998). *The gender of sexuality*. Thousand Oaks, CA: Pine Forge Press.

Skeggs, B. (1997). *Formations of class and gender: Becoming respectable*. London, Thousand Oaks, CA: Sage.

Sobo, E. J. (1993). Inner-city women and AIDS: The psycho-social benefits of unsafe sex. *Culture, Medicine & Psychiatry, 17*(4), 455–485.

Sobo, E. J. (1995). *Choosing unsafe sex: AIDS-risk denial among disadvantaged women*. Philadelphia: University of Pennsylvania Press.

Tolman, D. L. (2002). *Dilemmas of desire: Teenage girls talk about sexuality*. Cambridge, MA: Harvard University Press.

Tolman, D. L. & Diamond, L. M. (2001). Desegregating sexuality research: Cultural and biological perspectives on gender and desire. *Annual Review of Sex Research, 12*, 33–74.

Tolman, D. L., Striepe, M. I., & Harmon, T. (2003). Gender matters: Constructing a model of adolescent health. *Journal of Sex Research 40*(1), 4–9.

Ulin, P., Robinson, E. T., Tolley, E. E., & McNeill, E. T. (2002). *Qualitative methods: A field guide for applied research in sexual and reproductive health*. Research Triangle Park, NC: Family Health International.

Wente, M. (April 17, 2006). The trouble with Africa. *Globe and Mail*, p. A15.

West, C. (2001). *Race matters* (2nd Vintage Books ed.). New York: Vintage Books.

Worth, D. (1989). Sexual decision-making and AIDS: Why condom promotion among vulnerable women is likely to fail. *Studies in Family Planning, 20*(6), 297–307.

23 Gloria Martinez

"My Body Is Not the Same"
Body and Sexuality for White and Latina Long-Term Breast Cancer "Survivors"

Introduction

Surviving cancer has been described as "a tumultuous experience of balancing the elation of surviving life-threatening illness with the demands of chronic health concerns and altered life meaning" (Ferrell and Dow 1996). For many diagnosed with breast cancer, the illness involves a search for meaning and purpose to life in addition to physical challenges, stress and adversity. However, living through and surviving breast cancer can also be a catalyst for a greater appreciation of time, life and social relationships and for a healthier lifestyle and behavior (Carter 1993; Vickberg 2001; Hilton 1988).

Breast cancer not only impacts individuals, it extends to affect all their societal ties, interpersonal relationships, income, work, social status, and power. Breast cancer survivors face unique challenges to their social identities, their bodies, their social roles, their intimate relationships, and their families (Dow et al. 1996; Ferrell and Dow 1997; Oktay and Walter 1991).

Brief Review of the Literature

A psychosocial perspective on the meaning of illness assumes that women's perceptions and responses about the significance of illness and the social problems related to disease and illness are rooted in their life histories and personal value systems. Those histories and values impose unique meaning on women's individual experience of health and illness and, as such, potentially transform them with new meanings about themselves, their bodies, their health, and their future.

From a feminist perspective, researchers seek to understand how in medicine and in the health care system, the complexities and contradictions between the public and private meanings of illness get played out and how ideologies of gender and heterosexuality and sexism are socially reproduced and maintained (Kasper 1994; Ehrenreich and English 1978). Feminist research in particular seeks to explore the discrepancies between gender roles, sexuality, race and ethnicity as they are imposed on women by the dominant culture in their everyday lived experiences (Smith 1987). In the case of breast cancer "survivors," many women report changes to their perceived notions of femininity as they feel that "social assumptions which define them as women no longer match their own interior definition

Gloria Martinez, "'My Body Is Not the Same': Body and Sexuality for White and Latina Long-Term Breast Cancer 'Survivors'." Edited from a version first presented at the American Sociological Association Annual Meeting, August 2006. Reprinted by permission of the author.

of what it means to be a woman"; they experience a sense of loss (Kasper 1994).

This paper presents findings from research that aimed to understand how breast cancer affected White (non-Latina) and Latina (non-White) breast cancer survivors five years beyond their diagnosis and treatment. Specifically, this paper is part of a larger study that examined ethnic differences and similarities in long-term survivors' perceptions of the physical aspects of their bodies after having breast cancer surgery and treatment such as mastectomy, lumpectomy, chemotherapy, radiation, hormone therapy/tamoxifen and breast reconstruction, as well as long-term side effects. This study employed qualitative methodology to identify and describe (LTBCS) White (non-Latina) and Latina (non-White) long-term breast cancer survivors' consciousness about themselves and their health. In this paper I will describe White (non-Latina) and Latina (non-White) breast cancer survivors' perceptions about their bodies, selves, and femininity after surgery and treatment. I will also discuss the complexity of breast cancer survivors' "embodiment" after diagnosis, surgery (lumpectomy or mastectomy), and chemotherapy treatment.[1]

Methodology and Sample Demographics

Twenty-eight White (non-Hispanic) long-term breast cancer survivors living in the Midwest were interviewed. Respondents were telephoned and requested to participate in an in-person interview at their convenience and at a location of their choice, namely, home, office or the researcher's office. Most of the interviews were conducted at their homes and all of the interviews were tape-recorded. Following my interviews with White non-Latina women in Michigan, I conducted fieldwork among Latina (non-White) breast cancer survivors in California. I conducted all the interviews with 24 Latina long-term breast cancer survivors in California using a snowball sampling method. The snowball sampling method was helpful in accessing Latina breast cancer survivors because there still remains a great deal of fear, silence and stigma about breast cancer. Breast cancer is still perceived as a very personal and emotional experience and some women may feel ashamed or stigmatized of being identified; snowballing provided referrals from women who had already agreed to be interviewed.

Semi-structured interviews were conducted to allow survivors to tell their stories from their point of view; this allowed the women to expand and expound on their experiences. I aimed at being an empathetic and active listener when women began to tell their stories. I tried to avoid interrupting them and only interrupted if it seemed that they were going off on a tangent. I probed occasionally to get some more details about their experience. This method allowed me to be situated as a researcher who wanted to build knowledge from the standpoint of learning from women's perspectives, which may not be a fixed or uniform outcome among breast cancer survivors. I used many probes to gain a deeper understanding about what women said about sexuality, body image and intimacy by asking, "What side-effects do you have as a result of having had breast cancer?" "Can you tell me more?" and "What do you mean?" However, this was not an issue when interviewing over the telephone—topics such as sexuality and body image

TABLE 23.1 **Results and Discussions: Sample Demographics**

	White (non-Latina) (n=28)		Latina (n=25)	
Mean Current Age	66 (40–89)		57 (34–84)	
Mean Age at Diagnosis	54 (29–84)		47 (27–75)	
Mean Years Since Diagnosis	13		10	
Education	N	%	N	%
8th Grade or Less	–	–	5	20
Some High School	–	–	1	4
High School Graduate	4	15	4	16
Some College	8	31	2	8
Graduated College	4	15	6	24
Post-college Study	10	39	7	28
Employment				
Yes	12	44	15	60
No	15	56	10	40
Income				
<15,000	2	9	3	12
>15,000 <30,000	6	26	8	32
>30,000 <60,000	7	30	4	16
>60,000 <80,000	5	22	3	12
>80,000	3	13	7	28
Health Insurance				
Medicare	3	11	1	4
Medicaid	0	–	1	4
Medicare+Medicaid	1	4	–	–
Medicare+HMO	1	4	2	8
Medicare	7	27	2	8
+PPO/Private				
PPO/Private	12	46	10	40
HMO	2	8	8	32
Self-Pay/Uninsured	–	–	1	4
Type of Treatment				
Mastectomy	17	61	21	84
Lumpectomy	11	39	6	24
Breast Reconstruction	7	25	10	40
Radiation	12	43	4	16
Chemotherapy	7	25	15	60
Tamoxifen	5	18	8	32

were more openly discussed in this medium. Latinas (non-White) were more open to discussing issues of sexuality, intimacy and body image in person, except for women who were over age 60.

The White (non-Latina) sample consisted of a larger number of the women who were college-educated, earned high incomes, and had health insurance. Latinas were slightly younger at age of diagnosis— 47 years—and the mean age of the women in the study was 57. Most Latinas were bilingual (Spanish and English), but one-third of the women were monolingual Spanish speakers. Most Latinas were college-educated (60%), with 40% reporting incomes higher than $60,000; however, 44% reported earning less than $30,000. Most Latinas identified themselves as being of Mexican origin.

Women described their breast cancer as "devastating," "furious," a "wake-up call," or an "awakening," and said that breast cancer compromised their body and their health.

The cancer was horrifying to me because it felt as though an invader were in my body. White (non-Latina) LTBCS

Totally devastated. But it wasn't so much at the thought of breast cancer, cuz my mom had had it and there's 4 girls in the family and we always said we figured that a couple of us would get it. But I felt *not at 40 years old!* White (non-Latina) LTBCS

When breast cancer survivors were asked if they experienced any physical side effects, women who had had a mastectomy (compared to women who had had lumpectomy and radiation) reported negative permanent changes to their bodies. Only a few women who had lumpectomies reported perceiving their breasts as being deformed.

I don't feel like I've been a victim of any kind. I don't, you know, I think I was very fortunate to be able to have the lumpectomy rather than the mastectomy. That would be a constant reminder. This way my scar doesn't even show. People say, "Where was it?" It's that unobtrusive. I think you kind of forget about it. And somebody might, "Oh yeah, I did have that." White (non-Latina) LTBCS

(English translation)
I had a lumpectomy. For me it was difficult to see myself because I saw my breast deformed. It first signified to me a scar on my body. A deformation on my body. Secondly, imagine if they had removed my breast it would be a mutilation. For me it is a mutilation. It is not that the breast should be aesthetic or not aesthetic but that it is a mutilation on a part of your body! That what other women have on their bodies is missing on your body. I was always afraid of losing part of my organs or from my body. Let me tell you now, I am thankful that I was not large-breasted. I wanted to be like the girls on television. But now, I say that it was good that I was not large breasted because if I was, the lumpectomy would be more noticeable. I always fear losing a part of my body. Latina LTBCS

Women who had had breast reconstructions reported experiencing painful scarring and keloids, sagging skin, sagging or lopsided implants, inverted implants, or saline implants feeling hard and heavy. Some women who experienced chemotherapy-induced body changes, for example, pre-menopause conditions such as hot flashes, diminished menses, infertility, and fatigue. But both White (non-Latina) and Latina (non-White) women who had had a mastectomy, chemotherapy and breast reconstruction reported having more problems with their bodies:

Um, physically I still don't feel good about it [mastectomy]. There's nothing that will ever replace it. I just opted for an implant, but I absolutely love not having the prosthesis. You can finally get, you know, a nice bra and stuff but, nothing will ever replace the original. White (non-Latina) LTBCS

Women who had had mastectomies were more concerned about being treated differently and feeling different because they had a mastectomy scar, wore a prosthesis, or had a reconstructed "breast." Women who had chemotherapy talked about the negative effects of experiencing chemically induced menopause.

The impact of losing your breast for a woman is a big deal. My frame of mind was "I am not only a breast; I am more than a breast." So if this has to go, it has to go. I was given this prosthesis and this thing was heavy. I liked to come home and take my bra off and put on something comfortable so that way I feel good. . . . This empty space was in my chest so when I woke up or I am looking in the mirror there was emptiness there. At that moment I said, "well I am doing fine. Why not do a breast reconstruction?" I was doubtful, ay what for? I am already this age; do I need to do that? Then you know, "Yea, I do." I was up and down. My husband said, "For me don't do it. It doesn't make a difference to me. If I were you, I wouldn't do it. But you do whatever you want to." I went to the doctor and the plastic surgeon and I expressed my thoughts and my husband and he [the plastic surgeon] says, "I think you should do it. You are going to feel way better about yourself and everything." I said, "Ok, let's do it." Well everything was set and even the last day my husband is driving me to the clinic to have the surgery and he said, "Are you sure you want this? We can turn around." I said, "No, I decided that I want to." For other women this is not the case. I did it. But, for me, I know for me when I did it I felt better. So I am happy that I did it. Latina LTBCS

(thinking) I think sometimes I am, uh, saddened. My body doesn't look the same that it did. I think I had two very nice looking breasts. I am sorry that is not the case now. I do a lot of ballroom dancing and some of the Latin dancing dresses that are cut low in the front, you know what, it looks nice, but I will never be able to wear a dress like that, so there is a degree of grieving that went along with losing my breasts. I think that we use a very nice word when we talk about mastectomy. It's really a breast amputation. When you say amputation then suddenly there is a whole different focus on it. It is an amputation. I am saddened that my body has had to look different and I feel it is part of the sacrifice that one makes to get well. It's a sacrifice I did without any regret whatsoever. I did not want to have any obvious sign of cancer in my body, but yes, I am saddened that that breast is not there. Latina LTBCS

Women who had breast reconstructions reported still not feeling the same. Their sensitivity to touch and arousal during intimacy was described as a loss for themselves and for their intimate partners. Many women had to redefine their intimacy with their spouse or partners:

They said, "Well we could do it [breast reconstruction] right away, and you won't have to come in right away for surgery, you know, until after your chemo treatments." And I said, "Okay, why not?" I didn't look forward to being flat-chested. I was big-breasted, and that was another reason why I went ahead with the left [an unaffected breast] one, because it would be so lopsided, and they said, "Well, we can do a reduction [of the other breast]." But, there's a lot of scar tissue, and, they can't see on mammograms through scar tissue. So I just said forget it, just remove it. Much easier. I mean, I was done nursing my kids and stuff like that, and having kids, so, just, no big deal (Laughs) . . . My period stopped. I was on the pill, on the day I went in for surgery, on Valentine's Day, and they said, "That's it. No more." So that same week, my husband went in and had a vasectomy (Laughs). So we both were recouping at home. I mean, sometimes I come home, and he says, "Man, I miss 'em hon." (Laughs). "Yeah, I miss 'em too, dear." (Still laughing). You know, they're long gone. And he knows that, and you know, and he does miss 'em sometimes, but, and I do too, but, there are other things to do, and you know, you just kind of, oh well, that's life, and turn around, and let's see what else is facing you and what else you got to deal with. Keep moving. . . . White (non-Latina) LTBCS

Most women viewed wearing a prosthesis and having a breast reconstruction as necessary to help them restore their outer body image and overcome stigma and alienation in public space.

Breast cancer survivors framed their suffering as a result of the loss of their breasts in term of Western cultural meanings of femininity and social roles. Women who had a mastectomy perceived themselves as no longer looking like a "natural" person or as a "perfect" double-breasted body image, but instead as an amputated body deformed from scarring, and in some cases, with lymphedema arm swelling. Both the prosthesis and breast reconstruction served to hide the amputated breast and avoid the social stigma from looking "lopsided," "flat," or "empty." But the prosthesis and breast reconstruction only helped them restore their ability to wear body-contouring clothes and to portray a feminine-breasted image. However, the prosthesis and breast reconstruction have their limits. Most women who wore prostheses mentioned that they were not able to wear beautiful blouses, low cut or short sleeves.

Mastectomy was perceived as an amputation or a mutilation of the body that makes it look different and less aesthetic. Permanent changes to women's bodies affected their perceptions about corporeal femininity:

I appreciated being presented to the world as a beautiful breasted woman, and there was the value that people placed on me, and then losing my breasts meant that I was asking to be loved for myself, not for my breasts. My mother would say she has beautiful breasts and all look you know, and it was a big deal that I had breasts and it was a sense of femininity, and I remember at one time a man made an obscene remark about my breasts. My ex-husband loved my breasts. They were large and they were beautiful, but I felt like it was like people were looking at my breasts and not me, and I remember telling a friend that when they took my breasts it was as if my

heart opened. Everybody was looking at my breasts so nobody could look at my heart to love me. Latina LTBCS

The value and meaning of women's breasts had to be negotiated within themselves and others within a social context. It was not an easy process, especially given a patriarchal breast- and body-conscious Western society that privileges "well-endowed" two-breasted women.

I was big breasted, and they said, well, and at the time, I hadn't decided if I wanted the other mastectomy, the subcutaneous one, and so they said, "OK, we can go ahead." It was a kind of new thing, I think, at the time that, you know, the tissue expander. And, they said, "Well we could do it right away, and you won't have to come in right away for surgery, you know, until after your chemo treatments." And I said, "Okay, why not?" So, I mean, I didn't look forward to being *flat-chested*, but, I mean, right now, if it was the case, and they could do it, I would probably just say, "That's fine." I'm not, I'm not happy a hundred percent with my implants. White (non-Latina) LTBCS

The grief period, the loss of losing your breast or the possibility of losing the breast is very traumatic to all women. I had to come to grips with it because I decided to have a mastectomy. Everything that we see in magazines and all the cleavage and all the stuff you look at while you are shopping for groceries. It's there staring at you as if that is the most important thing about a woman and I had to come to grips with that. But, you tend to look at women's breasts a lot at first. If somebody's wearing something revealing. And your eyes just go and you catch yourself and you wonder what are you doing? Like it is the most important thing in the world. I had to come to grips with what does a breast represent to me? The breast meant breast feeding my child, pleasure to my husband but he didn't need two breasts at the same time, and it meant getting rid of the cancer. The only way that I can get rid of the cancer or feel like I am getting rid of it was to remove the breast that had the cancer. I saw it as my life. The grieving part wakes you up at night and makes you cry. I came to the realization that I am not a breast that I was a heart, that I was a mind, I was a mother, I was a wife, I was a professional, I was a cousin, I was a sister and so on just kind of helped me through the process. Men want to fix things. They want to fix it, and they want to tell their partner you look fine, its fine, it doesn't matter I don't see you that way blah blah blah not realizing that not until the woman sees herself that way, I mean for me its going to be 8 years on May 6th. I have to sometimes when I get out of the shower past my big mirror. I sometimes look at myself twice cause I almost see myself perfect, normal again, perfect, and two breasts. I have to stop and clear the mirror of the moisture and look again and see that, no. I don't see my breast and probably a man who has his head together probably doesn't either. He probably stops and sees his wife "deformed" or abnormal. Don't try to fix her way of thinking, uhm, telling them it's ok. Of course remind them tell them it's ok and love them through the process but allow them to grieve. He sees that the cancer is gone—everything is fixed—doesn't mean her heart is fixed, her mind is fixed until she goes through the grieving process. It took me a couple of years a few years you know to work it through. Latina LTBCS

Even my surgeon was not used to seeing young women with breast cancer because he forgot to ask me if I was planning to have a reconstruction afterwards, he just assumed that I was never going to have reconstruction. So he took all of my skin that they use for reconstruction. Even though at that time my whole goal was that I wanted to survive this cancer so I was not too worried about reconstruction or anything else you know. It was an option that was never given to me. Later on I remember someone asking me, "Hey, are you going to have a reconstruction?" I said, "Well I don't know. How do they do that?" I remember going to the surgeon and he said, "Well I never thought of asking you because most of the women that I have seen are over 45 and they don't really need reconstruction. They are already too old." He said, "Well you don't have much there to do a reconstruction because I took a lot of the skin out so it would be kind of hard to do a reconstruction." He says, "A prosthesis will work as well." (She laughs). I wanted to make sure that I went to the fifth year and thinking in five years if nothing has happened that means I am free of cancer so I didn't want to do any reconstruction until three years had passed. Latina LTBCS

Many women reported feeling stigmatized by their friends, family and coworkers about their "inappropriate" response to the changes of their body:

Now, my sister was very, um, I don't know why, I dealt with losing the breast probably better than expected just because my sister really wanted me to get reconstruction right away. She really pushed that and, that wasn't a main goal in my life. I had promised myself that, if I could stay 5 years cancer-free, that I would get some kind of reconstruction. Cuz all I could think of at the time was well, I should go through reconstruction and then 6 months later it happens all over again, you know, so that's what I did. I was not pleased in the respect of the prosthesis was a big nuisance. We have a pool in the back yard, my sisters are on a lake, we do a lot of swimming, and I just love, I absolutely love it that I can wear a bathing suit all the time now. Um, physically I still don't feel good about it. There's nothing that will ever replace it . . . I wasn't up for the trans flap, you know, I thought that was too much of a major surgery, sounded wonderful. Get a tummy tuck out of it and stuff but it sounded too much a major surgery and, so I just opted for a, but I absolutely love not having that. And then you can finally get, you know, a nice bra and stuff and, no, no, nothing will ever replace the original but, it helped immensely with . . . cuz the other thing was such a nuisance. (Laughs). White (non-Latinas) LTBCS

I didn't want anybody to see me. One dear friend looked at me and she say "Which one was it? Does it make any difference? That blew my mind! How can people be so insensitive? It's none of her damn business. White (non-Latina) LTBCS

Some of the people I thought would support me didn't, and some of the people I thought wouldn't do. So I was surprised about that . . . some of the people I worked with, I worked with a lot of women, and some of the women I worked with seemed to be angry about the choices I had made . . . about . . . getting a lumpectomy . . . instead of a mastectomy, and I had one woman tell me that I'd done the wrong thing. She suggested or said that it was just because I was vain, and I wanted to save my breast, and because of that I had a lumpectomy and that wasn't the right thing to do. I

was amazed. I was really was shocked. They seemed angry and frightened. I could tell they were frightened, I could tell that some people were frightened and didn't want to hear about it. No, didn't want to talk about it at all. White (non-Latina) LTBCS

There were lots of relationships before cancer that actually died while I was going through chemo. I just noticed a lot of—a sense of insensitivity on the part of some people. I remember reading about this one woman who was going through chemo and she said that there is just some relationships get stronger and some relationships just wilt and that was true for me. That was definitely true for me. The relationships that died were the relationships where people were afraid to make the phone call or to visit. I think it's really important to honor every person as an individual and to refrain from judgment. I am sure I looked like I was ready for the psych ward some days when I was there. I must have to some of them about the day I stood up and yelled "I have been a single parent on welfare this place isn't much better than County Hospital." I am sure they thought oh this lady needs some Prozac or something. All my senses were intact. I knew exactly what I was doing so I think it's really important to uh try to see things from the point of view of the person you are serving. They want to run the health care profession as though one size fits all. That is just not true. Everybody gets 350 mg of this and so therefore you will too. It's ridiculous and unfortunately it lowers their learning curve because if they were to get involved more intimately I think they would learn a lot. Latina LTBCS

(English translation)
R: Some people made some insensitive comments and they were often women.

One teacher when she learned that I had reconstructive surgery said, "How fortunate you are, how lucky you are." You know, "You got to pick your size" and I says, "You know what—I much rather have the ones God gave me, thank you very much" and I walked out of the room. And another one I tried to explain to her that I was grieving and that I was sad about the loss of my breast.

I: And what did she say?

R: And she said, "I didn't think you were into your body that way." And I said, "Well it wasn't a defining, it wasn't the defining factor of my being but it's still a loss your body" it is not the same as it was. It's just not the same, let alone people just don't understand it that when you have reconstructive surgery, you lose all the nerve endings . . . so that sense of touch is gone, it's gone, it's gone. It's a whole other ball game. That's a big loss. Maybe if I only lost one breast, it would be different, you know, getting over it would have been easier and faster. I don't know, but, uh, yea I think people try to minimize the effect just because it makes them more comfortable to do that. Latina LTBCS

Breast cancer survivors reported difficulty publicly communicating their unhappiness with the negative changes to their body, the limitations experienced as a result of losing a breast and fear of being "too into her body" or "vain." The women feared being perceived as selfish or "too into themselves," unappreciative of life, sinful, and identifying with their breasts—a sexualized part of their body.

For my fiancée breasts were very important and if I have one removed I knew that this was going to be more difficult for him to accept than the children issue because, even though this man was so much involved in the community and social justice issues, when it came to intimacy it was a different thing. Latina LTBCS

The impact of breast cancer on sexual expression was perceived as not being "a big deal," but it was qualified with statements about women's awareness of the negative impact that breast cancer can have on sexual intimacy. Single women often reported avoiding becoming intimately involved in a relationship because they were embarrassed by the way they looked and feared being rejected. They were concerned about how men would perceive them as not being "complete" or "perfect," and would perceive them as having nothing to offer sexually:

(English translation)

Well, for a woman, yes it has given me, well . . . I have not liked having relationships with another person. Even when I have had suitors, well, I feel, I feel bad, do you understand me? Because a man, when he sees one like this they say, "No, you are no longer complete." They make you ugly and it hurts oneself, you understand. "No, well you are no longer complete. You are no good for nothing or something like that." This is primarily caused by all those macho concepts from men. Latina LTBCS

A few breast cancer survivors shared information about their pain over being discriminated against and rejected as a result of having a mastectomy:

One boyfriend I had wanted me to have the breast surgery. I said, "Well, it's bothering you a hell of a lot more than it does me. Good-bye." I've gone with a couple of people, you know, it didn't seem to bother them. White (non-Latina) LTBCS

R: My fiancée, he started coming less around and calling me less and I knew that this was going to be the end. When he was asked why he had a problem with me missing a breast he just answered, "I don't know why I just can't deal with it." He finally admitted, "Yes, I am having a terrible time and maybe if they cut off your foot instead of your breast maybe that may have been different, maybe it may have had the same effect I don't know, I don't know but I can't deal with it." So after that we didn't see each other. He married somebody else. That was so painful. When I started a new relationship I realized how much I missed my breast because sometimes I felt like my capability to have pleasure had been removed. Sometimes I feel this tremendous sadness, like I have been castrated. I had this feeling that someone shortchanged me somewhere and yes I remember that doctor insisted that I shouldn't have that breast removed because I was too young. He never referred me the option to talk to someone that has gone through that and even though at that point my brain was not working because I was depressed.

I: What is it that you miss?

R: When I had sex with my partner that I have now it was like this big part of me that used to give me so much pleasure and I used to enjoy so much is gone now and it's never going to come back. And even though my partner never said anything that has made me feel uncomfortable or self-conscious or has done anything that will make me feel that way, I still miss my breasts. These are my feelings. I have implants now but there is no feeling there because my skin is dead. I don't have any sensation in parts of

my breast. I have feeling here, but everything else is dead. Latina LTBCS

I haven't gotten into a relationship in a long time. I would really feel awkward about it to think that those [the breast implants] are me and so those are the things I look at. I have been on dates but I haven't been intimate with anyone in years since my husband died over ten years ago. I'm looking for one that that doesn't matter. White non-Latina LTBCS

Rejection hindered women's intimacy. But women who emphasized that they were in a strong, loving relationship reported fewer problems with intimacy.

He's an emotional rock. He loves me and I know that. It made it clearer from the time he said, "I don't care if they remove your breasts I love you just the same." I knew he was serious about it. I know that he meant it. White (non-Latina) LTBCS

I would tell you that sexually actually of course when you go through surgeries and all that you don't even think about that but we have just celebrated 35 years of marriage and of course through life, you know you have more activity and less activity. Of course right now it's not what it used to be thirty years ago because we were younger and more active, but the depth of the emotional level we reach in our sexual moments is so so much deeper, right, it's less often but of so much value. It's more important the quality of the sexual interaction and the intimacy that you have with your husband is what matters. Latina LTBCS

Breast cancer survivors stated that they did find new meanings to their sexualities, through resisting against men's control and by ending hurtful relationships. A few breast cancer survivors shared information about having to redefine the meaning of their sexual intimacy and needing to discover how to affirm their own sexuality. As a result they were able to take control and embody new, intimate sexual relationships with men:

> I think I was very lucky that I met someone with whom I felt it was safe to express my feelings, using humor and with him I don't know why I didn't have any inhibitions and I felt so free. He allowed me to be free and say "I don't like this" or "I like this very much. Let's try this other thing." I was never afraid that he thought, "Oh this woman is crazy or kinky." He never judged me so I felt very free to experiment things. So when I was with that guy that was funny I only had one breast—I didn't miss anything about that and I never thought of anything that I was missing. Until I had sex with my present partner several years later and it was like, "Wow what happened here?" (She laughs). But I have been able to talk to him and say, "I don't have my breast now so I feel half of my joy is gone but why don't we make up this way?" More stimulation in other areas or whatever. I found that in other cases I do miss this other part but then again we also find other ways and he is the type of person that he is open to other things that I suggest. Sometimes he says, "I am not very creative but you tell me what to do." Latina LTBCS

> If I had been married with my former husband it would have totally have ruined our intimacy because he was a man who cared enormously about my appearance and he would be totally grossed. I had one baseball (pointed to her breast) and one normal breast so I was—this was hanging and this was up here. Here I am with no hair with no breast and this man [fiancée] makes me feel as I were the sexiest woman alive on earth. He was so loving you know and I could see that he really was crazy about me. It was really a tremendous love affair, even with all these things that drew away from my femininity. I survived but if it would have been the wrong relationship I mean with the person that couldn't handle that kind of stuff it would have been very devastating. We fell in love and we are going to get married. Latina LTBCS

In this study, White (non-Latina) women reported having few problems with their sexuality when compared to Latinas. In this sample more Latinas talked about how breast cancer impacted their intimacy and sexuality than did White non-Latinas. This may be because the Latinas were younger than the White (non-Latinas). Studies on Latina sexuality show that Latinas' ideology and behavior is changing and is heavily influenced by popular culture in the United States. Researcher Patricia Zavella (2003) argues that Latinas' sexuality is heavily influenced by traditional Catholic sexual ideology and by popular culture in the United States. This research suggests that Latinas' sexual attitudes and behavior might be heavily influenced by permanent and altering physical and social side effects after being diagnosed and treated with breast cancer.

Most breast cancer survivors reported being challenged to adjust to a new body image personally, interpersonally, and in society. They experienced stigma and personal suffering as a result of others objectifying their bodies and living in a society that equates breasts, especially large breasts, to women's beauty and femininity. Both White women and Latinas reported their sexuality and body images were impacted by the loss of their breasts and their "breasted self-image."

Conclusion

Breast cancer survivors face unique changes and challenges regarding the landscape of their bodies. After being diagnosed with breast cancer, the body is no longer perceived as being the same. Breast cancer survivors involuntarily are placed in a position to redefine and rearticulate their bodies to overcome looking and feeling "different." In her extensive qualitative study of long-term survivors of 25 breast cancer survivors, Barbara Carter (1996) argues that for breast cancer survivors, the sense of self is an ongoing interpretation over a lifetime, and the social context of an individual's life helps promote or impede psychosocial health. Similarly, Katrina Breaden (1997) found that breast cancer survivors described their survival process going from disembodiment between the mind and the body to regaining a feeling of being whole and becoming "embodied" again. The experience of embodiment, as Breaden notes (1997, p. 980), "refers to an intimacy between the body as an object and the body as it is lived, and it is this lived body that enables us to experience situations, interpret them, and interact with the world in a meaningful way. Disembodiment, on the other hand, refers to a perceived rift between the body we have and the body we are, a separation between the body and the self." Wilmoth (2000) indicated that breast cancer and its treatment

imposes a unique threat to self-concept through its impact on women's body image and sexual identity. Multiple factors, such as feelings about the body, self-esteem, sexual identity, femininity, and interpersonal relations play a role in sexuality after breast cancer. Susan Wilson, Robyn Andersen and Hendrika Meischke (2000) found that long-term breast cancer survivors (1–32 years since diagnosis) continued to have concerns about how their body looked after the surgery and treatment. Many of the breast cancer survivors in my study had to renegotiate their experiences of loss of sensitivity in their breasts, no longer looking like a "natural" woman, and thus reconstruct "new" gender identities around these losses.

Feminist research has argued that because Western society places so much value on a woman's breasts as a source of beauty, femininity and sexuality, breasts are an important component of body self-image. They are a part of a woman's identity and symbolize her unique femininity (Kasper 1994; Latteier, 1998; Langellier and Sullivan 1998). Women perceive that they are judged and evaluated based on how they look and less on how they feel about the loss of "breasted identity" (Young 1990). According to Iris Marion Young, "From the female subject, what matters most about her breasts is their feeling and sensitivity rather than how they look" (Young, 1990, p. 194). But the findings in this study also show that breast cancer survivors are concerned about how their bodies looked after breast cancer surgery. More research is needed to longitudinally assess long-term breast cancer survivors' body image, along with ethnic differences and similarities among breast cancer survivors. In this way we can more fully understand the long-term impact of breast cancer on women's body image and sexualities.

Notes

1. Today, there are two general types of surgeries, lumpectomy and mastectomy, and various combinations of treatment involving chemotherapy and hormonal therapy. A mastectomy can be a partial or segmental mastectomy or total mastectomy. The different types of breast reconstruction ranged from inserting silicon or saline implants to either moving tissue from the woman's own back, abdomen or buttocks to the chest area or having a saline or silicone implant.

Bibliography

Breaden, Katrina. 1997. "Cancer and Beyond: The Question of Survivorship." *Journal of Advanced Nursing* 26:978–984.

Carter, Barbara Jean. 1993. "Long-Term Survivors of Breast Cancer: A Qualitative Descriptive Study." *Cancer Nursing* 16(5):354–361.

———. 1996. "Understanding the Experiences of Long-Term Survivors of Breast Cancer: Story as a Way of Knowing." Pp. 151–159 in *Contemporary Issues in Breast Cancer*, edited by K. H. Dow. Boston, MA: Jones and Bartlett Publishers.

Dow, Karen Hassey, Betty R. Ferrell, Susan Leigh, John Ly and Pratheepan Gulasekaram. 1996. "An Evaluation of the Quality of Life Among Long-Term Survivors of Breast Cancer." *Breast Cancer Research and Treatment* 39:261–273.

Ehrenreich, Barbara, and Deidre English. 1978. *For Her Own Good.* New York: NY: Doubleday.

Ferrell, Betty and Karen H. Dow. 1996. "Portraits of Cancer Survivorship: A Glimpse Through the Lens of Survivors' Eyes." *Cancer Practice* 4(2):76–80.

Ferrell, Betty and Karen H. Dow. 1997. "Quality of Life Among Long-Term Cancer Survivors." *Oncology* 11(4):565–576.

Fredrickson, Barbara L. and Tomi-Ann Roberts. 1997. "Objectification Theory: Toward Understanding Women's Lived Experiences and Mental Health Risks." *Psychology of Women Quarterly* 21:173–206.

Hilton, B. Ann. 1988. "The Phenomenon of Uncertainty in Women with Breast Cancer." *Issues in Mental Health Nursing* 9:217–238.

Kasper, Anne. 1994. "A Feminist, Qualitative Methodology: A Study of Women with Breast Cancer." *Qualitative Sociology* 17(3):263–281.

Kasper, Anne S. and Susan J. Ferguson. 2000. *Breast Cancer: Society Shapes an Epidemic.* New York, NY: St. Martin's Press.

Langellier, Kristin and Claire F. Sullivan. 1998. "Breast Talk in Breast Cancer Narratives." *Qualitative Health Research* 8(1):76–94.

Latteier, Carolyn. 1998. *Breasts: The Women's Perspective on an American Obsession.* New York, NY: Harrington Park Press.

Oktay, Julianne S. and Carolyn A. Walter. 1991. *Breast Cancer in the Life Course.* New York, NY: Springer.

Smith, Dorothy E. 1987. *The Everyday World as Problematic: A Feminist Sociology.* Boston, MA: Northeastern University Press.

Vickberg, Suzanne M. J. 2001. "Fears About Breast Cancer Recurrence: Interviews with a Diverse Sample." *Cancer Practice* 9(5):236–243.

Wilson, Susan E., M. Robyn Andersen and Hendrika Meischke. 2000. "Meeting the Needs of Rural Breast Cancer Survivors: What Still Needs to be Done?" *Journal of Women's Health & Gender-Based Medicine* 9(6):667–677.

Young, Iris. 1990. *Throwing Like a Girl and Other Essays in Feminist Philosophy and Social Theory.* Bloomington, IN: Indiana University Press.

Zavella, Patricia. 2003. "Playing with Fire": The Gendered Construction of Chicana/Mexicana Sexuality." Pp. 229–244 in *Perspectives on Las Americas: A Reader in Culture, History, and Representation*, edited by Matthew C. Guttman, Felix V. Matos Rodriguez, Lynn Stephen and Patricia Zavella. Malden, MA: Blackwell Publishing.

24 Nadine Naber

Arab American Femininities
Beyond Arab Virgin/American(ized) Whore

It was a typical weeknight at my parents' home. My father was asleep since he wakes up at 4:00 a.m. to open his convenience store in downtown San Francisco. I joined my mother on the couch and we searched for something interesting to watch on TV. My mother held the remote control, flipping through the stations. Station after station a similar picture of an Anglo American male and female holding one another in romantic or sexual ways appeared on the screen. As she flipped the station, my mother remarked, "Sleep, Slept . . . Sleep, Slept . . . THAT is America!" She continued, "Al sex al hum, zay shurb al mai [Sex for them is as easy as drinking water]."

—Nadine Naber, journal entry, December 2, 1999

As I listened to my mother,[1] I recalled several experiences growing up within a bicultural Arab American familial and communal context. *Al Amerikan* (Americans) were often referred to in derogatory sexualized terms. It was the trash culture—degenerate, morally bankrupt, and not worth investing in. *Al Arab* (Arabs), on the other hand, were referred to positively and associated with Arab family values and hospitality. Similarly, throughout the period of my ethnographic research among middle-class Arab American family and community networks in San Francisco, California,[2] between January 1999 and August 2001, the theme of female sexuality circumscribed the ways my research participants imagined and contested culture, identity, and belonging. The theme of female sexuality tended to be utilized as part of some Arab immigrant families' selective assimilation strategy in which the preservation of Arab cultural identity and assimilation to American norms of "whiteness" were simultaneously desired. Within this strategy, the ideal of reproducing cultural identity was gendered and sexualized and disproportionately placed on daughters. A daughter's rejection of an idealized notion of Arab womanhood could signify cultural loss and thereby negate her potential as capital within this family strategy. In policing Arab American femininities, this family strategy deployed a cultural nationalist logic that represented the categories "Arab" and "American" in oppositional terms, such as "good Arab girls" vs. "bad American(ized) girls," or "Arab virgin" vs. "American(ized) whore." I coin the term Arab cultural re-authenticity to contextualize this process within Arab histories of transnational migration, assimilation, and racialization. Arab cultural re-authenticity,

Nadine Naber, "Arab American Femininities: Beyond Arab Virgin/American(ized) Whore," *Feminist Studies* 32, no. 1 (Spring 2006): 87–111. Copyright © 2006 Nadine Naber. Reprinted by permission of the author.

I suggest, is a localized, spoken, and unspoken figure of an imagined "true" Arab culture that emerges as a reaction or an alternative to the universalizing tendencies of hegemonic U.S. nationalism, the pressures of assimilation, and the gendered racialization of Arab women and men. I use the term hegemonic (white) U.S. nationalism to refer to the official discourses of the U.S. state and corporate media and the notion of a universalized abstract American citizen that "at the same time systematically produces sexualized, gendered, and racialized bodies and particularistic claims for recognition and justice by minoritized groups."[3]

This article focuses on the narratives of three of the thirty interviewees who are specifically activists who have worked within or supported Arab homeland struggles (i.e., Palestine and Iraq), radical Arab and Arab American feminist, queer Arab, and/or women of color feminist movements. Their location on the margins of both hegemonic U.S. nationalisms and Arab American cultural nationalisms provides a rich site from which to explore dominant discourses on gender and sexuality that circumscribe Arab American femininities. Their narratives represent historically specific contexts in which the gendered and sexualized discourses of assimilation, anti-Arab racism, and U.S. Orientalism emerge, as well as the multiple points at which they break down. Counter to dominant colonialist Western feminist approaches that highlight "religion" (Islam) as the primary determinant of Arab women's identities, this article demonstrates that religion (Christian or Muslim) alone does not determine the processes by which Arab American femininities are imagined and performed. Instead, it situates discussions on religious identity within the context of intersecting coordinates of power (race, class, nation, and so forth) and historical circumstances. Moreover, I do not present their narratives as sites from which to universalize the experiences of all Arab American women, but to provide an opportunity to think beyond misperceptions and stereotypes. I locate myself in the context of multiple, contradictory loyalties, such as Arab daughter, sister, and cousin, anthropologist, researcher, community activist, and feminist. This location rendered me at once "insider" and "outsider," collaboratively and individually deconstructing, contesting, and often reinforcing the cultural logics that circumscribed my research participants' identities.

This article focuses on the tense and often conflictual location of Arab American femininities at the intersections of two contradictory discourses: Arab cultural reauthenticity and hegemonic U.S. nationalism. I explore the ways that the theme of sexuality permeated many Arab immigrant families' engagements with the pressures of assimilation vis-à-vis a series of racial and cultural discourses on Arabness and Americanness. I argue that although my research participants (and their parents) perceived their cultural location within a binary of Arabness and Americanness, when lived and performed, this binary constantly broke down, particularly along the lines of race, class, gender, sexuality, religion, and nation. Yet binary terms for expressing the themes of family, gender, and sexuality persisted throughout my field sites as a discursive mechanism for explaining more complex processes that implicate my research participants and their parents within a desire for a stereotypical "Americanization" that is predicated on "Arabness" as the crucial Other. A binary cultural logic of "us" and "them" that was gendered and sexualized was then a discursive reaction to the complex dichotomies of hegemonic U.S. nationalism that at once pressure racialized immigrants to assimilate into a whitened middle-class U.S. national identity while positioning them outside the boundaries of "Americanness." Both generations were mutually invested in expressing the two racial-ethnic-national categories (Arab and American) in dichotomous terms because it provided a discursive mechanism for engaging with the processes of immigration and assimilation in which Arabness and Americanness absolutely depend on each other to exist—as opposites and in unison.

My research is based on intensive interviews and participant observation among thirty second-generation women between the ages of twenty and thirty, both Muslim and Christian, of Lebanese, Jordanian, Palestinian, and Syrian descent.[4] My research participants' parents emigrated to the U.S. in the 1960s, during a period of heightened secular Arab nationalism in the Arab world. Although most of my research participants were raised within secular families, religious affiliation (Muslim or Christian) was a key marker of identity and difference throughout my field sites. Most of my research participants of Muslim descent, for example, explained that growing up they understood Islam as part of their cultural identity. Most of my research participants who were from Christian backgrounds generally agreed that they were raised as "Christian Arabs" or that the "Arab community" that their parents identified with was comprised predominantly of Christian Arabs.

Before coming to the United States, most of my research participants' families were traders involved in small business enterprises who were either displaced to the San Francisco Bay area as a consequence of colonialism, neocolonialism, and war (i.e., Palestinians and Israeli colonization, or Lebanese and the Lebanese civil war) or emigrated to the San Francisco Bay area in the 1960s in search of economic mobility. Their parents did not integrate into culturally whitened middle-class corporate communities upon migration, but relied on familial and communal financial networks and support to eventually buy their own grocery and liquor stores. The internal pressures of tight-knit, familial, and communal networks and the external pressures of Americanization, assimilation, and racism have fostered an often reactionary bourgeois reproduction of Arab cultural identity. Cultural authorities—including parents, aunts, and uncles as well as the leaders of secular and religious community-based institutions—tended to generate a socially conservative and essentialized notion of "Arab culture" alongside a contradictory desire for the "American dream" and assimilation into American modes of whiteness.

This article, then, is not an analysis of *all* second-generation Arab Americans, but of how locational conditions (especially when it comes to racialized, gendered, class, and religious identities) mediate and break down an imagined "Arab" identity in the context of the San Francisco Bay area of California. It is an exploration of how binary oppositions within Arab American discourses on gender and sexuality take on particular form among my research participants, a group of educated, middle-class, young women active in progressive Arab, Arab feminist, and/or queer Arab political movements whose parents are ethnic entrepreneurs and immigrated, or were displaced, to the San Francisco Bay area—a traditionally liberal, racially/ethnically diverse location. Focusing on the narratives of three young Arab American women, this article highlights the processes by which discourses of Arab cultural re-authenticity and hegemonic U.S. nationalism police Arab American femininities circumstantially, depending on the types of "bad girl" behaviors to be controlled within a particular location. I argue that the phenomena of intersectionality cannot be generalized as taking one singular form for all Arab Americans; that one must be cautious about using the terms "Arab American" or "Arab American women" in a U.S. national sense; and that feminist theory and practice vis-à-vis Arab American communities should take the specific ways that the coordinates of race, class, gender, sexuality, religion, and national intersect in different contexts seriously. For example, perhaps part of the motivation behind the policing of an Arab daughter's behavior among middle-class business entrepreneurs invested in economic mobility and the selective reproduction of patriarchal cultural ideals is that San Francisco is home to some of the most vibrant progressive Arab, queer Arab, Arab feminist, and Arab student movements alongside some of the most vibrant civil rights, racial justice, feminist, and queer movements in the nation. In the San Francisco Bay area, multiracial coalition building, transgressive sexual politics, and critiques of classism, capitalism, U.S.-led imperialism, and war heavily inspire young people, such as my research participants, who are either active in or loyal to progressive politics.

Among my research participants, the performativity of an idealized "true" Arab culture emerged in the context of "regulatory ideals" that they associated with "being Arab" and distinguished from the regulatory ideals of "being American," such as: knowing what is *'abe* (shameful); knowing how to give *mujamalat* (flattery); knowing what you're supposed to do when someone greets you; drinking *shai* (tea) or coffee; talking about politics "sooo" much; getting up for an older person; respecting your elders; looking after your parents and taking care of them; judging people according to what family they are from; marrying through connections; gossiping and having a good reputation.[5]

Articulations of "selfhood" among my research participants were key sites where the oppositional logic of self/Other, us/them, Arab/American was reproduced among my research participants. Selfhood was often articulated in terms of a choice between "being an individual, being my own person, being an American," or "being connected, having family, and being 'Arab.'" Yet what ultimately distinguished "us" from "them," or *Al Arab* from *Al Amerikan*, among my research participants was a reiterated set of norms that were sexualized, gender specific, and performed in utterances such as *"banatna ma bitlaau fil lail"* (our girls don't stay out at night). Positioning the feminized subjectivities within my field sites in between the binary oppositions of good Arab daughter vs. bad American(ized) daughter, or Arab virgin vs. American(ized) whore, the discourse of Arab cultural re-authenticity reproduced a masculinist cultural nationalist assumption that if a daughter chooses to betray the regulatory demands of an idealized Arab womanhood, an imagined Arab community loses itself to the *Amerikan*. Jumana, recalling her parents' reinforcement of this distinction while she was growing up, explains,

My parents thought that being American was spending the night at a friend's house, wearing shorts, the guy-girl thing, wearing make-up, reading teen magazines, having pictures of guys in my room. My parents used to tell me, "If you go to an American's house, they're smoking, drinking . . . they offer you this and that. But if you go to an Arab house, you don't see as much of that. *Bi hafzu 'ala al banat* [They watch over their daughters].

My research participants generally agreed that virginity, followed by heterosexual (ethno-religious) endogamous marriage were the key demands of an idealized Arab womanhood that together, constituted the yardstick that policed female subjectivities in cultural nationalist terms. Here, discourses around Arab American femininities allow for a cultural, versus territorial, nationalist male Arab American perspective within the United States that emerges in opposition to hegemonic (white) U.S. nationalism and in the context of immigrant nostalgia. Here, an imagined notion of "Arab people" or an "Arab community" is inspired, in part, by a collective memory of immigrant displacement and romantic memories of "home" and "homeland culture." Among middle-class familial and communal networks in San Francisco, Arab American cultural nationalism was expressed in terms of an imagined Arab community or people that constituted "woman" as virgin or mother vis-à-vis an extended family context. Among Arab American cultural authorities in San Francisco, the ideal of marrying within one's kin group within the discourse of Arab cultural re-authenticity was refashioned in terms of marrying within the kin groups' religious group (Muslim or Christian); village of origin (Ramallah,

Al Salt), economic class, national (Jordanian, Lebanese, Palestinian, or Syrian), or racialized/ethnic (Arab) group. These categories were hierarchical, as "religious affiliation" tended to supersede "national origin" and "national origin" superseded "racial/ethnicity identity" as the boundary to be protected through a daughter's marriage. Although the regulatory demands of Arab womanhood were often framed as an alternative to assimilation and Americanization, the cultural discourses that controlled a daughter's marriageability simultaneously enabled a family strategy of assimilation to an appropriate American norm of whiteness that privileges heterosexual marriage—within particular boundaries of race and class—as capital.

The following narratives epitomize the processes by which discourses on Arabness and Americanness shifted depending on the kinds of power relations that set the stage for a daughter's expression and/or transgression of idealized notions of femininity within a given context. The first narrative centralizes intersections of race and class in the policing of Arab American femininities. The second narrative emphasizes intersections of religion and sexuality. The third narrative draws attention to intersections of Orientalism and religion. Together, these narratives highlight three different locations along a continuum of gendered experience among my research participants at the intersections of race and class; religion and sexuality; and Orientalism and religion. In doing so, they point to the process by which different sociohistorical circumstances produce shifting constructions of Arabness and Americanness in general and shifting constructions of Arab American femininity in particular. Although my research also illustrates that Arab cultural re-authenticity articulates masculinity and femininity as relational and mutually constitutive and implicates masculinity in binary terms that are contested, transformed, and often reproduced along the lines of race, gender, sexuality, religion, and nationality, an analysis of Arab American masculinities is beyond the scope of this article. Overall, this article argues for a historically situated, anti-essentialist approach to Arab and Arab American feminist studies that takes the locational conditions that mediate and break down an "imagined Arab American identity" seriously.

Race, Class, and the Double Life

Rime and I met at Arabian Nights, one of the few clubs in San Francisco where the DJ spins Arabic music. A mutual friend introduced us to one another and told her that I was doing research among young Arab Americans. As the DJ mixed hip-hop, reggae, and Arabic beats, Rime described herself as "living in two worlds . . . the 'Arab' world of [her] family . . . and the 'American' world outside of home." The next time we met, she explained that her parents emigrated to San Francisco from Jordan in the late 1960s in search of economic opportunity, that she was the oldest among five siblings, that her father owned a liquor store in one of San Francisco's poor black neighborhoods for the past fifteen years and that she graduated with a BA in nutrition and was pursuing a master's degree in public health.

—Naber, journal entry, June 18, 1999

Excerpts from Rime's Oral History: In high school, my parents didn't want me hanging out with my brother's friends because they got paranoid about my virginity and they didn't want me hanging out with my cousins' friends because they were Mexican and black. In high school, my mom got paranoid about my virginity. My dad used to tell me, "I had a nightmare that my daughter would marry a black man." That was because my dad owns a liquor store in the Tenderloin [neighborhood] and all his life he's been robbed and shot at, and his wife's been robbed by blacks. He blamed poor black communities for their situation without understanding it and he couldn't understand that I had a lot of black friends at school and that blacks were always the first ones out there supporting Arab student movements at school.

I remember when my cousin got pregnant with a guy who was half Mexican and half black. She lied and stayed out of the house for four years. Her family knew but kept it secret. The couple got in a big fight and the guy kicked my cousin out and she moved back to her parents' house. She did the most despicable thing a girl could ever do in Arab culture—and they took her back.

I was with Roger until recently. He was someone who I thought was total instant love but he was more of my support blanket because he was outside of the traditional Arab cultural realm. I lived in his house, and his parents accepted that 100 percent. As far as my parents were concerned, I was living with my cousin. But there was always the anxiety about getting caught for lying and I internalized hating being a woman. I would wake up at his house thinking about my father seeing me with a black guy. It was pure panic. Roger would touch my skin and be like, "You're so cold."

Because I was Arab I had to take care of my family's reputation and I was always reminded of it. I think my parents knew about him, but their attitude was, "Do what you do . . . don't let anybody find out." Then it was always my friends' fault—my American friends—"they're bad." And I couldn't work at the family store, because "American" men picked up on me there.

When I was graduating from college, I was partying a lot and I felt I needed to be more responsible. That's why I went back home to Jordan. In Jordan, my life completely turned around. I met Omar. All my life, the message was that I had to marry an Arab Christian man. I finally met an Arab Christian man who I love, and I thought the double life and the lying could be resolved . . . but my parents are not accepting him. Before he told his family or my family, he asked me to marry him, and traditionally, that was wrong. My mom is stuck on that issue. The thing that was really bugging her is that he's a communist and an atheist and against all the traditions. But what they focus on mostly is that . . . "the guy has no money—and you're going to go live with his family."

Traditionally if an Arab man is going to get married he should furnish and open a house for the girl and then get married, not get married and then worry about that stuff. My mom keeps saying *Batlee* [stop]. You're not getting married." It all comes down to our traditions—having Arab traditions, and then being raised here in the U.S. . . . Why does it have to be so difficult? Is it because I'm Arab? Is it because of my mother?"

I'm planning on moving to Jordan and marrying him. My parents will get over it. My cousin asked me, "Have you told him about birth control?" And when I said yes, she went crazy and said I was crazy for

telling him about birth control. They see him through a Western image of Arab men. They think I'm going to go back there from this independent, free spirit to be all the way across the world in this backward culture, like I'm going to be locked up at home rolling grape leaves all day. He says, "Don't worry, it won't be like that."

If we get married and I move back to Jordan and it doesn't work, I'll say, I'm going to get some milk, but then I'll get a ticket and go to New York. I won't even give them a phone number. I'll call them once a month—and tell them that I'm okay. Then I'll go and get all this freedom, but I'll be all alone. I'll be another lonely white CEO woman who's all alone and has no one: has no family, no brothers, no nothing. 'Cause that's what it's like in American culture.

Sometimes it can all make you crazy because you can't get out. I have so many worlds and every world is a whole other world. But in your mind they're totally separated, but then they're all there in your mind together. You get to a point that you are about to explode.

When Rime speaks of living in "two worlds," fixity and singularity underwrite her view of "culture." Rime speaks about "Arab culture" and "American culture" as though they already existed, transcending place, time, and relations of power. Yet as Trinh T. Minh-ha puts it, "categories always leak."[6] Rime's family's Christian religious affiliation and Omar's economic class, which disqualifies him as a suitable marriage partner, disrupt Rime's homogeneous "Arab world." Moreover, Omar's position as a "disappointment" to Rime's parents and his ironic foreignness reflects the instability of Arab cultural re-authenticity in that

Omar bursts the bubble of "authentic Arab-ness" that they left in the homeland and have tried to recreate in the United States. Here, Omar's forced presence in Rime's family's life exposes the nostalgia underlying Arab cultural re-authenticity for what it is.

Similarly, the racialized distinctions Mexican and black rupture Rime's essentialized "American" world. These discontinuities drive the present argument that while Rime sees herself between "two worlds," rupture and difference position her along the two axes of sameness and difference. At a critical distance from both "worlds," Rime decides to marry a Jordanian man of Christian descent who is an atheist. Yet her narrative reproduces a good girl versus bad girl binary in which "bad-girl behaviors" are signified by her desire to marry across lines of socioeconomic class and political affiliation. As she crafts an alternative plan to move to New York alone in case the marriage does not work, she invents tactics for transgression beyond the boundaries of a nostalgic "true" Arab culture.

Rime's "two (Arab and American) worlds" are not homogeneous or stable, but multiple and overlapping in the context of power, history and the changing intersections of class, race, gender, religion, and politics in different locations. Rime implies that the unacceptability of interracial marriage compounds the virginity ideal. Although prohibitions against mixed-race unions are common in the Arab world, Rime's interpretation of her community's prohibitions is mediated by historically based U.S. nationalist anxiety about interracial marriage. Rime's father's positionality as a liquor store owner in the Tenderloin neighborhood further shaped the racialized and gendered imperatives that policed Rime's sexuality. His nightmare over his daughter's potential interracial marriage emerges as a threat to securing white middle-class norms and implies the forging of a critical distance from the racial Other toward whiteness. Here, "Arab culture" is invoked as a strategy for harnessing markers of middle-class whiteness. Meanwhile, the regulatory ideal that forbids sex with the United States' racialized Other controls Arab daughters' sexuality while protecting Rime's family, and an imagined Arab people, from degeneracy in white middle-class terms. Binaries collapse in the context of a much greater complexity in that her father's attitude fits comfortably when he seems to be speaking (in his daughter's mind) to Arabness. Yet in fact, in policing Rime's sexuality, he is reinforcing the new identity he has had to develop in the United States, demonstrating the fiction of Arab cultural re-authenticity.

Rime's two worlds are similarly narrated in gendered and sexualized terms and her perception of a fixed and stable "Arab culture" is disrupted when her aunt and uncle take her cousin back after she "got pregnant with a guy who was half Mexican and half black." Here, her cousin's parents seem to care less about her mixed-race relationship and illegitimate pregnancy than with presenting the public face of an "authentic" or "traditional" Arab family. Through silence (that is, Rime's cousin staying out of the house for years; Rime living with her cousin) both "traditionalist" parents and their "Americanized" daughters are mutually implicated in keeping the idealized notions of Arabness and Americanness active and in opposition. These silences allow them to keep the binary intact and mask the fact that at different points the oppositions threaten to be one and the same.

Although Rime narrates herself as a split subject, her "worlds" "inside" and "outside"

(Arab and American) were not discreet. In bed, the boundaries between "inside" and "outside" collapse as her father's disapproving gaze interrupts the privacy of her boyfriend's bedroom while her boyfriend places his hand on her skin. Rime interprets the regulatory ideal of marrying "an Arab Christian man" as the central act that would render her embraceable or acceptable within the discourse of Arab cultural re-authenticity in between two seemingly distinct and homogeneous "Arab" and "American" worlds. Yet in learning of Omar's unacceptability as a communist atheist from a different socioeconomic class, Rime comes to terms with the heterogeneity of Arab cultural identity. Yet she also reproduces the notion of a normative "Arab cultural identity" when she interprets her reality as a choice between "having a family and community," or "being another lonely white CEO woman." Here, Rime's distinction between "having family and community" and "being a lonely white CEO woman" represents the reproduction of idealized notions of selfhood in the diaspora. As Rime critically receives cultural meanings, she associates "Arab" cultural identity with love, community, cohesiveness, and control and "American" cultural identity with individualism, autonomy, and alienation. Yet as Rime's parents render Omar unacceptable because he lives in the homeland, lacks money, and lacks Christian values, the fantasy of a romantic notion of "cultural authenticity" located in the homeland collapses along the lines of class, religion, and gender.

The Heterosexual Imperative

Waiting for a friend at Café Macondo, in San Francisco's Mission district, graffiti reading QUEER ARABS EXIST caught my attention. Later, in conversations among Arab women activists, I learned that the graffiti artist was a Syrian American woman named Lulu. Lulu was also the coproducer of a special issue of Bint Al Nas *on the theme of "sexuality."* Bint Al Nas *is a cyber magazine and network for queer Arab women and as part of this issue, Lulu designed the web art, "Virgin/Whore," where a collage representing herself as "virgin" (represented by drums, pita bread, camels, Allah, a Syrian flag, and a photograph of her family members wearing blindfolds) transforms into a second collage representing her as "whore" (represented by images of dildos next to her girlfriend's name written in Arabic, handcuffs, a blurred image of the picture that represents her parents, and a photo of Madonna). A few months later, Lulu and I made plans to meet at Café Flor, a queer hangout in the Castro district of San Francisco. I recognized Lulu from the tattoo of her girlfriend's name Amina in Arabic script on her arm and the Palestinian flag sewn onto her book bag. We talked about the collage and she explained, "What I am doing with the two images is showing how they are dichotomous, or at least they have felt that way, and how really, it has been an either/or situation. Also, I think it's how my mother would see my sexuality: dirty, sinful, dark. The reason for the roll over of images is to show that the two states can't coexist."*

—Naber, journal entry,
December 28, 2000

Excerpts from Lulu's Oral History: I grew up with this all the time: "Sex is an act of love in marriage. If you're not a virgin when you get married, you're in trouble." I fought that all the time. I would ask my mom about Syria. I would say, "If good Arab women are not having sex and Arab men can have sex, then who were the Arab men having sex with?" She would answer, "The Christian women." So the Christian women were the whores. That is very prevalent in my family, the Muslim virgin and the Christian whore. The whore is either American or Christian.

My family is unique because we talked about sex. My sister was really vocal about having boyfriends and they were always black, which was even more of a problem. My parents are into the idea that Arabs are white. I think it's more of a Syrian-Lebanese thing. But I didn't have the same problems with my parents about boyfriends as my sister because I knew I was queer since I was thirteen or fourteen. It was when I came out when things erupted for me. It got to the point where they were asking, "Don't you want to have a boyfriend?"

My mom won't come visit me at my house because she doesn't want to see that I live with a woman. The bottom line is premarital sex. Lesbian sex doesn't happen because Arab girls don't have premarital sex. When I came out, it was like, "That's fine that you're gay—but don't act on it. We don't want you having sex." Everyday I heard, "Get married with a guy and . . ." suppress it, basically. I said, "I can't do that." And I still get that . . . "We (Arabs) don't do that" . . . or "You're the only gay Arab in the world."

It became this thing that everyone was going to fix me. My uncles would come and take me out to lunch. They would say, "Let's talk. This doesn't happen in our culture. You've been brainwashed by Americans. You've taken too many feminist classes, you joined NOW, you hate men, you have a backlash against men. . . ." It was like . . . "This is what this American society has done to our daughter."

When that was the reaction I received, I totally disassociated myself from Arabs. I felt I couldn't be gay and Arab. I felt that either I have to go home and be straight or be totally out and pass as white. But later, I got a lot of support from queer Arab networks.

One of the first people I met was Samah. She was doing some research and asked if she could interview me. I did it and we both cried. Then I went to a queer Arab women's gathering. I was the youngest one and everyone knew that I came out a week after I turned eighteen and was kicked out by my parents four months later. I was the baby. They all supported me. Over the years, they've become my family.

Now my mom tells me, "Just go have sex with a man—maybe you'll change," and I say, "Maybe you should try it with a woman." She keeps finding ways to say I'm too Americanized . . . and when I tell her, "You don't know how many queer Arabs I know." She says, "They're American, they're American born, they're not Arab" or "They must be Christian," or "Their fathers must not be around because no father would accept his daughter being gay."

They blamed Western feminism and said I should go to a therapist. Then they changed their minds and said not to go because they don't want it on my hospital records that I am gay—because "You know," they would say, "After you change—someone might see on your hospital records that you were gay." Their idea was that they didn't want anyone finding out "after I change" and "once I get married," that I had this dark past. Then at the very end they did try to send me to a hospital. That was when the shit hit the fan, our big final fight. I was so strong in defending myself—and they thought that too was very American. So it became this thing of like—and they make it very clear—"You chose your sexuality over us. Sex is more important than your family." Which goes back to the tight-knit family Arab thing. It's all about group dynamics.

When Lulu's mother replaces the "American whore" with the "Christian Arab" she reveals the gaps and fissures within the idea of a unified Arab American nationalist identity and the ways that Arab cultural re-authenticity shifts depending on sociohistorical circumstances. Lulu's mother's association of the category "Syrian Christian" with the classification "Westernized Other" signifies the ways that the categories "Islam" and "Arabness" have often been conflated throughout Arab history and in several cases, juxtaposed against the notion of a Christian West. According to her mother, the Syrian-Muslim self is to be protected from the corrupted, Westernized, Syrian-Christian Other.

Intersections between national origin and racial identification in Lulu's narrative further complicate Arab cultural identity in the United States. Lulu, in remembering why her parents did not accept her sister's black boyfriends, explains that identifying as white is "a Syrian-Lebanese thing." The Syrian-Lebanese distinction is common within hegemonic Arab American discourses in San Francisco. Many of my research participants agree that Syrian and Lebanese Arab Americans have had more access to the privileges of middle-class whiteness compared to other Arab Ameri-

cans.[7] Steering Lulu's sister away from the racial Other, Lulu's mother, like Rime's father, secures a white middle-class positionality. Yet when it comes to Lulu's sexuality, the association of Syrians with whiteness is quickly disrupted as a sexualized, cultural, nationalist logic disassociates them as "Arabs" from the loose, sexually immoral American "feminist" Other in the name of controlling Lulu's sexuality. In Lulu's narrative, then, the *Al Arab/Al Amerikan* boundary is permeable and shifting. As Lulu explains, her parents uphold the normative demands of middle-class American whiteness to tame her sister's sexuality while they distinguish themselves from *Al Amerikan* when it comes to taming Lulu's behaviors.

Fissures in Arab cultural re-authenticity also emerge when Lulu's mother suggests that Lulu "try sex with a man." In the case of Lulu's queer identity, a heterosexual imperative becomes a more significant symbol of the Arab virgin/American whore boundary than the "virginity" ideal. Gloria Anzaldúa writes, "For the lesbian of color, the ultimate rebellion she can make against her native culture is through her sexual behavior. She goes against two moral prohibitions: sexuality and homosexuality."[8] Lulu's queerness, the central marker of her betrayal, underwrites her marginalization as traitor-outsider-American by cultural authorities such as her mother, her father, and her uncle. The extent to which she is seen as "unacceptable, faulty, damaged," culminate in her family's attempt to send her to a hospital to fix her so that she might return "straight" home. Here, the stance of their conservativism is made possible by their inculcation and reproduction of white American middle-class norms, such as "therapy," within the discourse of Arab cultural re-authenticity. Lulu's parents thus reinforce a particular kind of assimilation constituted by the ways that Arabness and Americanness operate both as opposites and in unison in the policing of Arab American femininities throughout my field sites.

In overriding the virginity ideal with the heterosexual imperative, Lulu's mother reinforces the control over women's sexual and marriage practices that underlie the heterosexual conjugal ideal in Arab and Western societies. Yet beyond reinforcing a heterosexual imperative, Lulu's mother is also reinforcing family ideals critically inherited from Arab homelands that are not only conjugal, but include extended kin that are inscribed beyond household or nuclear terms. In attempting to reinstate Lulu's heterosexuality, Lulu's mother seeks to protect Lulu's father's honor as well as the family honor of her nuclear and her extended family. Moreover, the intervention of Lulu's uncle can be interpreted in terms of the refashioning of a patrilineal ideal in the diaspora, in which males and elders remain responsible for female lineage members (even after marriage) and men are responsible for providing for their families, which includes their current wives and underage children and may include aged parents, unmarried sisters, younger brothers, and the orphaned children of their brothers.[9]

As a form of political critique directed against patriarchy and patrilineality, Lulu's chosen family is a sign of her resistance. In the act of choosing her family, Lulu challenges Arab and Anglo-European ideologies that read blood and heterosexual marriage ties as the key foundation of kinship, demonstrating that all families are contextually defined. In undermining the association of kinship with biology, Lulu overtly performs the social, ideological, political,

and historical constructedness of kinship. Yet when she meets Samah and joins queer Arab e-mail lists, Lulu finds an alternative to the Arab/American split in the coming together of what she understood to be her "queer" and her "Arab" identities. Lulu's insistence that QUEER ARABS EXIST is an act in resisting racism, homophobia, and patriarchy on multiple fronts: it undermines the Arab virgin/American(ized) whore that seeks to control women's sexuality by marking women who transgress the heterosexual imperative of Arab cultural authenticity as "American" and it disrupts the dualistic logic of hegemonic U.S. nationalist discourses that homogenize and subordinate Arab women as either veiled victims of misogynist terrorist Arab men or exotic erotic objects accessible to white/Western male heroes. Yet cultural identity, for Lulu, is more than "separate pieces merely coming together"—it is a site of tension, pain, and alienation that is constantly in motion.

Lulu's narrative signifies the critical inheritance of the polarization between Muslim and Christian Arabs from the homeland(s) to Arab San Francisco. It exemplifies the ways that this polarization took on local form among many bourgeois Arab American Muslims with whom I interacted. Throughout my field sites, hegemonic Arab Muslim discourses often privileged Arab Muslim women as the essence of cultural re-authenticity—as opposed to Arab Christian women who were often represented as promiscuous and therefore, "Americanized." Yet although cultural authorities often deployed religion as a framework for policing feminized subjectivities throughout my field sites, religious background alone did not determine the extent to which my research participants upheld, reconfigured, or transgressed the feminized imperatives of Arab cultural re-authenticity. My research participants who transgressed "good girl" behaviors through dating before marriage, interracial, and/or same-sex relationships were religiously diverse. In addition, religious affiliation alone did not determine the extent to which parents, aunts, or uncles circumscribed their daughters' behaviors and identities.

While Lulu explained that her mother deployed her Muslim identity to reinforce the normative demands of virginity, her parents' self-identification as "white" complexified their understanding of a "normative femininity." In addition, Lulu stated that her mother deployed a pan-ethnic "Arab" identity when she asked her to suppress her lesbian identity. Thus, while the discourse of the "Muslim virgin" and the "Christian whore" policed Lulu's femininity, the "virgin/whore" dichotomy was also constituted by a series of intersecting and contradictory discourses such as white versus non-white, Arab versus American. The ways that these discourses operated to police femininities depended on the different ways that coordinates of race, class, gender, sexuality, religion, and nation intersected in each of my research participants' lives.

U.S. Orientalism and the Religious Difference

Nicole and I agreed on Kan Zaman in San Francisco as our meeting spot since we heard they served argilah *[an Arabic water pipe]. Little did we know that on Thursday nights, it was the place to be for ex-hippie yuppies who enjoy mixing a little humus and a pita with a few drinks before a night of partying on the town. As we walked in, I greeted the owner Yousef, who goes by the name of Joe to his customers, as*

we watched two Anglo-American women who went by the names of Laila and Amina belly dancing with nose rings and sequined bikini tops. Sitting down on a bed of bright colorful pillows in a recreated imaginary Orient we began our first conversation. As daughters of Arab Christians, we had parents who similarly believed that emigration to the United States would mean further distancing themselves from the "backwards, uncivilized, Muslims." Over dinner, we confessed similar stories about our parents' comments about the Muslim Other and pondered the irony that our immigrant parents view us as "more Arab" than them because we interact with Muslims. For the following three months, Nicole and I continued meeting for dinner as she shared with me her struggles over gender, culture, and identity between and among the boundaries of "Arab" and "American."

—Naber, journal entry, August 16, 1999

Excerpts from Nicole's Oral History: One time I asked my uncle to send me an *argilah* from Lebanon. When it arrived in the mail, my mom hid it in the closet and started flipping out at me. She kept asking why her Western educated, Lebanese, Christian, civilized, modern daughter—and she used all these adjectives—who they gave the privilege of having a Western education—wanted to go back and smoke an *argilah* which is a backwards, dirty, horrible, uncivilized Muslim habit.

But when you grow up in the United States, all kinds of Arabs end up hanging out with each other and the Muslim Christian thing isn't as big. In college, the biggest movement was the Palestinian movement. I was involved because it was an Arab thing, even though growing up

Lebanese, the Palestinian struggle wasn't driven into you as much. In Lebanon, Palestinians, especially the Palestinian Muslims, were associated with being refugees, being radical politically, and trying to take over other Arab countries.

In college, my ethnicity bloomed. I felt more proud of being Arab—even though when I would tell people I was Arab, they wouldn't believe me because I go to parties and drink and they thought that if you were an Arab girl, you had to wear a veil and your parents never let you do anything. I remember once, when I told someone I was Arab, they said, "And your father let you go to college?" In college, my name and my look became cool because I was viewed as exotic. All of a sudden, you turn around with dark curly hair and dark lips and you're the item of the year. White men are confident to approach you. It's trendy. It's part of the boy talk with other boys. This one guy said to me, "I've been with a Sri Lankan, a Madagascan, a Somali. . . . It's like . . . I was with the Lebanese." People approach you because you are the vision of this exotic Arab woman goddess.

My parents were really liberal about guys. I would tell them when I had a boyfriend. In college, I started dating Ben. His mother is a Jewish lesbian. I told my father this over the dinner table. He was upset, but he got over it. They accepted him because no one else would have to find out about his mother. We could have told my dad's family that he is Christian.

Both my parents are Christian, but we were raised atheist. So why this reaction to Mohammed? After college, I met the love of my life, Mohammed. He's a Palestinian Muslim, and we've been dating seriously. My mom freaked out saying that meant he is Muslim and how dare I date a Muslim.

She went on to say, "Don't you know that there are 15,000 cases of Christian Western American women married to Muslim men and the women are in the States and the men have taken their children from them to the Muslim world and the women are in the States trying to get their children back from those horrible men?"

She learned this on *20/20*. Then she said, "Well you know, if you are sleeping with him, his family is going to kill you." The stereotypes never stop. She says that he will force me to sleep with him so I will have to marry him or that he will make me cover my hair, or he will marry more than one wife. After a few months she said, "Your father is freaking out because people in the community are talking about you. Even his friends in Lebanon heard you are dating a Muslim. He's saying that you've ruined his reputation." My dad called me and said, "You have to stop dating him right now." I told him that this doesn't make sense. I have aunts married to Palestinians. But even though Lebanese think they're better than Palestinians, that wasn't the issue. The issue was that he is Muslim. My dad is acting as if he's experiencing absolute betrayal and they're losing their daughter to the enemy.

What's crazy is my mom is Armenian and her Armenian parents let her marry my dad, an Arab! And my parents are atheists! So it's not really about religion per se, it's that they want me to marry someone Westernized, and Lebanese Christian falls into Western. Then there's this issue of land. My dad has all this land in the village. He's already discussed with my brother and [me] what land we get. And in the future, I want to build a house on that land. I know if I marry Mohammed my father is going to disown me and he won't give me that land. But I know that my brother will undo it. My brother told me he would give me the land but I know it's hard on him because he is also worried that he will get a bad reputation for sanctioning his sister to date a guy that is against his father's wish. I think my parents are doing all this to save face. I'll never forget the e-mail Mohammed sent me. It said, "How good is it that we love each other if we're going to allow Ottoman conventions to kill it?"

I have to figure out for myself if I can endure being rejected by my society and excluded from the social glue that keeps me tied to my roots and all the networks of social relations my family built here even though they're so reactionary. If I make the decision to marry him, I will be cut off from my lifeblood. Can I endure the pain and hardships of struggling against society for the sake of following my heart? But personal happiness extends way beyond the bond that ties man to woman. There are other ties . . . between an individual and her society, a daughter and her mother, and a girl . . . and the community that nurtured her. When I think about giving up Mohammed it's like giving up one kind of happiness to preserve another. My family and community's love has roots and gives me stability, whereas Mohammed symbolizes risk and daring and revolutionary uncertainty. That's what is causing my identity crisis. My life is bound up in the lives of others.

Within Nicole's narrative, her peers' Orientalist representation of Arab women as simultaneously veiled victim and exotic goddess, coupled with her mother's associations of Muslim habits with the terms "backwards, dirty, horrible, and uncivilized" and Muslim men with the themes of misogyny, illustrate the significance of Orientalism to middle-class U.S. notions of identity and modernity. Her peers reproduce an Orientalist logic that renders Arab women as requiring Western discovery, intervention, or liberation. Her mother, in aspiring to avoid identification with the Orientalist's Other, refashions Ottoman distinctions between Muslims and Christians and Lebanese nationalist distinctions between Lebanese and Palestinians in Orientalist terms. Here, Ottoman distinctions between Muslims and Christians are rooted in a framework for organizing social difference according to religious categories that persists in Arab states, despite the establishment of nation-states. (Within the Ottoman period of Middle East history, the categories "Muslims and non-Muslims" [with multiple subgroups] provided the predominant framework for organizing difference, and civil rights were assigned and administered by religious sect or rite.)[10]

At the intersections of Orientalism and Ottoman frameworks for organizing difference, the terms of Arab cultural re-authenticity shift. Nicole's mother deploys a selective assimilationist strategy that on the one hand operationalizes Arab cultural re-authenticity in terms of homeland notions of cultural difference, such as Ottoman distinctions between Muslims and Christians, while on the other hand, deploys Orientalist terms that denigrate behaviors and identities that are associated with pan-Arabism and Islam. This strategy disassociates Arab Christians from Arab Muslims, associates Arab Christians with the "West" and with "modernity," and articulates a desire for middle-class U.S. nationalist notions of identity that affirm that to be "modern" and "American" is to be "Orientalist." Nicole's mother thus pronounces a selective assimilationist strategy that reproduces the sexual politics of colonial discourse in terms of a rape/rescue fantasy in which the figure of the dark Arab Muslim male rapist threatens Western women (including Westernized Arab Christian women) and sex between Muslim men and Christian women can only involve rape.[11]

For Arab Christians, the possibilities for disassociating themselves from Orientalism have been made possible in that the "Western trope of the Muslim woman" articulated "as the ultimate victim of a timeless patriarchy defined by the barbarism of the Islamic religion, which is in need of civilizing" has permeated Orientalist discourses.[12] The significance of Islam within the refashioning of Orientalism among Nicole's Lebanese Christian family is particularly clear when Nicole recalls the difference between her parents' response to her ex-boyfriend Ben whose mother was a Jewish lesbian and their response to Mohammed. Although Ben's mother's Jewish and lesbian identities can be hidden, or conflated with Western or "American civilized identity," Mohammed's identity cannot.

Throughout her narrative, Nicole locates herself in between a series of binaries, such as American vs. Orientalized Other, Western modernity vs. religious discourse, Muslim vs. Christian, Lebanese vs. Palestinian, and individualism vs. "connectivity."[13] While she uses binaries as a coding for articulating her struggle between different kinds of happiness, she simultaneously articulates her identity at the intersections of a constellation of loyalties that are multiple, contradictory, constantly shifting, and overlapping. As these loyalties intersect, they produce a complex process that implicates her (and her parents) within a desire for being with the man she loves in the con-text of stereotypical Americanized norms such as freedom, individualism, and loneliness, and for maintaining her ties to her family, which are constituted by the multiple genealogies of Ottoman history, Western Christian modernity, U.S. Orientalism, multiculturalism, and racism. Nicole's narrative thus redraws the boundaries between "Arabness" and "Americanness" along multiple axes of power and control; affirms that binary formulations such as "Arabs" vs. "America," or "Christians" vs. "Muslims" are "always more complex than the straightjacket of identity politics might suggest";[14] and counters celebrations of hybridity that fail to account for the ways that essentialist categories, while constructed and fictive, operate to support hierarchies of privilege and domination and power and control.

Conclusion

Walking down the street between one of San Francisco's largest populations of homeless women and men and the new dot-com yuppies, I did my usual skim of graffiti on Café Macondo's walls. The "FOR" in LESBIANS FOR BUSH had been crossed out and replaced with the word "EAT." As I turned to the wall behind me to find out whether QUEER ARABS still EXIST[ed], my eyes followed an arrow, drawn in thick black marker that pointed to the words QUEER ARABS and was connected to the words, ONE OF MANY PROBLEMS.

Looking closer, I noticed another message superimposed over QUEER ARABS EXIST in faint blue ink. A line was drawn between the words QUEER and ARABS and the letter "S" was added to the beginning of the word "EXIST." I re-read it several times before I finally understood that superimposed upon QUEER ARABS EXIST, the new message, in coupling the words ARABS and SEXIST, implied that ARABS are SEXIST. I thought about my research and the resemblance between the images on the wall and my research participants' everyday experiences. While Lulu's graffiti confronted the lumping of Arabs into the homogeneous categories "veiled victim" or "polygamous terrorist," the defacement of QUEER ARABS EXIST reinforced the binary construction of "the Arab" as Other. Similarly, while Rime, Lulu, and Nicole burst the boundaries of hegemonic Arab American and U.S. nationalisms on multiple fronts, they also rearticulate hegemonic nationalisms in binary terms as a coding for a more complex process in which the categories "Arab" and "American" are mutually constitutive and exist both as opposites and in unison, in the context of immigration, assimilation, and racialization.

As I took another glance at ARABS ARE SEXIST, superimposed over QUEER ARABS EXIST, I noticed another message, a much smaller message written in black letters in Spanish and English that framed the top right side of QUEER ARABS EXIST. It read ES ALGO BUENO. IT'S A GOOD THING.

—Naber, journal entry, June 2001

Notes

I am grateful to Suad Joseph, Kent Ono, Ella Maria Ray, Martina Reiker, Minoo Moallem, Andrea Smith, Rabab Abdulhadi, and Evelyn Alsultany for providing me with invaluable feedback and support while I was developing this article. I would like to especially thank the editorial board members of *Feminist Studies* and the anonymous readers for their constructive suggestions and the immense time and effort they committed to seeing this article in publication. I am indebted to each and every person who participated in this project and I am grateful to Eman Desouky, Lillan Boctor, my mother, Firyal Naber, and my father, Suleiman Naber, for their persistent support and encouragement throughout the period of my field research.

1. This is not a literal translation, but conveys the message of my mother's words. Throughout the rest of this article, I have edited my research participants' quotes into a readable form, maintaining the originality of the quote as much as possible. The process included cutting repetitive words and statements, rearranging the order of the narratives, and simplifying elaborate explanations. I have also altered names and places in order to protect my research participants' privacy.

2. These networks included local chapters of the American Arab Anti-Discrimination Committee, the Arab Women's Solidarity Association, the Muslim Students' Association, Students for Justice in Palestine, and the Arab Cultural Center.

3. Minoo Moallem and Ian Boal, "Multicultural Nationalism and the Poetics of Inauguration," in *Between Woman and Nation: Nationalisms, Transnational Feminism, and the State*, ed. Caren Kaplan, Norma Alarcon, and Minoo Moallem (Durham, N.C.: Duke University Press, 1999), 243–64.

4. I first became acquainted with my research participants by joining community organizations and cultural/artistic collectives and by attending functions organized by Christian and Muslim religious institutions, Arabic language schools, and Arab and Muslim student groups. Fifteen of the women research participants were Palestinian, seven were Syrian, six were Jordanian, and two were Lebanese. The greater number of women of Palestinian descent whom I interviewed represent a pattern common within what my research participants refer to as San Francisco's "Arab American community," in which Palestinians make up the majority among those active in Arab American community affairs. Nevertheless, immigrants from the Levant (Lebanon, Jordan, Palestine, and Syria) comprised the majority of early Arab immigrants to San Francisco. They developed a variety of community networks through the establishment of a series of clubs and community associations. These networks have organized

"difference" in terms of village of origin (i.e., the Ramallah Club), country of origin (i.e., the Lebanese American Association) or pan-ethnic Arab identity (i.e., the Arab Cultural Center). Due to their early history of migration to San Francisco, the varieties of institutions they established, and their overall socioeconomic privileges compared to Arab immigrants and refugees living in the San Francisco Bay area from other countries (such as Yemen, Iraq, Tunisia, and Morocco), the term "Arab" or "Arab American" community often privileges Levantine Arabs, while either excluding or marginalizing "other Arabs."

5. Here, I use terms that were reiterated among my research participants to illustrate the ways that my research participants regularly associated "Americanness" with freedom and individualism and "Arabness" with family and connectivity.

6. See Trinh T. Min-ha, *Woman, Native, Other: Writing Postcoloniality and Feminism* (Bloomington: Indiana University Press, 1989).

7. Throughout my field sites, Palestinian and Jordanian Arab Americans tended to view Syrian and Lebanese Arab Americans as more "assimilated" than themselves. Several factors have produced this "difference." Historically, Syrian and Lebanese emigrated to the San Francisco Bay area in the early 1900s, before Palestinians and Jordanians, who first immigrated in the late 1950s.

8. Gloria Anzaldúa, *Borderlands: La Frontera* (San Francisco: Aunt Lute Books, 1987), 17.

9. Here, I build on Suad Joseph's definition of patrilineality in Arab families in "Gendering Citizenship in the Middle East," in *Gender and Citizenship in the Middle East*, ed. Suad Joseph (New York: Syracuse University Press, 2000), 3–32.

10. See Aaron Rodrigue, "Difference and Tolerance in the Ottoman Empire: Interview by Nancy Reynolds," ed. Nancy Reynolds and Sabra Mahmood, special issue, *Stanford Humanities Review* 5, no. 1 (1992): 81–92.

11. Here, I borrow from Ella Shohat and Robert Stam's three axes of sexualized, racialized, colonialist discourse. See Ella Shohat and Robert Stam, *Unthinking Eurocentrism: Multiculturalism and the Media* (New York: Routledge, 1992).

12. Minoo Moallem, *Between Warrior Brother and Veiled Sister: Islamic Fundamentalism and the Politics of Patriarchy in Iran* (Berkeley: University of California Press, 2005), 20.

13. "Connectivity" here is from Suad Joseph's definition of "patriarchal connectivity" in Lebanon. See Suad Joseph, "Gender and Rationality among Arab Families in Lebanon," *Feminist Studies* 19 (Fall 1993): 465–86.

14. Ella Shohat, introduction to *Talking Visions: Multicultural Feminism in a Transnational Age*, ed. Ella Shohat (New York: MIT Press, 1998), 6.

25 Peter Chua and Diane C. Fujino

Negotiating New Asian-American Masculinities
Attitudes and Gender Expectations

Historically, U.S. institutional practices have rendered Asian-American men as simultaneously hypermasculine and emasculated. Today, the model minority myth and asexual media representations have emphasized the feminized Asian-American male. Yet, no empirical study has examined how Asian-American men construct their own masculinities. Toward this end, this study sought to examine: (a) how college-age Asian-American and white men express their masculinities, (b) how Asian-American and white women perceive Asian-American masculinities, and (c) how Asian-American men negotiate their gender expectations. Through quantitative analysis of surveys, we found that U.S.-born and immigrant Asian men view their masculinity as distinct from white hegemonic masculinity. Unlike white men, Asian-American men did not view their masculinity in opposition to their femininity. Some Asian-American men, especially the U.S.-born, appeared to be creating a new, more flexible masculinity—one free from male dominance. U.S.-born Asian men linked their masculinity with certain caring characteristics and were the only men's group willing to do domestic tasks. Women viewed Asian-American men as having more traditional gender roles and being more nurturing, in contrast to their views of white men, which matched American norms of masculinity. Overall, these results contribute to the masculinity literature by showing how Asian-American men negotiate their contradictory positions as members of a privileged gender group and subordinate racial groups.

Changes in Asian-American heterosexual masculinity are of great interest within the Asian-American communities and to the general public. Historically, this racialized masculinity was both hypermasculinized and desexualized as a way to limit economic and racial opportunities in the United States (Espiritu, 1997). While these dichotomous ideas about Asian-American masculinities are still pervasive, new articulations of what it means to be male, straight, and Asian American are affecting different Asian-American communities and interpersonal relationships at home and in workplaces. Issues of Asian-American masculinities are brought up in relation to interracial dating and marriage, expectations about supporting the family and community, sexual violence within the home and sexual harassment in public spaces, racial violence stemming from economic scapegoating and white supremacist ideology,

Excerpted from the original. Peter Chua and Diane C. Fujino, "Negotiating New Asian-American Masculinities: Attitudes and Gender Expectations," *Journal of Men's Studies* 7, no. 3 (Spring 1999): 391–413. Reprinted by permission of Men's Studies Press, LLC.

mass media portrayals of Asian-American men, and complexities about ethnic identity and politics.

The present quantitative study uses survey data to examine, from a social psychological perspective, how college-age Asian-American and white men express their masculinities and how Asian-American and white women perceive Asian-American and white masculinities.[1] This study also explores how Asian-American men conceive and negotiate their expectations about gender relations.

This study contributes to our understanding of newer expressions of racial-ethnic masculinities by focusing on contemporary youth to expand the limited theoretical literature on Asian-American masculinity and by providing empirical evidence. There has been exciting fictional and artistic expressions of Asian-American masculinities but little quantitative analysis of these issues. Furthermore, this study enhances our understanding of racial-ethnic masculinities by focusing on changes in racial and gender power relations and expectations.

Social Construction of Male Masculinities

Masculinity is an important component in the social constructions of gender relations (Brod, 1987; Kimmel, 1987; Kimmel & Messner, 1995). Gender refers to the material and ideological relations and consequences based on social distinction made from female and male physical differences. Gender expectation refers to a normative conception of appropriate attitudes and activities for a particular racialized and gendered group. Gender embodies relations of power (Connell, 1987). This distinction functions to create and maintain unequal power relations between people of different biological sexes and results in the domination and exploitation of women as a group. It is not biology but patriarchal social institutions, interactions, and practices that limit each sex to those characteristics and activities defined as feminine and masculine. The ideas of what constitute masculinity and femininity are contingent on a given society and historical moment even though individuals are capable of the full range of abilities and emotions. No innate and universal gender qualities automatically accompany physical sex differences. In contrast, some believe gender qualities are strongly related to biological sex differences. These arguments rest on notions of racial and sexual superiorities. For instance, eugenicists like Rushton (1996) argue that Asians are more intelligent and less sexual than whites, who in turn are brighter and less sexual than blacks. They link race and masculinity to genetics, which we view as faulty arguments. This study is based on the former notion that gender embodies power. Sexist attitudes and actions valorize masculinity and accord men power and privileges. But if masculinities are socially constructed by and for each generation of men growing up rather than genetically inherited, then masculinities can change, and sexism in principle can be eradicated (Segal, 1990).

While masculinity is gendered, socially constituted, and intrinsically connected to power relations, it is also differentiated in its production, reproduction, and negotiation by everyone in society at the level of both group interactions and institutional practices. Masculinity is not one way of being for men; rather it takes a variety of forms. It is different for the working class and the upper class; for heterosexuals, gay men, and bisexuals; for blacks in Panama and in South Africa; and for the young and the elderly. Male masculinities are bound up with the complex weaving of race, sexuality, class, and other social distinctions used for domination and exploitation (Baca Zinn, 1982; Franklin, 1988; Kimmel, 1987; Mac an Ghaill, 1990). Moreover, male masculinities also relate to the ways some men have power over other men.

For example, in the U.S., Davis (1983), hooks (1981), and Wallace (1978) show how black men and black women have been sexualized during slavery and Reconstruction periods. White men used rape as a means of controlling and terrorizing black women during slavery, and the myth of the black male rapist was created to justify the lynching of black men. These events of rape and racism resulted in the social regulation of both black masculinity and femininity. However, these sexualized and racialized images never completely took hold, because when possible black men and women fought back against these images and acts of physical violence. These active struggles for control over their sexualized bodies offered possibilities to change gender relations.

Asian-American Heterosexual Masculinities

For Asian-American men, the masculinity issue is about who one is and how one relates to family and relatives, loved ones, emotional partners, close friends, and acquaintances. It is also related to the ways one presents oneself to the world at the workplace, at school, in leisure situations, and other public gatherings. It is in these ways Asian-American men reproduce and negotiate gender relations with women and other men in their lives. In this section, we discuss the historical context shaping their masculinities attending to issues of power relations. Here we focus on heterosexual masculinities given the scope of this study.[2]

Historically, racialized immigration policies, labor practices, and media images helped shape and regulate previous Asian-American masculinities and affect present forms of these masculinities. One set of practices involved the tension between recruitment and exclusion of Asian male laborers from 1850s to 1930s (Chan, 1991). On the one hand, these workers were recruited as a source of cheap labor to work in plantations, canneries, mines, and agricultural fields. On the other hand, hostility, race riots, and anti-Asian sentiments created an atmosphere of racial hatred against all Asians and resulted in the passage of race-based immigration laws and exclusionary policies. Moreover, the exclusionary policies were gendered by allowing a sizable number of Asian male laborers to enter, while restricting the entrance of Asian women, thus producing highly skewed sex ratios. Further, images of Asian people as members of inferior races, depraved heathens, opium addicts, and Yellow Peril invaders perpetuated popular media during this period. Not only did these images serve to heighten hostility against Asians in the U.S. and fuel the movement for their exclusion, these images also create lasting racialized Western narratives of the East and serve as one key justification for U.S. imperialist expansion into "foreign" lands.

These policies, practices, and images shape and regulate early Asian-American masculinities in several ways (Bulosan, 1946/1973; Espiritu, 1997; Okada, 1957/1976). The dominant society made these men to be perpetual outsiders, foreigners, different. Whites saw Asian-American men as treacherous, dirty, and criminals. They were viewed as sex-starved gangs of men lusting over white women, as potential rapists, and as hypersexualized invaders ready to produce Asian children in the U.S. if given the opportunity. They needed to be constantly monitored by employers, groups of white men, and the police to keep them docile and submissive. And the lives of these Asian-American men were highly dependent on their employers. In addition to being hypersexualized, Asian-American men were simultaneously emasculated. Many did "women's work," such as laboring as domestic servants, launderers, and cooks. Some were separated from their wives living in Asia and somehow maintained split households. Other men were able to have their wives enter the country through the picture bride system. For those not married, anti-miscegenation laws forbade these men from marrying white women in most states and made the formation of new families highly difficult. Most participated in bachelor societies outside the workplace. Here laws limited Asian-American men's interactions with white communities and especially white women. Religion, gambling, and visiting prostitutes served as some leisure and communal activities in an isolating, desolate, and unfriendly place.

In short, early Asian-American masculinity was constructed to be threatening and disempowering in relations to white employers and to the larger U.S. society. In regard to women, power relations were somewhat ambivalent. Patriarchal and unequal gender relations were reinforced in most U.S. households and split households. Relationships between Asian-American men and white women involved complex power relations; Asian-American men were simultaneously in dominant and subordinate positions in relation to their white partners.

The gender, ethnic, and economic compositions of U.S. Asians have changed with the shift to a less restrictive and discriminatory immigration policy in 1965 and the entry of political and military refugees resulting from U.S. military incursions into Korea and Southeast Asia. Since 1965, the majority of Asian immigrants have been women, resulting in a more similar number of men and women (Chan, 1991). This latest wave of refugees and immigrants brought new Asian ethnic groups, such as the Hmong as well as earlier Asian groups such as Filipinos. Larger numbers of middle-class professionals, along with people from working-class backgrounds, are changing communities built by the earlier generation of farm, manual, and domestic workers and small-business owners.

Recent changes in Asian-American masculinities cannot be accounted for merely by the more balanced gender ratio. Rather we posit that contemporary changes in these masculinities are linked with fundamental transformations in social relations resulting from the entry of recent Asian Americans and the concomitant economic, political, and cultural changes in these communities. First, the model minority myth is highly gendered and economic, and forms the basis of the dominant society's construction of Asian-American maleness (Cheng, 1996; U.S. Commission on Civil Rights, 1992).[3] This myth suggests that Asians are highly self-reliant, economically successful, and politically non-resisting. This myth is built on the sexist and heterosexist notions that Asian-American families instill "proper" work and moral values with the economically responsible father as the head of household. This is in contrast to previous stereotypes of Asian-American men as single, hypersexual, and docile males. The model minority image of Asian Americans is also used to minimize the effects of racism and to blame other racial minority and immigrant groups for their location with the economic hierarchy. In this sense, Asian-American masculinity is about being a good family man who provides for his family and does not ask for government economic assistance. This pressure to be a good provider impacts differentially for a variety of Asian-American men based on economic status, acculturation level, immigration and refugee status, and ethnic identity (Cheng & Thatchenkery, 1997; Lazur & Majors, 1995; Sue, 1990).

In addition to the model minority myth, the media generally create images of emasculated Asian-American men (Fong-Torres, 1995). The Asian-American men are not portrayed in sexual terms and are imputed with no sexual drive. They are characterized as brainy wimps, martial arts contenders, perpetual foreigners, or fatalistic, silent victims. In the rare times when they are portrayed in sexual encounters, they are usually hypersexualized as sex-starved rapists (Tajima, 1989). These portrayals simply recycle age-old stereotypes in contemporary roles through humor and horror.

In the past three decades, Asian-American heterosexual men have explored their own masculinities in search of new forms and expressions (Chan, 1998; Cheng, 1996; Chin, 1981; Fulbeck, 1990). Fictional narratives and experimental videos demonstrate some of the more public expressions of these changing masculinities. This search involves complex negotiations of certain gendered and sexualized practices rather than simply replicating dominant modes of white patriarchal heterosexual masculinity. Yet, other Asian-American men simply rely on male dominance to reclaim their neutered Asian masculinities. For example, some Asian-American men feel that their masculinity is challenged and undermined when Asian-American women date white men. This may be related to emotions of abandonment, rejection, and shame. Their perceptions of relatively high Asian female–white male unions are supported by empirical studies showing that Asian-American women marry and date whites at higher rates than do Asian-American men, a trend that has existed since the 1950s (Fujino, 1997; Kitano, Fujino & Takahashi, 1998; Shinagawa & Pang, 1996). For example in 1990 in California, 7.7 percent of Asian-American men were married to whites, compared to 16.2 percent of Asian-American women (Shinagawa & Pang, 1996). Among college students, Fujino (1997) found that 34.1 percent of Chinese-American men and 42.1 percent of Japanese-American men had dated at least one white partner, compared to 41.5 percent of Chinese-American women and 60.9 percent of Japanese-American women. While it is true that a higher percentage of Asian-American women date whites than do Asian-American men, these data indicate that Asian-American men date white women at fairly high rates, at least in a metropolitan, multicultural setting. Given this, it is possible that Asian female–white male unions challenge Asian-American masculinities, not because Asian-American men lack female dates, but rather because white dominant society and white men have already usurped Asian-American masculinities in so many ways. Clearly, redefining, renegotiating, and reconstructing Asian-American masculinity is a complex process, which has involved both resisting male dominance and privilege as well as using patriarchy to buttress a somewhat fragile and certainly racialized masculinity.

About Asian-American Male Masculinities

Social representation theory provides a way to examine how social groups negotiate in constructing their attitudes. The turn to social representation theory offers a social psychological approach to studying attitude formation by examining the expressed thinking of social individuals. Because this paper focuses on attitudes about Asian-American masculinities and takes seriously people's experiences, we view their attitudes as arguments about social representations. Moscovici (1984) posits that social representations are cognitive products about ideas or objects created by a social group. Social representations are structured by and anchored in ideological systems, and have emotional valences. Social representations communicate and create knowledge, and shape and are shaped by the relationships of domination and subordination in which they are embedded (Bhavnani, 1991). By considering them as representations, Moscovici highlights the active cognitive processes in which human beings structure their social environment. Moreover, Billig (1996) points to the argumentative context of attitudes. This argumentative context is social, rather than basing attitudes simply on individual's motives and beliefs. An attitude refers to an evaluation on matters of public debate, disagreement, and discussion. "In consequence, we can expect the possessors of attitudes to justify their stances, to criticize competing views, and to argue about the issues" (p. 207). In traditional cognition analysis, the perceiver re-

mains a lone individual, forming, apparently in isolation, her or his accounts of racial and gendered traits on the basis of the actual similarities and differences in the individual she or he meets. Here, we argue that attitudes in general, and attitudes about Asian-American masculinity, in particular, provide a way to understand the specific way gender and masculinity are socially conceived by the study's participants.

So far, we know of no quantitative study that examines how Asian-American men view their own masculinity. However regarding attitudes by others about Asian-American men, Niemann, Jennings, Rozelle, Baxter and Sullivan (1994) found that among University of Houston students, Asian-American men were considered intelligent, short, achievement oriented, soft spoken, and hard workers. From an augmentative social representation perspective, this suggests that Asian-American masculinity is socially constructed around "model minority" maleness and not in terms of the dominant construction of masculinity.

Moreover, the current literature on gender attitudes reveals contradictory findings about Asian-American men's views about gender expectations and women's rights. One study found that Chinese, Japanese, and Korean immigrant men, but not U.S.-born Asians, experienced gender-role conflicts in the areas of success, power, and competition as well as displays of emotions. In other words, immigrant Asian men tended to embrace hegemonic masculinity (Kim, O'Neil, & Owen, 1996). Based on the Attitudes Towards Women Scale, one study in Hawaii found that Chinese, Japanese, and Hawaiian men hold more conservative attitudes towards women's rights and roles than white men (Ullman, Freedland, & Warmsun, 1978), while another found that Chinese-American men hold more liberal views than white men (Braun & Chao, 1978).

Method

Procedure

The present study used data collected from a study on heterosexual college dating of Chinese, Japanese, and white Americans (see Fujino, 1992). The dating study recruited respondents from two sources: psychology courses and the registrar's listing of university students. Of the 319 (57 percent) from psychology courses, the majority came from introductory courses for which participation was one means to fulfill a course requirement, and a few students from upper division psychology courses participated for extra credit. To ensure an adequate number of Asians, the study also recruited 237 respondents (43 percent) from the university's listing of Chinese, Japanese, and white students. The dating study contacted these respondents randomly from the university telephone list. Participating respondents received a $5 gift certificate. Of the 405 individuals contacted by telephone and eligible to participate, 317 subjects agreed to participate, and 239 completed the questionnaire. For each ethnic gender group, a t-test analysis found no significant differences between samples, at the $p < .001$ criterion controlling for type 1 experimental-wide error rate, on any of the variables: age, parental socioeconomic status, parental education, and generation. So we decided to combine the two samples.

Measures

Respondents completed a 45-minute questionnaire dealing with demographic information and attitudes about themselves, women, and racial-ethnic gender groups. Measures specific to the present paper were as follows.

Demographic information. Respondents provided demographic information including ethnicity, sex/gender, age, marital status, sexual orientation, birthplace of self and parents, and mother's and father's educational and occupational backgrounds.

Attitudes about self. The study developed a list of 30 attributes to elicit ethnic and gender differences in heterosexual relationships to emphasize ethnic concerns, issues, and power relations from past studies of qualities desired in potential mates (Buss & Barnes, 1986) and of personality characteristics (Wiggins, 1979). The attributes include physical attractiveness (physical attractiveness, cute), sexual expectations (sexually exciting), personality characteristics (considerate, nurturing), and socioeconomic status (high occupational status potential). To explore respondents' attitudes of their own attributes, respondents reported the degree to which they possess each of the 30 attributes on a five-point Likert scale from "not at all" (1) to "a lot" (5).

Attitudes about others. The study presented the same list of 30 attributes to examine respondents' attitudes about Chinese, Japanese, and white members of the opposite sex. For example, women read: "Imagine that there were 100 Japanese-American men in the room. How many of these 100 men do you think possess each of the following characteristics?" Respondents indicated the number (from 0 to 100) of individuals perceived to possess each attribute. The study used the same procedure to assess the attitudes about Chinese-American and white men.

Attitudes about women's roles. The study assessed the attitudes towards the rights and roles of women with the Attitude Toward Women Scale (AWS; Spence, Helmreich, & Staff, 1973). The AWS short form consisted of 25 items, rated on a four-point Likert scale from "disagree strongly" to "agree strongly," that tap into six theme areas: vocational, educational, and intellectual roles; freedom and independence; dating, courtship, and etiquette; drinking, swearing, and jokes; sexual behavior; and marital relations and obligations. We used the AWS because it is the most commonly used measure of attitudes toward women, used in 371 published studies, and has a high internal-consistency reliability (coefficient alpha above .80 for various populations) and high validity (Beere, 1990).

Respondents

A total of 559 people responded to the survey questions: 55 immigrant Asian men, 90 U.S.-born Asian men, 92 white men, 67 immigrant Asian women, 96 U.S.-born Asian women, and 159 white women. The participants self-identified their ethnic background as solely Chinese, Japanese, or white/European. The study did not collect data on any other Asian-American groups, thus Asian Americans here refers to only those of Chinese and Japanese descent (see Note 1). The dating study also excluded married or homosexual individuals to provide an appropriate sample to examine interracial dating attitudes and practices of self-identified heterosexuals. The age ranged from 16 to 35, with a mean age of 19.8 years. We determined the respondent's generation using the country of birth of subjects and their parents. Over half of the Chinese Americans were immi-

grants, and another 40 percent were second generation. In contrast, most whites (80 percent) were at least third generation. Among Japanese Americans, 20 percent were first generation, 37 percent second generation, and 44 percent third generation or more. Participants generally came from families with above average socioeconomic levels. The Nam-Powers (Miller, 1991) socioeconomic status scores (0–100), derived from median education, median income, and occupation for women and men in the civilian labor force in 1980, yielded a mean SES score of 78 for fathers and 51 for mothers. On average, fathers had graduated from college and mothers had attended some college.

Data Reduction Analysis

We used principal components factor analysis with varimax rotation to determine the major factors underlying the 30 interpersonal characteristics of the Attitudes About Self and Attitudes About Others scales. First, we performed factor analyses separately on these scales to determine the number of factors to use. The scree procedure indicated a three-factor solution. We then performed factor analyses with varimax rotation, with the number of factors set to three, to determine the underlying factor structure. We included variables with eigenvalues greater than or equal to .30 in the factor, and yielded very similar factor patterns for each scale. Two attributes (quiet and expresses his/her feelings) did not consistently load on a single factor, and so we excluded them. We combined the two attribute scales imputed to Chinese and Japanese by taking the average scores for each of the 30 attributes because they were highly comparable. Note that the data suggest that there were no effects for the order in which subjects rated the three ethnic groups. If there was an order effect, the Chinese members of the opposite gender would consistently be rated highest (or lowest), followed by whites and then Japanese in descending (or ascending) order. What the data show is that Chinese and Japanese Americans were given consistently similar ratings, both of which differed from the ratings given to whites. This suggests that the respondents indeed responded to the ethnic backgrounds listed. The three-factor solution explains 47 percent of the observed variance of the Attitudes About Others scale.

The first factor, labeled Attractiveness, explains 22 percent of the observed variance for the Attitudes About Others scale. It consists of 11 items: sexually exciting, physically affectionate, physically attractive, outgoing/sociable, romantic, good sense of humor, exotic, values equal sex roles, strong personality, easy going, and cute. It exhibits a coefficient alpha reliability of .87.

The second factor, labeled Power, explains 16 percent of the observed variance for the Attitudes About Others scale. It consists of eight items: masculine, high occupational status potential, high income potential, ambitious, college graduate potential, dominant, independent, and feminine. The attribute feminine received a negative eigenvalue, and was thus negatively coded. This subscale, representing three aspects of power—dominance, socioeconomic status, and gender—has a coefficient alpha reliability of .88.

The third factor, labeled Caring, explains nine percent of the observed variance. It consists of nine items: considerate, polite, reliable, humble, obedient, sensitive to my feelings, nurturing, domestic, and tradi-

tional sex roles. It exhibits a coefficient alpha reliability of .87.

Results

Overall, the self-concept patterns for immigrant and U.S.-born Asian and white men differ substantively relative to each other. Compared to immigrant and U.S.-born Asian men, only white men list that they are sexually exciting, physically attractive, outgoing and sociable, and share feelings. More than 80 percent of white men report that they are masculine and physically affectionate, while between 60 percent and 80 percent of U.S.-born Asian men report so. Additional characteristics listed by both U.S.-born Asian and white men include nurturing, romantic, values equal sex roles, and strong personality. Only U.S.-born Asian men list that they will do domestic tasks. Immigrant Asian men construct the least distinctive self-concept: they listed the smallest number of characteristics, all of which were also common to U.S.-born Asian and white men.

All three groups have 11 characteristics in common, including college graduate, reliable, polite, good sense of humor, considerate, high-income potential, ambitious, sensitive to feelings, independent, easy-going, and high occupational status potential. Characteristics such as college graduate, high-income potential, and high occupational status potential show that these young male students knew their economic potentials because they attend a highly competitive university.

Attitudes Toward Asian-American Men by Asian-American and White Women

Overall, women impute a constellation of attributes to Asian-American men that differ substantially from the characteristics describing white men. Immigrant and U.S.-born Asian and white women share similarities in how they view Asian-American men. In contrast, immigrant and U.S.-born Asian women view white men slightly differently than do white women.

The three groups of women view Asian-American men as valuing traditional sex roles, college graduate, romantic, polite, nurturing, and exotic, and they ranked these characteristics in a similar order. Immigrant Asian and white women view more than 80 percent of Asian-American men as valuing traditional sex roles, college graduate and romantic while U.S.-born Asian women view between 60 percent and 80 percent of Asian-American men as having these traits. Only immigrant Asian women consider Asian-American men as dominant, and only white women consider Asian-American men as introverted/quiet, share feelings, and valuing equal sex roles.

The three groups of women view white men as independent, outgoing and sociable, ambitious, and having a strong personality. Both U.S.-born Asian and white women view white men as dominant and being college graduates. Both U.S.-born and immigrant Asian women view white men as easy-going, romantic, and having a good sense of humor. Only U.S.-born Asian women view white men as high occupational status potential, high-income potential, and physically affectionate. Also, only immigrant Asian women consider white men to share feelings.

Notice that U.S.-born Asian women impute more characteristics to white men than to Asian-American men. U.S.-born Asian women impute more characteristics to Asian-American or white men than do immigrant Asian and white women.

Asian-American Male Self-Concept of Attractiveness, Power and Caring

The attractiveness, power, and caring ratings resulted from the factor analysis of the 30 personal characteristics. The possible range of the ratings is from 0 (lowest) to 100 (highest). First, white men (60.7) view themselves as more attractive than do U.S.-born Asian men (54.8), followed by immigrant Asian men (49.6). Analysis of variance indicates that these means are statistically different, $F(2, 232) = 4.34$, p<.05. The mean ratings of attractiveness are statistically different between white men and U.S.-born Asian men, $F(1, 232) = 10.8$, p<.01, between white men and immigrant Asian men, $F(1, 232) = 27.33$, p<.01, and between U.S.-born Asian men and immigrant Asian men, $F(1, 232) = 5.45$, p<.05. Second, immigrant Asian (76.1), U.S. born Asian (76.2), and white (79.1) men view themselves similarly in terms of power. Analysis of variance indicates that these means are not statistically different, $F(2, 232) = 1.66$, p>.10. Third, immigrant Asian (56.7), U.S.-born Asian (59.7), and white (57.0) men view themselves similarly on the caring rating. Analysis of variance indicates that these means are not statistically different, $F(2, 232) = 2.10$, p>.10.

Attitudes About the Attractiveness, Power, and Caring of Asian-American Men

Two-way analysis of variance on the mean attractiveness, power, and caring scores indicates that the main effect of rated-male groups is significant, but the main effect for woman respondents is not significant. That is, first, the three groups of women view white men as more attractive than Asian-American men, $F(1, 320) = 313.01$, p < .01. Second, the three groups of women view Asian-American men as more powerful than white men, $F(1, 320) = 20.78$, p < .01. Third, the three groups of women view Asian-American men as more caring than white men, $F(1, 320) = 132.27$, p < .01.

In addition, all the women, on average, impute significantly lower attractiveness, power, and caring ratings than did the men. On average, these women impute men, both Asian American and white, with an attractive score of 42.1, while the men give themselves a score of 55.8. These women impute to men a power score of 66.1, while the men impute themselves with a score of 77.3. And these women impute to men a score on caring of 47.0 while the men impute to themselves a score of 57.9.

Negotiating Asian-American Masculinity

The most significant finding of the correlation analysis is that both U.S.-born and immigrant Asian men show no significant association between masculinity and femininity characteristics (for U.S.-born Asian men, rho = -.183, p>.05; for immigrant Asian men, rho = .004, p >.05). However there is a strong negative association between the white male masculinity and the "feminine" characteristic (rho = -0.621, p<.01).

Furthermore, there is a positive association between attractiveness and masculinity and between power and masculinity for all three male groups. In contrast, there exists a moderate association between caring and masculinity only for U.S.-born Asian men.

Immigrant Asian men associate masculinity with being physically attractive, physically affectionate, cute, sexually exciting, good sense of humor, and obedient (negative). U.S.-born Asian men associate masculinity with sexually exciting, outgoing/

sociable, high occupational status potential, polite, and reliable. White men associate masculinity with strong personality, sexually exciting, college graduate, independent, feminine (negative), high income potential, dominant, high occupational status potential, and values traditional sex roles.

Attitudes Toward Women and Asian-American Masculinity

Immigrant (2.03) and U.S.-born Asian men (2.05) are more conservative than white men (2.23), based on the composite AWS scale. Analysis of variance indicates that these scores are statistically different, $F(2, 234) = 9.17$, p<.01. Moreover, the mean score is statistically different between white and U.S.-born Asian men, $F(1, 234) = 13.75$, p<.01, and between white and immigrant Asian men, $F(1, 234) = 12.46$, p<.01; but there is no statistical difference between U.S.-born and immigrant Asian men, $F(1, 234) = 0.09$, p>.10.

This composite score pattern of the AWS scale by male groups reflects several distinct attitudes about women. The values for attitudes about vocation, education, and intellectual development of women for immigrant (2.10) and U.S.-born Asian men (2.08) are statistically lower than for white men (2.26), $F(2, 234) = 7.63$, p<.01. Likewise, the values for attitudes on women's drinking, swearing, and joking for immigrant (1.46) and U.S.-born Asian men (1.64) are statistically lower than for white men (1.85), $F(2, 234) = 6.02$, p<.01. The values for attitudes on women's sexual behavior for immigrant (1.62) and U.S.-born Asian men (1.84) are statistically lower than for white men (2.35), $F(2, 234) = 11.77$, p<.01. The values for attitudes on women's marital status and obligations for immigrant (2.19) and U.S.-born Asian men (2.30) are significantly lower than the white men (2.40), F(2, 234) = 5.20, p<.01.

However, the values for attitudes about women's freedom and independence did not differ among immigrant (2.07) and U.S.-born Asian men (2.04), and white men (2.16) are not statistically different, F(2, 234) = 1.58, p>.10. Likewise, the values for attitudes about women's dating, courtship, and etiquette did not differ among immigrant (2.23) and U.S.-born Asian men (2.13) and white men (2.25), F(2, 234) = .66, p>.10.

Moreover, a correlational analysis between masculinity and these attitudes toward women reveal no significant association for each male group, except for the correlation between attitudes about drinking, swearing, and joking and masculinity for U.S.-born Asian men (rho = -.283, p<.05).

Discussion

Strategies for Negotiating Asian-American Masculinity

Asian-American men construct their masculinity in unique ways. The college-age Asian-American men in our study did this in several ways by using strategies to negotiate their own masculinity and gendered identities through personal and social interactions. We infer these strategies from prior results by using social representation theory and the argumentative nature of attitudes in pointing to the ways social groups negotiate attitudes. One such strategy relates to the way Asian-American men differentiate their social representation—that is, a way of conceiving, engaging, and arguing about themselves as a group—of their masculinity from that of white hegemonic masculinity. This is an interesting social representation about a racialized masculinity.

First, while there are some similarities between Asian-American and white male self-concept, there are also substantive differences. Most white men consider masculinity as a highly important component of who they are. This is not so for U.S.-born Asian men and less so for immigrant Asian men in terms of how they view themselves. Only U.S.-born Asian men said that they would do domestic tasks, suggesting that these men would be more open to sharing household responsibilities, while others might not be. This is one indication of how they have a more expanded notion of masculinity and do not readily accept hegemonic masculine notions that view housework as women's work. Immigrant Asian men had the least number of characteristics as part of their self-concept profile, suggesting that there is no clear consensus among these immigrant men about their group profile. This indicates that there is a much greater variation in how they view their own masculinity that differs from U.S.-born Asian and white masculinity.

Second, unlike white men, both immigrant and U.S.-born Asian men view their masculinities not in opposition to their femininity. Asian-American men hold the view that maleness can contain elements of masculinity and femininity. This construction of Asian-American masculinity suggests a new formation, a more flexible masculinity. At the same time, other Asian-American men continue to construct a hegemonic masculinity. These two opposing strategies used by Asian-American men may be related to Asian-American men's contradictory position in U.S. society. As Messner (1993) argues, men with marginalized social status occupy positions of dominance and subordination simultaneously. Asian-American men hold male privilege at the same time they are racially subordinated. Because of their subordinated position, some Asian-American men try to counter the effeminate image of Asian-American men by emulating hegemonic masculinities, which include dominance over women. Though they can engage in patriarchy and obtain male privileges, they find that racism eventually prevents them from fully copying white hegemonic masculinity. Based on our findings, we suggest that Asian-American men today are at a critical site for redefining their masculinity, because of their own experience with subordination and because the women's movement has created the consciousness to challenge patriarchy. Men's studies scholars and activists suggest that it is time for all men to challenge hegemonic masculinities and redefine maleness (Baca Zinn, 1982; Chan, 1998; Cheng, 1996; Kimmel & Messner, 1995; Mac an Ghaill, 1990).

Our data suggest that Asian-American men, to some degree, are attempting to negotiate new forms of non-hegemonic masculinities. For example, U.S.-born Asian men linked their masculinity with certain caring characteristics such as being polite and obedient, and were the only men's group willing to do domestic tasks. These men were not effeminate; rather they view these caring attributes as part of their power and masculinity, again suggesting a more flexible construction of masculinity. This suggests that U.S.-born Asian men may relate with women differently through more caring and nurturing ways in their relationships, compared to white or immigrant Asian men. This tension in strategies is important, not because it suggests a contradiction in the results, but rather we argue that this is an important part of how these young Asian-American men negotiate their

masculinity. Given a history of emasculation and desexualization of U.S.-born Asian men, these men for the most part have been able to make a masculinity that does not completely resemble white hegemonic masculinity or a model minority masculinity that uses male privilege, power, and domination in relationship with a variety of racialized and class-stratified women and men.

Third, U.S.-born Asian men in our study rely on their ability to garner economic power, in terms of high occupational status potential, to build up their masculinity. They do not depend generally on being independent, dominant, and non-feminine for power; rather they rely on economic power. This finding suggests that, as university students, they leverage their economic ability for power and privileges within relationships more so than white men, though the latter also view economic power as part of their masculinity. In addition, unlike white men, U.S.-born Asian men also embrace caring as part of their masculinity. This further points to their flexible masculinity. In some ways, this reflects the model minority version of masculinity; however, these men do not draw on all aspects of this stereotype to construct their own masculinity. In contrast to U.S.-born Asians, immigrant Asian men do not link their masculinity with economic power or any other forms of power. They simply see their masculinity in terms of attractiveness.

Overall, these findings suggest Asian-American men construct a social representation of their masculinity through certain strategies through a series of negotiation regarding sameness and difference in relation to the norm of white masculinity in the U.S. While seemingly contradictory in construction, these collective social representations of power, attractiveness, and caring show how these men think about themselves and their maleness and how they relate to women.

Women's Constructions of Asian-American Masculinities

In contrast to the ways Asian-American men construct, negotiate, and practice their masculinity, Asian-American and white women present differing constructions of Asian-American masculinity. These women make clear distinctions between Asian-American and white masculinities. They tend to see Asian-American men as more traditional in their gender roles and more nurturing, and white men as more independent, masculine, and outgoing. Immigrant Asian women more so than U.S.-born Asian women view these Asian-American men as traditional. U.S.-born Asian women do not hold views about Asian-American men that are as strong as those held by immigrant Asian and white women. This indicates that there are more variations of the views, and there is not clear consensus presented in the U.S.-born women's group.

The findings suggest two key points. First, Asian-American and white women have ambivalent views toward Asian-American masculinity. On the one hand, they view Asian-American men as having traditional gender roles, yet they also consider these men as nurturing, romantic, polite, and exotic. (Given how the data was collected, there is no way to examine the potentially different ways Asian-American and white women use terms like "exotic" to refer to Asian-American men). This ambivalent relationship for immigrant and U.S.-born Asian and white women highlights some of their concerns about potential domineering actions of Asian-American men as compared to white men. Moreover, immigrant and U.S.-born Asian and white women view these Asian-American men not as masculine and physically attractive compared to white men, yet believe that they might receive more intimate types of personal relations with Asian-American men.

Second, U.S.-born Asian women do not hold strong views about Asian-American men as compared to immigrant Asian and white women. This might suggest that U.S.-born Asian women have stronger ambivalent feelings about Asian-American men and participate in more cautious relationships with them than compared to white women. U.S.-born Asian women however hold strong and more varied views about white men, while in contrast white women hold less varied views about white men. This further suggests that for U.S.-born Asian women, Asian-American masculinity is not as clearly articulated for them as compared to immigrant Asian women. In short, Asian-American and white women relate to Asian-American masculinity in a more ambivalent manner than previously expected. The women in the study do not see Asian-American masculinity in only stereotypical representations, yet they in their own personal ways engage actively in making for themselves their own views on Asian-American masculinity cautiously.

Concluding Remarks

In this article, we discuss some broad contours of Asian-American masculinity with emphasis on Asian-American men's agency and their changing construction of their masculinity and identity. Using quantitative methods, we begin to point to certain strategies used by Asian-American men and tensions in these strategies in dealing with their maleness and gender expectations as well as the ambivalent relationship women have with Asian-American masculinity. To explore these issues, detailed life histories and participant observations in a variety of locations would enhance our knowledge of the nuanced mechanics of Asian-American men's negotiations of their masculinity. We would like to offer some cautionary warning. First, it is important to consider the historical and situational limitations of this study, which focuses on Chinese and Japanese heterosexual college-aged respondents, and not to generalize beyond its scope. Given the limitations of the data collection, we can infer little about the masculinities of more recent Asian refugees in the U.S. and nothing about how other men and women of color view Asian-American masculinity as well as how Asian-American men view other people of color. This study serves as a necessary beginning by offering future studies important issues to explore. Second, we suggest that while our results and discussion highlight economic status as key in understanding Asian-American masculinity, this might not be so for working-class or poor Asian-American men. This may lead to simply reinforcing the gendered nature of the model minority stereotype. Third, we suggest that the categories of race, ethnicity, and national origins we used are not fixed. This points to the potential conflation of ethnicity, immigrant status, and acculturation levels in this study. Moreover, we want to caution against conflating cultural differences with differences in masculinities. This simply fosters reductionist thinking without considering the nuanced ways masculinities are constituted and maintained in our lives.

In closing, we suggest that it is important to think about Asian-American masculinity

as fluid and dynamic. Change is possible— not simply because this research suggests so, but because the historical record has shown that Asian masculinity has changed over time. Asian-American heterosexual men need to continue to dialogue about the kind of relations they want to have with the women and men in their lives. We all have to work through issues of power, privileges, and resistances to shape our personal, social, and workplace relationships. For some, this means finding a collective safe space to talk about these issues and deeply examining our emotions, beliefs, and actions that reproduce power inequalities. For others, it also means taking collective actions to create some change. It is our hope that this study contributes to the ongoing dialogue and collective action to redefine Asian-American masculinities in ways that value an Asian maleness that is not dependent on male and heterosexual dominance and privilege.

Notes

1. The term "Asian American" generally refers to a diverse group of Asians living in the United States, including Filipinos, Cambodians, and Asian Indians. However, this study's sample is limited to Chinese and Japanese. In an effort not to assume Asian-American groups would be viewed similarly, we had participants rate characteristics imputed to Chinese and Japanese men separately. It was logistically cumbersome to include even one or two more Asian groups. Caution must be exercised when generalizing to other Asian-American groups. Moreover, the term "masculinity" refers to male—and not female— versions of hegemonic masculinity.

2. Some issues addressed here are relevant to both heterosexual and homosexual males, such as sexual invisibility due to racism. Some Asian-American heterosexual and homosexual men choose to exhibit physical and interactional hypermasculinity

to oppose sexual invisibility. In contrast, some white sexual partners of gay Asian-American men consider youthful Asian-American men as exotically attractive. In this case, these Asian Americans are not sexually invisible but rather sexually objectified as objects of "Oriental" fantasies. We believe that the interconnections between gay male masculinity, economic class, and ethnicity are important topics for future research.

3. The notion of the "model minority" claims that Asian Americans have made it in U.S. society despite disadvantages. This image contrasts sharply with earlier stereotypes of Asian Americans as sneaky, manipulative, untrustworthy, manual laborers. The model minority stereotype, developed in the 1960s at the same time the black, Chicano, and Asian-American social movements were battling racism, functions to offer an assimilationist, non-resisting pathway to "success." The model minority stereotype functions to show that America is an open society, and that with enough hard work, any one can make it in the U.S. High levels of unemployment, incarceration, and poverty among African Americans, Chicanos, and Indigenous Peoples can then be explained by their own laziness and incompetence. This victim-blame explanation ignores the role systemic racism plays in creating marginalization within society as well as the hard work exerted by most working-class people.

References

Baca Zinn, M. (1982). Chicano men and masculinity. *Journal of Ethnic Studies*, 10, 29–44.

Beere, C. A. (1990). *Gender roles: A handbook of tests and measures*. New York: Greenwood Press.

Bhavnani, K. K. (1991). *Talking politics: A psychological framing for views from youth in Britain*. Cambridge: Cambridge University Press.

Billig, M. (1996). *Arguing and thinking: A rhetorical approach to social psychology* (2nd ed.). Cambridge: Cambridge University Press.

Brod, H. (Ed.). (1987). *The making of masculinity: The new men's studies*. Boston: Allen & Unwin.

Braun, J. S., & Chao, H. M. (1978). Attitudes toward women: A comparison of Asian-born Chinese and American Caucasians. *Psychology of Women Quarterly* 2, 195–201.

Bulosan, C. (1973). *America is in the heart*. Seattle: University of Washington Press. (Original work published 1946.)

Buss, D. M., & Barnes, M. (1986). Preferences in human mate selection. *Journal of Personality and Social Psychology* 50, 559–70.

Chan, J. W. (1998). Contemporary Asian American men's issues. In L. R. Hirabayashi (Ed.), *Teaching Asian America: Diversity and problems of community* (pp. 93–102). Lanham, MD: Rowman and Littlefield Publishers.

Chan, S. (1991). *Asian Americans: An Interpretive history*. Boston, MA: Twayne Publishers.

Cheng, C. (1996). "We choose not to compete": The "merit" discourse in the selection process, and Asian and Asian American Men and their masculinity. In C. Cheng (Ed.), *Masculinities in organizations* (pp. 177–200). Thousand Oaks, CA: Sage.

Cheng, C., & Thatchenkery, T. J. (1997). Why is there a lack of workplace diversity research on Asian Americans? *Journal of Applied Behavioral Science*, 33, 270–6.

Chin, F. (1981). *The chickencoop Chinaman*. Seattle: University of Washington Press.

Connell, R. W. (1987). *Gender and power*. Cambridge and Oxford: Polity and Cambridge University Press.

Davis, A. (1983). *Women, race, and class*. New York: Vintage Books.

Espiritu, Y. H. (1997). *Asian American women and men*. Thousand Oaks, CA: Sage Publications.

Fong-Torres, B. (1995). Why are there no male Asian anchormen on TV? In M. Kimmel & M. A. Messner (Eds.), *Men's lives* (3rd ed., pp. 256–260). New York: Macmillan Publishing.

Franklin, C., II. (1988). *Men and society*. Chicago, IL: Nelson Hall.

Fujino, D. C. (1992). Extending exchange theory: Effects of ethnicity and gender on Asian American heterosexual relationships. Ph.D. dissertation, Department of Psychology, University of California, Los Angeles, CA.

Fujino, D. C. (1997). The rates, patterns, and reasons for forming heterosexual interracial dating relationships among Asian Americans. *Journal of Social and Personal Relationships* 14, 809–28.

Fulbeck, K. (1990). *Banana split*. Experiment Video.

hooks, b. (1981). *Ain't I a woman: Black women and feminism*. Boston, MA: South End Press.

Kim, E. J., O'Neil, J. M., & Owen, S. V. (1996). Asian-American men's acculturation and gender-role conflict. *Psychological Reports* 79, 95–104.

Kimmel, M. (Ed.). (1987). *Changing men: New directions in research on men and masculinity*. London: Sage.

Kimmel, M., & Messner, M. A. (Eds.). (1995). *Men's lives* (3rd ed.). New York: Macmillan.

Kitano, H. H. L., Fujino, D. C., & Takahashi, J. S. (1998). Interracial marriage: Where are the Asian Americans and where are they going? In N. Zane & L. Lee (Eds.), *Handbook of Asian American psychology* (pp. 233–260). Newbury Park, CA: Sage.

Lazur, R. F., & Majors, R. (1995). Men of color: Ethnocultural variations of male gender role strain. In R. F. Levant & W. S. Pollack (Eds.), *A new psychology of men* (pp. 337–58). New York: Basic Books.

Mac an Ghaill, M. (1990). *Young, gifted, and black*. Milton Keynes: Open University Press.

Messner, M. A. (1993). "Changing men" and feminist politics in the United States. *Theory and Society*, 22, 723–37.

Miller, D. C. (1991). *Handbook of research design and social measurement* (5th ed.). Newbury Park, CA: Sage.

Moscovici, S. (1984). The phenomenon of social representation. In R. M. Farr & S. Moscovici (Eds.), *Social representation* (pp. 3–69). Cambridge: Cambridge University Press.

Niemann, Y. F., Jennings, L., Rozelle, R. M., Baxter, J. C., & Sullivan, E. (1994). Use of free response and cluster analysis to determine stereotypes of eight groups. *Personality and Social Psychology Bulletin* 20, 379–90.

Okada, J. (1976). *No-no boy*. San Francisco, CA: Charles E. Tuttle Co. (Original work published 1957.)

Rushton, J. P. (1996). Race, genetics, and human reproductive strategies. *Genetic, Social, and General Psychology Monographs* 122, 21–53.

Segal, L. (1990). *Slow motion: Changing masculinities, changing men*. London: Virago.

Shinagawa, L. H., & Pang, G. Y. (1996). Asian American panethnicity and intermarriage. *Amerasian Journal* 22, 127–152.

Spence, J. T., Helmreich, R. L., & Stapp, J. (1973). A short version of the attitude toward women scale (AWS). *Bulletin on the Psychonomic Society* 2, 219–20.

Sue, D. (1990). Culture in transition: Counseling Asian-American men. In D. Moore & F. Leafgren (Eds.), *Problem solving strategies and interventions of men in conflict* (pp. 153–165). Alexandria, VA: American Association for Counseling and Development.

Just a John?
Pornography and Men's Choices

There has been much talk at this conference about the need for men to love each other and be willing to speak openly about that love. This is important; we need to be able to get beyond the all-too-common male tendency to mute or deform our emotions, a tendency that is destructive not only to ourselves but to those around us. Many this weekend have spoken about our need to nurture each other, and that's important, too. But it's also crucial to remember that loving one another means challenging ourselves as well.

That's what I would like to do today, to challenge us—in harsh language—on men's use of pornography. In an unjust world, those of us with privilege must be harsh on ourselves, out of love.

This challenge is: Can we be more than just johns?

Let me start with a story that a female student at the University of Texas told me. She was riding from Austin to Dallas for a football game on a bus chartered by a fraternity, on which many of the passengers were women. During the trip, someone put into the bus' VCR a sexually explicit video. Uncomfortable with those hardcore sexual images of women being used by men, the female student began a discussion with the people around her about it, and one of the men on the bus agreed that it was inappropriate. He stood up and said to the other men, "You all know me and know I like porno as much as the next guy, but it's not right for us to play this tape when there are women on the bus."

No doubt it took some courage for that young man to confront his fraternity brothers on the issue, and we should honor that. But we should recognize that his statement also communicated to his fraternity brothers that he was one of them—"one of the guys"—who, being guys, naturally like pornography. His objection was not to pornography and men's routine purchase and use of women's bodies for sexual pleasure but to the viewing of it with women present. He was making it clear that his ultimate loyalty was to men and their right to use women sexually, though that use should conform to some type of code of chivalry about being polite about it in mixed company.

In doing that, he was announcing his own position in regard to sex. He was saying: I'm just a john.

Robert Jensen, "Just a John? Pornography and Men's Choices." Posted on http://uts.cc.utexas.edu/~rjensen/freelance/justajohn.pdf, 2005. Reprinted by permission of the author. Talk originally delivered to the second Annual Conference on the College Male, Saint John's University, Collegeville, Minnesota, February 26, 2005. This version reflects changes based on comments of conference participants.

Pimps and Johns

A john is a man who buys another human being for sex. Typically that other human being is sold through an intermediary known as a pimp.

Pimps sell the bodies of other people (most typically, a male pimp selling a woman) to a third person (who is almost always a man).

Men sell women to other men for sex: Pimps and johns.

There is much that could be said about the current cultural practice of using the term "pimp" in a wide variety of other contexts—for example, the MTV show "Pimp My Ride." We live in a world in which men who sell women are glorified. It also is a world in which the dominant white culture implicitly defines pimps as black and then alternately celebrates and denigrates them. The confluence of racism and sexism in these cultural trends deserves discussion. But today I want to concentrate not on the pimps but on the johns, on the men who buy women for sex.

I assume that lots of the men in this room use, or have used, pornography. I assume that lots of the men in this room masturbate, or have masturbated, to pornography. So, I assume there are lots of johns and former johns in this room.

I don't mean that most of us have necessarily bought a woman from a pimp in prostitution, though no doubt some in the audience have. I'm talking about the far more common experience of masturbating to pornography. In my childhood and young adulthood, I was sometimes a john. Virtually every man I know has been a john. Some number of you in this room no doubt still are johns.

In pornography, the pimp is called a publisher or a video producer, and the john is called a fan or a pornography consumer. But that doesn't change the nature of the relationships: One person (usually a man) selling another person (a woman) to a third person (usually a man).

So, pornography is pimps and johns, mass-mediated. When you masturbate to pornography, you are buying sexual pleasure. You are buying a woman. The fact that there are technologies of film or video between you and the pimp doesn't change the equation. Legally, it's not prostitution, but you're a john. Legally, you're not in trouble, but you're still just a john.

The Pornography That Johns Like

At this point, let me define a few terms. In this discussion, I'm using the term pornography to describe the graphic sexually explicit material that one finds in a pornographic video store that depicts primarily heterosexual sex and is consumed primarily, though not exclusively, by heterosexual men. Such material is also widely available on the Internet. There are, of course, other genres of pornography (such as gay or lesbian). But I'm speaking today of the material that I would suspect most of the men in the room have used most routinely—those DVDs and videos that are the bulk of the commercial pornography market.

There are three consistent themes in that pornography:

- All women want sex from all men at all times.
- Women naturally desire the kind of sex that men want, including sex that many women find degrading.

- Any woman who does not at first realize this can be turned with a little force (though force is rarely needed because most women in pornography instinctively understand their "true" sexual nature).

The pornography industry produces two major types of films, features and gonzo. Features mimic, however badly, the conventions of a Hollywood movie. There is some minimal plot, character development, and dialogue, all in the service of presenting the sex. Gonzo films have no such pretensions; they are simply recorded sex, often in a private home or on some minimal set. These films often start with an interview with the woman or women about their sexual desires before the man or men enter the scene.

All these films have a standard series of sex acts, including oral, vaginal, and anal penetration, often performed while the men call the women "bitch," "cunt," "whore," and similar names. As they are penetrated, the women are expected to say over and over how much they like the sex. As pornography like this has become increasingly normalized and mainstream—readily available throughout the country by increasingly sophisticated technology—pornographers have pushed the limits of what is acceptable in the mainstream.

One of the increasingly common types of sex in gonzo, and less common in features, is the double penetration—a scene in which a woman is penetrated anally and vaginally by two men at the same time. Another type of sex scene in gonzo is a "blow bang"—a scene in which a woman performs oral sex on a group of men, with each man in turn ejaculating onto the woman's face or into her mouth in standard pornographic fashion. Some gonzo tapes advertise "ATM," or

"ass-to-mouth," in which a man removes his penis from the woman's anus and she puts it directly into her mouth.

As one pornographic film director put it: "People want more. They want to know how many dicks you can shove up an ass. . . . Make it more hard, make it more nasty, make it more relentless."

How many dicks can you shove up an ass? It's rare, but there are films with double anals: Two men penetrating a woman anally at the same time.

In recent years, the pornography industry has produced about 11,000 new hardcore, graphic sexually explicit films a year. Estimates of the annual revenues of the pornography industry in the United States start at $10 billion. For comparison, the Hollywood box office—the amount Americans spend to go to the movies—was $9.5 billion in 2003.

That's a lot of johns and a lot of profit for the pimps.

Men's Choices and Responsibility

So, we live in a world in which men sell women to other men directly. And men also sell women to other men through mass media. These days, women are sometimes the buyers. And on rare occasions in recent years, women are the sellers. That is, there are women who consume pornography and a few women who make it. In this society, that's called progress. Feminism is advanced, we are told, when women can join the ranks of those who buy and sell other human beings.

All this is happening as a predictable result of the collaboration of capitalism and patriarchy. Take a system that values profit over everything, and combine it with a system of male supremacy: You get pimps and johns, and pornography that is increasingly normalized and mainstreamed, made into everyday experience. Because it's profitable in a capitalist world. And because men take it as their right to consume women's sexuality in a patriarchal world.

When confronted with this, men often suggest that because women in pornography choose to participate, there's no reason to critique men's use of pornography. We should avoid that temptation to take that easy way out. I'm going to say nothing in regard to what women should do, nor am I going to critique their choices. I don't take it as my place to inject myself in the discussion that women have about this. (A new book, *Not for Sale*, has interesting insights into those questions. http://www.spinifexpress.com.au/non-fict/nfs.htm)

I do, however, take it as my place to talk to men. I take it as a political/moral responsibility to engage in critical self-reflection and be accountable for my behavior, at the individual and the collective level. For men, the question is not about women's choices. It's about men's choices. Do you want to participate in this system in which women are sold for sexual pleasure, whether it's in prostitution, pornography, strip bars, or any other aspect of the sex industry? Do you want to live in a world in which some people are bought and sold for the sexual pleasure of others?

When one asks such questions, one of the first things one will hear is: These are important issues, but we shouldn't make men feel guilty about this. Why not? I agree that much of the guilt people feel—rooted in attempts to repress human sexuality that unfortunately are part of the cultural and theological history of our society—is destructive. But guilt also can be a healthy emotional and intellectual response to the world and one's actions in it.

Johns should feel guilty when they buy women. Guilt is a proper response to an act that is unjust. When we do things that are unjust, we should feel guilty. Guilt can be a sign that we have violated our own norms. It can be a part of a process of ending the injustice. Guilt can be healthy, if it is understood in political, not merely religious or psychological, terms.

Buying women is wrong not because of a society's repressive moral code or its effects on an individual's psychological process. It is wrong because it hurts people. It creates a world in which people get hurt. And the people who get hurt the most are women and children, the people with the least amount of power. When you create a class that can be bought and sold, the people in that group will inevitably be treated as lesser, as available to be controlled and abused.

The way out of this is not church or therapy, though you may engage in either or both of those practices for various reasons. The way out of being a john is political. The way out is feminism. I don't mean feminism as a superficial exercise in identifying a few "women's issues" that men can help with. I mean feminism as an avenue into what Karl Marx called "the ruthless criticism of the existing order, ruthless in that it will shrink neither from its own discoveries, nor from conflict with the powers that be."

We need to engage in some ruthless criticism. Let's start not just with pornography, but with sex more generally. One of those discoveries, I think, is not only that men often have johns, but that the way in which johns use women sexually is a window into other aspects of our sexual and intimate lives as well. For many men, sex is often a place where we both display and reinforce our power over women. By that, I don't mean that all men at all times use sex that way all the time, but that a pattern of such relationships is readily visible in this society. Women deal with it every day, and at some level most men understand it.

We can see that pornography not only raises issues about the buying and selling of women, but—if we can remain ruthless and not shrink from our own discoveries— about sex in general, about the way in which men and women in this culture are commonly trained to be sexual. It's not just about pimps and johns and the women prostituted. It's about men and women, and sex and power. If throughout this discussion you have been thinking, "Well, that's not me—I never pay for it," don't be so sure. It's not just about who pays for it and who doesn't. It's about the fundamental nature of the relationship between men and women, and how that plays out in sex and intimacy.

And if you think this doesn't affect you because you are one of the "good men," don't be so sure. I'm told that I am one of those good men. I work in a feminist movement. I have been part of groups that critique men's violence and the sex industry. And I struggle with these issues all the time. I was trained to be a man in this culture, and that training doesn't evaporate overnight. None of us is off the hook.

What Is Sex For?

No matter what our personal history or current practice, we all might want to ask a simple question: What is sex for?

A male friend once told me that he thought that sometimes sex can be like a warm handshake, nothing more than a greeting between friends. Many people assert that sex can be a purely physical interaction to produce pleasurable sensations in the body.

At the same time, sex is said to be the ultimate act of intimacy, the place in which we expose ourselves most fully, where we let another see us stripped down, not just physically but emotionally.

Certainly sex can be all those things to different people at different times. But is that not a lot to ask sex to carry? Can one human practice really carry such a range of meanings and purposes? And in such a context, in a male-supremacist culture in which men's violence is still tacitly accepted and men's control of women is often unchallenged, should we be surprised that sex becomes a place where that violence and control play out?

This isn't an argument for some imposition of a definition of sex. It's an invitation to confront what I believe is a crucial question for this culture. The conservative framework, often rooted in narrow religious views, for defining appropriate sex in order to control people is a disaster. The liberal/libertarian framework that avoids questions of gender and power has failed.

We live in a time of sexual crisis. That makes life difficult, but it also creates a space for invention and creativity. That is what drew me to feminism, to the possibility of a different way of understanding the world and myself, the possibility of escaping the masculinity trap set for me, that chance to become something more than a man, more than just a john—to become a human being.

27 Heidi M. Levitt, Elisabeth A. Gerrish, and Katherine R. Hiestand

The Misunderstood Gender
A Model of Modern Femme Identity

Butch–Femme History

Butch and femme lesbian genders first became visible in the United States in the late 1940s as bars allowed women to congregate without male escorts (Faderman, 1991). Butch women's more masculine clothing and short hair conflicted starkly with feminine norms at the time, and femme women exaggerated femininity and became known for their bright lipstick and seductive dress. Femme-butch couples resembled popular media images of heterosexual gender in the culture of that time, and increased public awareness of lesbianism through their discernable gender representation.

By the 1950s, it was imperative for a woman to identify as either femme or butch if she wanted to become integrated into this lesbian culture. At that time, these two genders "were the key structure for organizing against heterosexual dominance" (Lapovsky-Kennedy & Davis, 1993, p. 6). This gendering cast butch women as protectors and aggressors and femmes as seductresses and sources of emotional solace within a community geared for resistance. It offered a needed sense of belonging that helped to fortify the women against the harassments and arrests that were common at

the time—as well as offering a system of coupling that structured romantic pairing, in much the same way as physical sex does within heterosexual contexts.

Although to the outside world lesbians appeared to be mocking heterosexuality, femme–butch identities were very complex, and transcended and radicalized traditional gender roles (e.g., Feinberg, 1996). By appropriating the signs of masculinity, butch gender stretched the image of what it can mean to be a woman. Similarly, femme women gave feminine signifiers new meaning (Ruby, 1993). By orienting their sexuality toward a butch woman instead of a man, the femme women made lesbian desire public and challenged notions of female sexuality.

Although there were some similarities, relationships between women and men in the heterosexual community were transformed in the femme–butch relationship, as femme characteristics were not considered inferior but were granted respect and admiration (Laporte, 1992). Instead of being cast in the traditional feminine stereotype as weak or passive, they were known to be rebellious and courageous women—as they took the risks of being

Heidi M. Levitt, Elisabeth A. Gerrish, and Katherine R. Hiestand, "The Misunderstood Gender: A Model of Modern Femme Identity," *Sex Roles* 48, nos. 3/4 (February 2003): 99–113. Copyright © 2003 Springer Science + Business Media, LLC. With kind permission from Springer Science + Business Media.

seen publicly in the company of butch women and being caught in bar raids that could compromise both their employment and physical security. Also, as femmes sometimes had to support financially butch partners who had difficulty maintaining employment because of their masculine appearance (Faderman, 1991), their relationships had an economic basis characterized by greater equality than those of most heterosexual couples of that era.

Sexuality within butch–femme relationships was not based upon heterosexual sexuality (Lapovsky-Kennedy & Davis, 1993). The central focus of sexual relations was the femme partner's pleasure, as often a butch partner would not expect nor wish reciprocity and would receive satisfaction from the act of pleasuring. "Butch–femme was an erotic partnership serving both as a conspicuous flag of rebellion and as an intimate exploration of women's sexuality" (Nestle, 1993, p. 107).

By the late 1960s, however, feminism was emerging, and it brought with it a shift in gender politics. Feminists who desired to escape the constraints of gender, rejected butch–femme genders and embraced androgyny (Harris & Crocker, 1997). Feminists accused butch women of adopting male privilege and femme women of encouraging the patriarchal objectification of women. Nestle (1993) wrote that "We Lesbians from the fifties made a mistake in the early seventies; we allowed our lives to be trivialized and reinterpreted by feminists who did not share our culture" (p. 110). By the early 1980s attitudes had begun to change again, as women began to reclaim butch and femme identities. Yet as postfeminist lesbians reclaimed femme or butch identities, these roles developed new meanings. No longer a social necessity, claiming femme or butch roles became purely an act of self-definition in this decade, and these identities emerged into different social contexts.

Femme Literature

Although femmes and butches together formed the basis of the lesbian community in the 1950s, more public attention has been focused on butch identity, particularly as transgendered issues have come to the forefront of gender studies (e.g., Burana & Due, 1994; Halberstam, 1998; Hale, 1998). Femme identity has a history of being positioned as a complement of butch identity—to the chagrin of women who claim independent identities. Over the last decade, however, discussion of femme identity in its own right has increased as collections of theoretical and fictional essays from femme writers have come forth (see Harris & Crocker, 1997; Munt, 1998; Nestle, 1992; Newman, 1995).

These writings describe a diverse set of femme experiences, although some common themes seem to exist. Some authors defended femme identity as it is experienced as "so looked down on—especially in a [feminist] political community" (Austin, 1992, p. 363). They attempted to differentiate stereotypical, passive femininity from femme-inity and to respond to claims that androgyny is the only way to challenge patriarchy (e.g., Harris & Crocker, 1997; Nestle, 1992). Repeatedly, they asserted that femmes are "real" lesbians, and that their gender expression is not an attempt to pass as heterosexual (e.g., Newman, 1995).

The empirical studies of lesbian experience, however, rarely reflect the existence of femme women. Only a handful of studies have been done on femme identity—even fewer within the field of psychology. Bailey,

Kim, Hills, and Linsenmeier (1997), Smith and Stillman (2002) examined the tendency to specify femininity as a desired trait in lesbian personal advertisements (although not necessarily femme identity). Singh, Vidaurri, Zambarano, and Dabbs (1999) surveyed lesbian partners, and reported that the partner described to be more femme tended to be more gender typical, such as having a more feminine body shape and a stronger desire to give birth. Within lesbian relationships, partners seen as "more femme" tended to have lower levels of testosterone than "more butch" partners (Pearcey, Docherty, & Dabbs, 1996; Singh et al., 1999).

Levitt and Horne (2002) conducted a survey of queer women, and found that femme-identified women realized their sexual orientation at a much later age (22) than butch women (15) and significantly later than they realized their own preference for a feminine gender expression. Although traditionally this culture was associated with the working class (Weber, 1996), they found evidence to suggest that class divisions may be fading today. Levitt and Horne also suggested that femme women experience less discrimination than butch women, and they indicated that gender expression was more important to butch and femme-identified women than androgynous or "other" women when forming romantic relationships. Regardless of their gender expression, on average, all participants viewed both butch and femme identities as possible for both the community and the women themselves.

These studies add to the literature by researchers such as Kitzinger (1987) that distinguishes types of lesbian experience from one another. They inform readers about differences between groups that can allow for a more complex understanding of lesbian culture. They also point to the importance of gender within many lesbian communities. This body of research is just beginning, however, and many questions remain. This study was conducted to shed light upon the motivations to claim a femme identity and the meanings that it can hold.

Study Objectives

The purpose of this study was to develop an empirical model of femme-identity that is founded upon contemporary femme lesbians' descriptions of their own identities and experiences. Through the interpretation of exploratory interviews, we allowed participants to describe their construal of self and to communicate its complexity. We began this study to develop an understanding of how femme lesbians within a contemporary butch–femme community made sense of this gender category and to better understand how women reconciled feminist concerns about objectification within their own identities.

Method

Participants

As femme gender is rooted within unique lesbian contexts, it can be difficult to understand this construct without reference to specific butch–femme subcultures. The participants in this study were members of a lesbian community in Northern Florida. This community can be considered a lesbian separatist community to the extent that community activities (offered throughout each week) were open to women only, and it was assumed by the community that participating members identified as lesbian. Demographic information is presented in Table 27.1. Twelve participants were drawn

TABLE 27.1 Participant Demographics

Age	Years in community	Relational status	Ethnicity	Occupation
34	27	In relationship	White	Cosmetologist
25	03	Single	White	Scientist
27	02	In relationship	White	Interior decorator
39	08	In relationship	White	Painter
47	07	In relationship	White	Massage therapist
53	34	In relationship	White	Speech pathologist
41	05	In relationship	White	Health technician
34	28	Single	White	Health policy
33	05	Single	White	Mental health
34	04	Single	White	Graduate student
36	20	Single	White	Realtor
21	04	In relationship	White	Student

Note: Demographics are not listed in the order that they appear following quotes in this paper, in order to protect anonymity.

from a lesbian community that was predominantly made up of White women, and the composite of participants interviewed reflected this demographic. Participants varied in terms of their relationship status, age (range of 21–53 years), and length of time in the community (range of 2–34 years). Diversity in participant characteristics is a strength of grounded theory approaches wherein researchers seek to diversify sources of information in the service of developing results that are as rich and encompassing as possible (see Patton's principle of maximal variation; Patton, 1990). Advertisements were placed within the lesbian community newsletter to recruit interviewees who self-identified as femme. In addition, snowball recruitment occurred as some interviewees referred other participants to the project.

Interviews

The central question of the interview was: "What does it mean to you to be femme?" Prompts encouraged the women to describe the ways they experienced their identities within mainstream society, lesbian community, and romantic relationships. An exploratory style of interviewing was adopted; utilizing open ended questions and nonbiasing prompts. All interviews were conducted by the first author, who had been part of this community for approximately 1 year at the time and, as such, could bring an ethnographic experience to the hermeneutic interpretation of data. Interviews ranged from 1 to 3 hr in length.

Because the interviewer and the participants socialized within the same community, there was concern that the interview might create a potential imbalance in power as the interviewer would have access to personal information about participants at any future community meetings. Guided by a feminist ethic, the interviewer allowed participants to ask her about her gender experience at the end of the interviews. This exchange equalized the power within the data collection process and allowed for the mutual experience of learning. The less formal exchange also allowed the interviewer to develop a deeper sense of the participants' understanding of gender through the contrast and similarities in experiences discussed.

Grounded Theory Analysis

The analysis was conducted using grounded theory. This inductive approach allows investigators to compare units of interview transcript in order to identify and organize the common themes present. This method has been advanced in psychological research as a way to explore subjective experience and facilitate the development of theories (see Rennie, Phillips, & Quartaro, 1988).

First transcripts of the interview were divided into "meaning units," each of which expresses one idea (see Giorgi, 1970). Each unit was assigned a label that described the idea. Units were grouped into categories by using a process of constant comparison in which each label is compared with every other label. Categories were then compared to one another in a similar fashion, and higher order categories were created. These higher order categories were then compared and grouped, and in this way the process continued until one core category was created that reflected a concept that is central to the phenomenon. This analysis resulted in the creation of a hierarchical model.

Research notes were recorded throughout the analytical process to document shifts in hypotheses in an attempt to bracket theories that developed during the analysis, and so they did not influence the data sorting. Data collection was halted when saturation was reached, that is, when additional categories do not appear to be forthcoming despite the analysis of new data. In this analysis, the last three transcripts did not add new categories to the hierarchy, and so the model was considered to be saturated after nine transcripts.

Credibility Checks

Three checks were conducted to increase the credibility of the results. First, at the end of each interview, all participants were asked to reflect upon the process of the interview. They considered whether they would have said anything different to an interviewer with other demographic characteristics (e.g., an interviewer who was butch, Latina, or older) or whether they could envision questions that were not asked that would help elucidate their gender experience. Any information that was shared in response to these questions was incorporated into the hierarchy in order to reduce possible constraining effects of the interviewing context. Participants reported that they had shared their own experiences thoroughly, and said that they would not have been as forthcoming with an interviewer from outside the community. Two women doubted that their experience would be comprehended or well received by readers who might think that butch–femme was "un-PC."

The process of consensus between researchers strengthened the claim of credibility. While the analysis of this project was under way, the researchers met weekly for a period of one year to discuss the generation of categories and the labeling of concepts. The researchers offered different perspectives to this process of analysis: one is a femme-identified lesbian who had experience living in the community in question and interviewing the women, one does not identify as either butch or femme, and the other is a butch-identified lesbian. Although we took care to restrict the ways our individual biases and personal experiences might bring foreclosure to the process of

TABLE 27.2 Femme as Essential Within Two Fluid Continua

Categories	N^a	Subcategories
Homosexuality and butch–femme are continuous	7	No subcategories
Has had unfulfilling experiences with men	7	Has never wanted to be a man; has had negative experiences with men; made an educated choice to be a lesbian after abuse from men
Femme as essential or innate	11	Has always been femme; femme is who she is; being butch or femme is innate
Overall endorsement	12	

[a]Number of participants who contributed meaning units to this category.

conceptualization, it is congruent with a hermeneutic method to relate our research notes and interpersonal experiences to the phenomenon at hand as checks to maximize the thoroughness of the model after its conceptualization.

After the model was complete, the first author returned to the community and met with three women there (one butch-identified participant, one femme-identified, and one androgynous-identified woman) in order to seek feedback on the results of the study. The women all strongly endorsed the model and believed that it described their personal experiences of femme women. The femme consultant endorsed the core category with enthusiasm, and particularly appreciated the ways results of this study related to another similar study of butch experience (Levitt & Hiestand, 2002).

Results

Femme as Essential Within Two Fluid Continua

Participants discussed heterosexuality-homosexuality and butch–femme as two continua, upon which women could be positioned at any point (see Table 27.2). In general, participants thought that one's location along these continua was central to

the self, because of either early development or genetics. Accordingly, femmeness was experienced as an essential quality, if not an innate one.

Still, for most of the women interviewed, learning about their gender and sexuality was a continual process. All but one of the participants had a sexual and/or romantic history with men before she came out, and two had been married. Some of the interviewees reported having had unsatisfactory experiences with men in the past; most had dated men but never felt as comfortable or as happy as they felt with women. "I think some people are just born knowing, "God, I must be gay!" (laughs) And some people like me . . . probably have dated men most of my life, but I'm not as happy dating men . . . and I'm perfectly comfortable with that. It's an educated choice" (P-02).

The degree of distress in dating or being sexual with men differed between the women, as evidenced by another participant's description of her need to become intoxicated before being sexual with men. "I had sex with a lot of men and convinced myself that I was straight, but it never fit. It just never made any sense. I couldn't really stand to be with them, you know. I mean, once I sobered up in the morning, I'd be out of there" (P-07). The women did not

TABLE 27.3 **Femme as a Lesbian Label That Should Not Be Prescriptive**

Categories	N^a	Subcategories
Femme label as being positive or useful	11	People like having a construct that can describe experiences; being called femme opens up my experience of myself as lesbian; being femme fits my sense of self, feels happier; believes that the label femme describes certain patterns; identifying as femme was useful because it explained some interactions
Difficulties with the label femme when it is prescribing or superficial	11	Labels can be used to describe specific traits within overall general; butch–femme is extremely challenging to describe; being labeled as femme is often based upon your appearance alone; hesitant to use the label femme if it seems prescriptive; sometimes disagrees on what femme is
Butch–femme as uniquely lesbian constructs	8	Femme has different meaning in lesbian vs. popular culture; butch–femme do not correspond to male–female
There is not a language to describe femme	6	Being femme misunderstood as not lesbian; need to create a new language for femme experience; femme evokes a positive image of powerful females
Overall endorsement	12	

^{a}Number of participants who contributed meaning units to this category.

believe that these experiences determined their lesbianism but they provided confirmation that their sexual orientation was lesbian and that they would be happier with female partners.

Femme as a Lesbian Label That Should Not Be Prescriptive

The word *femme* was challenging to operationalize. Women said that lesbian gender needed to be "re-languaged," and they were concerned that femme is misunderstood as "not-butch" or as "not-typically-lesbian." For them, the label evoked a strong, positive image of feminine sexuality (see Table 27.3). "To me, femme is probably the word that evokes the powerful vitality of sexuality of the feminine flavor, rather than the 'Ooh, isn't she sweet' or 'Ooh, isn't she kind of slutty,' which are the derogatory ways to

be feminine and sexy. [Instead] it's a really powerful way to be sexy" (P-08). Femme was valued as a uniquely lesbian construct that could only be understood fully within a lesbian culture and vernacular.

This label was thought to have several purposes. It helped women to describe their experiences, to identify patterns that validated their experiences, and to make sense of themselves within the lesbian community. It allowed them to reconcile their "femininity" with their feminism and lesbian identity. Some women expressed hesitations about the label, however, when it was unclear what meaning was attributed to the word in a given context, when it was based upon appearances alone, or when it was used prescriptively in a way that confined or limited what a femme woman could be.

TABLE 27.4 Developmental Process of Becoming Femme

Categories	N^a	Subcategories
Memories of growing up femme; combining male and female gender traits	7	She was a tomboy as a child; sexual experiences or feelings during childhood; she began to dress more femininely in high school; she was more athletic in high school
Coming out as lesbian	12	Time of coming out differs; reactions for coming out range from discomfort to surprise; reasons for coming out include sincerity and political motivation; harder to come out to self as femme; coming out as confusing and scary
Learning about butch–femme	11	Deciding to explore butch–femme culture; discovering butch–femme culture; overcoming previous ideas; ways of understanding butch–femme culture
Coming out as femme	12	Coming out as femme as a scary identifying as process; identification came at different points for different women; reasons for identifying as femme; resistant and estranged reactions from others when came out as femme
Overall endorsement	12	

[a]Number of participants who contributed meaning units to this category.

Developmental Process of Becoming Femme

Four major stages emerged from participants' recounting of the development of their femme identity (see Table 27.4). First, women relayed childhood memories that included the mixing of masculine and feminine stereotypes: being a tomboy as a child but then becoming feminine as a teenager, having homosexual feelings or experiences despite dating men, and being athletic but feminine in high school.

Second, women described their process of coming out as lesbian as complicated by their femme gender, which conflicted with both butch stereotypes of lesbians and the feminine images of female beauty. Because images of masculine women are so stigmatized in our culture, some women described struggling to understand their attraction to others—dating men, trying to be butch, or trying to be attracted to femme women—

before they could recognize and accept their own attraction.

I didn't feel like I was lesbian. I didn't feel like I was heterosexual either . . . I said, "I don't want to have it [sex] with men anymore and [am] not feeling drawn to images of women that I see. . . ." That kind of [glamorous] woman didn't turn me on. I would not want to make love with a person that looked like that, but I did not want to make love with men either. So I didn't know what I was. (P-05)

Despite the difficulty in naming their sexual orientation, the participants thought that their youths were easier than butch women's childhoods, as they were not aware of their sexual orientations or gender differences until later.

Butch lesbians that I know work towards that feeling . . . "It's my birth right to be here and not be oppressed." . . . The courage and strength that it took for them to do that is incredible. . . . [They] were damaged by holding secrets, by being oppressed, feeling like you're the only one in the world. . . . It just blows me away. I've never had that feeling. By the time I started, you know, really naming what I was, there were, you know, lots of other lesbians I could go to. I didn't have to do that all by myself. They did. (P-06)

Still, at the same time as they saw butch childhoods as characterized by isolation, they also described being envious of butch women for knowing who they were earlier. "I feel like I was damaged by my heterosexual relationships . . . just the damage that comes from not knowing who you really are and always having this little 'not-being-happy,' you know . . . yearning, wanting to find a home when there wasn't one" (P-06).

After an awareness of their lesbian orientation developed, women reported experiencing a need to come out as lesbian, despite reactions from others that ranged from surprise (because their femininity conflicted with prevailing stereotypes of lesbians) to discomfort. This need for honesty was promoted by a strong sense of personal sincerity and integrity and the political motivation to challenge homophobia.

Usually, it was in or after their entrance into lesbian culture that women learned about butch–femme culture. On the whole, the participants described experiences of relief, excitement, and belonging, although some first had to overcome previous ideas about butch–femme (e.g., that these identities no longer existed or that being femme was weak or passive). "The first person that ever said anything to me about it . . . she

said, 'I am not going to cut off my hair. I'm not going to dress this way or that way. I'm just going to be a femme, like I am.' And I was so relieved. I was like, 'Oh, thank god!'" (P-09). They sought to understand butch–femme concepts through reading and by gradually contrasting and distinguishing butch–femme genders from heterosexual masculine–feminine genders.

Finally, the participants described the process of coming out as femme. The challenges in reconciling their gender with expected lesbian androgyny made it more difficult for them to self-identify as lesbian. Those women who did not initially identify as femme, however, faced a second process of coming out, which could be uncomfortable. "A few of them [friends] questioned me, "No, you're not femme." I can understand their reasoning. I mean, they'd seen me in the trenches a lot. And so they would identify me as butch . . . " (P-05).

Once femme-identified, they still had to negotiate acceptance in communities that most often were characterized by androgynous and butch members. Identifying as femme helped them to resist the pressures to adopt these dominant gender presentations and accept themselves as both feminine and lesbian. Affiliation with butch–femme community gave them a sense of desirability and connection with others who valued gender diversity. "I was so freed up to be all that I was. I didn't have to hold back anymore. When I was trying to operate in the straight world . . . I always felt I had to hold back. I always felt unsafe, like there'd be repercussions for being all that I was, for being as strong as I was, as truthful as I was, as honest as I was" (P-07). The women described a joy in being able to be aesthetically and sexually expressive in the manner in which they were most

TABLE 27.5 Enacting Femmeness—Components of Femmeness

Categories	N^a	Subcategories
Exceptions exist to any rule	12	Femme energy is expressed differently, from lesbian to lesbian; one can be being feminine but not femme; appearance is not reflective of her personality; femme roles as individual; femme with masculine characteristics
Aesthetic images of being femme	12	Has always looked femme because she feels happy/comfortable that way; being femme as presentation of self co-constructed with others; femme images; femininity as a sign of being femme; butch–femme is based on appearance
Femmes enacting femininity as having different meanings from straight women	7	Had to reexamine her reasons for looking femme; being femme in a way different from straight women
Femme archetype having certain interests	7	Chose hobbies based on how feminine they seemed; butch–femme is about exterior behaviors like male–female archetypes
The role of role-playing	9	Role-playing is secondary; butch–femme as a form of play; sometimes she and her partner step out of their roles; roles are not strict and are shaped by partners
Overall endorsement	12	

^{a}Number of participants who contributed meaning units to this category.

comfortable, while still being able to take pride in a lesbian identity.

Enacting Femmeness: The Components of Being Femme

Although there were exceptions to all rules, interviewees described femmes as having a general appreciation and identification with a feminine aesthetic quality, often associated with makeup, feminine clothing, and dressing provocatively (see Table 27.5). They described feeling most comfortable and sensual in this style. Interviewees said they were most commonly identified by their appearances or in contrast to butch partners. Both of these methods could be disturbing, as they negated the validity of their gender in its own right and ignored important values they associated with femmeness. They ascribed to femme identity the traits of strength, openness, and honesty that were neither necessary aspects nor common associations with heterosexual femininity.

Some participants described a process of self-examination to ensure that their enactments of femmeness differed from the heterosexual emphasis on women's appearance and did not result from a desire to pass as heterosexual or attract heterosexual attention. One woman described this process of questioning as follows:

"Who am I putting my makeup on for? Am I doing it for men and society?" And I had to deal with that. I had to look at that. Say, "What makes me who I am?" and "Why do I still wear high heels?". . . . I realized that it makes *me* very happy and comfortable. I love looking feminine. . . . I love being a woman and I'm very proud of that and I'm going to accentuate every little curve. (P-02)

TABLE 27.6 Social Relationships: Balancing Equality and Difference

Categories	N[a]	Subcategories
Social relationships within lesbian community: acceptance and pressures	12	Relations within lesbian community; acceptance and pressures; femme friendships with other lesbian genders
Romantic relationships: equality but difference	12	Butch–femme as sexual energies in interaction; dating preferences re: butch–femme; most believe that butches and femmes attract each other; power in femme–butch relationships is more equal; butches as being more defended emotionally
Femme sexuality: A strong and positive tension charged by differences	12	Flirting, sexual initiation, and sexual tension; being femme as an inherently sexual statement; butch–femme sexual interactions; heightening gender differences; femme perceptions of butches' physicality
Lesbian culture reclaiming butch–femme identity anew	12	In the mid-to-late 1980s, butch–femme started being talked about again; butch–femme being rejected in the 1970s–1980s or under liberal feminism; butch–femme as becoming more mainstream in lesbian culture; butch–femme as working or lower class; in mid-1980s lesbians began reclaiming butch–femme in new terms
Relations within straight culture: discrimination and difficulties	12	Discrimination for being femme; difficulties relating to straight women; difficulties relating to straight men; feeling safer from male power dynamics or abuse as femmes
Overall endorsement	12	

[a]Number of participants who contributed meaning units to this category.

Some women described being femme as a lesbian archetype that has associated behaviors and interests that communicated and resulted from their sexual and gender orientation. Although they thought that exaggeration or role playing could be a form of play between butch and femme partners, this meaning was secondary. In serious interactions, the butch and femme identities were not roles but identities that had flexibility and could be shaped by partners.

Social Relationships: Balancing Equality and Difference

In the interviews, women discussed their femme identities as influencing their friendships and romantic relationships within lesbian community and culture. They also reported that it affected their interactions within heterosexual contexts (see Table 27.6).

Lesbian contexts: Acceptance and pressures. Within the lesbian community at hand, most femmes interviewed said that their lesbian gender was accepted and embraced and that acceptance of femmes was growing across lesbian communities. They thought that when femmeness was not accepted within a lesbian context, it was because of either the misinterpretation of the meaning of being femme or a limited definition of lesbianism. Indeed, many participants had been accused by other lesbians of not being political, out, or lesbian "enough." They were concerned that being "lesbian" was made equivalent to being butch or androgynous so as to marginalize femme women.

One woman described a particularly harsh rejection from one lesbian community and the aftermath of her ensuing rape by one of its members.

I was called a "tourist" and not taken seriously for years . . . [I was] being called a "tourist" when that whole thing went down with that violence. Automatically . . . people who were very feminist were saying things like, "Well, look at what you were wearing. I mean you were wearing this little dress," and, "Look at the messages you give off." And I was like, "What? That I want to be raped? That I want to be beaten? Is that what a dress gives off?" . . . [They] would never say that to a straight woman." (P-07)

Lesbians who were not in a butch–femme culture judged her as aberrantly sexualized when she dressed in ways that were expected only of heterosexual women.

In addition to this expectation that "real" lesbians should be butch or androgynous, they also described expectations that a femme's romantic partner should be butch and that a femme's interests should be dominated by feminine activities. Although many of the women reported enjoying feminine activities, stereotypes about femme interests misrepresented the diversity of their interests and talents. All but one participant reported a principal attraction to butch women. They relayed an openness in modern-day butch–femme communities to femme–femme (or butch–butch) dating, however the expectation of butch–femme attraction structured many social interactions and at times could be constraining. "It's a little easier to relate to other femme women. I guess I don't feel as threatened. . . . Butch women, I guess . . . have more expectations as far as what a lesbian is supposed to be like . . . before they really take you seriously" (P-02).

Most interviewees cherished their sense of connection with other femmes and said that common experiences and interests were mutually validating. "The energy we exchanged has to do with almost celebrating our girliness" (P-01). Two women, however, did not share this experience. One younger woman was relatively new to the community and did not know other femme lesbians, and the other experienced a sense of competition with femmes that she disliked.

Friendships with androgynous women were comfortable, and participants appreciated androgyny as an aesthetic style. They saw butch friendships as potentially complicated because of the sexual energy that could exist, and they talked about the importance of monitoring and openly discussing sexual tension. Participants admired butch women for their bravery in maintaining their own gender expression despite the regular experiences of discrimination, and sought to support butch women's struggles.

They contrasted friendship behaviors: they described femme nurturing as providing emotional care and supportive confrontation and butch nurturing as oriented toward protection and providing assistance. "If I'm really depressed . . . I want to be held and patted on the back by my [butch] girlfriend or a butch friend—as in an 'I'll protect you' kind of way . . . but I would give all the dirty details to my good femme friend . . . I'd want to rehash and rehash the story with her" (P-08). Forms of nurturance were discussed as related to the interests and interactional styles of the different genders, and neither form was privileged over the other.

Romantic Relationships: Equal but Different. Throughout the interviews, butch and femme were described as sexual "energies" that characterize women. This metaphor was used frequently in descriptions of butch–femme flirting or romance—as energies that were "charged," "interacting," or "building."

> Her energy feels very different from mine, but they interact real good together . . . I just really notice that when I'm around women who are into their power [or identities] as butches, that I feel that energy and it gives me a charge. It makes me feel good inside, you know? Not necessarily like I'm crushed out on every butch, but I just really love butches, and I really like being around that energy (P-07).

Although most of the women interviewed were primarily attracted to butch women, some women reported feeling attraction to forms of "opposition" that were not based on lesbian gender but on another form of personality or behavior. Within these flirtations or relationships, however, women talked about maximizing existing gender differences to heighten their romantic attraction. When dating other femmes, some participants said that they would take on some "butch" qualities so that this tension could be maintained. With butch partners, women exaggerated differences in order to communicate respect for their partners' gender. "I just let my girlfriend be as male as she wants to be . . . I don't mind. . . . I'm like that with her because she's more comfortable—and, she will go to that [more vulnerable] place sometimes" (P-03). As butch women rarely have their genders recognized by others, signaling an awareness of gender difference allowed for a deeper level of connection and safety within the relationship.

Femmes described the power in their romantic relationships as being much more equal than in their own, or observed, heterosexual relationships. They said that housekeeping duties were divided more in accordance with personal preference than along gender lines. Also, they thought that divisions based on lesbian gender were not oppressive for femmes in the way male power could be for women.

> You can compare them [butch–femme interactions] with heterosexual ways, but they aren't heterosexual ways. Because there's more of an equality between women and an emotional base that's common to women. . . . Some of the sexism pieces are missing, you know. Because a butch, a butch lesbian doesn't really have the real power in the world and never has . . . never was raised that way. (P-05)

Butch partners were thought to need more defenses and to be "tougher" than femmes, both to cope with the daily discrimination they face and to fit into butch culture. As a result, the femme women understood them as being necessarily more emotionally guarded and comprehended their difficulty feeling comfortable with intimate relationships. "Women, especially life long butch women who have always known they were lesbian . . . they've had a much harder life . . . they often are a lot more stiff and rigid because of defenses that they've put up over the years" (P-08). By and large they respected butch partners' protection needs, which they described in terms of greater emotional rigidity and a slower process of becoming emotionally expressive, trusting, and interdependent. Some participants relayed struggles with resultant relationship issues, which stemmed from the conflict between wanting to increase intimacy, yet wanting to respect a butch partner's need for safety.

Femme sexuality: Strengthening the tension of difference. Similarly, many femmes interviewed thought that the lack of recognition or valuing of butch gender in mainstream culture created particular emotional vulnerability for butch partners during sexual interactions. During this time, femme women communicated respect for their partners' butch gender identity by valuing their partner's butch qualities over their feminine qualities. Strategies they used included heightening their gender differences so as to emphasize a partner's butchness, focusing caresses on body parts that were common to both men and women (e.g., shoulders, arms), or using fantasy or SM to make touch more comfortable. Respondents presented themselves within an emphatically feminine aesthetic during sexual interactions, for instance, by wearing lingerie. At times, they reported sexuality to be a difficult process of negotiation, as they could be unsure how to please their partners sexually without making them feel too feminine and negating their butch identities.

An identification as femme itself was a statement about sexuality for some. They described opposition as erotically compelling; however, opposition was defined within a lesbian context. None of the women interviewed confused "butchness" with "masculinity," instead, they valued and eroticized their partners' uniquely butch gender. They identified traits such as haircuts, body language, and piercings, among other butch gender signifiers. Although some participants were resistant to the idea of dating butch partners who pass as male regularly or who were transitioning to become men, others were more accepting—seeing these partners as transgendered instead of as men.

Many participants enjoyed being admired physically and being the primary recipient of physical pleasure. There were mixed responses about femme initiation and aggression: some women thought that flirting to invite advances, then allowing butch women to initiate sexual behavior, was typical of being femme, but other women reported initiating sex as well. Both "top" and "bottom" roles were described.

The meaning of being sexually receptive or "bottoming" was experienced as strikingly different within a butch–femme context than within a heterosexual context.

> I don't feel like I'm invoking all the historical oppression against women and feeling truly degraded or something, by having a surrendering moment or by dressing up on a butch's arm for the evening. I can get into that and find the excitement and sexiness of that and sort of get off on being an ornament or something. It would just feel completely different if I were on a man's arm. (P-08)

Women cited many other reasons for this distinction, including the relative physical, social, and economic equality between two women, shared feminist beliefs, and their desire to be sensitive to butch women's repeated experiences of discrimination and invisibility. By proffering symbols of femininity, the femme women enjoyed being appreciated as objects of beauty, and consciously allowed partners to claim symbols of power that affirmed their own marginalized gender identity.

Lesbian culture: Reclaiming femme identity. Those interviewees who had longstanding identities as femme shared their experiences of changes in femme-identity within lesbian culture. They talked about the rejection of butch–femme by liberal feminism in the 1970s. Within these contexts, some of the participants described their own misunderstandings of femme identity as subordination. "There was this blooming feminist in me that was like, 'I wouldn't bow down to a man. Why should I bow down to a woman?' I saw it [femmeness] as a weakness" (P-11). Participants described their own experience of reclaiming this identity and the importance of femme icons in that process. They described this reemergence of "femmes" as transformed by the feminist consciousness that now pervades lesbian culture. They examined the meaning of being femme in butch–femme discussion groups within their community and rid it of connotations of weakness. Although still known to be the object of disapproval in some lesbian communities, femme and butch identities were seen to be gaining acceptance and becoming more fluid and less rule-bound. Lesbian community at present was described as evolving and "validating this particular part of lesbian culture" (P-06).

Heterosexual contexts: Discrimination and difficulties. The women described their heterosexual relationships as being influenced by their gender in a number of ways. Participants reported that relationships with men were complicated by the common assumption that lesbians dislike men, which resulted in defensiveness or distance from men. Also, as they did not fit mainstream cultural stereotyped images of lesbians, they are approached by interested men and have to negotiate refusals.

As the participants' gender did not allow them to relate to men as "one of the guys"—in the way butch women can at times—they were expected to relate to men as heterosexual women or as potential objects of desire. They described actively resisting flirtatious, subordinate, apologetic, mothering, or conciliatory roles that are often expected of feminine women and are associated with positions of lesser power.

I got pretty severely punished by men for being how I was. . . . They definitely responded to me differently than they did to your typical straight female because I was like "head on" all the time. . . . [I was] not holding their dicks and confronting them at the same time, which is that tight rope that I see straight women walk on all the time, and I just never walked it. . . . [I was] mostly called too assertive, or too aggressive, crazy, overemotional, too personally involved in the subject. All those things that are just really about not being willing to lie. (P-07)

Some of the participants described feeling safer from these gendered dynamics within the lesbian community, and limited their interactions with men to avoid power struggles. It was important to the participants to act in accordance with their beliefs that they should not adopt a passive position when interacting within heterosexual contexts.

Being Femme Is Inherently Political

For many of the women, being femme was inherently political (see Table 27.7). Their consciousness about their femme and lesbian identities empowered them to speak out when they thought that their status as lesbian was not recognized. Participants actively confronted femmephobia in the lesbian community by refusing to stand for "femme-bashing" and by pointing out stereotypes and images of lesbians that excluded their experience. For instance, they

TABLE 27.7 **Being Femme Is Inherently Political**

Categories	N[a]	Subcategories
To fight femme phobia in lesbian community	7	Believes it is important to be political and active in community; femmes coming out as femmes helps fight femmephobia
Indicates commitment to live one's life with integrity vs. the status quo	10	Being strong enough to be yourself; standing by your politics and coming out as femme; challenging the status quo; she is not going to change her appearance and society must accept her or not
To educate others and fight homophobia within heterosexual world	11	Being visible as femme is important and difficult; it is easier to break down prejudices as femme; she likes educating people about lesbians and broader stereotypes; subversive to be out with a passing butch
Overall endorsement	12	

[a]Number of participants who contributed meaning units to this category.

contested hypotheses that boyish-looking women were lesbian, by pointing out that a feminine-looking woman could be as well. They said that femmes needed to come out as often as possible, within and outside of the lesbian community, so that they would become more visible.

Outside the lesbian community, coming out was a continual process for femmes, as they usually were assumed to be heterosexual. Unlike butch women whom they believed were identified more often as lesbian by appearance, femmes who were politically committed to coming out, verbally had to come out to people with whom they interacted, which was challenging at times. They thought that it was important to be out for reasons of lesbian visibility, limiting potential misunderstandings, broadening the image of lesbians, and promoting honest relationships. One entrepreneur would not work for anyone who did not know her sexual orientation, regardless of the financial loss.

I have to go around saying I'm a lesbian all the time . . . if I didn't people wouldn't know because it [femmeness] is subtle and straight people don't pick up on it. . . . So consequently they're oblivious to many many femme women that go around in the world. I make sure that people I work for know I'm a lesbian, mostly before I work for them. I just tell them as soon as I can. (P-04)

Many of the women described this verbal coming out as a particularly femme concern that could be difficult and dangerous at times, although many saw taking the risk as preferable for the community, if not for their own personal benefit.

Most interviewees saw this political work as vital, as they could educate people on a deeper level and challenge the attribution of "difference" ascribed to lesbians. Their feminine appearances made it easier for them first to be known by people who were homophobic and then, afterward, to break down prejudices.

I get to sneak up on them. It's not so in your face. It's kinda like, "Oh, by the way, I date women." A lot of those people would've been shut right off to me had they known maybe from the beginning that I was different, or a little more masculine, whatever. But this way they couldn't put up their defenses because they had no idea they had to. (P-02)

Ironically, their activism could promote a sense of "lesbian visibility," as by coming out they provided evidence of the many "nonidentifiable" lesbians that may be encountered unknowingly. At the same time, they appreciated Butch political work as broadening the ways femininity can be displayed within heterosexual society, and some reported enjoying the subversiveness of visibly being in a butch–femme couple.

Most of the women interviewed thought that being femme indicated a commitment to live one's life with the integrity to challenge the status quo, both within the lesbian community and without. In social relationships, they saw femmes as the ones to confront others with the complexity of truths, even when they were difficult to hear. Femmes said that they were determined not to change the way they wanted to look, even if others accused them of being apolitical, not-lesbian, or aesthetically unpleasant. One interviewee described her experience of pride: "[I'm] just being me. Being true to myself at last. I'm just now discovering about integrity and pulling all of the pieces of me together and being okay with who I am, totally" (P-09). These women had the courage to stand by their personal values of prizing diversity in gender presentation and sexual orientation and to work to be seen and acknowledged in their entirety.

Core Category

The core category is the theme that represents an important motif that runs across the other categories. The core category of the analysis was that of "Maintaining integrity: Upholding beliefs about sexual desire and gender representation." Across many of the themes discussed, femme women were concerned with being recognized for their beliefs within both the culture at large and their personal relationships. The celebration of diversity in gender representation was a central aspect of their femmeness, which integrated their decision to retain a feminine appearance and their conscious structuring of their relationships and social encounters by activist values.

Discussion

An empirically derived model of femme gender has been derived on the basis of modern femme women's descriptions of their identities. This model allows for a greater appreciation of lesbian experience and for an understanding of how gender categories can be constructed within a social community. It also deconstructs a variety of gendered behaviors by attributing contextually based meanings to their performances. In doing so, it exemplifies a subculture in which the enactment of traditional aesthetics of femininity can have a radical meaning. It expands the stereotypes of lesbianism and feminism, and celebrates a powerful feminine aesthetic and sexuality.

Although the participants had diverse geographical origins, ages, socioeconomic classes, and occupations, readers should exercise caution when generalizing findings to other communities. It is important to note that many lesbians or bisexual women who appear feminine do not claim a femme identity and may not share a sense of gender with these participants. Not all femme sexuality is in reference to butch partners, although we stressed the dynamics within this pairing as all but one of the participants described their sexuality within a butch–femme context, which was the dominant form of relational coupling in the community.

The implications of this model of modern femme identity are broad and bring to light the complexity of gender experiences and identities. Analyses were based on life experiences narrated by femme-lesbians who have reconciled their feminism with a reclaiming of stereotypical feminine beauty and sexuality. Participants described a social system of complex gendered interactions shared by members of their community. The resultant model describes health, empowered understandings, and experiences of femme identities and butch–femme relationships, which often are absent from a psychological literature that tends to pathologize difference (see Kitzinger, 1987).

Becoming Visible as Femme

Across the various content areas, the women interviewed discussed the effort to be visible as a femme lesbian. Attempts were impaired by difficulties in describing femme gender so that it could be understood as a gender separate from stereotypical connotations of femininity. An understanding of femme identity within a context of difference is echoed in other narratives of femme experience. For instance, Vaisseau (1995) wrote that "I am not a straight girl; I am femme. There is a *huge* difference" (p. 30).

It can be difficult for those unfamiliar with butch–femme culture to comprehend the difference between heterosexual and femme sexuality and to reinterpret gender signifiers. Butler (1990) succinctly elucidated this point: "Lesbian femmes may recall the heterosexual scene, as it were, but also displace it at the same time. In both butch and femme identities the very notion of an original or natural identity is put into question; indeed, it is precisely that question as it is embodied in these identities that becomes one source of their erotic significance" (p. 123). As gender theorists and psychotherapists (e.g., Levitt & Bigler, 2003) work to understand and develop strategies to promote positive femme-identity, an understanding of differently gendered women's lived experiences becomes of central importance.

In our interviews, women emphasized the differences in the meaning of the same behaviors in heterosexual and butch–femme contexts. These differences were attributed to a basic equality between women, the integration of feminist thought and identity by both partners, a wish to honor partners' genders that typically may be not recognized or valued, and an understanding that gendered behaviors are presented consciously and have political meaning. This social construal of femme identity empowered them and supported their conscious decision to maintain a gender presentation that felt coherent with their sexualities and values.

The Assumption of Privilege

A survey study (Levitt & Horne, 2002) of this same community indicated that femme identities were thought to benefit femme women more than butch identities benefited butch women. Indeed, compared to similar interviews with butch lesbians (Levitt & Hiestand, 2002), femme women reported less heterosexist discrimination and stranger harassment. Still, the ascription of heterosexual privilege to femme women appears inaccurate, even under a cursory examination of this model.

Although they did not experience the regularity of stranger harassment that butch lesbians reported, many participants still experienced personal risk regularly, as their values tended to demand that they come out verbally. This communication entailed unique challenges as they had to face anger, disbelief, or suspicion at times from people who might have avoided them had their lesbianism been apparent. In addition, many femme women reported facing sexist harassment, such as catcalls, come-ons, and sexual comments, which butch women reported more rarely (Levitt & Hiestand, 2002).

Participants described some experiences of rejection within heterosexual cultures for *being* lesbian; they also faced suspicion from some lesbians for not being lesbian-*enough*. As a result, they described experiences of marginalization in both contexts. Some of the women described femme-only gatherings, or support groups, to discuss femme experiences, to support one another, to reinforce their political activism as lesbians, and to celebrate their sexuality together.

Objectification Revisited

In essays on femme-identity, women repeatedly describe how their femmeness influences their sexuality. These writers (e.g., Newman, 1995) often convey a seductive feminine power that is distinct from passivity, but results in others' admiration and desire. This wish to be admired was not described by participants as connected to a lack of self-esteem, but, rather, as a desire to exchange sexual energy. It was through signaling a mutual recognition of gender difference that a sexual appreciation and tension was built. It was partners' dis-

tinctly butch gender that was recognized when femmes allowed them to open doors or to pay on dates. In turn, femme women enjoyed tributes to their femmeness, such as being pleasured sexually, having doors held open, and being complimented or admired.

Participants described a transformed meaning of being the recipient of romantic adoration. By offering themselves as objects for butch gaze alone, femme women took control of their status as such. The admiring subject could only be another woman of her choice. It took a social foundation of equality and a shared valuing of the courage to relinquish the position of the viewer to elect to be the object of another's gaze.

Indeed, butch women have reported (Levitt & Hiestand, 2002) appreciating femme women's comfort in being observed while enacting femininity. Ironically, this ability signaled both the power of beauty and a sense of self or subjectivity confident enough to house the vulnerability of objectivity. Although femme women described aesthetically appraising butch partners as sexual objects, they were cautious not to do so during acts of sexuality, as they did not wish to negate the butch partner's gender identity. This interaction afforded to the butch partner a sense of security that mitigated the vulnerability sometimes associated with sexuality or intimacy.

In being admired then, the femme partner consciously offered the safety of subjectivity to her partner. Femme partners' conscious self-objectification altered the roles of both participants by placing volition, care, and power in the role of the "object." They did not describe an unexamined etiquette performed between sets of individuals with differing social power, but a conscious adoption of mutually empowering interpersonal rites that was consistent with their feminist values.

Throughout these interviews, women relayed the formation of interpersonal dynamics that prized diversity in gender presentation and sexuality, and was guided by values of respect and quality. These considerations were at play within friendships and romances and were evidenced within both lesbian and heterosexual contexts. The core of femme relating appeared to be a process of structuring relationships so that they incorporate care for others' vulnerabilities with a sense of personal integrity.

Acknowledgments

The authors thank the Social Services and Humanities Council of Canada for their support. As well, we thank the bright and courageous women who shared their experiences in this project.

References

Austin, P. (1992). Femme-inism. In J. Nestle (Ed.), *The persistent desire: A femme–butch reader* (pp. 362–366). Boston: Alyson.

Bailey, J. M., Kim, P., Hills, A., & Linsenmeier, J. A. W. (1997). Butch, femme, or straight-acting? Partner preferences of gay men and lesbians. *Journal of Personality and Social Psychology, 73*, 960–973.

Burana, L., & Due, L. R. (Eds.). (1994). *Dagger: On butch women*. San Francisco: Cleis Press.

Butler, J. (1990). *Gender trouble: Feminism and the subversion of identity*. New York: Routledge.

Faderman, L. (1991). *Odd girls and twilight lovers: A history of lesbian life in twentieth century America*. New York: Columbia University Press.

Feinberg, L. (1996). *Transgender warriors: Making history from Joan of Arc to Dennis Rodman*. Boston: Beacon Press.

Giorgi, A. (1970). *Psychology as a human science: A phenomenological approach*. New York: Harper & Row.

Glaser, B. J., & Strauss, A. (1967). *The discovery of grounded theory: Strategies for qualitative research*. Chicago: Aldine.

Halberstam, J. (1998). *Female masculinity*. Durham, NC: Duke University Press.

Hale, C. J. (1998). Consumering the living: Dis(re)membering the dead in the butch/FTM borderlands. *Journal of Lesbian and Gay Studies, 4*, 311–348.

Harris, L., & Crocker, E. (1997). *Femme: Feminists, lesbians, and bad girls*. New York: Routledge.

Kitzinger, D. (1987). *The social construction of lesbianism*. Thousand Oaks, CA: Sage.

Laporte, R. (1992). The butch–femme question. In J. Nestle (Ed.), *The persistent desire: A femme–butch reader* (pp. 208–219). Boston: Alyson.

Lapovsky-Kennedy, E., & Davis, M. D. (1993). *Boots of leather, slippers of gold: The history of a lesbian community*. New York: Penguin.

Levitt, H. M., & Bigler, M. (2003). Facilitating lesbian gender exploration. In J. S. Whitman & C. J. Boyd (Eds.), *The therapist's notebook for lesbian, gay, and bisexual clients*. Binghamton, NY: Haworth Press.

Levitt, H., & Hiestand, K. (2002). *A quest for authenticity: Contemporary butch gender*. Manuscript under review.

Levitt, H. M., & Horne, S. G. (2002). Explorations of lesbian-queer genders. *Journal of Lesbian Studies, 6*(2), 25–39.

Munt, S. (1998). *Butch/femme: Inside lesbian gender*. Washington, DC: Cassell.

Nestle, J. (1992). *The persistent desire: A femme-butch reader*. Boston: Alyson.

Nestle, J. (1993). Butch–femme relationships: Sexual courage in the 1950s. In J. Penelope & S. Wolfe (Eds.), *Lesbian culture: An anthology* (pp. 107–111). Freedom, CA: The Crossing Press.

Newman, L. (1995). *The femme mystique*. Boston: Alyson.

Patton, M. Q. (1990). *Evaluation and research methods* (2nd ed.) Newbury Park, CA: Sage.

Pearcey, S. M., Docherty, K. J., & Dabbs, J. M., Jr. (1996). Testosterone and sex role identification in lesbian couples. *Physiology and Behavior, 60*, 1033–1035.

Rennie, D. L., Phillips, J. R., & Quartaro, G. K. (1988). Grounded theory: A promising approach to conceptualization in psychology? *Canadian Psychology, 29*, 139–150.

Ruby, J. (1993). A lesbian feminist fucks with gender. *Off Our Backs*, 28(8, pt.1), 4.

Singh, D., Vidaurri, M., Zambarano, R. J., & Dabbs, J. M., Jr. (1999). Lesbian erotic role identification: Behavioral, morphological, and hormonal correlates. *Journal of Personality and Social Psychology, 76*, 1035–1049.

Smith, C. A., & Stillman, S. (2002). Butch/Femme in the personal advertisements of lesbians. *Journal of Lesbian Studies, 6*, 45–51.

Vaisseau, R. (1995). I am not a straight girl. In L. Newman (Ed.), *The femme mystique* (pp. 30–32). Los Angeles: Alyson.

Weber, J. C. (1996). Social class as a correlate of gender identity among lesbian women. *Sex Roles, 35*, 271–280.

CHAPTER 4 STUDY QUESTIONS

1. Have you ever considered the ways in which social class might relate to sexualities? What arguments do Jenny A. Higgins and Irene Browne make about class (Reading 22)?

2. In Chapter Three you read about gendered bodies. What connections can you draw between bodies and sexualities, besides the obvious (namely, that some of our sexuality resides in our physiology)?

3. Gloria Martinez (Reading 23) describes a study of White (non-Latina) women and Latina (non-White) women and breast cancer. Do the women seem to have similar experiences in processing the effects of the disease? Are their sexualities similar? Does "difference" inspire us to look for difference while ignoring similarities?

4. What point of view do these authors take? How can you tell what each one's point of view is? Does a clear statement of point of view change your perception of a reading?

SECTION III

The Macrocosm of Gender: Institutions, Structures, and Politics

CHAPTER **5** Doing Gender Diversity: At Home and at Work

28 Judith E. Owen Blakemore, Carol A. Lawton, and Lesa Rae Vartanian

I Can't Wait to Get Married
Gender Differences in Drive to Marry

Whereas married people of both genders are evaluated more favorably than are unmarried people (Etaugh & Birdoes, 1991; Etaugh & Hoehn, 1995; Etaugh & Stern, 1984; Ganong, Coleman, & Mapes, 1990; Russell & Rush, 1987), women appear to be subject to social pressures to marry in ways that men are not (Nilsen, 1977). Although some single women report that they enjoy their independence and the freedom to focus on their own careers, others express anxiety about remaining single and report pressure from family members and others to marry and have children (Kaslow, 1992; Lewis & Moon, 1997). Although the normal aging process decreases both male and female fertility, it places no absolute limit on men's ability to father children, but clearly defines parameters for women's childbearing—creating a particular pressure for women to marry. It is also the case that single women often report feeling that they are responsible for the success of romantic relationships—that they are to blame and that others blame them when heterosexual relationships fail. They also tend to think that women who have not married are perceived as deficient (Reynolds & Wetherell, 2003; Sandfield & Percy, 2003). Finally, fear for personal safety when alone in public is not likely to be a concern of single men, but it is a concern often expressed by single women

Judith E. Owen Blakemore, Carol A. Lawton, and Lesa Rae Vartanian, "I Can't Wait to Get Married: Gender Differences in Drive to Marry," *Sex Roles* 53, nos. 5/6 (September 2005): 327–335. Copyright © 2005 Springer Science + Business Media, LLC. With kind permission from Springer Science + Business Media.

An earlier version of this paper was presented at the annual meeting of the Midwestern Psychological Association in May 2004.

(Chasteen, 1994). Thus it is reasonable to assume that women's desire to marry would be expected to be especially strong.

As opportunities for women have expanded and feminist attitudes have gained acceptance (Huddy, Neely, & Lafay, 2000), attitudes toward marriage and women's roles have changed in some respects, but not others. Marriage role expectations of female college students from the 1960s to the present have become more egalitarian (Botkin, Weeks, & Morris, 2000). Young women regard favorably the roles of both worker and mother for married women (Bridges, 1987; Hoffnung, 2004), and young women and men place similar importance on anticipated career and marital identities (Kerpelman & Schvaneveldt, 1999). Yet when asked whether they would choose marriage or career if they could only pick one, women college students are more likely than men to choose marriage (38% vs. 18%), and more women than men say they would be willing to make sacrifices, such as moving to a new city, in order to advance a future spouse's career (Novack & Novack, 1996). Young women also place greater importance than do young men on their future parental identity (Kerpelman & Schvaneveldt, 1999), are more likely to consider the possibility of an extended work interruption to manage future family concerns (Peake & Harris, 2002), and expect to be the parent who will stay at home with a newborn infant (Novack & Novack, 1996).

The significance of marital identity for women is reflected in the fact that the majority of women still use or intend to use the title "Mrs." upon marriage (Brightman, 1994; Twenge, 1997). Young women, in particular, show little understanding of or desire to adopt the title "Ms.," which was intended to be neutral with regard to marital status (Atkinson, 1987; Lawton, Blakemore, & Vartanian, 2002; Pauwels, 2001). Apparently somewhat older unmarried or divorced women do understand the meaning of the title, as they say that they prefer to use "Ms." because they do not wish to reveal their marital status. However, many young single women prefer to use "Miss" to signal their availability, and many married women prefer "Mrs." because they are proud to be married and want others to know they are married (Foss & Edson, 1989; Lawton et al., 2003).

In addition to using the title "Mrs.," the majority of married women also adopt their husband's surnames. Only a minority of women keep their birth names when they marry, and there are notable differences among those who do and those who do not adopt their husband's names (Brightman, 1994; Duggan, Cota, & Dion, 1993; Foss & Edson, 1989; Fowler & Fuehrer, 1997; Intons-Peterson & Crawford, 1985; Kline, Stafford, & Miklosovic, 1996; Twenge, 1997). Generally, women who have adopted or plan to adopt their husband's name are more traditional, less concerned with equality in their marital relationships, and more focused on relationships with husbands and children as the central part of their identities. Some mention that the adoption of a husband's name is an important symbol of their new identity as a family unit (or part of becoming "one"). Women who keep their birth names are more likely to be explicitly feminist, concerned with equality in their marital relationships, and to see their individual and professional identities as central. It is interesting that when the issue has been studied (e.g., Kline et al., 1996), both groups of women value their marriages, and there appear to be no differences in marital quality between them. We do not know, however, whether women who plan to adopt their husbands' names are also more likely to want to marry in the first place.

In this study, we examined three issues. First, we wanted to determine if there were differences between young women and men in their eagerness or desire to get married. Therefore, we developed a "Drive to Marry" scale. This scale was intended to measure feelings of pride or excitement about getting married, rather than the value of, or commitment to, the marital role and its responsibilities (e.g., as examined by Amatea, Cross, Clark, & Bobby, 1986). We hypothesized that women would show a greater drive to marry than would men based on previous research that demonstrated that women are more likely than men to choose marriage over career, if they have to make a choice; to make sacrifices for marriage; to feel a sense of failure if they are unable to maintain a satisfactory intimate relationship; and to feel safer when they have a male partner.

In addition to examining gender differences in the drive to marry, we also wanted to study predictors of individual differences in the drive to marry within each gender. Certainly some young people, women and men alike, are less likely than others to want to marry. As potential factors related to individual differences in the drive to marry, we examined public self-consciousness (the extent to which people are concerned about others' views of them), traditional versus feminist attitudes, and the value of future parental and occupational roles. Consistent with the external pressure to marry that is reported by many single women, we hypothesized that women who are more concerned about what others think of them would have a stronger drive to marry. We also expected that women

who highly value their future role as a parent would have a stronger drive to marry. In contrast, a lower drive to marry was predicted for women who more highly value their future occupational role. Finally, we predicted that traditional women would have a stronger drive to marry. We also examined the drive to marry in men, but made no specific predictions about what factors would be related to it.

We also wanted to examine the relationship between drive to marry and women's desire to adopt their husband's name, use the title "Mrs.," and wear a wedding ring. Therefore, we developed a second measure to examine these issues. On the basis of the previous research, we expected that scores on this measure would be predicted by the value of the parental and occupational roles, and by the Attitudes Toward Women Scale (AWS; Spence & Helmreich, 1978). We also predicted that young women with a higher drive to marry would have higher scores on this "name and ring" scale.

Method

Participants

There were 395 (149 men and 246 women) never-married participants, who ranged in age from 18 to 31 years ($M = 19.75$; $SD = 2.25$). Data from 15 additional participants who indicated that they were not heterosexual (below 3 on a 5-point scale; 1 = *not-at-all heterosexual*, 5 = *strongly heterosexual*) were not included in the analyses. The majority (88.6%) of the 395 participants identified themselves as White. Most of the other participants identified themselves as Black (6.1%), Hispanic (2%), or Asian (1.5%). The participants were Introductory Psychology students from a regional commuter campus of a state university in the Midwestern

United States, who took part in partial fulfillment of a course requirement. The majority of the students on the campus are from working to middle class backgrounds; many are first generation college students.

Materials

Demographics. Participants first completed several demographic questions (e.g., gender, age, ethnic background, current relationship status, sexual orientation).

The Drive to Marry Scale. The participants were asked 13 questions concerning their desire to get engaged and married, as well as excitement and pride in achieving marital status. Participants were asked to rate these items on a 5-point scale (1 = *disagree strongly*; 5 = *agree strongly*) with the following instructions: "The following questions concern your views about marrying. To answer them, think about marriage itself, as much as possible without considering either its potential economic benefits or your relationship with a particular partner."

These questions were analyzed with a series of factor analyses, including the principal components analysis and varimax rotation. As a result of those analyses, a final "Drive to Marry" (DTM) scale was constructed that consisted of five items, with a Cronbach's alpha of .86. The final scale score was a mean score of these five items. The five items and their factor loadings can be seen in Table 28.1.

Name and Ring Scale. We next asked female participants about their desire to wear a wedding ring, to keep their birth name, to adopt their husband's surname, and to use either the title "Ms." or the title "Mrs." These five items were all rated on 5-point scales that ranged from 1 = "*not at all*" to 5 = "*very*

TABLE 28.1 **Items in the Drive to Marry Scale with Factor Loadings**

Item	Factor Loading
I can't wait to get married	.85
Being married will make me feel proud	.80
I feel I will have achieved a major life goal when I get married	.79
Becoming engaged would be one of the most exciting things that could happen to me	.79
Getting married is not one of my top priorities[a]	.79

[a]Reverse scored.

much." The items were factor analyzed by principal components analysis and varimax rotation. The items loaded onto a single factor (Cronbach's alpha = .70), which we call the "Name and Ring Scale." The items that asked about keeping one's birth name and using the title "Ms." were reverse-scored. Therefore, higher scores on this scale reflect a greater desire to wear a wedding ring, to use the title "Mrs.," and to adopt a husband's surname. The final scale score was a mean score of these five items. The items and their factor loadings can be seen in Table 28.2.

TABLE 28.2 **Items in the Name and Ring Scale with Factor Loadings[a]**

Item	Factor Loading
If you were to become married How much would you want to adopt your spouse's last name?	.81
How much you would prefer to use "Mrs."?	.76
How much would you want to keep your birth name?[b]	.67
How much you would prefer to use "Ms."?[b]	.65
How much you would want to wear a wedding ring?	.53

[a]Female participants only.
[b]Reverse scored.

Value of Future Identities in Careers, Parenthood, and Marital Role. Participants also completed three subscales from the Life Role Salience Scales (LRSS; Amatea et al., 1986). This instrument measures the importance or reward value that people assign to various life roles.

There are five items on each of these subscales, and each item is rated on a 5-point scale ranging from 1 = *disagree strongly*, to 5 = *agree strongly*. Each scale has a maximum score of 25; higher scores reflect greater commitment to the role.

We were especially interested in the extent to which people valued their future roles as workers and as parents. We wanted to examine whether the desire to get married, as measured by the DTM, would be predicted by the extent to which participants value these two roles. Hence, we used the Parental Role Value (PRV) and Occupational Role Value (ORV) subscales as possible predictors of DTM.

We also examined the participants' scores on the Marital Role Value (MRV subscale), which measures the extent to which people value the marital role, to establish construct validity of the DTM scale. The measures did, in fact, correlate ($r = .74$). Therefore, our new measure (the DTM) demonstrated a strong and positive relationship with a previously published measure of the extent to which people value the marital role. Because the overlap is not complete, the measures are clearly assessing somewhat different aspects of the phenomenon. We did not, however, use the MRV as a predictor of DTM because of the partial overlap between the two scales.

Self-consciousness. In addition to completing the Drive to Marry (DTM) scale and the LRSS, participants completed the Self-Consciousness scale (Fenigstein, Scheier, & Buss,

1975). For the purposes of this study we considered only the public self-consciousness (PUBSC) subscale, which assesses the extent to which participants are concerned with others' opinions about them (e.g., "I usually worry about making a good impression"). The seven items on this subscale are rated on a 5-point scale ranging from 1 (*not at all like me*) to 5 (*a lot like me*); the overall score is a mean score.

Attitudes toward Women. To assess traditional versus feminist attitudes, participants completed the short version of the Attitudes toward Women Scale (AWS; Spence & Helmreich, 1978). This scale includes items such as "a woman should not expect to go exactly the same places or have quite the same freedom of action as a man." The 15 items on the short version of the scale are each rated on 4-point scales ranging from 0 (*disagree strongly*) to 3 (*agree strongly*). Items reflecting traditional attitudes are reverse coded; scores on the scale can range from 0 (*very traditional*) through 45 (*very pro-feminist*).

Procedure

A female undergraduate research assistant administered the questionnaire to participants in groups. All participants were administered the scales in the same order: demographic information, Drive to Marry scale, Name and Ring scale, the LRSS, the PUBSC, and the AWS.

Results

Gender Differences in the Measures

ANOVA was used to compare the scores of men and women on all of the major scales (except the Name and Ring scale, which was examined for women only). The mean scores and the results of ANOVAs can be found in

TABLE 28.3 Men's and Women's Scores on the Scales

	Men	Women		
Scale	M (SD)	M (SD)	F(1, 389)[a]	p
Drive to Marry (DTM)	3.54 (0.96)	3.76 (0.95)	5.18	.023
Parental Role Value (PRV)	20.28 (4.34)	21.24 (4.10)	5.10	.025
Attitudes Toward Women (AWS)	30.23 (7.60)	35.20 (5.65)	48.27	<.001
Marital Role Value (MRV)	19.16 (4.53)	19.36 (4.55)		ns
Occupational Role Value (ORV)	17.08 (3.40)	17.00 (3.65)		ns
Public Self-Consciousness (PUBSC)	3.47 (0.77)	3.55 (0.71)		ns

[a]The residual degrees of freedom varied slightly because of missing data on some analyses.

Table 28.3. Women had significantly more liberal or feminist attitudes on the AWS, higher scores on the parental role value subscale, and higher scores on the Drive to Marry scale (DTM). Men and women were not different in their public self-consciousness or in their scores on the occupational role value subscale. Also, despite the fact that women had a higher DTM, men and women did not differ in their scores on the marital role value subscale.

Although our non-White sample was not large enough to statistically test racial or ethnic differences in drive to marry, there appeared to be an interesting trend among different groups of women. The mean DTM scores were 3.81 for White women (N = 219); 3.8 for both Hispanic and Asian women (Ns = 2 and 3, respectively); and 3.12 for Black women (N = 15). These scores illustrate the potential importance of ethnicity in women's DTM, although a larger sample would be needed to further explore this issue.

Correlations Among the Measures in Men and Women

We examined the simple correlations between our DTM scale and all of the other measures. Because we were interested in these relationships independently in men and women, the correlations are presented separately for each gender in Table 28.4. An examination of the correlations demonstrates that women's scores on DTM were significantly related to their scores on all the other measures. Women with high DTM scores gave greater value to the parental and marital roles (PRV & MRV), were more concerned about others' opinions of them (PUBSC), gave less value to the occupational role (ORV), and were more conservative on the AWS.

TABLE 28.4 Correlations Among the Measures, Separately for Men and Women

	DTM	ORV	PRV	MRV	PUBSC	AWS
DTM	1.00	−.14	.66***	.79***	.15	.00
ORV	−.23***	1.00	−.19*	−.15	.27***	−.09
PRV	.41***	−.23***	1.00	.72***	−.02	−.14
MRV	.72***	−.32***	.48***	1.00	.08	.04
PUBSC	.20**	.06	.11	.14*	1.00	−.01
AWS	−.24***	.41***	−.13*	−.28***	−.01	1.00
Name/Ring	.43***	−.21***	.30***	.45***	.06	−.28***

[a]Men are above the diagonal, and women are below the diagonal.

*p < .05. **p < .005. ***p < .001.

For men, the only significant correlation (other than the obvious one between DTM and MRV) was between DTM and PRV. Men who valued the parental role were more likely to have a stronger drive to marry. It is interesting that the relationship between DTM and Parental Role Value was very high in men ($r = .66$, $p < .001$), and, although it was significant and positive in women, the correlation was smaller ($r = .41$, $p < .001$). A statistical test of the difference in these two correlations (Ferguson, 1976) was significant, $z = 3.39$, $p < .001$.

The correlations between the Name and Ring scale and the other measures in women can also be seen in Table 28.4. This measure was significantly correlated with all of the other measures except public self-consciousness.

Individual Differences in Women's and Men's Drive to Marry

Many of the predictor variables were intercorrelated, therefore simultaneous multiple regression analyses were conducted to assess the unique contributions of Parental Role Value, Occupational Role Value, Public Self-Consciousness, and the AWS separately for women's and men's DTM scores.

The model explained a significant amount of variance in DTM for women, $F(4, 231) = 18.82$, $p < .001$, adjusted $R^2 = .23$. AWS, Public Self-Consciousness, and Parental Role Value were significant predictors of women's DTM, and Occupational Role Value was a marginally significant predictor (see Table 28.5). More traditional women, women more concerned about others' opinions of them, and women who valued the parental role more highly all had high DTM scores, and there was a trend for women who valued the occupational role more highly to have somewhat lower DTM

scores. An examination of the squared semi-partial correlation coefficients (see Table 28.5) demonstrates that, among the predictors, Parental Role Value accounted for the most variance in DTM, but that the other variables also accounted for unique and modest portions of the variance.

TABLE 28.5 **Predictors of Women's Drive to Marry**

Predictor	β	t	p	sr^2
Parental role value	.36	5.98	.001	.34
Occupational role value	−.12	−1.79	.075	−.10
Public self-consciousness	.18	3.08	.002	.18
AWS	−.14	−2.24	.026	−.13

Note: sr²: squared semi-partial correlations.

For men, even more of the variance in DTM was accounted for by the model, which had fewer significant predictors, $F(4, 134) = 32.84$, $p < .001$, adjusted $R^2 = .48$. In men, only Public Self-Consciousness and Parental Role Value emerged as significant predictors (see Table 28.6). An examination of the squared semi-partial correlations shown in Table 28.6 clearly demonstrates that, for men, Parental Role Value accounted for a great deal of the variance in DTM, and Public Self-Consciousness accounted for a modest amount.

TABLE 28.6 **Predictors of Men's Drive to Marry**

Predictor	β	t	p	sr^2
Parental role value	.67	10.49	.001	.64
Public self-consciousness	.21	3.29	.001	.20

Note: sr²: squared semi-partial correlations.

Thus, for women, being more conservative, being more concerned with other's opinions of them, placing higher value on the parental role, and placing a somewhat lower value on the occupational role predicted a higher drive to marry. For men, only the value of the parental role and concern about others' opinions of them predicted drive to marry.

Individual Differences in Title, Name, and Ring Use in Women

We also examined parental role value, occupational role value, public self-consciousness, AWS, and DTM as predictors of women's desire, upon marriage, to adopt their husband's last name, to use the title Mrs., and to wear a wedding ring (Name and Ring scale). The model accounted for a significant amount of variance, $F(5, 229) = 13.87$, $p < .001$, adjusted $R^2 = .22$; DTM, AWS, and Parental Role Value emerged as significant predictors. That is, women with a stronger drive to marry, women who value the parental role, and more traditional women had higher scores on the Name and Ring Scale (see Table 28.7). An examination of the squared semi-partial correlations demonstrates that DTM accounted for approximately twice as much of the variance as the other predictors did. We had also predicted that women who were less likely to value the occupational role would have higher scores on the Name and Ring scale, but they did not.

TABLE 28.7 **Predictors of Women's Desire to Wear Wedding Ring, Use Title "Mrs.," and Adopt Husband's Surname**

Predictor	ß	t	p	sr²
Drive to marry	.31	4.64	.001	.27
Parental role value	.14	2.19	.029	.13
AWS	−.16	−2.42	.017	−.14

Note: sr²: squared semi-partial correlations.

Discussion

Marriage represents a significant and normative adult role for men and women alike, but being married appears to hold special significance for women. Although changes during the last two decades have brought more flexible gender role attitudes and beliefs, and more opportunities for women to adopt roles other than "wife" and "mother," results of many studies have suggested a continuing greater regard among women than men for being married. In this study we sought to answer three key questions: "Do women have a higher 'drive to marry' than do men?," "What variables account for individual differences in the desire to marry?," and "Do similar variables account for individual differences in the desire of women to adopt their husband's name, to use the title 'Mrs.,' and to wear a wedding ring?"

On the basis of previous research that indicates that women experience various social pressures to marry (Chasteen, 1994; Kaslow, 1992; Lewis & Moon, 1997), we predicted that women would show more eagerness and excitement about getting married (i.e., have a higher "drive to marry") than would men. Whereas previous researchers have compared men and women in terms of the value placed on a future marital role (Amatea et al., 1986; Kerpelman & Schvaneveldt, 1999; Stone & McKee, 2000), no researchers have considered the extent to which women and men are enthusiastically looking forward to getting married. As predicted, we did demonstrate a higher "drive to marry" in women. We found a higher drive to marry in women despite the fact that the men and women in our sample valued the marital role equally.

Also, as predicted, the women who were most eager to marry were those who placed a higher value on their future parental role, had more conservative attitudes toward women's roles, and were more concerned about others' opinions of them. There was also a tendency for women who value the occupational role to have a lower drive to marry. These findings resonate with past research, which has demonstrated that women expect career and family roles to compete with one another (Bridges, 1987; Mennino & Brayfield, 2002; Novack & Novack, 1996) and that others may view them less positively if they do not marry (Etaugh & Birdoes, 1991; Etaugh & Hoehn, 1995; Etaugh & Stern, 1984; Ganong et al., 1990).

We did not make predictions about individual differences in men's drive to marry. We found that it was related to only two of the variables we measured: the value of the parental role and public self-consciousness. Apparently, young men and women share these two factors as underlying reasons for their desire to get married. The fact that men and women who are concerned about others' views of them have a higher drive to marry is consistent with previous research that demonstrated that both men and women who are married are viewed more positively by others (Etaugh & Birdoes, 1991; Etaugh & Hoehn, 1995; Etaugh & Stern, 1984; Ganong et al., 1990; Russell & Rush, 1987). These young people appear to sense that they will be held in higher esteem once they get married.

That the value of the parental role was linked with drive to marry is certainly reasonable—parenthood and marriage are obviously linked. It is interesting that the amount of variance accounted for by parental role

value was larger in men than in women. This suggests that, for men, wanting to become fathers is an especially compelling reason to want to marry, whereas for women, it is an important reason, but only one of many. Because women bear children, and because they often have custody of them following the breakup of a relationship, it is logical that men would benefit from the close availability of a partner with whom they may share parenthood. Thus, it may be especially evident to young men who want to be fathers that they will have a greater opportunity to actively engage in this role if they get married.

For women, there was also evidence that the value given to the parental role positively correlated with their drive to marry. However, the value given by women to the occupational role was negatively correlated with their drive to marry. Despite the fact that it is no longer uncommon for women to choose both "spouse" and "worker" roles for themselves, we can also see that there remains a tendency for these roles to exist in relative opposition to one another in the minds of young women in a way that they do not in young men.

Finally, we hypothesized that a higher drive to marry, traditional attitudes, high parental role value, and low occupational role value would predict women's willingness to adopt their husband's surname, use the title "Mrs.," and wear a wedding ring (Name and Ring scale). As hypothesized, scores on all of these measures did correlate with scores on the Name and Ring scale. However, value given to the occupational role did not uniquely contribute to scores on the Name and Ring scale once all predictors were entered simultaneously in the regression, most likely because of the shared variance of ORV and both PRV and the AWS.

One important limitation of the study is its sample. This was a single sample of college students from the Midwestern United States. They are predominantly first generation college students who are somewhat politically conservative. Most commute to campus and many live with their parents. It is important to replicate the gender difference in drive to marry in other samples. Given that we found that conservative attitudes about gender roles and the value given to the parental role were related to higher drive to marry scores in women, it is possible that among less conservative or traditional samples, men and women's drive to marry might, in fact, be similar. It is also possible that the drive to marry might increase in men as they grow older, especially considering that men typically marry at slightly older ages than do women (Kreider & Simmons, 2003). This could potentially be examined in a future sample with greater diversity in age.

Another important limitation of the sample is that the participants were predominantly White. Black women who attend college have been found to have lower expectations that they will marry and to be less likely to marry. They are also less likely to think that occupational and parental roles are in conflict and to adopt their husbands' names (Hoffnung, 2004; Murrell, Frieze, & Frost, 1991; Twenge, 1997). Hence, the drive to marry might well be lower in Black women than in White women. Our sample of Black women was not large enough to do a statistical test of this potentially important difference, but the mean DTM score appeared to be lower in the 15 Black women who took part in this study. This certainly suggests an important avenue for further research.

In conclusion, in this study we constructed a Drive to Marry scale to measure young people's eager anticipation about the possibility of getting married. We found that women had a higher drive to marry and that drive to marry in women was related to more variables than was drive to marry in men. Both men and women who had a stronger desire to become parents and who were concerned about others' views about them also had a stronger drive to marry. Women, on the other hand, also had a stronger drive to marry when they were less feminist and when they were somewhat less focused on a future career. Such women were also more likely to want to adopt a husband's name, be called Mrs., and wear a wedding ring.

Acknowledgments

The authors thank Samantha Lauer for her assistance in collecting data.

References

Amatea, E. S., Cross, E. G., Clark, J. E., & Bobby, C. L. (1986). Assessing the work and family role expectations of career-oriented men and women: The Life Role Salience Scales. *Journal of Marriage and the Family, 48,* 831–838.

Atkinson, D. L. (1987). Names and titles: Maiden name retention and the use of Ms. *Journal of the Atlantic Provinces Linguistic Association, 9,* 56–83.

Botkin, D. R., Weeks, M. O. N., & Morris, J. E. (2000). Changing marriage role expectations, 1961–1996. *Sex Roles, 42,* 933–942.

Bridges, J. S. (1987). College females' perceptions of adult roles and occupational fields for women. *Sex Roles, 16,* 591–604.

Brightman, J. (1994). Why Hillary chooses Rodham Clinton. *American Demographics, 16,* 9–11.

Chasteen, A. L. (1994). "The world around me": The environment and single women. *Sex Roles, 31*, 309–328.

Duggan, D. A., Cota, A. A., & Dion, K. L. (1993). Taking thy husband's name: What might it mean? *Names, 41*, 87–102.

Etaugh, C., & Birdoes, L. N. (1991). Effects of age, sex, and marital status on person perception. *Perceptual and Motor Skills, 72*, 491–497.

Etaugh, C., & Hoehn, S. (1995). Perceiving women: Effects of marital, parental, and occupational sex-typing variables. *Perceptual and Motor Skills, 80*, 320–322.

Etaugh, C., & Stern, J. (1984). Person perception: Effects of sex, marital status, and sex-typed occupation. *Sex Roles, 11*, 413–424.

Fenigstein, A., Scheier, M. F., & Buss, A. H. (1975). Public and private self-consciousness: Assessment and theory. *Journal of Consulting and Clinical Psychology, 43*, 522–527.

Ferguson, G. (1976). *Statistical analysis in psychology and education.* New York: McGraw-Hill.

Foss, K. A., & Edson, B. A. (1989). What's in a name? Accounts of married women's name choices. *Western Journal of Speech Communication, 53*, 356–373.

Fowler, R. I., & Fuehrer, A. (1997). Women's marital names: An interpretive study of name retainers' concepts of marriage. *Feminism and Psychology, 7*, 315–320.

Ganong, L. H., Coleman, M., & Mapes, D. (1990). A meta-analytic review of family structure stereotypes. *Journal of Marriage and the Family, 52*, 287–297.

Hoffnung, M. (2004). Wanting it all: Career, marriage, and motherhood during college-educated women's 20s. *Sex Roles, 50*, 711–723.

Huddy, L., Neely, F., & Lafay, M. R. (2000). The polls—Trends: Support for the women's movement. *Public Opinion Quarterly, 64*, 309–350.

Intons-Peterson, M. J., & Crawford, J. (1985). The meanings of marital surnames. *Sex Roles, 12*, 1163–1171.

Kaslow, F. W. (1992). Thirty-plus and not married. In B. R. Wainrib (Ed.), *Gender issues across the life cycle* (pp. 77–94). New York: Springer.

Kerpelman, J. L., & Schvaneveldt, P. L. (1999). Young adults' anticipated identity importance of career, marital, and parental roles: Comparisons of men and women with different role balance orientations. *Sex Roles, 41*, 189–217.

Kline, S. L., Stafford, L., & Miklosovic, J. C. (1996). Women's surnames: Decisions, interpretations and associations with relational qualities. *Journal of Social and Personal Relationships, 13*, 593–617.

Kreider, R. M., & Simmons, T. (2003). *Marital status: 2000.* Retrieved March 15, 2005, from http://www.census.gov/prod/2003pubs/c2kbr-30.pdf

Lawton, C. A., Blakemore, J. E. O., & Vartanian, L. R. (2003). The new meaning of Ms.: Single, but too old for Miss. *Psychology of Women Quarterly, 27*, 215.

Lewis, K. G., & Moon, S. (1997). Always single and single again women: A qualitative study. *Journal of Marital and Family Therapy, 23*, 115–134.

Mennino, S. F., & Brayfield, A. (2002). Job-family trade-offs: The multidimensional effects of gender. *Work and Occupations, 29*, 226–256.

Murrell, A. J., Frieze, I. H., & Frost, J. L. (1991). Aspiring to careers in male- and female-dominated professions: A study of Black and White college women. *Psychology of Women Quarterly, 15*, 103–126.

Nilsen, A. P. (1977). Sexism in the language of marriage. In A. P. Nilsen, H. Bosmajian, H. L. Gershuny, & J. P. Stanley (Eds.), *Sexism and language* (pp. 131–140). Urbana, IL: National Council of Teachers of English.

Novack, L. L., & Novack, D. R. (1996). Being female in the eighties and nineties: Conflicts between new opportunities and traditional expectations among White, middle class, heterosexual college women. *Sex Roles, 35*, 57–78.

Pauwels, A. (2001). Spreading the feminist word: The case of the new courtesy title Ms. in Australian English. In M. Hellinger & H. Bussmann (Eds.), *Gender across languages: The linguistic representation of women and men, Vol. 1: Impact, studies in language and society* (pp. 137–151). Amsterdam: John Benjamins.

Peake, A., & Harris, K. L. (2002). Young adults' attitudes toward multiple role planning: The influence of gender, career traditionality and marriage plans. *Journal of Vocational Behavior, 60,* 405–421.

Reynolds, J., & Wetherell, M. (2003). The discursive climate of singleness: The consequences for women's negotiation of a single identity. *Feminism and Psychology, 13,* 489–510.

Russell, J. E., & Rush, M. C. (1987). The effects of sex and marital/parental status on performance evaluations and attributions. *Sex Roles, 17,* 221–236.

Sandfield, A., & Percy, C. (2003). Accounting for single status: Heterosexism and ageism in heterosexual women's talk about marriage. *Feminism and Psychology, 13,* 475–488.

Spence, J. T., & Helmreich, R. L. (1978). *Masculinity and femininity: Their psychological dimensions, correlates, and antecedents.* Austin: University of Texas Press.

Stone, L., & McKee, N. P. (2000). Gendered futures: Student visions of career and family on a college campus. *Anthropology and Education Quarterly, 31,* 67–89.

Twenge, J. M. (1997). "Mrs. His Name": Women's preferences for married names. *Psychology of Women Quarterly, 21,* 417–429.

29 Sally Hines

Intimate Transitions

Transgender Practices of Partnering and Parenting

Introduction

The term "transgender" may refer to individuals who have undergone hormone treatment or surgery to reconstruct their bodies, or to those who transgress gender categories in ways which are less permanent. The term thus includes people who are at different stages of gender transformation: physically, emotionally and temporally.

Although sociological interest in transgender has increased over recent years, the dominant framework of discussion remains focused upon the construction of transgender as a theoretical category. Thus the broader social context of gender transitioning remains under explored. Conversely, whilst there has been an expansion of research into shifting familial and partnering structures within sociology and social policy, experiences of intimacy are largely analysed in relation to congruent expressions of gender identity. This article aims to overcome this lacuna by exploring the experiences of intimacy within the context of gender transition. In doing so the article has two aims. First, I hope to bring a sociological analytic to transgender theory and, second, to encourage a non-normative gender inquiry within sociological studies of intimacy.

Research Notes

The research on which this article draws is linked to the ESRC project "CAVA" ("Care, Values and the Future of Welfare") at the University of Leeds, which is exploring changes in the meanings and practices of care and intimacy, the ethical practices associated with these, and the implications of these for future social policies. Data was generated through in-depth interviews with 30 transgender men and women. Participants were purposively selected in relation to the variables of gender, age, sexuality, "race" and ethnicity,[1] occupation, geographical location, relationship and parenting status, and levels of involvement in transgender community organizations. Thirteen participants were trans men and 17 were trans women; the age range of the sample was from 26 years to 75 years old; a little under half of the sample lived in rural towns or villages, while just over half lived in urban localities; 15 members of the sample group identified as heterosexual, while 15 members identified as gay, lesbian, bisexual or queer; 8 participants were single, while the remainder were in relationships; 7 members of the sample group were parents. All of the participants resided in the UK.

The Case Studies

The article now explores the partnering and parenting experiences of three research participants in the form of case studies. Following Platt (1998), Roseneil and Budgeon (2004) suggest that case studies are useful because "if these practices are possible in these cases, they must exist in other cases, and (that) they must be taken into account in the formulation of general propositions about intimate life" (Roseneil and Budgeon, 2004: 153). Although each of these case studies represents individual biographies, they are useful for the purpose of this article as they portray broader research findings of how gender transition impacts upon experiences and practices of partnering and parenting. Thus while this article is based upon three cases that have been chosen for particular reflection, the analysis is based upon wider knowledge and narratives.

Bernadette is in her seventies and describes herself as a transsexual woman. She is of Celtic descent and lives in a small rural village. She identifies as heterosexual and lives with the woman she has been married to for 40 years. She had a stepson who died and has an adult stepdaughter. She is a retired physicist and government communications advisor, and remains Chairperson of her local council. Bernadette transitioned 10 years ago.

Dan is in his thirties and considers his gender identity as FtM (female-to-male). Dan is white British and lives in a rural town. He identifies as heterosexual and lives with his female partner of five years. He has a teenage son. He is a civil engineer. Dan transitioned six years ago.

Cheryl is in her forties and considers her gender as MtF (male-to-female). She is white British and lives in a city. She identifies as bisexual and is living temporarily with her female partner of five months. She has two young children who live with her ex-wife. She is a craft technician. At the time of interview Cheryl was waiting for her first appointment at a gender clinic, and was hoping that this would lead to hormone therapy and to her being placed on the NHS waiting list for surgical reconstruction.

The similarities within the case studies are that Bernadette, Dan and Cheryl all live with their partners and all are parents. While Dan is the primary carer of his child, Bernadette and Cheryl no longer live with their children on a full-time basis. Other key differences between the case studies relate to age and transitional time span.

Practices of Partnering

Reconfigured Partnerships

A recurring theme in the narratives of research participants who transition later in life is long-standing professional and relationship commitments. Bernadette, for example, had a high-profile career and a marriage of 30 years prior to transition. Bernadette says:

> I had a wife and children to support and I became chairman of various investigative boards and had a busy time for eleven years [. . .] I suppose it was a matter of subjugating my feelings to professional success and it worked. You couldn't walk around with the Prime Minister and suddenly one day change gender, it isn't on. And I ac-

cepted that I was playing a fairly crucial role in Government service at that time and it would have been irresponsible to vast numbers of people and organizations if I'd have said "Oh to hell with you, I'm going to go off and do what I've always wanted to do." So that necessity made me plan things and wait until I had got to a point where I thought I could wind that service down.

In this narrative, professional and relationship commitments are understood as coping mechanisms for dealing with complex feelings around gender identity, and are presented as an explanation for late transition. Bernadette's transition can thus be seen to be reflexively negotiated and performed within the context of work and family life.

When Bernadette was in her thirties her best friend of many years died. A few years after the death of her friend, Bernadette married his wife. Although it would be 30 years before she took the decision to transition, Bernadette was open with her partner about her feelings around gender identity. As Bernadette articulates in the following quotation, her partner was to become a central source of emotional support in the years before her transition:

I had a very helpful wife who supported me. She knew there was something very strange about me but found it something she could cope with. I had known her for twenty years before we got married. I got to know her as my best friend's wife in the early 1940s. So we got to know all about each other. She has supported me in every aspect and she supports me still.

Bernadette and her wife moved to the village where they currently live four years be-fore Bernadette's transition. Bernadette became well known in the village. She was an active member of the village church and was elected Chairperson of the local council. As the population of the village fluctuated over the last decade, Bernadette believes that her transition has become less of a public issue and that she and her partner are no longer perceived as a previously heterosexual couple. Rather Bernadette believes that "everybody thinks of us as sisters. A lot of people think we are sisters." Thus, subjective understandings of the relationship are located as shifting beyond a sexual framework, to be repositioned within the context of kinship bonds. Bernadette was unconcerned that some people in her community may view the relationship as a lesbian one and focused upon the shifting meanings of intimacy throughout the relationship's life span, as shown in this section of the interview:

Sally: Do you think some people see your relationship as a lesbian relationship?

B. Oh, some people might, but that is their concept of it. I have a relationship with my wife which is very intimate and loving and has been for the past umpteen years—forty years—and it isn't any different now than it has ever been and it's very good.

Bernadette suggests that the continued emotional bond between herself and her partner has been possible due to the lack of emphasis placed on sex within the relationship prior to transition. Bernadette says:

I suppose, in the case of physical aspects of sexuality, I always seemed myself to be more of an observer, than a participant and in that respect that's the problem I had throughout all my married life, but that was okay with her.

In de-centring sex within her relationship, Bernadette challenges the notion that sex is central to partnering and emphasizes the role of emotional care. A further theme within Bernadette's narrative is the significant positioning of age within shifting experiences of sexual intimacy. Bernadette says:

After one is in one's mid-fifties one can deal with their sexuality in a different way. I couldn't contemplate how we would have reacted had we been twenty years younger. So where my wife was concerned, no problem of physical relationship arose simply because I think we'd always had it in the right sort of context from when we got married in our early forties to the time of my transition in my late fifties.

This relationship cannot be smoothly characterized as either a sexual relationship or as a friendship. Rather, the meanings of intimacy transgress either framework to illustrate how intimate practices may be revitalized across time and situation. There are connections here with Roseneil and Budgeon's (2004) recent work on friendship and non-conventional partnerships, which suggests that contemporary practices of intimacy represent a blurring of the demarcation between lovers and friends. However, the narrative may also be seen to be characteristic of a common-sense perception of long-term partnerships and, particularly, heterosexual partnerships, whereby emotional closeness is seen as more significant than sexual desire.

Although Bernadette does not believe that her transition has altered the level of emotional intimacy with her partner, she suggests that a key change within their relationship has been a greater level of domestic equality. Bernadette says:

Now we have a largish house and grounds here. She's five years older than me but we can split all this up between us, so we have a good working relationship, two old women running a nice house [. . .] We ended up getting married after we'd been together for a couple of years and we're still together now [. . .] Although it's not a traditional marriage relationship we're glad we did it and we are married. I think we've been through everything together now. It's been hard at times. She's had to put up with me not being as interested in sex as I was previously, I was quite highly sexed before. I felt guilty because I wanted to go to sleep at night rather than do anything else. My feelings changed as my body changed. She's had to be strong and we've had to be strong together. I think the trust has grown.

Bernadette's discussion of increased levels of domestic equality post-transition resonates with findings from previously discussed studies of same-sex relationships (Dunne, 1999; Weeks et al., 2001). Research findings thus suggest that gendered, as well as sexual, non-normative practices may enable a space beyond conventional assumptions of gender roles in which to negotiate equal relationships. Within the context of this long-standing partnership, the meanings and lived experiences of intimacy can be seen to be fluid and adaptable to transformations of gender identity. Moreover, practices of emotional care and the values of honesty and trust are emphasized above sexual desire. However, there are apparent tensions in Bernadette's narrative concerning the role of sex in her marriage. In the previous quotations, Bernadette can be seen to shift between competing accounts of her marriage: while she initially positions sex as unimportant in her marriage, she proceeds to describe her pre-transition identity as "highly sexed." Such tensions show the value of discourse analysis, which views interview data as socially constructed and momentarily situated, rather than as a fixed "truth" (Plummer, 1995). The complexities of shifting experiences of intimacy within the changing context of gender transition are also apparent in narratives of relationship separation.

Relationship Separation

Findings show that the process of gender transition might initiate irreconcilable shifts in partnering roles, leading to relationship break-up. However, intimacy remains located as a fluid rather than a fixed process, which is frequently able to transgress the boundaries of sexual relationships and friendship.

Cheryl cross-dressed for many years, though had decided to begin the process of gender transition only six months before our interview. She has been married twice, though both relationships ended. Cheryl was open with her partners about her feelings around gender identity, saying that she "told them both probably within a month so that when we got married they were fully aware that I would cross-dress." Cheryl said that her first marriage ended because she and her wife "drifted apart," although she also said that "she (her first wife) couldn't really handle the situation very well." By the time she met her second wife, she had made friends with other trans people and often spent weekends away at transgender social events where, initially, her wife would accompany her. Cheryl says:

My second wife and I got on very well. She could handle it all and she came away with me for a couple of our weekends and she said they were some of the best weekends she's had. Everybody was so friendly. We used to get really close when I was dressed.

Yet Cheryl also discusses how her partner's initial acceptance of her gender transformation was unrealizable, and her marriage broke up when her wife found that she could no longer manage the shift in gender roles. Cheryl says:

And then basically last November things were getting more and more intense [. . .] And my wife said I should see a doctor and she said "If you are TS (transsexual) I can't live with you any more because I married a man and you don't fulfill that role anymore." It was hard for both of us.

Cheryl has been able to build a friendship with her ex-partner, who now has a new partner. She says:

Her (Cheryl's wife) friend from across the road has moved in with her now [. . .] They're together now and I couldn't wish for a better person to be around my kids. I'm really pleased for her. My wife has said that she'll support me as much as she can and we are good friends.

Within this narrative, a range of affective possibilities are illustrated and the boundaries between sexual relationships and friendship are seen to oscillate. This resonates with Roseneil's (2000), Weeks et al.'s (2001) and Roseneil and Budgeon's (2004) discussions of a continuum of sexual desire and friendship that fluctuates across time and circumstance.

Issues around sexual desire and practice, however, are often of key importance when it comes to forming new relationships after transition.

Forming New Relationships

Findings show that the formation of new relationships after transition is a significant theme within narratives of intimacy. After several years of being single, Dan felt that he wanted to begin a relationship, though he was fearful of being rejected by a prospective partner once he told them about his transition. Dan says:

> I didn't have a relationship for many years for several reasons, one of which was because the situation didn't present itself. Secondly I didn't know what sort of relationship I wanted and thirdly I was so shy of my body. I'd had chest surgery quite early on but it's just a real fear about if someone will accept your body.

Dan met his current partner through an Internet dating site and they communicated for a few weeks by e-mail and phone before meeting. It was important for Dan to discuss his transition with this woman once he knew that he wanted the relationship to progress:

> I'd decided before we met that if I really liked her and we clicked I was going to tell her that night. And so I told her and I just rabbited and rabbited and she was quiet for about five minutes, didn't say a word, and I just thought "oh no, I've blown it, I've blown it" and then she just said "well it doesn't make any difference."

Despite these reassurances, Dan worried that his new partner's feelings towards him would change once the relationship became sexual. Dan says:

> You know, she was saying everything was fine, but how was it going to be when things started getting physical? And eventually we did, well it wasn't that long anyway (laugh) and it was just [pause]. I was also really worried about, you know, would I know what to do? So I was really worried and I was worried that she wouldn't like my body, that she wouldn't like it because I didn't have a willy. But I did know what to do (laugh) and for her [pause]. She wanted [pause]. She did want to be with a man but what she didn't like was, you know, the penis side of sex. So she was happy, I was happy.

Bodily acceptance as a man is positioned as central within Dan's experience of forming a new relationship following transition. The interplay between (trans)gender and sexuality is complex, and Dan's narrative reflects the significance of gendered embodiment within trans subjectivities (Hines, 2005). Similarly, the earlier tension around the changing priority of sex in Bernadette's narrative can be understood in relation to shifting experiences of gendered embodiment, as Bernadette's sexual identity changed from a heterosexual man to a heterosexual woman. While the issues here indicate that gender "matters," suggesting that desire may be "inherently gendered" (Jackson, 1999: 4), trans gendered identifications clearly question the constitutional qualities of gender itself. MacCowan's argument that "Gender *per se* is not the problem [. . .]" (1992: 318), but the "correlation between biological sex, gender identity, gender or sex roles, sexual object choice, sexual identity. . . . It is this system and the denial of any other constructions of gender (which is problematic)" (1992: 318), is useful for an analysis of transgender identities, which act to untie biological sex and gender identity, and bring new meanings to sexual identity categories. While Dan's narrative questions normative understandings of gender and sexuality as experienced and practiced through biological "sex," there is, however, an investment in a discourse of romance, whereby non-normative gendered bodies "make no difference." Such a discourse is different from a discourse of realism, whereby non-normative bodily status would be acknowledged and negotiated. Moreover, a trans romance discourse contrasts with a queer discourse, in which non-normative bodies would be a site of celebration and pleasure in their own right.[2]

Cheryl met her current partner, a trans woman, shortly after her marriage ended. In the following quotation, Cheryl discusses the importance of emotional support within her new relationship:

> It's a very close relationship and she's been so supportive. She's there for me when times are hard. She's been a rock, she really has. We are having a relationship but it's also about our friendship.

Cheryl's broader story articulates the fluidity and complexities of gender and sexuality as theoretical categories and as lived experiences. Within her life history, Cheryl's gender and partnering identities have shifted from a married man in a heterosexual relationship, to a female lover of a lesbian-identifying woman. Thus the binaries of male/female and hetero/homo are complicated and a diversity of intimate subject positions are reflected.

Practices of Parenting

Although many trans people are parents, there is an absence of sociological research on the experiences of transitioning parents. Outside of sociology, Green's (1978, 1998) clinical studies on the impact of gender transition upon the children of transsexual people remain the only UK studies within this area.[3] Moreover, while lesbian and gay parenting sparks much debate within contemporary society, there is a cultural reticence to speak about trans people as parents, which leaves the practices of transgender parenting largely invisible. For the three participants of this article, relationships with children are pivotal to narratives of intimacy.

Telling Children

Decisions around when and how to tell children about their forthcoming gender transition were central to the narratives of trans parents. While the issues of disclosure here relate to gender and not to sexuality, there are links with the experiences of "coming out" to children within the context of lesbian and gay parenting. Gabb comments that "heterosexual parents do not need to make 'proud' declarations of their heterosexuality. The image of such parents routinely 'coming out' to their children as heterosexual is almost beyond our imagination" (Gabb, 2001: 347). Similarly the "inside/out" (Fuss, 1991) gender binary naturalizes non-transgender identity as that which does not have to be articulated, while trans identity as the outsider to the silent norm is forced to speak its name.

Dan was in his thirties and the lone parent of a nine-year-old son when he decided to transition. Dan felt dissonance with his gender identity as a young child. In his twenties, he married and had a child. In the following quotation, Dan's decision to become a parent is articulated as an attempt to manage his conflicting feelings around gender:

> I didn't start dealing with it, well, talking about it, until I was in my thirties but I went through lots and lots of denial in that time and I got married because I thought it would make it go away. One of the reasons for having a child was that it would make it go away, it would make me whole. You destroy all this stuff that was doing my head in, but it didn't.

Dan's marriage broke up when his child was a baby and being a parent did not stop Dan questioning his gender identity, as he wished at the time. Parenting commitments, however, moderated his decision to transition during this time. Dan says:

> I had my son when I was in a can of worms. That was the hardest bit whilst I was sorting my head out, it was "I need to do this for me, but what impact is this going to have on him? Will I lose him? Will he hate me? Will I have to face a custody battle?"

As his son grew up, Dan began to change the way he viewed the link between transitioning and parenting. Dan says:

> My point of view then was that I was becoming so screwed up in my head that I was starting to fail my son as a parent and if I didn't sort my head out and live as me, as how I felt, then I would totally fail him because I didn't have it in me to love him and provide for him and, you know, I'd end up on tranquilizers and god knows what. So he would have ended up without

a parent 'cos he wouldn't have had a parent to support him.

Thus rather than seeing transitioning as problematizing his relationship with his son, Dan began to see it as a process which would enable them to have a more successful relationship. Initially Dan's son found the situation hard to understand, as Dan describes:

> He was very distressed when I told him, he was nine, just nine. His first reaction was that it'd messed his life up. But after two weeks he came back and said "Ok if it's got to be, it's got to be." I think to start off he was worried that he'd go to school on Monday morning with me as his mum and I'd pick him up on the night as his dad. And I explained to him that you started off very slow and he realized it was going to be slowly.

Dan's openness about the procedures involved in gender reassignment can be seen to have enabled his son to more fully understand the changing situation. The importance of open dialogue is also stressed in terms of enabling children to adapt to the changes initiated by gender transition.

Open Dialogue

As Dan began hormone therapy, open dialogue with his son enabled a close relationship through the first stages of transition. Dan says:

> And he'd known that something was troubling me, but he didn't know what it was. So I'd hidden a lot from him during that time and once I'd opened up and was honest I told him everything that had happened since that time and he actually started ask-

ing some really, really pertinent questions. But he was brilliant, especially at the beginning, if I needed to go to the loo he'd insist on going into the loo first so that he could find out where the cubicle was for me. So he was very protective of me which was brilliant. It was nice to know he cared that much [. . .] We've always been in a close relationship and it's been tested along the way and we talk and we've always talked.

Dan's narrative suggests that open dialogue can enable a climate of emotional care in which support is generated not only from parent to child, but also from child to parent. Reciprocal caring between parent and child, however, may mean that the child cares for the parent by not revealing the full extent of what is happening in his/her emotional life. Children may feel more internally conflicted, or face more external conflict than they feel willing or able to reveal to their parents. Thus it is important to note that the children in question were not interviewed and to acknowledge that children may offer different accounts.

Support between parent and child is also articulated within Bernadette's narrative. When Bernadette married she became stepparent to two teenagers. In the following quotation, she discusses her relationship with her stepchildren and talks about the support she received from them when she decided to transition:

My stepdaughter is one of my best friends [. . .] Unfortunately, my stepson died, but he again was someone who was totally supportive of me. I was always entirely honest with them and it's been very good.

Here we can see fluidity between parenting and friendship, which supports Pahl and

Spencer's (2004) thesis of a fusion between friends and family within people's "personal communities." Moreover, as in discussions of significant values within partnering relationships, emotional support and honesty are emphasized.

Although at the time of the interview, Cheryl's children did not know that she was about to transition, she too related to the importance of openly discussing the process of gender reassignment. As Cheryl's wife is the main carer of the children, Cheryl's situation with her children is more complex than that of Dan. While Cheryl's wife supports Cheryl's decision to transition and they remain friends, she is unhappy about telling the children. Cheryl says:

She (Cheryl's wife) doesn't want to tell them yet. I'd love to live my life as I do when I'm seeing them but I respect her wishes on that. In time when I start taking hormones and my body starts to change obviously things will change. To start with it won't be a problem 'cos it's such a slow process so we're probably taking a minimum of eighteen months and they'll be seven and nine. I want to talk to them about it, but for now the important thing is that I keep seeing them.

Although Cheryl is pragmatic here about not discussing her transition with her children at present, she indicates later in the interview that she experiences the situation as problematic. Cheryl continues:

I live at home as Cheryl and I see myself now as a cross-dresser from female to male because I cross-dress to go to work and to see the kids. Before, her clothes were in a suitcase in the loft, now his clothes are tucked away and I have to get them out to go to work. And it's the same with family and I think with kids honesty matters and is important but I'm not able to be honest. I feel resentful about that sometimes but it is going away because things are happening and the goal is getting nearer.

Here, open dialogue with children not only signifies an emphasis upon honesty within parenting relationships, but is also linked to the affirmation of Cheryl's identity as a woman.

A significant component effecting relationships between trans parents and their children relates back to partnering relationships. Findings from this research suggest that the relationship between a child's parents significantly impacts upon how the child accepts gender transformation. Partnership breakdown can thus problematize parenting relationships for trans people, especially if the child lives with the other parent. Similarly, Green's (1998) clinically based study reported that children of transsexual parents stated that they were affected more by the breakdown of their relationship with their transitioning parent following parental divorce, than with the issue of gender transition itself.

Amicability between ex-partners who are parents can thus be seen to significantly affect a child's emotional well being. Moreover, the parents interviewed in this research project were aware of the importance of maintaining an amicable relationship with their child's other parent. The maintenance of positive relationships between separated parents can thus be identified as a key objective within transgender practices of care in relation to parenting. This corresponds with the work of Smart and Neale (1999, 2003, cited in Williams, 2004), which finds that parents frequently

sustained their relationships following separation: "practical ethics which are important in these situations are based on attentiveness to others' needs, adaptability to new identities, and a spirit of reparation" (Williams, 2004: 45). Balancing self-identity with emotional care for children can be complex (Lawler, 2000), however, and the process of negotiation between the two is a significant theme in the narratives of trans parents.

Negotiating Transition with Children

A significant issue discussed in relation to helping children come to terms with gender transition concerns the linguistic shifts which accompany changes in gender identity. Rather than reversing the parenting nouns of "mum" or "dad," each of the parents I spoke to had suggested that their child call them by their new first name or a nickname, which was often a variation of their pre-transition name. Dan, for example, says:

> He doesn't call me dad, he calls me "Danny" and I think that made things a hell of a lot easier for him. And at the school he was at the headmaster talked to all the staff and they were instructed that from that moment they were to call me "Danny," nothing else, you know, never to say to my son "when's your mum coming?" or "when's your dad coming?" just "when's 'Danny' coming?" That really helped things as well. And it helped with the pronouns, but for a couple of months I heard the most convoluted conversations, you know, "ask Danny whether Danny wants a cup of tea" and it was quite interesting (laugh). But I think that really helped him. I think one of the main issues children have problems with is changing that. A few people in the

group (FtM network), when they've been talking about problems with children, I've said "don't try and get them to go from 'mummy' to 'daddy' try a nickname, even if it's not something you want to be known by, some androgynous nickname."

Similarly, Bernadette's stepchildren called her "Bernie." Considerations about how children would address their transitioning parent are thus reflexively situated in relation to enabling children to adapt to the changing gender status of parents.

A further theme within discussions of negotiating the process of transition with children relates to how children experience the changes in their parents' appearance once they begin to take hormones and/or have surgical procedures. Findings suggest that children of parents who transition from female-to-male may find the process easier to adapt to, as their parent was more able to present androgynously before transition than were MtF (male-to-female) parents. Dan, for example, says:

I always wore a shirt and a tie to work before anyway. That's what everybody else wore and that's what I wore and I've still got clothes now that I was wearing seven or eight years ago and that shows how male stroke androgynous they were. So my clothes hadn't changed. So it wasn't like one day I was taking him to school in make up and the next day I was in a shirt and tie.

Greater cultural acceptance of female androgyny compared to male femininity can thus be seen to impact upon the experiences of children to benefit the children of trans men.

Children's experiences of their parents' transition, however, are not only affected by the ways in which their parents negotiate the process. In the following quotation, Dan discusses how the understanding of the head teacher at his son's school smoothed the process for his son:

Obviously his peer group were going to be an issue at some point, but again the school dealt with that. It got to the point where some people, some of the boys, were starting to question why I was looking more masculine and the headmaster rang me up and said "I'm telling the boys tonight." We'd agreed it would happen at some point, and we don't know what he told them but they sent my son off on an errand and told the boys [. . .] All I know is that some of the parents rang me up the next day and said "my son has come home and told me what's happening and you've got our total support." We don't know what the headmaster said but he said something that really bound them together in a protective network and as far as I know my son has never had any difficulty.

Here Dan articulates the significance of the head teacher's role as a mediating agent. For parents of young children, the school environment and particularly the reaction of teachers, parents and other children, are raised as important factors that impact upon a child's adaptation to parental gender transition.

Corresponding with the narratives of partnering relationships, a central theme to arise from narratives of trans parenting relationships is the reflexive negotiation of the process of gender transition within the context of relationships with children. Thus, rather than representing an individualized process, decisions around the timing, disclosure and management of gender transition are considered and realized in relation to parenting concerns and responsibilities. Key values in negotiating the process of gender transition with children can be identified as trust, honesty and care.

Sandell's point in the early 1990s that: " . . . men and women have, for years, formed committed same-sex relationships, and had children, but what is relatively new is for men and women to self-identify as being part of a gay or lesbian family, and to have children with that identity" (Sandell, 1994: 2) is pertinent to the current state of play in relation to trans parenting. Thus historically, while many cross-dressing and cross-gender-identifying men and women would have been parents, self-identifying as a trans parent is a recent social development. Further, as social and legislative debates around lesbian and gay parenting have contributed to the growing public profile of lesbian and gay families (Sandell, 1994: 2), the Gender Recognition Bill[4] is drawing public attention to the existence of transgender families.

Shifts in gendered parenting roles problematize normative assumptions of the link between biology and parenting identity, which firmly situates motherhood with female biology and fatherhood with male. Castells argues that technological developments, such as surrogacy, sperm banks and in vitro fertilization, have led to increased reproductive possibilities and choices, representing "growing control over child bearing and, over the reproduction of the human species" (1997: 241). Developments in reproduction technology additionally present increased parenting possibilities for surgically reassigned trans people. Moreover, developments in reconstructive surgery and endocrinology further sever gender identity from biology. Castells' premise that technological transformations have effected a "whole new area of social experimentation" (1997: 241) can thus be expanded to take account of transgender practices of parenting in order to address the issues these practices raise for theories of social change.

Conclusion

The findings from this research suggest that studies of transgender practices of partnering and parenting enable a richer understanding of the dynamics of contemporary "life experiments" (Weeks et al., 2001). Notions of agency and choice run through the accounts of partnering to illustrate how complex decisions around gender transition are negotiated within the context of partnering relationships and family commitments. The meanings and experiences of sexual identity and sexual desire and practice can be seen to shift in relation to the performance of gender diversity. Boundaries of sexual intimacy and friendship are traversed as emotional support and care is emphasized within current partnering relationships, and in relationships with ex-partners. The impact of gender transition upon parenting relationships is reflexively explored, and the notions of openness and honesty are frequently stressed as important responsibilities within practices of parenting. Understandings and experiences of intimacy are thus fluidly situated, and a range of affective practices are constructed. Research findings thus show that practices of intimacy within transgender partnering and parenting relationships are amenable to complex shifts in gendered meaning and expression.

While these case studies articulate personal creativity and agency, I would like to situate them beyond an individualized context. I suggest that these stories talk not only about individual change over time, but that they speak also of socio-historical changes in the diversification of meanings and experiences of gender, and the impact of these shifts upon intimate lives and social frameworks. The incorporation of transgender practices of partnering and parenting into analyses of contemporary patterns of sociality thus sheds further light upon the ways in which intimate relationships are subject to ongoing contest, negotiation and innovation.

Notes

1. All the participants interviewed, however, were white and British. "Informal" discussions with one member of a support group for racially and ethnically diverse transgender people highlighted the specific issues faced by transgender people from minority ethnic communities, and the complexities between transgender, ethnicity and "race" represent a greatly under-researched area (Roen, 1996).

2. There are also complex questions to be asked here about the heterosexual eroticization of FtM bodies, which is, however, beyond the scope of this article.

3. Richard Green is a prominent psychiatrist at the Gender Identity Clinic (GIC) at Charing Cross Hospital. Green's first study in 1978 was based on interviews with 16 children of transsexual parents who were in attendance at Charing Cross GIC. His second study in 1998 focused upon 18 children of transsexual parents in the same setting.

4. The Gender Recognition Act (GRA) gives transsexual people legal recognition in their gender of choice. The Bill was passed by the House of Lords on 10 February 2004.

References

Beck, U. and E. Beck-Gersheim (1995) *The Normal Chaos of Love*. Cambridge: Polity Press.

Castells, M. (1997) *The Power of Identity*. Oxford: Blackwell.

Dunne, G. (1999) "A Passion for 'Sameness'?: Sexuality and Gender Accountability," in E. B. Silva and C. Smart (eds.) *The New Family?* London: Sage.

Fuss, D. (ed.) (1991) *Inside/Out: Lesbian Theories, Gay Theories*. New York: Routledge.

Gabb, J. (2001) "Desirous Subjects and Parental Identities: Constructing a Radical Discourse on (Lesbian) Family Sexuality," *Sexualities*, 4(3): 333–52.

Giddens, A. (1992) *The Transformation of Intimacy: Sexuality, Love and Eroticism in Modern Societies*. Cambridge: Polity Press.

Green, R. (1978) "Sexual Identity of 37 Children Raised by Homosexual or Transsexual Parents," *American Journal of Psychiatry* 135: 692–7.

Green, R. (1998) "Transsexuals' Children," *The International Journal of Transgenderism* 2(4), URL (consulted Nov. 2005): www.symposion.com/ijt/ijtc0601.htm

Hines, S. (2005) "'I am a Feminist but . . .': Transgender Men, Women and Feminism," in J. Reger (eds.) *Different Wavelengths: Studies of the Contemporary Women's Movement*. New York: Routledge.

Jackson, S. and S. Scott (eds.) (1996) *Feminism and Sexuality: A Reader*. Edinburgh: Edinburgh University Press.

Jamieson, L. (1999) *Intimacy: Personal Relationships in Modern Societies*. Cambridge: Polity Press.

Lawler, S. (2000). *Mothering the Self: Mothers, Daughters, Subjects*. London: Routledge.

MacCowan, L. (1992) "Re-collecting History, Renaming Lives: Femme Stigma and the Feminist Seventies and Eighties," in J. Nestle (ed.) *The Persistent Desire: A Femme–Butch Reader*, Boston, MA: Alyson Publications.

Pahl, R. and L. Spencer (2004) "Personal Communities: Not Simply Families of 'Fate' or 'Choice,'" *Current Sociology* 52(5): 199–221.

Platt, J. (1998) "What Can Case Studies Do?," in R. G. Burgess (ed.) *Studies in Qualitative Methodology: A Research Annual*, Vol. 1. London: JAI Press.

Plummer, K. (1995) *Telling Sexual Stories: Power, Change and Social Worlds*. London: Routledge.

Roen, K. (2001) "Transgender Theory and Embodiment: The Risk of Racial Marginalisation," *Journal of Gender Studies* 10(3): 253–63.

Roseneil, S. (2000) "Queer Frameworks and Queer Tendencies: Towards an Understanding of Postmodern Transformations of Sexuality," *Sociological Research Online* 5(3), URL (consulted Nov. 2005): www.socresonline.org.uk/5/3/roseneil.html

Roseneil, S. and S. Budgeon (2004) "Cultures of Intimacy and Care Beyond 'the Family': Personal Life and Social Change in the Early 21st Century," *Current Sociology* 52(2): 135–59.

Sandell, J. (1994) "The Cultural Necessity of Queer Families," *Bad Subjects* 12, URL (consulted Nov. 2005): http://eserver.org/bs/12/Sandell.html.

Stacey, J. (1996) *In the Name of the Family: Rethinking Family Families in the Post-modern Age*. Boston, MA: Beacon Press.

Weeks, J. (1995) *Invented Moralities: Sexual Values in an Age of Uncertainty*. Cambridge: Polity Press.

Weeks, J., B. Heaphy and C. Donovan (2001) *Same Sex Intimacies: Families of Choice and Life Experiments*. London: Routledge.

Weston, K. (1991) *Families We Choose: Lesbians, Gay Men and Kinship*. New York: Columbia University Press.

Williams, F. (2004) *Rethinking Families*. London: Calouste Gulbenkian Foundation.

30 Dana Berkowitz

Can a Gay Man Be a Housewife?
Gay Fathers Doing Gender, Family, and Parenting

Heteronormative assumptions about appropriate parents, gender norms, and child socialization continue to underpin the hegemonic view of family. Lesbian and gay families challenge these gender and heteronormative assumptions and expose the widening gap between the complex reality of contemporary families and the simplistic ideology that pervades modern family thought, scholarship, rhetoric, and policies. This paper advances theoretical understanding on how gay men discursively construct their procreative consciousness and fathering experiences. I maintain that attention to such discourse opens doors to new understandings of how societal surveillance fueled by heterosexism, homophobia, and constricting gender norms shapes gay men's fathering thoughts and experiences.

I draw upon my current research that explores the narratives of 22 gay fathers and 19 childless gay men. I detail how many of the men I spoke with relied upon dominant narratives of gender, kinship, biogenetics, and responsibility in the context of the interview setting. Participants described how they negotiate gender, sexuality, and real or imagined families within explicit gendered and heterosexist social boundaries; ultimately reifying certain discourses that I ex- pected them to subvert or at least transgress. I argue that because these men and their families are under extreme surveillance and public scrutiny, they are forced to draw upon the very discourses that many family scholars expect them to reject.

Background

I expand upon the procreative identity framework—a conceptual lens that was initially developed to explain how heterosexual men experience the procreative arena (Marsiglio & Hutchinson, 2002). The procreative identity framework is a useful conceptual lens to explore gay men's experiences in the reproductive realm because procreative consciousness is viewed as the cognitive and emotional awareness and expression of self as a person capable of creating and caring for life. Moreover, the framework treats this self-expression as a process-oriented phenomenon tied to situational contingencies, global sentiments, and romantic relationships. Although gay men's experiences are distinct in some ways, the basic conceptual lens is relevant to gay men because it accentuates how men's procreative consciousness is activated and evolves. Furthermore, the model's emphasis

Dana Berkowitz, "Can a Gay Man Be a Housewife? Gay Fathers Doing Gender, Family, and Parenting." Edited from a version first presented at the American Sociological Association Annual Meeting, August 2007. Reprinted by permission of the author.

on both individual-based and relationship-based modes for expressing procreative consciousness draws attention to how gay men, on their own and in conjunction with partners, learn to frame their view about becoming fathers.

While it is sensible to extend the procreative identity framework to the experiences of gay men, extending a model originally conceptualized for heterosexual men is complicated. I hesitate to take knowledge developed by and for heterosexual men and risk incorrectly extending this knowledge to the experience of gay men. Although gay men's desire for parenthood may be similar in some situations to heterosexuals' feelings, gay men's access to fatherhood and fathering experiences are constructed within a heterosexually defined realm embedded with ideological proscriptions. To address this consideration, I draw upon the theoretical contributions of feminist sociologist Dorothy Smith. Smith maintains that women's consciousness has been created by men occupying positions of power (1987, 1990). I borrow from and expand on this framework positing that gay men's procreative consciousness has been constructed within a world that has traditionally assumed heterosexuality and continues to privilege heterosexual parenting. Smith maintains that consciousness is not merely something going on in people's heads, rather it is produced by people and it is a social product (Smith, 1990). Thus, in order to more completely understand gay men's procreative consciousness and their possible fantasies of fathering, there is a necessity to link this consciousness with the institutions that create, maintain, challenge, and eventually change how gay men have historically imagined fatherhood and families. Smith's framework helps to anchor

gay men's personal thoughts and experiences about fatherhood within the political, historical, economic, and social process that shapes them. Smith's theoretical paradigm highlights how certain institutions and ruling relations, such as adoption and fertility agencies, and the institutionalization of both fatherhood and the gay subculture shape the processes by which gay men contemplate and experience fatherhood. For example, even though gay men's desire for parenthood and experiences of fathering may be similar in some situations to heterosexuals' feelings, gay men's access to adoption and assisted reproductive technologies is mediated by a bureaucratic apparatus that affects the conditions under which they can father (Lewis, 2006). This is especially important for this study because the majority of data were collected in Florida and New York. The former is currently one of the only states with explicit statutes prohibiting adoption by gay men and lesbians and in the latter state all use of surrogate mothers is illegal (Horowitz & Maruyama, 1995; Mallon, 2004; Weltman, 2005).

I also draw upon the concept of *doing fathering* to show how men engage in fathering actions, behaviors, and processes. This concept emerges from West and Zimmerman's construct of *doing gender* (1987). The metaphor of *doing gender* was one of the first to reconceptualize gender as not so much a set of traits residing with individuals, but as something people do in their social interactions. "A person's gender is not simply an aspect of what one is, but more fundamentally, it is something that one does, recurrently, in interaction with others" (West and Zimmerman, 1987: 126). By using this conceptual lens to frame my analysis, fathering and more broadly family are viewed as situated accomplishments of my participants, and when fathering and family are viewed as such, the focus of analysis moves from matters internal to the individual to interactional and eventually institutional arenas. Thus, one is not only a father but one does fathering, just as one does gender. The concept of accountability is of primary significance here because given that much of society still defines family as a heterosexual two-parent nuclear structure, the families in my study came to be held accountable for every action each member performed. Accountability is relevant to both those actions that conform and deviate from prevailing normative conceptions about family. I stress that while individuals are the ones who do fathering and family, the process of rendering something accountable is both interactional and institutional.

The concept of accountability becomes critical as I move into a theoretical discussion of how heterosexual domination influences how gay men discursively do fathering and family. Accountability is of primary importance in the specific context of gay and lesbian headed families. Gay fathers are consistently viewed with suspicion because of myths surrounding issues of pedophilia, a desire to "replicate their lifestyle" and a perceived lack of ability to properly socialize children and inscribe them with stereotypical gendered norms.

Gay men's thoughts about fatherhood and fathering experiences are complex and dynamic. Thus, each of these theoretical lenses is necessary to expand the procreative identity framework and disentangle the convoluted web of gay men's fathering talk.

Method

As a qualitative method, in-depth interviewing accentuates the subjective quality of different life experiences, the contextual nature of knowledge, the production of social meanings, and the interactive character of human action. I use this interviewing technique to study the process by which gay men express their procreative consciousness, father identities, and fathering experiences.

Recruitment

Analysis draws on audiotaped, in-depth interviews conducted with a sample of 19 childless gay men and 22 gay fathers who have created families through nonheterosexual means. The participants were recruited through a variety of methods in diverse locales from 2004–2006. In South and North Central Florida, I used both snowball sampling and posted fliers in areas frequented by members of the gay community such as gay community centers, shopping malls, eating and drinking establishments, hair salons, and gay activist organizations. The fliers for the recruitment of childless gay men were a broad call for participants who might be interested in discussing their thoughts about fatherhood, without screening them for whether they intended to have children. The fliers for gay fathers specified that we were searching for men who had become fathers through any means other than heterosexual intercourse.

Participants

The group of childless gay men differed substantially from those who chose to become fathers through nonheterosexual means. These differences should not be regarded as a substantive finding of my research, but an artifact of my recruitment strategies. The childless gay participants were more racially, ethnically, and economically diverse than the fathers. Three of the childless men were African American, 1 was

Chinese-American, 2 were Latino, and 13 were White. Three participants had not completed college, 5 were enrolled in college with the intentions of graduating, 7 had graduated from a four-year university, and 4 had an advanced graduate degree. Two participants were Jewish, 1 was Presbyterian, 3 were Christian, 4 were Catholic, 1 was Buddhist and Catholic and 8 reported to have no religious affiliation. Six participants were students and the remaining participants were employed in either the service sector or the professional sector. Annual income for these men ranged from under $15,000 to over $75,000 annually. Ages of the childless men ranged from 19–53 and the mean age was 31.

Consistent with other research on gay fathers (Johnson & Connor, 2002; Mallon, 2004), the gay fathers participating in this research were White and predominantly upper middle class. All but 2 of these men earned over $75,000 annually, the remaining 2 earned between $30,000–$60,000, and the majority of participants were employed in the professional sector. Similarly, all participants except 2 had completed college and 8 had an advanced graduate degree. Fathers' ages ranged from 33–55 with a mean age of 43.5. Nine participants were Jewish, 5 were Catholic, 4 were Christian, 2 were Unitarian, and 3 claimed to have no religious affiliation. Participants created their families in diverse ways, including various forms of adoption, traditional and gestational surrogacy arrangements, and co-parenting with a lesbian woman or women.

Interviews

Semi-structured interviews were conducted that lasted from 45–120 minutes. They took place in a variety of settings (e.g., participants' households or work offices, coffee shops, eating and drinking establishments, the researcher's office, and over the telephone). Although it was my intention to conduct all interviews individually, 6 men who were coupled and had young children opted to be interviewed together. The qualitative interviews were preceded by a brief sociodemographic background survey. Interviews were open-ended and designed to generate rich, detailed information. Participants were encouraged to discuss their thoughts, feelings, experiences, and personal narratives regarding their images and decisions about fatherhood. Interviews were designed to explore the men's emerging identity as a prospective or real father, including how their father identity emerged out of interactions with other children, friends, family members, birth mothers, agency coordinators, and romantic partners.

Analysis

The initial textual material was analyzed with grounded theory methodology for qualitative data analysis (Glaser & Strauss, 1967; Strauss & Corbin, 1998). As ideas, terms, moods, and so on surfaced in multiple interviews, they were coded and given tentative labels during the open phase of coding. Open coding is a process of comparing concepts found in the text for classification as examples of some phenomenon. As similarities in experience, patterns, and emergent themes appeared, categories of phenomena were labeled and entered into a code list. This process of open coding enabled me to create an analytic process for identifying key categories and their properties (Strauss & Corbin, 1998).

My final stage of selective coding allowed me to compare themes identified in this study to existing literature exploring fathering talk among both gay and heterosexual men. The themes derived from this work unveil the dynamic and complex process of how gay men discursively construct their procreative and father identities in a socially constructed world that privileges heterosexuality.

Findings

The remainder of this paper addresses how the men I spoke with drew upon dominant gender and familial discourses. First, I explore how men's descriptions of their procreative consciousness was framed within an essentialized context. Next, I move to a discussion of how men described their ideal fathering experiences and detail aspects related to the privileging of biological ties and the dominant two-parent nuclear family. Finally, I examine how participants narrated their thoughts about engendering their children and their experiences of gender accountability. In each and every phase of procreative and fathering talk, men drew upon a discourse associated with the hegemonic family and/or normative gender stereotypes.

An Essentialized Procreative Consciousness

Regardless of one's sexuality, parenthood has become a reflective process in contemporary Western society. "Paths to parenthood no longer appear natural, obligatory, or uniform, but are necessarily reflexive, uncertain, self-fashioning, plural, and politically embattled" (Stacey, 2006, p. 28). Children have moved from an economic asset to an economic responsibility and even a liability. Thus, "an emotional rather than economic calculus governs the pursuit of parenthood" (Stacey, 2006, p. 28). Openly identified gay men who seek fa-

therhood face these dimensions of postmodern parenting in an exaggerated way. Furthermore, it has been documented that the thought processes that gay men undergo to become fathers are quite different from those experienced by their heterosexual counterparts (Barret & Robinson, 2000; Bigner & Jacobsen, 1989; Mallon, 2004). Many of the men I spoke with were well aware of emerging legal and reproductive opportunities that made their once outlandish daydreams of becoming a father now a viable reality. Yet, they also were well aware of how structural and institutional constraints shaped their experiences in the procreative realm.

More interestingly however was how some men explained their fathering desires within the constraints of dominant gender discourse. Nick, a soft-spoken 26-year-old who moved from the Midwest to Miami Beach a year earlier eloquently discussed his burning desire to father as equivalent to a woman's natural drive to mother:

Because I was always gay and I did have some maternal instinct. Maybe at the time that women first, whenever, somewhere in adolescence, was when I first started thinking I want to have a child . . . the older I got the more I considered it the same way as finding Mr. Right . . . this very important thing that would complete me. The only thing that could [complete me].

Nick cited identifying as gay as being tantamount to having a maternal urge. Further, he recognized that as a human being, the only thing that would fully complete him was creating a family of his own. Ross, a childless single man, echoed Nick's sentiments regarding a desire to father. He asserted that fatherhood is "the greatest thing that somebody can do. I think it enriches your life . . . you can give back to someone your good experiences, so they can become a good person."

That men discussed their procreative fantasies in terms of having a "maternal instinct," "the greatest thing that somebody can do" and "needing something to complete me" clearly speaks to our contemporary pronatalist milieu. It also touches on the notion of generativity, or the nurturing quality in individuals whereby they seek to "create and guide younger generations" (Marsiglio, 1995, p. 84). While some refer to gay men choosing fatherhood as postmodern pioneers (Stacey, 2006), the yearning to procreate, father, nurture, and have someone depend on you is a particularly modern characteristic. What is unique about this desire is only that it is being articulated by gay men, a population who because of gender and heterosexist norms are not expected to have these yearnings. Clearly, because gay men are raised within a socially constructed society that stresses pronatalism and generativity, their procreative desires and discourses are not so different from their heterosexual counterparts.

However, when we listen to how gay men negotiate these modern desires for fatherhood with their gay identity, essential ideologies associated with gender and sexuality surface. For example, while Luke wanted children in his future, he maintained that:

Gay men were not meant to be that way, if it was meant to be that way then two people would have stood beside each other and had a baby. Obviously there is a reason that our bodies are built to procreate and for a woman to go through that process.

Luke described his procreative urges within the constraints of a heteronormative discourse. If we take Luke's statement and juxtapose it against those of Nick and Ross, it illuminates how gay men's reliance on dominant familial, heterosexual, and gender discourse underscores the need for a more inclusive way of talking about parenting. Furthermore, because we live in a society that conflates and confuses gender and sexuality, gay men's procreative fantasies are narrated within the constraining framework of Western conceptions of gender and sexuality. Yet while many of the men describe their procreative desires within a gendered and heteronormative context, there were a few exceptions. Not surprisingly, one of these exceptions surfaced in my conversation with Segal, a fellow sociologist who is a leading scholar on gender and sexuality. He mentioned that my study should critically examine how heterosexism "hinders and hurts gay men." This reliance upon dominant gender and familial discourse is a theme that surfaced more than I would have ever imagined and confirms Segal's statement of how heterosexism constrains gay men's narrative abilities.

Essentializing Biology

The formation of a father identity for some of the men is mediated by the anticipated or actual presence of biological ties. Childless participants diverged in whether they desired a child who was biologically related to them. Some men explained that they preferred a child who would have blood ties to them, whereas others talked about wanting to adopt their future child. Zach, a childless 33-year-old Chinese-American restaurant manager, confessed that the only way he would have a child was if that child was biologically related to him. He elaborated:

> I would love more than anything to have a child. My own as well. . . . If I am going to have a child, I want it to be a part of me . . . I want it to have some of my characteristics . . . I want to have a little piece of me . . . I think that if anything, that is really what drives all of it. I do want to have someone, a little piece of me out there doing a little something to contribute to the world.

Zach was one of the few childless men who was so explicit in his desire for a biological child. A handful of other childless men claimed that although a biological tie was preferred, adoption would be a second option. Taylor, also childless, explained, "adoption would just be the second option, like a fall back . . . I'd rather conceive a child with someone I know and trust . . . I guess I would rather have my own . . . but if that's not an option, adoption wouldn't change anything." Although Taylor and a few other men ideally preferred a biological relation between themselves and their child, as gay men and as prospective fathers, they realized their options were quite limited. Many other men, both childless and fathers, questioned their ability to feel the same level of affection for a child not biologically related to them as compared to a genetically related child. These statements illuminate how the men I spoke with still greatly valued biogenetic ties. Although I found a great deal of creative negotiation within these families, it is significant to recognize that such negotiations were regulated with the conventional privileging of biological relatedness at the forefront of these men's consciousness.

The Essential Family

The majority of childless men I spoke with perceived their futures as residing in an intimate partnership raising children. Noah articulated that, "I know that that's going to be the only way for me to have a kid, but I would like to, I would like to provide that child with more of a structured family than just a single parent." Walter echoed Noah's sentiments when he explained, "I'm not religious, but I think God made it so that two people have to create a child because it usually takes two people to parent a child." In an ideal family, most of these men saw themselves raising children in a (post)modern nuclear family: two men, two children, a pet, a suburban style house and a white picket fence. While gay men are marginalized from traditional family arrangements, my participants' narratives underscore that their ideal visions of family and fatherhood are forged within a dominant understanding of normative images of family. Moreover, men's visions of an ideal family were fashioned with the dominant mother as nurturer, father as provider familial ideology.

Noah fantasized his ideal parenting experience:

> I definitely see myself being like the quintessential little housewife, if a gay man can be a housewife. Like, I very much and like take on the maternal role in the family, and in a relationship, I'm very much like the little wife. And I'm always cooking and cleaning for them, and like taking care of them, and so I think it's, when I think of myself having kids, I very much think of myself being like the soccer mom . . . I think about . . . where we would live and our family and I'd have my

Volvo Sedan, my Sedan, my Volvo SUV with my SLK hardtop convertible, for when I want to have like mommy time, and be the soccer mom.

Noah's ideal fathering—or rather, mothering—visions take place within a 1950s glorified and somewhat postmodern conception of a *Leave It to Beaver*–esque family. The reliance by so many men on a dominant gender and family discourse points to a very uninclusive way of speaking about family. That Noah envisioned his parenting roles as a caretaker and nurturer and automatically equates these roles with taking on the role of a soccer mom speaks to the insidiousness of socially constructed gender norms within the family.

Gender Essentialism

A final theme that surfaced was how men spoke about negotiating the real or imagined gender of children. Many of the gay men's narratives underscored uncertainty with regards to how they envisioned coping with public bathroom issues, menstruation, bra-shopping, and the first dates of their future or present daughters. A vast majority of gay fathers painted a mental picture of a menstruating, bra-shopping, sexually active teenager and I heard constant concern from these men wondering if two dads could adequately deal with the "harsh" realities of a thirteen-year-old girl's pubescent phase. Rick and Art, fathers of a three-year-old boy spoke about how they fantasized about the challenges of having a little girl because, "We knew boy issues; we knew what to expect . . . we also thought girls were more difficult in terms of later on, with puberty and all that." Both Rick and Art questioned if two dads could ade-

quately deal with the realities of a 13-year-old girl's pubescent phase.

When envisioning raising a girl child, many men discussed the importance of securing a suitable role model for her, particularly during her pubescent phase. Noah explained:

> I like to think that like my mother or my partner's mother or my female friends would be there and that they would . . . like help her out and like if she's having like maybe, if I had a daughter and she's 12 years old, and she's got her period, and like I'd like to have help with that, but I understand where she would feel uncomfortable coming to me, so, I see that you know the presence of like other women or a mother or someone who'd be involved is beneficial.

When men envisioned taking up the tasks of raising a girl, preparation and planning become critical. Such planning always includes guaranteeing a suitable role model for their girl children to assist with milestones like menstruation.

If I were to follow a folk logic, it makes sense that two men would have anxiety about raising a girl child because in their minds, their own experiences would not easily parallel hers. However, some participants wondered how their gender and sexuality would interact to negatively affect their boy children's future socialization. Marc, the proud single father of a four-year-old girl explained, "If I have a boy, will I be as good as a role model? You know, dads take their sons to ball games and things like that, which I am just not into . . . if I had a boy, it might be somewhat difficult to do that 'macho' role model." Because Marc was never the stereotypical masculine athlete, he questioned whether he could participate with his imagined son in "normal" male-bonding activities. In most cases, it is taken for granted that someone can appropriately raise a child of the same gender, but in some cases, like Marc's own, gender atypical behavior is cited as a reason for not being a suitable role model for children of the same gender. Hence, the men's perceptions of their future children's gender socialization helped forge the men's child and fathering visions as well as their procreative and father identities. However, such considerations were clearly framed within rigid gender stereotypes.

Sanctions against gay men for doing gender incorrectly are rampant in heterosexist U.S. society. These sanctions are exacerbated in the case of gay parents, in that they have a unique type of surveillance surrounding both their own normative gendered behavior as well as their children's gendered actions and attitudes. Because the heterosexual nuclear family has become institutionalized as an "ideological code" (Smith, 1993), gay fathers are held accountable for the gendered outcomes of their children. Thus, the panoptic gaze of the heterosexual eye serves as a surveillance mechanism that commands these fathers to engage in self-monitoring their children's gendered actions, to become per Foucault (1977) "docile bodies" inscribed with normative gender standards.

This becomes more lucid when we explore how men spoke about *how* they actually did fathering. Lawrence is a gay father with two teenage sons who never doubted his own ability to instill his teenage boys with "proper" masculine ideals. Nevertheless, he recalled a scenario when an outsider who happened to be in close proximity to him and his son scrutinized his fathering skills:

> I remember once Issac [older son] was crying, he was like 3-years-old, and he hurt himself and he was crying, and there was this painter in the house, and the painter kept saying, "be a man, be a man." And my instinct is to hug him and wait until he stopped crying, and let him sit there and calm down, you know. But this man's thing was "be a man" which is I think what many people would say. . . . So, I just took him away, and I didn't say any more.

Gender scholars have argued that normative definitions such as No Sissy Stuff, The Big Wheel, The Sturdy Oak, and Give 'em Hell give men a blueprint for how to live their lives (Brannon, as cited in Connell, 1995 and Kimmel, 1994). As an adult gay man reared with these gendered blueprints, Lawrence was acutely aware of the rigid definitions of masculinity in contemporary society. As such, he was keenly attentive to the pressures of raising a man in a socially constructed world that defines masculinity in such strict terms. In contemporary society, raising a boy to be a "proper" and "suitable" man is simultaneous with preparing him to fit into the historically and socially constructed version of hegemonic masculinity that is culturally dominant (Connell, 1995, 2000).

Lawrence also elaborated on another time when an outsider commented on his son's masculine development. Many years prior to the interview, Lawrence was with his two young sons at a local playground. He clearly remembered another father approaching his younger son, who had recently been wounded and was wailing at the pain. The man exclaimed, "Oh stop crying, you're acting like a girl" to the young boy. Although Lawrence was tempted to retort "What is wrong with being a girl?" he quickly stopped himself from succumbing to his immediate response and simply picked up his boy and walked away. Lawrence explained that he was uncomfortable with having another adult man fill his son's head with stereotypical masculine ideals. At the same time, Lawrence clearly did not want to get in a verbal argument in a public playground about the unfairness of the expectation that boys should not display emotion. Furthermore, Lawrence was in a paradoxical dilemma: he should not want his son to have to act in accordance with hegemonic ideals of masculinity, yet he understood that in order to survive as a man in contemporary society, one needs to adapt to certain normative gender standards.

Discussion

This paper details how gay men discursively construct their procreative and father identities within the constrictions of a gendered and heteronormative discourse. My analysis underscores the needs to move beyond the social and structural constraints in attaining fatherhood to distinguish what type of father identities and families are produced in these distinct settings. Expanding the procreative identity framework developed for heterosexual men with Smith's feminist sociology, West and Zimmerman's (1987) concept of accountability and a Foucaultian power/knowledge (1977) framework brings us closer to grasping the insidious effects of heterosexual surveillance on gay and lesbian parents.

Whereas the closet as a strategy of accommodating to heterosexual domination is be-coming less salient, this does not necessarily denote that heterosexual domination is a remnant of the past. The discourses of my participants demonstrate that whether it is the 1970s, 80s, 90s or today, gay men are still growing up in a world organized by heterosexuality. Although many individuals today can choose to live beyond the closet, they must still reside in a world where most institutions maintain heterosexual domination. My conversations with these men show how heterosexual dominance is deeply rooted in the institutions and culture of American society and must be understood as not simply a product of laws or individual prejudice, but institutionalized pervasive dominance (Seidman, 2004).

The insights I generate about gay men and their fathering talk should be viewed in context and their limitations noted. Meanwhile, because the process of becoming a gay father through nonheterosexual means is often financially costly, and because of my recruitment strategies, the fathers who participated in my study were primarily white and in the professional class. Regrettably, I am unable to speak to how minority men and gay men of more limited financial means discursively construct their procreative and father identities. That is an area for further research.

Literature Cited

Barret, R. L., & Robinson, B. E. (2000). *Gay Fathers*. San Francisco: Jossey-Bass.

Bigner, J. J., & Jacobsen, R. B. (1989). The value of children to gay and heterosexual fathers. *Journal of Homosexuality, 18*:12, 163–172.

Connell, R. W. (1995). *Masculinities*. Berkeley: University of California Press.

Foucault, M. (1977). *Power/Knowledge: Selected interviews and other writings, 1972–1977*. New York: Pantheon.

Glaser, B. G., & Strauss, A. L. (1967). *The discovery of grounded theory: Strategies for qualitative research.* Hawthorne, NY: Aldine de Gruyter.

Horowitz, R. M., & Maruyama, H. (1995). *Legal issues in gay and lesbian adoption: Proceedings from the Fourth Annual Pierce-Warwick Adoption Symposium.* Washington, DC: Child Welfare League of America.

Johnson, S. M., & Connor, E. M. (2002). *The gay baby boom: The psychology of gay parenthood.* New York: New York University Press.

Kimmel, M. (1994). Masculinity as homophobia: Fear, shame, and silence in the construction of gender identity. In Harry Brod and Michael Kaufman (Eds.), *Theorizing masculinities* (pp. 119–141). Thousand Oaks, CA: Sage.

Lewin, E. (2006). Family values: Gay men and adoption in America. In K. Wegar (Ed.) *Adoptive families in a diverse society* (pp. 129–145). New Brunswick, NJ: Rutgers University Press.

Mallon, G. P. (2004). *Gay men choosing parenthood.* New York: Columbia University Press.

Marsiglio, W. (1995). *Procreative man.* New York: New York University Press.

Marsiglio, W., & Hutchinson, S. (2002). *Sex, men, and babies: Stories of awareness and responsibility.* New York: New York University Press.

Seidman, S. (2004). *Beyond the closet: The transformation of gay and lesbian life.* New York: Routledge.

Smith, D. (1987). *The everyday world as problematic: A feminist sociology.* Toronto: University of Toronto Press.

Smith, D. (1990). Conceptual practices of power: Toward a feminist sociology of knowledge. Boston: Northeastern University Press.

Stacey, J. (2006). Gay parenthood and the decline of paternity as we knew it. *Sexualities, 9,* 27–55.

Strauss, A., & Corbin, J. (1998). *Basics of qualitative research: Techniques and procedures for developing grounded theory* (2nd ed.). Newbury Park, CA: Sage.

Weltman, J. J. (2004, August 26). Surrogacy in New York. *Resolve of New York.* Retrieved September 1, 2005, from http://www.surrogacy.com/Articles/news_view.asp?ID=128.

West, C., and Zimmerman, D. (1987). Doing gender. *Gender & Society, 1,* 2: 125–151.

31 Shirley A. Hill

Teaching and Doing Gender in African American Families

Family processes and structures are now widely recognized as pivotal in the construction and the maintenance of gender ideologies and roles. Marriage itself, noted Risman (1998), is a linchpin of gender inequality, as it usually assigns rights and responsibilities on the basis of sex. Children learn gendered behaviors by observing marital roles and through social interactions and gender-typing in families (Bem, 1983; Block, 1983; Deutsch & Saxon, 1998; Ex & Janssens, 1998; Leaper, Leve, Strasser, & Schwartz, 1995; Leve & Fagot, 1997; Slavkin & Stright, 2000; Wright & Young, 1998), and these behaviors are perpetuated by social structures and interactions in the broader society (Risman, 1998; West & Zimmerman, 1987). As West and Zimmerman (1987) explained, gender is both a cultural construct and a feature of the social structure, perpetuated because we are continually "doing gender." In this paper, I use qualitative data to offer some preliminary findings on how gender "gets done" in African American families. Assuming that both race and social class affect parental notions about gender equality, I examine what parents teach their children about gender and how gender shapes the distribution of work in their own families.

Gender is a vital component of family organization and child development, yet it has rarely been the explicit focus of research on African American families. In general, the gender discussion concerns the extent to which Black people embrace the traditional gender norms[1] of American society, use them to organize family responsibilities, and/or teach them to their children. Most Black scholars have contended that, at least historically, African Americans were not expected or even allowed to conform to the gender norms of White Americans (Billingsley, 1992; P. H. Collins, 1990; Dill, 1979, 1988). Slavery forced Black women to devote most of their energies to work rather than to family life (Giddings, 1984; Jones, 1985) and essentially deprived Black men of their roles as breadwinners, protectors, and heads of the family. Afrocentric scholars have agreed that gender role distinctions among Blacks have been negated to some extent, but explained it as originating from the African cultural heritage, where the low status of women was elevated by their economic roles and the existence of female-centered kin networks (Asante, 1987; Burgess, 1994; Caldwell, 1996; Nobles, 1985; Scanzoni, 1977). In-

Shirley A. Hill, "Teaching and Doing Gender in African American Families," *Sex Roles* 47, nos. 11/12 (December 2002): 493–506. Copyright © 2002 Springer Science + Business Media. With kind permission from Springer Science + Business Media.

Earlier versions of this paper were presented at the Sociologists for Women in Society meeting in February 1999 and at the Association for Black Sociologists meeting in August 1999.

deed, the strongest argument of Black divergence from rigid gender roles is found in analysis of the roles of African American women, whom scholars have argued are taught to be strong and independent (P. H. Collins, 1987), to prepare for careers rather than to rely on marriage for economic security (Higginbotham, 1981; Higginbotham & Weber, 1992), and are often given priority when parents decide which child to send to college (Blau, 1981). There is less evidence, however, that African American sons are socialized into accepting gender role flexibility and/or nontraditional gender roles; to the contrary, many scholars have implied that the difficulties faced by young Black men are a product of their inability, because of structural obstacles such as low wages and unemployment, to assume traditional masculine roles in their families (cf. Blake & Darling, 1994; Gibbs, 1988; Hunter & Davis, 1992; W. J. Wilson, 1997).

The Black feminist and/or Afrocentric contention of gender equality among African Americans is also challenged by survey research. For example, some researchers have found that Black people have more traditional and/or sexist views than do Whites (Binion, 1990; Smith & Seltzer, 1992), and Black women, even those who are employed, have not achieved gender equality in the domestic arena (Hossain & Roopnarine, 1993; M. N. Wilson, Tolson, Hinton, & Kierman, 1990). Only a few scholars have examined gender socialization in African American families, and they also reported contradictory findings: Some have claimed that gender plays only a minimal role in the child socialization practices of Black parents (Lewis, 1975; Peters, 1997; Scott, 1993), yet others, such as Black cultural theorist hooks (1992), have

refuted that claim. Sharing her own personal experience, hooks made it clear that traditional gender norms were expected in her family:

> As young children, we were brother and sister, comrades, in it together. As adolescents, he was forced to become a boy and I was forced to become a girl. In our southern black Baptist patriarchal home, being a boy meant learning to be tough, to mask one's feelings, to stand one's ground and fight—being a girl meant learning to obey, to be quiet, to clean, to recognize that you had no ground to stand on. I was tough, he was not. I was strong willed, he was easygoing. We were both a disappointment. (1992, p. 87)

Gender is clearly implicated in most of the issues faced by African American parents and their children, yet its significance is often overshadowed by studies that focus exclusively on the impacts of racism and poverty. Additional factors that obscure a better understanding of gender are relying more on autobiographical/experiential data than on systematic research; focusing on the experiences of poor, single mothers; ignoring the growing class diversity among Blacks; and omitting the experiences of men from the study of gender. In this study, which focuses on the gender socialization of African American children in their families, I address some of these shortcomings. Guided by multiracial feminism, a perspective that sees gender as a social and cultural construct with norms and expectations that are shaped and defined in racial and class context (Brewer, 1993; P. H. Collins, 1998; Hill & Sprague, 1999; King, 1988), I analyze interview data from a class-diverse sample of 35

African American mothers and fathers to learn what they are teaching their children about gender and how they organize gender in their own families.

Gender in African American Families

Gender role socialization assumes that "individuals observe, imitate, and eventually internalize the specific attitudes and behaviors that the culture defines as gender appropriate by using other males and females as role models" (Ickes, 1993, p. 79). Although gender is defined and reproduced in a variety of institutions, the traditional gender roles approach has emphasized the important role of families in this process; indeed, some have argued that the family is the most important setting for the construction and perpetuation of gender (Crouter, McHale, & Bartko, 1993; West & Zimmerman, 1987). Gender-typing typically begins at the moment of birth, and by age 4 or 5, most children have developed gender stereotypic attitudes and beliefs (Bem, 1983; Bigler, 1997; Blakemore, 1998). The traditional pattern of gender role socialization, as summarized in a review essay by Block (1983), shows that parents want their sons to be "independent, self-reliant, highly educated, ambitious, hard-working, career-oriented, intelligent, and strong-willed" and their daughters to be "kind, unselfish, attractive, loving, well-mannered, and to have a good marriage and to be a good parent" (p. 1341). These gender norms have been criticized by feminists as privileging boys and disadvantaging girls; however, the extent to which they are embraced and/or taught in African American families is an issue of some debate.

Gender is socially constructed, and multiracial feminists argue that race and social class are key factors in how gender gets defined and enacted. Black feminists, according to Brewer (1993), have been central in theorizing the race–class–gender dynamic and using it to describe how the prescribed gender roles for Black and White women have differed. Like other women, African American women have had a secondary and disadvantaged status in society based on gender; however, race and class have interacted to produce distinctly different roles and stereotypes for Black women (Baca Zinn & Dill, 1996; P. H. Collins, 1990; King, 1988). For example, White women were portrayed as innately domestic, submissive, and dependent, whereas Black women endured relentless paid and unpaid labor, and were often seen as unusually strong (Jones, 1985; King, 1988). Their economic roles undermined the establishment of patriarchal families (Dill, 1988), negated the notion of femininity among Black women, and broadened their concept of womanhood (Giddings, 1984). But do these historic experiences still inform gender practices in Black families today? And how have growing class diversity and social mobility among African Americans affected their gender views and practices?

Research on the gender role training of Black children is sparse, and offers contradictory findings. Most scholars have focused on the gender socialization experiences of African American girls, arguing that they are socialized to see themselves as strong and self-reliant. P. H. Collins (1990) and Higginbotham and Weber (1992), for example, pointed out that girls are taught to expect to work, get an education, and carry responsibilities for their families and communities. Scott (1993) echoed a similar theme, contending that Black girls "are socialized to be at once independent and assertive as well as familistic and nurturant . . .

to be sexually assertive . . . to be as authoritative, individualistic, and confident as African American sons are, and as economically self-sufficient and personally autonomous as sons are" (p. 73). This concurs with an early paper in which Lewis (1975) argued that the gender socialization of children in Black families was minimal, a position more recently reiterated by Peters (1997), who found that age and competency, rather than biological sex, shape the behavioral expectations of Black parents. An observational study of preadolescent children by Reid and Trotter (1993) supported this finding: Black children exhibited fewer gender stereotypical behaviors than did White children.

Studies used to support the hypothesis of a minimal influence of gender in the socializing of Black children typically fail to consider social class diversity among Blacks or the importance of other factors that shape gender socialization, such as religion and family structure. Class diversity has increased sharply among African Americans since the 1960s. For example, S. M. Collins (1997) pointed out that the proportion of Blacks in white-collar jobs increased by 80% between 1960 and 1970 and by another 44% in the following decade. Although many Blacks are moving into professional/managerial jobs, however, others are experiencing greater poverty and hardship due to the loss of industrial jobs, continuing racial segregation, and inner-city decline (S. M. Collins, 1997; Hurst, 2001; W. J. Wilson, 1997). Thus, it is increasingly difficult to view Blacks as a monolithic group simply on the basis of their racial status; moreover, emerging research shows that this growing diversity influences attitudes about gender in child rearing (Hill & Sprague, 1999). In the current study, a preliminary investigation into gender socialization in African American families, I examine what parents are teaching their children about gender and how they are organizing gender in their own homes.

A Multiracial Feminist Perspective on Gender Socialization

This study was guided by the premises of multiracial feminism,[2] a perspective that builds on the feminist assertion that gender is a social construct that has typically prized men and masculinity and devalued women and femininity (cf. Lorber, 1994). Multiracial feminism provides further evidence of the socially constructed nature of gender by showing that race and social class are key factors in defining gender, as evident from the historically divergent gender roles and stereotypes of Black and White women (P. H. Collins, 1990; Dill, 1979; Giddings, 1984). King (1988), an early proponent of the perspective, argued that African American women experienced "multiple jeopardies" based on their gender, race, and class position. Others have noted that race, class, and gender are interlocking systems of oppression that form a matrix of domination (P. H. Collins, 1990), and that the three operate simultaneously in a way that is irreducible to individual attributes (Andersen & Collins, 1998; Baca Zinn & Dill, 1996). The multiracial feminist perspective encompasses the interaction between social structure and human agency, and also notes that the way race inequality is played out depends on one's position in the class structure. Although the perspective at least tacitly recognizes that social class is not always a "jeopardy," little work has been done to explore how class advantage shapes gender ideologies.

The current research builds on multiracial feminism by focusing on the growing class diversity of African Americans. In addition, although the perspective has often been validated by examining the origins of gender divergent roles in the historic experiences of Black women, I look more at contemporary patterns of gender by focusing on the socialization of children and the organization of gender in families. I begin with the premise that racial status has been a unifying experience for African Americans, historically overriding both class and gender in determining their place in American society. Like gender, race is a social construct, and being Black has been defined in terms of inferiority and undeservingness. Racism and segregation have impeded the educational and employment opportunities for African Americans, have contributed heavily to their high rates of poverty and low-class position, and have been key factors in Blacks' inability to conform to the marital and gender norms of White Americans. That Black parents acknowledge and actively respond to the structural barriers of race is evident in research showing that the majority of African American parents engage in racial socialization, an attempt to prepare their children for the realities of being Black in America (Billingsley, 1992). Racial and gender socialization intersect, as both are social processes enacted simultaneously. Just as Black boys learn a racialized form of masculinity consistent with their social class position (Hill & Zimmerman, 1995), Black girls learn racialized gender roles that often emphasize a combination of traditional gender-typed values along with teaching the value of economic self-reliance, community activism, and assertiveness.

The impact of class on these ideologies is less clear, and is thus the focus of this study.

Method

The objective of this study is to understand the gender ideologies and practices that shape African American parents' socialization of their children. More specifically, I sought to examine whether parents professed gender equality as an explicit norm in the socialization of children, how class shaped their gender views, and whether the gender context in which children were being reared supported the norms expressed by their parents. The study includes indepth interviews with a nonrandom sample of 35 African American parents, 25 mothers and 10 fathers, all of whom were actively involved in raising their children. The interviews were semistructured with open-ended questions. They were conducted in the homes ($N = 32$) or workplaces ($N = 3$) of the respondents and were audiotaped and transcribed verbatim. The interviews were the qualitative component of a broader study that surveyed African American parents with elementary-school-age children in a large, urban, Midwestern city. Students took the surveys home with a request that parents complete and return them to the school. A few surveys included a request for a personal interview to discuss child-rearing issues further, and interviews were conducted with those parents who volunteered. Nearly all parents had multiple children but answered the questions mostly by focusing on a specific "target" child, usually the one who brought the survey home from school.

Two married couples were interviewed jointly, and 31 parents were interviewed individually. Parents ranged in age from 21 to 52 years, with an average age of 36 (see Table 31.1). Most of the parents were married (63%, or 22 of the 35), and most expressed a relatively high level of religiosity. A majority (21) had at least some college, including 12 with a 4-year college degree or more, and most had household incomes above $15,000. For the purpose of exploring social class, I divided the parents into two groups, those who were "more educated" (e.g., had at least some college) and those who were "less educated" (e.g., had a high school degree or less). Education is a vital (although imperfect) measure of social class; indeed, it is included in the two major measures of social class[3] in sociology, whereas income is included in neither. Moreover, Kerbo (2000) argued that education has become more important to social class than occupation, achievement, or ascription. Education is an especially relevant indicator of social class in the current study because, although income and education correlate to a large extent (see Table 31.1), income for these respondents is largely affected by family structure; for example, "less education," dual-income, married couples have higher family incomes than do "more educated" single mothers.

Finally, I selected an ethnographic/qualitative approach on the basis of interview data to gain a fuller understanding of the parents' gender socialization ideologies and their explanations of their actual behaviors. Qualitative and/or ethnographic research has been widely used to study racial minority populations (see, for example, Burton, 1990; Jarrett, 1994), and it often uncovers data difficult to capture in survey/quantitative studies. A grounded theory approach was used in the collection and analysis of

TABLE 31.1 Characteristics of Participants (N = 35)

	N	%
Parents		
Mothers	25	71
Fathers	10	29
Ages of parents (range = 21–52)		
21–34 years old	12	34
35–44 years old	21	60
45 years old and over	2	6
Marital status		
Married	22	63
Single, never married	7	20
Divorced/separated/widowed	6	17
Education		
High school or less	14	40
Some college	9	26
4-year degree or more	12	34
Family income		
Less than $15,000	9	26
$15,001–30,000	12	34
$30,001–50,000	7	20
More than $50,000	7	20
Religiosity		
How important is religion in your life?		
Very important	21	60
Somewhat important	10	29
Not very important at all	4	11
Income of less educated parents (N = 14)		
Les than $15,000	9	64
$15,000–30,000	3	22
$30,001–50,000	1	7
More than $50,000	1	7
Income of more educated parents (N = 21)		
Less than $15,000	—	—
$15,000–30,000	9	42
$30,001–50,000	6	29
More than $50,000	6	29

Less educated parents = high school degree or less; more educated parents = at least some college.

these data (Glaser & Straus, 1967; Strauss & Corbin, 1990; Tesch, 1990). This approach is based on inductive analysis, with no preconceived categories or hypotheses. Data analysis consists of carefully reading/ rereading interviews, exploring and coding responses, and allowing new themes, issues, and questions to emerge during the process.

Results

Teaching Gender: Parental Socialization of Children

I began my interviews by asking parents whether they thought there should be differences in the ways girls and boys are raised. Then, parents were asked to evaluate their own child-rearing practices in terms of whether the sex of the "target" child was influencing how the child was being raised. The answers to these questions were analyzed in terms of what parents believe and are teaching about gender. My analysis of the interview data revealed widespread verbal support for gender equality in child socialization among these parents, regardless of the sex of the parent, the sex of the child, or the social class of the parent. One divorced mother, for example, strongly emphasized the importance of teaching her 9-year-old son egalitarian marital roles and participation in domestic work, which she pointed out was similar to what she had been taught:

> I will definitely teach my son that men and women are equal; he is not the head of anybody. His wife will always have input and say-so in whatever is going on in their lives. And he needs to know that . . . when we were growing up, boys washed dishes, boys cooked; girls washed dishes, girls cooked. My mother taught us pretty

equally to do everything, just in case you were on your own you wouldn't have to depend on somebody.

Although parents overall favored gender equality in raising their children, social class, as measured by education, was a key factor in enhancing that support. Parents who had at least some college education ($N = 21$) were most adamant in articulating their support for instilling norms of gender equality in their children. One college-educated mother of two sons said,

> No gender roles for me—my husband says I traumatized the kids by talking so much about what they're going to do when they get older . . . we treat all able bodies the same: work is work, and anybody can do it. I plan to have him help with anything that needs to be done. I wouldn't care if he did feminine things, like take dancing. He wanted to take dancing lessons a long time ago, and he loves to brush and fix hair, but lately he's turned toward male stuff, playing ball. But I tell him I'll love him regardless of what he does; be happy with his life, [and] I won't have a problem with it.

Studies have mostly focused on whether African American girls are taught traditional gender roles, but these data show that educated parents of sons also support egalitarian gender roles, including teaching sons gender equality in the home. I asked a married, employed mother of two daughters and a son whether she ever found herself having different expectations of her children on the basis of their sex. She replied that gender played at best a small role in her child socialization practices, and emphasized the importance of teaching both girls and boys independence. Describing her expectations for her 12-year-old son, she noted,

> I have the same expectations of him as I do from my daughters . . . I tell my daughters that they should be able to take care of themselves, and he should be able to take care of himself, whether he's married or not. He should know how to wash his clothes, keep his house, take care of his books—he should be able to be independent, just like the girls should . . . we talk about this all the time, and when I forget, my girls remind me!

Fathers were equally supportive of gender equality, especially in wanting their daughters to get an education and have a career outside of the home. One 42-year-old respondent, a schoolteacher and the father of three children, including an adolescent daughter, said,

> I'm teaching my daughter to have a career. If she then chooses to go back in the home, a decision between her and her future spouse, then that's fine . . . my daughter wanted to be a doctor . . . if my daughter wants to be a doctor, we're going to find the money to pay for it.

Nearly all parents had high educational expectations for their children, and the sex of the child did not influence these aspirations. Although their sons often aspired to become professional athletes, parents tried to steer their sons away from those aspirations. As one mother said of her 9-year-old son,

> He wants to play basketball, but we try to stress right now that he's going to Harvard, and he's going to be a doctor. . . . It's a form of brainwashing, but they need that. And I

had a brother who went to Harvard and became a doctor, so he has a good role model.

As theorized by multiracial feminism, analyses of these data did reveal some class-based differences in support for gender equality, despite the tendency for all parents to want both sons and daughters to succeed academically and occupationally. For example, I noted that some parents described as middle-class on the basis of their education were a bit more hesitant in their support for complete gender equality. Although they had high expectations for their sons and daughters alike, a careful analysis of their interviews revealed some ambivalence in their support for gender equality. For example, one 35-year-old college-educated mother, asked what she expected of her 11-year-old daughter, emphasized that she was teaching her to be a "warrior," carrying on "the struggle [for racial justice] by fighting everyday of her life for the respect of Black people," and her own personal respect. Although this reflects a strong and even "nontraditional" image of womanhood, this mother also emphasized the value of more traditionally feminine characteristics, such as being "ladylike":

> I tell her that she has to carry herself well, and she can't go around being loud and screaming and yelling because that is one thing she likes to do. I tell her she has to sit properly and is expected to act like a lady by carrying herself well—when you go somewhere, you have to sit properly . . . so I speak to that a lot, that she's a girl and these are the kinds of things girls should do, like being ladylike . . .

A "warrior" and a "lady"? The view of a woman as a warrior certainly contradicted the feminine-typed attributes traditionally instilled in daughters (cf. Block, 1983; Ireson & Gill, 1988), and it seemed quite inconsistent with being a "lady." This contradiction led me to explore why some educated parents were more tentative in their support for gender equality, or at least seemed to have a narrower view of what it entailed.

To explain these differences in parents' strength of support for gender equality, I analyzed the background information on parents, especially their discussion of their own growing-up experiences. This analysis revealed that first-generation, middle-class parents[4] (i.e., educated parents who came from poor and/or disadvantaged families) were usually also more ambivalent in their support for gender equality than were others. I argue that these parents held a transitional position in the middle class and are likely to see embracing traditional gender norms as consistent with their new status. This observation is supported by a growing literature showing that Blacks have historically sought acceptance, middle-class standing, and "respectability" by conforming to the gender and marital norms of the dominant society (Higginbotham, 1993). Moreover, general class analysis literature documents the status anxiety the upwardly mobile experience as they either abandon their previous status for a middle-class standing or strive to find a comfortable niche between the two (cf. Gardner, 1993). Given the stigma of race and the historical focus on Black families as poor, female-headed, and pathological, African Americans who have recently achieved success are likely to want to distance themselves from stereotypical racial images (cf. Kaplan, 1997). Within this context, I read the ambivalence and/or contradictory support for gender equality as stemming from wanting their children to embrace the norms they view as consistent with middle-class "respectability," without sacrificing the cultural tradition of strength and activism as characteristic of Black woman. In some cases, these newly middle-class parents stress traditional gender roles in the home and equality in the workplace. The mother quoted previously, asked if she would teach her adolescent daughter that men and women should have equal rights and equal responsibilities, was quite equivocal:

> I will in one sense, but not in another. In terms of the family, I'm teaching her that a man is supposed to take care of her . . . but in the workplace, I'm teaching her that they are equal.

Support for gender equality in the workplace and tradition at home also shows how racial and gender socialization messages intersect, for example, the articulation of racialized gender norms that support Black girls as "warriors" for the cause of racial justice while teaching them that "a man is supposed to take care" of them at home. Despite differences in their levels of support for gender equality, the parents in this study, especially the mothers, were united in a racial ideology that emphasized the need for daughters to be successful in the labor market. For example, parents assumed that their children would face racial barriers to success, and they articulated a vision of Black women as striving and succeeding despite these obstacles. They rejected the notion that African American women have higher levels of education and placement in professional occupations simply because they are "less threatening" than Black men and thus have more opportunities. Mothers emphasized

that the success of Black women was a result of their own effort and hard work. As
one widowed mother said,

> [Black women] are just more go-getters
> than Black men are—I can't think of the
> right word—but she'd be more of a driving
> force to succeed in what she wants to do,
> because Black women overall are like that
> compared to Black men.

Another mother emphasized that Black
women succeeded despite facing even more
barriers than did Black men, as women were
often responsible for jobs and children.

> I hear that Black women are able to do
> more, move better through the work force
> and things like that. I *hear* that, but I don't
> *see* that, you know? . . . "if you're Black, get
> back," and it almost doesn't matter if
> you're a woman or a man . . . Black people
> just have it rough. Okay, I'm going to be
> biased here: women might have it a bit
> rougher because a lot of times we have the
> mother role, and we can't step out of that,
> and men can.

Black women define themselves as strong
and, as this mother did, explain the difficult relationship between men and women
in terms of men's unwillingness to accept
women's strength:

> Well, if a person cannot handle your
> strength, that means [he's] insecure. And
> it's sad to say, but we do have a lot of inse-
> cure Black males. I don't want my daughter
> to limit herself so that this man will be nice
> to her. . . . And I don't want my son to go
> and treat a woman badly because she's sure
> of herself, instead of checking out himself
> to see what he's all about. I think Black fe-

male strength could be a reason why there's
such a problem, but it's because of [men's]
insecurities.

Whatever their views of gender roles, the
historic racial experiences of African American women continue to unify them in
their views of their own strength and capa-
bilities. Thus, parents offer daughters a
racialized gender socialization message that
often seems contradictory. For example,
one first-generation, middle-class, single
mother emphasized teaching her 13-year-
old daughter assertiveness, yet her racial socialization message reflects a concern that
her daughter learn to deal with the realities
of White power and privilege:

> I tell her that she has to learn . . . that
> White people are going to be here, wher-
> ever she goes, and they're *always* going to
> tell her what to do. No matter what, there
> is always going to be some White person
> telling you what to do, and 9 times out of
> 10 you're going to have to do it, and do it
> with the right attitude.

In her effort to prepare her daughter for
racism and help her to manage it, she
stresses the need for submissiveness to and
respect for White authority as necessary for
success. Moreover, such conformity seems
consistent with the values of the newly
middle class, who are aware of the negative
stereotypes that are associated with lower-
income African Americans (cf. Ingrassia,
1993). Evidence of this is implied in the
distinction that one first-generation, middle-
class mother made between being middle
class and lower class. For her, class position was less about education or income
than it was about behaving in a "respectable" way:

I guess I'm tying to instill—quote/unquote—a lot of middle-class values in her. And to me that means you don't steal, don't destroy other people's property, you work for what you have, and you don't expect something for nothing. . . . Those are the kinds of things I consider middle-class values.

Recent class mobility created subtle but important differences among similarly educated parents in their support for gender equality, and being in this "transitional" class also coincided with stronger support for religion and less tolerance for homosexuality. Both of these factors pushed parents toward less support for gender equality in the way children are raised. A majority of respondents in the study (60%) indicated that religion was very important in their lives. Although religion can be a catalyst for progressive social change, the most religious respondents in this study supported traditional roles for women and men in the family. One mother emphasized that what she wants most for her daughter is "to present herself as a Christian lady"—a value that was often mentioned by respondents.

Concern over homosexuality also produced more ambivalent support for gender equality in socialization. Because feminine traits are devalued, boys are more likely to be stigmatized for being "sissies" than girls are for being "tomboys." Leaper et al. (1995), for example, found mothers to be much more tolerant of cross-gender-typed behavior in daughters than sons. In a similar study, McCreary (1994) found that boys and men are punished more for gender role transgressions than girls and women are, and concluded that the underlying reason is concern over the sexual orientation of men.

African Americans are even less tolerant of homosexuality than are other racial groups (Battle & Bennett, 2000; P. H. Collins, 1990), which may explain why some of the parents in this study, when asked about teaching gender roles, immediately responded by talking about sexual orientation. One mother of two sons and a daughter, asked if there should be differences in the way girls and boys are reared, rejected any biological/genetic explanation of homosexuality, implying that it could result from socialization:

I watch my kids . . . they say how kids are born homosexuals? I find that hard to believe, you know . . . but I've watched my kids, and my boys are boys and my girl is a girl. But when [my son] liked to play with dolls, I caught myself saying "No, you don't need to play with that!" . . . so I don't really encourage [boys playing with dolls]. But he only did that for a little while; it's not that he acts prissy or anything, it's just the fact that he had that doll that bothered me a little bit.

The gender teachings of parents with a high school education or less (N = 14) revealed even more mitigated support for gender equality in child socialization, and especially more concern that the failure to teach masculinity might result in homosexuality. Fathers were more likely than mothers to express this concern. One couple who was interviewed jointly talked about the father's fear that feminine-typed toys could affect their son's sexual orientation. They explained,

[Mother] Our son wanted a stove and refrigerator for Christmas once and I was going to get it, but he [the father] wouldn't let me, even though he's a cook. [Father] Well, today I know which way he's going, so I would. [*You mean his sexuality?*] Yeah . . . if he wants to play with girl things now, it's okay, because I know which way he's going.

For less educated parents, gender equality is endorsed in the public arena, specifically the workplace, but much less in the home, and none of the less educated parents in this study opted for fundamental changes in the way sons are socialized. Although they were frequently single mothers, they emphasized the value of traditional marriages. As one single, employed, high school educated mother of a 13-year-old daughter pointed out,

> I am very marriage minded! I believe in the cooking and the cleaning . . . I'm an old-fashioned woman, right out of Proverbs 31. I believe in going to the sales and making sure I get the best for my family, fixing breakfast, and ironing clothes. I am not the modern woman!

Asked to explain why so many Black mothers are single, another mother emphasized marriage and the importance of men taking responsibility for their families, and she blamed mothers for not teaching them to do so:

> Since most women don't mind being married, it must be the men. I would imagine that men, Black men [aren't being] taught to take responsibility for the family . . . the Black man has seen, too much of the time, women being so responsible that he doesn't even feel responsible, nor is he taught that he's responsible. . . . Not just the teaching, but just seeing so many Black women take responsibility, what's to encourage him to take on that role?

Doing Gender: The Organization of Gender in Families

In addition to what parents say they are teaching their children about gender equality, I sought to understand how gender was organized in their families, specifically the distribution of responsibility for domestic work and child care. Parents' gender ideologies show overall support for gender equality in child rearing; however, that support is mediated by their education, family background, religion, and homophobia. There was also often a gap between their ideologies and how gender was actually done in families. Structural factors, such as social class, marital status, and wives' employment, were more important than was gender ideology in shaping the actual distribution of work in families. Although gender role socialization plays an early and important role in shaping the beliefs of children, research has shown that gendered social structures may be even more powerful in the perpetuation of gender inequality. The family is the prototype of a gendered organization, as roles and responsibilities are typically assigned on the basis of sex (Risman, 1998). In this section, I explore how parents explain the division of housework and child care in their own families as an additional indicator of what children are taught about gender. Studies have shown that family structure can influence gender role socialization; for example, children growing up in single-parent families are often exposed to less traditional gender roles (Leve & Fagot, 1997), and they seem more likely to define themselves in terms of independence, self-reliance, and aggressiveness (Slavkin & Stright, 2000). In the present study I also found family structure to be an important predictor of both income (e.g., dual-income parents had higher incomes than did single parents) and the distribution of family work.

Marriage, secure middle-class status, and women's participation in the labor force produce a great deal of verbal support for gender equality in the home. Both fathers and mothers in dual-income families were enthusiastic about sharing domestic work and child care; indeed, the married men in this study seemed to take a special pride in their participation in the home. One wife explained the division of housework in this way:

> Primarily, [my husband] does about everything. He has always cooked—he's a better cook than I am . . . I think men and women should share equally in the responsibility of the home, but it depends on what the strengths and weaknesses of the two people are. But I think there should be an equal sharing.

In a joint interview with parents of two young sons, it was clear that both parents were extremely involved in caring for the children, but they had to negotiate to agree that the sharing was equal. When asked who had the primary responsibility of taking care of the children, they said,

> [Father] As far as rearing the children— total rearing? That even includes cooking? [Mother] I would have to take a bigger rank in it, simply because I take them to school and pick them up . . . but, nevertheless, he is responsible for dressing them.

I do most of the cooking, but he does all the bathing. So it's probably . . . well, I do the laundry and I do the clothes. I think that's where I'm going to get the upper hand. [Father] Give me that question again? I would say 50/50. [Mother] Do you think so? [Father] I would say so, because I think we're pretty even. [Mother] Well, 51/49, because I do the laundry. But really, it's pretty even. [Father] Well, I used to do the laundry, but I got fired. [Mother] . . . okay, it's probably 50/50.

One mother indicated that she enjoyed taking care of her children so much that she had to struggle to share the work with her husband, who was also eager to participate:

> I love to take care of my children—but I'm learning in just the last few years to share it. But I just really enjoy doing it, [but] my husband is incredible . . . he's just a great help. He loves to help the kids with their homework; as they get older he takes more responsibility. And he loves to plan our vacations and go on field trips with the kids at school.

Sharing child care was common, although, as indicated in the quote above, there was often a gender division in the type of child care performed by fathers and mothers: Mothers do most of the routine care tasks and discipline, and fathers spend more recreational/educational time with children. As one mother said, "he does help with their homework, but he wants to do more of the fun things—play basketball, take them places like to the movies. I'm the disciplinarian."

The married women who were full-time housewives ($N = 5$) freely admitted that they do most of the housework and child care, but they believed that this gender division of labor was fair. One mother of three elementary-school-age children, when asked who did most of the domestic work and child care, said,

> I think I do, because I'm here, and because right now he's working a full-time job and trying to start a business. And when he's done with that job he usually goes to the office . . . but I'm trying to get him to where he'll have some input in what they do.

Married women in this study expressed very little dissatisfaction with the gender division of labor at home. Some housewives wanted their husbands to be more involved with the children, but they were homemakers by choice and pleased with the opportunity to assume that role. Thus, parental support for gender equality was modeled more in dual-earner families than in the more traditional breadwinner–homemaker family.

Less educated, single mothers were least enthusiastic in their ideological support for gender equality, but quite likely to embrace it in raising their children. Single parents were not faced with the challenge of sharing housework with a spouse: As one single mother pointed out, "I do it all." Ideologically, these parents supported traditional marriage and gender arrangements, yet their ideology and behavior were in sharp contrast. For example, the sons of single mothers were more involved in family and child care work than were sons of married mothers. One divorced mother said of her son,

> My son, when he was 3-years old, was setting the table and I [didn't expect] to have to tell him everyday. He was taught

where to put the plates and the silverware at age 3.

Similarly, a father who grew up in a single-mother home noted he had to assume the responsibility of helping his mother:

> I had to be more of an adult. I loved my mother a lot, and I didn't want to see her take all of the pressure. So I tried to make sure . . . that we cleaned up the house. I had to play two roles. I had to watch out for my sisters, had to watch out for my mother. I had to play that role, because we didn't have a father image.

These findings suggest that, regardless of the actual gender ideology of parents, the practical realities of everyday life shape how gender gets done in the family.

Discussion

This research, based on in-depth interviews with 35 African American parents, examines the extent to which parents think gender influences the ways in which they socialize their children and the distribution of housework and child care in the home. Despite a proliferation of interdisciplinary research on the topic, I argue that gender has remained one of the least studied aspects of African American family life, especially as it pertains to the socialization of children.

This preliminary research allows us to begin to see how race and class shape gender roles and ideologies in Black American families. Examining the gender ideologies that parents say influence their socialization of children, I found that all parents expressed some level of support for gender equality, regardless of the sex of the parent, the sex of the child, or their social class position. Indeed, researchers have noted that it is common today for people to express a belief in gender equality, regardless of their actual behaviors (Risman, 1998; Warner & Steel, 1999). Still, class does matter. Using education as a measure of social class position, I divided parents into two groups—those who are "more educated" (i.e., have at least some college education) and those who are "less educated" (i.e., have a high school degree or less). On the basis of an analysis of differences in support for gender equality among the "more educated," I made a further distinction between those who are second-generation, "securely middle-class" and those who are first-generation parents who are in a sense "transitioning" into the middle class. These class distinctions affect parents' thinking about gender, with increasing ideological support for gender equality as one ascends the class hierarchy. Securely middle-class parents, for example, had the strongest support for gender equality in socializing their children, and they also had the broadest view of the meaning of gender equality and support equality at home and in the workplace. These findings support the results of other research that the gendering of childhood experiences diminishes as the education of parents increases (cf. Peterson, Bodman, Rush, & Madden-Derdich, 2000).

Support for gender equality among first-generation, transitional middle-class African American parents waned, I argue, because of recent class mobility and status anxiety. Substantial class mobility in recent decades has created a large group of "first-generation," middle-class Blacks—a "transitional" class still in the process of distancing themselves from negative racial images by conforming to what they see as the "respectable"

marital and gender conventions. Although upward economic mobility is the essence of the American Dream, many people bring into their new class location internalized classism, racism, and sexism that leaves them feeling marginal, estranged, and alienated and, as Gardner (1993) has pointed out, afraid of being exposed as imposters. The notion that newly middle-class Blacks experience status anxiety is also corroborated by the research of Kaplan (1997), who found it to be a major factor in the responses of Black middle-class mothers to pregnancy in their single, teenage daughters. This transitional status also coincides with higher levels of religiosity and homophobia, which push parents to embrace traditional gender ideologies. Despite abundant research, the dominant image of the Black family has been the domineering, single, poor, welfare-dependent mother—a denigrating racial stereotype that newly middle-class parents want to shed in favor of the respectability of conventional families and gender norms.

Religious fundamentalism and concern over homosexuality also shape gender socialization practices. Parents in general tend to be more supportive when their children engage in gender-typed behaviors rather than in cross-gender behaviors (Gallagher & Smith, 1999; Leaper et al., 1995). McCreary (1994) explained why boys are taught to avoid feminine-typed behaviors and punished more for gender role transgressions than are girls by concluding that the underlying concern was not social status, but sexual orientation. In the present study, these views were even stronger among those who were less educated, as they were more likely to see homosexuality as resulting from childhood experiences. Studies show that African Americans have disproportionately negative attitudes toward homosexuality; indeed, some Blacks have argued that it was unknown in Africa and is a White strategy for destroying the Black race (Battle & Bennett, 2000).

Less educated parents (i.e., those with high school education or less) had the narrowest view of gender equality: They wanted equality for daughters in the workplace but held traditional gender roles in the family as ideal. Black fathers, for example, were especially supportive of their daughters' career aspirations (see also Staples & Johnson, 1993), but resistant to the notion of their sons engaging in feminine-typed behaviors. Other researchers have found the intergenerational transmission of traditional gender ideologies from mothers to daughters to be especially strong (Blakemore, 1998; Ex & Janssens, 1998); however, the racialized gender socialization messages of the parents in this study, especially the mothers, combined teaching traditional gender roles in the home with an emphasis on strength, striving, and success in the public arena, despite the expectation of racial and gender barriers.

Turning to the issue of how parents say gender affects the distribution of housework and child care in families, I examined whether the lived experiences of these parents coincided with their gender beliefs. Despite growing support for the ideology of gender equality, researchers question whether that support is being translated into a reduction in gender-typed behaviors (Benokraitis & Feagin, 1995; Wright & Young, 1998). I found that family structure and middle-class status affected the organization of gender in the family: gender equity was strongest among married, middle-class, dual-income parents; thus, their strong support for gender equality coincided with

their actual behaviors. The level of sharing in these households is the greatest, although only one couple claimed complete equality in the domestic arena. This lends credence to the results of other studies that showed men's increasing participation in family work, but also that, among Black husbands and wives, women are still responsible for most of the housework and child care (Wilson et al., 1990). In addition, the sharing of domestic work, especially child care, falls along gender lines: Women do most of the day-to-day work of caring for children, and men spend more recreation time with children.

Married women who are full-time homemakers experienced the greatest contradiction between their gender ideology of equality and lived experiences, as they clearly were responsible for most of the family work. But as King (1988) pointed out, Black women often see being a full-time wife and mother as a privilege rather than a source of gender oppression. Married mothers in the present study were clearly pleased with the freedom to engage domesticity on a full-time basis, despite their desire to have fathers more involved in child care.

Less educated parents supported traditional gender roles in the family and gender equality in the workplace, but were least able to live their gender ideology at home. These parents were more likely to be single, employed mothers with less education and lower incomes. Of necessity, they and their children seemed to engage in more gender flexible behaviors, yet they clung to the notion of traditional gender roles as proper. Yet, as Deutsch and Saxon (1998) have pointed out, it is not uncommon for people to reconcile traditional ideologies and identities with nontraditional roles. Despite their traditional ideologies, these mothers modeled women's independence and assigned their children household tasks in a gender-neutral fashion. Moreover, researchers have argued that growing up in single-mother families encourages nontraditional gender-typed behaviors, especially in daughters (Leaper et al., 1995; Leve & Fagot, 1997), despite the ideological views of the families.

Because this study focused on gender socialization among a small, nonrandom sample of African Americans, its findings are preliminary and cannot be widely generalized. These findings do, however, speak to the need for more research, and they provide some interesting directions that such research might take. First, scholars have noted that the concept of gender role socialization suggests a unilateral, linear process with parental teachings increasingly embraced by children. The reality is, however, that socialization processes are bilateral, with parents and children influencing each other, and children taking an active role in creating, accepting, and negotiating engendered behaviors (Moore, 2001; Peterson et al., 2000). Thus, broader approaches to understanding how gender is defined and transmitted must take into consideration a broader array of socializing groups and institutions as well as the multiple ways in which gender is mediated in microsocial relationships. Second, it may be valuable to rethink the meaning of gender equality, especially because gender oppression is so commonly linked with and measured by factors such as traditional family roles and the exclusion of women from the labor market. Yet, as multiracial feminists have argued (cf. King, 1988), for Blacks, conforming to traditional family roles may be

evidence of middle-class status and mobility; indeed, as P. H. Collins (1990) has argued, given the historic necessity of Black women's participation in the labor market, being a full-time wife and mother can be seen as an act of resistance. Despite their embrace of some "traditional" gender ideologies and practices, African American women may define themselves in ways that contradict Eurocentric views of femininity and womanhood, such as the emphasis on strength as a feminine or woman's characteristic. Also, it has long been recognized that Black and White women may have different opinions about key feminist issues, such as motherhood (Polatnick, 1996).

A related issue is the growing class diversity among African Americans and its impact on gender ideologies and behaviors. Research on African American families has focused heavily on poor, single mother families, and even the multiracial feminist perspective sometimes tacitly assumes that class (along with race and gender) is one of the "jeopardies" faced by Black women. Although a few scholars have explored the issue of class in families (Landry, 1987; Willie, 1988), most recent studies have focused heavily on the growing poverty of the underclass (W. J. Wilson, 1997), leaving race the dominant discourse in studies of African Americans (Ortner, 1998). Yet class polarization has grown dramatically among African Americans since the 1980s (S. M. Collins, 1997; Hurst, 2001), and, although Blacks do share some common historic experiences, it is increasingly difficult to see them as a monolithic group. The classic child-rearing studies of Kohn (1963, 1977) emphasized the importance of class in the values parents teach, yet offered much less in the way of race and gender analysis.

Emerging research, however, shows the validity of a race–class–gender dynamic in understanding childhood socialization (Hill & Sprague, 1999) and the importance of class mobility and status anxiety in shaping family relations among African Americans (Kaplan, 1996).

Finally, I have argued that gender is implicated in most of the issues that face African American children today, and thus deserves more attention. For example, how are childhood activities and outcomes related to how gender is taught and organized in Black families? Does support for androgynous gender roles benefit boys and girls equally? Are traditional gender teachings related to the tendency of poor Black girls to see motherhood as evidence of womanhood (Ladner, 1971), or of Black boys to try to achieve masculinity through violence and hypersexuality when other routes are not available (P. H. Collins, 1990; Hill & Zimmerman, 1995)? The race–gender–class dynamic of multiracial feminism offers a promising framework for exploring the increasing diverse ways in which gender is defined and influencing lives.

Acknowledgments

I thank the University of Kansas Office of Research and Graduate Studies for their financial support of this project.

Notes

1. The use of the concept "traditional gender norms" in no way suggests that these norms are still the tradition for White families, nor are the data in this study used for a racial comparison.

2. Also referred to as multicultural feminism by those who emphasize cultural differences that exist between White women and Women of Color.

3. The Warner Index of Social Standing includes dwelling area, dwelling type, occupation, and education in assessing social class, and the Hollingshead Scale, the most commonly used, includes education and occupation (see Hurst, 2001).

4. This was assessed primarily on the basis of the portions of the interview where parents were asked to describe their own growing-up experiences and relationships with their own parents.

References

Andersen, M. L., & Collins, P. H. (1998). *Race, class, and gender: An anthology* (3rd ed.). Belmont, CA: Wadsworth.

Asante, M. K. (1987). *The Afrocentric idea*. Philadelphia: Temple University Press.

Baca Zinn, M., & Dill, B. T. (1996). Theorizing difference from multiracial feminism. *Feminist Studies, 22*, 321–331.

Battle, J., & Bennett, M. (2000). Research on lesbian and gay populations within the African American community: What have we learned? *African American Perspectives, 6*(2), 35–47.

Bem, S. L. (1983). Gender schema theory and its implications for child development: Raising gender-aschematic children in a gender-schematic society. *Signs, 8*, 598–616.

Benokraitis, N. V., & Feagin, J. R. (1995). *Modern sexism: Blatant, subtle, and covert discrimination* (2nd ed.). Upper Saddle River, NJ: Prentice-Hall.

Bigler, R. S. (1997). Conceptual and methodological issues in the measurement of children's sex typing. *Psychology of Women Quarterly, 21*, 53–69.

Billingsley, A. (1992). *Climbing Jacob's ladder: The enduring legacy of African-American families*. New York: Simon & Schuster.

Binion, V. J. (1990). Psychological androgyny: A Black female perspective. *Sex Roles, 22*, 487–507.

Blake, W. M., & Darling, C. A. (1994). The dilemmas of the African American male. *Journal of Black Studies, 24*, 402–415.

Blakemore, J. E. O. (1998). The influence of gender and parental attitudes on preschool children's interest in babies: Observations in natural settings. *Sex Roles, 38,* 331–358.

Blau, Z. S. (1981). *Black children/White children: Competence, socialization, and social structure.* New York: Free Press.

Block, J. H. (1983). Differential premises arising from differential socialization of the sexes: Some conjectures. *Child Development, 54,* 1334–1354.

Brewer, R. M. (1993). Theorizing race, class, and gender: The new scholarship of Black feminist intellectuals and Black women's labor. In S. M. James & A. P. A. Busia (Eds.), *Theorizing Black feminisms* (pp. 13–30). New York: Routledge.

Burgess, N. (1994). Gender roles revisited: The development of the "woman's place" among African American women in the United States. *Journal of Black Studies, 24,* 391–401.

Burton, L. M. (1990). Teenage childbearing as an alternative life-course strategy in multigenerational Black families. *Human Nature, 1,* 123–143.

Caldwell, J. C. (1996). The demographic implications of West African family systems. *Journal of Comparative Family Studies, 27,* 331–352.

Collins, P. H. (1987). The meaning of motherhood in Black culture and Black mother-daughter relationships. *Sage, 4,* 3–10.

Collins, P. H. (1990). *Black feminist thought: Knowledge, consciousness, and the politics of empowerment.* Boston: Unwin Hyman.

Collins, P. H. (1998). It's all in the family: Intersections of gender, race, and nation. *Hypatia, 13,* 62–82.

Collins, S. M. (1997). *Black corporate executives: The making and breaking of the Black middle class.* Philadelphia: Temple University Press.

Crouter, A. C., McHale, S. M., & Bartko, W. T. (1993). Gender as an organizing feature in parent-child relationships. *Journal of Social Issues, 49,* 161–174.

Deutsch, F. M., & Saxon, S. E. (1998). Traditional ideologies, nontraditional lives. *Sex Roles, 38,* 331–362.

Dill, B. T. (1979). The dialectic of Black womanhood. *Signs, 4,* 545–555.

Dill, B. T. (1988). Our mother's grief: Racial ethnic women and the maintenance of families. *Journal of Family History, 13,* 415–431.

Ex, C. T. G. M., & Janssens, J. M. A. M. (1998). Maternal influences on daughters' gender role attitudes. *Sex Roles, 38,* 171–186.

Gallagher, S. K., & Smith, C. (1999). Symbolic traditionalism and pragmatic egalitarianism: Contemporary evangelicals, families, and gender. *Gender and Society, 13,* 211–233.

Gardner, S. (1993). What's a nice working-class girl like you doing in a place like this? In M. M. Tokarczyk & E. A. Fay (Eds.), *Working-class women in the academy: Laborers in the knowledge factory* (pp. 49–59). Amherst: University of Massachusetts Press.

Glaser, G. G., & Straus, A. L. (1967). *The discovery of grounded theory.* Chicago: Aldine.

Gibbs, J. T. (1988). Young Black males in America: Endangered, embittered, and embattled. In J. T. Gibbs (Ed.), *Young, Black, and male in America: An endangered species* (pp. 1–36). Dover, MA: Auburn House.

Giddings, P. (1984). *When and where I enter: The impact of Black women on race and sex in America.* New York: Bantam Books.

Higginbotham, E. (1981). Is marriage a priority? Class differences in marital options of educated Black women. In P. Stein (Ed.), *Single life: Unmarried adults in social context* (pp. 133–176). Ann Arbor, MI: Institute for Social Research.

Higginbotham, E. B. (1993). *Righteous discontent: The women's movement in the Black Baptist church, 1880–1920.* Cambridge, MA: Harvard University Press.

Higginbotham, E., & Weber, L. (1992). Moving up with kin and community: Upward social mobility for Black and White women. *Gender and Society, 6,* 416–440.

Hill, S. A., & Sprague, J. (1999). Parenting in Black and White families: The interaction of gender with race and class. *Gender and Society, 13,* 480–502.

Hills, S. A., & Zimmerman, M. K. (1995). Valiant girls and vulnerable boys: The impact of sex and race on caring for chronically ill children. *Journal of Marriage and the Family,* *57*, 43–53.

hooks, b. (1992). *Black looks: Race and representation.* Boston: South End Press.

Hossain, Z., & Roopnarine, J. L. (1993). Division of household labor and child care in dual-earner African-American families with infants. *Sex Roles, 29,* 571–583.

Hunter, A. G., & Davis, J. E. (1992). Constructing gender: An exploration of Afro-American men's conceptualization of manhood. *Gender and Society, 6,* 464–479.

Hurst, C. E. (2001). *Social inequality: Forms, causes, and consequences* (5th ed.). Boston: Allyn and Bacon.

Ickes, W. (1993). Traditional gender roles: Do they make, and then break, our relationships? *Journal of Social Issues, 49,* 71–85.

Ingrassia, M. (1993, August 3). Endangered families. *Newsweek,* pp. 17–27.

Ireson, C., & S. Gill. (1988). Girls' socialization for work. In A. H. Stromberg & S. Harkess (Eds.), *Women working: Theories and facts in perspective* (2nd ed.). Mountain View, CA: Mayfield.

Jarrett, R. L. (1994). Living poor: Family life among single parents. African American women. *Social Problems, 41,* 30–47.

Jones, J. (1985). *Labor of love, labor of sorrow: Black women, work and the family from slavery to the present.* New York: Vintage Books.

Kaplan, E. B. (1996). Black teenage mothers and their mothers: The impact of adolescent child-bearing on daughters' relations with mothers. *Social Problems, 43,* 427–443.

Kaplan, E. B. (1997). *Not our kind of girl.* Berkeley: University of California Press.

Kerbo, H. R. (2000). *Social stratification and inequality* (4th ed.). Boston: McGraw-Hill.

King, D. K. (1988). Multiple jeopardy, multiple consciousness: The context of Black feminist ideology. *Signs, 14,* 42–72.

Kohn, M. L. (1963). Social class and parent-child relationships. *American Journal of Sociology, 63,* 471–480.

Kohn, M. L. (1977). *Class and conformity: A study of values* (2nd ed.). Chicago: University of Chicago Press.

Ladner, J. A. (1971). *Tomorrow's tomorrow: The Black women.* Garden City, NY: Doubleday.

Landry, B. (1987). *The new Black middle class.* Berkeley: University of California Press.

Leaper, C., Leve, L., Strasser, T., and Schwartz, R. (1995). Mother-child communication and sequences: Play activity, child gender, and marital status effects. *Merrill-Palmer Quarterly, 41,* 307–327.

Leve, L. D., & Fagot, B. I. (1997). Gender-role socialization and discipline processes in one- and two-parent families. *Sex Roles, 36,* 1–21.

Lewis, D. K. (1975). The Black family: Socialization and sex roles. *Phylon, 36,* 221–238.

Lorber, J. (1994). *Paradoxes of gender.* New Haven, CT: Yale University Press.

McCreary, D. R. (1994). The male role and avoiding femininity. *Sex Roles, 31,* 517–531.

Moore, V. A. (2001). "Doing" racialized and gendered age to organize peer relations. *Gender and Society, 15,* 835–858.

Nobles, W. W. (1985). *Africanity and the Black family: The development of a theoretical model* (2nd ed.). Oakland, CA: Institute for the Advanced Study of Black Family Life and Culture.

Ortner, S. B. (1998). Identities: The hidden life of class. *Journal of Anthropological Research, 54,* 1–17.

Peters, M. F. (1997). Parenting of young children in Black families. In H. P. McAdoo (Ed.), *Black families* (3rd ed., pp. 167–182). Thousand Oaks, CA: Sage.

Peterson, G. W., Bodman, D. A., Rush, K. R., & Madden-Derdich, D. (2000). Gender and parent-child relationships. In D. H. Demo, K. R. Allen, & M. A. Fine (Eds.), *Handbook of family diversity* (pp. 82–103). New York: Oxford University Press.

Polatnick, M. R. (1996). Diversity in women's liberation ideology: How a Black and a White group of the 1960s viewed motherhood. *Signs, 21,* 679–706.

Reid, P. T., & Trotter, K. H. (1993). Children's self-presentations with infants: Gender and ethnic comparisons. *Sex Roles, 29,* 171–181.

Risman, B. J. (1998). *Gender vertigo: American families in transition.* New Haven, CT: Yale University Press.

Scanzoni, J. (1977). *The Black family in modern society: Patterns of stability and security.* Chicago: University of Chicago Press.

Scott, J. W. (1993). African American daughter-mother relations and teenage pregnancy: Two faces of premarital teenage pregnancy. *Western Journal of Black Studies, 17,* 73–81.

Slavkin, M., & Stright, A. D. (2000). Gender role differences in college students from one- and two-parent families. *Sex Roles, 42,* 23–30.

Smith, R. C., & Seltzer, R. (1992). *Race, class, and culture: A study of Afro-American mass opinion.* Albany: State University of New York Press.

Staples, R., & Johnson, L. B. (1993). *Black families at the crossroads: Challenges and prospects.* San Francisco: Jossey-Bass.

Strauss, A., & Corbin, J. (1990). *Basics of qualitative research: Grounded theory procedures and techniques.* Newbury Park, CA: Sage.

Tesch, R. (1990). *Qualitative research: Analysis types and software tools.* New York: Falmer Press.

Warner, R. L., & Steel, B. S. (1999). Childrearing as a mechanism for social change: The relationship of child gender to parents' commitment to gender equity. *Gender and Society, 13,* 503–517.

West, C., & Zimmerman, D. (1987). Doing gender. *Gender and Society, 1,* 125–151.

Willie, C. V. (1988). *A new look at Black families* (3rd ed.). Bayside, NY: General Hall.

Wilson, M. N., Tolson, T. F. J., Hinton, I. D., & Kierman, M. (1990). Flexibility and sharing of childcare duties in Black families. *Sex Roles, 22,* 409–425.

Wilson, W. J. (1997). *When work disappears: The world of the new urban poor.* New York: Vintage.

Wright, D. W., & Young, R. (1998). The effects of family structure and maternal employment on the development of gender-related attitudes among men and women. *Journal of Family Issues, 19,* 300–314.

32 Joan Acker

Gender, Capitalism and Globalization

Feminist scholars have been producing research and theoretical reflections on women, gender, and global transformations at least since 1970, the date of publication of Ester Boserup's ground-breaking *Woman's Role in Economic Development*. In this essay, I discuss some aspects of the mostly Western feminist scholarship on gender and globalization to provide a context for the papers in this volume. Although I do not attempt to summarize what is now a very large literature,[1] I briefly look at how gender is implicated in globalization processes, asking whether and how these processes are gendered and what gendered effects result from these processes. Because both "globalization" and "gender" are contested concepts, I begin with a discussion of how I define them.

Gendering Globalization

"Globalization" captures a multiplicity of changes that are, it is claimed, altering the contours of economies, polities, and social life in general at the end of the 20th Century and the beginning of the 21st Century. Influential male theorists in the social sciences argue about the meaning of the term, the processes involved and the likely outcomes (e.g., Giddens 1999; Bauman 1998;

Beck 2000; Sen 2002; Wallerstein 1974; Hardt and Negri 2000). Disagreements exist about whether present globalization is a new stage in capitalist development or a continuation of globalizing processes that have been characteristic of capitalism from its emergence in the 15th Century. Or, possibly, globalizing processes began much earlier and are not inevitably tied to capitalism (Sen 2002). Other disagreements have to do with how total is the economic and cultural penetration of global capitalism, how fundamental are the transformations of economic and social processes, how much these changes improve or undermine conditions of daily life, how central are technological innovations to other changes, and how much have global forces overwhelmed the autonomy of nation states. Many writers link the concept of a "new economy" to the concept of globalization, seeing new technology-based production and communication as necessary to and facilitating the expansions and penetrations of globalization.

Granting that capitalism has always been "global," there do seem to be identifiable changes in global processes in the past 30 years or so. As I understand it, globalization

Excerpted from the original. Joan Acker, "Gender, Capitalism and Globalization," *Critical Sociology* 30, no. 1 (January 2004): 17–41. Copyright © 2004 Koninklijke Brill NV, Leiden. Reprinted by permission of SAGE Publications.

I want to thank Heidi Gottfried for suggesting I write this introduction and for her excellent editorial suggestions.

refers to the increasing pace and penetrations of movements of capital, production, and people across boundaries of many kinds and on a global basis. This view emphasizes that globalization is processual and contradictory as well as complex and multifaceted (e.g., Lenz 2002). Globalization is about class, race/ethnic, and gender relations: it is political and cultural, as well as economic.[2] The growth and consolidation of transnational corporations, along with new forms of decentralization, relocation and reorganization of production and subcontracting are parts of the process. "Free marketization," or the reduction of old state and contractual controls with the substitution of other controls, and the potential commodification of almost everything are other aspects of present changes.[3] The old controls that have either disappeared or are under attack include those that protected local/national firms and industries, enacted welfare state supports and constrained capitalist actions to oppose unions, to endanger workers' health and safety, or to pollute the environment. New controls, on the other hand, may regulate new categories of workers, constrain opponents of unlimited corporate freedom, or reinforce neo-liberal ideology, such as mandates in the U.S. that impoverished single mothers must work for pay without regard for the welfare of their children. Organizational restructuring, downsizing, new forms of flexibility and new forms of employment relations are parts of free marketization. Finally, there is the emergence of new leading sectors of global capitalism based on technological innovations, the "new economy." As identified in the business literature, these are computer and information technology, global finance, and biotechnological innovation. All of these changes are interrelated and shaped by the ideological dominance of neo-liberal thought.

The dominant discourse on globalization that describes and theorizes the above changes has a hidden commonality: gender and often race are invisible. Globalization is presented as gender neutral, even though some theorists do pay some attention to women, the family and women's employment (e.g., Castells 2000). This ostensible gender neutrality masks the "implicit masculinization of these macro-structural models" (Freeman 2001; see also Ward 1993). The implicit masculine standpoint in the ruling relations (Smith 1987) from which theories of society have been constructed impedes adequate analysis. For example, unpaid caring, household, and agricultural labor, along with much informal economic activity that maintains human life (Elson 1994; Mies 1986), do not enter the analyses or are assumed to be in unlimited supply. The omission of mostly women's unpaid work seriously biases discussions of the penetration of capitalist globalizing processes and limits understanding of both negative consequences and potentials for opposition (Bergeron 2001; Gibson-Graham 2002).

"Gendering" the discourse of globalization exposes the discontinuities between the realities of women's and men's lives and mainstream scholarly work about global processes. Combined with integral attention to race and ethnic processes, "gendering" should produce a better understanding of contemporary global issues. Before presenting some of the extensive feminist work that has gendered globalization research and theory, I briefly examine the concept of gender. Gender as used here is defined as inequalities, divisions, and differences socially constructed around assumed distinctions between female and male. Gender is a basic organizing principle in social life, a principle for allocation of duties, rights, rewards, and power, including the means of violence. Gender is a factor in organizing daily life for individuals, families, communities, and societies as large structures. Women are usually disadvantaged in terms of power and material and status rewards. Gender is neither an essential attribute of individuals nor a constant in social life, but consists of material and symbolic aspects of existence, constantly produced and reproduced in the course of ongoing social activities and practices. Gender necessarily involves bodies of actual people and the ways that they see and experience themselves, their identities. This implies that there are many versions of gender, different masculinities and femininities, lived differently in different times and places, but also varying within particular times and places. Although there are many versions of masculinity and femininity and many ways of organizing gender differences, heterosexual gender is the norm almost everywhere. Most feminist analysts of gender and globalization use some such notion of gender as socially produced and highly variable, while recognizing the predominant subordination of women within gender relations.

Although gender includes female and male, masculine and feminine, women and men, in scholarly and everyday practice, including discussions of globalization, gender often means women. Much of the work on gender and globalization is actually research on women, work, and family under contemporary conditions of economic transformations. This gender research may include men as their actions and practices shape the worlds of women, but the bulk of the research on men, work, and economy is cast as gender-neutral, with the implicit assumption that to talk about men is to talk about the general situation. Much research in which men are the principle actors can be interpreted from a gender perspective, and fairly recent work on masculinity is helpful (e.g., Connell 1987, 2000; Hooper 2000). However, this is another long-existing conceptual problem and one that has been difficult to solve. I suspect that part of the problem has to do with the gender structure of research institutions: the specialization in which "gender" understandings are the domain of women researchers and of little interest to researchers who are men (or women working within a masculinized frame of reference).[4]

Is Globalization Gendered?

"Is globalization gendered?" could be answered in many ways. I have chosen to first look at how gender is embedded in the structuring and ongoing practices of globalizing capitalism, and second, to examine the impacts of some of the changes linked to globalization on women, men, families, and gender relations.

Gender as Embedded in Globalizing Capitalism

I argue that gender is intrinsic to globalizing capitalist processes and relations by discussing first, the gendered construction of a separation between capitalist production and human reproduction and continuing corporate claims of non-responsibility for reproduction that are linked to that separation. Second, I discuss the role of masculinities in globalizing capitalism. Third, I look at gender as a resource for globalizing capital.

The gendered construction of a division between capitalist production and human reproduction. The division between commodity production in the capitalist economy and reproduction of human beings and their ability to labor has long been identified by feminists as a fundamental process in women's subordination in capitalist societies.[5] This organization of social life carries contradictory potentials: production is organized around goals of capital accumulation, not around meeting the reproductive and survival needs of people. Women have been subordinate in both domains, held responsible for unpaid reproductive labor and consigned to positions with less power and lower pay than men within the sphere of production. Men, unburdened by reproduction responsibilities and already the major wielders of power, built the factories and railroads and managed the developing capitalist enterprises. Thus, the structural and ideological division between production and reproduction was shaped along lines of gender and contributed to continuing gendered inequalities. This division emerged in the historical development of Euro-American capitalism, and contributed to a particular cultural/structural form of masculine dominance that was exported in the early phases of globalization. As Connell (2000) argues, "The colonial world saw the installation, on a very large scale, of institutions on the North Atlantic model: armies, states, bureaucracies, corporations, capital markets, labour markets, schools, law courts, transport systems. These are gendered institutions, and their functioning has directly reconstituted masculinities in the periphery" (p. 45).[6]

These gendered institutions assume a particular gendered organization of society, which may or may not have been consistent with that of the colonized. Thus, functioning of these institutions also reconstituted (to varying extent) the lives of women. Or, at least, an overlay of Euro-American gender relations was established in many parts of the world as men from the North carried out their colonizing projects. As European and then American capital established dominance through colonization, empire, and today's globalization, one of the cultural/structural forms embedded in that dominance has been the identification of the male/masculine with production in the money economy and the identification of the female/feminine with reproduction and the domestic. This ideological construction starkly contrasts with the actual organization of production and reproduction, as women were often as much "producers" as "reproducers."

The gender-coded separation between production and reproduction became, over time, an underlying principle in the conceptual and actual physical organization of work, the spatial and time relationships between unpaid domestic and paid work, bodily movements through time and space, the general organization of daily life, and the ways that groups and individuals constructed meaning and identities. For example, the rules and expectations of ordinary capitalist workplaces are built on hidden assumptions about a separation of production and reproduction (Acker 1990).

This gendered organization of social life provides the grounds for the reproduction of different and unequal lives of women and men, and for the reproduction of images and ideologies that support difference and inequality, long after the ideals and actualities of separate spheres for some have been weakened or, in some cases, have disappeared altogether. Gender was and is thus built into the organization of daily life, but not in the same ways or with the same consequences for everyone. Class and race/ethnic differences, embedded in different histories, mediate the gendered organization of daily life and identity and the gendered deployment of power in the Euro-American capitalist centers and in other countries and areas brought into their orbit through conquest, settlement, colonization, empire, and today's "globalization."[7]

The contradictory goals of production and reproduction contribute to another gendered aspect of globalizing capitalist processes. This is the frequent corporate practice, on national and global levels, of claiming non-responsibility for reproduction of human life and reproduction of the natural environment. Here I find it useful to use Diane Elson's (1994) description in economic terms of the separation between production and reproduction as a division between the monetary "productive" economy and the non-monetary "reproductive" economy.[8] "The ability of money to mobilize labour power for 'productive work' depends on the operation of some non-monetary set of social relations to mobilize labour power for 'reproductive work.' These non-monetary social relations are subordinate to money in the sense that they cannot function and sustain themselves without an input of money; and they are reshaped in response in the power of money. Nevertheless, neither can the monetary economy sustain itself without an input of unpaid labour, an input shaped by the structures of gender relations" (Elson 1994, 40). Elson emphasizes the interdependence of the monetary and non-monetary economies, although she recognizes that macro-economic policy considers only the monetary economy, ignoring the non-

monetary economy, in which women perform most of the work. In addition, macro-economic policy, representing the interests and perspectives of production, implicitly assumes that "there is an unlimited supply of unpaid female labour, able to compensate for any adverse changes resulting from macro-economic policy, so as to continue to meet the basic needs of their families and communities and sustain them as social organizations" (Elson 1994, 42).

Although the monetary and non-monetary economies are interdependent, their interests are also often contradictory and conflicting: maximizing profit and capital accumulation may undermine the reproduction and maintenance of human life, given that an adequate labor supply still exists. At the very least, capitalist expansion has often involved the subordination of the aims of reproduction to the aims of production, either through explicit policies and practices or through un-benign neglect or non-responsibility. I think it is very important to see non-responsibility as actively constructed through organizational inventions and state actions, such as legislation in the 19th and 20th centuries that created the rights of corporations to act in their own interests, as their leaders defined those interests.

The establishment in the 19th Century of *laissez-faire* ideology with rational economic man as the iconic figure supported denial of responsibility by economic organizations. Rational economic man acted purposively in his own interest, his decisions contributing to positive outcomes for the community and national.[9] The needs of reproduction, to the extent that they were visible, would be provided for by positive economic outcomes. This did not happen automatically: the history of Anglo-American capitalism can be read as a series of ongoing battles between workers and employers over issues related to reproduction such as the payment of starvation wages, the refusal to provide safe working conditions, insistence on long working hours, or the destruction of environments and indigenous communities. Under some conditions, capitalist firms did take some (paternal) responsibility for workers, families, and communities, as exemplified by company towns founded in the U.S. This usually occurred when the firm was well established in a particular place and dependent on a local labor supply. However, historically, men in control of the monetary economy, the sphere of production, have often denied that they or their firms have any responsibility for reproduction. The human needs of colonized peoples were also of no concern, as their non-monetized economies were routinely weakened or destroyed in the processes of empire and later globalization.

Capitalist organizations continued to ignore the needs of their own workers and their families and people in general unless forced to pay attention, either because a critical need arose for certain labor power or because social movements, responding to crises of reproduction as in the 1930s, either directly or through state intervention challenged corporate power (Acker 1988). The development of welfare states after World War II, especially in the rich Northern countries, diluted this power by establishing state supports for reproduction and forcing firms to also take some responsibility. Although outcomes varied, welfare states were usually based on the assumption that women still provide the unpaid work of caring. In the same period in the U.S., under pressures of the labor movement, large corporations negotiated higher wages, medical care, vacations and other benefits with their workers, even as they may have still opposed national and state legislation for welfare programs.

Subsequent history abounds with corporate efforts to protect and restore non-responsibility, with considerable success in the 1990s. The restoration of neo-liberalism as the dominating economic discourse has provided legitimacy for reducing welfare state programs and restoring corporate non-responsibility in most countries, although this varies greatly. At the same time, some parts of reproductive services move into the capitalist economy, becoming available only to those able to pay. In the U.S., from opposition to worker efforts to raise wages to refusals to support paid parental leave legislation or public day care, corporations escalate their denial of responsibility for anything but the bottom line. Caring and nurturing, unless a source of profit, are not important, in spite of rhetoric to the contrary. ("Leave no child behind" is a cynical and dishonest goal in this context.) As caring work is devalued, so are those who primarily do that work. Claims to non-responsibility reinforce the underlying gender divisions between production and reproduction and the gendered understructure of capitalist production, as they continually relegate reproduction to the unpaid work of women or to the low paid work of women in the for-profit economy.

These gendered elements in fundamental capitalist processes are exacerbated in present globalizing changes. "Development" in third world countries often, perhaps usually, disrupts the reproduction of daily life through the non-monetary economy as peasant agriculture continues to be displaced by corporate farming, cheap agricultural imports, or deforestation. Demands for structural adjustment by the International Monetary Fund (IMF) force the sharp reduction of welfare state social protections for reproduction and increase poverty and inequality (Marchand and Runyan 2002; Stiglitz 2002). Women's unpaid labor keeps life going under these conditions. The transnational organization of production builds non-responsibility into the structure of capitalist processes. As corporations such as Nike or Liz Claiborne contract production to firms in other countries, the corporation has relatively few workers of its own, thus few who might demand responsibility. As Applebaum and Gereffi (1990: 44) say, "Contracting means that the so-called manufacturer need not employ any production workers, run the risk of unionization or wages pressures, or be concerned with layoffs resulting from changes in product demands." Thus, downloading responsibility in the interest of accumulation underlies corporate decisions to continually move production to the location with the cheapest labor. Non-responsibility is built into globalizing processes, indeed the opportunities for production and gain without challenges to non-responsibility probably constitute a major incentive for moving production from rich, capitalist countries to poorer, low wage locations. At the same time, back in corporate headquarters in the U.S. or other rich countries, where design, marketing, and production decisions are made, a significant degree of gender and race/ethnic equality may emerge as skilled professionals are hired to do this work. It may even be good business for Nike, for example, to have an Asian-American woman as a public spokesperson. Her work conditions, and possibilities for meeting obligations of home and reproduc-

tion are probably quite different than those of the non-employees making the company's products.

Although claims to non-responsibility have been loud and persistent during the recent period of the triumph of neo-liberalism and global capitalism, they are beginning to be challenged in many different arenas, including Seattle, Davos, etc., by feminist and women's organizing in many parts of the world (Bergeron 2002; Mohanty 2002; Gibson-Graham 2002), and potentially by the widespread discrediting of U.S. corporations in recent scandals.

Masculinities in globalizing capital. In the history of modern globalization, beginning with the expansion of England and other European countries in colonial conquest, agents of globalization, leaders and troops, have been men, but not just any men. They have been particular men whose locations within gendered social relations and practices can be captured by the concept of masculinity. "Masculinity" is a contested term.[10] As Connell (1987, 2000), Hearn (1996), and others have pointed out, it should be pluralized as "masculinities," because in any society at any time there are several ways of being a man. Connell (2000) defines masculinities as "configurations of practice within gender relations, a structure that includes large-scale institutions and economic relations as well as face-to-face relationships and sexuality" (p. 29). Masculinities are reproduced through organizational/institutional practices, social interaction, and through images, ideals, myths or representations of behaviors and emotions. Hegemonic masculinity is the most desired and admired form, attributed to leaders and other influential figures at particular historical times. More than one type of hegemonic masculinity may exist simultaneously, although they may share characteristics, as do the business leader and the sports star at the present time.

Connell (2000) identifies "globalizing masculinities," beginning with the masculinities of conquest and settlement of the 18th and 19th Centuries that combined "an unusual level of violence and egocentric individualism" (p. 47) among the conquerors. Masculinities of empire cast the male colonizers as more manly and more virile than the colonized, thus emasculating colonized others, and, at the same time, legitimating violence in the interests of empire. Globalizing masculinities organized around violence and domination seems to have been predominant in these two periods of conquest and settlement. As corporate capitalism developed, Connell and others (for example Collinson and Hearn 1996) argue, a hegemonic masculinity based on claims to expertise developed along with masculinities still organized around domination. Hegemonic masculinity relying on claims to expertise does not necessarily lead to economic organizations free of domination and violence, however (Hearn and Parkin 2002). Hearn and Parkin (2002) argue that controls relying on both explicit and implicit violence exist in a wide variety of organizations.

In today's organizing for globalization, we can see the emergence of a hegemonic hyper-masculinity that is aggressive, ruthless, competitive, and adversarial. Think of Rupert Murdoch (Reed 1996), Phil Knight (Strasser and Beklund 1993), or Bill Gates. Gates, who represents a younger generation than Murdoch and Knight, may seem to be more gently aggressive and more socially responsible than the other two examples, with his contributions to good causes around the globe. However, his actions made public in the anti-trust lawsuits against Microsoft seem to still exhibit the ruthlessness, competitiveness and adversarialness of hyper-masculinity. This masculinity is supported and reinforced by the ethos of the free market, competition, and a "win or die" environment. This is the masculine image of those who organize and lead the drive to global control and the opening of markets to international competition. Masculinities embedded in collective practices are part of the context within which certain men make the organizational decisions that drive and shape what is called "globalization" and the "new economy." We can speculate that how these men see themselves, what actions and choices they feel compelled to make and they think are legitimate, how they and the world around them define desirable masculinity, enter into that decision-making. Decisions made at the very top reaches of (masculine) corporate power have consequences that are experienced as inevitable economic forces or disembodied social trends. At the same time, they symbolize and enact varying hegemonic masculinities (Connell 1998).

Researchers rarely study how gender, or masculinity, influences the orchestration of contemporary globalizing processes, probably because access to those levels of corporate, international agency (e.g., IMF, World Bank), and state decision-making is difficult to obtain for scholars interested in masculinity. An exception is Alison Woodward's (1996) study of the gendered nature of the European Commission, revealing a highly masculinized bureaucracy dominated by engineers and lawyers with a miserable record on opportunities for women. Press reports of international financial scandals and novels describing the machinations of Wall Street bond salesmen and currency traders give additional insight into the organizing practices, passions, and illusions of men involved in the globalization of financial markets. In a book about the world of (mostly male) corporate managers, Robert Jackall (1988) chronicles the competition, ambitions, and defeats inherent in life at the near top and top of corporate hierarchies. Although he discusses gender in only one section in which he describes the difficulties experienced by women in presenting themselves as competent managers, most of the book can be read as an account about men with money and power who are desperately hanging on to that money and power. Similar studies of masculinities in globalizing organizations would be instructive.

The new hegemonic masculinity, which may differ from that revealed in studies such as Jackall's, represents neo-liberal ideology. *The Economist* talks about the Davos Man,[11] a term that includes businessmen, bankers, officials, and intellectuals (Benería 1999; see also Hooper 2000). "In many ways, he is the rational economic man gone global" (Benería 1999: 68). R. W. Connell (1998) describes a "trans-national business masculinity" as "marked by increasing egocentrism, very conditional loyalties (even to the corporation), and a declining sense of responsibility for others (except for purposes of image making)" (p. 16). This masculinity also seems marked by arrogance, a passion to control, ruthlessness, and aggression. I suspect that excitement and pleasure, perhaps bordering on the erotic (Hacker 1989), are also part of this hegemonic masculinity, including the intertwined pleasures of technology and power. We may have failed to take adequate notice of pleasures as we have considered the role that emotions and gender identities play in organizations, and by

extension in the globalizing process of capitalism. Arlie Hochschild's (1997) description of the pleasures of being at work, pleasures that make the workplace a more desirable place to be than the home, is an exception. Pleasure may extend to domination (Hearn 1993). To dominate may produce a rush of exhilaration. Sally Hacker argued that the pleasures of technology often become "harnessed to domination, and passion becomes directed toward power over nature, the machine, and other people, particularly women, in the work hierarchy" (Acker 1990, p. 153).

Transnational business masculinity, although it may involve the pleasures of domination, does not need to be openly violent because the means of violence are institutionalized in seemingly neutral, rational business practices (Hearn and Parkin 2002). The violence of leaving people without resources for survival through downsizing or moving production from one low-wage locale to another lower-wage locale is simply business necessity. Conceptualized through accounting and strategic planning, no human bodies appear on the books, thus such violences are accomplished as gender neutral and abstracted from actual human consequences. This is another way that corporate non-responsibility and its gendered consequences are embedded in ordinary practices.

Will men and various forms of hegemonic masculinity continue to dominate and symbolize the organizations leading and profiting from globalization? Women, at least a few, are represented among business and political leaders, but they are rare and usually must perform in terms of prescriptions gendered as masculine. However, there are indications that the "new economy" is emerging in a form as male-dominated as the "old economy." The new dominant growth sectors, information technology, biotech innovation, and global finance, are all heavily male-dominated, although women fill some of the jobs in the middle and at the bottom, as is usual in many old economy sectors. Numerically these are small sectors, but their importance far out-distances their size. Much of the evidence for the male dominance of these sectors is anecdotal and comes from the press, from novels, and from TV images. There is, however, some systematic data on gender in computer science and computer technology, occupations that are fundamental to the new economy sectors; without computers these sectors would not exist.

In the U.S., women are a decreasing proportion of those being educated in computer science as well as a decreasing proportion of those working as computer scientists and analysts. The National Science Foundation reports (NSF 2000) that in 1984 women constituted 37 percent of those graduating with a BS in computer science, 29 percent of those graduating with a MS in the field, and 12 percent of those obtaining a Ph.D. By 1996, women had dropped to 28 percent of BS graduates and 27 percent of MS graduates, but had slightly increased their proportions at the Ph.D. level to 15 percent. It could be that fewer women are entering the field, but that those who enter persist more doggedly. Employment in the field follows similar patterns. Women as a proportion of Computer/mathematical Scientists (this includes all those employed regardless of their academic degrees) seem to have hit a high point in 1990 when they were 36.5 percent of those employed in the field (NSF 2000). By 1997, their proportion had dropped to 27.3 percent. Women are a much smaller proportion of those employed as electrical and electronic engineers, having expanded their representation from 8.7 percent to 9.1 percent of these categories in the period between 1990 and 1997 (NSF 2000). In computer programming, a similar pattern occurred. While the numbers of computer programmers increased between 1991 and 1999, women's representation in the field dropped by 6.42 percent (Bureau of Labor Statistics 2000). A recent *New York Times* article confirms that the relative scarcity of women in computer science is still being replicated in U.S. high schools. For example, in Los Angeles, "more than 19,000 boys took the Advanced Placement computer science examination in 2001, compared with just over 2,400 girls" (Stabiner 2003: 35).

Although no one has definitive answers to why computer science and technology remains so male dominated, a primary factor seems to be the identification of computer work with forms of masculinity that exclude women and emphasize obsessive concentration and/or violence and self-absorption. The culture of computer science and technology heavily emphasizes total commitment to the work to the exclusion of the rest of life. Many news stories about Silicon Valley dramatize the round-the-clock work lives there. Henry Nicholas, an electrical engineering Ph.D. and co-founder of Broadcom is quoted as explaining the 18-hour days he often works, "You have to take yourself to the absolute limits of human behavior. The whole concept is you leave nothing in reserve" (*International Herald Tribune*, June 27, 2000). Tracy Kidder documented this peculiarity of computer designers in *The Soul of a New Machine* in 1982. Apparently, little has changed. In addition, computer science emerged in close connection to engineering, which has always been a male-identified and dominated field. Although as this is written in 2003, the IT and computer industry is in a deep recession, there are no indications that this technology will become less important for globalizing transnational firms.

Male dominance and a masculine ethos of computer science have an importance that goes beyond the new economy sectors and extends to the global society as a whole.

Computer scientists and technologists may not be the Information Technology managers of the future. Instead, they may be people trained in business administration, but with a broad grasp of technology issues, which might mean that more women could move into such positions. However, the gendered expectations and behaviors of top corporate leaders seem to continue to be defined in terms set by hegemonic masculinities even when women fill these positions, as noted above.

Gender as a resource for globalizing capital. Women's labor is a resource for capital, as documented in the very large literature on women and development and gender and economic policy, detailing research on the working lives of poor women, especially women in non-Northern countries, makes clear (for example, Bakker 1994; Benería and Roldán 1987; Boserup 1970; Nash and Fernández-Kelly 1983; Rowbotham and Mitter 1994). Gender has been a resource for globalizing firms as they seek out new sources of low-wage labor. In country after country, women and often children have been drawn into production for the world market and into wage labor in transnational organizations. Although such employment often provides welcome income for poor families, much research also exposes how exploitive it is. Multinationals

may find it particularly profitable to locate production where labor laws and unions are weak and women workers are still attached to peasant families. For example, Ong (1983) describes these processes in rural Malaysia in the late 1970s. Where the state and women's lack of power are not sufficient to maintain low wages, transnational corporations or their local contractors may, of course, resort to more blatant methods. In a later example from Malaysia, Bhopal (1997) details the campaign of intimidation orchestrated by a U.S. company against strong union organizing among electronics workers in Malaysia. The author notes that 85 percent of the workers were Malaysian women, but does not examine the role that gender might have played in their struggle or the gender consequences of the loss of union rights.

Literature on Third World women workers also reveals the great variety of ways in which women are incorporated into transnational capitalist production and the ways in which existing local gender relations are a resource for capital. For example, production may be done in the home, with the family organized as an entrepreneurial enterprise, as in the satellite factory system in Taiwan (Hsiung 1996). In such cases, class, gender, production, and reproduction meld in different ways than in Western societies, with employer/supervisory control folded into existing patriarchal family controls. In other cases, for example in China, some industrial production for the world market is carried out by mostly women workers living in large dormitories reminiscent of the dormitories set up for women textile workers in New England at the beginning of the nineteenth Century (Lee 1998). In other cases, young women workers live at home and contribute their cash incomes for the support of parents and siblings, while they remain under the traditional control of parents (Wolf 1992). These examples do not begin to reflect the complex and multifaceted ways in which gender relations, mediated by race/ethnic and class relations, are integrated into the relations of capitalist production as globalization progresses.

Capitalism can prosper from many different gender and race/ethnic patterns. While the above examples come from "developing" countries, gender, along with immigration, continues to be a resource for employers in the rich Euro-American countries. Gender is particularly a resource for the provision of the multiple support services that make possible the existence of the centers of transnational business in "global cities" as Saskia Sassen (1998) argues. In global cities the work of provisioning, cleaning the offices, child tending, and caring for bodies and homes must be done so that global managers and other members of the global elite can go easily about their business. The labor power for these tasks is to a large extent provided by immigrants, disproportionately women, from Third World countries.

Evelyn Nakano Glenn (1998) and others discuss the transnational gender relations that exist in caring work. For example, Filipinas and Guatemalan women migrate to the United States to become domestic workers for affluent women whose professional careers are thus facilitated. Transnational migration of domestic and caring workers is also nothing new for the United States. Forced migration of African slaves included women who became house servants and child minders. Waves of European immigrant women worked first as domestics in the cities of America in the late 19th and early 20th Centuries.

Gendered images and ideologies of femininity and masculinity are used in various sectors of international capital to construct desirable workers (and managers) and desired behaviors. Working class and Third World women are often seen as docile, cheap to employ, and able to endure boring, repetitive work, whether or not women see themselves in these ways. The "feminization of labor" (Standing 1989), or the increasing insecurity, low pay, and routine tasks of jobs and other forms of employment, confirms such images of women workers.

In the rich "developed" countries, gender images continue to help shape sex segregation, the continuing gender stereotyping of jobs, and the symbolic construction of desirable workers. Images of successful professionals and managers in global businesses are sexualized and gendered as they are presented in the media. These images are not uniform, but seem to present a variety of ways in which to be assertive, smart, competitive, and in control. Some of these images are depictions of feminine success, the young and sexy woman who is beautiful as well as on top in the business world. Such images suggest the changing class configurations of gender in the centers of capitalist global power. Changing gender images seem to have also been part of the transition from socialism to market capitalism in Eastern Europe. For example, the image of the male worker as the hero of socialism has been replaced by the entrepreneur (True 2000).

The Gendered Effects of Globalization

Globalization has had gendered impacts on the lives of women, men, and their families. The following is a very brief summary of some of these effects. One of the most visible impacts has been the increased participation of women in the paid labor market almost everywhere, except in the former socialist countries, while for men labor market participation has decreased (Standing 1999). At the same time, Standing (1999) and others argue, the old full-time, secure, with-benefits kind of employment is eroding as new "feminized" jobs, low-paid, temporary or part-time, insecure, and without benefits are created. However, these new jobs are often much better than no jobs and they do improve the lives of many of the women who have them. In addition, in many countries educated middle-class women have had in the 1980s and 1990s increased opportunities for professional and managerial employment, contributing to increased affluence for their families, while exacerbating class differences among women. Another general impact is that unemployment has also risen around the globe (Standing 1999), with some indications that men's unemployment rates are rising to the levels of those of women.[12] Inequality and dire poverty are gendered outcomes of globalization. Inequality and poverty contribute to the apparent increase in the international trafficking in women for prostitution and trafficking in both women and men for other kinds of labor (NIKK 2002).

Generalization about the effects of changes in the structure of employment and welfare state protections is difficult and problematic because they vary tremendously over time, over nations, over economic sectors, and over class and race/ethnic as well as gender lines. However, it seems that women may be more negatively affected than men.

Global changes also affect personal gender relations and identities. For some

women, increased opportunity for paid employment may mean greater autonomy and equality in personal life, or avenues out of oppressive relationships. For others, these changes lead to less security, greater difficulties in taking care of themselves and their families, and, perhaps, the necessity to remain in unsupportive or violent relationships with men. The old Euro-American gender contract in which men earned the family income and women did the unpaid work of maintaining home and family is substantially gone, although still an ideal for many. To the extent that a secure job and a living wage were supports for a stable masculinity, that masculinity may be threatened by the increasing difficulty in finding such work, as men are extruded from good jobs into less skilled jobs, unemployment, or early retirement. This is probably a particularly severe problem for young men who are trying to establish a satisfactory masculine identity. These examples only touch on a few of the possible consequences of global restructuring for the destabilizing of gender identities.

Some things remain the same. In spite of the erosion of the economic base for the old male/provider—female/carer model in the rich industrial countries of the North, work has been and still is organized on a masculine model of the worker. This model has a fundamental lack of fit with the more complex demands for nurturing and earning money of most women's lives. This model for work organization is predicated upon the separation of production from other aspects of life, as I argued above. The reorganization of work and demands for increased productivity, increased intensity of work, and longer or irregular hours, increase the lack of fit with women's lives (Hochschild 1997) and the lives of men who desire to share family work. (Few men are as yet required to share this work.) These increasing demands stretch across levels of skill and hierarchy, although varying in terms of specific pressures. In the lowest paid female-typed service jobs, such as elder or child care, serving in fast food restaurants, or routine clerical jobs, work invades life through irregular schedules, required overtime and/or required part-time. Thus, increased stress for many workers, especially women, is another consequence of the complex changes that are summarized under the concept "globalization."

Notes

1. Valentine M. Moghadam (1999) has written a recent overview of research and theoretical issues in the field. See also, Chandra Talpade Mohanty (2002) and Marianne Marchand and Anne Sisson Runyan (eds., 2000). See also Basu et al. (2001) and Zillah Eisenstein (1998).

2. This statement, by implication, maintains conceptual distinctions between these large institutional areas. But, these distinctions are discursive as well as anchored in some concrete organizational arrangements. As discursive distinctions, the separation of economy, polity, and the rest of social life may impede rather than facilitate understanding by posing connections as particular objects of investigation rather than as integral to the ongoing functioning of social relations as a whole that extend across discursively constructed boundaries. Feminist deconstructions have long argued that boundaries, such as those between the public (male) and the private (female), are part of the conceptual practices of power (Smith 1990) that maintain the dominance of certain men. Conceptual boundaries may also be part of the practices of power that maintain the dominance of globalizing, gendered capitalism.

3. In some countries, there are also new controls that protect workers rights, particularly those of women to equal opportunities and equal pay with men, as Walby (2002) has pointed out.

4. *A Historical/Methodological note:* I have the sense that the term "globalization" began to be used as the dominance of neo-liberal capitalism began to be proclaimed in the late 1980s and certainly by the time of the demise of the USSR and communist regimes in other countries around 1989–90. At that time political leaders in the Northern, rich capitalist countries began to proclaim triumphantly, "There Is No Alternative" (TINA) to their form of capitalism. Until then, one could have argued that there were two competing global systems, but with only one remaining, TINA seemed obvious. "Globalization" as an area of research and publication exploded once there seemed to be only one global playing field. A bibliographical search for articles on globalization confirms this surmise. Academic Search Elite lists 5 articles on globalization for the ten years from January 1978 to January 1988. From February 1988 to December 1995 (8 years), 52 articles with this subject appear, while in the seven-year period from January 1996 to December 2002, 2,287 articles on globalization were indexed.

5. See, for example, the work of Maria Mies (1987).

6. North Atlantic masculinities were not, however, simply transferred to diverse colonial worlds, as Mohanty (2002) and others point out. In some colonizing efforts, colonized men were "feminized" by European occupiers as weak and compliant, not sufficiently masculine.

7. A large literature on these processes now exists. See, for example Mies 1986; Mohanty, Russo, and Torres 1991; Connell 2000.

8. The idea of a "productive" and a "reproductive" economy in uneasy interdependence is in some ways similar to the much earlier Marxist feminist argument that housework was necessary to the reproduction of labor power and thus necessary to the production of surplus value. This argument disappeared partly because of its functional nature—i.e., housework exists because it is necessary or functional for capital. The notion of productive and reproductive economies seems not to have this problem of circularity. However, this formulation is an oversimplified abstraction that does not provide space for the increasing role of the state in both production and

reproduction in the history of capitalism in Euro-American countries.

9. See Lourdes Benería (1999) for another analysis focusing on the development of market society.

10. Much of this discussion is based on the work of R. W. Connell (1987, 2000).

11. Davos is the town in Switzerland where world business, economic, and political leaders meet yearly to discuss the world economy.

12. Unemployment is defined and measured differently in different countries. See Standing (1999), Chapter 5 for a discussion of some of the difficulties in measurement and suggestions of solutions.

References

Acker, Joan. (1990). Hierarchies, Jobs, Bodies: A Theory of Gendered Organizations. *Gender & Society*, 4,2: 139–158.

———. (1988). Class, Gender, and the Relations of Distribution. *Signs: Journal of Women in Culture and Society* 13,3: 473–497.

Acker, Joan, Sandra Morgen, and Lisa Gonzales. (2002). *Welfare Restructuring, Work & Poverty.* Eugene, Oregon: University of Oregon, Center for the Study of Women in Society.

Applebaum, Richard P. and Gary Gereffi. (1994). "Power and Profits in the Apparel Commodity Chain." In Edna Bonacich, Lucie Cheng, Norma Chinchilla, Nora Hamilton, and Paul Ong, Eds., *Global Production: The Apparel Industry in the Pacific Rim.* Philadelphia: Temple University Press.

Bakker, Isabella (ed.). (1994). *The Strategic Silence: Gender and Economic Policy.* London: Zed Books.

Basu, Amrita, Inderpal Grewal, Caren Kaplan, and Liisa Malkki. (2001). *Globalization and Gender, special issue of Signs* 26,4.

Bauman, Zygmund. (1998). *Globalization: The Human Consequences.* Cambridge: Polity.

Beck, Ulrich. (2000). *What Is Globalization?* Cambridge: Polity.

Benería, Lourdes. (1999). Globalization, Gender and the Davos Man. *Feminist Economics* 5,3: 61–83.

Benería, Lourdes and Martha Roldán. (1987). *The Crossroads of Class & Gender: Industrial Homework, Subcontracting, and Household Dynamics in Mexico City.* Chicago: University of Chicago Press.

Bergeron, Suzanne. (2001). Political Economy Discourses of Globalization and Feminist Politics. *Signs* 26,4: 983–1006.

Bhopal, Mhinder. (1997). Industrial Relations in Malaysia—Multinational Preferences and State Concessions in Dependent Development: A Case Study of the Electronics Industry. *Economic and Industrial Democracy* 18,4: 567–596.

Boserup, Ester. (1970). *Woman's Role in Economic Development.* London: George Allen and Unwin Ltd.

Bureau of Labor Statistics, Current Population Survey. (1983–1999). Employed Persons by Detailed Occupations and Sex. Washington, DC: GPO.

Castells, Manuel. (1997). *The Power of Identity. The Information Age: Economy, Society and Culture*, Volume II. Oxford: Blackwell.

Collinson, David L. and Jeff Hearn (eds.). (1996). *Men as Managers, Managers as Men.* London: Sage.

Connell, R. W. (1987). *Gender & Power.* Stanford, CA: Stanford University Press.

Connell, R. W. (2000). *The Men and the Boys.* Berkeley: University of California Press.

Eisenstein, Zillah. (1998). *Global Obscenities: Patriarchy, Capitalism, and the Lure of Cyberfantasy.* New York: New York University Press.

Elson, Diane. (1994). "Micro, Meso, Macro: Gender and Economic Analysis in the Context of Policy Reform." In Isabella Bakker, ed., *The Strategic Silence: Gender and Economic Policy.* London: Zed.

Freeman, Carla. (2001). Is Local: Global as Feminine: Masculine: Rethinking the Gender of Globalization. *Signs* 26,4: 1007–1038.

Gibson-Graham, J. K. (2002). "Beyond Global vs. Local: Economic Politics Outside the Binary Frame." In A. Herod and M. Wrights, eds., *Geographies of Power: Placing Scale.* Oxford: Blackwell Publishers.

Giddens, Anthony. (1999). *Runaway World.* London: Profile Books.

Glenn, Evelyn Nakano. (1999). "The Social Construction and Institutionalization of Gender and Race: An Integrative Framework." In Myra Marx Ferree, Judith Lorber, and Beth B. Hess, eds., *Revisioning Gender*. Thousand Oaks: Sage.

Hacker, Sally. (1989). *Pleasure, Power, and Technology*. Boston: Unwin Hyman.

Harcourt, Wendy (ed.). (2002). Place, Politics and Justice: Women Negotiating Globalization. *Development* 45,1.

Hardt, Michael and Antonio Negri. (2000). *Empire*. Cambridge, MA: Harvard University Press.

Hearn, Jeff. (1993). "Emotive Subjects: Organizational Men, Organizational Masculinities and the (De)construction of 'Emotions.'" In Stephen Fineman, ed., *Emotions in Organizations*. London: Sage.

Hearn, Jeff and Wendy Parkin. (2001). *Gender, Sexuality and Violence in Organizations*. London: Sage.

Hochschild, Arlie. (1997). *The Time Bind: When Work Becomes Home and Home Becomes Work*. New York: Metropolitan Books.

Hooper, Charlotte. (2000). "Masculinities in Transition: The Case of Globalizations." In Marianne H. Marchand and Anne Sisson Runyan, eds., *Gender and Global Restructuring: Sightings, Sites and Resistances*. London and New York: Routledge.

Hsiung, Ping-Chun. (1996). *Living Rooms as Factories: Class, Gender and the Satellite Factory System in Taiwan*. Philadelphia: Temple University Press.

Jackall, Robert. (1988). *Moral Mazes: The World of Corporate Managers*. New York: Oxford University Press.

Kidder, Tracy. (1981). *The Soul of a New Machine*. New York: Avon Books.

Lee, Ching Kwan. (1998). *Gender and the South China Miracle: Two Worlds of Factory Women*. Berkeley: University of California Press.

Lenz, Ilse. (2002). Globalization, Gender and Work: Perspectives on Global Regulation. Working Paper.

Marchand, Marianne H. and Anne Sisson Runyan. (2000). "Introduction. Feminist Sightings of Global Restructuring: Conceptualizations and Reconceptualizations." In Marianne H. Marchand and Anne Sisson Runyan, eds., *Gender and Global Restructuring: Sightings, Sites and Resistances*. London and New York: Routledge.

Mies, Maria. (1986). *Patriarchy and Accumulation on a World Scale*. London: Zed Books.

Moghadam, Valentine M. (1999). "Gender and the Global Economy." In Myra Marx Ferree, Judith Lorber, and Beth B. Hess, eds., *Revisioning Gender*. Thousand Oaks, CA: Sage.

Mohanty, Chandra Talpade. (2002). "Under Western Eyes" Revisited: Feminist Solidarity through Anticapitalist Struggles. *Signs* 28,2: 500–535.

———. (1991). "Cartographies of Struggle: Third World Women and the Politics of Feminism." In Chandra Talpade Mohanty, Ann Russo, and Lourdes Torres, eds., *Third World Women and the Politics of Feminism*. Bloomington and Indianapolis: Indiana University Press.

Mohanty, Chandra Talpade, Ann Russo, and Lourdes Torres (eds.). (1991). *Third World Women and the Politics of Feminism*. Bloomington and Indianapolis: Indiana University Press.

Nash, June and Fernández-Kelly, María Patricia (eds.). (1983). *Women, Men, and the International Division of Labor*. Albany: SUNY Press.

National Science Foundation/Division of Science Resources Studies. (1997). SESTAT (Scientists and Engineers Statistical Data System), 2000. *Women, Minorities and Persons With Disabilities in Science and Engineering: 2000*.

NIKK. (2002). *Bodies Across Borders—Prostitution and Trafficking in Women*. Oslo, Norway: Nordic Institute for Women's Studies and Gender Research.

Ong, Aihwa. (1983). "Global Industries and Malay Peasants in Peninsular Malaysia." In June Nash and María Patricia Fernández-Kelly, eds., *Women, Men, and the International Division of Labor*. Albany: SUNY Press.

Reed, Rosslyn. (1996). "Entrepreneurialism and Paternalism in Australian Management: A Gender Critique of the 'Self-Made' Man." In

David L. Collinson and Jeff Hearn, eds., *Men as Managers, Managers as Men*. London: Sage.

Rowbotham, Sheila and Swasti Mitter. (1994). *Dignity and Daily Bread*. London and New York: Routledge.

Sassen, Saskia. (1998). *Globalization and Its Discontents*. New York: The New Press.

Sen, Amartya. (2002). How to Judge Globalism. *The American Prospect, Special Supplement: Globalism and the World's Poor*, Winter: 2–6.

Smith, Dorothy. (1987). *The Everyday World as Problematic*. Boston: Northeastern University Press.

———. (1990). *The Conceptual Practices of Power*. Toronto: University of Toronto Press.

Stabiner, Karen. (2003). Where the Girls Aren't. *New York Times*, January 12, Section 4A: 35.

Standing, Guy. (1988). Global Feminization through Flexible Labor. *World Development* 17: 1077–1095.

———. (1999). *Global Labour Flexibility*. New York: St. Martin's Press.

Stiglitz, Joseph E. (2002). Globalism's Discontents. *The American Prospect, Special Supplement: Globalism and the World's Poor*, Winter: 16–21.

Strasser, J. B. and Laurie Becklund. (1993). *Swoosh: The Unauthorized Story of Nike and the Men Who Played There*. New York: Harper Business.

True, Jacqui. (2000). "Gendering Post-Socialist Transitions." In Marianne H. Marchand and Anne Sisson Runyan, eds., *Gender and Global Restructuring: Sightings, Sites and Resistances*. London and New York: Routledge.

Walby, Sylvia. (2002). Gender and the New Economy: Towards a Framework for Comparative Analysis. Paper presented at workshop of the Globalization, Gender and Work Transformation Research Groups, Tokyo, Aug. 29–Sept. 1.

Walby, Sylvia and Heidi Gottfried. (2003). *Gendering the New Economy: Theorizing the Trajectories of the G-4Y, Regulation and Gender*. London: Palgrave.

Wallerstein, Immanuel. (1974). *The Modern World System*. New York: Academic Press.

Ward, Kathryn B. (1993). "Reconceptualizing World System Theory to Include Women." In Paula England, ed., *Theory on Gender/Feminism on Theory*. New York: Aldine de Gruyter.

Wolf, Diane. (1992). *Factory Daughters: Gender, Household Dynamics, and Rural Industrialization in Java*. Berkeley: University of California Press.

Woodward, Alison E. (1996). "Multinational Masculinities and European Bureaucracies." In David L. Collinson and Jeff Hearn, eds., *Men as Managers, Managers as Men*. London: Sage.

33 Mary Nell Trautner

Doing Gender, Doing Class
The Performance of Sexuality in Exotic Dance Clubs

One of the key findings of contemporary feminist scholarship is that organizations and occupations are often gendered—that is, they draw on notions of femininity or masculinity that are hegemonically defined. Building on the idea of gender as performance (Butler 1990; Moloney and Fenstermaker 2002; West and Zimmerman 1987), scholars find that workers in a wide range of occupations and organizations "do gender" in particular ways, based on assumptions about what customers like, motivations, and "normal" interactive behaviors (Acker 1990). Particularly in service-oriented occupations, women work as women, as femininity is constructed and reified in ways that reinforce heterosexuality and male dominance and "naturalize" stereotypical images of women (Dellinger 2002; Dellinger and Williams 2002; Hall 1993; Leidner 1991; Loe 1996; Williams, Giuffre, and Dellinger 1999). Through the continual performance and institutionalization of gender and gendered behaviors and rituals, gender and sexuality become central features of organizational culture—those shared understandings, beliefs, behaviors, and symbols that emerge through interactions between organizational actors (Dellinger 2004; Dellinger and Williams 2002; Gherardi 1995; Hallett 2003; Trice 1993).

While the concept of the gendered organization has been critical to our understanding of how and why sexuality and gender are core features of many jobs, what has received less attention is why some organizations—particularly those that are very similar to one another—exhibit different forms of gender and sexuality (Britton 2003; Dellinger 2004). To examine this question, this article builds on the idea of gendered organizations. I argue that gender in organizations interacts with other major features of stratification—such as class and race—to construct unique organizational cultures that project distinctive images of gender and sexuality that are fitted to their particular organizational settings. I show that the activities and practices of strip clubs construct forms of sexuality that are not only gendered but also distinctively classed—that is, they articulate ideas and presentations of gender that are mediated

Excerpted from the original. Mary Nell Trautner, "Doing Gender, Doing Class: The Performance of Sexuality in Exotic Dance Clubs," *Gender & Society* 19, no. 6 (December 2005): 771–788. Copyright © 2005 Sociologists for Women in Society. Reprinted by permission of SAGE Publications.

AUTHOR'S NOTE: I would especially like to thank Ronald Breiger and Elizabeth Borland for their advice and suggestions on earlier versions of this article, as well as Tim Bartley, Joseph Galaskiewicz, Andrew Jones, Samantha Kwan, Calvin Morrill, Wade Roberts, Louise Roth, and David A. Snow. I would also like to thank Christine Bose, Christine Williams, the anonymous reviewers from *Gender & Society*, my research "escorts," and finally, the three women whom I interviewed for this article.

by class position. I explore this idea of organizations as gendered and classed through a comparative ethnographic analysis of the performance of sexuality in four exotic dance clubs in the southwestern United States.

In exotic dance clubs, women at work must act like women by embodying traditionally female behavior and roles as well as by dressing and behaving femininely. Because the central features of the organizational culture within exotic dance clubs are the commodification and commercialization of women's sexuality, the clubs are premised on the consumption of women's bodies and the presence of those bodies in hegemonic male fantasies. Thus, women work not only as women but as sexualized women. Yet despite having similar underlying institutional logics, clubs offer noticeably different presentations and performances of gender and sexuality. My data demonstrate that exotic dance clubs have different organizational cultures based on distinctions made by the perceived social class of customers. Clubs construct sexuality to be consistent with client class norms and assumptions and with how the clubs and dancers think working-class or middle-class sexuality should be expressed. Those clubs that cater to a middle-class audience present one version of sexuality, while a quite different type of display can be found at working-class clubs. As a result, women in exotic dance clubs work not only as sexualized women but as classed women.

Before reviewing the context and methods of the present study, I briefly address two literatures that inform my analysis: the literature on gendered organizational cultures and the literature on the relationship between gender, sexuality, and class. I then present my findings on how organizational

culture influences the performance of sexuality in strip clubs. I argue that exotic dance clubs and the actors within them do class much like organizations and their actors also do gender. As West and Fenstermaker (1995, p. 13) have argued, "no person can experience gender without simultaneously experiencing race and class." I am asserting that the same is true of organizations by locating class performance as a central feature of organizational culture. Finally, I consider the implications of this study for future research.

Organizational Culture and Gender

Organizational culture refers to the shared understandings and behaviors of a work environment as well as informal or symbolic interpersonal norms such as those that promote or prohibit particular sexual interactions and sexual behaviors (Dellinger and Williams, 2002; Hearn and Parkin 1995). Organizational cultures contain strong symbolic orders of gender that provide clues to men and women about how to behave properly (Gherardi 1995). Gender in organizations thus becomes simultaneously and continually performed and institutionalized. While organizational actors may believe they are expressing purely personal, preexisting tendencies and tastes when they dress in a particular way, manage disputes, or interact with their clients or colleagues, their behaviors and inclinations are strongly influenced by their surrounding organizational culture—what "matches" or "clashes" with the organization's style (Dellinger and Williams, 2002; Gherardi 1995; Morrill 1995).

While a number of studies have examined the ways in which particular organizational and occupational cultures are gendered, there is generally little research that compares gender across organizational cultures to understand gender as dynamic, interactional, and context specific (see Britton 2003; Dellinger 2004). Comparing the experiences of male accountants in the magazine publishing industry, Dellinger (2004) found that workers "do masculinity" differently, depending on the particular gender ideologies supported by the organizational cultures in which they are embedded. Similarly, Britton (2003) found that among prison guards, the construction of gender varies across organizational contexts. Thus, when it comes to the social construction of gender in the workplace, these authors support the idea that "where you work matters just as much as what you do" (Dellinger 2004, 546). In this article, I build on and contribute to this idea of gender as context specific by examining the role of social class in the construction and consumption of gender and sexuality.

Gender, Sexuality, and Class

In addition to structuring opportunities and life chances, social class structures gender and sexuality in important ways and is itself constructed and performed in relation to gender and race (Bettie 2000, 2003). As Bettie (2000, 15) argued, women perform "different versions of femininity that [are] integrally linked and inseparable from their class and race performances." I draw from the results of several ethnographies of American high schools to inform my analysis of exotic dance clubs because the construction of gender difference and the performance of gender in both locations are magnified and exaggerated. Moreover, these ethnographies highlight that distinc-

tions between middle-class and working-class groups are marked in a range of ways: through clothing, vocabularies, grammar and accents, hairstyles, cosmetics, attitudes toward teachers, and perhaps most important, through attitudes toward and practices of sexual behavior (Bettie 2000, 2003; Morrill et al. 2000; Ortner 1991). The middle-class teens in Bettie's (2000, 2003) California school (most of whom were white) saw tight-fitting clothing and heavy cosmetic use as signals that their working-class peers (most of whom were racial minorities) were sexually promiscuous, even if they were not. Working-class girls, aware of these perceptions, reinforced their class identity by exaggerating the appearance differences between themselves and the white middle-class girls. In this way, as Ortner pointed out, "class differences are largely represented as *sexual* differences" (1991, 178, emphasis added).

Recent comparative work in exotic dance clubs has found a similar relationship between gender, sexuality, and social class as they intersect in women's appearance. Frank (2002) found that customers perceive the appearance of dancers to be related to the position of the club in the class hierarchy. Dancers in lower-class clubs, who were more racially diverse, were considered by male customers to be "overweight," to be "out of shape," and to wear too much makeup and perfume. In contrast, clubs in the upper tier of the class hierarchy consisted of mostly white dancers who tanned and had breast implants. Based on these appearance cues, men imagine the dancers to have different amounts of cultural and educational capital—and it is this distinction that motivates their club choices (Frank 2002). Although Frank's work is a major contribution to the study of exotic dance clubs, her approach, like Bettie's (2000, 2003), primarily emphasizes individuals. As a result, sexuality and class remain individual characteristics and performances rather than central features of organizational culture. In this article, I combine insights from both of these literatures. I examine the multiple ways in which social class, as a core feature of organizational culture, is constructed and institutionalized in the performance of gendered sexuality in exotic dance clubs.

Method

To explore the ways in which social class and organizational culture influence the performance of sexuality within strip clubs, I made a total of five visits each to four exotic dance clubs in Pueblo,[1] resulting in more than 40 hours spent in the field. The advantage of a prolonged direct observation technique in this setting is that I was able to experience the club settings and routines as both a first-time club goer and a more seasoned customer, familiar with the settings, members, and activities. These four clubs, The Oasis, The Hourglass, The Treasure Chest, and Perfections Showclub, are the busiest, most well-known, and most popular clubs in town. Each of these clubs serves alcohol, which by state law means that they are topless only, as opposed to fully nude. Because my sample is derived from just one city in one state, my findings highlight differences within the boundaries of this particular state's laws. While clubs in other locations would no doubt be responsive to variations in state and city laws, I believe that variations in social class norms would continue to be as salient as I found them to be in Pueblo.

Most clubs in Pueblo allow a woman to enter as a customer only when accompanied by a man. Although it is commonly believed that rules governing the admittance of women were created to prohibit prostitutes and lesbians from entering the club, a private conversation with a club manager in Texas (Trautner 1998) revealed that an additional function of these rules may be to prevent jealous wives and girlfriends from entering the clubs and physically harming dancers and/or customers. Consequently, I presented myself not only as a paying customer but also as either the girlfriend or friend of my male escort(s) to observe naturally occurring interactions and club routines. Like many women researchers who enter strip clubs, my presence in the club did seem to be noticeable to both customers and dancers. To minimize the intrusiveness of my presence, I followed the techniques outlined by Wood (2000): I visited each club frequently (five times each) and for long periods of time (at least two hours each visit), which allowed me to blend into the scene and become less conspicuous to those around me.

At each site, I assumed the role of the naïve stranger to blend in with the crowd as much as possible by looking and acting much like the typical woman customer and also to learn as much as possible about how each club operated. This role involves acting naïve, curious, and responsive but very unknowledgeable about the setting, unspoken rules, and activities taking place, which encouraged members to explain and elaborate on the customs and expectations of the club (Morrill 1995; Snow, Benford, and Anderson 1986). I paid particular attention to interactions between dancers and customers, appearances of dancers, and styles of stage and table dances. A dance is the length of one song, which is usually about three minutes long. This means that on any particular stage, about 40 dances occur in the space of two hours. Field data were collected between January and July of 2001.

The drawback to my covert position is my lack of insight into the club employees' thoughts and feelings toward, and explanations of, the routines in which they participate. In an attempt to sort out this issue, I conducted supplemental in-depth interviews with three exotic dancers in the summer of 2002. These women work at the clubs I observed while in the field and were selected based on prior personal contacts.

Sexuality in the Strip Club

The four clubs I visited serve two distinct clientele: Perfections Showclub and The Oasis market themselves to a middle- and business-class clientele, while The Hourglass and The Treasure Chest serve primarily working-class and military audiences. While the focus of this article is on how these clubs do class through the performance of sexuality, I should note that they do class in other ways as well. Generally, the middle-class clubs price everything higher than do the working-class clubs, although the differences are often minimal (i.e., a bottle of beer costs fifty cents more at the middle-class clubs, and the cost of admission is $6 and $7, in contrast to $3 and $4 for the working-class clubs).

Clubs also do class in large part through their physical characteristics. These characteristics, such as the state of the parking lot, quality of the lighting and sound systems, club furnishings, amenities offered to customers, and physical layout of the club, signal to potential customers what kind of club it is and what kinds of sexual experiences customers might expect. In doing so, they also encourage customers to become middle-

class or working-class "performers" (Bettie 2003). That is, regardless of their own class background, customers can experience a middle- or working-classed event and be seen as a middle- or working-classed individual through their consumption of sexuality as organized by the exotic dance club. By providing their customers with cigars, gourmet meals, soundproof phone booths (presumable to call home or the workplace without revealing the nature of their location), and plush, relaxing arm chairs, the middle-class clubs make the club-going experience about more than just sex, more than just viewing unclothed women. They appear to make every effort to insulate customers from everyday reality by providing them with a safe haven in which they can desire and appreciate women and act and be treated like "gentlemen" (Edgley 1989). These clubs, as I will demonstrate, are characterized by performances of desire and gazing at the female form from a distance, constructed to appear as admiration and respect. I refer to this as "voyeuristic sexuality."

In contrast, the working-class clubs create an atmosphere conducive to pure physical pleasure and lust. Gone are the amenities, high-quality equipment, and soft, comfortable furniture. Customers, who are mostly working-class performers, are able to come to these clubs for vicarious sexual experiences and little else, as the sexuality that is on display is often more interactive than is seen at middle-class clubs. These clubs are havens for the viewing of women as sex objects, for the imagining of these women as sexual partners, and for the enactment of male power (Liepe-Levinson 1998; Wood 2000). This form of sexuality I call "cheap thrills" sexuality.

In addition to the physical characteristics of the clubs, these two forms of sexuality and gender—voyeuristic and cheap thrills—are constructed and institutionalized in various performative aspects of the clubs as well. I argue that these performative aspects—the appearances of the dancers and other staff, the dancing and performance styles, and the interactions that take place between dancers and customers—are as indicative of class and classed expectations as they are of sexuality.

Images of Attractiveness

There is a general difference in the appearance of the women at the middle-class and working-class clubs. Dancers conform much more closely to the hegemonic cultural ideals of attractiveness at Perfections and The Oasis than do dancers at the working-class clubs. In these middle-class clubs, there is a narrowly restricted range of women's body types. For example, there are very few overweight dancers, women with short hair, older women, women with strong musculature, or nonwhite women. About half of the dancers at each middle-class club appear to have breast implants, and most of the others have naturally large breasts. In fact, one woman I interviewed, Mandy, commented that The Oasis, where she works, "is known for the most . . . for all the girls having them. They call it 'Silicone Valley.'" While there are some small-breasted women, there are comparatively fewer working in these clubs, approximately 10 to 15 percent (as compared to approximately 40 percent in the working-class clubs). Most of the women wear their hair styled in some way (i.e., curled, gelled, sprayed), but all wear their hair loose, flowing down their shoulders and back. Only occasionally will a dancer wear her hair in pigtails to match a schoolgirl costume. All of the women wear makeup, and the majority of the dancers heavily accentuate their eyes with glitter, eyeliner, or eye shadows. Most have long fingernails painted in light or neon shades that reflect the black lights of the club. Mandy says these features describe women who are "classy looking" (at least in this context) and that this is a look that develops over time, as the women become accustomed to the ways in which "Oasis girls" look and "take care of themselves": "Some girls start out and they are so ghetto looking, but then she works and she starts to look better and starts to take more appreciation in what she looks like—tanning, and doing her hair more, and just . . . *changing*. As they are around the other girls and see how the girls keep up themselves, they start to change themselves, because they have the money to also take care of themselves."

According to Mandy, one reason the dancers pay such attention to makeup use and hairstyle is that the amount of money they make from customers is contingent on how sexy, attractive, and feminine they appear to their audience (see Price 1998). While this is true of any club, for middle-class clubs, there is a heavy emphasis on conforming to middle-class cultural ideals. Marina, a dancer at The Treasure Chest, one of the working-class clubs, also recognizes this feature of the middle-class clubs as she comments that "The Oasis and Perfections are probably the best for girls that have ideal bodies according to standards by society today . . . like mainstream standards, pop culture standards."

Fixing their hair, tanning, wearing perfume, and applying particular kinds and shades of makeup not only symbolize doing heterosexuality and femininity—practices that reproduce and naturalize the dominant cultural norms of heterosexual (Dellinger and Williams, 1997; Giuffre and Williams

390 | Chapter 5: Doing Gender Diversity: At Home and at Work

1994)—they symbolize doing class as well, as the performers distance themselves from women who are "ghetto looking." By using their appearances to simultaneously do gender, heterosexuality, and class, these women increase their financial gains while at the same time conforming to, legitimating, and perpetuating dominant cultural ideals.

At The Treasure Chest and The Hourglass, however, there is a much broader spectrum of female bodies on display. There are several overweight women, as well as some women who are so thin their entire skeletal structure is visible through their skin. There are a few older women working at each club (40-ish), and there is a greater diversity of dancers in terms of race. In contrast to the middle-class clubs, which feature predominantly white women, each of the working-class clubs employs a (relatively) large proportion of Latina dancers, with a few Black and Asian women. On a typical night with 30 dancers, approximately 15 are women of color, compared to about 5 of 30 in the middle-class clubs, thus more accurately reflecting the racial composition of Pueblo. Most women also tend to have long hair, and nearly all the white women have bleached-blond hair. Women are also more creative with their hairstyles. One woman at The Hourglass has a completely shaved head, and other women wear their hair in braids or pulled back into ponytails or barrettes. Marina notes that at "blue-collar" clubs such as The Treasure Chest, "you can see more of the personalities of all these people, which is what I am really interested in. The girls can do whatever they want, and do." Women apply heavy makeup that accentuates their mouths, rather than their eyes as in the middle-class clubs. Most wear dark or bright red lipstick and paint their long fingernails to match, styles typically associated with working-class women (Bettie 2003).

Another aspect of attractiveness is the types of clothing that dancers wear. While by law all dancers must wear a G-string, there are considerable differences in the other types of clothing and accessories worn. Dancers at the middle-class clubs tends to wear outfits—either themed costumes such as a dominatrix or a Catholic schoolgirl outfit or pieces of lingerie like a satin chemise or teddy that covers both the breasts and the buttocks. A few of the dancers wear much more elaborate outfits, such as bodysuits or minidresses. Some dancers choose to wear accessories to appeal to particular members of the audience, like cowboy hats or baseball caps, and some accessorize with thigh-hi stockings or a garter. Veronica, who dances at The Oasis, captures all of these themes as she describes her outfits to me:

Well, I usually do "the schoolgirl." Ninety-nine percent of the time I wear a plaid schoolgirl skirt with a white top, knee-hi socks. It is the most profitable outfit that I have. And I have a lot of outfits. But tonight, I'm not going to be the schoolgirl. Tonight I brought lingerie; I'll wear black thigh-his and a black bra and this really pretty black robe that one of the girls sold me. I do have one other outfit, like hip-hugger pants that kind of flair out at the bottom, and a little bikini top that's really cute. For a while, on Sundays only, because on Sundays a lot of people are out riding their motorcycles and they'll come into the club, I have a little shirt with sequins and a motorcycle, and it says "Born to Ride." I don't remember if it says "Harley Davidson" on it, but it's my biker shirt for the motorcycle people. But my main thing is the schoolgirl.

All the dancers wear high heels, but they wear the chunky heeled platform shoes that were in fashion at the time, rather than traditional stilettos, as worn in the working-class clubs. Dancers at these clubs wear more jewelry than seen at other places, and many even wear wristwatches. Mandy and Veronica both revealed that there was a time when all the dancers were required to wear evening gowns. Veronica says, "When [the present owner] first bought The Oasis, he really wanted to target like age 30 and up, white-collared-class businessmen. So he said that all the girls had to wear gowns or dresses on stage, and we're only going to play 80s music. That was his way to appeal to that age group."

Few of the dancers at The Hourglass or The Treasure Chest wear costumes or anything that could be dubbed an outfit. Most of the dancers wear a bra-like top and their G-string, with nothing else. Occasionally, a dancer will wear some type of lingerie or dress that covers both the buttocks and the breasts, but it is rare. As one of my escorts commented, "It feels like we're at the beach!" Marina agrees but notes that she dresses a little differently than do most of the other dancers at The Treasure Chest, emphasizing how clothing—"covering up"—reinforces and reproduces classed expectations: "A lot of girls will just walk around in just a bikini," she says, "but I'll wear dresses, I'll cover up more and be more like . . . classy. Not that I *am* more classy, but I have that façade." Note also that Marina is highlighting the difference between class as a material location ("not that I *am* more classy") and class as a symbolic performance ("but I have that façade").

What these body images amount to is a complete catering to the cultural ideals and perceived fantasies in the middle-class clubs and a wider array of images of women's sexuality and appearance in the working-class clubs. That the dancers at The Oasis and Perfections draw attention to their eyes suggests an invitation to look and an aura of mystery—they are meant to see and be seen. The red lipstick that accentuates the lips of the dancers at the working-class clubs oozes sensuality, fire, and excitement. In a sense, the dancers draw from two different yet equally stereotyped images of femininity: the good girl (who looks but does not touch, "innocent" in her sexualized schoolgirl outfit) and the bad girl (who falls outside the hegemonic beauty ideals and flaunts her exaggerated sexuality). Yet as Ortner (1991), Bettie (2000, 2003), and others have pointed out, these stereotypes are as much about class as they are about femininity.

Stage Performances: Constructing the Gaze

The stage is perhaps the most visible and obvious place in which sexuality is performed. On a main, center stage of a club, nearly everyone in the audience has a view of the show, and as such, performing on the main stage is a dancer's main method of being seen, making eye contact with customers, and finding people for whom she may perform table dances later in the evening (Ronai and Trautner 2001). For many customers, the stage area is their only experience with dancers, as many patrons never purchase table dances at all, preferring to watch the constant and varied entertainment provided on the stage. This is where dancers can show off their bodies, show off their athletic and dance abilities, and show customers, through their dance style and choice of music, the personalities they have constructed for their performances.

There is a distinct dissimilarity between the styles of music featured at each of the clubs. While all the women are allowed to choose their music for dancing, there is much less variation than there would be if organizational cultures had no effect on music style. The songs heard at Perfections and The Oasis, the middle-class clubs, are generally contemporary pop music, such as one would find on the Billboard Top-40 or on the television station VH-1 (recall that the club owner at The Oasis required all dancers to perform to hits from the 1980s a few years ago). The songs are for the most part slower, with lyrics that are decipherable. Most of the songs feature male vocalists (such as songs by Third Eye Blind or Matchbox 20), although some instrumental techno songs, as well as some music by Madonna and Janet Jackson, are played. Veronica reveals that a few years ago, "no rap was allowed. None. No rap. But now they play some. You really gotta appeal to everyone." A typical evening, however, features only one or two rap songs.

In contrast, the music at The Hourglass and The Treasure Chest is remarkably different from the middle-class clubs. Most of the songs played are rap songs, heavy metal, and classic rock. There are very few pop songs played, and even fewer songs with women vocalists. Marina describes the music in similar terms, stating that "there's girls who dance to rap music and they'll have more of a 'tough' side. There's girls who do country, and there's girls that do really angry, evil music. And it doesn't necessarily mean that the girl *is* that way, it's just the style that she dances. She'll, like, appeal to the S&M crowd." At the working-

class Treasure Chest, where they "can do whatever they want," dancers exercise even more control over the music in the club, while simultaneously playing up their classed, sexualized, "bad girl" image. Marina describes scenes in which "girls will go up on stage and if they don't like the music the DJ is playing, they might tell him 'fuck you,' or they might just lay there and not dance. It is *crazy*." In other words, dancers exercise social control over each other, DJs, and managers by not dancing to songs that fall outside the club's regular style of music.

Tipping and Table Dances: Interacting with Customers

Dancers expect to receive tips while performing on stage. The stage tip is a customer's way of communicating that he likes what he sees and perhaps that he may be willing to purchase a table dance from the dancer later in the evening. For the dancer, accepting a stage tip simultaneously functions as a way for her to advertise herself to the entire audience and for them to imagine what getting a table dance from her might be like (Ronai and Ellis 1989). Much like the dancing routines themselves, the styles by which dancers accepted tips were characteristic of very different forms of sexuality.

Dancers at The Oasis and Perfections, the middle-class clubs, were much more likely to accept tips without permitting any sort of touching between themselves and the customers, consistent with the passive dancing style. Even when customers attempted to touch dancers, the women enforced voyeuristic sexuality. One customer at The Oasis, for instance, held his dollar between his teeth for the dancer (presumably so that she would use her mouth or breasts to retrieve the bill, a method often seen at working-class clubs), but the woman, with perhaps a smidge of disdain, simply used her hands to pluck the bill out of his mouth.

Many dancers at the middle-class clubs, instead of touching or allowing contact between themselves and patrons, will perform a "mini-show" for the tipping customer to view, as Kayla at Perfections does (as illustrated by my field notes): "A man wearing dark slacks and a polo-style shirt approached the stage during Kayla's dance, with a crisp one-dollar bill held firmly in his hand. He stood patiently at the side of the stage, waiting for her to notice him. She saw him as she turned around, and strolled over to where he was standing, smiling and making eye contact. She lay down on the stage, and for 10-15 seconds, rolled around on the stage, moving her legs in the air in a scissors-like fashion before lifting the side of her G-string for dollar placement." Other dancers, instead of giving the customer a special performance, will lightly place their hands on the man's shoulders and lean over him, throwing their hair over his head and then whisper something in his ear, before removing their hair, stepping back, and lifting the side of their G-strings. Several times I asked my male escorts to tip these women and let me know what kinds of things the dancers were whispering to the patrons. By those reports, they were whispering light conversational fare: "What's your name?" "Are you having a good time?" "Is that your girlfriend with you?" None of these comments are inherently sexy, but in this context, the way in which these questions are whispered leaves men feeling somewhat special, like the dancer thinks he is interesting enough to have been noticed, or that she wants to know his name.[2] If the trick

works, perhaps he will purchase a table dance from her after she leaves the stage (Ronai and Ellis 1989).

In contrast, the dancers at the working-class clubs accept tips and perform the dances in very different ways. In these clubs, stage tips and the table dances appear to be driven by the desire to give a "cheap thrill," a term that merges sexuality and social class. There is much contact between dancer and customer, and the seemingly most popular dancers are those who touch the customers in some way with their breasts or genital region. One widespread method of accepting tips is demonstrated by Sara at The Hourglass (from my field notes): "She bent down so that her breasts were directly in front of his face, moved close to him, and then grabbed the back of his head, pulling his face into the space between her breasts, and shook her body from side to side. There was not enough space between the man's face and her breasts to see how the man responded, so he might have kissed or licked her breasts and no one would have seen." Another popular method of receiving tips from customers is to grab the back of the man's head and shove it into the dancer's genital region while shaking his head from side to side. Trina, a dancer at The Treasure Chest, thanked a man for his $1 tip by holding the back of his neck with her left hand, whispering in his ear, and grabbing his bottom with her right hand. She then slapped his rear end with an open hand and poked him with her index finger in the space right between his cheeks.

Likewise, table dances simulate sex and sexual acts in dramatic ways. I observed several dancers at both working-class clubs who spent at least one-third of each song sitting on her knees facing the customer, with her face directly inside the man's legs, simulating oral sex. Marina is one dancer who uses this trick, and she describes in detail just what it is she is doing down there: "If the guy seems clean and seems all right, I will go down like I'm going to give him a blow job, and I'll do this thing where I'll blow warm arm through his pants and I'll roll my Rs so that it feels like a vibrator." It also appears that many of the dancers will very lightly run one of their hands over the man's genital region. Most dancers sit on a customer's lap, facing away from him, grinding their buttocks in a circular motion over his genitals. Dancers also will stand with one foot firmly on the floor, the other resting on the man's shoulder, leaning in toward the man's face so as to give him a close view of her crotch. About a year ago, Marina got in trouble with regulatory agents for "flashing," quickly pushing her G-string over to the side to reveal her genitalia to the customer, a practice she asserts is common (and even condoned) at The Treasure Chest: "When I got in trouble for flashing, the manager told me, 'Well, 95 percent of the girls here flash, so don't feel bad. They just happened to catch you. You should probably just be more careful.'"

These examples make it clear that very different styles of dancing and interacting with customers are taking place at these strip clubs. The middle-class clubs are characterized by performances of passive desire and distance, while the working-class clubs are marked with explicit allusions to sex and sexuality, physical activity and exertion, and contact between patron and dancer.

Conclusion

In this article, I have emphasized the ways that exotic dancers perform gendered and classed sexuality. Of course, women's performances are both a reflection and an interpre-

tation of other core features of organizational culture such as management styles and organizational rules. Had I interviewed managers, more dancers, or customers, or had I become an employee of these clubs, my perspective on the performance of class and the performance of sexuality might perhaps be more focused on those features that constrain or enable women's agency. Yet the strength of my observational approach and small sample is that as an outsider, I am able to make sense of the variations in one city's club experiences much as any customer or potential customer might. Consumers, when faced with an array of seemingly similar services, such as those found in exotic dance clubs, make distinctions based on the frontstage of organizational culture (i.e., the performance of sexuality and class) not based on the backstage constraints that produce them.

Expressions and performances of sexuality, I have argued, are not homogeneous. Clubs construct distinctive working-class and middle-class performances and performers of sexuality that are consistent with popular ideas of how class and sexuality intersect. In this way, my analysis shows that social class is a central feature of organizational culture. Others have examined the ways in which the performance of gender in organizations is context specific (Britton 2003; Dellinger 2004), but they have not examined the role that social class plays in creating different organizational cultures and the effects of those classed cultures on the expression of gender and sexuality. Indeed, just as social class was an invisible category of identity for the young women studied by Bettie (2003), class differences can be overlooked by organizations and gender scholars. In this article, I have argued that exotic dance clubs are not only gendered organizations but also classed organizations. That is, they articulate ideas and presentations of gender that are mediated by class position.

Class differences are thus represented as sexual differences in very concrete ways: in the appearance of dancers and other staff, dancing and performance styles, and the interactions that take place between dancers and customers. Middle-class clubs are associated with a sexuality that is voyeuristic, characterized by distance, gazing, and a formal sexual atmosphere, while working-class clubs are associated with cheap thrills, contact, and a casual sexual atmosphere. These types of sexuality are consistent with and further specify popular images of femininity and masculinity that are also mediated by social class (and race): sexually restrained middle-class white men and women and sexually promiscuous working-class men and women of color. Sex as performance, class, race, power, and gender are thus all intertwined.

Thus, sexuality is much more than an individual attribute, and social class is much more than simply a material location. As women and men construct, perform, and consume gender and sexuality in exotic dance clubs, they are simultaneously constructing, performing, and consuming social class. The task for gender scholars is to examine this understudied intersection between gender, sexuality, and class more fully and in more institutional and organizational contexts, as Bettie (2000, 2003) has done in contemporary high schools. This study of exotic dance clubs, in which gender and sexuality are explicit and exaggerated features of organizational life, provides a rich context in which to view the organizational performance and construction of class. But these processes are at play in other organizational contexts as well, just perhaps more hidden (as class often is). Attention to the simultaneous performance of gender and class will lead us to a richer, more textured understanding of gender and gender inequality, especially in organizational settings. While the indicators of class difference that I highlight here (images of attractiveness, distance/the gaze, and interactions) may be specific to this organizational setting, they may be useful places to proceed as others seek to develop this intersectional approach into other arenas.

Notes

1. Pueblo is a mid-sized city in the southwestern United States (population approximately 500,000). Pseudonyms have been used in place of the names of the city, clubs, and dancers throughout.

2. Most of my male escorts reported feeling this way, even though they also said they "knew better." That is, they were aware that the dancers were interested in a potential financial opportunity, not in a date, yet each still left the stage with a rush of excitement and feeling "special."

References

Acker, Joan. 1990. Hierarchies, jobs, bodies: A theory of gendered organizations. *Gender & Society* 4:139–58.

Bettie, Julie. 2000. Women without class: Chicas, cholas, trash, and the presence/absence of class identity. *Signs: Journal of Women in Culture and Society* 26:1–35.

———. 2003. *Women without class: Girls, race, and identity.* Berkeley: University of California Press.

Britton, Dana. 2003. *At work in the iron cage: The prison as a gendered organization.* New York: New York University Press.

Butler, Judith. 1990. *Gender trouble.* New York: Routledge.

Dellinger, Kirsten. 2002. Wearing gender and sexuality "on your sleeve": Dress norms and the importance of occupational and organizational culture at work. *Gender Issues* 20:3–25.

———. 2004. Masculinities in "safe" and "embattled" organizations: Accounting for pornographic and feminist magazines. *Gender & Society* 18:545–66.

Dellinger, Kirsten and Christine L. Williams. 1997. Makeup at work: Negotiating appearance rules in the workplace. *Gender & Society* 11:51–77.

———. 2002. The locker room and the dorm room: Workplace norms and the boundaries of sexual harassment in magazine editing. *Social Problems* 49:242–57.

Edgley, Charles. 1989. Commercial sex: Pornography, prostitution, and advertising. In *Human sexuality: The societal and interpersonal context*, edited by Kathleen McKinney and Susan Sprecher. Norwood, NJ: Ablex.

Frank, Katherine. 2002. *G-strings and sympathy: Strip club regulars and male desire.* Durham, NC: Duke University Press.

Gherardi, Sylvia. 1995. *Gender, symbolism and organizational culture.* London: Sage.

Giuffre, Patti A., and Christine L. Williams. 1994. Boundary lines: Labeling sexual harassment in the workplace. *Gender & Society* 8:378–401.

Hall, Elaine J. 1993. Smiling, deferring, and flirting: Doing gender by giving "good service." *Work and Occupations* 20:452–71.

Hallett, Tim. 2003. Symbolic power and organizational culture. *Sociological Theory* 21:128–49.

Hearn, Jeff, and Wendy Parkin. 1995. *"Sex" at "work": The power and paradox of organisation sexuality.* 2d ed. New York: St. Martin's.

Leidner, Robin. 1991. Serving hamburgers and selling insurance: Gender, work, and identity in interactive service work. *Gender & Society* 5:154–77.

Liepe-Levinson, Katherine. 1998. Striptease: Desire, mimetic jeopardy, and performing spectators. *The Drama Review: TDR* 42:9–29.

Loe, Meika. 1996. Working for men: At the intersection of power, gender, and sexuality. *Sociological Inquiry* 66:399–421.

Moloney, Molly, and Sarah Fenstermaker. 2002. Performance and accomplishment: Reconciling feminist conceptions of gender. In *Doing gender, doing difference: Inequality, power, and institutional change*, edited by Sarah Fenstermaker and Candace West. New York: Routledge.

Morrill, Calvin. 1995. *The executive way: Conflict management in corporations.* Chicago: University of Chicago Press.

Morrill, Calvin, Christine Yalda, Madalaine Adelman, Michael Musheno, and Cindy Bejarano. 2000. Telling tales in school: Youth culture and conflict narrative. *Law & Society Review* 34:521–65.

Ortner, Sherry B. 1991. Reading America: Preliminary notes on class and culture. In *Recapturing anthropology: Working in the present*, edited by Richard G. Fox. Santa Fe, NM: School of American Research Press.

Price, Kim. 1998. Stripping work: Women's labor power in strip clubs. Paper presented at the annual meetings of the American Sociological Association, San Francisco, August.

Ronai, Carol Rambo, and Carolyn Ellis. 1989. Turn-ons for money: Interactional strategies of the table dancer. *Journal of Contemporary Ethnography* 16:271–98.

Ronai, Carol Rambo, and Mary Nell Trautner. 2001. Table and lap dancing. *Encyclopedia of criminology and deviant behavior*, vol. 3, edited by Nanette Davis and Gilbert Geis. Philadelphia: Taylor and Francis.

Snow, David A., Robert Benford, and Leon Anderson. 1986. Fieldwork roles and informational yield: A comparison of alternative settings and roles. *Urban Life* 15:377–408.

Trautner, Mary Nell. 1998. When you are a scholar and a sex object: The conflicting identities of female college students who strip for a living. Sociology honors thesis, Southwestern University, Georgetown, TX.

Trice, Harrison M. 1993. *Occupational subcultures in the workplace.* Ithaca, NY: ILR Press.

West, Candace, and Sarah Fenstermaker. 1995. Doing difference. *Gender & Society* 9:8–37.

West, Candace, and Don H. Zimmerman. 1987. Doing gender. *Gender & Society* 1:125–51.

Williams, Christine, Patti Giuffre, and Kirsten Dellinger. 1999. Sexuality in the workplace: Organizational control, sexual harassment, and the pursuit of pleasure. *Annual Review of Sociology* 25:73–93.

Wood, Elizabeth Anne. 2000. Working in the fantasy factory: The attention hypothesis and the enacting of masculine power in strip clubs. *Journal of Contemporary Ethnography* 29:5–31

34 David Iacuone

"Real Men Are Tough Guys"
Hegemonic Masculinity and Safety in the Construction Industry

There is considerable debate in the field of industrial sociology concerning the precise impact that the culture of masculinity has on the lives of working-class men. There are different opinions about it depending which theorist you read. Lynch (1997), citing Connell (1995), argues that manual labourers embody an "ideal type" of manliness called "protest masculinity." This gender culture is characterized by horseplay and aggressiveness. In his analysis of the British building industry circa 1918, Hayes (2002) reveals that workers impeded the development of welfarism (amenities, annual leave, etc.) because they believed that "true men" should be able to tolerate harsh working conditions (Hayes, 2002; p. 238). Williams (1993) and Hopkins (1995) reject the notion of masculinity altogether arguing that blue-collar workers' thinking is conditioned by their class position. During the six months I spent on building sites as an undisclosed ethnographic researcher and the 20 interviews I conducted, I developed my own interpretation regarding the manner in which this culture functions. In this article, I examine how a particular network of dominant social relations functions in the construction industry. The major argument put forward here is that the hegemonic masculine construct most commonly found on building sites in Victoria (Australia) serves to create a gender hierarchy, and this informal power matrix influences builders' perceptions of occupational health and safety (OH&S) so that they become less concerned about their welfare. This article is divided into (1) dimensions of masculinity, (2) the gender hierarchy, (3) one-upmanship, and finally (4) hegemonic masculinity and perceptions of OH&S.

Dimensions of Masculinity on Construction Sites

In this section, I explore masculinity on building sites. The masculine culture in this situation consists of five distinct but not completely unrelated dimensions: (1) gender identity and sexuality, (2) girl-watching, (3) risk and physical prowess, (4) horseplay and larrikinism, and (5) alcohol consumption. I draw upon my field observations and interviews to demonstrate how they function.

Gender Identity and Sexuality

The construction worker's world is not only designated as male, it is also defined as heterosexual (Paap, 1999; p. 9). A substantial

Excerpted from the original. David Iacuone, "'Real Men Are Tough Guys': Hegemonic Masculinity and Safety in the Construction Industry," *Journal of Men's Studies* 13, no. 2 (Winter 2005): 247–266. Copyright © 2005 Men's Studies Press, LLC. Reprinted by permission of Men's Studies Press.

amount of general discussion between construction workers centres on the issues of heterosexuality and men's genitalia. Five weeks into my ethnography, I was working on a supermarket refurbishment. I encountered Dave in the toilet at 15 past 11, and he commented, "I once read in a book about a prostitute that a tradesman's tools only operate as well as he uses them." This comment was a generic reference to heterosexuality. As he explained it, the point he was trying to get across was that "it is not the size of a man's penis that counts; it is how he utilizes it."

Four days later, I was sitting in the lunch shed for morning tea. I observed a construction worker as he read two stories out of the newspaper loud enough to allow everybody to hear. The common theme in the news articles was the discussion of male genitalia. The first story involved a vindictive 33-year-old wife who cut off her 81-year-old husband's penis before murdering him. The second case depicted a male streaker who was pursued by police. Upon his apprehension, he was thrust into a wire fence. "Boy, that must've really hurt his testicles," exclaimed the tradesman after he finished regaling us with this story.

On day 34, I was sent to work on a site where factories were being constructed. At lunchtime, I was sitting in the lunch shed with Karl (the foreman) and Allen and David (labourers). Karl turned to me and said, "Allen wants to go work in a morgue." "Why?" I asked. "Why do you think?" "You're sick, Allen, isn't that called necrophilia?" I cried out. "Yeah, I think that's what it's called," said David. "At least if you work in a place like that, there's little chance you'll get knocked back by any women," I said while grinning. The trio found this remark humorous.

The importance of heterosexuality, sexual prowess, and the value placed on a man's penis was not only conveyed to me in workplace discussions. When I strolled around building sites, I encountered many drawings of oversized penises and pictures of objectified women in compromising sexual positions. Here are some of the examples of the scrawlings. The first example was found on a site in Caulfield where a series of apartments were being erected.

There was a scrawling of a naked man with a bushy chest and an oversized penis on a concrete pillar in the lunchroom. A scrawling of a naked woman with long hair and an accentuated vagina appeared below the man. Below her, there was a crude drawing of a penis the size of her entire body. (Fieldnotes)

I spotted the remaining scrawlings while I was working for On-time Labour Hire. I discovered them in the toilets of a six-storey building that was nearing completion:

A crude drawing of a penis with a ruler appeared on the wall. "My 9 inch long" was written below. In the second cubicle of the toilets on the fourth floor, there are several crude drawings of penises. There is also a picture of a man ejaculating over a naked woman with her legs spread open. (Fieldnotes)

These examples provide insight into the construction worker's psyche. They reveal that the men pay a lot of attention to their genitalia and have specific ideas about women's function in society. It is conceivable that they were uncensored expressions because these scrawlings were not made in the presence of others. They provide insight into workers' perceptions of gender relations and how tradesmen's masculine identities are linked to virility and sexual conquest.

Girl-Watching

Over many decades, girl-watching had been a common pastime on construction sites. Many tradesmen will observe women who walk by their workplace and comment about their physical parameters to their peers (or even to the women) every chance they get. This practice gives rise to a whole series of issues. Sometimes the women are within earshot of the workers and find their remarks abhorrent. In a minority of cases, the tradesmen can take their harassment too far, resulting in legal charges. The construction, forestry, mining, and energy union (CFMEU) has tried to stamp out this practice by introducing sanctions for anybody caught making offensive comments to bystanders. Upon arrival at many sites, you are informed that sexual harassment of any kind will not be tolerated. On one occasion, I worked on a site that was located in a private girls' school. I was told by the shop steward that if I were to make any sexual innuendos to the girls, I would be asked to leave the site. But I soon discovered that despite building companies' best efforts, this practice still occurs.

On the first day of my participant-observation research, I was sent to work on a site where they were erecting a large factory. I partook in two instances of girl-watching with three other men who worked for Jupiter's (a labour hire company). We were located on the second-floor office section of the construction site, which overlooked a road. On two occasions, young women walked by, and we all ran over to ogle them. Tony, a middle-aged carpenter, said, "Have a look at the tits on her."

Making a reference to a woman's physical attributes was very common and it normally occurred moments after all the workers had huddled together to partake in this act of voyeurism. On day 48 of my research, I was stationed at a Jewish girls' school that was undergoing a partial renovation. At lunchtime, Neil (the site foreman) and I were walking to a 7-Eleven. We passed a female pedestrian. Neil looked at me and said, "Boy, did you see the size of her tits?"

In his research on voyeurism in the building industry, the American sociologist Feigelman (1974) discovered that remaining undetected was a fundamental rule of girl-watching (Feigelman, 1974; p. 41). Feigelman spent three months on a construction site in a large city as a participant-observer. The key findings of his research are as follows: voyeurism is determined by social variables, a worker's proclivity to peep is influenced by group dynamics, and girl-watching performs the function of encouraging social integration (Feigelman, 1974; p. 36).

Feigelman's notion of the importance of going unnoticed was reinforced by my own observations. Five months into my ethnography, I was working on a series of offices in Kew. One day after my morning break, Robert (the OH&S officer) and I continued pulling down a wire fence at the rear of the building site. Robert was standing on a ladder, and he began to peek though a crack in the corrugated iron fence behind the one we were tearing down. He noticed a young woman washing her automobile in the car wash on the adjacent property. He looked at me and said, "Boy, she's a nice-looking girl. Here, come up this ladder and take a look."

Another important issue that Feigelman raises is that, in the construction industry, peeping serves a critical social function. It brings people together who would not otherwise fraternise with one another. A worker may not have the strongest desire to scrutinise a woman's physical characteristics. But he is more likely to do so if his peers are already engaged in this behavior (Feigelman, 1974; pp. 42–45). Furthermore, this voyeuristic activity has an important intergroup dimension. Workers have an obligation to facilitate each other's peeping experiences. When a worker spots a woman and makes a remark about her to his coworkers, they are in a moral position to validate his actions by agreeing that the female is attractive or sexually desirable. In the late stages of my fieldwork, I was working on a site where a series of flats were being erected. After morning tea, John and I were labouring on the third-storey scaffolding located at the front of the building site. A female jogger who appeared to be in her late 30s to early 40s ran past. I looked over at him and made him aware of her presence with a motion of my head. John smiled at me and said, "I'd bend that over, I suppose." In this instance, I was complicit in reinforcing the masculine culture. This is because I had undergone socialisation into an environment where such behaviour was the norm.

The Importance of Risk and Physical Prowess in Men's Activities

On a building site, there is a belief that men need to be tough and should not be afraid to partake in physically demanding tasks. Men should also value what are considered "real sports" (e.g., football) and need to embody a daredevil attitude. The first time I observed the importance of this was one week after I was stationed on the supermarket renovation. I was sitting in the lunchroom with three electricians during lunchtime. The three men were sharing their fondness for water-skiing. One electrician in particular gained excitement from reaching high speeds on water-skis. Men's need to recklessly pilot motor vehicles at high velocities is supported by Australian statistics on fatalities and injuries. Walker (1998) reports that young males are overrepresented in motor vehicle related deaths.

Two days later, I was digging in the partitioned area at the rear of the supermarket. From 10:00 to 12:30, Dominic and Joel discussed the topic of snow sports. They then spoke about altercations for an additional 40 minutes. The discourse focused on ingenious ways of defeating enemies when they possess greater strength than you. For the major proportion of our lunchtime recess, Joel and Dominic shared instances when they had witnessed violence on the football field. This next discussion occurred several days later during "smoko" (colloquial for morning break). In the course of our morning break, Dave and I began discussing the weekend's English football results. "How did you like Manchester United's performance? 3-0, a good result, hey?" Dave asked me. "You're not talking about soccer again, are you? Find another topic," Joel cried out. This comment ignited a debate between the workers who supported soccer (Dave and I) and those who disliked the sport and preferred Australian-rules football (everybody else). Soccer in Australia was condemned for producing dull contests and not demanding a sufficient level of physical endurance from its players.

Construction workers don't only value machismo behaviour and physical toughness in the field of athleticism. Many tradesmen believe that involving oneself in an altercation is an acceptable means of resolving a grievance. Indeed, many tradesmen placed a high value on fisticuffs. Take the third-year apprentice Joel as an example. Joel was raised in an environment where the use of physical force to solve one's disputes was commonplace. He boasted that he could have defeated the "Greek tiler" (with whom he had a verbal joust prior to starting on the supermarket renovation). He also divulged that he had frequently been involved in physical struggles with his siblings.

In July 2002, I was assisting in the construction of a library at an exclusive girls' school. When I arrived at the site one morning, I had a conversation with John (site foreman) on the topic of fighting. John said, "If I'm backed into a corner by five guys trying to bash me, I use the element of surprise to my advantage. I'll knock one of the bastards out, and the rest will run away."

Horseplay and Larrikinism

This constitutes the fourth dimension of masculinity on building sites. This cultural component encompasses activities ranging from playing minor pranks on people, such as affixing a sticker on their back and allowing them to walk around with it (in view of others) for the rest of the day, to more elaborate farces such as this one:

> Other sort of jokes, I ride a pushbike when I can to my site, and one day my bike was completely gone, and I found it wired inside the ceiling space, and the ladders were all chained up so I couldn't go home. (Interviewee's recollection)

Larrikinism or mischievous behaviour has been a subject of interest for sociologists. In his classic study of a Ford car manufacturing plant, Beynon (1973) found that young men's machismo behaviour created life-threatening situations. In the late 1960s, the Halewood plant was forced to lower the minimum age of employment to 18, consequently employing a larger number of adolescents. As is the case among many young people, they participated in practical jokes. For example, the "lads" crafted hand grenades made by combining flammable adhesives and hurled them into nearby rubbish bins. The resulting explosion produced flame 20 feet high. Someone could have easily been killed by this practice (Beynon, 1973; p. 139).

Willis (1977) examined the behaviour of a specific group of male school children who were designated "the lads." These boys embraced a "counter school culture" that emphasized the use of force to dominate weaker adolescents, heterosexual promiscuity, and a dislike for formal authority.

Years later, the University of Newcastle academic Lynch (1997) studied larrikinism in N.S.W.'s construction industry. Adapting Connell's (1995) theory, Lynch distinguishes between two different types of masculinity. He calls the first "protest masculinity," which on a building site manifests itself as larrikin-style behaviour. The second is called "complicit masculinity," more associated with domination via institutional power (Lynch, 1997; p. 76). Lynch argues that the working class embraces protest masculinity and the middle class is complicit with it. The complicit male defines his masculinity through institutional power obtained through education and hard work. The protest man defines his manhood through the use of physical force and an aversion for management. In Lynch's conceptualisation, these two groups are in conflict with one another. The complicit male wages a battle against the protest man by controlling the division of labour and through the utilization of academic and social capital. Through the media, he depicts the protest man as unruly and troublesome, wishing only to bring the building industry to a standstill (Lynch, 1997; pp. 79–83).

Having briefly reviewed the literature, I now discuss occasions when I observed this practice. This incident took place three weeks after I had been stationed on the supermarket refurbishment. I was walking down a thoroughfare. Dave was proceeding up the walkway (presumably to the foreman's office). As he passed me, I noticed that he had a large sticker glued to his back. I got his attention, approached him, and removed the label from his left shoulder. "Thank you, David, for removing that sticker!" exclaimed Dave. Several minutes later, I encountered Dave at the rear of the construction site. He was working with Bill and John (the concreter). He turned to me and said in a loud voice, "Dave, I bet you it was one of these bastards that stuck that sticker on my back." Both John and Bill vehemently denied the accusation.

In June of 2002, I was helping a group of shopfitters outfit a large factory. I was working for Ron, who was the leading hand of the shop-fitters. Ron was a jovial man who would continually engage in minor acts of horseplay. For example, when I asked him the location of the site toilets, he said that there were none and that I would have to cross the street. After a brief pause, he told me he was not being serious and pointed me in the right direction. Another shop-fitter would constantly joke about the size of the vacuum cleaner I was using (it was the variety that you strap onto your back). He lamented that it had insufficient suction, and he urged me to find a more powerful one.

The aforementioned field observations demonstrate that horseplay encompasses a broad range of activities. My interviewees also reported many occasions when they had observed acts of bravado. For example, Ian, a 48-year-old asbestos worker, discusses some of the kinds of larrikinism that occurred on the sites he worked on:

> Ian: We used a lot of tape and all that sort of stuff, and people went up ladders, and you would put tape around their legs so they couldn't get down from the ladders, things like that, you know?
>
> David: So you've actually seen that happen?
>
> Ian: I've done it to people, and people have done it to me, you know; you do payback, you say, "Payback's a bitch. I'll get you sooner or later," you know?
>
> David: And what sort of reaction does that person have when you do that?
>
> Ian: A bit of swearing. "You bastard." They chase you down and say, "When I get down from here I'll have you."

Alcohol Consumption

Alcohol consumption is the final dimension of masculinity. Generally speaking, it is a significant part of men's lives. Fletcher (1997) reports that 62 percent of men in the general population compared with 40 percent of women drink alcohol at least once per week. Additionally, men are more than three times as likely to be drinking in excess amounts. Alcohol consumption is an important aspect of the masculine culture found in the building industry. According to many construction workers, "real men" look forward to occasions when they can drink beer, and men who do not are considered to be effeminate. Riemer (1979) discovered that the practice of consuming copious amount of alcohol figured prominently in American construction workers' perceptions of themselves as genuine and working-class males. In the time I spent in the field, tradesmen devoted a lot of time to planning collective drinking sessions. On the first day of my research, I was sent to assist in the construction of a factory in Scorsby. Craig, a labourer from Jupiter's, commented on many occasions that he was looking forward to the evening because he would be free to consume a large amount of alcohol. He suggested that after we had completed the day's work, we should all head down to the nearest hotel.

On another occasion, I was working on a girls' school. During "smoko," the following discussion transpired. "Are you going to the pub tonight?" asked Peter (a young demolition worker) of Trevor (the leading hand). "I'm not sure," he replied. "Of course you are. Where else would you go on a Friday night?" remarked Peter.

When tradesmen were not planning the next occasion when they would drink beer to the point of paralysis, *alcohol* would arise as the topic in other ways. This discussion took place between two tradesmen who were working at the supermarket refurbishment. During "smoko," I was sitting in the first lunch shed. The refrigeration man was reading the newspaper and made the following comment. "Not another story about a drunk driver. Why don't they leave them alone? Why don't they pick on all the people who take heroine and then drive? You should be able to take a test where you can get a license to drive around drunk," said Joel with a smirk. "This permit should only be given to people who can prove that they are capable of safely driving a car whilst under the influence." This comment made the refrigeration man laugh.

In the construction industry, there is pressure placed on the nondrinker to become one and ultimately a peer-group member. The following event occurred on a building site in Kew. At the end of a particular day, Robert and I entered the underground car park to access our vehicles. As I entered, I noticed that 12 tradesmen had congregated in the car park, and they were consuming beer. They offered Robert a beer, and he picked up a can and joined the group. Two days later, Nigel (another labourer from Jupiter's) and I were heading towards our cars at the end of the day. We encountered eight tradesmen sitting on big rolls of carpet drinking alcohol. As we walked past, they offered us a beer each. Nigel and I accepted, and we joined them. By Nigel's own admission, he does not like beer, but in this case he accepted their invitation because of the peer-group situation.

The Gender Hierarchy

Having explored the masculine culture in the construction industry, I will now take this picture one step further and argue that gender-based practices serve to create a hierarchy among tradesmen. This pecking order is established by the men's subscription to a particular configuration of male culture called *hegemonic masculinity*. Hegemonic masculinity is the most common blueprint in Western culture regarding the way men should behave and the goals they should aspire to. It is an imagined construct rather than a practical one. Only a select few actually possess all the traits associated with this gender ideology. However, the majority still holds its principles in the highest esteem (Paap, 1999; p. 190). It is my contention that different versions of this cultural architecture exist in different socioeconomic groups and in various organisations, often fed by the same messages via advertising and the mass media.

The hegemonic masculine construct found on building sites is characterised by Cheng (1999), whose article *Marginalised Masculinities and Hegemonic Masculinity* is an introduction to the theoretical debates concerning this topic. He defines the dominant masculine culture with these adjectives:

> . . . [D]omination, aggressiveness, competitiveness, athletic prowess, stoicism, and control. Aggressive behaviour if not outright physical violence is important to the presentation of hegemonic masculinity. . . . Love, affection, pain, and grief are improper displays of emotion. (p. 298)

This description of hegemonic masculinity suits the gender performances that thrive in the construction industry, but Cheng overstates his case by assuming that these are the characteristics of the hegemonic culture in general. While office and white-collar workers subscribe to overt heterosexual displays, an integral part of the dominant male culture, I do not believe they value physical toughness and fisticuffs as much as manual labourers do.

Subordinated Gender Constructs

Hegemonic masculinity in the construction industry is developed in conjunction with femininities and subordinated masculine configurations such as effeminate gender performances. The heterosexual man's self-identity depends on his dislike of these other gender constructs (Cheng, 1999; p. 297). In this case, I am using the term "subordinated gender constructs" to denote the various gender configurations on building sites that are targeted by the workers who subscribe to the hegemonic male culture. I acknowledge that Tolson (1977), Connell (1982), Donaldson (1991), and Pease (2002) depict working-class masculinity as a subordinated gender construct in itself. However, this issue is not the focus here, and I am more concerned about the dissemination of power within organisations in the spirit of social theorists like Tausky (1970).

In my field observations, the notion of gender subordination was conveyed to me in the guise of attitudes and practices toward women. The blue-collar workers had specific ideas about women's place in relation to men and how they should be treated. On the first day of my field observations, I was stationed on a site in Scorsby where a factory was under construction. At morning tea, I purchased some food from a van. A construction worker told the rest of us that he wanted to receive fellatio from the woman who operated the food van.

Several weeks into my research, I was working on a supermarket renovation. One day, we started work at four in the morning because our work crew needed to cut the floor inside the store with a deafening machine. It would have been too disruptive to the normal functioning of the supermarket if we did it during business hours. The man operating the cutting device made the following remark to Rob. "Smash that slab really hard. Pretend it's your girlfriend." At that moment, Rob was attempting to upend a freshly cut concrete slab with a long crowbar.

In the afternoon, Joel and I were dumping concrete slabs into the refuse, which was located in the loading bay. The large bricks were coated in a thick greyish paste, so I was using a pair of gloves. Joel was reluctant to carry them because he had no gloves. "Surely you own a pair of gloves," I asked. "Don't you use gloves when you clean the dishes at home?" "Clean the dishes?" Joel answered in bewilderment. "I never set foot in either the kitchen or the laundry. They're the places where the bitches work." "Who are you talking about?" I inquired with growing alarm. "My mother and my girlfriend," replied Joel.

The next day, I was sitting in front of the lunch shed during our midday break. Five tilers were sprawled in front of the lunchroom. One tiler said, "You know, I'd fuck anything that moves. Don't you just hate it when you're fucking a girl and she starts talking to you? You just give her a slap in the face and say, 'Shut up and let me finish my business.'"

When I finished working at the supermarket renovation site, I was sent to work on a group of apartments in Balaclava. One afternoon, it began to rain heavily. The deluge forced two scaffolders and me to seek refuge in a lunch shed. As they waited for the rain to subside, they engaged in a discussion about their sexual experiences. "Have you ever had sex with a mother?" one scaffolder said to the other. "No, have you ever had a threesome?" "Yes, this one time. . . ."

A month after this, I was sent to work on the construction of a library at an exclusive girls' school. Ben (a labourer from Jupiter's) made a comment about his relationship with his girlfriend: "I'm the Alfa-dog, and she's the Beta-dog. Do you know what I mean by that David?" "Yes," I said and nodded my head, "you're the boss, and she's the one who takes orders."

After I finished up at this school, I worked in yet another girls' private college. After visiting the convenience store, I sat down in the lunchroom with Neil and the two Italian bricklayers. As we consumed our sustenance, we had a conversation about street prostitution in St. Kilda. "They're better off working in a licensed brothel than on the streets. Anything can happen to them there. They can get raped," I said. "They don't mind getting raped," replied one of the bricklayers in a serious tone.

The next two events occurred on an office block in Kew during August of 2002. At lunchtime, I was sitting in a lunch shed with Robert, Karl, and a plumber (corpulent with a shaved head). The plumber entertained us with a story about a car accident he was involved in. A mother of two crashed into his vehicle, and she was unable to pay for the damage. This is how the plumber explained it. "This woman, she started telling me about her whole life story. How she couldn't pay because she was raising two kids." "So she had your dick in her mouth, did she?" asked Karl. In this case, Karl characterised the woman's desire to appease the plumber in a misogynistic fashion.

These final examples both occurred while I was employed by On-time Labour Hire. Glen, the lanky lift operator, made this remark to me in relation to his sexual interactions. "When I bring a woman back to my house, I fuck her and then I tell her to get the fuck out of my house." The next morning, I was riding the elevator with Glen. He said, "Everybody wants to ride my life, even the Sheilas." "There are no sheilas around, mate, only blokes," I replied with a wry smile. "There's one walking around the site from Schevello [an interior decorating company]," said Glen. "I tell you what, if I get her in my lift, it will be out of service for an hour while I rape her."

As can be seen in these excerpts, construction workers have particular views about women's place in the world. I overheard many conversations where women were objectified, depicted as servile, and viewed as best suited to domestic duties and only being of value to men in a sexual capacity. In some cases, the notion of sexual assault was apparently acceptable. However, not all men on building sites are complicit in sustaining the dominant masculine culture. In fact, these two examples will demonstrate that a minority is not. The first involves Detlef, a carpenter I met while I was working on an office block in Kew:

> At smoko, Detlef was reading *The Age* and began talking to me about a report on a recent gang rape in Melbourne. The report stated that the "ring leader" received 55 years of imprisonment for his role in the crime. Detlef felt that the gang rape of the 20-year-old girl was a crime of unspeakable brutality. (Fieldnotes)

Detlef's view indicates that he feels sympathy for the victims of such crimes. This final comment was made by a labourer I encountered while I was assisting in the renovation of a storey of a city building:

> At lunchtime, the older construction worker was reading the *Herald Sun* and came across a report about the DNA analysis of a man who raped two women. The test was a police effort to link the man to another crime. He said, "How's that? The police are testing this guy's DNA to see if he committed a rape in another state, and his lawyer is claiming that

it's an invasion of his privacy. What about the privacy of the girls he raped? Isn't that important?" (Fieldnotes)

These examples are significant because they indicate that a small portion of men try to resist the influences of the hegemonic masculine culture. This trend can be seen as part of a general development where men are challenging traditional patriarchal relations in order to improve women's welfare. This is exemplified by men's groups such as the Victorian-based "No to Violence," which provides counseling services for men who harm their partners (*No to Violence*, 2004).

Homosexuality as an Insult

On building sites, if a worker wishes to insult another man, he will often question the individual's membership in the dominant masculine culture. The tradesman will achieve this by accusing the man of being in possession of qualities typically associated with subordinate gender constructions. On a building site in Kew, there was a handwritten notice posted next to the fridge in the second lunch shed that read, "For those of you with limp wrists, if you find that the milk carton is too heavy to return to the fridge, please ask for assistance." This notice was evidently made by an individual who became annoyed when he continually found the communal milk carton outside of the fridge. Such a practice ensured that the milk would spoil and the tradesmen would be left without milk to put in their coffee. After this notice was put up, nobody left the dairy product out again. This sanction functioned because physical strength is valued in the hegemonic masculine culture, and anybody who is found lacking it is viewed as effeminate.

The allegation of homosexuality was frequently used as another way to insult a person. This incident occurred while I was working at the supermarket renovation. Joel made this remark moments after a *Savage Garden* song was on the radio, "Oh, no, not that poncey guy [i.e.: Darren Hayes, lead singer]. He's a pillow-biter." "Pillow-biter" is a colloquial term for homosexuality.

Women on Building Sites

Australian Bureau of Statistics (ABS) figures reveal that women only constitute 12 percent of the industry's workforce. Those women employed in the industry are concentrated in administrative and accounting positions with only eight percent involved in physical work (ABS, 2002). When women who work on building sites embody the values of masculinity, they are accepted by other men (Eisenberg, 1998; pp. 82–83). Although I did not encounter any female manual workers during my field observations, some of the men who participated in my interviews did. Craig, a 22-year-old carpenter, recalled a case where a female labourer was on site:

> Craig: On the Sheraton in Geelong, there was a woman labourer there.
> David: O really? What sort of relationship would the men have with the female labourer? I mean, would they say anything particular to her?
> Craig: Na, she had obviously worked with the company for a while; she was just part of the crew.
> David: She was treated? . . .
> Craig: She was treated pretty good, actually.
> David: Ok, so no one ever made any jokes about her or anything like that?

> Craig: Not really; she fitted in. The boys went to the pub after work, and she'd go the pub with the boys. Yeah, she was just one of them.

In this excerpt, the female labourer in question was spared from being ostracised because her gender performance was consistent with the one prescribed to construction workers by hegemonic masculinity. By Craig's own admission, she was just "one of the boys" and even engaged in ritualistic masculine behaviour by devoting her evenings to alcohol consumption with her all-male work crew. However, had she behaved in a manner that was more consistent with conventional femininity, she would have become the subject of ridicule. Cameron, a 39-year-old ex-foreman, has worked on a site where there were eight female construction workers:

> David: How were they treated?
> Cameron: Oh, poorly, I think. . . . Yeah, look, some of them could hold their own, so they were all right, but the others couldn't hold their own, really; they were more feminine than the others, and they were the butts of many jokes.
> David: Were they like sexist jokes?
> Cameron: Yeah, mainly sexist jokes and even about lifting things, you know, things like that. You know, they'd be given equipment that would be miniature in size. You might be using scrubbing brushes or something like that. They'd be given a tiny one, a bottle brush, "Here, this is yours because you're weak."
> David: So basically they were constantly reminded that in a physical sense they were weaker than the rest?
> Cameron: Some of them weren't. I tell you what—there was some there that could

mix it with the guys and certainly give it out as much as they took. . . . They were referred to in derogatory terms as being butch, and they would then stir the other weaker females or the more feminine females like the guys would, and they were accepted.

David: So they would actually end up stirring the weaker females?

Cameron: Yeah, they wouldn't protect them at all; they'd certainly give them heaps as well.

In Cameron's example, the female workers' inability to embody the hegemonic masculine value of physical strength cost them dearly. They were the subject of ridicule and systematic mocking as exemplified by the gift of the small equipment to remind them of their physical inferiority. On Cameron's building site, a gender hierarchy also came to exist between female labourers. Once again, a worker's location on this hierarchy depended on her gender performance in relation to the dominant masculine culture. All things said, it is certain that the women who were situated at the apex of this all-female hierarchy would have been perceived by the men as most closely embodying the dominant masculine values. Indeed, this was so deeply entrenched in the women's psyche that they believed that this was the correct form of behavior, and they punished other women ("they would give them heaps") for not acting in accordance with these conventions.

One-Upmanship

Hegemonic masculinity is about control and domination. Men who subscribe to this way of thinking have a strong desire to subordinate weaker men and women. Consequently, competition for power becomes a common practice. On the building site, this contest takes the shape of an activity referred to as *one-upmanship*. One-upmanship is the cultural practice whereby construction workers vie for status, recognition, and self-reassurance of their masculine attributes. This activity has to occur in a group because a person's peers need to acknowledge his achievements. If a worker makes a remark about his association to hegemonic masculinity and there is nobody around to acknowledge it, this action would not be as gratifying because he has no audience. An audience also ensures that the worker's status in his peer group will rise incrementally each time his accomplishments in the realm of being male are recognised. One-upmanship is also a crucial element of complicity in hegemonic masculinity. It operates as a mechanism that guarantees that the majority continues to subscribe to the values of the dominant male culture. In this section, I draw on my interviewees' experiences of one-upmanship to illustrate how it functions. I provide two common examples. The first excerpt is from an interview with a 37-year-old carpenter:

David: Have you ever seen a worker lift an object that is too heavy for him in order to show his friends that he's not a "wimp"?

Toni: Yeah, I remember one time one guy lifted a bag of cement, and another guy said, "I'm stronger than you; I'll take two bags of cement," so he lifted two bags of cement.

David: So they were competing with one another? So what happened in the end?

TABLE 34.1 A Summary of Different Types of One-Upmanship Based on Interviewees' Experiences

Types of one-upmanship	No. of interviewees who had seen these contests at least once	No. of interviewees who felt they occurred frequently
Frequency of sexual encounters	0	5
Demonstration of virility	1	0
Wages and job performance	4	0
Alcohol consumption capacity	0	2
Demonstrations of physical strength	4	6

They just kept on competing until they couldn't lift anymore?

Toni: No, it's just a sort of a joke thing, you know? And you just sort of end it there. Just to prove who's stronger, I suppose, that's all it was.

Craig, a 22-year-old carpenter, recalls an incident where his boss felt an urge to demonstrate his physical strength and needed an audience to validate the experience:

Craig: My last boss, he was a pretty big sort of a bloke. You know these six-meter beams—six-by-four beams—he had one of them; he was trying to get three; actually he had one of them on each shoulder, which, you know, you should have two blokes lifting them up.

David: And how heavy would that be, three on your back, like how many kilograms in weight? Are we talking like 35 kilograms, 40?

Craig: Probably, they're probably forty kilo each. . . . Yeah, he was lifting two of them, and he was going for this third he had, yeah.

David: And were people watching him do it?

Craig: Yeah, he gathered up a few people just to say, "Look at me do this." He got two up, and he didn't get three.

David: What did the people say around him?

Craig: Nothing, he was just called an idiot, didn't achieve him anything; he didn't get heroic status.

This example illustrates that construction workers need an audience to witness their acts of physical strength in order to validate their efforts. Possibly, Craig's boss may have not attempted to pick up three 40-kilogram beams had his peers not been in the vicinity. Table 34.1 is a summary of the various kinds of one-upmanship that take place on construction sites, as reported by my interviewees.

As can be seen, the type of one-upmanship that most frequently occurred involved contests of physical strength. This highlights the connection between OH&S and hegemonic masculinity. The interviewees recalled instances where people tussled for status by engaging in dangerous behaviour. In most cases, tradesmen attempted to demonstrate their manhood by outshining others by participating in impromptu contests of strength. My respondents reported that individuals who had no desire to partake in these competitions would be provoked by remarks such as, "Come on, what are you, a girl?" Most important, such games can have dangerous consequences.

At this point, I will turn my attention to the nexus between hegemonic masculinity and OH&S.

Hegemonic Masculinity and Workers' Perceptions of OH&S

The dominant masculine culture influences construction workers' attitudes towards OH&S. Hegemonic masculinity prescribes that men should be tough, dominate over others, and should not be afraid of danger. Consequently, this social environment is conducive to risk taking. In fact, in certain situations it is demanded of people. Two events I observed while I was working at the supermarket refurbishment constitute critical junctures[1] regarding the way masculinity relates to safety. Several weeks after I was stationed on this construction site, Joel and I were working in a barricaded area at the rear of the supermarket. Bill entered the enclosure and remarked, "Be careful when you lift that slab. I did my back in the other day doing a similar job." Joel then said, "That's because you're a 20-year-old pussy. Here, Dave, let's toss another concrete slab on the trolley" [the trolley was already holding two slabs]. In this case, Joel viewed Bill's preoccupation with safety as a quality of a subordinated gender construct (conventional femininity) and insulted him by bringing his association with the dominant masculine culture into question.

Two weeks later, Joel, Rob, and I were standing near the doorway of the office area. Rob began drilling a hole in the wall. The drill emitted a loud, high-pitched noise. I clasped my ears to muffle out the sound. Joel saw me and said, "Oh, come on, Dave. I can't believe that's too loud for you. What are you, a man or a mouse?" At this point, Rob said, "Has he put on his earmuffs again, Joel?" "No, he's holding his ears," he replied in an irritated tone. "That's because he's a pussy," said Rob. In this scenario, I was verbally reprimanded because I was concerned about damaging my hearing and took appropriate measures to protect it. In Joel's and Rob's opinions, I exhibited behaviour that was not fitting for a "true male." These kinds of scenarios take place in the building industry on a daily basis, and it is easy to see how tradesmen ensure that malcontents fall into line with the hegemonic masculine culture.

The tradesmen I interviewed also highlighted the connection between masculinity and OH&S. In many cases, men engaged in dangerous behaviour as a way of reinforcing their association with the dominant masculine culture. A 54-year-old carpenter recalled this incident:

Alex: It happened that one chappie was balancing to walk across a frame, on the highest structural point that was about 12 feet in the air and he was sort of balancing around.

David: So, he was walking on top of the frame?

Alex: Which is only 90 mil wide.

David: How high is that?

Alex: Twelve feet in the air or 3,600 millimetres to four meters in the air.

David: You're kidding me? He was walking on that?

Alex: Well, they get pretty confident, but I always remind them, "Don't get too confident because you can have an accident."

David: Did anyone say anything to him?

Alex: Not really, you think he's stupid. You tell him just to be careful, take it easy;

there's no need to do it. You don't say, "What are you doing up there, you? . . ."

David: You didn't try to directly tell him off?

Alex: You just advise him to do it another way rather than just walking across from one end of the room to the other on the top place. . . . Unfortunately, with carpenters to do that is a sign of macho. To be able to stand up and walk on top plates, it can have devastating results.

This is an example of the health-related risks that some tradesmen take in the name of masculinity. In a second example, a 39-year-old boilermaker became highly concerned when one of his coworkers did something dangerous in an effort to be macho:

David: Have you ever witnessed any cases where guys will do something dangerous on building sites in order to impress their mates?

Dave: Dangerous? Yeah, actually I did witness something once, and I wasn't very happy about it. . . . We were working at a Navy depot that had actually been decommissioned; we were demolishing it. It was sort of like a demolition/asbestos removal job. Yeah, we found some old, um . . . compressed air, a bit like scuba tanks and um . . . this particular gentleman said, "What's this?" And he belted the tap off the end of it, and it shot off the ground like a torpedo. I mean you could fit one hundred cubic foot of air in a small area, and of course it went across the ground like a torpedo and um . . . he or anyone else didn't realise how far it would go and in fact how much damage it would cause. Luckily no one was injured.

The hegemonic masculine culture prescribes that men should engage in reckless behaviour with little regard for their own or others' well-being. In this case, a worker attempted to demonstrate his manhood and caused a tank of compressed air to shoot off like a rocket. This could have easily ended someone's life. In a second example, an on-site OH&S officer described an incident where a worker's demonstration of stature and physical prowess could have resulted in a fatality:

Mark: I've seen bricks thrown from scaffolds at people's heads to show that they were tougher than the bloke down three flights below.

David: So someone actually threw a brick off a scaffold three stories high?

Mark: At the bloke, yeah.

David: But they had a hardhat on, didn't they?

Mark: No, it would have killed him if it had hit him.

David: My god! For what reason?

Mark: Because he parked his truck in a way that the other vehicle couldn't get off the site. But the whole object the next day of throwing the brick was to show himself to be better and tougher than the people he had the dispute with.

David: Why are workers compelled to do these sorts of things?

Mark: A predominately male environment means that boys will be boys and the boys have got to show off to each other. It's an industry where we all try to beat each other in some fashion and so therefore a dangerous act can be seen by workers to be one way of showing that they're better than the next bloke. It's a way of producing a pecking order. Um . . . dangerous acts of course include direct violence against others to show themselves to be better, so if I knock the bloke out, it's a dangerous act that shows me to be better than he.

Mark's comments indicate that he possesses an awareness of the gender hierarchy that exists on his construction site. Additionally, Mark's case is a perfect example of how notions of masculinity and safety intersect. The tradesman in question had been involved in a minor altercation with another man and, as prescribed by the dominant male culture, had to prove himself to be the superior and physically stronger male. He attempted to achieve this by dropping a brick on the other man's head.

Notes

1. A "critical juncture" is an event or a situation that provides an unprecedented understanding of a particular issue under investigation.

References

ABS (2002). *Labour Force, August 2002: Australia* (Cat no. 6302.0) Canberra.

Beynon, H. (1973). *Working for Ford*. London: Penguin Books.

Cheng, C. (1999). Marginalised masculinities and hegemonic masculinity: An introduction. *Journal of Men's Studies, 7*(3), 295–315.

Connell, R. (1982). Men and socialism. In G. Evans & J. Reeves (Eds.) *Labour essays* (pp. 53–64). Melbourne: Drummond.

Connell, R. (1995). *Masculinities*. London: Polity Press.

Donaldson, M. (1991). *Time of our lives: Labour and love in the working class*. Sydney: Allen & Unwin.

Eisenberg, S. (1998). *We'll call you if we need you: Experiences of women working construction*. Ithaca, New York: ILR Press.

Feigelman, W. (1974). The pattern of voyeurism among construction workers. *Urban Life and Culture, 3*(1), 35–51.

Fletcher, R. (1997). *Australian men and boys: A picture of health?* NSW: University of Newcastle.

Hayes, N. (2002). Did manual workers want industrial welfare? Canteens, latrines and masculinity on British building sites, 1918–1970. *Journal of Social History, 35*(3), 637–671.

Hopkins, A. (1995). *Making safety work: Getting management's commitment to occupational health and safety*. St. Leonards: Allen & Unwin.

LeMasters, E. (1974). *Blue-collar aristocrats*. Wisconsin: University of Wisconsin Press.

Lynch, C. (1997). Larrikins in the labour market: Masculinity, class struggle and union leadership in the NSW building industry. *Journal of Interdisciplinary Gender Studies, 2*(2), 75–88.

No to Violence's homepage. (1994). Retrieved 26 April, 2004, from www.ntv.net.au.

Paap, K. (1999). *Masculinity under construction: Gender, class and race in the construction industry*. PhD thesis, Madison: University of Wisconsin.

Pease, B. (2002). *Men and gender relations*. Melbourne: Tertiary Press.

Riemer, J. (1979). *Hard hats: The work world of construction workers*. Beverly Hills: Sage Publications.

Tausky, C. (1970). *Work organisations: Major theoretical perspectives*. Illinois: F. E. Publishers.

Tolson, A. (1977). *The limits of masculinity*. London: Tavistock Publications.

Walker, L. (1998). Under the bonnet: Car culture, technological dominance and young men of the working class. *Journal of Interdisciplinary Gender Studies, 3*(2), 23–43.

Williams, C. (1993). Class, gender and the body: The occupational health and safety concerns of blue collar workers in the South Australian timber industry. In M. Quinlan (Ed.) *Work and safety: The origins, management and regulation of occupational illness* (pp. 57–91). Melbourne: Macmillan.

Willis, P. (1977). *Learning to labour: How working class kids get working class jobs*. Farnborough: Saxon House.

CHAPTER 5 STUDY QUESTIONS

1. Are you surprised by the arguments and findings in the Judith E. Owen Blakemore et al. article (Reading 28) on marriage? Why or why not?

2. What role does hegemonic gender play in constructing families? What about the role of "mother" or "father"? What role does language play in shaping our perceptions of these roles?

3. How does intersectionality matter in a systematic study of families? In what ways does "the family" interact with broader social structures?

4. Joan Acker (Reading 32) describes numerous ways in which global systems and social structures are gendered. What examples of globalization, gender, and capitalism can you find?

5. Have you ever been to an "exotic dance club"? What kind of labor occurs there? Can you "see" class in the average exotic dance club? What about race?

6. Mary Nell Trautner (Reading 33) and David Iacuone (Reading 34) describe two different occupational settings, both highly gendered and classed. What other occupations or job settings can you describe that are similarly gendered and classed?

Thinking Critically about Structures and Institutions in Our World

35 Transgender Law Center

Peeing in Peace

A Resource Guide for Transgender Activists and Allies

This Resource Guide is a first of its kind publication combining basic information about how someone (or some group of someones) can protect themselves with common sense steps that can be taken to change the way in which an employer, school administrator, business owner, or government official handles bathroom access issues. It provides basic tools you can use to affect how someone sees the issue of bathroom access and safety by questioning who should be able to access which bathroom and why we divide most public bathrooms into Men's and Women's facilities in the first place.

The Transgender Law Center receives numerous complaints each year from community members around the state about bathroom related harassment and discrimination. We also hear regularly from people who want to do something beyond responding to individual examples of discrimination in order to make bathrooms more accessible to everyone.

Started in 2003, our Safe Bathroom Access Campaign (SBAC) focuses on the real world problems that are created for transgender people and our partners, families and friends because of the way that society views gender and the stereotypes associated with it. Working closely with People in Search of Safe Restrooms (PISSR), SBAC has been able to open a dialogue in California about this important issue. Many of the lessons we have learned through that work and the solutions that we have helped to devise are encompassed in this resource guide. It is our hope that the hundreds of people who have contacted us about this issue since we opened our doors in 2002 will be able to take all or some of the information in this guide and share it with

Transgender Law Center, "Peeing in Peace." Excerpted from original posting at http://www.transgender lawcenter.org/pdf/PIP%20Resource%20Guide.pdf. Every effort was made to contact the rightsholder.

friends and allies who are also interested in challenging the current bathroom situation.

Language and Definitions

Because the transgender community does not have uniform agreement on terms, we take just a minute to define some of the words that we use in this guide. As with all definitions of this type, these are not the only "right" definitions or the only way to talk about certain kinds of identities or bathrooms. We are providing them to create a common base of knowledge. In the real world, many people identify in different ways and use different terms. We recognize that it's important not to force people to use language that isn't comfortable for them.

Gender-Neutral or All-Gender Bathroom: a bathroom that anyone with any gender can use.

Gender-Specific or Gender-Segregated Bathroom: a bathroom intended for people who identify with a particular gender (for instance, a women's room or a men's room).

Multi-Stall Bathroom: a bathroom with multiple toilets and/or urinals.

Single-Stall Bathroom: a bathroom with only one urinal and/or toilet that is meant to be used by only one person at a time (unless that person is being accompanied by a parent, family member, and/or attendant).

Transgender: a term that is being used in this guide to refer to people whose gender identity or expression is different than the gender they were assigned at birth or different than the stereotypes that go with that gender. This includes people who identify as MTF (male-to-female), FTM (female-to-male), butch, genderqueer, tranny, transsexual, sissy boy, etc.

Transition: the steps that some transgender people take to express their gender identity. "Transition" can be as simple as adopting a new name and wearing clothes that are more stereotypically male or female (depending on the way someone is transitioning). Some people get help from a doctor in transitioning and use hormone therapy, mental health services, or surgical procedures. However, in this guide, we are not using transition to imply that anyone has to have taken any of these steps. It simply means that period after which someone has claimed their gender identity as their gender. For simplicity sake, we'll often use the term "post-transition."

Historical Bathroom Activism

Bathrooms have long been a place where people with authority, power, or wealth have denied access to other people. Over 150 years ago, only wealthy people could afford bathrooms in their homes and poor people were forced to use insufficient, non-hygienic public toilets. For far too long, public bathrooms here in the United States were segregated between "white" and "colored" facilities. "Colored" bathrooms, along with colored sections of restaurants and buses to name only two more instances, were less sanitary and convenient than "white" bathrooms. One of the hard fought victories of the Civil Rights Movement was the elimination of these "colored" bathrooms because it was determined that "separate" was never equal. Women working in the construction trades struggled in the 1970s to create women's bathrooms on job sites where before there had been only men's rooms. After decades of struggle, people with disabilities succeeded in passing the Americans with Disabilities Act in the 1980s, part of which included guidelines for the creation of accessible public bathrooms.

Despite all of the great work mentioned above, bathrooms continue to be unsafe for some people. Because of this, the work described in this guide is a continuation of the work of each of these past movements. One important thing that can be learned from past bathroom activism is that, unless we work on this issue with a variety of needs in mind the bathroom revolution will never work for everybody.

Working to create safe bathrooms for transgender people and our partners, families and friends also means taking into consideration the many ways that bathrooms are made unsafe for people. If we only focus on gender-identity based harassment and discrimination, we fail to meet the needs of those people in our community who face discrimination on other grounds (race, income level, disability, etc.). For that reason, bathroom activism is a natural place to work in coalition with other groups. . . . Doing so is a great way to make sure that the work you are doing better meets the needs of all people in our community as well as the needs of other marginalized people outside of the community.

The Problem

Safe bathroom access is not a luxury or a special right. Without safe access to public bathrooms, transgender people are denied full participation in public life. For example, transgender youth may be unable to complete school due to a lack of safe bathroom access. Due to bathroom discrimina-

tion in the workplace, transgender people may quit or be fired from their jobs.

For many transgender people, finding a safe place to use the bathroom is a daily struggle. Even in cities or towns that are generally considered good places to be transgender (like San Francisco or Los Angeles), many transgender people are harassed, beaten and questioned by authorities in both women's and men's rooms. In a 2002 survey conducted by the San Francisco Human Rights Commission, nearly 50% of respondents reported having been harassed or assaulted in a public bathroom. Because of this, many transgender people avoid public bathrooms altogether and can develop health problems as a result. This not only affects people who think of themselves as transgender, but also many others who express their gender in a non-stereotypical way but who may not identify as transgender (for instance, a masculine woman or an effeminate man).

Of course, some transgender people are able to use the bathroom of their choosing pre- or post-transition with relative ease (for instance, someone who is female-to-male using the men's bathroom). For other transgender people this is not the case for a variety of reasons. Some people do not "pass" well (meaning, for example, someone who is perceived to be a woman even though he has transitioned from female to male). Others do not necessarily identify as male or female and are harassed in both the men's and the women's bathroom. Many transgender people also face discrimination and harassment because of other parts of their identities (for instance, they are young, homeless, low-income, and/or people of color).

Many non-transgender people also experience difficulty and inconvenience in gender-specific bathrooms. Parents with differently-gendered children are not able to accompany them in gender-segregated bathrooms (for instance, a mother taking her young son into a multi-stall women's room). Disabled people with differently gendered attendants or family members are not able to bring them into gender-specific, multi-stall bathrooms. (And these difficulties are compounded when a public bathroom is not one that has been made accessible for people with disabilities to begin with.)

Discrimination comes in many forms and it is not always easy to know why someone is asking you questions or telling you to leave a bathroom. In the end, it really doesn't matter. Everyone should be able to use a safe public bathroom so that they can pee in peace.

Legal Landscape

One of the most common questions we get is: what are my rights around the bathroom? Unfortunately, this is not always an easy question to answer. Some answers are easy. If you're ever assaulted in the bathroom, you have the right to report the person to the police and sue them in civil court. You cannot be told that you cannot use any bathroom (i.e., you have to be allowed to use at least one bathroom). You cannot be fired from a job, kicked out of school, or evicted from an apartment because your boss, principal, or landlord cannot figure out what bathroom you should use.

In San Francisco and Oakland, it is clear that you have a right to use the bathroom that corresponds to your gender identity (for instance, if you are male-to-female, you have the right to use the women's bathroom). You have this right because local laws in each city either clearly address the bathroom issue or some city agency has al-ready decided what a general non-discrimination law means in that city.

Of course, if you do not identify as male or female, this still doesn't solve your problem. However, in San Francisco at least, the Human Rights Commission recommends that all businesses have at least one gender-neutral bathroom.

But, if you live outside of one of these cities, what are your rights? Clearly, you cannot be discriminated against in employment, housing, education, and public accommodation (this means using a business like a hotel or clothing store or a government building like a court house, for example) simply because you are transgender (along with a number of other characteristics). At TLC, we strongly believe that this means that you must be able to use the bathroom that corresponds to your gender identity.

Women and Children's Safety

One of the questions that is often asked is: "does changing the way we think about restrooms compromise women and children's safety?" We think that it does not. Because we live in a society in which both women and youth regularly face discrimination and oppression, however, it is important to take this question seriously.

At the root of this question is the idea that bathrooms cannot be safe for women, children *and* transgender people. This idea is inaccurate and it puts women and children on one side and transgender people on the other. When marginalized groups are pitted against each other like this, coalition building becomes difficult (if not impossible) and the political power of all the groups is weakened. And that is a shame because nothing about allowing people to use the bathroom that is appropriate for their gender identity or creating gender neutral bathrooms makes those bathrooms more unsafe for women and children.

The truth is that the current bathroom situation does not adequately ensure women's safety. Putting a sign that says "women" on the door of a bathroom does not stop people who want to harm women from entering. Thinking that a sign will create protection might actually increase the potential for violence in bathrooms because if someone did intend to assault a woman in a bathroom, they would certainly know where to look. In doing bathroom activism, it is important that we help people realize that something as symbolic as a sign on a door does not provide any real safety or protection.

The current bathroom situation is not particularly safe for children either. Many opponents of bathroom activism have stated that making bathrooms safer for transgender people will make them less safe for children. However, gender-neutral bathrooms can actually be safer for children because parents or other caretakers would be able to accompany them to any public bathroom thus personally ensuring their safety.

Another idea that we hear a lot is that making bathrooms safe for transgender people decreases the privacy that women and men need when using the bathroom. If people are worried about privacy, it is entirely possible that bathrooms could be built in a way that provide more privacy than most bathrooms currently do. For example, stall doors could extend all the way to the ground and locks on individual stalls could function more effectively. Most people have become used to using public bathrooms only with other people who have the same birth-assigned gender. The thought of carrying out one's bodily functions in the same facility as the "opposite sex" makes many people feel embarrassed and uncomfortable. However, considering that the current bathroom situation does not adequately provide for the safety of many people including transgender people, women and children, embarrassment should be considered secondary. Change is often uncomfortable, even when it is for the better, but if bathrooms are going to be made safe for all people, minor discomfort is a small price to pay.

One final idea that we hear is that creating gender neutral bathrooms will lead to less cleanliness. This argument assumes that men are inherently messy in the bathroom and are thus incapable of sharing a bathroom with women who are supposedly neater. For one thing, most people know by experience that all public bathrooms get messy sometimes whether those bathrooms are marked for use by men or women. Secondly, many people live in mixed-gender homes and are able to share their home bathroom with other members of the household with minimal problems. That people of different genders are able to share residential bathrooms with relative ease indicates that people of different genders could learn to share public bathrooms as well.

Handling Harassment

If possible, it is best to try to handle bathroom incidents directly with the person who is harassing you before bringing in a third party. In situations in which you cannot deal with the person directly, we recommend contacting someone who may be able to positively influence that person such as a supervisor. Sometimes an advocate can help you figure out who that person might be (see resources section for more info).

TABLE 35.1 Steps for Dealing with Harassment in the Bathroom

In general:

- If it is safe to do so, confront the person harassing you.
- If you are being harassed in a particular bathroom, try going to a different bathroom in another part of the building for the short-term, but do not feel as if this is a permanent solution.
- Write down the dates, times and individuals involved in the incident as well as names of any witnesses.
- Seek allies—if you know of anyone in that particular location who would support your right to safe bathroom access.
- Report any incidents to the appropriate person in authority and/or make a complaint to a local or state agency (see list in the Resource section). Follow up any verbal complaint in writing.
- Provide educational materials to people at that location.
- Ask the proper person at that location about creating a gender neutral restroom option.

In a government-owned building:	*In a shelter:*	*In a restaurant or store:*	*If you are harassed at school:*	*If you are harassed at work:*
Government-owned buildings include welfare offices, city hall, libraries, and the social security office. Let security know what is happening if you feel safe doing so. If you have a case manager in that office, try talking to them about it. Encourage them to put up a sign urging people to respect other folks when using the restroom.	Do what you feel is comfortable without jeopardizing your shelter spot. If you feel safe doing so you can make a complaint to the employees who work at the shelter.	Let an employee or manager know what is happening if you feel safe doing so. Encourage them to put up a sign urging people to respect other folks when using the restroom. If none of the above steps are successful, consider taking legal action. Contact a legal advocacy organization for assistance.	Get the support of understanding faculty and staff. Report the incident to your principal or district. If your school has a GSA or LGBT student group, talk to them about doing activist work around the issue. If possible, tell a parent or guardian what is happening and ask them to help advocate for you.	Make a complaint to your supervisor and/or the appropriate person in the Human Resources office. If the situation is not resolved, you should follow your employer's or union's grievance process. Don't sign anything your employer gives you without first consulting a lawyer. If you are planning to transition on the job, talk to your employer about it beforehand and make sure that bathroom access is a part of the conversation.

If the harassment becomes threatening or violent you might need to contact a police officer. Unfortunately, the police are not always helpful. Too many transgender people have reported that they have been harassed by police officers even when they were the person calling for help.

Table 35.1 is one way to think about how to defend yourself when harassment occurs. Keep in mind that these are only suggestions and that they may not always be the right steps to take in every situation.

Assault in Bathrooms

By "assault" we mean that someone has touched you (grabbed you, pushed you, punched you, kicked you, etc.). Many of the steps you should follow are the same as the steps to follow if you are harassed but here are some additional suggestions:

- Document any injuries you receive by taking photographs and/or getting a letter from any doctor who treats you.
- If you feel comfortable doing so, report incidents of assault to the police.
- Practice self-care. Assault can be both physically and psychologically traumatizing. Seek medical care. If you are uninsured, find a local free clinic. Find a support group or low cost therapy clinic if you are experiencing post-traumatic stress.
- If you decide to bring a suit against someone, you have two years from the date of the incident to file a claim in California. You do not have to be represented by an attorney in order to file a suit, but it is a good idea to try to find someone to take your case.

Security Guards or Police Officers

Police officers and security guards frequently detain, question and, in very rare cases, arrest transgender people who they believe to be in the "wrong" bathroom. A study conducted by the National Coalition of Anti-Violence Programs in 2002 showed that in 50% of the hate violence claims submitted by transgender people in San Francisco, police officers and security guards were the perpetrators. While the numbers have dropped in more recent years, they are still far too high.

When dealing with the police, everybody needs to act according to their life situation. If you are on parole or probation, an officer could use this as an excuse to take you into custody. If there is a warrant out for your arrest, being caught in the "wrong" bathroom provides the police with an opportunity to run a record check and bring you into custody. People of color, non–U.S. citizens, homeless people, and youth also face specific risks when dealing with law enforcement agents. If you fit into one or more of these categories you can find helpful information in the resources section of this guide.

Avoiding Conflict

If you need to use a bathroom in a location where there are police or security guards present and you are worried about a confrontation, leave and go to the bathroom somewhere else.

If a security guard or officer comes in and tells you that you're in the wrong bathroom, respectfully tell them you are in the correct room and are just trying to use the facilities. If they are not satisfied by that answer, offer to leave and use the bathroom elsewhere.

Being Detained and Remaining Silent

Being detained means that you are not allowed to leave a situation. A security guard only has a limited right to detain you. And while police officers cannot detain you in every situation, they do have many ways of holding you to ask you questions. If you are being questioned, you should always politely ask if you are free to leave. If they say you can leave, do, but remember or write down the name of the officer or guard on your way out of the bathroom.

If not, it's best to only share with the guard or officer the most basic information. If you have an ID with the correct gender marker on it, show it to the guard or officer.

If the guard or officer begins to ask you a lot of questions about what you are doing in a certain location or what your plans are for the evening, you have a choice to make:

1. You can answer the questions or tell the person you'll only answer the questions with a lawyer present. If you do answer the questions, make sure you only say things that you'd want said in a courtroom. Everything you say can be used in a case against you and police officers will often find a way to turn any answers you give against you later on.

2. If you do not answer the questions, it's important to understand that this might prompt a guard to detain you for the police and an officer to arrest you. However, both of these things might also happen if you do answer the questions.

Searches

Security guards have a very limited right to search you. If they begin to do so, be aware that they are probably breaking the law. Again, police officers have more rights, but those rights are limited (except if you are on probation or parole). Make sure any officer who is searching you knows that you do not want to be searched by politely but clearly stating the words, "I do not consent to this search." Unless they have what is called "probable cause" for the search, anything they find can't be used against you.

Arrest

In very rare cases, people are arrested by officers who think that they are using the wrong bathroom or who just want to harass them. If this happens to you, make sure to remain silent until you have representation from an attorney (it may take up to 72 hours to get an attorney). You should not sign any documents that an officer gives you unless you are sure it does not contain any details of the arrest or waive your Fifth Amendment right to remain silent. It is okay to sign a sheet for your belongings or a Promise to Appear notice if you are being released.

If you have been arrested, it is quite possible (depending on local laws) that you were arrested falsely and on a bogus charge. In most places, it is not illegal to use the "wrong" bathroom. You were not there with criminal intent, you were just trying to pee. Meet with your lawyer or a court appointed attorney as soon as possible.

Transgender people often feel uncomfortable and are subject to harassment and violence when using male- or female-specific campus restrooms. "Gender-neutral" bathrooms—typically single-stall, lockable restrooms available to people of all genders—provide a safe facility for transgender people. These restrooms also help families with children (such as mothers bringing sons, or fathers bringing daughters, to a restroom) and people with disabilities who need the assistance of an attendant of a different gender. Single-stall restrooms also more easily meet the accessibility regulations of the Americans with Disabilities Act (ADA).[1]

A rapidly growing number of colleges and universities are creating gender-neutral bathrooms, either through renovations or by simply changing the signs on single-stall male/female restrooms. Currently, more than 150 campuses have gender-neutral bathrooms, including Oberlin College, which has two gender-neutral bathrooms in its student union and at least one in every residence hall; the University of California, San Diego, which has changed male/female signs on 88 single-stall restrooms in campus buildings; and the New College of California, where all campus bathrooms are gender-neutral.

Many of the colleges and universities with gender-neutral bathrooms list the locations of these restrooms on their websites. See, for example:

New York University: http://www.nyu
.edu/lgbt/restroom.html
Ohio University: http://pages.ohio.edu/
lgbt/resources/transrestrooms.cfm
UCLA: http://www.lgbt.ucla.edu/bath
rooms.htm
University of Colorado, Boulder: http://
www.colorado.edu/glbtrc/resources/
restrooms.html

Along with developing gender-neutral restrooms, some institutions, such as American University, Kent State University, Ohio State University, the University of California, Santa Barbara, and Washington State University, have implemented or are in the process of implementing policies requiring that all extensively renovated and newly constructed buildings include at least one gender-neutral bathroom.

The University of Arizona has established a bathroom policy that affirms that individuals have the right to use the bathroom that corresponds with their gender identity. The statement is available at http://fp.arizona.edu/affirm/restroomaccess.htm.

Resources

Sylvia Rivera Law Project: http://www.srlp
.org/index.php?sec=03C&page=genderseg

Transgender Law and Policy Institute: http://www.transgenderlaw.org/college/index.htm

---

"Gender-Neutral Restrooms." Originally posted at http://www.umass.edu/stonewall/uploads/listWidget/8749/bathroom%20FAQ.pdf. Every effort was made to contact the rightsholder.

Frequently Asked Questions About Gender-Neutral Bathrooms

Taken from the University of Chicago's Gender-Neutral Bathrooms Campaign: http://queeraction.uchicago.edu/statement.html

What are the problems created by only having sex-segregated bathrooms in a particular location?

Bathrooms segregated by sex are potentially unsafe and intimidating places for a variety of people.

Persons who are not easily legible as male or female often experience various forms of intimidation in these places. If a woman in a women's-only restroom is assumed to be a man, there may be real threats to her comfort and even safety. For example, one woman on our campus had security called on her while she was in the women's restroom of her workplace because a client through she was "a man in a women's bathroom." Assault, insults, and police intervention are frequently part of the reality of sex-segregated bathrooms for butch women, transgender people, and others. Many people have had the experience of being harassed or threatened in public bathrooms; though this is not as strong of a factor on campus, it contributes to a feeling of discomfort with the single-sex bathroom setting.

Certain people feel threatened in single-sex bathrooms based on their presumed sexual orientation rather than gender identity. Students have faced gay-baiting comments in our university's sex-segregated bathrooms. Men's bathrooms may be particular sites for this sort of harassment because of their image as queer cruising grounds. Regardless of whether those making the comments intended to act on the threats made, people were made uncomfortable and felt unsafe.

Bathroom comfort issues are most acute for transgender and trans-questioning people on campus. Members of the transgender community face specific concerns and threats to safety depending on how they are read in certain situations. Choosing a sex-coded restroom is one of the most frequently reported sources of anxiety in this community: often, transgender people will go far out of their way to gain access to bathrooms that are more private or comfortable. For instance, one gender-transgressive graduate student reports waiting to go home rather than using public bathrooms on campus; this is a response to frequent hostility in that setting. Access to public single-occupancy bathrooms would be ideal for undercutting this source of intimidation, but converting existing multi-stall bathrooms to gender neutrality is an excellent, and easy, intermediate step.

It is important to realize that this is not simply a language or labeling issue: the initiative to create gender-neutral bathrooms is not driven by an avoidance of the angst of choosing an icon for one's gender identity. It is, rather, centered on the kinds of interactions that actually occur when some members of our community make either one of the available choices.

The most significant problem that arises in a gendered space is one of intimidation. When that gendered space is one like a restroom, a place that everyone should be able to go without incident and without feeling intimidated, addressing this problem becomes increasingly significant.

Will adding gender-neutral bathrooms help to alleviate these problems?

Yes! If a space is not segregated into male and female categories, it significantly reduces the possibility for gender- and sex-based intimidation toward those whose appearance and presentation does not fit within the traditional male/female paradigm.

While it is not possible to entirely remove safety risks in any space, intimidation in public bathrooms generally happens because queer and gender-transgressive people are perceived to be trespassing on others' sense of space. This would not happen in gender-neutral bathrooms, which would significantly reduce the risk involved in using the facilities.

*Ironically, many of the people who are most resistant to creating gender-neutral bathrooms on the grounds that they constitute "special rights for transsexuals" are also uncomfortable with **either** of the choices a trans person might make about use of conventional sex-segregated public bathrooms.*

It is also important to note that many people in the U.S. are questioning their sexuality and gender identity and coming out at younger ages as lesbian, gay, bisexual, and/or transgender. The University must realize that many potential students and faculty are looking for a campus which is proactively supportive of queer concerns. Transgender and allied people in particular want to know how their needs will be met in terms of comfortable restroom options, because it is a real concern in many day-to-day lives.

Notes

1. University of Chicago QueerAction, "Gender-Neutral Bathrooms Campaign: A QueerSafeCampus Initiative," http://queeraction.uchicago.edu/statement.html.

37 Gretchen M. Herrmann

His and Hers
Gender and Garage Sales

It's traditional. The household and household management is women's responsibility more so than men. And I think that still is even though we have families where both people work. Whether or not to sell the spatula still seems to be the woman's decision. And because she decides to sell it, she plans the garage sale and then she ends up taking the responsibility for the sale and she also keeps the money. Now, I've known men to have garage sales, men who live alone. I don't know if I've known many men to have a garage sale when they're married. I just think because it comes out of the household it goes back into the household. It has been the woman's domain.

—Lisa McFarren, 36, married, artist,
homemaker, mother, garage sale seller

The home and the family have long been considered women's responsibility (e.g., Coontz; Rubin, *Families*), so it is not surprising that women comprise about two-thirds of the shoppers and sellers in the garage sale. Garage sale trade takes place at private residences; it is a kind of quasi-commercial exchange that grows directly from the home. Many of the activities involved in holding a sale are direct extensions of housekeeping: cleaning house to select items; cleaning, folding and arranging items; and creating an attractive display. Such tasks fall among those traditionally assigned to women (Oakley). Shopping, too, is mainly performed by women as part of the "consumption work" for their families and themselves (Krafft; Oakley; Weinbaum and Bridges).

Lisa McFarren's opening quotation is a clear acknowledgment that traditional patterns still govern most domestic behavior despite the large number of married women in the paid labor force. Studies on the household division of labor demonstrate that women continue to perform the overwhelming majority of cooking, cleaning, child care, and shopping work for the

Gretchen M. Herrmann, "His and Hers: Gender and Garage Sales," *Journal of Popular Culture* 29, no. 1 (Summer 1995): 127–145. Reprinted by permission of Wiley-Blackwell.

An earlier version of this article was presented at the Second Gender and Consumer Behavior Conference, sponsored by the Department of Marketing, David Eccles School of Business, University of Utah, in June 1993, in Salt Lake City. Much of the research for this article was made possible by New York State/United University Professions Professional Development and Quality of Work Life Study Leaves during portions of 1985 and 1987–1988. I am very grateful for their support.

household even when they work outside the home; one study estimates that working women, even managers and professionals, perform about 79 percent of the housework (Berardo et al.). While many husbands spend more time caring for their children than in the past, most of the household labor is still performed by women (Lamphere et al.; Rubin, *Families*). Hartmann even concludes that men are a net drain on household labor, in that more labor is required to maintain them than they contribute. Women perform so much housework on the "second shift" that sociologist Arlie Hochschild estimates that they put in an additional month of twenty-four-hour days a year above their paid jobs. Women who cohabitate with men also perform more housework than do the men, although less than women who are married (Shelton and John).

This essay will focus on differences between men and women in their styles of shopping and selling in garage sales. It will delineate how their garage sale activities reflect the traditional division of labor by sex, emphasizing how the major components of the socially constructed male gender role help to explain differences in male behavior and sensibilities from those of women in the garage sale. The paper addresses "male" and "female" sales, the frequent peripheral involvement by men in selling and shopping and the opposing style of serious and purposeful involvement by men. In short, men are more concerned with money and their time, while women are more concerned with creating relationships through this informal trade. The gender differences outlined here are *generalizations*. Individuals—female or male—can and do behave in ways that do not fit the generalizations, but there is

enough of an observable difference in these patterns of behavior to delineate them here.[1]

My field research indicates that, for heterosexual couples, the activities involved in holding a sale follow traditional patterns of the division of labor by gender (Herrmann). Women are in charge of household management and inventories, except for such male domains as shops and garages; they procure most of the household items (Weinbaum and Bridges) and get rid of those they deem are no longer needed. The closet cleaning aspect of garage sale preparation falls almost entirely to women, as does the cleaning and displaying merchandise. Women generally do most of the shopping (e.g., Krafft; Oakley), so they do most of the pricing of the items and they are usually in charge of household budgets (Rubin, *Worlds*; Whitehead; Zelizer). However, women frequently discuss prices with their husbands or knowledgeable (usually female) friends because pricing is difficult to gauge.

Men commonly take out the trash and are in charge of household repairs. Their contributions to garage sale preparation mirror these traditional tasks and the conventional attitude of "helping out" (e.g., Berheide et al.) rather than taking responsibility for most household chores (Herrmann). Men carry the heavy items and set up display areas, largely under the direction of their wives and girlfriends. Women, usually in charge of the aesthetics, arrange the actual displays. Men may select a few items from their personal belongings (clothes or tools), but often only after their wives prod them to do so, and sometimes not even then, as Lisa recalls telling her husband:

> I told you for a week to take the clothes you wanted for the sale and you didn't do it, so

I'm going to your closet and taking out your clothes that I don't like anymore to sell.

Men usually put up the signs, and, since some feel they have more "pressing" commitments (be they work or recreation), leave their wives to run the sales once they have helped set up. Men often help to dismantle the sale at the end. Many men do, of course, operate sales with their wives. This is particularly so for younger men with a more egalitarian ideology—couples with hyphenated last names are often equal partners in selling—and for older men who have retired and have more uncommitted time. These patterns are so common that reversals are striking, such as the male seller in his twenties who was "minding the sale" while his wife, seven months pregnant, was putting up signs in the neighborhood.

His and Hers Sales

It is a common perception that men and women operate different kinds of sales. One kind of "male sale," especially for younger men leaving town, could uncharitably be characterized as "chaos on the lawn." There is not very much merchandise, especially in the housewares department. Items for sale might include some cassette tapes, CDs, books, an old saw, a few shopworn shirts, and a jacket. Often these things are jumbled on top of one another and sometimes dirty. Recently, two men in their twenties held a country sale that had some of the dirtiest stuff I remember seeing—everything was in decaying old boxes. As with many "male sales," theirs had no prices on merchandise; often men prefer negotiation, or just do not get around to pricing thing. Other men are super-salesmen, explaining at great length

how their old computer or table saw works and drumming up enthusiasm among shoppers. This engaged male style echoes Tannen's characterization of men as experts who must explain things to others.

Steve Redman holds another kind of "male" garage sale, one that has developed a following. He refurbishes old tools (purchased at garage sales), and at an annual sale resells those he does not either use or give to relatives. Most of his customers are men. George Rolfe, a seller and shopper in his thirties, admires Redman's sales:

His sales have been an inspiration to me. It's a wonderful thing to go buy junky tools and fix them up and sharpen them up and sell them at a reasonable price. It's a public service. You just can't find tools like that anymore except in garage sales and things. It's just wonderful to see somebody who really takes the time to fix them up and recycle them and get them back into the community.

While this sale of tools has a distinctly male character in American culture, smaller versions of the same thing occur at other sales.

The quintessential "female sale" is quite different. Clean, carefully displayed tables of merchandise await the shopper. All the items—glassware, jewelry, Avon bottles, tidy piles of folded clothes—are priced and the seller is prepared with exact change. Or, there may be a profusion of children's clothes and paraphernalia. In contrast to the "male sale," everything is neat and clean. The proprietor is friendly, but low-key, or there may be several women enjoying the day together while selling their household extras. These stylistic differences reflect stereotypic differences between male and female sensibilities in American society, such that women are expected to be neat, clean, and prepared, while men are often granted license to be messy and "just wing it" (Lott, *Women's*).

We can even speak of objects as "gendered" in the garage sale setting, just as they are "gendered" in the rest of society (e.g., Allison et al.; Debevec and Iyer). Typically, the man of the house sells some tools, recreation gear and perhaps even some computer equipment, which attracts male shoppers. At the same time, the woman of the house sells children's items, household goods, fabric remnants, and house plants. This is where most of the female shoppers spend their time. Csikszentmihalyi and Rochberg-Halton discovered a similar gender-typing of objects in American society. Men find television sets, stereo equipment, sports equipment, vehicles, and trophies to be important in their lives, while women value photographs, sculpture, plants, glass, and textiles more than do the men. Women also express more interest in the interpersonal components and emotional attachment related to things than do men (e.g., Dittmar).

In the garage sale, gender-typed items (e.g., tools for men or kitchenware for women) attract shoppers of the appropriate gender. Sellers even direct men and women to the expected grouping of objects; I have been steered away from the tool area more than once by well-meaning sellers. It is quite common for a male-female couple shopping together to actually shop in parallel, so that the man surveys the "masculine" items and the woman looks over the traditional "feminine" ones. Marsha Harris, who holds an annual sale, describes how this behavior pattern occurs at her sales:

It's interesting when couples come because they separate and they shop and then they come back. They quite often even pay separately. It's not that the man cares what the woman buys. I don't think he is concerned, but it's almost like they're shopping for their own separate interests.

Such a couple may shop together for items of mutual interest, such as toasters, carpets or furniture. Otherwise, there is often a "his" and a "hers" experience of shopping at sales.

Peripheral Involvement by Men: The Oblique Look

Many men are actively involved in garage sales, as shoppers and sellers, and they enjoy what they do and take pride in it. For others, it is an "acquired taste," if it ever becomes palatable at all. Many men, husbands and boyfriends, become involved, peripherally and with considerable hesitation, in garage sales because of the women in their lives. Their aversion is seen in trivializing participation, making jokes, avoiding public association with sales (e.g., remaining in the house or car) and other detectable manifestations of embarrassment. They look askance at the practice— what I refer to as the "oblique look." While it is true that members of both genders may manifest similar behavior, it is done predominantly by males. An article in a Sunday supplement, written by a man, captures this characteristically male aversion to sales, this one in Georgetown:

I stopped. The couple who own the house are acquaintances of mine. He is a well-known physician. She is a former network executive. She stood behind her household items, hawking them in an understated fashion. He lurked inside the house, occasionally peering out the window. The yard sale was not his idea, his wife said with a giggle. My heart went out to him. (Cohen 7)

This male embarrassment about garage sale activities can be viewed as an offshoot of men's role as primary breadwinner. David and Brannon outline four major aspects of the male role in U.S. society:

1. No Sissy Stuff: The stigma of all stereotyped feminine characteristics and qualities, including openness and vulnerability;
2. The Big Wheel: Success, status, and the need to be looked up to;
3. The Sturdy Oak: A manly air of toughness, confidence, and self-reliance;
4. Give 'Em Hell!: The aura of aggression, violence, and daring. (12)

The fact that the garage sale, a female-dominated institution, is an extension of traditional women's work, can consciously or unconsciously disturb men. Studies have demonstrated repeatedly that males define themselves as "other than female," even at an early age (e.g., Maccoby and Jacklin 284). David and Brannon also cite the cardinal theme in the definition of masculinity: "A 'real man' must never, never resemble women, or strongly display stereotyped feminine characteristics" (14). Many male participants do not even like to be reminded that women outnumber men as garage sale participants, presumably because their masculinity then feels threatened.

Garage sales are also "marked" from the traditional male perspective because they publicly question the man's ability to provide adequately for his family and himself. Someone might think, after all, that they actually *need* the money from a sale; male

self-esteem is closely linked with the ability to make money. The ability to provide is a part of how most men derive a sense of status (Gould; Rubin, *Families*; "The Big Wheel" above); Susan Faludi notes that the leading definition of masculinity among American men is being a "good provider" (65).

Our puzzled male journalist goes on to try to understand why the Georgetown couple would hold a sale and why it bothered him so much that they did so:

Like the husband who would not come out of the house, I have no desire to appear mercenary, to seem to care about money. Indeed, maybe because my parents were born poor and seemed to save $2 for every $1 they earned, I have affected a nonchalance about money that, besides being a total lie, has left me in considerable debt. For one thing, I will not bargain, and bargaining is what yard sales are all about. (Cohen 7)

This sort of male chagrin about garage sale participation, then, is linked to preserving a sense of social status, one that is predicated on the notion that one's income is comfortable and one's position in the society is stable. A middle-class seller in her thirties described her husband's aversion to sales like this:

It's kind of hard to explain. I can sort of feel it with my husband. I can tell he's kind of embarrassed to do it. I really think he is. He hasn't really verbalized it though. I think he feels embarrassed to have all this junk in his yard and try to sell it, where I'm not at all. I think he thinks it's just a lot of junk.

To him, holding a garage sale may make him look impecunious to the general public, a loss of status (Tannen 1990: "The Big Wheel" above). No words need be spoken to detect this attitude. Even strangers can pick up on the aversion of others. Marge Robertson, aged fifty, described a situation where the man of the house was clearly avoiding his wife's sale:

We got there when the sale was just starting. It was obvious he was just leaving because of the sale and he wasn't planning to come back until it was over. I wonder if there's something there for some men, that it's not quite okay to sell stuff.

My field research revealed numerous men who look askance at or who are only peripherally involved in garage sale activities. When Lisa McFarren and Meagan Kraft held their sale, both of their husbands remained in the house and "hung out," not even watching the children. Once, for a while, they came out and talked a bit, but they never became part of the activities, despite the fact that ten years earlier, Lisa's husband operated garage sales to sell antiques. But that was commercial, to make *real* money, and this sale was to clean house. Cathy Vanderbuilt's husband, in his thirties, came by her sale near the end of the day, but kept a healthy distance. He had to go to work, so he was not available, or interested in, helping out with the garage sale. Cathy depicted the attitude of many men as like that of her husband:

Some of them are *embarrassed* to get involved, I think. Here we are putting all our junk out for the neighborhood and they don't see its value and I think there's a certain kind of embarrassment. It's also that guys may not recognize that their junk would have value to anyone else.

Cathy's husband did help to count the money and was very impressed with how well they had done. This changed his attitude somewhat towards sales.

When husbands and boyfriends help to operate a sale, the emphasis tends to be on "help" rather than "operate." Most often, the female partner is in charge. The male frequently resists taking an active role, such as determining prices on unmarked items, even if they belonged to him. Terry Parker, a shopper in her twenties, carefully describes these gendered differences:

The sales that are selling fishing poles and stuff usually have a guy on the scene. But if it is a sale that is run by a husband and wife, the guy does tend to recede into the background a lot. The women almost always take the money. Almost always. Even with that guy I bought the lantern from, I kept trying to hand him the money and he kept saying, "Well, I don't have my glasses on," so I had to wait until his wife came out. She didn't know how much it was, but she was in charge, he told me. So there was this little role playing thing that has been duplicated in other sales. The one where I bought some fabric, the man was right next to me and the price was right there and he made no effort to come and look at the price. The woman had to walk all the way from the other end of that sale.

This male resistance to, or lack of touch with, aspects of selling is common. I witnessed a male seller, a professional in his forties, squirm and avoid pricing his own clothes. Because his wife was involved elsewhere at the sale, he eventually was forced to come up with a figure.

The other side of female responsibility for garage sales is that they are the *bosses* of the events. Women direct men in such activities as pricing items, putting up the signs, and displaying items. Responsibility for operating a sale can provide an opportunity for women to demonstrate competence in areas such as the cost of items or knowledge of people. It can also be the arena of conflict between traditional male and female sensibilities. I have even seen women "chastise" men for such transgressions as creating a price sticker that was unattractive and making them do it over. The imposition of such "feminine" aesthetics is what led one female seller in her thirties to speak of women being "mean" to men, a pattern she was trying to avoid in her garage sale. She compared this behavior to wives criticizing grocery shopping done by their husbands, when they bring home bags of such essential items as olives and doughnuts.

Very often the men—husbands, brothers, and boyfriends—assist in setting up the sale. Their assistance is primarily in physical activities associated with the male role (an aspect of the "Sturdy Oak" theme): setting up tables, carrying heavy items, putting up clothes lines, and tacking up signs. Some men will "help out" in setting things up and then leave during the actual sale. One woman in her thirties with two young children described her husband's behavior, with an edge in her voice. He had prevailed upon her to hold the sale and she ended up missing two days of substitute teaching to do so. In her words:

My husband helped—somewhat. He doesn't get into it quite as much, I guess. When he mentioned having the garage sale, I told him that with the children I would probably need more help if we were going to do it. So, he's playing tennis. . . . He pulled out the things he wanted to sell,

his tools and some other items. He helps me put up the tables, but basically I'm the one that puts it *on* the tables. He had his tool table. I said, "There's *your* table. You do what you want there." And he'll go around and tell me if he doesn't like the prices.

A female proprietor in her fifties, originally from Australia, was fascinated with sales since, when she had lived there, they did not have any in her native country. Her husband was not minding the sale with her because, according to her:

He had to work, actually. But he wasn't too crazy about staying around for it anyway. He's a businessman—he probably thinks this is pretty petty stuff. . . . He's just like a lot of men. He thinks these are just for women. He's going to be *surprised* when he sees how much money I made.

Her husband apparently did joke with her about the profits of the first day, a joking that can be interpreted as trivializing female involvement in garage sales. He reportedly said, "Seeing you've made all that money, you can buy me a couple of drinks!"

While the examples mentioned here illustrate different forms of male aversion to sales, the men here were at least peripherally involved. Some men find the practice so distasteful that their wives must hold sales while their husbands are out of town. A woman in her thirties, a teacher off for the summer, confided that the timing of her sale was to take advantage of her husband's business trip; he could not tolerate holding one. Beatrice Winter, a seller in her seventies, described once waiting to hold a sale until her husband, a lawyer, had gone on a fishing trip because he was so embarrassed.

There are, of course, instances in which the woman is the unwilling partner in holding a garage sale, but this is less common. Steve Redman's wife would routinely leave the house when he held his annual tool sale. Marsha Harris told of a couple she knew who would have an annual sale, initiated by the wife, who insisted her husband run it because she was shy:

> Every year her husband asks her how much he has to pay her to not have them. He hates it. She sets up and he works the sale. She will not deal with the people. She sets up and he does it.

Do Men Lack the Shopping Gene?

Male distaste for shopping is so well known it has become the stuff of comedy routines (*Syracuse Post-Standard*). One shopper in her early thirties, a Ph.D. candidate in biology, described her husband's loathing of the activity:

> Frank hates stores, he hates being in them, he hates the mall with a passion! Think of all the women who go there to kill the time or to window shop or whatever. Frank wouldn't be caught dead doing it. Many times I've dragged him in there for some purpose and he always complains and tells me how he hates it. I guess yard sales fall into the same domain.

It is easier for a man (or woman) to avoid shopping at sales than to avoid involvement in one held at home. These men simply do not have to go to the sales or, if for some reason they are out with their wives, they can remain in the car. Susan Katz's husband, a professor, would remain in the car on the rare Saturdays he accompanied her. Men may joke with their wives about sales by "putting their foot on the accelerator" as they happen to pass one, a form of "torture" some women attribute to their husbands.

The most common form of male aversion is to joke about shopping at garage sales and the items bought there. Such joking trivializes shopping, especially second-hand shopping, while it distances the men from an activity perceived as feminine. Male joking about what women bring home from shopping expeditions is a staple of comic strips and television sitcoms; it is firmly embedded in the culture. One "Hi and Lois" cartoon, for example, depicts Hi with a look of concern, worrying, "I knew I shouldn't have let your mother go out in the car today." When his son asks why, the scene shifts to the driveway where Lois is unloading lamps, furniture, rugs and paintings. Hi explains, "It's tag sale season again." Male aversion, and even condescension, is accentuated by the nature of items at garage sales; there are some truly strange and unusual things that can lend themselves to ridicule more readily than most new merchandise. As the husband (an insurance agent comfortably well-off and near retirement) of one shopper said, "She brings home the most God-awful things." His sentiment is quite common. Another husband spoke of garage sale shopping as a disease.

Men who do not like sales can make it uncomfortable for spouses by giving them "grief" about their purchases. Some women literally smuggle in their goods. Cindy Banner, aged thirty-seven, shows her husband only the really good things she gets at sales, rather than take the kidding she knows she would get if she brought home something so unworthy as a pocketbook. Sally James' husband keeps garage sales at arm's length by joking with his wife upon her return from sales: "Okay, show me the loot." Marsha Harris worries about what her husband will say when she comes home:

> When I go to a garage sale, I always worry, "What is Frank going to say when I get home?" I'm always concerned that he is going to say, "Why didn't you just go and buy a new one?" I'm the type, and he's not. I think women are more shopper oriented and bargain oriented than men are anyway.

Later in the interview, she described her husband's general dislike of second-hand goods. Jean Vanek attributes male embarrassment about garage sale purchases to their "bigger egos":

> I think that men, generally, have a lot bigger egos than women. I think that every man likes to think he makes enough money that his wife doesn't have to go buy second-hand stuff. A man wants to think he can provide everything for his family.

This observation echoes the point that male status is derived through the ability to provide.

Some men have a "breakthrough" and learn to appreciate the value of garage sale shopping. Leslie Howard is a woman in her thirties who claims she could not have survived without garage sales (*literally!*), yet, the man she has lived with for many years had to be hauled to the sales "howling and complaining and whatever." But a couple of years ago, he had a "conversion" experience about shopping at sales. In Leslie's words:

> It was the sale of a retired insurance man who was moving to Florida. David got a really, really nice wool three-piece suit for $6. It fit him. The man made David go in

the house, try it on, had David come out, show me, show the man's wife, and was telling David how to dress in a suit, what color shirts, what color ties. David ended up buying a topcoat from him for $2 and he threw in a couple of shirts. And ever since then, I think David has been *convinced* and will pick things up. He still will not go out of his way to go to one, but if we're going by one, he's willing to stop.

Leslie feels David's affluent background accounts for his initial reluctance to shop at sales.

Super Involvement by Men: Getting Serious

The quality of male participation in garage sales is often colored by concerns associated with this historic role as primary breadwinner (David and Brannon; Ehrenreich; Faludi) and their need for status (Goode; Tannen). The men that *do* become involved in garage sales—as both shoppers and sellers—frequently do so with a degree of purposiveness less often found among women. Men focus on the monetary aspects of sales and are keenly aware of money's corollary—time. Their participation tends to be more commercialized. Men's motives for participating places financial considerations closer to the top, although they do participate for reasons of housecleaning, socializing (especially older men), recycling, amusement and the like. Men are more often found at sales of greater size (which generate larger profits), at sales where more expensive (e.g., large furniture or appliances) or "manly" (e.g., sports equipment or tools) items are sold, and at sales that are operated primarily to generate profits. Michael Krantz, aged thirty-eight, put it this way:

You'll see guys involved in selling when there are large and expensive items for sale. Men are much less likely to be at sales when there are a lot of little gizmos and *tchotchkes* than when there is a dresser or stereo, not to mention manly stuff like tire irons or old tires.

The fact that so many of the sales in which making money is a primary motive are operated by men indicates the importance of profits to their participation. Even men who are not running mini-businesses are likely to keep a keen eye on the likely proceeds of a sale to determine if it is worth their time to run one. Steve Redman states:

During this spring, we had a sale that got $400, which is fairly significant for a garage sale. I will not hold a garage sale if I don't think I can make at least $400. I'm not going to spend a day unless I can get that kind of money, with all the work that goes into it.

Given that the proceeds from the average sale in the area are about $150 to $175 (and can be considerably less), this amount of money is substantial.

Couples who hold sales together often find the husband is more interested in making money and in pricing items higher than is the wife. Michael Krantz, for example, described his approach as different from his wife's in this way:

Sarah wanted to price everything low enough to get rid of it. Just wanting the things out of the house. My feeling is really strong, if we're going to sell stuff, to sell it at a price to make it worthwhile to get the money. Better to sell half as many things for twice as much money than to price every-

thing to move. Mostly we've been going with the prices I have been suggesting. The stuff we sold was at *real* prices not nickel and dime prices. We went to the store and checked with the stuff that was selling new, like the Lennox china, and priced it at half of that, not 10 percent of it.

This was describing a sale they once held to clear out, among other things, unused wedding gifts. Later, Sarah compared her orientation to holding the sale to Michael's:

Michael was more interested in making enough money to make it worth the time. I'm more interested in getting rid of the stuff and making sure they get to a good home. And the people can be really interesting.

While Michael was interested in making money, Sarah was more concerned with making an emotional connection with shoppers. These respective goals conform to Deborah Tannen's (1990) depiction of male concern with independence (e.g., money), contrasting to female concern with intimacy (e.g., connection).

Some men become "sale proud" or otherwise proud of their competence or achievements in garage sales. This attitude is not limited to men of course, but it goes along with a common male attitude that sales should be worth their investment of time and effort. A mathematics professor in his forties exemplifies this pride in hosting a high quality sale, one that is worthwhile to attend:

It was good. I sold about $300 or $400 worth of stuff. I had a lot better stuff than most people have. I had a church pew I sold for $90. Stuff was priced well. I got rid of some excess building supply stuff. I gave a guy about a third off the price at Grossman's on some fence sections and so it was good for him and good for me. So, I sold about $350 worth of stuff. The main thing I needed was more space and it was stuff I had accumulated over a long period of time. It was fun. I think I had a better sale than a lot of people because I had a lot of good stuff. I had a treadle sewing machine that I think I had a good price on. I had some duck decoys, but I priced them at the high end and everybody knew that. I had some interesting things. . . . I just don't like to waste people's time. You like to put out a lot of stuff. It is embarrassing if you go out of your way, you drive, and you go in and the person having a garage sale really doesn't have all that much stuff.

There is a lot embedded in this extended discourse. The emphasis on money is apparent from the number of times it is mentioned and from the fact it was mentioned first. Other motivations for having the sale are there—those of cleaning and having "fun"—but they are overshadowed by a preoccupation with profits, pride in the quality of the sale and the competence with which he priced things. It is also clear he is sensitive to the issue of status in that he would be *embarrassed* to hold a sale with few or low quality items.

Rather than merely "helping out" some male sellers become super-salesmen. They latch onto prospective customers and shepherd them from item to item, demonstrating how things work and sometimes trying to convince shoppers to buy things. This style of selling is more aggressive than that of most women. In addition to gaining increased control over the situation, the super-salesman often engages in more conversation, playful fantasy, joking, and even manipulation than most sellers. One male seller tried to hype his wife's jewelry by saying it came "directly from the sultan's harem in Baghdad." Another tried to convince every shopper to purchase his old stereo. This predominantly male style is highly engaged and *in charge* (Tannen). Other men run the sale and have their wives running back and forth to get okays on prices or to tend to the needs of customers.

Men are often more reluctant to spend time shopping at garage sales than are women. For example, men often plan routes on the basis of strict, "rational" criteria, such as location of sales and items sought, leaving little room for spontaneity. One male shopper in his forties described himself as "all business" when he was shopping. If their wives linger, men may become impatient, especially over items they do not consider interesting. Sharon Bonn's husband, in his twenties, shopped regularly with her and enthusiastically shared in their search for antiques and collectibles to resell for profit. But Jim could not tolerate it when Sharon wanted to look at clothing or household items. If she wanted to buy clothes at a sale, she had to return later, after dropping off her husband. Sharon used these terms to describe why men are reluctant to go to sales:

> Because a woman won't leave when they want to. They want to stay to look at clothing or jewelry or dishware, where the man doesn't want to. The man wants to be where the man wants to be. If you're looking at something, he wants to leave. Just like Jim, he won't want to come because he says I stay too long. I tell him they have men's stuff at garage sales. He says I look at junk.

Jim was very interested in the profits to be made from collectibles they purchased, but he had no patience for domestic consumption; in his working-class background that was women's work.

Male impatience, probably related to a strong value placed on their time, is suggested by male rejection rates to a shoppers' questionnaire I administered. I kept track of those who declined to fill them out by gender. At three of the four sales, the male refusal rate was about twice as high as that of women. Their comments upon declining often had to do with impatience—"Not now, I'm looking for the next sale" or "I don't have the time." Often they tried to pass the questionnaires on to their wives instead of filling them out themselves— "Maybe my wife will do it." In contrast, women shoppers who declined to fill out the questionnaire often mentioned constraints of relationships, such as their husband was leaving or their baby was in the car, for not filling out the questionnaire.

Value of their time can also enter into the calculus of whether a male shopper chooses to purchase an item. Terry Parker describes her live-in boyfriend in these terms:

> He tells me all the time, "It is not worth my time." It is one of his favorite phrases. It is a statement that I have said, but not very often. He says it a lot more often. Just grunt work, like repairs on something at a yard sale or something, if I wanted to pick it up he would say, "It's not worth the time to fix it." But I'll say that I'll never see another one of these again and it is unique or that it is exactly what I wanted. Unfortunately, it is broken, but it is worth the time because it is irreplaceable.

She notes that when *he* feels like repairing an item from a garage sale, his sense of the value of his time changes.

Garage Sale Participation as Extensions of Traditional Gender Roles

What emerges from my field research is that participation in garage sales often follows traditional gender roles for men and women. The predominance of female participants in the garage sale can be attributed to its close link to traditionally defined female activities, such as shopping, cleaning, and socially engaging others. Their style of participation in sales is colored by the "female values"[2] of creating connections, community and consensus (Tannen).

Male's participation in garage sales, and their reluctance to participate, can also be viewed as an extension of their traditional roles as primary breadwinners. They are concerned with money and time, both of which are strongly associated with the breadwinner role. These concerns color male participation in sales, and serve as the reasons for them *not* to participate—"They're not worth my time," or "It's too penny-ante." Similarly, male concern with status ("The Big Wheel") in the garage sale is associated with breadwinner anxiety about job hierarchies, public perceptions, and social prestige. The factor of status can manifest as male reluctance to become involved in sales (e.g., embarrassment) or can translate into claiming special status within sales (e.g., hosting a really *good* sale). Drawing on Tannen's delineation, they are interested in status, hierarchy and power.

Male participation often focuses on physical strength, such as lifting, or construction-type skills, such as putting up clotheslines.

These are activities associated with the male role, and which, at least partially, derive from the fact that most males are physically stronger than most females. Issues of competence ("The Sturdy Oak") may characterize male participation. They are likely to undertake garage sale activities with a degree of completeness and purposefulness not as commonly found among women. Also, an element of "Give 'Em Hell" can be seen in those males who bargain for sport.

As with most distinctions of gender differences in behavior, the similarities far outweigh the differences (Lott, "Dual"). What has been emphasized here are gendered patterns. Overall, both men and women engage in garage sale activities with similar motivations, friendliness and enjoyment. Character differences can color the style of participation of men and women, along with factors such as ethnicity, class, religion, race and sexual preference. Further, generational differences can play a big part in the style of garage sale participation. Grown sons of fathers who would never hold a sale can be seen hawking their things along with mothers, friends, and wives. Younger men, in general, are more likely to be full participants, that is, equally "in charge" of holding sales and equally involved in shopping at them. Retired men, with time on their hands and looking for company, are also often active garage sale participants.

Notes

1. This essay is part of a much larger body of work (Herrmann; Herrmann and Soiffer; Soiffer and Herrmann), based on over a decade of ethnographic research on the garage sale and its participants. I have interviewed, often with a tape recorder, over 200 shoppers and sellers and attended over 1,500 garage sales. I have observed numerous sales and accompanied shoppers on their rounds. Most of those interviewed are European-Americans, but some are African-Americans, Asian-Americans and Hispanic-Americans. The vast majority of shoppers and sellers are middle-class, stable working-class or students. I tallied the gender and approximate age of the participants, which indicates that approximately two-thirds of the shoppers and sellers are women. A major focus of the research has been the participation of women, in contrast to that of men, in the female dominated institution of the garage sale. Pseudonyms are used to protect the identities of informants.

2. I am not referring to an essentialized notion of female values, or what has at times been called cultural or difference feminism. I am speaking here of values that women tend to internalize by virtue of their socialization and their disproportionate experience as nurturers and caretakers.

Works Cited

Allison, Neil K., Linda L. Golden, Gary M. Mullet, and Donna Coogan. "Sex-Typed Product Images: The Effects of Sex, Sex-Role Self-Concept and Measurement Implications." *Advances in Consumer Research*, vol. 7. Ed. J. Olson. Ann Arbor: Association for Consumer Research, 1979. 604–09.

Berardo, Donna H., Constance L. Shehan, and Gerald R. Leslie. "A Residue of Tradition: Jobs, Careers, and Spouses' Time in Housework." *Journal of Marriage and the Family* 49 (1987): 381–90.

Berheide, Catherine, Sarah Berk, and Richard Berk. "Household Work in the Suburbs: The Job and Its Participants." *Pacific Sociological Review* 19 (1976): 491–518.

Cohen, Richard. "Who Stoops to Bargain." *Washington Post Sunday Magazine* (11 Oct. 1987): 7.

Coontz, Stephanie. *The Way We Never Were: American Families and the Nostalgia Trap.* New York: Basic, 1992.

Csikszentmihalyi, Mihaly, and Eugene Rochberg-Halton. *The Meaning of Things.* New York: Cambridge UP, 1981.

David, Deborah S., and Robert Brannon. "The Male Sex Role." *The Forty-Nine Percent Majority*. Ed. D. David and R. Brannon. New York: Addison-Wesley, 1976. 7–45.

Debevec, Kathleen, and Easwar Iyer. "Sex Roles and Consumer Perceptions of Promotions, Products, and Self: What Do We Need to Know and Where Should We Be Headed?" *Advances in Consumer Research*, vol. 13. Ed. R. J. Lutz. Provo, UT: Association for Consumer Research, 1988. 210–14.

Dittmar, Helga. "Meanings of Material Possessions as Reflections of Identity: Gender and Social-Material Position in Society." *To Have Possessions: A Handbook of Ownership and Property*. Ed. F. Rudmin. Special Issue of *The Journal of Social Behavior and Personality* (1991): 165–86.

Ehrenreich, Barbara. *The Hearts of Men*. Garden City, NY: Anchor, 1984.

Faludi, Susan. *Backlash*. New York: Crown, 1991.

Goode, William J. "Why Men Resist." *Rethinking the Family*. Ed. B. Thorne and M. Yalom. New York: Longman, 1982. 131–50.

Gould, Robert E. "Measuring Masculinity by the Size of a Paycheck." *Men and Masculinity*. Ed. J. H. Pleck and J. Sawyer. Englewood Cliffs, NJ: Prentice-Hall, 1974. 96–100.

Hartmann, Heidi L. "The Family as the Locus of Gender, Class and Political Struggle: The Example of Housework." *Signs* 6.3 (1981): 366–94.

Herrmann, Gretchen M. *Garage Sales as Practice: Ideologies of Women, Work and Community in Daily Life*. Ph.D. dissertation, SUNY at Binghamton, 1990.

Herrmann, Gretchen M., and Stephen M. Soiffer. "For Fun and Profit: An Analysis of the American Garage Sale." *Urban Life* 12.4 (1984): 397–421.

Hochschild, Arlie, with Anne Machung. *The Second Shift: Working Parents and the Revolution at Home*. New York: Viking, 1989.

Krafft, Susan. "How Shoppers Get Satisfaction." *American Demographics* 15 (1993): 13–16.

Lamphere, Louise, Patricia Zavella, Felipe Gonzales, with Peter B. Evans. *Sunbelt Working Mothers*. Ithaca: Cornell UP, 1993.

Lott, Bernice. *Women's Lives: Themes and Variations in Gender Learning*. Monterey, CA: Brooks/Cole, 1987.

Lott, Bernice. "Dual Natures or Learned Behavior: It Makes a Difference." Unpublished paper presented at Feminist Transformations of the Social Sciences, Hamilton College, 1988.

Maccoby, Eleanor E., and Carol N. Jacklin. *The Psychology of Sex Differences*. Stanford: Stanford University Press, 1974.

Oakley, Anne. *The Sociology of Housework*. New York: Pantheon, 1974.

Rubin, Lillian. *Families on the Faultline*. New York: Harper Collins, 1994.

Rubin, Lillian. *Worlds of Pain*. New York: Vintage, 1976.

Shelton, Beth Anne, and John Daphne. "Does Marital Status Make a Difference?: Housework among Married and Cohabiting Men and Women." *Journal of Family Issues* 14.3 (1993): 401–20.

Soiffer, Stephen M., and Gretchen M. Herrmann. "Visions of Power: Ideology and Practice in the American Garage Sale." *The Sociological Review* 35 (1987): 48–83.

Syracuse Post-Standard. "Experts: Women Born, Men Bored to Shop." 20 Apr. 1991: A,1.

Tannen, Deborah. *You Just Don't Understand: Men and Women in Conversation*. New York: Ballantine, 1990.

Weinbaum, Batya, and Amy Bridges. "The Other Side of the Paycheck: Monopoly Capitalism and the Structure of Consumption." *Capitalist Patriarchy and the Case for Socialist Feminism*. Ed. Z. Eisenstein. New York: Monthly Review, 1979. 190–205.

Whitehead, Ann. "The Politics of Domestic Budgeting." *Of Marriage and the Market*. Ed. K. Young and R. McCullagh. Boston: Routledge & Kegan Paul, 1984. 93–116.

Zelizer, Viviana A. *The Social Meaning of Money*. New York: Basic, 1994.

I'd Rather Go Along and Be Considered a Man
Masculinity and Bystander Intervention

In October of 2002, the gang rape of an unconscious 15-year-old girl took place at an out of control party. The parents, having left their 21-year-old son in charge, were away for the weekend. The semi-conscious girl was led out of one room and directed to lie down on a pool table. After she passed out, she was assaulted by four perpetrators (one adult and three juveniles) in the presence of six bystanders. When interviewed about the crime, the District Attorney said that the reason none of the bystanders intervened was because they did not want to be considered "wusses" or "be made fun of." The idea the bystanders were more afraid of their masculinity being called into question than the violence potentially turning on them is essential to understanding the perplexing dynamics between gender, power, and violence. This research seeks to answer the question: What role does masculinity play in bystander intervention in crises situations? For the purposes of this research, a crisis situation is defined as one in which violence is being directed toward another individual in the presence of bystanders or onlookers.

The Bystander Studies

Rosenthal's (1964) landmark book detailed the tragic death of Kitty Genovese, who was raped and stabbed to death in the presence of 38 witnesses. The book is a descriptive narrative of the killing and its aftermath, and is the most cited work on an actual case of bystander apathy. In response to the Genovese killing and Rosenthal's published account, John Darley and Bibb Latane (1968) conducted several psychological experiments, considered seminal for later research on bystander intervention. Some of the features noted in their research was that the number of bystanders a research subject saw during a crisis had an important effect on whether the research subject would intervene (e.g., the more bystanders the less likely a research participant would intervene). However, contrary to the perception that non-intervention demonstrated a lack of empathy for the victim, they found that the non-interveners *were still in a state of indecision and conflict* about whether to intervene (Darley & Latane, 1968, emphasis added). In other words, their non-responsiveness was a sign of their moral dilemma. For the subjects who knew there were other bystanders present, the cost of nonintervention was lowered, meaning that if no one acted, then no one specific individual could be blamed for their non-intervention. However, the individual conflict over what to do was far more acute than was previously thought. Darley and Latane term this bystander conflict the "diffusion of responsibility" (p. 90).

Shotland and Straw (1976) found that if a man attacks a woman, bystanders are less likely to intervene, if they are perceived to be married. Further, when the bystanders were given no information about the attack, they assumed a relationship between the man and the woman and, therefore, were less likely to intervene. In a comparable study with similar results, Borofsky, Stollak, and Messe (1971) asserted that male bystanders receive sexual gratification from seeing a woman being attacked. To test these findings, Harari, Harari, and White (1985) staged a series of simulated rapes on one college campus in areas where real rapes had occurred. They found most males did intervene to assist the women victims. Thus, the researchers argued that not all bystanders behave in the same ways and that this should be considered when conducting field research. One study found that the primary factor influencing men's willingness to intervene to prevent sexual assault was the men's perception of other men's willingness to intervene (Fabiano, Perkins, Berkowitz, Linkenbach, & Stark, 2004).

An important variable affecting bystander intervention is the status of the victim. If the victim is perceived to be of high status or in the "in-group," then they are more likely to receive aid from bystanders (Levine, Cassidy, & Brazier, 2002; Ridgeway & Diekema, 1989; Tisak & Tisak, 1996). Piliavin, Rodin, and Piliavin (1969) found that an apparently drunk person will not receive help even after collapsing because they might be "dirty or disgusting" (p. 290). Further, Piliavin, Rodin, and Pili-

avin found that bystanders are less likely to directly intervene, if intervention appears to have an unwanted physical or psychological consequence such as exposing oneself to danger or verbal harassment.

Interviews

The study was based on qualitative interviews during which participants had three scenarios read to them. Each was based on real-life occurrences. The scenarios were:

On a typical Friday night, you are out walking around on Main St. A fight has broken out between three guys. Two of the guys have ganged up on the third one, and he is definitely losing. Other people are standing around paying some attention, but they are not intervening in the situation. You think the fight is unfair because it is two against one.

On a typical Friday night you are out walking around on Main St. You happen to see a guy shoving a girl around. The girl is crying and asking him to stop. He does not. Other people are standing around paying some attention, but they are not intervening in the situation.

You are at a party. You go upstairs to just sort of look around in the rooms. You decide to walk into one room. When you step into the room you see several guys standing around a table. One guy is having sex with a naked and unconscious woman on top of the table. Other guys are standing around watching and saying nothing. Still others are cheering him on and appear as if they are waiting to take their turn to have sex with her.

After reading each scenario individually, I asked the participants a series of open-ended questions based on their reactions to the hypothetical situations. The starting question was always what the participants thought about the male bystanders in each situation. I usually followed up with what they thought about the female bystanders in each situation, with the intention of discovering if they held different gender expectations of male and female bystanders. Subsequent questions were generated by the answers that each participant gave. I also asked them some open-ended questions about masculinity, i.e., how they defined masculinity and what pressures they feel they are under from their peers and society to act in a manly or masculine way. The interviews lasted between 20 and 90 minutes. The average interview lasted approximately 45 minutes, though I always endeavored to elicit longer interviews in order to generate as much of their experiences and viewpoints as possible.

I judged the participants' answers to be truthful because many of them struggled with the answers they gave. The majority of participants took time to formulate their answers and asked for clarification if they did not understand what I was asking. Although some of them could readily answer certain questions, such as what they thought society and peers thought of their behavior, other questions were more difficult. The questions that the participants found most challenging to answer were those that asked about their own personal definitions of masculinity and what they think society's messages about masculinity mean to them in their personal lives.

Participants

The participants were all men ages 18 or 19 who were college freshmen or sophomores at California State University, Chico (CSUC).[1] Seventeen of them were Caucasian, one Philippino, one Southeast Asian, and one participant describes himself as half-Asian. None were African-American or Latino. All except one is from California. Three come from inner cities, nine come from rural areas in Northern California, with eight coming from suburban Southern California. Only three of the participants mentioned having girlfriends.

Findings

Many of the findings deal with men who would hypothetically intervene in a variety of crisis situations, not all of which focus on sexual assault. However, regardless of the type of violent situation, certain aspects of masculinity that the participants reported are highly relevant to the levels of aggression and violence that are acceptable to the participants. For example, the majority of participants in this study reported that they did not want to look weak in front of other men, which is an important finding when thinking about how male bystanders might weigh the consequences of intervening in a gang-rape. As some researchers have asserted, gang-rape is a male-bonding activity that reinforces alliances between men and boys, the participants' desire to be seen as manly by other men is relevant to the phenomenon of gang-rape (e.g., Messerschmidt, 1993; O'Sullivan, 1998). Further, for a majority of these participants, the context of how a violent situation starts determines whether or not they will intervene. Many of the participants asserted that they would not intervene in the fight scenario, because the guy might have "deserved it" or "asked for it." These same attitudes have often been cited as reasons why women are raped and blamed for their attacks. Accordingly, asking questions about violence aimed toward men and aimed at women enabled me to understand how men view aggression directed toward both genders and if they account for it in different ways.

Several themes emerged: men must not cry, men must be big and powerful, men must fight, men must be conscious of their physical stature, men must protect women, men must engage in heavy drinking, and many men think that they are different from their peers. However, one dominant theme became apparent and appeared to influence all other subsequent masculine ideals: Men must not be weak, appear weak, or show weakness of any kind. Participant John Smith[2] illustrated this with his remarks, "I think that's, like, pretty much the general theme . . . is just don't be weak. You know weak means being a pussy, being a wuss, being a crybaby."

The men in this study defined certain behaviors as weak and therefore unmasculine. Traits that adhered to traditional prescribed behaviors for females, such as compassion, crying, indecisiveness, or passivity are considered unmasculine and undesirable. Not responding to any perceived infringement of his rights or not responding to a demonstrated lack of respect from another man is also considered weak. For example, Steele said, "You can't be weak in the sense that you give up too easily, or you back down too much . . . you have to stand up." Paul further exemplified this by stating, "You know, being tough, the whole tough thing . . . like standing up in situations, rather than like bowing down, even when it's smart, you

know." These quotes exemplify the expectations about masculinity that the participants have, and those expectations influence how they think they should behave.

In addition to acting tough and not backing down, another set of behaviors are defined as masculine. Men are expected to be decisive and should not appear to regret their decisions; Juco's comments illustrate these ideals:

To me being a man means basically having balls, that's what I think. I mean it doesn't matter what you believe, but like if you do something and you regret that decision move on . . . basically you're not scared and you're not a pussy. You don't really care about the consequences for what you did.

Another weak behavior is crying. James' comments illustrate this belief: "Because from their standpoint they would definitely be like, 'Oh, you are a fag, you cried,' like only fags cry."

Besides not crying and seeking to avoid the verbal consequences of unmasculine behavior, these men are also receiving the message from society and their peers that to be masculine means to have muscled bodies and to be physically more impressive. Mike's comment illustrates this belief perfectly, "I am not a 'gym rat' but the guys in my fraternity talked me into it, so I feel very manly today as I worked out last night and my arms hurt." Being physically big and powerful is another example of how men must not appear weak, and Mike's quote demonstrates how these men are influenced by their peers to conform to perceived standards of masculinity.

The men were also conscious of how their size affects their behavior. Body consciousness influences whether or not they would intervene in certain situations. Five of the participants echoed the ideas that intervention would depend on how much bigger the other guys are. Wheaties stated, "Well, I'm not that large of a guy, so I wouldn't step in because I don't think I could offer any help. . . . If you are a big person, you're kind of generally supposed to step in."

In addition to avoiding outward displays of certain emotions and wanting to be physically impressive, many of the participants believe that men are naturally aggressive and that fighting is a normal expression of this aggression. George's comments illustrate this notion:

I don't know. I personally . . . I don't really like to watch the fights that much. I think it's just because they . . . I don't know . . . it's the *male thing* to do I guess, to watch fights. That's what they want to go do. . . . Because it's like you know, I'm tough, I want to see someone get beat up, you know . . . I don't know, *I would beat that guy too if I was him* kind of like that image that they're trying to portray. (Emphasis added)

Some of the participants did accept that this is not an inherent biological feature of being male but the result of how boys are socialized in American culture. John Smith demonstrates this belief, "Guys like fights. I don't know . . . maybe uh, that's what we've been socialized to think or something. We watch wrestling and watch you know USC fights and get into it. And we like fighting and wrestling with our friends, you know." Zack also mentioned this socialization, "It's been kind of reinforced that men are allowed to be violent in circumstantial settings, wrestling, boxing, events like that, hockey, for example, which is really violent."

The context of the fight also appears to be an important factor in whether a man will intervene. In their mind the possibility that the victim may have instigated their assault renders them at fault for their "beat down," a phrase commonly used on campus. Rusty's question is clearly illustrative of this rationale, "Was the losing person jumped or did he provoke the other two people?" Since it appears that violence is considered a normal and natural part of the male life experience, it is seen as the appropriate way to handle transgressions and exhibit masculinity.

Many of the participants draw the line at a certain level of violence. The criteria for intervention, regardless of how or who started the fight, is when the one being beaten has stopped moving, fighting back, or it appears to the observer that bones are being broken. Wheaties' statement acknowledges this conviction, "If they were seriously hurting him, like anything where like the police would have to be involved or he has to go to the hospital or anything like that, that's crossing a certain point." At that point, then intervention is deemed necessary.

Throughout the research, whenever the participants made the decision to hypothetically get involved, they consistently reported that they would choose direct intervention. Direct intervention is defined as getting directly involved in the situation (e.g., getting in the middle of the fight to stop it) to assist in a crisis (Darley & Latane, 1970). Bystander research has consistently shown that men use the direct form to intervene, as opposed to women who use indirect methods such as calling 911.

The existing research does not shed light on why men choose direct intervention over non-direct methods. However, given that men are socialized to see action as the appropriate response in many situations, it logically follows that they would engage in an action-oriented behavior during a crisis (Connell, 1987). Pauly echoed that masculinity is about action with his comments, "It's basically action not like sitting back and, uh, I'll deal with that tomorrow or something. It's go out, get it done."

One participant was the exception to this "rule." In regards to the fighting, Kevin never asked about the specifics of the fight. He very calmly stated that an unfair fight was wrong, and he would step in and attempt to break up the fight without "getting too involved." Once again we see how the type of intervention used is direct involvement, something that the majority of the participants reported as the chosen behavior.

Another significant masculine activity that men must engage in is to drink alcohol and to drink heavily. Steele asserted, "You have to drink, if you don't drink you're kinda considered weak." One consequence of not drinking or drinking heavily is commentary from the men's peers. For example, if these men do not drink or do not engage in heavy drinking, then they will have their masculinity called into question verbally. Not drinking or being a light drinker is associated with femininity and therefore considered weak. James' comments show this belief, "I like to drink. I like to go party but if I tell my friends I got smashed off of three shots. Like dude that's all you can handle? I'm expected to party more because I'm male. Totally."

Given these beliefs about masculinity, it is logical to conclude that the drinking also fuels the fighting associated with masculinity. Simply put, the link between alcohol consumption and violence is well-documented, and as fighting is considered a manly behavior, this combination appears to produce drunken fights that are often excused as just another "guy thing." As there seems to be a rationale that determines when it is a guy thing or when the victim has brought it on himself, I believe that this is partially why the context of how a fight starts is important to these men.

For some, drinking further fuels the level of aggressiveness should they decide to intervene. Note how once again intervention is in the direct form, a further example of how masculinity is demonstrated by the male bystander. Rusty stated:

> If I wasn't intoxicated, I would hurry over there quickly grab the guy and push him away. If I was intoxicated, I'd run up there and beat the crap out of him. . . . Because I'd be under the influence and, like I said, I have a short temper and sometimes the alcohol takes things to the extreme.

Mike's remarks also support the relationship between drinking and fighting. Further, his comments also illustrate how a certain level of violence is tolerable. As stated earlier, after a certain level of violence has been reached in a fight between two men, intervention is deemed acceptable.

> If it got to the point where someone was unconscious, I gotta say honestly what we'd probably do is do equal damage to the well not equal damage we'd probably just beat the other guy so he wouldn't be able to move and then we'd call the police. Say look there's a guy wearing this who was the instigator and we got him. But he got the other guy so we'd probably do it anonymously. I gotta say *most of the time we're probably a little drunk* so we're not going to do the most rational thing we should do. (Emphasis added)

Adding to the belief that being a man means demonstrating behavior that is action-oriented, several of the participants told me that they believe part of their masculinity means protecting women. When I asked Steele about his beliefs concerning masculinity, he told me, "I kinda have this, uh, weakness toward women so it's like I gotta protect them. Part of being a man is to protect women."

Many of the participants indicated that while men fighting each other is considered normal masculine behavior, men acting aggressively toward a woman is not. Some of the participants expressed this belief by talking about what they saw as the unequal physical attributes of men and women, or by stating feelings of anger toward the male aggressor. When I asked him why he would intervene on behalf of a woman being pushed around by a man, Rob echoed this principle plainly, "It just seems like the right thing to do. I mean someone who's defenseless, or can't really fight back for themselves."

Despite some of the participants expressing a responsibility to protect women, several of them asserted they understood why real-life bystanders to the gang-rape did not intervene. As evidenced by the quotes below, they comprehended the pressure the bystanders felt to avoid looking weak in front of their friends. This conflict between protecting women but at the same time feeling forced to avoid looking weak or sensitive in front of their peers is another important component of the relationship between masculinity and bystander intervention. When I asked Zack if he thought he would lose respect from his peers if he were to intervene in a gang-rape he responded by saying, "Oh definitely. . . . Because I entered another man's territory. The

man's territory being his girl and henceforth by entering his domain I've desecrated his territory supposedly." John Smith also said, "They're not going to leave; they're not going to do anything about it. 'Cuz they're too scared to look like a pussy leaving the room." George did as well, "I think they're pressured to cheer him on because they don't want to look weak in front of their other friends." Juco's comments are also quite clear on what the possible consequences might be, "Basically, if they tried to stop it, you know it would be over for them. People would give them shit about it all the time. They'd probably be looked down upon. They'd be viewed as too sensitive." These remarks are another example of how some men believe masculinity means avoiding the appearance of weakness, and how showing weakness is perceived to have undesirable consequences. These comments are telling in how men might weigh their options, should they find themselves in a situation where the need to preserve their masculine reputations may outweigh the victim's needs.

Though the majority of men in this study stated they would protect women in the aforementioned situation, some seemed to waiver in their conviction to intervene in the rape scenario. Thus, it appears as if a distinction is apparently made between women who are being abused in a public venue and women who are raped in a private setting. As a result, two of these participants, asserted that they would not intervene in the hypothetical rape, even though these two participants were very clear that a hypothetical rape was being committed. A large majority said they would intervene in the hypothetical, with three more who seemed to waiver as to whether they would intervene or not.

Another important issue I noticed is something I call *gender distancing*. Simply put, some of the men in this study see themselves as different from other men and often stated so in various ways. Many of the participants told me verbally that they are not like other men, or that others do not hold certain values as highly as they do. Again, Zack's comments are illuminating:

I don't know. I would never ever ever have a situation like this at all like I would never forcibly do anything my girlfriend would not want to do but that's just me and I have a different set of morals than most people in my generation. . . . Other people do not hold this virtue as highly and because of that they may find themselves in these situations.

Tom echoed this need for not being just like other men, "I just—I kinda try to hold myself to a different standard and just live my life the way I feel that it should be lived."

Though these men believed that they did not exhibit these behaviors and indeed, that they were different from their peers, as evidenced by their previous remarks they did engage in many of the behaviors associated with masculinity. Nevertheless, when examining their comments more closely, the men who professed to be different did, in fact, still conform to expected gender ideals. Accordingly, they did not seem to be significantly different from their peers.

Though some of these men believe that they are different from their peers, they are still aware of the penalties of engaging in behavior perceived to be less masculine. In this study the men repeatedly used certain words to describe behaviors they considered unmasculine and weak. Words such as "fag," "gay," and "pussy" are the primary

chosen vocabulary used to call the men's behavior into question. As George's comments show, he is one man who is aware of the consequences of "weak" behavior and how these words are used for this purpose:

I do think that guys in general have to like, kind of put up with a little bit more of a tougher image, or else they might get called like names like "gay" or something similar . . . and everyone starts ganging up on—you get ganged up on by your friends or your peers or whatnot and people don't want to feel that way.

For one man these labels are painful and induce anger. James stated that for him:

It makes you feel terrible. Damn am I really viewed like that? I think like the word "fag" totally provokes a different mindset. That puts me at the mindset of, "Like dude, you need to stop, 'cause I'm going to start to get pissed."

Although some of the men believed that socialization played a role in how some men act, others believed that men and women were biologically programmed for certain roles and behaviors. This biological determinism is seen by the participants as the reason why men and women act in certain ways, and it is used to explain the many behaviors defined as masculine. Mike's statement illustrates this well:

Oh well, it's like because of the presence of testosterone in men and testosterone is responsible for a lot of different things, because of that like women tend to be more interpersonal or at least with children like when little girls play in nursery schools they are always playing house and exploring relationships, whereas boys are more like physical and then they're more like things that do things like they like to play with trucks that can move sand. There's obvious differences, it's across other cultures too. There's biological needs for one sex to do one thing and the other sex to do other things.

Although some men in this study recognize the role that socialization plays, Mike's comments are highly indicative of the pervasive belief that men are the way they are because of their hormones. These beliefs are used to support the idea that men are supposed to act in certain ways, and when they do not, they are considered less masculine. Therefore, when men fail to act in gender appropriate ways, their competence as men is questioned. Further, as these men do not want to be viewed as less masculine, this complicated gender performance is something they feel they must engage in, in order to be viewed as masculine by their peers and society. Should they be seen as less masculine, they might suffer the consequences. Here Wheaties is describing the social cost to his roommate who decided he did not want to engage in a traditionally masculine activity:

He was telling me about this . . . he went hunting with his dad like every day. And he was like finally, "Dad, you know I like shooting, I like going out and hunting with you. But it's just not my thing. I'd rather be riding dirt bikes or something." And it's just spread all around town like within a week, that this guy's son didn't like hunting and he was like, disowned, like just by these people's thoughts, just 'cuz he didn't like hunting.

Wheaties' story demonstrates these men believe and have heard real-life experiences

to support their fear of consequences from unmasculine behavior. Should they be seen as weak or unmanly, the participants believe they will suffer at the hands of their peers and society. More importantly, they have some real-life experience to support these fears.

The importance these men attach to these beliefs cannot be dismissed. If these men's greatest fear is having their masculinity called into question, then they are arguably enslaved to a gender ideal that is dangerous to them and to the women they profess to feel responsible for protecting. These men appear to believe their masculinity centers on drinking, engaging in personal violence, and appearing physically larger than everyone else. Consequently, socially constructed gender expectations are often being excused away as a natural male behavior, even in the face of their obvious policing of each other's masculine identities.

In spite of the real and perceived consequences, not all of the men fit completely into these prescribed behaviors and patterns. One participant named Ian never mentioned drinking in his interview, and did not feel that it was any of his business to intervene in a fight between other males. His feelings were strong enough that even if the male fight victim was injured badly enough to need medical care, he was insistent that he still would not intervene, directly or otherwise. Still in keeping with the expectation that women must be protected, he stated he would intervene if a woman was being abused in a public venue. Though he could not explain his logic as to why the victim's gender would yield a different response, his statement, "[G]irls tend to not be so aggressive, so if she's getting beat up, it's usually because of some aggressive boyfriend. . . . I would take it automatically as, 'He is an asshole. . . . So, I would want to break that up,'" is a telling one. As it appears to him that men tend to be more aggressive, perhaps this is the reason why he would not intervene on behalf of another man. By that same logic, if women tend to be less aggressive, it might seem more appropriate to him to protect a woman from another man.

Conversely, Pauly does not conform to any of the "typical" behaviors for men. While the majority of the participants drink and fight, he does not. Nor did he ever mention protecting women as a masculine behavior. Indeed, like many of the other participants in this study, Pauly asserts that he is different and from his account, he is. Pauly is a self-described "band geek" so arguably his standards of masculinity are different from the other men in this study. Nevertheless, when I asked him about looking weak in front of other men he replied, "There were times when I didn't fit in and didn't feel cool. But I made an effort to put myself out there and be the opposite of the rule." Pauly's account shows that though he does not engage in certain defined masculine behaviors, he is aware that there are "rules" about masculinity and, in the past, he has modified his behavior in an attempt to prove those rules wrong.

Discussion

The findings in this study demonstrate that masculinity may be another factor in the complex behavior of bystanders to violent situations. The most important finding is that these men feel they must not be weak and, perhaps more importantly, must not appear weak to others, especially to other men. In addition, the desire to avoid looking weak also appears to serve as the foundation for other subsequent behaviors such as drinking and fighting. Furthermore, the pressures the participants feel to be big and powerful, to act aggressively, to fight, and to drink heavily, are all potential factors in a gang-rape situation.

Another issue to consider is that apparently intervening in a public setting where both males and females are present is considered masculine, but for some of the participants intervening in a private setting where only other men are present is considered too weak and therefore unmasculine behavior. Further, the participants who stated they understood why the bystanders to the real-life rape did not intervene illuminates that masculinity may be a factor in a bystander's decision-making process. Therefore, it appears that when a man is exclusively in the presence of other men, he may feel he cannot risk intervening for fear of looking weak or unmasculine.

Another potential factor to consider is that should a male bystander intervene in a gang-rape, he may have to account for his heterosexuality. Some researchers have asserted that gang-rape is a test of manhood (O'Sullivan, 1998; Sanday, 1990). With that assertion in mind, it is possible that a man who intervenes to stop a gang-rape may find himself in the position of having to defend his sexual orientation. Both Connell (1995) and Kimmel (1994) have argued homophobia and maintaining a heterosexual identity are central organizing principles of masculinity. Accordingly, the role of masculinity in bystander intervention is situational. For that reason the answers the participants gave help to shape a clearer understanding of why some men may choose not to intervene in a gang-rape situation.

The fighting and other behaviors that are accounted for as gender appropriate activities say a great deal about the participants' beliefs about masculinity. One could argue that since the participants' principle concern is avoiding the appearance of weakness, and aggression is constructed as normal male behavior, these two issues feed into each other. Further, if men are supposed to be aggressive, cannot be seen as weak, and must sexually pursue women, then does it not follow that rape is the "logical" outcome of this gender enforced dynamic? Several theorists have argued this exact point (Connell, 1995; Katz, 1999; Kimmel, 1994; Messerschmidt, 1993; O'Sullivan, 1998).

Previous research has asserted a victim's gender plays a role in how the victim is perceived (Chancer, 1998; Levine, Cassidy, & Brazier, 2002; Tisak & Tisak, 1996). The current research has a slightly different outcome than the previous scholarly work. Herein, the participants reported the hypothetical victim's gender in the gang-rape scenario did not appear to be as much of a mitigating factor to the degree it has been in real-life incidents. However, in the second scenario where a woman is being abused in a public venue, the majority of participants seemed much more firm in their conviction to intervene. They also expressed more anger at that particular situation, whereas only two expressed anger at the gang-rape incident. In the gang-rape scenario, another three participants expressed shock, but not anger at the hypothetical gang-rape. Overall, most of the participants took the gang-rape in stride and accounted for their lack of shock or anger by telling me they had heard of this type of scenario in the news and from their friends.

My research both supports and is also supported by the theory of "doing gender."

West and Zimmerman (1987) argue that, "gender is the product of social doings of some kind of sort" (p. 129). They also argue that, "a person's actions are often designed with an eye to their accountability and how they might look and how they might be categorized by others" (p. 136). The participants reported they must avoid the appearance of weakness in its various forms because they do not want to be categorized as unmasculine. This is a main example of West and Zimmerman's assertion that "a person engaged in virtually any activity may be held accountable for performance of that activity as a *man*" (p. 136).

West and Zimmerman (1987) also argue that doing gender means creating differences between women and men and that these differences are not natural, essential or biological. Differences that are constructed are used to reinforce the essentialness of gender. Several of the participants cited biological differences to support why men and women engage in certain behaviors. West and Zimmerman argue these supposed biological differences are seen as normal and natural behavior for men and women, but, in fact, these behaviors are constructed and then used to reinforce fundamental beliefs about gender.

Conclusion

Masculinity, as the participants define it, comes with serious physical, psychological, and social costs to men and women. For men, it is hard to imagine they are not being injured from the fighting and heavy drinking that appears to be taking place. This assertion is especially important when considering that the participants in this study stated that, hypothetically, they would not intervene in a fight unless someone has stopped moving or bones had been broken. Furthermore, men who cannot back down for fear of being seen as weak could potentially be more likely to engage in other types of violence to prove their manhood. Sabo (2006) argues that activities such as hazing, gang wars, and homicide are just some of the violent pursuits some men engage in to prove their masculinity. Other costs to men are emotionally shallow relationships, depression, poor health from being too masculine to go to the doctor for physicals, and higher morbidity rates (Harrison, Chin, & Ficarroto, 1992; Sabo, 2004).

For women, there are several potential consequences of masculinity. One possible consequence is that a rape culture is largely sustained by violent masculinity; therefore as a result of living in a rape culture, rape will continue to be a serious problem (Buchwald, Fletcher, & Roth, 2004; Sanday, 1996; Scully, 1995). However, one consequence that should be considered is the possibility a woman may find herself in a situation that puts her at risk for rape and discovering she does not have the male allies she may need to avoid a rape. Because showing empathy or sensitivity might be construed as weakness, a man may not feel he can risk showing these emotions. Indeed, the male bystander may feel he has too much to lose by showing any understanding of the potential victim's predicament. Consideration should also be given to how a man may have to account for his heterosexuality were he to intervene to stop a gang-rape. With these issues in mind, the male bystander may decide against protecting a woman for fear of being seen as weak or gay by his male peers.

As the previous research into bystander intervention has not explicitly investigated the role of masculinity, my study fills some of this gap in the literature. These findings should serve to illuminate how masculinity may be influencing the male bystanders' decision making processes.

Notes

1. This study was approved by the Institutional Review Board at California State University, Chico. Each participant gave informed consent, was paid $10.00, and was promised full confidentiality.

2. Participants' names have been changed to protect anonymity and confidentiality.

References

Borofsky, G., Stollak, G., & Messe, L. (1971). Sex differences in bystander reactions to physical assault. *Journal of Experimental Social Psychology, 7,* 313–318.

Buchwald, E., Fletcher, P., & Roth, M. (2004). *Transforming a rape culture.* Minneapolis: Milkweed Editions.

Chancer, L. (1998). Gender, class and race in three high profile crimes: The cases of New Bedford, Central Park and Benson Hurst. In S. Miller (Ed.), *Crime control and women: Feminist implications of criminal justice policy* (pp. 20–31). Thousand Oaks, CA: Sage Publications.

Connell, R. W. (1987). *Gender and power.* Stanford: Stanford University Press.

Connell, R. W. (1995). *Masculinities.* Berkeley: University of California Press.

Darley, J., & Latane, B. (1970). *The unresponsive bystander: Why doesn't he help?* New York: Appleton-Century-Crofts.

Fabiano, P., Perkins, H., Berkowitz, A., Linkenbach, J., & Stark, C. (2004). Engaging men as social justice allies in ending violence against women: Evidence for a social norms approach. *Journal of American College Health, 52*(3), 105–112.

Harari, H., Harari, O., & White, R. (1985). The reaction to rape by American male bystanders.

The Journal of Social Psychology, 125(5), 653–658.

Harrison, I., Chin, I., & Ficarroto, I. (1992). Warning: The male sex-role may be dangerous to your health. In M. Kimmel & M. Messner (Eds.), *Men's lives* (2nd ed., pp. 271–285). Boston: Allyn and Bacon.

Katz, J. (Producer), & Jhally, S. (Director). (1999). *Tough guise: Violence, media, and the crisis in masculinity* (Documentary). Northampton: Media Educational Foundation.

Kimmel, M. (1994). Masculinity as homophobia. In Estelle Disch (Ed.), *Reconstructing gender: A multicultural anthology* (pp. 132–139). Mountain View: Mayfield Publishing Company.

Levine, M., Cassidy, C., & Brazier, G. (2002). Self-categorization and bystander non-intervention: Two experimental studies. *Journal of Applied Social Psychology, 32*, 1452–1454.

Messerschmidt, J. (1993). *Masculinities and crime*. Lanham: Rowman & Littlefield.

O'Sullivan, C. (1998). Ladykillers: Similarities and divergences of masculinities in gang rape and wife battery. In L. Bowker (Ed.), *Masculinities and violence* (pp. 82–105). Thousand Oaks: Sage.

Piliavin, I., Rodin, J., & Piliavin, J. (1969). Good samaritanism: An underground phenomenon? *Journal of Personality and Social Psychology, 13*, 289–299.

Ridgeway, C., & Diekema, D. (1989). Dominance and collective hierarchy formation in male and female task groups. *American Sociological Review, 54*, 79–93.

Rosenthal, A. M. (1999). *Thirty-eight witnesses: The Kitty Genovese case*. Berkeley: University of California Press.

Sabo, D. (2006). Masculinities and men's health: Moving toward post-superman era prevention. In E. Disch (Ed.), *Reconstructing gender: A multicultural anthology* (4th ed., pp. 541–558). Mountain View: Mayfield Publishing Company.

Sanday, P. (1990). *Fraternity gang rape: Sex, brotherhood, and privilege on campus*. New York: New York University Press.

Sanday, P. (1996). *A woman scorned: Acquaintance rape on trial*. Berkeley: University of California Press.

Scully, D. (1995). Rape is the problem. In B. R. Price & N. Sokoloff (Eds.), *The criminal justice system and women: Offenders, victims, and workers* (2nd ed., pp. 197–215). New York: McGraw-Hill.

Shotland, L., & Straw, M. (1976). Bystander response to an assault: Can a woman attract help? *Journal of Personality and Social Psychology, 34*, 990–999.

Tisak, M., & Tisak, J. (1996). Expectations and judgments regarding bystanders' and victims' response to peer aggression among early adolescents. *Journal of Adolescence, 19*, 383–392.

West, C., & Zimmerman, D. (1987). Doing gender. *Gender & Society, 1*, 125–151.

39 Sinikka Elliott

Men, Race, and Emotions
Men of Color and Masculine Productions

What does it mean to be a man? Although most scholars agree that being a man means different things to different men, most researchers also find patterns and similarities among men. A consistent finding is that the production and reproduction of masculinity frequently involves the need to differentiate self from others, especially women and "weak" men, the need to be independent and self-reliant, and the need to be superior and more powerful than others (Connell, 1995, 2000; Harrison, Chin, and Ficarrotto, 1995; Kimmel, 1994). When we begin to think about these elements of masculinity, it becomes clear that masculinity exacts a huge toll, especially in terms of men's emotional lives.

Indeed, empirical studies have shown that the control of emotions is an integral aspect in the construction of masculinity (see review by Connell, 1995: 39). Gender is not only embedded in power, production, and symbolic relations, but also works on the emotional and sexual levels (Connell, 1995, 2000). Through a complex process that involves psychological and sociocultural forces, boys learn that some emotions are unmanly—such as fear, compassion, and sadness—while others are ac-

ceptable in men, such as aggression, steadfastness, and courage. Most men, however, experience a host of contradictory feelings and emotions on a daily basis and not all men accept the "grin and bear it" mentality. Thus, deciding how to *be*, as a man, is itself an emotional process that individual men grapple with throughout their lives within the context of their everyday interactions. Yet, despite having profound effects on everyday lives, emotions are frequently overlooked in studies of masculinities.

This paper seeks to redress this gap by exploring what it means to be a man of color in the U.S., focusing specifically on the emotional aspects of masculine construction. By men of color, I mean Native American, Asian American, Chicano/Latino, and African American men. I acknowledge, however, the great diversity that exists within this overly simplistic category. Not only does this group include men of different skin tone, racial/ethnic background, age, sexuality, and nationality, but also men of varying socioeconomic statuses. Although men of color constitute a disproportionate number of the poor in the U.S., they are located at all levels of the class structure. I first present a broad overview of

Sinikka Elliott, "Men, Race, and Emotions: Men of Color and Masculine Productions." Edited from a version presented at the American Sociological Association Annual Meeting, August 2004. Reprinted by permission of the author.

current thinking on masculinities. Next, I review the literature on emotions and masculinities, focusing specifically on studies of men of color. And lastly, I offer a summary of critique of these studies and call for a new theoretical approach to the study of men, race, and emotions, such as that advocated by multiracial feminism.

Masculinities in Context

Although sex role theory, popular in the seventies and eighties, theorized "the male role," more recent research indicates that there is no one universal male role—indeed, research and theory on men and masculinity now emphasize the multiplicity of meanings of manhood (Connell, 1995, 2000; Kimmel, 1996; Messner, 1995). Current research also points to masculinities as ongoing achievements, rather than as static possessions, and stresses the importance of context in the development and production of masculinity. Structural, interpersonal, and individual dynamics all affect the *forms* of masculinity that are produced and reproduced. As Connell (2000: 12) puts it, masculinities "are actively produced, using the resources and strategies available in a given social setting."

Men do not merely define themselves in relation to other men; they also delineate alliances, domination, and subordination between different *kinds* of masculinity. Gender interacts with race, class, sexuality, age, citizenship, and so on in producing a hierarchal *gender order*. Connell (1995, 2000) identifies four forms of masculinity: hegemonic, subordinated, complicit, and marginalized. *Hegemonic masculinity*, according to Connell, is the form of masculinity that holds the most sociocultural authority at a given point in time, even if

few men actually personify this version of masculinity. Hegemonic masculinity is an historical construct that varies across time and place. In the U.S., the masculinity that currently occupies the hegemonic position is middle-class, white, and heterosexual (Kimmel and Messner, 1998).

Because hegemonic masculinity in the U.S. and most everywhere is heterosexual, gay men and men who do not embody or embrace the masculine ideal (e.g., effeminate men) are subordinated to straight and masculine men (Connell, 1995: 78–9). These men compose the category of *subordinate masculinities. Complicit masculinities* include those men who passively accept the patriarchal dividend—the gains men reap in sexist society. They are, for example, the men on the sidelines, cheering on the football players (Connell, 1995: 79–80) and (in some cases) ogling the cheerleaders. *Marginalized masculinities*, according to Connell, include working-class men and men of color and reflect the interplay of gender with class and race relations. This form of masculinity includes "gender forms produced in exploited or oppressed groups such as ethnic minorities, which may share many features with hegemonic masculinity but are socially de-authorized" (Connell, 2000: 30).

What does it mean to be a socially de-authorized man—to lack social power, status, and authority? For a man of color, to be a socially de-authorized man means to live in a society in which you may be treated as an exotic or dangerous "other," a threat or a pet (e.g., Espada, 1996; Fong-Torres, 1995; Kelley, 2001). For men of color, being de-authorized means being seen as different from white Americans in tangible and intangible ways. They constitute the "other" in U.S. society.

Despite variations within and between different types of masculinities, many masculinities scholars argue that there is "a singular vision of masculinity, a particular definition that is held up as the model against which we all measure ourselves" (Kimmel, 1996: 5); suggesting that, over all men's heads hangs a rubric of what they, as men, can and should be, or at least aspire to be: what Connell (1995, 2000) terms hegemonic masculinity. Men's relationship to hegemonic masculinity is, however, variable—not all men want to acquire this form of masculinity; indeed, many reject it. Connell emphasizes the contradictions, conflicts, and emotional compromises involved in the production and reproduction of masculinities and stresses that "the masculinity that occupies the hegemonic position in a given pattern of gender relations is always contestable" (1995: 76). This is partly because most men do not embody the masculine ideal and partly because the achievement of masculinity relies on proving superiority— over women and over alternative or "inferior" masculinities (Connell, 1995, 2000). Masculine construction is an ongoing emotional process.

Emotions and Marginalized Masculinities

Emotion is a complex concept for which there is no simple definition. Emotions include anger, sadness, fear, happiness, anxiety, and so on. But emotion is more than a feeling; it is also the perception of and reaction towards feeling. We may feel tired, for example, but our emotional response towards our tiredness can differ dramatically: we may angrily reject our exhausted state, mentally commanding ourselves to "buck up," or we may react with acceptance and

sympathy, telling ourselves we deserve a good night's sleep. Hence, emotion involves both mind and feeling. The notion that emotions are private, inner drives and desires, something we have little control over, is misleading: emotions have a profoundly social character. Hochschild (1983: 7) coined the term "emotional labor" to describe the work that is involved in inducing or suppressing feeling in order to maintain a desired outward countenance. According to Hochschild (1983: 27), feelings are not just something we have, they are also something we do: "The very act of managing emotion can be seen as part of what the emotion becomes."

We relate to each other as human beings from an emotional core. Race and gender exist within emotional contexts that influence the ways we react to one another and ourselves. For example, people typically hold preconceived ideas about how men "should act" and how women "should act." We also hold stereotypes about how people of color "should act." Thus, race and gender can inspire a host of emotional responses.

Yet, very few studies specifically focus on the emotional lives of men of color. Several written works, however, point to the emotional work that is involved in managing "difference" in a discriminatory, racist context—in this case, American society (Brod, 1994; Espada, 1996; Espiritu, 2001; Fong-Torres, 1995; Franklin, 2000; Fung, 2001; Hanchard, 2001; Kelley, 2001; Mac an Ghaill, 1994; Majors, 1995; Marable, 2001). Men of color in the U.S. confront a variety of (most often negative) myths and stereotypes concerning every aspect of their lives on a daily basis. Navigating through the labyrinth of these negative beliefs can take its toll. For many men, managing emotions becomes part of who they *are* as men. For men of color, this emotional process may take on an even greater urgency because of the racist, discriminatory contexts in which they live.

Some men of color, most notably Latino/ Chicano men, for example, confront the social stereotype that they are hot-blooded and irrational. Other men of color, especially Asian American men, in an equally damaging stereotype, are caricatured as emotionally cold and without feeling. Stereotypes typically put those stereotyped in a double-bind—either you fit the stereotype and confirm people's fears or you do not fit the stereotype and are seen as the "exception"—as being different from others like you. Either way, you are not allowed simply *to be*. As Espada (1996: 88) puts it, "any assertiveness on the part of Latino males, especially any form of resistance to Anglo authority, is labeled macho and instantly discredited." Similarly, Kelley (2001: 299), a self-identified "soft-sensitive" black man, argues "the 'nice Negro,' like the model-minority myth pinned on Asian Americans, renders the war on those 'other' niggas justifiable and even palatable." This double-bind situation may lead some marginalized men to exaggerate negative stereotypes in a rejection of "white" culture (Mac an Ghaill, 1994). Resistance can take many forms, including those that paradoxically reinforce the resister's oppressive conditions: "Oppressed groups both actively participate in their own domination and actively resist that domination" (Hondagneu-Sotelo and Messner, 1994: 203).

For example, Majors (1995: 82–5) finds that in coping with the legacy and continued persistence of racism, African American men may adopt a "cool pose": a posture that denotes control, toughness and detachment. The cool pose is a defense mechanism, Majors argues, adopted by oppressed men that, in effect, tells the world, "I can take it." "I'm strong, not weak." "I'm a survivor." But, while being cool encourages pride and inner strength and protects one's dignity, in acting cool, African American men must hide all feelings that may be seen as a form of weakness, and this, Majors asserts, may severely limit their intimate relationships. Ultimately, according to Majors, guarding against oppression in white society makes it very difficult for men of color to let their guard down around people they care about, creating difficulties in their intimate relationships.

Some argue that socially de-authorized men who do not automatically hold power and prestige in society may experience a stronger need to *prove* their masculinity. This has been called "compensatory masculinity" (Harrison et al., 1995: 238)—a way of coping with anxiety surrounding the achievement of masculinity. The need to prove the *right* to male status can result in destructive behaviors such as excessive drinking, violence, and competitiveness, among others. Sexuality can also become a mechanism for proving masculinity. The more sexual conquests one has, the more of a man one is. This holds potentially serious negative consequences for men's (and women's) intimate lives.

Critique of the Literature on Men of Color and Emotions

Where Have All the Women Gone?

The few studies that consider the emotional labor of men of color, like Majors', however, tend to have the alarming effect of erasing women from the picture. In an effort to examine how masculinities interact with racism, relations between men and women are, paradoxically, ignored. In fact, research shows that, in protesting racism, some men of color may promote sexism (Bourgois, 2001; Espiritu, 2001; Franklin, 2000; Mac an Ghaill, 1994). Franklin (2000), for example, traces the emergence of the "new manhood" movement that sprung up in African American communities following World War I as a response to racial inequality, and notes that while this movement promoted the rights of African Americans, it did so at the expense of African American women. The call issued by (black male) leaders of the movement was for black women to return to the domestic front and be submissive—to effectively prop up their struggling black brothers.

Are White Men the Model upon Which All Men Are Judged?

Similarly, a narrow focus on marginalized men's need to prove themselves suggests that the masculine identities of privileged men are exemplary. This serves to reinforce negative stereotypes of less privileged men without fully gripping the complexities and nuances of men's lives. Indeed, President George Bush, arguably one of the most powerful men in the world and someone who was born with a silver spoon in his mouth, is clearly intent on proving his manhood. This has involved personally destructive behaviors such as alcohol and drug abuse to waging war in the Middle East. But the consequences of privileged men's destructive behaviors often do not impact them personally—many will die as a result of George Bush's military agenda, but Bush himself probably will not pay with his life for his extreme enactments of masculinity. In fact, as Connell indicates, most men, to a certain extent, engage in

some form of compensatory masculinity. This is because masculinity is not a given, it is always precarious, always dependent upon the subordination and inferiority of others. Hence, it is paramount to examine masculinities in a relational context—including all intersecting oppressions—race, class, age, gender, sexuality, nationality, citizenship, and so on (Baca Zinn and Thornton Dill, 1996).

How Does Change Come About?

My final critique is that the majority of the reviewed studies tend to characterize men of color as victims of racist society, and thus neglect to capture the complex, contradictory, and ever-changing ways that men produce and reproduce masculinities. By contrast, *Muy Macho* (1996), an anthology of personal essays by Latino writers on the topic of masculinity, exposes the multiple marginalized identities that emerge within contexts of inequality. Many of the stories touch upon the difficulties first and second generation men of color encounter in straddling two identities—in this instance, Latino and American. A constant theme in the contributors' personal narratives is their relationships with their fathers—many of whom were distant, absent, detached, and sometimes violent men. In *Muy Macho*, we meet a father who so fears his son's effeminacy that he subjects his son to repeated humiliations in the hopes of "reforming" him (Munoz, 1996). We meet fathers who are and always will be in a mental state of exile—in the U.S. in body but not spirit, and who do not understand, and in some cases, do not accept their sons' lives and choices (Lopez, 1996; Munoz, 1996). Overall, we hear the voices of men who were rarely, if ever, intimate with their fathers (Gonzalez, 1996; Rios, 1996; Rodriguez, 1996; Quintana, 1996).

But change is the only constant. Thus, for example, in *Muy Macho* we are also introduced to fathers who make a conscious effort to be present for their own children—to be active, involved, emotionally connected parents (Espada, 1996; Quintana, 1996). In parenting their children, they learn to parent themselves. Similarly, we see sons rejecting their fathers' violence. As poet and novelist Elias Miguel Munoz (1996: 31) writes: "My father will also incarnate machismo, while I will always try to deconstruct the macho archetype."

The stories in *Muy Macho* highlight the nuanced and sometimes contradictory ways in which marginalized and subordinated masculinities are changing, an important step in understanding the emotional lives of men of color. These stories do not merely portray men of color as victims of racist society, but rather as active agents, working with the resources and materials available to them. And yet, in most of these stories, just as in most masculinities studies, women are absent, or are present only as victims or as bit players, not central to the drama between men. Again race and masculinity trump male/female relations.

Discussion

The sociology of emotions emphasizes that what we know and *feel* about ourselves is mediated through historical and sociocultural forces. Attitudes, emotions, and behaviors reflect individuals' unique positions and experiences in society. In this paper, I have reviewed studies that focus on the emotional aspects of masculine construction in the lives of men of color. I have argued that these studies tend to either ignore women or only include them as victims or bit players, that they frequently focus on the emotional deficiencies of men of color thereby implicitly promoting the notion that white men's emotional responses are exemplary, and that in focusing primarily on structural barriers, such as racism, these studies deny men of color agency. I conclude by suggesting that multiracial feminism offers a theoretical approach that addresses some of the limitations found in previous studies of the emotional lives of men of color.

Baca Zinn and Thornton Dill (1996) argue that multiracial feminism is distinguished by six themes: the belief that (1) gender is constructed by a range of interlocking inequalities, (2) hierarchies are intersectional and contextual, and (3) privilege and subordination are interrelated; (4) an emphasis on agency with a focus on resistance and change, (5) the use of diverse methodologies and theoretical approaches, and (6) a commitment to diversity.

An analysis that includes the notions of interlocking inequalities, intersectional hierarchies, and the relational nature of domination and subordination would address how the oppression of women intricately links masculinities together; how the marginalization of certain masculinities is an important component of the reproduction of male power over women (Kimmel and Messner, 1998: xix). Studies find, for example, that in resisting other men's power over their lives, some men assert power over women. "To the extent that systems of social inequality limit men's access to societally valued resources, they also contribute to sexual stratification. Men in some social categories will continue to draw upon and accentuate their masculinity as a socially valued resource" (Baca Zinn, 1995: 40). When racial oppression is seen as more important than gender oppression, women often suffer, both in terms of research and real life. As Hondagneu-Sotelo and Messner (1994: 215–16) assert, "to avoid reverting to the tendency to view masculinity simply as a defensive reaction to other forms of oppression, it is crucial . . . to keep women's experiences of gender oppression as close to the center of analysis as possible."

Thus, research on emotions and masculinities must not only account for relations between men of different race/ethnicity, class, sexuality, age, etc., but also relations between men and women. Studies of heterosexual couples, for example, reveal the contradictory emotions that lie at the heart of intimate relationships—love and hate, trust and jealousy, compassion and rivalry—all co-reside, to name just a few, making it far more difficult to generalize about certain characteristics or behaviors of one partner or the other (Coltrane, 2001; Franklin, 2000; Gutmann, 1996; Hondagneu-Sotelo, 1992).

A multiracial feminist approach also leads to a critical awareness of the ways in which privilege and subordination are interrelated. Hondagneu-Sotelo and Messner (1994), for example, point out that while an important aspect of hegemonic masculinity in the past was stoicism and emotional inexpressivity, the "New Man" is seen as sensitive and "in touch with his feelings." But the aspects of traditional hegemonic masculinity the New Man has rejected, they argue, are "increasingly projected onto less privileged groups of men: working class, gay body-builders, black athletes, Latinos, and immigrant men" (Hondagneu-Sotelo and Messner, 1994: 207). Thus, it is paramount to remain critical of the ways in which difference is constructed in the U.S. based on "whiteness" as the standard or norm and how difference is then made into inferiority. In this way, the emotional expressions of marginalized men are seen as dysfunctional while those of privileged men are considered exemplary.

Finally, because men (and women) of color are the theoretical underpinnings and starting points of multiracial feminism, this approach emphasizes agency in these men and women's lives and actions. As Matthew Gutmann (1996, 18) reminds us, "Although the assertion of identity can be used to exclude and control oppressed peoples, it can also be used by these peoples to counter such domination as well." Thus, for example, the contributors to *Muy Macho* document the process of personal growth toward positive self-definitions that occurs through a critical examination of their lived experiences. A multiracial feminist analysis highlights resistance and change in the emotional lives of men of color (Hondagneu-Sotelo and Messner, 1994).

In sum, masculine construction is an emotional process that hinges on both resistance to, and demands for, masculinity—masculinities are contradictory and contested. Since masculinities are not constructed in a social vacuum, but are, rather, products of our everyday lives and interactions, historical, social, and cultural forces play a role in the construction of masculinities. Thus, as Connell, notes, in theorizing the gender order and multiple masculinities, it is important to examine relations *between* men and masculinities, not to subscribe to the notion of *a black masculinity*, for example. By examining the relationships between men, we can better see the historical and sociocultural forces that shape individual behaviors and emotions as well as seeing that not all men benefit equally from gender inequality. But, as a multiracial feminist approach emphasizes, women must also be included in masculinity studies—privilege and subordination are interrelated, not just in terms of the hierarchal ordering of masculinities but also in terms of men and women. In coming to grips with oppression and moving towards change, it is paramount to treat race, class, gender, sexuality, age, and so on as a system of domination in which individuals construct unique identities given the resources and strategies available at any given time.

References

Baca Zinn, Maxine. 1995. "Chicano Men and Masculinity." Pp. 33–41 in Kimmel, Michael S. and Michael A. Messner (Eds.), *Men's Lives*, Third Edition. Boston: Allyn and Bacon.

Baca Zinn, Maxine and Bonnie Thornton Dill. 1996. "Theorizing Difference from Multiracial Feminism." *Feminist Studies*, 22: 321–31.

Bourgois, Philippe. 2001. "In Search of Masculinity: Violence, Respect, and Sexuality among Puerto Rican Crack Dealers in East Harlem." Pp. 42–55 in Kimmel, Michael S. and Michael A. Messner (Eds.), *Men's Lives*, Fifth Edition. Boston: Allyn and Bacon.

Brod, Harry. 1994. "Some Thoughts on Some Histories of Some Masculinities: Jews and Other Others." Pp. 82–96 in Brod, Harry and Michael Kaufman (Eds.), *Theorizing Masculinities*. Thousand Oaks: Sage Publications.

Collins, Patricia Hill. 2000. *Black Feminist Thought: Knowledge, Consciousness, and the Politics of Empowerment*, Second Edition. New York and London: Routledge.

Coltrane, Scott. 2001. "Stability and Change in Chicano Men's Family Lives." Pp. 451–466 in Kimmel, Michael S. and Michael A. Messner (Eds.), *Men's Lives*, Fifth Edition. Boston: Allyn and Bacon.

Connell, R. W. 1995. *Masculinities*. Berkeley: University of California Press.

———. 2000. *The Men and the Boys*. Berkeley: University of California Press.

Espada, Martin. 1996. "The Puerto Rican Dummy and the Merciful Son." Pp. 75–90 in Gonzalez, Ray (Ed.), *Muy Macho*. New York: Anchor Books, Doubleday.

Espiritu, Yen Le. 2001. "All Men Are *Not* Created Equal: Asian Men in U.S. History." Pp. 33–41 in Kimmel, Michael S. and Michael A. Messner (Eds.), *Men's Lives*, Fifth Edition. Boston: Allyn and Bacon.

Fong-Torres, Ben. 1995. "Why Are There No Male Asian Anchor*men* on TV?" Pp. 208–211 in Kimmel, Michael S. and Michael A. Messner (Eds.), *Men's Lives*, Third Edition. Boston: Allyn and Bacon.

Franklin, Donna L. 2000. *What's Love Got to Do With It? Understanding and Healing the Rift Between Black Men and Women*. New York: Simon and Schuster.

Fung, Richard. 2001. "Looking for My Penis: The Eroticized Asian in Gay Video Porn." Pp. 515–524 in Kimmel, Michael S. and Michael A. Messner (Eds.), *Men's Lives*, Fifth Edition. Boston: Allyn and Bacon.

Gonzalez, Ray. 1996. "My Literary Fathers." Pp. 165–186 in Gonzalez, Ray (Ed.), *Muy Macho*. New York: Anchor Books, Doubleday.

Gutmann, Matthew C. 1996. *The Meanings of Macho: Being a Man in Mexico City*. Berkeley: University of California Press.

Hanchard, Michael C. 2001. "On 'Good' Black Fathers." Pp. 467–474 in Kimmel, Michael S. and Michael A. Messner (Eds.), *Men's Lives*, Fifth Edition. Boston: Allyn and Bacon.

Harrison, James, James Chin, and Thomas Ficarrotto. 1995. "Warning: Masculinity May Be Dangerous to Your Health." Pp. 237–249 in Kimmel, Michael S. and Michael A. Messner (Eds.), *Men's Lives*, Third Edition. Boston: Allyn and Bacon.

Hochschild, Arlie Russell. 1983. *The Managed Heart: Commercialization of Human Feeling*. Berkeley, LA, London: University of California Press.

Hondagneu-Sotelo, Pierrette. 1992. "Overcoming Patriarchal Constraints: The Reconstruction of Gender Relations Among Mexican Immigrant Women and Men." *Gender & Society*, 6: 393–415.

Hondagneu-Sotelo, Pierrette and Michael A. Messner. 1994. "Gender Displays and Men's Power: The 'New Man' and the Mexican Immigrant Man." Pp. 200–218 in Brod, Harry and Michael Kaufman (Eds.), *Theorizing Masculinities*. Thousand Oaks: Sage Publications.

Kelley, Robin D. G. 2001. "Confessions of a Nice Negro, or Why I Shaved My Head." Pp. 299–305 in Kimmel, Michael S. and Michael A. Messner (Eds.), *Men's Lives*, Fifth Edition. Boston: Allyn and Bacon.

Kimmel, Michael S. 1994. "Masculinity as Homophobia: Fear, Shame, and Silence in the Construction of Gender Identity." Pp. 119–141 in Brod, Harry and Michael Kaufman (Eds.), *Theorizing Masculinities*. Thousand Oaks: Sage Publications.

Kimmel, Michael S. 1996. *Manhood in America: A Cultural History*. New York: The Free Press.

Kimmel, Michael S. and Michael A. Messner (eds). 1998. *Men's Lives*. Fourth Edition. Boston: Allyn and Bacon.

Lopez, Jack. 1996. "Of *Cholos* and Surfers." Pp. 91–98 in Gonzalez, Ray (Ed.), *Muy Macho*. New York: Anchor Books, Doubleday.

Majors, Richard. 1995. "Cool Pose: The Proud Signature of Black Survival." Pp. 82–85 in Kimmel, Michael S. and Michael A. Messner (Eds.), *Men's Lives*, Third Edition. Boston: Allyn and Bacon.

Marable, Manning. 2001. "The Black Male: Searching Beyond Stereotypes." Pp. 17–23 in Kimmel, Michael S. and Michael A. Messner (Eds.), *Men's Lives*, Fifth Edition. Boston: Allyn and Bacon.

Mac an Ghaill, Mairtin. 1994. "The Making of Black English Masculinities." Pp. 183–199 in Brod, Harry and Michael Kaufman (Eds.), *Theorizing Masculinities*. Thousand Oaks: Sage Publications.

Messner, Michael A. 1995. "Boyhood, Organized Sports, and the Construction of Masculinities." Pp. 102–114 in Kimmel, Michael S. and Michael A. Messner (Eds.), *Men's Lives*, Third Edition. Boston: Allyn and Bacon.

Munoz, Elias Miguel. 1996. "From the Land of Machos: Journey to Oz With My Father." Pp. 17–34 in Gonzalez, Ray (Ed.), *Muy Macho*. New York: Anchor Books, Doubleday.

Quintana, Leroy V. 1996. "Bless Me, Father." Pp. 131–142 in Gonzalez, Ray (Ed.), *Muy Macho*. New York: Anchor Books, Doubleday.

Rios, Alberto Alvaro. 1996. "My Father and the Snow." Pp. 221–230 in Gonzalez, Ray (Ed.), *Muy Macho*. New York: Anchor Books, Doubleday.

Rodriguez, Luis J. 1996. "On Macho." Pp. 187–202 in Gonzalez, Ray (Ed.), *Muy Macho*. New York: Anchor Books, Doubleday.

40 Thomas Rogers

What the Pregnant Man Didn't Deliver

By the time Thomas Beatie, "the Pregnant Man," strode across Oprah Winfrey's stage on April 3, his story had already become a worldwide phenomenon. Beatie—a transgendered man who was born a woman and became pregnant through artificial insemination—had captured headlines, and worldwide attention, in the preceding weeks. On the show, Oprah clutched Beatie's belly like a touchy aunt and asked him nosy questions about his family, his sex life and the appearance of his clitoris. ("It looks like a penis," he answered uncomfortably.)

The episode—which garnered a 45 percent audience increase compared to the same time slot in the previous week—was actually one of the more nuanced moments in a bizarre uproar over a bizarre pregnancy that became fodder for news anchors and late-night comedians. The night before, David Letterman had aired a top 10 list of "messages left on the pregnant man's answering machine." No. 1 was, "Michael Jackson here—just wanted to reach out to another androgynous freak show."

The transgender community has often been caught in the shadow of its gay and lesbian brethren, and Beatie's story offered an opportunity for some much-needed attention. But with the spotlight hopelessly focused on such salacious details as Beatie's genitalia, and the story becoming little more than a punch line, it has left many transgender activists wishing the Thomas Beatie media circus would simply go away.

Unfortunately, that's unlikely to happen. Beatie is due to give birth Thursday, July 3, via Caesarean section, an event likely to ignite a new wave of media coverage and unfortunately puns, and once again raise some prickly questions: What does the media's treatment of Thomas Beatie tell us about the way America thinks about the transgender community? Why do we even care about him? And what, if anything, can the pregnant man teach us about the changing nature of gender in America?

The story of the pregnant man began, demurely enough, with an essay in the *Advocate*, a gay and lesbian magazine, describing Beatie's pregnancy and his trouble finding a doctor. It told the poignant tale of Beatie's transition, his wife Nancy's hysterectomy, and his decision to become pregnant with a child. There was little that was medically remarkable about Beatie's pregnancy—facial hair excepted—and, as a matter of fact, he is not the first transgendered man to carry a child. (The *Village Voice* published an article about a transgendered male pregnancy as far back as 2000.)

Then why did Beatie become the focus of so much attention? It's partly because, unlike other pregnant men, Beatie has

Thomas Rogers, "What the Pregnant Man Didn't Deliver." Originally posted at www.salon.com, July 3, 2008. Reprinted by kind permission of Salon.com.

demonstrated a remarkable willingness to speak to the press (including dubious tabloids like the *News of the World*). And, according to Paisley Currah, a transgendered associate professor of political science at Brooklyn College and the author of the upcoming "The United States of Gender," "the idea that seems to draw the public is the idea of the supposed freakish body of the transgendered man." In other words, people are attracted to the story because staring at Beatie's body—the large stomach protruding from his manly chest—is both an unsettling and captivating experience, and Beatie, for whatever reason, doesn't seem to mind the attention.

While transgendered people have become increasingly visible in popular culture in recent years—with films like "Transamerica," about a shrill transgendered woman traveling across the country, and TV shows like "Dirty Sexy Money," featuring a character with a transgendered mistress, and "Ugly Betty," with Rebecca Romijn as the recipient of some very convincing surgery—most characters have been middle-aged transsexual women. Transgendered men, like Beatie, have remained largely invisible, and this, apparently, has led to confusion in the press. Many journalists don't seem to know how to talk about him, and some, like Diane Sawyer, have had trouble keeping their pronouns straight. "I don't get the sense that people have correlated female-to-male with male-to-female," says Jamison Green, a transgender policy advisor. "They really see Thomas Beatie as a woman."

The highly respected *International Herald Tribune*, for example, published an opinion piece by Jeff Jacoby (under the headline "Pregnant, Yes—but Not a Man"), which referred to Beatie as "her" and argued that

"there is no 'pregnant man' . . . there is only a confused and unsettled woman who proclaims that surgery, hormones and clothing made her a man, and is clinging to that fiction even as the baby growing in her womb announces her womanhood to the world." Dramatic, yes; informed, not so much.

Part of what seems to have unsettled Jacoby, in particular, is the way that advances in technology have made physical gender far more malleable than ever before. People can use surgery to remove—or add—breasts, and use hormones to change their voice and facial hair, while leaving other parts of their body intact. In Beatie's case, Currah says, "gender ideology is colliding with the materiality of bodies." Or, in slightly less abstruse terms, Beatie reminds us that sometimes our bodies and our gender don't necessarily align in black-and-white terms—an unsettling feeling that some men encounter when they gain weight and grow breasts, or when women discover unsightly facial hair—and the pregnant man is such an extreme case that it's almost impossible to look away.

According to Judith Halberstam, a gender theorist at the University of Southern California and the author of "Female Masculinity," Beatie's pregnancy also feeds into a more fundamental discomfort with the ways that medical technology has changed pregnancy. "It seems like the real reason it appeals to people is because the pregnant body is so sacred," she says, "and the pregnant woman still represents something to people about nature." Beatie's protruding stomach, when combined with his male body, destroys the fantasy that pregnancy is a purely natural process. "His pregnant body is evidence that pregnancy has become another site of human engineering."

The pregnancy also points to the way that perspectives on gender are changing within the transgender community itself. An increasingly visible minority of transgendered people—primarily in large urban centers—are becoming comfortable living outside of either gender. "I definitely think there's been an increased visibility of that kind of fluidity," says Green. Some are using hormones without surgery, or surgery without hormones to create the body in which they feel most comfortable, or going by gender-neutral pronouns like "ze" and "zir."

For the vast majority of transgendered people, however, who are content to live their life "passing" in their new gender, there are far more pressing issues than a pregnant man—like keeping their jobs. Last year, a heated debate about the inclusion of "gender identity" in the Employment Non-Discrimination Act (a bill prohibiting job discrimination on the basis of sexual orientation) created widespread rancor between some transgender and gay and lesbian activists. The bill eventually passed the house without a gender identity clause, but the transgender rights movement has had other successes in past years, often in smaller jurisdictions. In New York, for example, it's now legal for a transgendered person to change the gender on his or her birth certificate.

Mara Keisling, the executive director of the National Center for Transgender Equality, resents the way that the Thomas Beatie flap has overshadowed more important developments. "The media hasn't gotten a message yet that they ought to get a life," she snaps. Last week, Congress held its first-ever hearing on discrimination against transgender employees, and on June 17, the American Medical Association passed a resolution stating that it "supports public and private health insurance coverage for treatment of gender identity disorder," but these items have received nowhere near Beatie's media attention.

While Beatie's profile has diminished in recent weeks, he has still managed to pop up in tabloid photos ("Pregnant man mows lawn at seven months"), and recently announced a planned memoir for St. Martin's Press (it has since been shelved). But the breadth of coverage from here on out probably depends on whether he agrees to publish baby photos. If he doesn't, and the pregnant man disappears from the world's headlines, what does the transgendered community take away from this brief phenomenon?

"The only positive thing that's come out of this is that the Beaties get to have a baby," Keisling says. "I don't see this as a cause for celebration among transgendered people," Halberstam concurs. In fact, she's worried that Beatie's publicity may have endangered people's abilities to access hormones or sexual reassignment surgery. His story may allow doctors to point to him as an example of why such surgery isn't even necessary or advisable. "I don't see how this helps anybody except to publicize that [people like Beatie] exist," says Halberstam.

Green, however, is slightly more enthusiastic, and believes the story will lead to some positive changes. For the time being, though, he thinks Beatie should stop focusing on the media and start thinking about himself. "The best thing that Thomas Beatie can do for the trans community is live his life as honestly as he can, and worry about what his immediate neighbors think of him, and how successful he is in his local community." Green adds, "If people go back to accepting him as a man, that would be a big plus."

41 Heather Worth

Bad-Assed Honeys with a Difference
South Auckland Fa'afafine Talk about Identity

Heather Worth, "Bad-Assed Honeys with a Difference: South Auckland Fa'afafine Talk about Identity," Intersections: Gender, History and Culture in the Asian Context 6 (August 2001). Please access this article online at http://intersections.anu.edu.au/issue6/worth.html.

42 Joane Nagel and Lindsey Feitz

Deploying Race, Gender, Class, and Sexuality in the Iraq War

At about 0700 hours (local time) on 23 March 2003, while moving through the outskirts of the city of An Nasiriyah in southeastern Iraq, an element of the 507th Maintenance Company was attacked by Iraqi forces and irregulars. There were 33 U.S. Soldiers in the 18-vehicle convoy. . . . The Iraqi forces in An Nasiriyah conducted fierce attacks against the convoy. Of the 22 Soldiers who survived, nine were wounded in action. Although all details of the battle could not be determined with certainty, it is clear that every U.S. Soldier did their duty (U.S. Army, 2003).

There were three women soldiers serving with the 507th who were taken prisoner by the Iraqis:

Private First Class Jessica Lynch of Palestine, West Virginia, was born in April, 1983. When the Humvee she was riding in crashed, this 19-year-old supply clerk suffered lacerations, a broken arm, broken leg, and head and back injuries. She was taken by Iraqis to a hospital, treated for her injuries, and rescued on April 1 by U.S. forces. Jessica's rescue was filmed by the U.S. military and was widely circulated in the U.S. media. Seven months later 500,000 copies of her biography, *I Am a Soldier, Too: The Jessica Lynch Story*, were released; during the next week she was interviewed by Diane Sawyer on ABC's "20–20," by Katie Couric on NBC's "Today" show, by David Letterman on CBS's "Late Night Show," and by Larry King on CNN's "Larry King Live." On August 23, 2003, Jessica Lynch received a medical honorable discharge from the Army and an 80 percent disability benefit.

Army Specialist Shoshana Johnson of El Paso, Texas, was born in January, 1973.

Joane Nagel and Lindsey Feitz, "Deploying Race, Gender, Class, and Sexuality in the Iraq War," *Race, Gender & Class* 14, nos. 3/4 (2007): 28–47. Reprinted by permission of *Race, Gender & Class*.

We would like to thank the Institute for Policy & Social Research at the University of Kansas for its support and Monique Laney and Erik Nielsen for their help in researching this paper.

During her capture outside Nasiriyah the 31-year-old cook was shot in the ankle and injured in both legs. She was held by the Iraqis until she and six others were rescued on April 13 by U.S. forces. Johnson was the first African American woman POW. During the next few months Shoshana received awards and invitations to speak from a number of organizations including *Essence* magazine, the NAACP, the Rainbow Push Coalition, the Congressional Hispanic and Black Caucuses, the Olender Foundation, and the historically black institution of higher education, Fayetteville State University. On December 12, 2003, Shoshana Johnson retired from the Army with a temporary disability honorable discharge and a 30 percent disability benefit.

Private First Class Lori Piestewa of Tuba City, Arizona, and member of the Hopi Nation, was born in December, 1979. The 23-year-old supply clerk was driving the same Humvee carrying Jessica Lynch when they were attacked by Iraqi forces near Nasiriyah. According to eye witness accounts (including that of Jessica Lynch) Piestewa maneuvered the Humvee around firing Iraqi troops and debris, circling around crippled vehicles in an effort to give aid to her fellow soldiers until her vehicle was struck by a rocket-propelled grenade and crashed (Shaffer, 2003). She was wounded in the head and died a few hours later in captivity. Lori was the first Native American woman to die in combat while serving with the U.S. military. She was posthumously promoted to Specialist by the Army, the Arizona state government renamed "Squaw Peak" in the Phoenix Mountains "Piestewa Peak," the Grand Canyon Games organizers instituted annual Lori Piestewa National Native American Games, an Arizona freeway has been named for her, and a plaque bearing her name is located at the White Sands Missile Range in New Mexico.

Race, Gender, Class, and Sexuality in the Iraq War Narrative

We expect that readers will be much more familiar, as we were when we started this research, with the story and image of Jessica Lynch than with those of Shoshana Johnson or Lori Piestewa. It certainly can be argued that the bravery and actions under fire of Johnson and Piestewa were more newsworthy than the passive role played by Lynch who reported she was knocked unconscious when her Humvee crashed. The fame and treatment of the three women constitute a kind of natural experiment for examining how race, gender, class, and sexuality operate in the U.S. military and in the larger society. Gender and class are "controlled for" in this experiment, but race and sexuality are variables. All three soldiers were from working class backgrounds, were of similar rank, and all three were women. They differed by race: Lynch was white; Johnson was black; Piestewa was native. They also differed in terms of their sexual backgrounds: Lynch was unmarried with no children; Johnson was a single mother with one child; Piestewa was divorced with two children. What also differed were the circumstances of their rescue and, more important, their treatment by the military and the media after their ordeals. Investigations in the months following the women's capture and release have revealed that Jessica Lynch's rescue was dramatized, if not entirely staged, by the U.S. military, that it was filmed and promoted for media and public consumption, and that the U.S. military did not attempt to correct the record when the excesses and distortions of the media were pointed out to them, including by Lynch herself. The discovery of Shoshana Johnson and her six co-POWs during a search of houses in Nasiriyah three weeks after their capture was much less made-for-primetime, in fact it was somewhat accidental; it was not filmed, nor has it been the subject of made-for-TV movies, books, or extensive television interviews. There was virtually no national news coverage of Lori Piestewa's capture and death.

Before moving to our analysis of the ways in which racial and sexual depictions of these three service women were deployed by the U.S. military and media to narrate the Iraq war, we would like to locate the Jessica Lynch story in the larger media landscape of embedded reporting, military censorship, official secrecy, and news media collaboration with the U.S. government's "official story" about the war in Iraq (see Smith, 2003). The U.S. military has learned well the media lessons of Vietnam, in particular, how to control the visual images coming out of a war. Although the Iraq war is approaching its sixth year with thousands of military and civilian deaths and casualties, we see virtually no body bags, no rows of flag-draped coffins, no helicopters medevacing dying and wounded GIs, no Americans gunning down Iraqis, no blood, no suffering. We are struck by how very few images of death and mayhem in Iraq haunt the evening news. Those few pictures from Abu Ghraib circulated in late 2003, all of which have yet to be released officially, were all the more shocking not only because of their content, but also because of their rarity. Embedded reporters seem to have forgotten their cameras and misplaced their keyboards. Michael Weisskopf (2006), a reporter with *Time* magazine, was embedded

with the First Armored Division in Iraq in 2003, when he lost his hands tossing a bomb out of his armored vehicle; he identifies that as the moment when the line between reporter and soldier began to blur for him. Critics of the embedding process argue that even when such drastic injuries do not occur, it is inevitable that reporters will come to identify with the troops who protect them. This dependency has led Hess and Kalb (2003) to ask whether war reporting is distorted by a "Stockholm syndrome" in which the journalists start to "identify with the soldiers and lose their professional detachment?"

News releases from the U.S. military and government control the message and camouflage the violence associated with the Iraq war. We *hear* about the daily deaths, but we see almost nothing despite the fact that nearly 4,000 service personnel and an estimated 80,625 to 88,048 civilians had been killed in Iraq by the end of January, 2008 (U.S. Defense Department, 2007a; Iraq Body Count, 2008). There are very few pictures to replace the thousands of words. We are, instead, treated to optimistic appraisals: we were told that we were witnessing the "last throes of the insurgency," the "evildoers" are losing, and "mission accomplished." And we are regaled with tales of the heroic rescue of damsels in distress—brave American men saving white American women from sexual ravishment and murder by brown Iraqis. As we noted above, the hyperdramatized story of saving Private Jessica Lynch was the U.S. military's, American government's, and U.S. news media's story, and it went unchallenged for several weeks after its initial release.

The first major assault on the veracity of the Lynch rescue account was aired on BBC television on May 18, 2003, in a documentary entitled, "War Spin," in which correspondent John Kampfiner referred to the story of saving Jessica Lynch as "one of the most stunning pieces of news management ever conceived." In the broadcast he questioned the entire "rescue"—from the storming of the Iraqi hospital by U.S. Special Operations forces to the filming of the operation on a night vision camera. Kampfiner (2003) reported:

> witnesses told us that the special forces knew the Iraqi military had fled a day before they swooped on the hospital. . . . Dr. Anmar Uday [reported]: "There were no [Iraqi] soldiers in the hospital. . . . It was like a Hollywood film. They cried, "go, go, go," with guns and blanks without bullets . . . and the sound of explosions. They made a show for the American attack on the hospital—action movies like Sylvester Stallone or Jackie Chan.

In fact, according to Kampfiner (2003),

> Two days before the snatch squad arrived, [Dr.] Harith [a-Houssona] had arranged to deliver Jessica to the Americans in an ambulance. But as the ambulance, with Private Lynch inside, approached a checkpoint American troops opened fire, forcing it to flee back to the hospital. . . . When footage of the rescue was released, General Vincent Brooks, U.S. spokesman in Doha, said, "Some brave souls put their lives on the line to make this happen, loyal to a creed that they know that they'll never leave a fallen comrade."

Kampfiner's recounting of Iraqis' efforts to return Lynch to the Americans was confirmed by Jessica Lynch herself in her April 25, 2007, testimony before the U.S. Congress: "We were fired upon at a checkpoint, and the driver of the ambulance had to turn around and brought me back to the hospital" (U.S. House of Representatives, 2007).

There was no dramatized or even particularly well-documented rescue of Shoshana Johnson and her six fellow male POWs, and no saga of the brave death of Lori Piestewa. Only the rescue of pretty young Jessica Lynch made it to the front pages of American newspapers and opening stories of news broadcasts. Although *Glamour* magazine named both Jessica Lynch and Shoshana Johnson as its 2003 Women of the Year (Lori Piestewa apparently was not on their radar), critics have pointed out a number of disparities in the treatment, coverage, and rewards given to the two women: Lynch became a poster girl for the U.S. military and her rescue not only was planned and filmed, it was reenacted on network television as a dramatized spectacle of U.S. Special Operations derring-do; she received a one million dollar advance on the first book published about her (Bragg, 2003). Johnson has become neither a poster girl nor a millionaire; there were no instant book deals, movie contracts, or primetime interviews for Shoshana.[1] Lynch and Johnson also differed in how the U.S. Army assessed their injuries. Although both women have lingering physical problems from the incident and both have difficulty walking, the Army has classified Johnson as 30 percent disabled and Lynch as 80 percent disabled. This is a difference worth several hundred dollars more a month for Lynch—one that has not been lost on many observers (see Grundy, 2003; Douglas, 2003; Wise, 2003).

Both Jessica Lynch and Shoshana Johnson have been modest about their actions during their capture. Lynch has disavowed initial government and media reports that she attempted to shoot her way out of captivity testifying that she blamed "the military for not setting the record straight and the media for spreading it and not seeking the true facts. . . . My weapon had jammed, and I didn't even get a shot off. I'm still confused as to why they chose to lie and try to make me a legend" (U.S. House of Representatives, 2007); she says she does not recall being raped as the book written right after her release reported (Bragg, 2003). Johnson has not confirmed reports that she violently attempted to resist her capture: "I got off one round and then my gun jammed. . . . All of our weapons jammed because of the sand, so we had no way to return fire"; she credits the bravery of her fellow servicemen who rescued her: "I'm a survivor, not a hero. . . . The heroes are the soldiers who paid the ultimate price and the Marines who risked their lives to rescue us. Who knows what they could have walked into? It could have been a trap. But just the thought of getting us out was enough. They took a chance, and because they did, I'm here" (Byrd, 2004). The national media have remained mute on the subject of Piestewa's bravery under fire, although to her credit, Lynch has told the story of her friend's heroism and efforts to help her fellow soldiers, stating that Piestewa fought to her death (CNN, 2003; Kirkpatrick, 2003; U.S. House of Representatives, 2007).

As a point of reference, the men who were killed and captured on March 23, 2003, remain largely unnamed—they were not photographed, dramatized, or even reported about. So, gender matters—women appear to be more valuable media commodities than men where dramatic rescues

are concerned. And as the treatment of the three women above indicates, race also matters. William Smith, a Vietnam veteran and media advisor for the National Association for Black Veterans laid the race card squarely on the table in his comparison of the treatment of Johnson and Lynch: "There before you is the American dilemma: We are unfair in treatment and view when it comes to people of color" (Douglas, 2003). Robert Thompson, a professor of television and popular culture at Syracuse University, isn't so sure. He doubts "that race was the reason Lynch became a media celebrity"; instead he attributes her celebrity to the tastes of those presumably colorblind casting executives in Hollywood: "with her good looks and compelling story, Lynch looked like a figure from Central Casting at a time when the Pentagon, under heavy criticism over its war plan, desperately needed one" (Douglas, 2003). Consistent with this analysis is the conclusion that the American Indian woman who died trying to aid her comrades, Lori Piestewa, also simply was not as visible or attractive to Central Casting as the pretty white girl who, in her own words, "was just there in that spot, you know, the wrong place, the wrong time" (CNN, 2003).

Sexuality also matters in the comparative publicity and outcomes of the capture and release of these three servicewomen. Both Shoshana Johnson and Lori Piestewa were single mothers. Jessica Lynch had no such history: no children, no marriages, no divorces. Sexual purity is an important qualifier for the successful deployment of even déclassé female whiteness in the war of words that accompanies military operations. Not only Lynch's race, but her youth and presumed innocence made her an attractive candidate for the role of damsel in distress. Her sexual and moral worth were easy to market, especially since her story reproduced familiar images from U.S. history and reflected longstanding popular media accounts of other damsels in distress. McAlister (2003) describes Lynch's rescue as an updated version of seventeenth century captivity narratives which featured white women in peril, captured by savage Indians, rescued by heroic American men. She argues that foregrounding Lynch's physical and sexual vulnerability provided America with a historically comfortable moral justification for the war in Iraq because now one of *our* brave, sexually chaste, and virtuous American women needed rescuing from *their* dangerous, sexually alien, evil-doing foreign men. McAllister notes that this mediated script could only be enacted by a white woman because captivity narratives (and in this case, Special Operations rescue missions) do not exist for women of color like Johnson and Piestewa. The lesson here: not all gender is equally deployable to pique the national interest; race matters and sex is the most valuable commodity in political and media markets.

The importance of Lynch's persona as a "girl next door" is emphasized by Howard and Prividera (2004:92) who find that the majority of media reports following Lynch's rescue focused primarily on her femininity rather than her soldier identity. They note that little was said about the duties Lynch performed in the military and instead the authors report that she was repeatedly described as "cute," "young," "attractive," "blonde," and a winner of "Miss Congeniality" who loved her hairbrush. In addition to her physical appearance, they found that Lynch's sexuality also was widely discussed, especially ruminations about reports of her being sexually assaulted while held captive. Together, the military and the media represented Jessica Lynch as a hero of circumstance rather than a war hero honored for her military skill and prowess. Howard and Prividera (2004:96) also argue that the rhetorical significance of Lynch's rescue and her public transformation from a brave warrior to a female victim/captive in need of male rescuers perpetuates dangerous dichotomous gender stereotypes within the military and the media and illustrates the exploitive power of patriarchy "as the identities of and relationships between 'Jessica' and her rescuers were constructed for the media public."

Masculinity, Femininity, and War

The Iraq war constitutes an important case study of the deployment of gender, race, class, and sexuality in military conflicts. The militarization of race and class illustrated by these three women soldiers draws on familiar themes in U.S. culture and history. In their images and biographies we can see evidence of the military's reliance on and reproduction of class and race relations in the larger society: the recruitment of working class individuals for low-level, low-status, dangerous military work, the valorization of whiteness, and the devaluation of the contributions and sacrifices of soldiers of color. What is new in these pictures and the stories behind them is the militarization of gender and sexuality. We argue that these women's images and the circumstances by which they came to our attention reveal disturbing new implications of increasing enlistments of women in the U.S. armed forces.

Although we focus here on the "damsels in distress" narrative, we note and have written elsewhere that this story represents only one episode in the saga of deploying of gender and sexuality in the Iraq war (Feitz, 2005; Feitz & Nagel, 2008). Other installments include what we title "chicks with guns"—the use of female sexuality as an instrument of torture at Abu Ghraib and Guantánamo prisons, "comrades in arms"—the recurrent scandals involving women's sexual abuse at the hands of their fellow servicemen, and "fall gals"—the strategy of blaming servicewomen, especially female officers, and protecting servicemen, especially male officers, when problems become public.[2] These cases provide evidence of the military's assignment of women soldiers to various special duties—as propaganda tools (e.g., the rescue of women soldiers to showcase masculine military bravery), as instruments of torture (e.g., the use of female sexuality to assault and humiliate the enemy), as emotional and sexual workers (e.g., women soldiers expected to service the servicemen), and as scapegoats (e.g., women officers blamed for military failures).

In order to understand what these representations of women in uniform tell us, and in order to identify what is new and what is important about the experiences of these and other women serving in the U.S. military and in the Iraq war, we look first to scholarship on masculinity and the military. Studies of masculinity and war provide some insight into the contemporary deployment of femininity in war. This research emphasizes masculinism and its cultural fit with militarism, nationalism, and patriotism, with male codes of honor, with warrior ideologies, with hierarchical military organization, with officially sanctioned and unofficially enacted aggression in conflicts (e.g., rape, torture, other rituals of manliness), and with manly posturing in national politics and international relations (see Mosse, 1996; Nagel, 1998, 2003; Enloe, 2000; 2004; Connell, 2005; Hutchins, 2007). Scholars note that war is intimately linked to nationalism, patriotism, and masculinity, and as Enloe (1990:45) comments, "nationalism [and nationalist conflicts have] typically sprung up from masculinized memory, masculinized humiliation, and masculinized hope."

Given this emphasis on men and masculinity in matters of patriotism, nationalism, and militarism, it is no surprise that sexuality also is central to understanding both women and men at war. In her work on "gendering war talk," Cohn (1993) has documented the use of sexual insults, threats, and homophobia in national "defense" and war discourse. Men use homosexual jokes and banter and misogynistic humor and insults, such as calling one another "faggots," or "ladies" or "girls," to foster solidarity and enforce moral boundaries (see also Goldstein, 2003; Winslow, 1999). During the first war with Iraq—the Gulf war in 1990/91—for instance, a commonly reported phrase alleged to have been written on U.S. missiles targeted on Iraqi positions was, "Bend over, Saddam" (Cohn, 1993:236).

This scholarship, with its emphasis on the masculinist aspects of war, has tended to depict women in historically passive rather than active roles: as the objects of national defense—what Enloe (1993:165) calls the "womenandchildren" category, as support staff on home fronts and in the military itself for the real work undertaken by men, as sources of emotional, physical, and sexual comfort for men at war. Women have been shown historically to be central to the *justification* for war—as the source of the warm and fuzzy feelings and moral mobilization of warriors defending home and hearth. Women also are recognized as important contributors to war efforts as workers in industry and in service sectors such as medicine, sex work, domestic work, and childcare, and until recently, only occasionally as actual combatants (see Apeles, 2004; Fenner & DeYoung, 2001; Zimbabwe Women Writers, 2001).

The military may be a man's world ruled by masculine codes of honor with women cast primarily in historical roles as objects of defense, but women's place in the U.S. military is changing (Stiehm, 1989; 1996; Herbert, 1998; Skaine, 1999; Solaro, 2006). These changes are reflected in growing numbers of women in uniform, expansion of women's military roles, and ambiguities associated with defining combat and locating battlefronts in contemporary peacekeeping duty and military conflicts such as the Iraq war.[3] Since the early 1970s the U.S. armed forces have adopted two policies that increased the recruitment of women: the elimination of a 2 percent cap on women's enlistment and the adoption of gender-neutral recruiting policies.[4] The result has been a steady increase in the proportion of women serving in the U.S. military (Segal & Segal, 2004). Table 42.1 shows the number and percentage of women in the U.S. armed forces from 1970 to 2006. As the table shows, in 1970, before the new policies were adopted, there were 27,948 women in the four armed services (Army, Navy, Marine Corps, Air Force); they comprised 1.1 percent of active service personnel. In the two decades after the 1973 lifting of the 2 percent cap, but before gender-neutral recruiting was instituted, women's representation in the armed forces grew ten-fold, rising to 8.5 percent

in 1980 and 10.9 percent in 1990. After the implementation of gender-neutral recruitment in the early 1990s, women's representation in the military increased again to 14.7 percent in 2000. In 2006, there were 197,622 women serving in the four U.S. military services comprising 14.5 percent of active service personnel (U.S. Defense Department, 2002; 2006). Women constituted 7 percent of the troops deployed in the 1991 Gulf war (Quester & Gilroy, 2002) and 14 percent of the troops deployed in Iraq in 2003 (Curphey, 2003). Women's duties and rank have expanded as their numbers have grown. In 1973 women constituted 4.2 percent of the officers in the four military services; in the past three decades that proportion has more than tripled: in 2002, 15.6 percent of officers were women (U.S. Defense Department, 2002). Although women are still officially restricted to non-combat roles, they serve in virtually all areas of the military, including as pilots of combat aircraft (Hurrell et al., 2002).[5]

TABLE 42.1 Women Serving in the U.S. Armed Forces (Army, Navy, Marines, Air Force), 1970–2006

Year	Number	Percent
1970	27,948	1.1
1980	148,771	8.5
1990	188,913	10.9
2000	169,084	14.7
2006	197,622	14.5

Sources: U.S. Defense Department (2002, 2006).

Women are not only a growing presence in the military because of their sheer numbers and responsibilities associated with rank. Despite prohibitions against combat duty for women, most military observers report that women are involved in military violence and combat situations on a daily basis in Iraq (see Skiba, 2005; Williams & Staub, 2005; Jervis, 2005; Walters, 2005). This is partly because there is no clear "front line" in the Iraq occupation since urban warfare and guerrilla tactics defy conventional notions of battle zones. It is also the case that women's expanded police and guard roles bring them into close contact with Iraqi combatants and prisoners, further blurring the line between combat and non-combat duty. Despite its continued insistence on women's official exclusion from combat, the military has been quick to capitalize on the presence of women soldiers in a variety of military settings in Iraq—as police and security workers searching women and men Iraqi civilians, as prison guards, as pilots, and as wives and lovers of servicemen (Scarborough, 2005).

It remains to be seen what are the implications of the increased number and role of women in the U.S. military. Do women who join the military become "men"? Or if enough women join the military, will they "feminize" it? Is there a critical mass—a point at which women cease to become masculinized in male-dominated institutions and begin to transform the institutions according to the feminine interests and culture they bring with them? In other words, do women who participate in masculine organizations or situations "feminize" those institutions and settings, or do they conform to manly codes of conduct or to masculinist definitions of women's proper places? What does the increased number of servicewomen mean for the experiences of women soldiers in Iraq?

The answer to the question of women becoming masculinized or masculine institutions becoming feminized is an important one not only for understanding the place of women in the Iraq war, but also for making sense of national and international politics. As women enter the political realm in greater numbers around the world, will we see a shifting of state agendas and a decoupling of nationalism and militarism from masculinity—will state politics emphasize guns or butter? Enloe (1990) is skeptical about the prospects of butter rising to the top of national politics any time soon. She notes the limited change that has resulted from the many nationalist independence movements around the world, and observes that in most post–World War II states it is "business as usual" with indigenous masculinities replacing colonial masculinities at the helms of states and employing local and global patriarchal and masculinist logics in governance and international relations:

> Given the scores of nationalist movements which have managed to topple empires and create new ones, it is surprising that the international political system hasn't been more radically altered than it has. But a nationalist movement informed by masculinist pride and holding a patriarchal vision of the new nation-state is likely to produce just one more actor in the international arena. A dozen new patriarchal nation-states may make the international bargaining table a bit more crowded, but it won't change the international game being played at that table (Enloe 1990:64).

If the Iraq war is any indication of the shape of military things to come, we are seeing support for Enloe's observations about the entrenched institutionalization of patriarchy and masculinism—not only in the international system, but in the way the U.S. interacts with that system. Critics long have complained about the militarization of U.S. politics in the post–Second World War period. Mills (1956) referred to the mentality of perpetual conflict that characterized the Cold War as "military metaphysics." Despite the end of the Cold War and the anticipated "peace dividend," the speed and magnitude of U.S. militarization in the post-Soviet era, especially during the unending "War on Terror," has alarmed scholars and policy analysts on the political Left and Right. Johnson (2004) argues that the shift in the locus of U.S. foreign policy from the State Department to the Defense Department threatens to destroy both the American republic and the U.S. economy. The rush to military "solutions" to a variety of problems marks what Bacevich (2005) refers to as "the new American militarism" and leads Andreas (2004) to conclude that the U.S. is "addicted to war."

The end of the military draft in 1973 necessitated the often difficult recruitment of young Americans disaffected by the dangers of military service. In order to meet its staffing needs, the military has shown an elastic institutional capacity to stretch its boundaries to include women in a broad array of roles. What is ironic, but predictable from Enloe's analysis, is that as women have entered deeper and higher into the military's ranks, the patriarchal, gendered institutional character of the military as a male cultural and political space has remained intact (for a discussion of gendered institutions, see Wharton, 2002). Instead of being feminized, the military has found new ways to take advantage of femininity and of women's symbolic and material presence.

Conclusion

We have argued here that all war is raced, gendered, classed, and sexualized and that wars are primarily masculinist undertakings defined by manly codes of honor and justified by appeals to men to protect home, hearth, and the women and children waiting there. We have noted the growing numbers and roles of women in the U.S. military, and we recognize that the expanded opportunities for servicewomen are greater than at any time in U.S. history. Despite these changes, we have concluded that the war in Iraq is no exception to the historical masculinist rules of war. We find that the U.S. military has deployed women and femininity to achieve public relations and combat goals, and we conclude that, despite much official rhetoric about the limitations of women in combat, the deployment of women's gender and sexuality has been integrated into the U.S. military's structure and operations.

Women who choose military service are paying their dues and then some. Not only are they entering male domains, working at men's jobs, and facing serious injury and death just like their male comrades, they also are serving a military second shift, deployed as symbolic and service workers in propaganda campaigns, prison abuse programs, and the military-sexual complex. We find that when women enter longstanding, entrenched masculinist spaces like military organizations, even when their numbers grow and they are promoted to positions of authority, the racial, gender, class, and sexual politics of the U.S. military and American society shape the policies and realities of day-to-day operations in war zones. The deployment of race, gender, class, and sexuality in the Iraq war suggests strongly that racial and gender integration are not guarantees of racial and gender equality. The recent experiences of servicewomen in the Iraq war illustrate the capacity of U.S. military organization to incorporate difference and maintain established power relations even in the face of demographic changes in its personnel.

Notes

1. Johnson signed a contract with Kensington Publishing for her story in 2006, but the contract was cancelled; she has a new contract with Simon & Schuster for a book slated for publication in 2008 (Pride 2007).

2. Servicewomen's post-traumatic stress associated with their sexual harassment and assault by their mostly male comrades has been labeled officially, "military sexual trauma" or "MST" and the U.S. Veterans Affairs Administration has instituted special treatment programs at VA hospitals (U.S. Veterans Administration, 2007); for a list of major U.S. Defense Department investigations into sexual abuse scandals, see U.S. Department of Defense (2003, 2004, 2005, 2007b). One of the most egregious examples of scapegoating women is the case of former Brigadier General Janis Karpinski. Karpinski, who had no prior experience in the field of corrections, was put in charge of 15 military prisons in Iraq; she was blamed for the Abu Ghraib scandal, lost her command, and was demoted to Colonel. We compare Karpinski's treatment to the lack of disciplinary action against Major General Geoffrey Miller, who commanded the U.S. detention facility at Guantánamo Bay, traveled to Iraq in 2003 to help "Gitmo-ize" operations at Abu Ghraib, and received a Distinguished Service Medal from the Army when he retired in 2005 (White, 2005; see also Karpinski, 2006).

3. For a discussion of the ambiguities of women's role in combat zones, see Nantais and Lee (1999); Miller and Moskos (1995); for a discussion of women in peacekeeping, see DeGroot

(2001); for a discussion of the problems of locating battlefronts and, some argue, impossibility of keeping women out of combat situations, see Jervis (2005); Agostini (2005); CNN (2005).

4. In 1973 the 2 percent cap was eliminated and in the 1990s the various services adopted gender-neutral recruitment policies; the Navy later rescinded its gender-neutral policy because of constrained berthing policies on Navy vessels—as a result there was a 6 percent drop in women's recruitment from 20 percent in 1995 to 14 percent in 1997, though the percentage of women recruited increased to between 17–20 percent after 1997 (Department of Defense, 2002).

5. The U.S. Air Force began training women as fighter pilots in 1993; in 2005 4.1 percent of USAF pilots were women (Wilson, 2005).

References

Agostini, L. (2005). Women's combat support role could end in Iraq. http://www.marines.mil/marinelink/mcn2000.nsf/0/BEBFFC30B3A4917A85257006005AF8E8?opendocument (accessed 7/20/05).

Andreas, J. (2004). *Addicted to war: Why the U.S. can't kick militarism.* Oakland, CA: AK Press.

Apeles, T. (2004). *Women warriors: Adventures from history's greatest female fighters.* Emoryville, CA: Seal Press.

Bacevich, A. (2005). *The new American militarism: How Americans are seduced by war.* New York: Oxford University Press.

Bragg, R. (2003). *I am a soldier, too: The Jessica Lynch story.* New York: Knopf.

Byrd, V. (2004). Shoshana Johnson's "to hell and back." *Essence* (March). http://www.essence.com/essence/print/0,14882,590888,00.html (accessed 11/29/07).

CNN. (2003, November 7). Lynch: Military played up rescue too much. *CNN.com.* http://www.cnn.com/2003/US/11/07/lynch.interview/ (accessed 7/18/05).

———. (2005, June 28). Female troops in Iraq exposed to combat. *CNN.com* http://www.cnn.com/2005/WORLD/meast/06/25/women.combat/ (accessed 7/21/05).

Cohn, C. (1993). Wars, wimps, and women: Talking gender and thinking war. In M. Cooke & A. Woollacott (eds.), *Gendering war talk*, pp. 227–246. Princeton, NJ: Princeton University Press.

Connell, R. W. (2005). *Masculinities*. 2nd edition. Berkeley: University of California Press.

Curphey, S. (2003). 1 in 7 U.S. military personnel in Iraq is female. *Women's E-News*. http://www.womensenews.org/article.cfm/dyn/aid/1265/context/cover/ (accessed 7/21/05).

DeGroot, G. (2001). A few good women: Gender stereotypes, the military and peacekeeping. *International Peacekeeping*, 8:23–38.

Douglas, W. (2003, November 9). A case of race? One POW acclaimed, another ignored. *Seattle Times*. http://seattletimes.nwsource.com/html/nationworld/2001786800_shoshana09.html (accessed 7/12, 2005).

Enloe, C. (1990). *Bananas, beaches, and bases: Making feminist sense of international politics*. Berkeley: University of California Press.

———. (1993). *The morning after: Sexual politics at the end of the cold war*. Berkeley: University of California Press.

———. (2000). *Maneuvers: The international politics of militarizing women's lives*. Berkeley: University of California Press.

———. (2004). *The curious feminist: Searching for women in a new age of empire*. Berkeley: University of California Press.

Feitz, L. (2005). The U.S. military's deployment of female sexuality as an instrument of torture at Abu Ghraib. Paper presented at the Hall Center for the Humanities, University of Kansas, Lawrence, Kansas, March 3.

Feitz, L. & Nagel, J. (2008). The militarization of gender and sexuality in the Iraq War. In C. H. Carreiras & G. Kümmel (eds.), *Women, violence and the military*, Wiesbaden, Germany: VS Verlag.

Fenner, L. M. & De Young, M. (2001). *Women in combat: Civic duty or military liability?* Washington, DC: Georgetown University Press.

Goldstein, J. (2003). *War and gender: How gender shapes the war system and vice versa*. New York: Cambridge University Press.

Grundy, G. (2003, November 6). Three-fifths of a heroine. *The record* (Harvard Law School). http://www.hlrecord.org/media/paper609/news/2003/11/06/Opinion/ThreeFifths.Of.A.Heroine-551069.shtml (accessed 6/28/05).

Herbert, M. S. (1998). *Camouflage isn't only for combat: Gender, sexuality, and women in the military*. New York: New York University Press.

Hess, S. & Kalb, M. (2003). *The media and the war on terrorism*. Washington, DC: Brookings Institution Press.

Howard, J. W. III & Prividera, L. C. (2004). Rescuing patriarchy or saving "Jessica Lynch": The rhetorical construction of the American woman soldier. *Women and Language*, 27:89–97.

Hurrell, M. C., Beckett, M. K., Chien, C. S., & Sollinger, J. M. (2002). *The status of gender integration in the military: Analysis of selected occupations*. Santa Monica, CA: The Rand Corporation.

Hutchings, K. (2007). Making sense of masculinity and war. Men and Masculinities Online, First(10):1–16. http://jmm.sagepub.com.www2.lib.ku.edu:2048/cgi/rapidpdf/1097184X07306740v1 (accessed 11/29/07).

Iraq Body Count. (2007). Documented civilian deaths from violence. http://www.iraqbodycount.net (accessed 1/25/08).

Jervis, R. (2005, June 27). Despite rule, U.S. women on front line in Iraq war. *USAToday.com*. http://www.marines.mil/marinelink/mcn2000.nsf/0/BEBFFC30B3A4917A85257006005AF8E8?opendocument (accessed 7/5/05).

Johnson, C. (2000). *Blowback: The costs and consequences of American empire*. New York: Henry Holt.

Kampfiner, J. (2003, May 18). Saving private Lynch story "flawed." *BBC.News* http://news.bbc.co.uk/2/hi/programmes/correspondent/3028585.stm (accessed 7/19/05).

Karpinski, J. (2006). *One woman's army: The commanding general of Abu Ghraib tells her story*. New York: Miramax Books.

Kirkpatrick, D. (2003, November 7). Jessica Lynch criticizes U.S. accounts of her ordeal. *New York Times*. http://query.nytimes.com/gst/fullpage.html?res=9D02E4DB1539F934A35752C1A9659C8B63 (accessed July 7, 2005).

McAlister, M. (2003, April 6). Saving private Lynch. *New York Times*, pp. 4, 14.

Miller, L. & Moskos, C. (1995). Humanitarians or warriors? Race, gender, and combat status in operation restore hope. *Armed Forces and Society*, 21:615–635.

Mills, C. W. (1956). *The power elite*. New York: Oxford University Press.

Mosse, G. L. (1996). *The image of man: The creation of modern masculinity*. New York: Oxford University Press.

Nagel, J. (1998). Masculinity and nationalism: Gender and sexuality in the making of nations. *Ethnic and Racial Studies*, 21:242–269.

———. (2003). *Race, ethnicity, and sexuality: Intimate intersections, forbidden frontiers*. New York: Oxford University Press.

Nantais, C. & Lee, M. F. (1999). Women in the United States military: Protectors or protected? The case of prisoner of war Melissa Rathbun-Nealy. *Journal of Gender Studies*, 8:181–191.

New York Times. (2005, July 15). The woman of Gitmo. *New York Times.com*. http://www.nytimes.com/2005/07/15/opinion/15fril.html (accessed 7/15/05).

Pride, F. (2007, June 18). Shoshana Johnson title lands at S&S. *Publishers Weekly*. http://www.publishersweekly.com/article/CA6452847.html (accessed 11/24/07).

Quester, A. O. & Gilroy, C. L. (2002). Women and minorities in America's volunteer military. *Contemporary Economic Policy*, 20:111–121. http://www.dtic.mil/dacowits/research/Women_Minorities_in_Amer_Vol_Military.pdf (accessed 7/21/05).

Scarborough, R. (2005, July 11). Iraq lacks women trained in security. *Washington Times*. http://washingtontimes.com/national/2005 0711-122346-9856r.htm (accessed 7/11/05).

Segal, D. & Segal, M. (2004). America's military population. *Population Bulletin* 59(4). http://www.prb.org/Source/ACF1396.pdf (accessed 11/25/407).

Shaffer, M. (2003, November 12). Piestewa went to war for Lynch, books says. *Arizona Republic*. http://www.azcentral.com/news/special/veterans/articles/piestewa-3.html (accessed 7/5/05).

Skaine, R. (1999). *Women at war: Gender issues of Americans in combat*. Jefferson, NC: McFarland Publishers.

Skiba, K. M. (2005). *Sister in the band of brothers: Embedded with the 101st airborne in Iraq*. Lawrence: University Press of Kansas.

Smith, T. (2003, June 3). Saving private Lynch. *On-line Newshour*. http://www.pbs.org/newshour/bb/media/jan-june03/lynch_0610.html (accessed 7/20/05).

Solaro, E. (2006). *Women in the line of fire: What you should know about women in the military*. Emeryville, CA: Seal Press.

Stiehm, Judith H. 1989. *Arms and the enlisted woman*. Philadelphia: Temple University Press.

———. 1996. *It's our military too! Women in the U.S. military*. Philadelphia: Temple University Press.

U.S. Army. 2003. *Special report: Attack on the 507th Maintenance Company*. http://www.army.mil/features/507thMaintCmpy/AttackOnThe507MaintCmpy.pdf (accessed 7/13/05).

———. (2005). *Army sexual assault prevention and response program*. http://www.sexualassault.army.mil/ (accessed 7/22/05).

U.S. Department of Defense. (2002). *Population representation in the military services*. http://www.dod.mil/prhome/poprep2002/index.htm (accessed 7/21/05).

———. (2003). *Defense task force report on domestic violence*. http://www.dtic.mil/domesticviolence/reports/DV_RPT3.PDF (accessed 7/18/05).

———. (2004). *Task force report on sexual assault policies*. http://www.asmra.army.mil/eo/eo_docs/Army%20Report%20(May%2027%20 2004).pdf (accessed 7/8/05).

———. (2005). *Confidentiality policy for victims of sexual assault* (March 31). http://www.defenselink.mil/news/Mar2005/d20050318dsd.pdf (accessed 7/22/05).

———. (2006). Statistics on women in the military: Women serving today. Women in Military Service for America Memorial Foundation. http://www.womensmemorial.org/Press/stats.html (accessed 11/26/07).

———. (2007a). Operation Iraqi Freedom: U.S. casualty status and fatalities as of November

29, 2007. http://www.defenselink.mil/news/casualty.pdf (accessed 11/29/07).

———. (2007b). Annual report on military services sexual assault for CY2006" (March 15). http://www.sapr.mil/contents/references/2006%20ANnual%20Report.pdf (accessed 11/26/07).

U.S. House of Representatives. (2007). Testimony before house oversight and government reform committee (April 25). http://oversight.house.gov/documents/20070424110022.pdf (accessed 11/25/07).

U.S. Veterans Administration. (2007). Military sexual trauma program. http://www1.va.gov/wvhp/page.cfm?pg=20 (accessed 11/26/07).

Walters, J. (2005, April 30). As casualties soar, America's women face reality of front line. *The Guardian.* http://www.buzzle.com/editorials/4-30-2005-69348.asp (accessed 7/11/05).

Weisskopf, M. (2006). *Blood brothers: Among the soldiers of ward 57.* New York: Henry Holt & Company.

Wharton, A. (2002). Gender, institutions, and difference: The continuing importance of social structure in understanding gender inequality in organizations. In S. C. Chew & J. D. Knottnerus, *Structure, culture, and history: Recent issues in social theory,* pp. 257–270. New York: Rowman and Littlefield.

White, J. (2005, July 14). Abu Ghraib tactics were first used at Guantánamo. *Washington Post,* A1.

Williams, K. & Staub, M. E. (2005). *Love my rifle more than you: Young and female in the U.S. Army.* New York: W. W. Norton.

Wilson, Capt. B. A. (1996). Military women pilots. http://userpages.aug.com/captbarb/pilots.html (accessed 7/21/05).

Winslow, D. (1999). Rites of passage and group bonding in the Canadian airborne. *Armed Forces and Society,* 25:429–457.

Wise, B. S. (2003, October 28). On Shoshana Johnson, Jessica Lynch and disability. *Dissent.* http://www.intellectualconservative.com/article2798.html (accessed 7/5/05).

Zimbabwe Women Writers. (2001). *Women of resilience: The voices of women combatants.* London & Harare: African Books Collective.

CHAPTER 6 STUDY QUESTIONS

1. Have you ever considered how we do gender in public bathrooms? Do you see people doing gender in dormitory bathrooms? How else is gender connected to bathroom behavior?

2. If you wanted to mount a public information or a social change campaign about gender-neutral restrooms, what would you do? What steps would you take to design your message, target your audience, and create change?

3. Three of the articles in this chapter ask you to (re)consider the social construction of masculinity (Melanie Carlson [Reading 38], Sinikka Elliott [Reading 39], and Thomas Rogers [Reading 40]). In what ways does social context define how men do gender in the seemingly individual and intimate ways the authors describe?

4. Which structures and institutions will you now think critically about? What actions or steps will you take to extend your critique?

CHAPTER 7 Rattling the Cage: Social Change

43 What Is Gender-Normative Privilege?

If I am gender normative (or, in some cases, simply perceived as gender normative):

- My validity as a man/woman/human is not based on how much surgery I have had or how well I "pass" as a non-transgender person.
- When initiating sex with someone, I do not have to worry that they will not be able to deal with my parts, or that having sex with me will cause my partner to question his or her own sexual orientation.
- I am not excluded from events which are either explicitly or de facto (because of nudity) for men-born-men or women-born-women only.
- My politics are not questioned based on the choices I make with regard to my body.

- I do not have to hear "so have you had *the* surgery?" or "oh, so you're *really* a [incorrect gender]?" each time I come out to someone.
- Strangers do not ask me what my "real name" [birth name] is and then assume that they have a right to call me by that name.
- People do not disrespect me by using incorrect pronouns even after they have been corrected.
- I do not have to worry about whether I will experience harassment or violence for using a bathroom or whether I will be safe changing in a locker room.
- I do not have to defend my right to be part of "queer," and gay men and lesbians will not try to exclude me from *our* movement in order to gain political legitimacy for themselves.

Anonymous, "What Is Gender-Normative Privilege?" Originally posted at www.umass.edu/stonewall/uploads/listWidget/8942/trans%20packet.pdf. Every effort was made to contact the rightsholder.

- I do not have to choose between being invisible ("passing") or being "othered" and/or tokenized based on my gender.
- When I go to the gym or a public pool, I can use the showers.
- If I go to the emergency room, I do not have to worry that my gender will keep me from receiving appropriate treatment, or that all of my medical issues will be seen as a result of my gender.

- My health insurance provider (or public health system) does not specifically exclude me from receiving benefits or treatments available to others because of my gender.
- My identity is not considered "mentally ill" by the medical establishment.
- The medical establishment does not serve as a "gatekeeper," determining what happens to my body.

But You're So Queer for a Straight Guy!
Affirming Complexities of Gendered Sexualities in Men

Affirming Complexities of Gendered Sexualities in Men

Questions of whether Abe Lincoln was gay or whether Heath Ledger and Jake Gyllenhall, the actors portraying Ennis and Jack in *Brokeback Mountain*, found some personal pleasure in their on-screen kissing and sexual play reflect an on-going curiosity—most often found in gay men's publications—about whether straight guys (particularly those who have public identities as heterosexuals), are really, *really* gay just beneath the surface, the belt (or just past the lips!). Of course there isn't a way of knowing unless the straight man himself announces that he has experienced homoerotic attractions, or forms an identity that is intentionally associated with being gay. When it comes to public figures like Lincoln, Ledger and Gyllenhall, speculation is primary—wherein the individuals themselves don't say, won't say, or, in the case of Lincoln, can't say. At the same time much of the discourse on sexual orientation as it relates to male intimacy, or the appearance of intimacy, relies on a gay-straight dichotomy, labeling men who might be sexually expressive in relation to another man as likely bisexuals, a label that struggles for de-finition. Was Lincoln "bi" because he was married and produced children, while seeming to prefer sharing his bed with other men? Did Ledger and Gyllenhall experience a "bi-moment" in the midst of their passionate kisses? The questions (and possibilities) are seemingly endless in part because the categories of straight, bi, and gay themselves don't adequately represent the possible variations, particularly when it comes to the intersection of sex and gender.

Using a typology of sexualities of queer straight men (Heasley, 2003, 2005), a broader representation of this intersection is possible, and notably so for those men who "bend" away from hegemonic hetero-masculinity and are open to a hetero-feminist-gay identity of being *queer straight males*.

Queer-straight males are men who disrupt both heterosexuality and hegemonic masculinity—who make a contribution to the expansion of the conceptualization of straightness and of masculinity (Heasley, 2003). In the process, they represent a more honest picture than has been articulated of straight men's experiences and ways of being. This is particularly important given the absence of positive imagery in the culture of men who do not fit the hegemonic type of

Robert Heasley, "But You're So Queer for a Straight Guy! Affirming Complexities of Gendered Sexualities in Men." Edited from a version presented at the American Sociological Association Annual Meeting, August 2007. Reprinted by permission of the author.

hetero-masculine. It is also important to trouble gender and sexuality, as suggested by Judith Butler (1990) and Michel Foucault (1979). Men who do not conform are perceived as "non traditional," as noted in an earlier article (Heasley 2003, 2005). "Non" implies the absence of a quality—"non" implies the negative, suggesting that "traditional" men have qualities that are desired, and that "non" traditional men are missing those qualities. Consider the following:

The "non-traditional" male, however, presents an unknown, unfamiliar package, even if qualities the male exhibits are desirable, his difference demands justification, explanation. Being "non" means "not having." Applied to gender and sexuality, the implications are profound. The very labeling of a subject as the absence of something (such as labeling women as "non-men") reifies the dominant group while subjugating the subordinate. "Non" erases. And in the process it problematizes other. For a straight queer man, there is no place for awareness of self in relation to what is. He becomes the deviant, he is isolated, and in the process, vulnerable to reactions in the form, for instance, of stigma and labeling by the dominant group. "Non" has no history, no literature, no power, no community. "Non" requires an invention of self. By creating a typology of queer masculinities of straight males, we give space and language to lived experience, and set the stage upon which narratives of straight-queer men can find a home (Heasley, 2003).

Thus, when Ennis and Jack make love for the first time, the audience is led to question their sexual orientation, from presumed straight (they are, after all, ranchers), to presumed gay (they do, after all, have anal sex). But neither is true necessarily; they may represent a type of straight masculinity that goes undocumented, unacknowledged, and often hidden from history and from view. But straight men are more complex than the hegemonic hetero-masculine construction suggests. To step out of the paradigm does not mean stepping into the only alternatives—becoming "non" traditional in their masculinity and non-straight in their sexuality. We need to, as Bem (1995) suggests, turn the volume up, but also, to provide clarity on new, previously unacknowledged "sounds."

Typology of Queer Straight Men: Affirming the "Other"

Despite the absence of history, legitimacy, and often, agency, many straight men experience and demonstrate "queer masculinity," though for some, qualities associated with the queer masculine may be kept from view. Queer straight masculinity is defined here as "ways of being masculine outside of the hetero-normative constructions of masculinity that disrupt, or have the potential to disrupt, traditional images of the hegemonic heterosexual masculine" (Heasley, 2003). There are a number of ways this disruption occurs, many of which are captured in a typology of characteristics, and include:

(1) Straight sissy boys: Straight men who cannot "do" straight masculinity due to physical or personality qualities that do not meet the normative standards. These are men who might have high-pitched voices, small builds, no interest in traditional male activities, and/or be more comfortable in association with females and what is perceived feminine.

(2) Social-justice straight-queers: These are straight identified males who actively and publicly support feminist and/or gay rights, and ways of being. They may risk discrimination or threat for their actions and beliefs, but are determined to take a stand and prefer (or at least pursue) identity with women and gays, rather than with those forces which represent the dominant sexual/gender order.

(3) Elective straight-queers: The category represents straight men who take on the performance of being non-straight, who associate with and are willing to be perceived as gay. Men in this category elect to move into queer masculinity as a means of liberating the self from the constrictions of heteronormative masculinity. Unlike the sissy, they can move into and out of the role of perceived gay; they can also move in and out of gay space, dancing at a gay bar, having and being with close gay friends—but dissociating from these encounters when they select.

(4) Committed straight queer: Different from the elective queers, these men practice at being queer—at being in and experiencing gay-ness and the feminine—with the intention of benefiting personally from that experience. This may also be a social justice action, and involve some aspects of "elective" queerness, but the overriding difference is that straight males who are committed to being queer open themselves up to a master identity of queer.

(5) Stylistic straight-queers: Men in this category intentionally take on a presentation of masculinity that goes against some elements of the hegemonic masculine—pursuing fashion that is associated with gay-ness, relationships that have qualities associated with being female (dinner dates with male friends rather than meeting at a

bar for a beer). While not necessarily politically active in support of women's or gay rights, and not necessarily comfortable with women's or gay space, the representation of the male-ness serves to disrupt the normative measures of masculinity and perception of heterosexuality.

(6) Men living in the shadow of masculinity: This category encompasses a range of males who share a common experience of dissatisfaction with hegemonic heteromasculinity, for whatever reason, but live in a way that avoids encountering the effects or the environment itself. They may be inadequate to "do" the hegemonic heteromasculine performance, or simply reject it, but don't have awareness of legitimized options. Ennis comes to mind as representing a character for whom the standards of both heterosexual and masculinity don't seem to "fit"—but with Jack's taking the risk of inviting him into a romantic relationship, he doesn't experience his alternative form of the hetero-masculine. It isn't a surprise that until Jack and Ennis have become sexual and romantic in their relationship, that there is nothing in Ennis' character that displays his playful side, that permits him to wrestle with Jack, to laugh, to relax his male-ness.

This typology attempts to capture ways straight men express non-conformity that associates them with, and represents their affinity for, that which is perceived feminine *and* homosexual in areas such as gender attitude, beliefs, and behaviors.

Consider two male college students who identify as heterosexual, yet have come to find themselves in agreement that they are bothered by—and don't like hanging around with—other straight men, particularly those whose straightness is associated with, say, homophobia and misogyny, sexualizing females, obsessing about sports and NASCAR. Over time they become more open about their lives, displaying vulnerabilities, expressing their appreciation for each other. They spend time alone in the dorm room of one of the young men, sitting on a bed, talking, sharing a joint, a glass of wine or a beer. They lay together as they talk, eventually finding themselves cuddling, one's arm around the other, and falling asleep as the night grows late. If they tell others the next day about their experience together—the romance suggested in the privacy and quiet of the setting, the shared intimate feelings, the tenderness of their touch, the gentleness of falling asleep in each other's arms, the response is likely to be something to the effect that they are "so gay" (from peers) or "at risk" of becoming gay, as perceived by parents and other elders. Even those who might be open and supportive if the young men were gay would likely see the "potential" for gay-ness in their interactions. But, are they really so gay? At risk? Or even expressing a homosexual side?

These two men, who were in my class on sexuality a few years ago, asked themselves these same questions. Over time, even with an additional attempt to make out with each other, and engage in French kissing, fondling each others' genitals, and continuing to sleep together, they simply didn't become "sexual" partners. As radical feminists and activists, they began wearing skirts to classes, holding hands when they walked in public, kissing on the lips when greeting at the student union. Indeed, these men referred to themselves as straight queers for not being (or wanting to be) part of the hegemonic hetero-masculine. They also came to see themselves as "non-orgasmic" partners—meaning to them, that they were

sexual with each other—through touching, kissing, being open to romanticizing their love, but their experience was not arousing, and not orgasmic. They were, as the title of this paper suggests, *so queer for two straight guys*. Yet they weren't gay, or bi, they were queer-straight guys in a way that fits a number of categories in the typology.

For instance, these men performed their relationship in public spaces because of the feminist ideology and commitment to challenging stereotypes and homophobia. They fit the criteria of the second category in the typology presented above. They are *social-justice straight-queers*—willing to take on not only the intellectual and political arguments about sexual orientation and misogyny, but, by wearing skirts, holding hands, kissing in public places, they select to make political statements by being together in public in ways that they are in private—their actions are based on private, intimate connections and not just public performance, and thus serve to make public that which is personal, and most often revealed only in privacy.

These students also exhibit qualities of those fitting the category of *elective straight-queers*. These men can practice being sexual with each other, can select when and where to appear feminine by wearing skirts, holding hands, displaying elements of their sexual closeness and gender openness in public, not just private space. Because they are not gay, are not women, they retain the privilege of where and when they display behaviors that are perceived queer, they *elect* to move into and out of queer.

Finally, these men represent another category—that of *committed straight queers*. Men in this category hold onto their beliefs, values and commitments to queer identity over time, taking political action, and refusing to adapt to the dominant forms of the hetero-masculine. For these two friends, working with gay and feminist organizations to advance social justice was core to their identity—and yet, unlike many straight men who share similar commitments (and are more likely to fit the category of *social-justice straight queers*), they were themselves actively engaged in challenging their personal boundaries around sex and gender, and presenting their very personal consciousness in public settings. They not only were joining the movement for gay and women's rights, they were experiencing the movement at a personal level through activity "queering" their relationship.

Unlike the intentionality behind the two young men above, some men limit the degree to which they disrupt the normative, either by choice or by chance, yet are still participating in the queering of hetero-masculinity. Their non-conformity is important to recognize. *Straight sissy boys*, for instance, may be more vulnerable to attack by other boys in school, have less sexual capital when it comes to being desirable to women, and are more likely to be perceived as gay until proven otherwise. They may compensate for missing the physical and behavioral qualities that are valued and associated with straight masculinity. As a result they may avoid places and spaces that are dominated by the hegemonic-hetero male, or they may over-compensate by adopting some qualities that might place them more squarely in a presentation of self that is acceptable to the dominant society. They may avoid any association with that which is considered either gay or feminine, expressing, for instance, a high degree of homophobia or sexism, qualities which align them more closely with the hegemonic masculine. For those who don't over-compensate, who don't attempt to adapt but rather pursue their lives without participating in the hegemonic hetero-masculine, they succeed in presenting an alternative model of straightness and masculinity for others to witness.

On the other hand, *stylistic straight queers* (often referred to as metro-sexuals), like their counterparts in other categories, challenge the status quo through their appearance and presentation of self. Just being non-normative introduces an alternative presentation of the straight masculine. Such men are seldom seen as "regular guys." Rather, like men fitting the other categories, stylistic straight queers are viewed as exceptions—exceptions to the "rule" of hetero-normative masculinity. Note that even the term "regular guy" reflects the norm of the hetero-masculine that suggests "regular" masculinity is not sissy, not social-justice oriented in terms of gay and women's rights, unlikely to find men "electing" or risking being perceived as gay or feminine, and even less likely to be committed to, or practice behaviors that are gay or reflect feminine qualities.

Shifting Paradigms, Shifting Gears

For many men the categories of straight and masculine have become problematic and self-limiting. There is a need to broaden the range of ways we think about both masculinity and men's sexuality—creating new expanded categories that affirm those men who move into what Halberstam calls queer space and time (2005). The problem of men's heterosexuality is not the existence of sexual attractions to women, but the way these attractions are acted out by limitations on men's expression of self and their relation to others—including other men. Maintenance of the hegemonic hetero-masculine has meant amplifying homophobia—distancing men from each other except for the purpose of competition and isolation from that which is perceived feminine, including limited access to such qualities as emotional intelligence, same-sex intimacy, and vulnerability.

In his book *Picturing Men: A Century of Male Relationships in Everyday American Photography*, John Ibson (2002) presents portraits of men in relationship with other men that glow under the light of closeness, with expressions of warmth, tenderness and love. In his introduction Ibson laments the loss of emotional awareness that has become one of the defining characteristics of the hetero-masculine. Pollack (1998) equates men's homophobia as the secular successor to the witchcraft mania of any earlier time in U.S. history. We fear having boys appear or be gay; we do not, as men and women who raise male children, know how to negotiate the desperate need men have for closeness, tenderness, and arms to lie in when we sleep. This is true for the arms of the women in our lives (mothers, lovers and friends)—or the men in our lives, our "buddies"—a euphemism that creates a barrier to the feelings that inhabit men's lives, the very same needs for touch, closeness, connection that many women experience.

A recent art exhibit, a visual sociology project entitled "Shifting Gears: Finding Intimacy in Men's Friendships" (Halpern, 2005), attempts to address the need for a broader representation of men's sexuality and masculinity. The exhibit outlines the intention and need for variations of the representation of men's relationship, with themselves, and with other men. It is a project about "queering" hetero-masculinity,

highlighting the qualities that expand the notion of hetero-masculinity, moving it closer (and in ways *into*) the space of the feminine and that perceived to be gay. The exhibit:

. . . portrays close and intimate relationships between male friends. It is about making visible what is possible. It is about men who tell each other about their lives, sharing their struggles and their joys, are able to be vulnerable and be physically close. Because such relationships are rarely portrayed in popular culture and run counter to many common images of "being a man," there is little opportunity for men in our culture to find models for these friendships or to experience the value they can have. Sadly most people do not know that such relationships exist, or are possible.

Often, for males, the process of "maturing" is associated with a process of creating barriers *that discourage* such closeness. As a result, the world of adult male relationships often focuses on interactions based in the external world—sharing activities or talking about events. Although enjoyable, what is often missing is any focus on the internal world, the world of feelings, of caring and *emotional* connection, *touch*, and of simply having time to share, to talk and to listen.

Still, we don't believe that all such elements of male friendship disappear in adulthood, rather they become limited, often unspoken and hidden. Unsure of their acceptance by themselves as well as by wider society, moments of tenderness between men do not often appear in public spaces. If they happen, they take place off-stage, where tears can flow, where silliness is safe, or where listening without interruption or distractions from the larger world becomes possible—**And** even where the words, *I love you*, can be spoken.

Far too often, these intimate moments are rare, scattered among and behind those barriers—both internal and external—that burgeon as men move from childhood to adults. And even when such moments do take place, the expectation is that the relationship will continue with the pretense that they had never happened—*such closeness among men becomes fleeting.*

We have attempted to capture these relationships through a combination of photographs and narratives. ("Shifting Gears: Finding Intimate Relationships in Men's Friendships," 2005).

Creating images for queer straight men in itself is a queering of hegemonic heteromasculinity. It is an attempt to change social attitudes around both men's sexuality and masculinity and provide support for both those in the trenches of queerness and those men who are in the shadows. It turns the volume up, giving legitimacy and voice to a way of being for queer straight men (Heasley, 2003).

References

Bem, S. (1995). Dismantling gender polarization and compulsory heterosexuality: Should we turn the volume down or up? *Journal of Sex Research, 32*(4), 329–334.

Butler, J. (1990). *Gender Trouble.* New York: Routledge.

Foucault, M. (1978). *The History of Sexuality. Vol. 1.* New York: Pantheon.

Halpern, D., Heasley, R., and Wecker, N. (2005). *Shifting Gears: Finding intimacy in men's friendships: A photo-narrative project.* Funded by: Community Arts Partnership of Tompkins County/New York State Council on the Arts Decentralized Program.

Heasley, R. (2004). Crossing the borders of gendered sexuality: Queer masculinities of straight men. In C. Ingraham, (ed.). *Thinking Straight: The Promise, the Power, and the Paradox of Heterosexuality.* New York: Routledge.

Heasley, Robert B. (2005). Queer masculinities of straight men: A typology. *Men and Masculinities,* 7.3. Sage.

Hulbertam, J. (2005). *In a queer time and place: Transgender bodies, subcultural lives.* New York: New York University Press.

Ibson, J. (2002). *Picturing Men: A century of male relationships in everyday American photography.* Washington, D.C.: Smithsonian.

Pollack, W. (1999). *Real Boys: Rescuing our sons from the myths of boyhood.* New York: Henry Holt.

45 Barbara J. Risman

Gender as a Social Structure
Theory Wrestling with Activism

Gender has become a growth industry in the academy. In the years between my own college education and today, we have moved from not enough having been published in 1972 to justify my writing a literature review for an undergraduate course paper to more sociologist's studying and teaching about gender than any other single substantive area in American society. In 1998, I published *Gender Vertigo: American Families in Transition* (Risman 1998), which offered both a historical narrative about how the field of gender had developed and an integrative theoretical explanation for the tenacity of gender stratification in families. In this article, I briefly summarize my earlier argument that gender should be conceptualized as a social structure (Risman 1998) and extend it with an attempt to classify the mechanisms that help produce gendered outcomes within each dimension of the social structure. I then provide evidence from my own and others' research to support the usefulness of this theoretical schema. Finally, using gender structure as a starting point, I engage in conversation with ideas currently emerging about intersectionality and wrestle with how we might use theory in the service of social change.

Gender as Social Structure

With this theory of *gender as a social structure*, I offer a conceptual framework, a scheme to organize the confusing, almost limitless, ways in which gender has come to be defined in contemporary social science. Four distinct social scientific theoretical traditions have developed to explain gender. The first tradition focuses on how individual sex differences originate, whether biological (Udry 2000) or social in origin (Bem 1993). The second tradition, perhaps portrayed best in Epstein's (1988) *Deceptive Distinctions*, emerged as a reaction to the first and focuses on how the social structure (as opposed to biology or individual learning) creates gendered behavior. The third tradition, also a reaction to the individualist thinking of the

Excerpted from the original. Barbara J. Risman, "Gender as a Social Structure: Theory Wrestling with Activism," *Gender & Society* 18, no. 4 (August 2004): 429–450. Copyright © 2004 Sociologists for Women in Society. Reprinted by permission of SAGE Publications.

AUTHOR'S NOTE: There are too many scholars who have read this work and helped to improve it to thank each and every one. I do owe a great deal to the feminist intellectual community of Sociologists for Women in Society. Special thanks are due to Shannon Davis, Patricia Yancey Martin, Michael Schwalbe, Donald Tomaskovic-Devey, and the students in my 2003 and 2004 graduate seminars in sociology of the family, sociology of gender, and feminist thought.

first, emphasizes social interaction and accountability to others' expectations, with a focus on how "doing gender" creates and reproduces inequality (West and Zimmerman 1987). The sex-differences literature, the doing gender interactional analyses, and the structural perspectives have been portrayed as incompatible in my own early writings as well as in that of others (Fuchs Epstein 1988; Kanter 1977; Ferree 1990; Risman 1987; Risman and Schwartz 1989). England and Browne (1992) argued persuasively that this incompatibility is an illusion: All structural theories must make assumptions about individuals, and individualist theories must make presumptions about external social control. While we do gender in every social interaction, it seems naïve to ignore the gendered selves and cognitive schemas that children develop as they become cultural natives in a patriarchal world (Bem 1993). The more recent integrative approaches (Connell 2002; Lorber 1994; Ferree, Lorber, and Hess 1999; Risman 1998) treat gender as a socially constructed stratification system. This article fit squarely in the current integration tradition.

Lorber (1994) argued that gender is an institution that is embedded in all the social processes of everyday life and social organizations. She further argued that gender difference is primarily a means to justify sexual stratification. Gender is so endemic because unless we see difference, we cannot justify inequality. Lorber provided much cross-cultural, literary, and scientific evidence to show that gender difference is socially constructed and yet is universally used to justify stratification. She wrote that "the continuing purpose of gender as a modern social institution is to construct women as a group to be subordinate to men as a group" (p.

33). I share this presumption that the creation of difference is the very foundation on which inequality rests.

Martin (forthcoming) extended Lorber's (1994) use of the term "institution" in her argument that gender should be conceptualized as such. She identified the criteria for a social institution as follows: (1) Characteristic of groups; (2) persists over time and space; (3) includes distinct social practices; (4) constrains and facilitates behavior/action; (5) includes expectations, rules/norms; (6) is constituted and reconstituted by embodied agents; (7) is internalized as identities and selves; (8) includes a legitimating ideology; (9) is contradictory, rife with conflict; (10) changes continuously; (11) is organized by and permeated with power; and (12) is mutually constituted at different levels of analysis. I build on this notion of gender as an institution but find the institutional language distracting. The word "institution" is too commonly used to refer to particular aspects of society, for example, the family as an institution or corporations as institutions. My notion of gender structure meets the criteria offered by Martin (forthcoming) as well. While the language we use may differ, our goals are complementary, as we seek to situate gender as embedded not only in individuals but throughout social life (Patricia Martin, personal communication).

I prefer to define gender as a social structure because this brings gender to the same analytic plane as politics and economics, where the focus has long been on political and economic structures. While the language of structure suits my purposes, it is not ideal because despite ubiquitous usage in sociological discourse, no definition of the term "structure" is widely shared. Smelser (1988) suggested that all structuralists share the presumption that social structures exist outside individual desires or motives and that social structures at least partially explain human action. Beyond that, consensus dissipates. Blau (1977) focused solely on the constraint collective life imposes on the individual. In their influential work, Blau and his colleagues (e.g., Blau 1977; Rytina et al. 1988) argued that the concept of structure is trivialized if it is located inside an individual's head in the form of internalized norms and values. Blau focused solely on the constraint collective life imposes on the individual; structure must be conceptualized, in his view, as a force opposing individual motivation. Structural concepts must be observable, external to the individual, and independent of individual motivation. This definition of "structure" imposes a clear dualism between structure and action, with structure as constraint and action as choice.

Constraint is, of course, an important function of structure, but to focus only on structure as constraint minimizes its importance. Not only are women and men coerced into differential social roles; they often choose their gendered paths. A social structural analysis must help us understand how and why actors choose one alternative over another. A structural theory of action (e.g., Burt 1982) suggests that actors compare themselves and their options to those in structurally similar positions. From this viewpoint, actors are purposive, rationally seeking to maximize their self-perceived well-being under social-structural constraints. As Burt (1982) suggested, one can assume that actors choose the best alternatives without presuming they have either enough information to do it well or the options available to make choices that effectively serve their own interests. For example, married women may choose to do considerably more than their equitable share of child care rather than have their children do without whatever "good enough" parenting means to them if they see no likely alternative that the children's father will pick up the slack.

While actions are a function of interests, the ability to choose is patterned by the social structure. Burt (1982) suggested that norms develop when actors occupy similar network positions in the social structure and evaluate their own options vis-à-vis the alternatives of similarly situated others. From such comparisons, both norms and feelings of relative deprivation or advantage evolve. The social structure as the context of daily life creates action indirectly by shaping actors' perceptions of their interests and directly by constraining choice. Notice the phrase "similarly situated others" above. As long as women and men see themselves as different kinds of people, then women will be unlikely to compare their life options to those of men. Therein lies the power of gender. In a world where sexual anatomy is used to dichotomize human beings into types, the differentiation itself diffuses both claims to and expectations for gender equality. The social structure is not experienced as oppressive if men and women do not see themselves as similarly situated.

While structural perspectives have been applied to gender in the past (Epstein 1988; Kanter 1977), there has been a fundamental flaw in these applications. Generic structural theories applied to gender presume that if women and men were to experience identical structural conditions and role expectations, empirically observable gender differences would disappear. But this ignores not only internalized gender at the individual level (which indeed purely structural theorists deny exists) but the cultural interactional expectations that remain attached to women and men because of their gender category. A structural perspective on gender is accurate only if we realize that gender itself is a structure deeply embedded in society.

Giddens's (1984) structuration theory adds considerably more depth to this analysis of gender as a social structure with his emphasis on the recursive relationship between social structure and individuals. That is, social structures shape individuals, but simultaneously, individuals shape the social structure. Giddens embraced the transformative power of human action. He insisted that any structural theory must be concerned with reflexivity and actors' interpretations of their own lives. Social structures not only act on people; people act on social structures. Indeed, social structures are created not by mysterious forces but by human action. When people act on structure, they do so for their own reasons. We must, therefore, be concerned with why actors choose their acts. Giddens insisted that concern with meaning must go beyond the verbal justification easily available from actors because so much of social life is routine and so taken for granted that actors will not articulate, or even consider, why they act.

Gender is deeply embedded as a basis for stratification not just in our personalities, our cultural roles, or institutions but in all these, and in complicated ways. The gender structure differentiates opportunities and constraints based on sex category and thus has consequences on three dimensions: (1) At the individual level, for the development of gendered selves; (2) during interaction as men and women face different cultural expectations even when they fill the identical structural positions; and (3) in institutional domains where explicit regulations regarding resource distribution and material goods are gender specific.

Social Processes Located by Dimension in the Gender Structure

When we conceptualize gender as a social structure, we can begin to identify under what conditions and how gender inequality is being produced within each dimension. The "how" is important because without knowing the mechanisms, we cannot intervene. If indeed gender inequality in the division of household labor at this historical moment were primarily explained (and I do not suggest that it is) by gendered selves, then we would do well to consider the most effective socialization mechanisms to create fewer gender-schematic children and resocialization for adults. If, however, the gendered division of household labor is primarily constrained today by cultural expectations and moral accountability, it is those cultural images we must work to alter. But then again, if the reason many men do not equitably do their share of family labor is that men's jobs are organized so they cannot succeed at work and do their share at home, it is the contemporary American workplace that must change (Williams 2000). We may never find a universal theoretical explanation for the gendered division of household labor because universal social laws may be an illusion of twentieth-century empiricism. But in any given moment for any particular setting, the causal processes should be identifiable empirically. Gender complexity goes beyond historical specificity, as the particular causal processes that constrain men and women to do gender may be strong in one institutional setting (e.g., at home) and weaker in another (e.g., at work).

Schwalbe and his colleagues (2000, 419) suggested that there are other "generic interactive processes through which inequalities are created and reproduced in everyday life." Some of these processes include othering, subordinate adaptation, boundary maintenance, and emotion management. Schwalbe and his colleagues suggested that subordinates' adaptation plays an essential role in their own disadvantage. Subordinate adaptation helps to explain women's strategy to adapt to the gender structure. Perhaps the most common adaptation of women to subordination is "trading power for patronage" (Schwalbe et al. 2000, 426). Women, as wives and daughters, often derive significant compensatory benefits from relationships with the men in their families. Stombler and Martin (1994) similarly showed how little sisters in a fraternity trade affiliation for secondary status. In yet another setting, elite country clubs, Sherwood (2004) showed how women accept subordinate status as "B" members of clubs, in exchange for men's approval, and how when a few wives challenge men's privilege, they are threatened with social ostracism, as are their husbands. Women often gain the economic benefits of patronage for themselves and their children in exchange for their subordinate status.

One can hardly analyze the cultural expectations and interactional processes that construct gender inequality without attention to the actions of members of the dominant group. We must pay close attention to what men do to preserve their power and privilege. Schwalbe et al. (2000) suggested that one process involved is when subordinate groups effectively "other" those who they want to define as subordinate, creating devalued statuses and expectations for them. Men effectively do this in subversive ways through "politeness" norms, which construct women as "others" in need of special favors, such as protection. By opening doors and walking closer to the dirty street, men construct women as an "other" category, different and less than independent autonomous men. The cultural significance attached to male bodies signifies the capacity to dominate, to control, and to elicit deference, and such expectations are perhaps at the core of what it means for men to do gender (Michael Schwalbe, personal communication).

These are only some of the processes that might be identified for understanding how we create gender inequality based on embodied cultural expectations. None are determinative causal predictors, but instead, these are possible leads to reasonable and testable hypotheses about the production of gender. I offer them as part of a conceptual scheme to help us think about how different kinds of processes are implicated at each dimension of the gender structure. Martin's (2003) research on men and women workers in a corporate setting can help illustrate how much a conceptual scheme might work. She wrote about a male vice-president asking his female counterpart to pick up a phone call, which she does unreflectively, but she soon thereafter identifies this request as problematic. Martin presented this as an example of how interactional status expectations attached to sex category create inequality within professional relationships. This empirical example supports the thesis that shared but routine cultural expectations re-create inequality even without the conscious intent of the actors. Gender structure theory does not presume that this man and women do not bring gendered selves to the office to accept Martin's analysis. In fact, one might suggest that a vice-president who had more thoroughly internalized traditional femininity norms would not have noticed the inequity at all.

Nor does one need to have a company that has purged all discriminatory practices from its policies to see the import of the cultural expectations that Martin identified. A meta-analysis that looks at the effects of gender inequality in the workplace should integrate findings about social processes at the level of individual identities, cultural expectations, and organizational practices. In the next section of this article, I provide empirical illustrations of this conceptual scheme of gender as a social structure.

Empirical Illustrations

I begin with an example from my own work of how conceptualizing gender as a social structure helps to organize the findings and even push forward an understanding of the resistance toward an egalitarian division of family work among contemporary American heterosexual couples. This is an area of research that incorporates a concern with nurturing children, housework, and emotional labor. My own question, from as early as graduate school, was whether men could mother well enough that those who care about children's well-being would want them to do so. Trained in the warfare model of science, my dissertation was a test of structural versus individualist theories (Kanter 1977) of men's mothering. As someone who considered herself a structuralist of some generic sort, I hypothesized (Risman 1983) that when men were forced into the social role of primary parent, they could become just like mothers: The parenting role (e.g., a measure of family structure) would wipe out the effects of individual gendered selves in my models. What I found was, alas, more complicated. At the time, I concluded that men could "mother" but did not do so in ways identical to women (Risman 1983). After having been influenced by studies

showing that tokenism worked differently when men were the tokens (Williams 1992; Zimmer 1988) and that money could not buy power in marriage for women quite as it seemed to for men (Brines 1994; Ferree 1990), I came to the realization that gender itself was a structure and would not disappear when men and women were distributed across the variety of structural positions that organize our social world.

To ask the question, Can men mother, presuming that gender itself is a social structure leads us to look at all the ways that gender constrains men's mothering and under what conditions those change. Indeed, one of my most surprising, and unanticipated, findings was that single fathers who were primary caretakers came to describe themselves more often than other men with adjectives such as "nurturant," "warm," and "child oriented," those adjectives we social scientists use to measure femininity. Single fathers' identities changed based on their experiences as primary parents. In my research, men whose wives worked full-time did not, apparently, do enough mothering to have such experiences influence their own sense of selves. Most married fathers hoard the opportunity for leisure that frees them from the responsibilities of parenting that might create such identity change. My questions became more complicated but more useful when I conceptualized gender as a social structure. When and under what conditions do gendered selves matter? When do interactional expectations have the power to overcome previously internalized predispositions? What must change at the institutional level to allow for expectations to change at the interactional level? Does enough change on the interactional dimension shift the moral accountability that then leads to collective action in social organizations? Could feminist parents organize and create a social movement that forces workplaces to presume that valuable workers also have family responsibilities?

These questions led me to try to identify the conditions that enable women and men to actually succeed in creating egalitarian relationships. My next research project was an in-depth interview and qualitative study of heterosexual couples raising children who equally shared the work of earning a living and the family labor of child care, homemaking, and emotional work. The first interesting piece of data was how hard it was to find such people in the end of the twentieth century, even when recruiting at daycare centers, parent-teacher associations, university venues, and feminist newsletters (all in the southeastern United States). Three out of four volunteer couples failed the quite generous criteria for inclusion: Working approximately the same number of hours in the labor force (within five hours per week), sharing the household labor and child care tasks within a 60/40 split, and both partners' describing the relationship as equitable. There are clearly fewer couples who live equal lives than those who wish fervently that they did so.

What I did find from intensive interviews and home observations with 20 such couples was that the conditions that enabled their success spread across each dimension of the gender structure. Although I would have predicted otherwise (having once been committed to a purely structural theory of human behavior), selves and personalities matter. The women in my sample were strong, directive women married to relatively laidback men. Given the overwhelming gendered expectations for men's privilege in heterosexual marriage, this should have been expected, but to someone with my theoretical background, it was not. Less surprising to me, the women in these couples also had at least the income and career status of their partners and often bettered them. But this is not usually enough to dent men's privilege, or we would have far more egalitarian marriages by now. In addition, these couples were ideologically committed to equality and to sharing. They often tried explicitly to create social relationships with others who held similar values, for example, by joining liberal churches to meet like-minded others. Atypical gendered selves and shared feminist-inspired cultural expectations were important conditions for equality, but they were not enough. Men's workplace flexibility mattered as well. Nearly every father in this sample was employed in a job with flexible working hours. Many women worked in jobs with flexibility as well, but not as uniformly as their male partners. These were privileged, educated workers for whom workplace flexibility was sometimes simply luck (e.g., a father who lost a corporate job and decided to sell real estate) but more often was a conscious choice (e.g., clinical psychologists choosing to teach at a small college to have more control over working hours despite decreased earning power). Thus, these couples experienced enabling contexts at the level of their individual selves, feminist ideology to help shape the cultural expectations in their most immediate environments (within the dyad and among at least some friends), and the privilege within the economy to have or find flexible jobs. By attending to each dimension of the gender structure, I amassed a more effective explanation for their ability to negotiate fair relationships than I could have without attention to selves, couple interaction, and their workplaces. The implications for feminist social change are direct: We cannot simply attend to socializing children differently, nor creating moral accountability for men to share family work, nor fighting for flexible, family-friendly workplaces. We must attend to all simultaneously.

The research on gender in occupational settings (Williams 1992; Zimmer 1988) and quantitative studies of household division of labor (Brines 1994; Greenstein 2000) also provide good examples of how using gender structure as a conceptual framework can help organize meta-analytic reviews of the literature to create cumulative knowledge. Kanter's (1977) early structural hypotheses presumed that tokenism per se was an important mechanism that explained women's and men of color's continued subordination in the labor force. But as research testing this tokenism hypothesis expanded to include men in women's jobs, it became clear that the theory was not indeed only about numbers. Tokenism did not work the same way for white men. Men tokens rode glass escalators while women and racial minorities hit glass ceilings (Reskin 1998; Williams 1992; Yoder 1991). Gender and race remained important; the cultural interactional expectations remained different even in integrated work settings. Status expectations (Ridgeway 1991; Ridgeway et al. 1998) favored men and devalued women, whatever their numbers. We can conceptualize this as the interactional cultural level impeding further changes that realignments on the institutional dimension would predict.

Similarly, quantitative research findings about the household division of labor have made it quite clear that even when women work outside the home full-time, they shoulder the majority of household and child care. Over time, researchers have tested a variety of theories for why, sometimes presuming that as time pressures and resources equal-

ized between husbands and wives, so too would the burden of household labor (Bianchi et al. 2000; Coverman 1985; Pleck 1985; Presser 1994; Shelton 1992). Not so. The data are unequivocal. Even in dual worker families, women do considerably more work and retain the majority of responsibility, even if they do share (or perhaps delegate) some of the family work to husbands and children. Sociology has provided solid evidence (Fenstermaker Berk 1985; Greenstein 1996, 2000; Robinson and Milkie 1998; Twiggs, McQuillan, and Ferree 1999) that domestic work, whether cleaning toilets or changing diapers, is as much about the production and display of gender as it is about clean toilets and dry bottoms. But such information only gets us so far analytically. We can integrate such research by asking questions about when and how the different effects of the gender structure remain resistant to change and when some progressive feminist change has occurred. Do young women in the twenty-first century, raised by feminists, successfully negotiate fair families? Or does the moral accountability to do gender as mothers and wives combined with devalued status in the workplace still defeat even women socialized for equality? Does workplace flexibility for men allow feminist women more success in their negotiations at the family level? The conceptualization of gender as a structure, and attention to the mechanisms at work in each dimension of the gender structure, helps to frame the kind of research that might answer such queries.

Gender structure theory allows us to try to disentangle the "how" questions without presuming that there is one right answer for all places, times, and contexts. It is easy to illustrate that a combination of gender wage gap and the organization of careers requiring inflexible hours and full-time commitment pushes married mothers outside the labor force and creates stressful lives for mothers who remain within it, married or not. But we must still ask why this is true for women but not men. Perhaps, under some conditions, women socialized for emphasized femininity do indeed hold themselves accountable for being personally responsible for more than good enough mothering and sparkling households. Research should identify under what conditions and to what extent gendered selves help to account for objective inequalities (e.g., women working more hours a day than their partners) and when other factors are more significant. My own hypothesis is that feminist women are often defeated in their attempt at egalitarian heterosexual relationship by cultural gendered interactional expectations. Within the past year, memoirs have been written by young feminists, academics, and daughters of famous women's movement leaders (Fox 2003; Hanauer 2002) bemoaning the impossible expectations facing career women who choose motherhood as well. Similarly, a recent feminist cyberspace conversation on the Listserve of Sociologists for Women in Society described the struggle to combine motherhood and career in the academy in nearly as despairing a tone as did Arlie Hochschild (1975) in her classic article first published three decades ago. I have yet to see recent memoirs, or hear of painful listserver conversations, among twenty-first-century fathers. Little cultural change has occurred around fathering. Most men are still not morally responsible for the quality of family life, and women have yet to discover how to avoid being held accountable.

Gender structures are even more complicated than my discussion suggests thus far because how gender identities are constructed on the individual and cultural dimensions vary tremendously over time and space. Even within contemporary American society, gender structures vary by community, social class, ethnicity, and race.

Theory Wrestling with Activism

Within any structure of inequality, perhaps the most important question a critical scholar must ask is, What mechanisms are currently constructing inequality, and how can these be transformed to create a more just world? If as critical scholars, we forget to keep our eye on social transformation, we may slip without intention into the implicitly value-free role of social scientists who study gender merely to satisfy intellectual curiosity (Risman 2003). The central questions for feminists must include a focus on social transformation, reducing inequality, and improving the status of women. A concern with social change brings us to the thorny and as yet too little explored issue of agency. When do subordinate groups collectively organize to challenge their oppression? When do superordinate groups mobilize to resist? How do we know agency when we see it, and how can we support feminist versions of it?

Feminist scholarship must seek to understand how and why gender gets done, consciously or not, to help those who hope to stop doing it. I end by focusing our attention on what I see as the next frontier for feminist change agents: A focus on the processes that might spur change at the interactional or cultural dimension of the gender structure. We have begun to socialize our children differently, and while identities are hardly postgender, the sexism inherent in gender socialization is now widely recognized. Similarly, the organizational rules and institutional laws have by now often been rewritten to be gender neutral, at least in some nations. While gender-neutral laws in a gender-stratified society may have short-term negative consequences (e.g., displaced homemakers who never imagined having to support themselves after marriage), we can hardly retreat from equity in the law or organizations. It is the interactional and cultural dimension of gender that has yet to be tackled with a social change agenda.

Cognitive bias is one of the mechanisms by which inequality is re-created in everyday life. There are, however, documented mechanisms for decreasing the salience of such bias (Bielby 2000; Reskin 2000; Ridgeway and Correll 2000). When we consciously manipulate the status expectations attached to those in subordinate groups, by highlighting their legitimate expertise beyond the others in the immediate social setting, we can begin to challenge the nonconscious hierarchy that often goes unnoticed. Similarly, although many subordinates adapt to their situation by trading power for patronage, when they refuse to do so, interaction no longer flows smoothly, and change may result. Surely, when wives refuse to trade power for patronage, they can rock the boat as well as the cradle.

These are only a few examples of interactive processes that can help to explain the reproduction of inequality and to envision strategies for disrupting inequality. We need to understand when and how inequality is constructed and reproduced to deconstruct it. I have argued before (Risman 1998) that because the gender structure so defines the category woman as subordinate, the deconstruction of the category itself is the best, indeed the only sure way, to end gender subordination. There is no reason, except the transitional vertigo that will accompany the process to dismantle it, that a utopian vision

of a just world involves any gender structure at all. Why should we need to elaborate on the biological distinction between the sexes? We must accommodate reproductive differences for the process of biological replacement, but there is no a priori reason we should accept any other role differentiation simply based on biological sex category. Before accepting any gender elaboration around biological sex category, we ought to search suspiciously for the possibly subtle ways such differentiation supports men's privilege. Once two salient groups exist, the process of in-group and out-group distinctions and in-group opportunity hoarding become possible. While it may be that for some competitive sports, single-sex teams are necessary, beyond that, it seems unlikely that any differentiation or cultural elaboration around sex category has a purpose beyond differentiation in support of stratification.

Feminist scholarship always wrestles with the questions of how one can use the knowledge we create in the interest of social transformation. As feminist scholars, we must talk beyond our own borders. This kind of theoretical work becomes meaningful if we can eventually take it public. Feminist sociology must be public sociology (Burawoy forthcoming). We must eventually take what we have learned from our theories and research beyond professional journals to our students and to those activists who seek to disrupt and so transform gender relations. We must consider how the knowledge we create can help those who desire a more egalitarian social world to refuse to do gender at all, or to do it with rebellious reflexiveness to help transform the world around them. For those without a sociological perspective, social change through socialization and through legislation are the easiest to envision. We need to shine a spotlight on the dimension of cultural interactional expectations as it is here that work needs to begin.

We must remember, however, that much doing gender at the individual and interactional levels gives pleasure as well as reproduces inequality, and until we find other socially acceptable means to replace that opportunity for pleasure, we can hardly advocate for its cessation. The question of how gender elaboration has been woven culturally into the fabric of sexual desire deserves more attention. Many of our allies believe that "viva la difference" is required for sexual passion, and few would find a postgender society much of a feminist utopia if it came at the cost of sexual play. No one wants to be part of a revolution where she or he cannot dirty dance.

In conclusion, I have made the argument that we need to conceptualize gender as a social structure, and by doing so, we can analyze the ways in which gender is embedded at the individual, interactional, and institutional dimensions of our society. This situates gender at the same level of significance as the economy and the polity. In addition, this framework helps us to disentangle the relative strength of a variety of causal mechanisms for explaining any given outcome without dismissing the possible relevance of other processes that are situated at different dimensions of analysis. Once we have a conceptual tool to organize the encyclopedic research on gender, we can systematically build on our knowledge and progress to understanding the strength and direction of causal processes within a complicated multidimensional recursive theory. I have also argued that our concern with intersectionality must continue to be paramount but that different structures of inequality have different infrastructures and perhaps different influential causal mechanisms at any given historical moment. Therefore, we need to follow a both/and strategy, to understand gender structure, race structure, and other structures of inequality as they currently operate, while also systematically paying attention to how these axes of domination intersect. Finally, I have suggested that we pay more attention to doing research and writing theory with explicit attention to how our work can come to be "fighting words" (Collins 1998) to help transform as well as inform society. If we can identify the mechanisms that create gender, perhaps we can offer alternatives to them and so use our scholarly work to contribute to envisioning a feminist utopia.

References

Andersen, Margaret, and Patricia Hill Collins. 1994. *Race, class, and gender: An anthology.* Belmont, CA: Wadsworth.

Baca Zinn, Maxine, and Bonnie Thornton Dill. 1994. *Women of color in U.S. society.* Philadelphia: Temple University Press.

Bem, Sandra. 1993. *The lenses of gender.* New Haven, CT: Yale University Press.

Bianchi, Suzanne M., Melissa A. Milkie, Liana C. Sayer, and John P. Robinson. 2000. Is anyone doing the housework? Trends in the gender division of household labor. *Social Forces* 79(1):191–228.

Bielby, William T. 2000. Minimizing workplace gender and racial bias. *Contemporary Sociology* 29(1):120–29.

Blau, Peter. 1977. *Inequality and heterogeneity.* New York: Free Press.

Bonilla-Silva, Eduardo. 1997. Rethinking racism: Toward a structural interpretation. *American Sociological Review* 62(3):465–80.

Brines, Julie. 1994. Economic dependency, gender, and the division of labor at home. *American Journal of Sociology* 100(3):652–88.

Burawoy, Michael. Forthcoming. Public sociologies contradictions, dilemmas and possibilities. *Social Forces.*

Burt, Ronald S. 1982. *Toward a structural theory of action*. New York: Academic Press.

Calhoun, Cheshire. 2000. *Feminism, the family, and the politics of the closet: Lesbian and gay displacement*. New York: Oxford University Press.

Collins, Patricia Hill. 1990. *Black feminist thought: Knowledge, consciousness, and the politics of empowerment*. New York: Routledge.

———. 1998. *Fighting words: Black women and the search for justice*. Minneapolis: University of Minnesota Press.

———. 2004. *Black sexual politics: African Americans, gender, and the new racism*. New York: Routledge.

Connell, R. W. 1987. *Gender and power: Society, the person, and sexual politics*. Stanford, CA: Stanford University Press.

———. 2002. *Gender: Short introductions*. Malden, MA: Blackwell.

Coverman, Shelley. 1985. Explaining husbands' participation in domestic labor. *Sociological Quarterly* 26(1):81–97.

England, Paula, and Irene Browne. 1992. Internalization and constraint in women's subordination. *Current Perspectives in Social Theory* 12:97–123.

Espiritu, Yen Le. 1997. *Asian American women and men: Labor, laws, and love*. Thousand Oaks, CA: Sage.

Fenstermaker Berk, Sarah. 1985. *The gender factory: The apportionment of work in American households*. New York: Plenum.

Ferree, Myra Marx. 1990. Beyond separate spheres: Feminism and family research. *Journal of Marriage and the Family* 53(4):866–84.

Ferree, Myra Marx, Judith Lorber, and Beth Hess. 1999. *Revisioning gender*. Thousand Oaks, CA: Sage.

Fox, Faulkner. 2003. *Dispatches from a not-so-perfect life: On how I learned to love the house, the man, the child*. New York: Harmony Books.

Fuchs Epstein, Cynthia. 1988. *Deceptive distinctions: Sex, gender, and the social order*. New Haven, CT: Yale University Press.

Giddens, Anthony. 1984. *The constitution of society: Outline of the theory of structuration*. Berkeley: University of California Press.

Greenstein, Theodore N. 1996. Husbands' participation in domestic labor: Interactive effects of wives' and husbands' gender ideologies. *Journal of Marriage and the Family* 58:585–95.

———. 2000. Economic dependence, gender, and the division of labor in the home: A replication and extension. *Journal of Marriage and the Family* 62(2):322–35.

Hanauer, Cathi. 2002. *The bitch in the house: 26 women tell the truth about sex, solitude, work, motherhood, and marriage*. New York: William Morrow.

Hochschild, Arlie. 1975. Inside the clockwork of male careers. In *Women and the power to change*, edited by Florence Howe. New York: McGraw Hill. Repr. in *The commercialization of intimate life*. Berkeley: University of California Press, 2003.

Kanter, Rosabeth. 1977. *Men and women of the corporation*. New York: Basic Books.

Lorber, Judith. 1994. *Paradoxes of gender*. New Haven, CT: Yale University Press.

Martin, Patricia. 2003. "Said and done" versus "saying and doing": Gendering practices, practicing gender at work. *Gender & Society* 17:342–66.

———. Forthcoming. Gender as a social institution. *Social Forces*.

Myers, Kristen A., Cynthia D. Anderson, and Barbara J. Risman, eds. 1998. *Feminist foundations: Toward transforming society*. Thousand Oaks, CA: Sage.

Pleck, Joseph H. 1985. *Working wives/working husbands*. Beverly Hills, CA: Sage.

Presser, Harriet B. 1994. Employment schedules among dual-earner spouses and the division of household labor by gender. *American Sociological Review* 59(3):348–64.

Reskin, Barbara. 1998. *The realities of affirmative action in employment*. Washington, DC: ASA.

———. 2000. The proximate causes of employment discrimination. *Contemporary Sociology* 29(2):319–28.

———. 2002. How did the poison get in Mr. Bartlett's stomach? Motives and mechanisms in explaining inequality. Presidential address given at the 97th annual meetings of the

American Sociological Association, Chicago, August.

Rich, Adrienne. 1980. Compulsory heterosexuality and lesbian existence. *Signs: Journal of Women in Culture and Society* 5(4):631–60.

Ridgeway, Cecilia L. 1991. The social construction of status value: Gender and other nominal characteristics. *Social Forces* 70(2):367–86.

———. 1997. Interaction and the conservation of gender inequality: Considering employment. *American Sociological Review* 62(2):218–35.

———. 2001. Gender, status, and leadership. *Journal of Social Issues* 57(4):637–55.

Ridgeway, Cecilia L., and Shelley J. Correll. 2000. Limiting inequality through interaction: The end(s) of gender. *Contemporary Sociology* 29:110–20.

Ridgeway, Cecilia L., Kathy J. Kuipers, Elizabeth Heger Boyle, and Dawn T. Robinson. 1998. How do status beliefs develop? The role of resources and interactional experience. *American Sociological Review* 63:331–50.

Ridgeway, Cecilia L., and Lynn Smith-Lovin. 1999. The gender system and interaction. *Annual Review of Sociology* 25:191–216.

Risman, Barbara J. 1983. Necessity and the invention of mothering. Ph.D. diss., University of Washington.

———. 1987. Intimate relationships from a microstructural perspective: Mothering men. *Gender & Society* 1:6–32.

———. 1998. *Gender vertigo: American families in transition*. New Haven, CT: Yale University Press.

———. 2003. Valuing all flavors of feminist sociology. *Gender & Society* 17:659–63.

Risman, Barbara J., and Pepper Schwartz. 1989. *Gender in intimate relationships*. Belmont, CA: Wadsworth.

Robinson, John P., and Melissa A. Milkie. 1998. Back to the basics: Trends in and role determinants of women's attitudes toward housework. *Journal of Marriage and the Family* 60(1):205–18.

Rytina, Steve, Peter Blau, Jenny Blum, and Joseph Schwartz. 1988. Inequality and intermarriage: Paradox of motive and constraint. *Social Forces* 66:645–75.

Schwalbe, Michael, Sandra Godwin, Daphne Holden, Douglas Schrock, Shealy Thompson, and Michele Wolkomir. 2000. Generic processes in the reproduction of inequality: An interactionist analysis. *Social Forces* 79(2):419–52.

Scott, Joan Wallach. 1997. Comment on Hawkesworth's "Confounding Gender." *Signs: Journal of Women in Culture and Society* 22(3):697–702.

Shelton, Beth Anne. 1992. *Women, men and time: Gender differences in paid work, housework and leisure*. Westport, CT: Greenwood.

Sherwood, Jessica. 2004. Talk about country clubs: Ideology and the reproduction of privilege. Ph.D. diss., North Carolina State University.

Smelser, Neil J. 1988. Social structure. In *Handbook of sociology*, edited by Neil J. Smelser. Beverly Hills, CA: Sage.

Staples, Robert. 1990. Social inequality and Black sexual pathology: The essential relationship. *Black Scholar* 21(3):29–37.

Stombler, Mindy, and Patricia Yancey Martin. 1994. Bring women in, keeping women down: Fraternity "little sister" organizations. *Journal of Contemporary Ethnography* 23:150–84.

Tilly, Charles. 1999. *Durable inequality*. Berkeley: University of California Press.

Twiggs, Joan E., Julia McQuillan, and Myra Marx Ferree. 1999. Meaning and measurement: Reconceptualizing measures of the division of household labor. *Journal of Marriage and the Family* 61(3):712–24.

Udry, J. Richard. 2000. Biological limits of gender construction. *American Sociological Review* 65:443–57.

West, Candace, and Don Zimmerman. 1987. Doing gender. *Gender & Society* 1:125–51.

Williams, Christine. 1992. The glass escalator: Hidden advantages for men in the "female" professions. *Social Problems* 39:253–67.

Williams, Joan. 2000. *Unbending gender: Why family and work conflict and what to do about it*. New York: Oxford University Press.

Yoder, Janice. 1991. Rethinking tokenism. *Social Problems* 5:178–92.

Zimmer, Lynn. 1988. Tokenism and women in the workplace: The limits of gender-neutral theory. *Social Problems* 35:64–77.

When the Girls Are Men

Negotiating Gender and Sexual Dynamics in a Study of Drag Queens

The dilemmas of feminist research were never more apparent to us than when we, as lesbian activists, spent more than three years hanging out with and studying drag queens. "Strangers in a strange land" is how one reviewer described our "fieldwork, focus groups, and tribal living in the wilds of Key West," where we came to count "a randy band of gay men" as our friends.[1] We could never have written our book, *Drag Queens at the 801 Cabaret* (Rupp and Taylor 2003b), without the kind of participatory and collaborative methods that have played such a central role in feminist research. But the experience also led us to reflect on the complex gender and sexual dynamics at play in such a project. Ironically, we eventually realized that being women and lesbians facilitated rather than hampered our entrée into the world of the drag queens, even as our gender and sexuality also complicated the research process. We were also keenly aware that the ways in which we were different from the drag queens contributed to a continually shifting balance of power between them as men and the stars of the show and us as the tellers of their stories. And, since facilitating as well as documenting social change is central to feminist research, we came to understand how much gender and sexuality entered into those aspects of the study.

Our consideration of the power dynamics in and the social change goals of our project builds on a rich body of literature on feminist research.[2] We agree with Shulamit Reinharz (1992) that feminist research encompasses a plurality of methods or techniques for collecting evidence—such as ethnography, interviews, surveys, oral histories, discourse analysis, archival research, experimental research, content analysis, action research, genealogical analysis, and other modes of inquiry—none inherently more feminist than the others. What is distinctive about feminist methodology is not the use of particular techniques but rather an epistemological understanding of how knowledge is generated, how it is reported, and how it is used (Harding 1987, 1991; Fonow and Cook 1991; Naples 2003). In particular, self-reflexivity about the impact of researchers' gender and—if only recently much attended to—sexual identity on the research process is crucial.[3]

Scholars such as Esther Newton (1972, 1993, 1996), Walter Williams (1986, 1996), Sabine Lang (1990, 1996), Kath Weston (1991, 1996), Elizabeth Kennedy

---

Excerpted from the original. Verta Taylor and Leila J. Rupp, "When the Girls Are Men: Negotiating Gender and Sexual Dynamics in a Study of Drag Queens," *Signs* 30, no. 4 (2005): 2115–2139. Copyright © 2005 by the University of Chicago. Reprinted by permission of the University of Chicago.

and Madeline Davis (1993, 1996), Stephen Murray (1987, 1996), Don Kulick (1998), and Annick Prieur (1998), who have studied gay, lesbian, and transgender communities through participatory and engaged methods, have had to negotiate relationships fraught with gender, sexual, and other tensions. These writings suggest that gender and sexuality can impede understanding and rapport, on the one hand, and enrich interpretation, on the other, in some of the same ways that differences of race and class can. In this article we explore the impact of our negotiations of complex power relationships on the course and outcome of our research on the 801 Girls, a troupe of self-identified gay men who perform as drag queens in Key West, Florida. We begin by introducing the drag queens, their role in the community, and their public performances, which challenge excessively restrictive and oppressive gender and sexual categories. We then discuss the methods we used to conduct the research and the ways that gender and sexuality came into play in every phase of the project. The heart of our consideration of the dilemmas of feminist research focuses on the gender and sexual dynamics involved in negotiating the power relationships between us as researchers and the drag queens as research participants and in structuring the research to facilitate social change.

The 801 Girls

Key West is a quirky tropical community almost entirely dependent on tourism, closer to Cuba than to Miami, and tenuously attached to the rest of the United States by a highway stretching across a chain of tiny islands. Diverse communities coexist in Key West—Cuban, Bahamian,

hippie, gay—and the unofficial philosophy calls for tolerance, recognition that we are all, as an omnipresent bumper sticker puts it, "one human family." Although a place unto itself, Key West is not unlike other gay tourist destinations. And the drag shows at the 801 Cabaret, although notable for the extent of interaction with the audience, represent a style of drag that can be found throughout the United States and even around the globe.

However, what is not so typical is that drag queens are part of the daily life and even part of the lure of Key West. During tourist season the city holds a "drag race" in which drag queens run down the street teetering on their high-heeled shoes. On New Year's Eve, Sushi, the house queen at the 801 Cabaret, sits in a giant red high-heeled shoe dangling over Duval Street, the main street that runs from the Atlantic Ocean to the Gulf of Mexico, and on the stroke of midnight descends to mark the start of the new year. What started as a gay alternative to the conch shell lowered at Sloppy Joe's at the other end of town was in 2003 broadcast live on CNN. This is just one sign of the centrality of drag queens to Key West's tourist industry.

The 801 Girls are full-time drag queens, some of whom perform every night of the year. They are a fixture on Duval Street, where every night before the show they drum up business by handing out flyers and bantering with passersby. Their regular appearances at holiday events, gay pride celebrations, local festivities, and fund-raisers make them celebrities in Key West and beyond. They are central to community life.

But if the drag queens are celebrities, they are also marginal, both economically and socially. They generally earn salaries of less than $200 a week, and their tips, which they pool, vary wildly from night to night and season to season. And to some extent an unsavory reputation clings to them. "Freaks, we're still considered that," says Milla. "Some are just looking at freaks," adds Inga. It is an odd combination of celebrity and hostility. In the community of Key West, there are some who point to the drag queens as a symbol of the town's diversity and openness. However, drag queens here as elsewhere meet with a mixed reception even in the queer movement. Up against the assimilationist tendency of gay and lesbian activism, from the homophile movement of the 1950s to the present, drag queens have been an embarrassment (D'Emilio 1983; Adam 1995). In the confrontational wing of the movement, however, drag has long played a central role in the construction of a public gay identity and has often been used as a political tactic in marches and demonstrations (Newton 1972; Rupp 1999).

The group of drag queens known as the 801 Girls has changed and grown in size over time, but during our research it consisted of eight regulars. Sushi, whose mother is Japanese and late father was from Texas, has a beautiful tall, slender body with thin but muscled arms and a dancer's legs. She never really looks much like a man, even when dressed as Gary, and in the shows she talks about her "mangina" and asks the audience if she should get breasts.[4] Sushi in fact passed as a woman for a period of time, including while hooking on the streets of Los Angeles, but then realized that wanting to wear women's clothes did not mean that she wanted to be a woman, or, as she often puts it, "to cut off her dick." It just meant that she was a drag queen. Sushi is the house queen: she is responsible for hiring and paying the girls and keeping

them in line, and, as a talented seamstress, she also makes most of the costumes.

Milla, who left Key West shortly after we completed the research, is, like Sushi, beautiful in drag. Her mother is Italian, and her late father was a military man from Florida. With her olive skin and dark eyes and fondness for Erykah Badu numbers, Milla is often taken onstage for African American, and she sometimes describes herself as a white gay man trapped in a black woman's body. She also describes herself as "omnisexual," as Milla is attractive to (and her devoted fans include) men and women of all sexual identities.

Kylie is Sushi's best friend from his hometown of Kaiser, Oregon, as Sushi announces in nearly every show. They began dressing in drag together in high school as a way both to attract attention and to hide behind a costume and makeup. For a time, Sushi lived secretly in the closet of Kylie's parents' apartment in Los Angeles, and when Sushi went out hooking, Kylie went along to keep her company. They are incredibly close. Kylie hosts the Saturday Night Sex Show, where, at the end of the night, she strips to "Queen of the Night," leaving on her wig and makeup.

R. V. Beaumont, who grew up in a small town in Ohio, has a background in theater and learned to do drag while working at Disney World. She has a penchant for Bette Midler numbers. At the end of the weekend shows, she also performs "What Makes a Man a Man," a plaintive ballad about the difficult life of a drag queen, while removing her wig, makeup, and dress and transforming herself back into a man.

Margo is a painfully thin, deep-voiced sixty-something New Yorker who only began performing drag at the age of fiftynine, after raising a black adopted child as a single gay Jewish man and succeeding in a variety of careers, from interior design to teaching. She is introduced in the shows as "the oldest living drag queen in captivity," and her commentary includes talk about Stonewall and gay pride. Out of drag, as David Felstein, he writes a column for the local gay paper.

Scabola Feces, from Providence, Rhode Island, has no intention of looking beautiful, as her name suggests. She is HIV-positive, very thin, has large expressive eyes, a raspy smoker's voice, and a big evil-sounding laugh. Scabby's numbers are clever and outrageous critiques of conventional gender and sexual norms: she performs, for example, Karen Carpenter as a vomiting bulimic, a scorned woman wearing a ripped-up bridal gown in "Wedding Bell Blues," and Monica Lewinsky clutching a photo of Bill Clinton.

Inga, the "Swedish bombshell," like R. R., Scabby, and Milla, comes from a theater background. She really is Swedish, tall, blond, big, soft, and adorable, with deep dimples. She did the choreography for the troupe before she left the 801 to perform at Divas (now called Aqua), a club down the street, but she frequently comes by to visit.

Gugi Gomez joined the troupe when Inga left. She's Puerto Rican, from Chicago, and as Rov is handsome, with black curly hair, beautiful dark eyes, and a sweet face. Rov is shy, while Gugi is aggressive and outgoing. She moves and dances seductively, and she performs as Cuban, hosting a show called "A Night in Havana." Gugi, like Sushi and Milla, lived for a while as a woman.

After our first few times at the cabaret, we were convinced that what was taking place in the shows was a genre of political theater. Elsewhere we argue that the drag shows at the 801 affirm gay, lesbian, bisexual, transgendered, and transsexual identi-

ties; empower participants and audience members; and educate heterosexuals in attendance about gay life (Rupp and Taylor 2003b; Taylor, Rupp, and Gamson 2004). The drag queens regularly express pride in their own identities. "Did I tell you that I'm a drag queen?" Sushi asks the audience. Another night, using her performance to trouble gender and sexuality, she explains, "A drag queen is somebody who knows he has a dick and two balls." Moving out from their own identities as drag queens, the performers embrace other queer identities. Margo performs "I Am What I Am," a gay anthem that concludes with her removing her wig as a sign of pride in her identity as a gay man in drag. Her introduction to the number reaches out to all audience members: "The next song I'm going to do for you will explain to everyone who, what, and why we are. . . . We are drag queens, and we are proud of what we do. Whether you are gay or straight, lesbian, bisexual, trisexual, transgender, asexual, or whatever in between, be proud of who you are!"

Their public pronouncements and banter during the shows reflect the conviction that their performances have the potential to change people's thinking about gay life and the world of drag. Interviewed in the Key West newspaper for a story about drag queens, Sushi commented, "We're not just lip-synching up here, we're changing lives by showing people what we're all about" (Schmida 2001, 1C). To us she confided, "I have a platform now to teach the world." R. V. thinks that when straight people leave the bar, "they have a better, more tolerant understanding of what we're all about, what gay people are about. We change their lives." Sushi says, "They come from all over and fan out, to Idaho and Oklahoma, and we make a difference. We liberate them a little bit." In all these ways, the 801 Girls enact queer theory's troubling of gender and sexuality.[5] We took as our theoretical project the development of a framework for evaluating when cultural performances such as drag shows are political and when not (see Taylor, Rupp, and Gamson 2004).

The Research Process

Studying the drag queens required immersion in their world in a number of ways. In the course of our research, we attended their weekly meetings, visited with them on the street and in their dressing room before the show, attended social functions and shared meals, went to the beach together, talked with them on the phone, and attended community events where they performed. We conducted, tape-recorded, and transcribed life histories of twelve performers. We also observed, tape-recorded, and transcribed fifty performances, including the dialogue, music, and audience interactions.

To assess the role of the 801 performers in the larger gay and lesbian and Key West communities, we examined over a three-year period all stories that contained references to the drag queens in the weekly gay newspaper *Celebrate!* and in the mainstream Key West media. In addition, we structured the research process to bring the drag queens, gay and lesbian community members, and wider community into conversations about the drag queens' performances. We conducted twelve focus groups with forty audience members who attended the performances, and we held informal conversations and short interviews with fifty-five additional spectators. We also followed up by holding individual and group discussions with the drag queens about their reactions to the book.

Like anthropologists who travel to study cultures very different from their own, we probably should have been far more worried about whether we as women academics, even if lesbians, could really get to know a troupe of gay male drag queens who were different from us in so many ways. Most of them have no more than a high school education, and they live economically precarious lives. The drag queen life involves heavy drinking, drug use, sexual promiscuity. But despite the chasms of gender, class, education, lifestyle, and ethnicity, we developed close personal relationships, with some of the performers more than others, that allowed us to understand their world.

At some point, in fact, we realized that our differences of gender and sexuality actually eased our entrée into this world and made participation easier. It had not escaped our notice that the classic work on drag queens, *Mother Camp* (Newton 1972), was also written by a lesbian. Recently we asked the girls if they thought our being lesbians affected our ability to study them. Although they didn't really address the question, their responses suggest that what we are not, as well as how they feel about us (and us about them), proved to be crucial. As Margo put it, "You weren't bitchy. We gave you the interviews, which I think proves how we feel about you." "You weren't bitchy queens," added Desiray, one of the cast members who joined at the end of our research. Piped up Scabby, "We love you girls." Kylie, who took a while to trust us, commented, "You guys were interesting to talk to. And it was obvious that you liked us, but I didn't know, really, what to think of you, it took a while." From our perspective, in ways that we discuss below, the drag queens' maleness helped to balance the power we held as educated and privileged researchers. We were in so many ways outside their normal social worlds and for that reason, paradoxically, could participate without too much disruption. If, as Newton (1996) describes, there is an "erotic equation in fieldwork" and we, like her, came to love some of our subjects and were not immune to their charms in drag, they evinced none of the sexual interest in us that they lavish on men, especially handsome masculine men. In that sense there were no sexual tensions between them and us to get in the way of the research.

Working for Social Change

Knowing the controversy over drag among both scholars and activists—whether it troubles or reifies gender—we hoped to engage the drag queens and the larger community in considering whether the visible public presence of drag in Key West accomplishes the drag queens' intent to destabilize gender and sexual categories and undermine stereotypical attitudes about gay, lesbian, bisexual, and transgender people. The drag queens wanted to know as much as we did what people took away from the shows and how audiences reacted to their performances. As Nancy Naples (2003) has argued, research projects can empower participants—both when they promote dialogues that allow people to explore the way their practices are shaped and constrained by wider social, economic, and political structures and when they lead participants to work to alter practices and structures that promote inequality. To this end we structured the research process to bring the drag queens, gay and lesbian community members, and the wider community into conversations about the drag queens' role in Key West. We devised two main strategies: organizing focus groups and holding more informal conversations with audience members and disseminating our research findings in the local community both while we were engaged in the research and after the publication of the book. Like other researchers, we found that our gender and sexual identities came into play and sometimes presented a barrier to the kind of interaction necessary to engage with the ideas and practices of both the participants and other members of the Key West community. Throughout the project, the drag queens, audiences, and community members often took our gender and sexuality as a cue to our opinions and responded to the research within that context.

In recruiting individuals for focus groups, we sought diversity in terms of gender, sexual identity, race, ethnicity, class, and age, some of these characteristics more readily apparent than others. At the shows we handed out flyers to fifteen to twenty audience members, asking them to return the next afternoon and offering, courtesy of the bar owners, a free drink for those who showed up (for more on the focus groups, see Blee and Taylor 2002). Early on we realized that we, as women, might have trouble recruiting gay men, and that heterosexual audience members might be reluctant to participate. We invited sociologist and sexuality scholar Josh Gamson, a gay man with experience conducting focus groups, to participate in this part of the research. It was the right decision. The first time the three of us went to the show to recruit for a focus group, the fact that Josh was male, handsome, and not obviously gay helped to recruit a diverse group of participants, including heterosexual married couples. He also conducted a focus group composed entirely of gay men. Every group produced a different kind of discussion, depending on the participants, so the mixed and all-gay groups added to the richness of our data. When the drag queens introduced us at the show as "the professors of lesbian love" or worse, "the pussy lickers," we found that the only audience members likely to show up were lesbians. Clearly, our gender and sexual identities affected our ability to recruit diverse focus groups. To compensate for the fact that heterosexual men were underrepresented in the groups, we sought them out for informal interviews about their reactions to the shows. The drag queens helped by introducing us to heterosexual men and couples who regularly attended their shows.

Gender and sexuality also shaped the course of discussion in the focus groups. Some heterosexual participants talked about how it felt to walk into a gay bar to see the show. As one young straight woman put it, it can be "scary going into a gay bar" because "you walk into a gay bar, you're gay." The focus groups also had the potential to be intimidating, since at times it was evident that heterosexual members had never conversed with a gay man or lesbian about the kinds of issues that came up in the discussions. We asked the groups to talk about why they came to the shows, what they liked and didn't like, and what they say in the performances. Yet some of the most interesting conversations took place between people who disagreed about such things as whether they thought of the drag queens as women or men, which girls were most attractive, and whether they enjoyed the performances more or were made uncomfortable when the drag queens deliberately broke the illusion of femininity by accentuating their identities as gay men.

As difficult as they might be, these discussions across lines of gender, sexual iden-

tity, class, and ethnicity were not only productive for us as researchers; they also had the potential to stimulate participants' thinking about the experiences of gay, lesbian, bisexual, and transgender people and about the socially scripted nature of gender and sexuality. Gay and lesbian focus group members often speculated on what impact attending the show might have on straight people in the audience. A group of gay men thought that the performances and the audience interaction would cause straight people to open up a little bit. One said, "Right, they have a whole new perspective," to which another added, "And I think that helps open up a lot of people's eyes as far as they go back home and run across somebody and they find out they're gay, they're going to be a little bit less judgmental of that gay person." Added one more, "It's like taking the blinders off the horse."

And in fact many audience members concluded that the labels of "gay" and "straight" (or "female" and "male") just don't fit. Almost all of our focus group members made reference to this aspect of the shows. According to one gay man, "You leave them at the door." Another gay man thought the show "really pushes gender identity and gender role and homophobia issues with straight people to have that kind of interaction with drag queens." Because straight men are supposed to suppress any femininity, he said, "the drag show really gives them an opportunity to kind of delve into, ever so slightly, that side of their personality." A straight male tourist put it this way: "I think that one of the beauties of attending a show like this is that you do realize that you . . . shouldn't walk out and say 'I only like men' and you shouldn't say 'I only like women' and it all kind of blends together a lot more so than maybe what we want to live in our normal daily lives." A young gay man thought the performers were "challenging the whole idea of gender and so forth and they're breaking that down." These kinds of responses indicate that the focus groups themselves—despite or perhaps because of the complex gender and sexual dynamics—facilitated new ways of thinking about sexual and gender identity.

The focus groups, then, initiated the process of stimulating discussion about our research in the community. Even while the research was in progress, participants grappled with the complex meanings of drag in the lives of the 801 Girls, continually asking whether drag was an identity or a performance. Focus group members were sometimes willing to participate because they hoped to meet the girls out of drag, and they often got their wish because we held the groups in the cabaret at a time when the girls arrived to get dressed. One group asked Kylie about her stripping on Saturday night, and Kylie responded that she performs the way she does because leaving on the wig and makeup "confounds people. It baffles them and it does make them think." In this way, the focus groups stimulated interaction between the drag queens and audience members as well as among audience members.

Perhaps the most dramatic example of the ways that the focus groups fostered thought about the meaning of drag and created the potential for personal change is the fact that we first met Desiray as a member of a focus group of local gay men. As Joel, he had originally come to the show as a tourist, becoming so enthralled that he quit his job and moved to Key West. When Sushi found that he was sleeping on a lawn chair behind the bar because he had no money for rent, she got him a job as a cock-tail server. One night Gugi put Joel in drag, and Desiray was born. As if to illustrate the educative functions of drag that were so central to the focus group discussions, Desiray now hosts the Friday night show, called "Good Boys Gone Drag," featuring the girls as teachers. Desiray, the home-room teacher, introduces the history teacher to cover the disco era, the school nurse to talk about AIDS, and all the girls to teach sex education.

Issues of gender and sexuality affected not only recruitment to focus groups and conversations among the focus group members but also ongoing discussions in the community about the meaning of drag. As a result of local publicity and the drag queens' talk about the research at the shows, people in Key West frequently engaged us in conversation about the book, drag queens, and the 801 Girls in particular. Some local women told us in no uncertain terms that they did not go to the show because they found drag queens demeaning, assuming that we as women, feminists, and lesbians might share their perspective. We encountered criticism as well from staff members at the Women's Center at our university when we brought the drag queens to campus. The resulting dialogue with feminists, whose experiences with drag were for the most part theoretical, exposed them to the feminist project on drag.

However, some gay men who distanced themselves from drag as embarrassing or who disliked the 801 Girls as too "in-your-face" assumed that we were so involved with the girls that we would view them through rose-colored glasses. A former editor of *Celebrate!* made no secret of the fact that he had no use for some of the 801 Girls. When the book came out, he wrote us a letter acknowledging that he had not expected to like it but had decided to give it a try: "The result I will express in this old cliché: I couldn't put it down. You have given Key West a wonderful gift. You have not let yourselves become 'stonewalled' by these 'girlz.'" He admitted having unpleasant experiences with several of the drag queens when he worked for the paper but told us that "as I read your book, I found myself shedding those thoughts." The stories about the drag queens' struggles with gender and sexuality as boys and young men made him think about gay students he had encountered when he taught high school and prompted him to wonder what had happened to them. "Thank you for allowing me to become more focused upon the reasons I moved to Key West, to be part of a culture that does not represent the repression that occurs in so much of this country," he added. His letter was a powerful statement about the wide-ranging significance of drag for gay and lesbian lives and activism.

Ongoing discussion in the Key West community about gender, sexuality, and drag is taking place because we continue to go back to the site of our research and to engage with the drag queens, audiences, and community members. As Mitch Duneier (2001) points out with reference to his own ethnography of urban street vendors in New York City, it is relatively rare for ethnographers to maintain ongoing relationships with research participants. Despite the difficulties of negotiating the boundaries of gender and sexuality in our focus group research and in our continuing discussions about the impact of drag on the community, we think that our research strategy succeeded in fostering dialogue that promotes social change. Our focus groups facilitated interactions among the audience members across boundaries of gender and sexuality, stimulating thought

about the meaning of the shows and about the injustices experienced by gay, lesbian, bisexual, and transgender people. And the book itself, and our discussions of it in various venues, both scholarly and with the general public, contribute, we hope, to our feminist vision of change by challenging conventional thinking about the rigidity and biological nature of gender and sexuality and by stimulating debate about the political significance of drag performances.

That such conversations are not confined to the Key West community became evident when Sushi, Kylie, and Gugi came to Santa Barbara. After two performances, one in Verta's seven-hundred-student introductory sociology class, the student newspaper devoted a front-page article and a back page of photographs to the drag queen visit (Gonzalez 2004; Lewis 2004). Then one of Verta's students wrote an opinion piece titled "Drag Queens Present a Day of Scantily Clad, Eye-Opening Education," beginning with the great line, "When you see your lesbian sociology professor touch a naked drag queen's penis, you know it's going to be a good day" (Sikola 2004). That provoked a right-wing response arguing that drag queens are suffering from gender identity disorder and should be treated, not celebrated (Hastings 2004). This was followed by an indignant denial that drag queens are mentally diseased, written by a student herself diagnosed with gender identity disorder (Boyden 2004). And then the local alternative paper reviewed the drag show at the Multicultural Center, noting that the girls "made sex less taboo and more faboo (as in fabulous)" and "were true performers who dared to push the limits of their audience" (Ingersoll 2004). At the end of the quarter, we received student papers that made it clear that, as one put it, "the drag queens opened my eyes and my heart to the myriad of people that fill this earth."

After the book came out, Kylie told us that, although the 801 Girls had always intended to challenge the way people think, our research had made them realize that they did in fact have an impact on people, that they did make audience members think in a more complex way about gender and sexual categories and about the oppression that queer people experience in their daily lives. Response to the book and to the shows suggests that they have succeeded in their mission.

Conclusion

We approached our research on the drag queens from the perspective of what Sandra Harding (1991, 1993) calls "strong objectivity." That is, we scrutinized the ways that our positions as researchers, with particular attention to gender and sexuality, affected the research process, and we acknowledged the impact of our complicated relationships with the drag queens on the analysis we produced in working with them. Instead of ignoring the tensions between us as feminist researchers and the drag queens as gay men, we foregrounded them.

We encountered dilemmas in negotiating the dynamics of gender and sexuality in our dealings with the drag queens, audience members, and the Key West community, and these difficulties made us more aware of the power relations that are central to every aspect of feminist research, from the collaboration that is essential to participatory research to the social change agenda that is the heart of feminist research. Our being women and lesbians had a complex impact on the project, ironically easing our entrée and creating a delicate and shifting balance of power with the drag queens but sometimes making

recruitment to focus groups difficult and leading audience and community members to make assumptions about our perspectives on the drag queens and sometimes even to challenge us because we are feminist researchers. In trying to get across the message that drag shows are not merely entertaining performances, which was one of Sushi's central goals in collaborating with us, we were sometimes accused of partiality by members of the gay and lesbian community, the audiences at the shows, and the wider Key West community.

Yet the tensions and contradictions we encountered in the research process were not just problems to be overcome; they also proved to be productive for our thinking about how the drag queens play with and deconstruct gender and sexual categories in their performances and the way this makes gender and sexual fluidity and oppression visible. If being introduced as "pussy lickers" limited the diversity of our focus groups, it also led us to see how the drag queens use vulgar expressions for sexual acts to categorize people and then tear down the boundaries by suggesting that one sexual act, and thus any sexual actor, is pretty much like another. And it also demanded that we wear these labels as proudly as the drag queens bear the stigma of gay male femininity, revealing in a profoundly personal way the role drag queens play in making visible gay and transgender identities. If the letter writers to *Celebrate!* implied that lesbians could not appreciate the beauty of Colby's new breasts, they were also engaging in the kind of public discussion of what drag means that we had hoped to stimulate. In talking with the drag queens about our research, Sushi once quipped, "You're like modern Oscar Wildes, you descended into a den of iniquity and emerged with a new view of the world." That we did, and, much to our surprise, it is one that has made us think more deeply about the dilemmas and promises of feminist research.

Notes

1. Syndicated review by Richard Labonte, e-mailed from University of Chicago Press, June 2003.

2. In particular, we situate our analysis in the literature that considers the ways that feminist research pays attention to the relationship between the researcher and the researched, the social change goal of feminist research, and the impact of gender and sexuality on the research process. See Golde 1970; Guerney 1985; Harding 1987, 1991, 1993, 2004; Riessman 1987; Hondagneu-Sotelo 1988; DeVault 1990, 1999; Acker, Barry, and Esseveld 1991; Fonow and Cook 1991; Oakley 1991; Taylor and Rupp 1991, 1996, forthcoming; Cancian 1992, 1996; Bell, Caplan, and Karim 1993; Mies 1993; Williams and Heikes 1993; Kennedy with Davis 1996; Lewin and Leap 1996; Newton 1996; Wafer 1996; Lincoln 1997; Taylor 1998; Gamson 2000; Oleson 2000; Naples 2003; Errante 2004; Geiger 2004; Hesse-Biber, Nagy, and Yaiser 2004; Rubenstein 2004; Weston 2004.

3. See especially Guerney 1985; Riessman 1987; Simon 1987; Hondagneu-Sotelo 1988; Taylor and Rupp 1991, 1996; Williams and Heikes 1993; Kennedy with Davis 1996; Lewin and Leap 1996; Newton 1996; Wafer 1996; Rupp and Taylor 2002; Weston 2004.

4. Following the linguistic practices of the drag queens, we switch between female and male pronouns, but with a preference for drag names and the feminine gender.

5. Drag has long interested scholars writing about the destabilization of gender and sexual categories. See Newton 1972; Dolan 1985; Butler 1990, 1993; Garber 1992; Halberstam 1998; Lorber 1999; Muñoz 1999; Schacht 2002.

References

Acker, Joan, Kate Barry, and Johanna Esseveld. 1991. "Objectivity and Truth: Problems in Doing Feminist Research." In Fonow and Cook 1991, 133–53.

Adam, Barry D. 1995. *The Rise of a Gay and Lesbian Movement*. Rev. ed. New York: Twayne.

Bell, Diane, Pat Caplan, and Wazir Jahan Karim, eds. 1993. *Gendered Fields: Women, Men, and Ethnography*. London: Routledge.

Blee, Kathleen M., and Verta Taylor. 2002. "Semi-structured Interviewing in Social Movement Research." In *Methods in Social Movement Research*, ed. Bert Klandermans and Suzanne Staggenborg, 92–117. Minneapolis: University of Minnesota Press.

Boyden, Alina. 2004. "Don't Mislabel Drag Queens, Kings as Mentally Diseased." *Daily Nexus Online* 83(134). Available online at http://www.dailynexus.com/opinion/2004/7596.html. Last accessed March 28, 2004.

Butler, Judith. 1990. *Gender Trouble: Feminism and the Subversion of Identity*. New York: Routledge.

———. 1993. *Bodies That Matter: On the Discursive Limits of "Sex."* New York: Routledge.

Cancian, Francesca M. 1992. "Feminist Science: Methodologies That Challenge Inequality." *Gender and Society* 6(4):623–42.

———. 1996. "Participatory Research and Alternative Strategies for Activist Sociology." In *Feminism and Social Change: Bridging Theory and Practice*, ed. Heidi Gottfried, 187–205. Urbana: University of Illinois Press.

Cannon, Lynn Weber, Elizabeth Higginbotham, and Marianne L. A. Leung. 1991. "Race and Class Bias in Qualitative Research on Women." In Fonow and Cook 1991, 107–18.

Collins, Patricia Hill. 1990. *Black Feminist Thought: Knowledge, Consciousness, and the Politics of Empowerment*. New York: Routledge.

Crenshaw, Kimberlé. 1991. "Mapping the Margins: Intersectionality, Identity Politics, and Violence against Women of Color." *Stanford Law Review* 43(6):1241–99.

D'Emilio, John. 1983. *Sexual Politics, Sexual Communities: The Making of a Homosexual Minority in the United States, 1940–1970*. Chicago: University of Chicago Press.

DeVault, Marjorie L. 1990. "Talking and Listening from Women's Standpoint: Feminist Strategies for Interviewing and Analysis." *Social Problems* 37(1):96–116.

——. 1999. *Liberating Method: Feminism and Social Research*. Philadelphia: Temple University Press.

Dolan, Jill. 1985. "Gender Impersonation Onstage: Destroying or Maintaining the Mirror of Gender Roles?" *Women and Performances: A Journal of Feminist Theory* 2(4):5–11.

Duneier, Mitchell. 2001. "On the Evolution of *Sidewalk*." In *Contemporary Field Research: Perspectives and Formulations*, ed. Robert M. Emerson, 167–87. 2nd ed. Prospect Heights, IL: Waveland.

Errante, Antoinette. 2004. "But Sometimes You're Not Part of the Story: Oral Histories and Ways of Remembering and Telling." In Hesse-Biber, Nagy, and Yaiser 2004, 411–34.

Fonow, Mary Margaret, and Judith A. Cook, eds. 1991. *Beyond Methodology: Feminist Scholarship as Lived Research*. Bloomington: Indiana University Press.

Gamson, Joshua. 2000. "Sexualities, Queer Theory, and Qualitative Research." In *Handbook of Qualitative Research*, ed. Norman K. Denzin and Yvonna S. Lincoln, 347–65. 2nd ed. Thousand Oaks, CA: Sage.

Garber, Marjorie. 1992. *Vested Interests: Cross-Dressing and Cultural Anxiety*. New York: Routledge.

Geiger, Susan. 2004. "What's So Feminist about Women's Oral History?" In Hesse-Biber, Nagy, and Yaiser 2004, 399–410.

Gilbert, Constance. 2003a. "Teasers Come to the 801." *Celebrate!* September 4–17, 10.

——. 2003b. "The Writer Replies." *Celebrate!* September 18–October 1, 12.

Golde, Peggy, ed. 1970. *Woman in the Field: Anthropological Experiences*. Chicago: Aldine.

Gonzalez, Jessica. 2004. "Kings, Queens Hold Audience at MCC." *Daily Nexus* 84(130):1.

Guerney, Joan Neff. 1985. "Not One of the Guys: The Female Researcher in a Male-Dominated Setting." *Qualitative Sociology* 8(1):42–62.

Halberstam, Judith. 1998. *Female Masculinity*. Durham, NC: Duke University Press.

Hamilton, Henry. 2003. "Hamilton Raises Hackles." *Celebrate!* September 18–October 1, 12.

Harding, Sandra, ed. 1987. *Feminism and Methodology: Social Science Issues*. Bloomington: Indiana University Press.

——. 1991. *Whose Science? Whose Knowledge? Thinking from Women's Lives*. Ithaca, NY: Cornell University Press.

——. 1993. "Rethinking Standpoint Epistemology: What Is Strong Objectivity?" In *Feminist Epistemologies*, ed. Linda Alcoff and Elizabeth Potter, 49–82. New York: Routledge.

——. 2004. "Can Men Be Subjects of Feminist Thought?" In Hesse-Biber, Nagy, and Yaiser 2004, 177–97.

Hastings, Ted. 2004. "Praising Drag Queens Perpetuates Lack of Treatment for Mentally Ill." *Daily Nexus Online* 83(133). Available online at http://www.dailynexus.com/opinion/2004/7590.html. Last accessed March 28, 2005.

Hesse-Biber, Sharlene Nagy, and Michelle L. Yaiser. 2004. *Feminist Perspectives on Social Research*. New York: Oxford University Press.

Hill, Shirley A., and Joey Sprague. 2004. "Parenting in Black and White Families: The Interaction of Gender with Race and Class." In Hesse-Biber, Nagy, and Yaiser 2004, 155–76.

Hondagneu-Sotelo, Pierrette. 1988. "Gender and Fieldwork: Review Essay." *Women's Studies International Forum* 11(6):611–18.

Ingersoll, Holland. 2004. "Dude Looks Like a Diva." *The Independent*, May 20, 63.

Kennedy, Elizabeth Lapovsky, and Madeline D. Davis. 1993. *Boots of Leather, Slippers of Gold: The History of a Lesbian Community*. New York: Routledge.

——. 1996. "Constructing an Ethnohistory of the Buffalo Lesbian Community: Reflexivity, Dialogue, and Politics." In Lewin and Leap 1996, 171–99.

Kulick, Don. 1998. *Travesti: Sex, Gender, and Culture among Brazilian Transgendered Prostitutes*. Chicago: University of Chicago Press.

Lang, Sabine. 1990. *Männer als Frauen, Frauen als Männer: Geschlechtsrollen-wechsel bei den Indianern Nordamerikas*. Hamburg: Wayasbah-Verlag.

——. 1996. "Traveling Woman: Conducting a Fieldwork Project on Gender Variance and

Homosexuality among North American Indians." In Lewin and Leap 1996, 86–107.

Lewin, Ellen, and William L. Leap, eds. 1996. *Out in the Field: Reflections of Lesbian and Gay Anthropologists.* Urbana: University of Illinois Press.

Lewis, Danny. 2004. "Photo Essay: Drag Queens Sushi, Kylie and Gugi Strut Their Stuff for a Sociology Class." *Daily Nexus* 84(130):12.

Lincoln, Yvonna S. 1997. "Self, Subject, Audience, Text: Living at the Edge, Writing in the Margins." In *Representation and the Text: Reframing the Narrative Voice*, ed. William G. Tierney and Yvonna S. Lincoln, 37–56. Albany, NY: SUNY Press.

Lorber, Judith. 1999. "Crossing Borders and Erasing Boundaries: Paradoxes of Identity Politics." *Sociological Focus* 32(4):355–70.

Mies, Maria. 1993. "Towards a Methodology for Feminist Research." In *Social Research: Philosophy, Politics and Practice*, ed. Martyn Hammersley, 64–82. London: Sage.

Muñoz, José Esteban. 1999. *Disidentifications: Queers of Color and the Performance of Politics.* Minneapolis: University of Minnesota Press.

Murray, Stephen O. 1987. *Male Homosexuality in Central and South America.* New York: Gay Academic Union.

———. 1996. "Male Homosexuality in Guatemala: Possible Insights and Certain Confusions from Sleeping with the Natives." In Lewin and Leap 1996, 236–60.

Naples, Nancy A. 2003. *Feminism and Method: Ethnography, Discourse Analysis, and Activist Research.* New York: Routledge.

Newton, Esther. 1972. *Mother Camp: Female Impersonators in America.* Chicago: University of Chicago Press.

———. 1993. *Cherry Grove, Fire Island: Sixty Years in America's First Gay and Lesbian Town.* Boston: Beacon.

———. 1996. "My Best Informant's Dress: The Erotic Equation in Field Work." In Lewin and Leap 1996, 212–35.

Oakley, Ann. 1991. "Interviewing Women: A Contradiction in Terms." In *Doing Feminist Research*, ed. Helen Roberts, 30–61. London: Routledge.

Oleson, Virginia L. 2000. "Feminisms and Qualitative Research at and into the Millennium." In *Handbook of Qualitative Research*, ed. Norman K. Denzin and Yvonna S. Lincoln, 215–56. 2nd ed. Thousand Oaks, CA: Sage.

Phoenix, Ann. 1994. "Practicing Feminist Research: The Intersection of Gender and Race in the Research Process." In *Researching Women's Lives from a Feminist Perspective*, ed. Mary Maynard and June Purvis, 35–45. London: Taylor & Francis.

Prieur, Annick. 1998. *Mama's House, Mexico City: On Transvestites, Queens, and Machos.* Chicago: University of Chicago Press.

Reay, Diane. 1998. "Classifying Feminist Research: Exploring the Psychological Impact of Social Class on Mothers' Involvement in Children's Schooling." *Feminism and Psychology* 8(2):155–71.

———. 2004. "Rethinking Social Class: Qualitative Perspectives on Class and Gender." In Hesse-Biber, Nagy, and Yaiser 2004, 140–54.

Reinharz, Shulamit. 1992. *Feminist Methods in Social Research.* New York: Oxford University Press.

Richardson, Laurel. 1993. "The Case of the Skipped Line: Poetics, Dramatics, and Transgressive Validity." *Sociological Quarterly* 34(4):695–710.

Riessman, Catherine K. 1987. "When Gender Is Not Enough: Women Interviewing Women." *Gender and Society* 1(2):172–207.

Rubenstein, Steven L. 2004. "Fieldwork and the Erotic Economy on the Colonial Frontier." *Signs: Journal of Women in Culture and Society* 29(4):1041–71.

Rupp, Leila J. 1999. *A Desired Past: A Short History of Same-Sex Love in America.* Chicago: University of Chicago Press.

Rupp, Leila J., and Verta Taylor. 2002. "Pauli Murray: The Unasked Question." *Journal of Women's History* 14(2):83–87.

———. 2003a. "Authors Saddened by Misogynic [*sic*] Remarks." *Celebrate!* October 30–November 12, 17.

———. 2003b. *Drag Queens at the 801 Cabaret.* Chicago: University of Chicago Press.

Schacht, Steven. 2002. "Four Renditions of Doing Female Drag: Feminine Appearing Conceptual Variations of a Masculine Theme." In *Gendered Sexualities*, ed. Patricia Gagné and Richard Tewksbury, 157–80. New York: JAI Press.

Schacht, Steven, and Lisa Underwood. 2004. *The Drag Queen Anthology: The Absolutely Fabulous but Flawlessly Customary World of Female Impersonators*. New York: Harrington Park Press.

Schiller, Stephen. 2003. "801 Cabaret Commentary Draws Flack." *Celebrate!* September 18–October 1, 12.

Schippers, Mimi. 2004. "The Social Organization of Sexuality and Gender in Alternative Hard Rock: An Analysis of Intersectionality." In Hesse-Biber, Nagy, and Yaiser 2004, 382–98.

Schmida, Terry. 2001. "When Life's a Drag." *Key West Citizen*, June 3, 1C+.

Sikola, Karen. 2004. "Drag Queens Present a Day of Scantily Clad, Eye-Opening Education." *Daily Nexus Online* 83(131). Available online at http://www.dailynexus.com/opinion/2004/7567.html. Last accessed March 29, 2005.

Simon, Barbara Levy. 1987. *Never Married Women*. Philadelphia: Temple University Press.

Taylor, Verta. 1998. "Feminist Methodology in Social Movements Research." *Qualitative Sociology* 21(4):357–79.

Taylor, Verta, and Leila J. Rupp. 1991. "Researching the Women's Movement: We Make Our Own History, but Not Just as We Please." In Fonow and Cook 1991, 119–32.

———. 1996. "Lesbian Existence and the Women's Movement: Researching the 'Lavender Herring.'" In *Feminism and Social Change: Bridging Theory and Practice*, ed. Heidi Gottfried, 143–59. Urbana: University of Illinois Press.

———. 2005. "Participatory Action Research in the Study of Social Movements: Drag Queens and the Performance of Protest." In *Rhyming Hope and History: Activism and Social Movement Scholarship*, ed. David Croteau, William Hoynes, and Charlotte Ryan, 362–98. Minneapolis: University of Minnesota Press.

Taylor, Verta, Leila J. Rupp, and Josh Gamson. 2004. "Performing Protest: Drag Shows as Tactical Repertoire of the Gay and Lesbian Movement." *Research in Social Movements, Conflict, and Change*, 25:105–37.

Troka, Donna, Kathleen LeBesco, and Jean Noble. 2002. *The Drag King Anthology*. New York: Harrington Park Press.

Twine, France Winddance, and Jonathan W. Warren, eds. 2000. *Racing Research, Researching Race: Methodological Dilemmas in Critical Race Studies*. New York: New York University Press.

Wafer, James. 1996. "Out of the Closet and into Print: Sexual Identity in the Textual Field." In Lewin and Leap 1996, 261–73.

Weber, Lynn. 2004. "A Conceptual Framework for Understanding Race, Class, Gender, and Sexuality." In Hesse-Biber, Nagy, and Yaiser 2004, 121–39.

West, Candace, and Sarah Fenstermaker. 1995. "Doing Difference." *Gender and Society* 9(1):8–37.

Weston, Kath. 1991. *Families We Choose: Lesbians, Gays, Kinship*. New York: Columbia University Press.

———. 1996. "Requiem for a Street Fighter." In Lewin and Leap 1996, 274–285.

———. 2004. "Fieldwork in Lesbian and Gay Communities." In Hesse-Biber, Nagy, and Yaiser 2004, 198–205.

Williams, Christine L., and E. Joel Heikes. 1993. "The Importance of Researcher's Gender in the In-Depth Interview: Evidence from Two Case Studies of Male Nurses." *Gender and Society* 7(2):280–91.

Williams, Walter L. 1986. *The Spirit and the Flesh: Sexual Diversity in American Indian Culture*. Boston: Beacon Press.

———. 1996. "Being Gay and Doing Fieldwork." In Lewin and Leap 1996, 70–85.

47 Eli Clare

Sex, Celebration, and Justice
The Queerness and Disability Conference

Introduction

In the last three decades disabled people and lesbian, gay, bisexual, and transgender peoples have taken to the streets and entered the academy. We've built movements for social change, created culture and community, and shape our own theory and analysis. But the issues, concerns, and experiences of queer disabled people have rarely been placed front and center. With these thoughts about marginalization, identity politics, and community building, a small group of activists—myself included—organized the first-ever Queerness and Disability Conference at San Francisco State University in 2002. The event brought together artists, activists, and scholars to explore a whole host of issues, ranging from the medicalization of bodies to sex, from using personal attendant care to queer performance, crip style. Three hundred people gathered for an intense, high energy two days where the sparks of connection and challenge, community and conflict, flew. Those 48 hours were fueled by an explosion of energy that often happens when people who have lived in immense isolation first find each other. The readings, presentations, and performances provoked tears, excitement, hunger, discomfort, anger, dis-

appointment. Many of us felt relief not having to explain homophobia to straight disabled people or ableism to non-disabled queer people. The sheer, stunning variety of bodily differences was both ordinary and awesome.

Intertwined with this energy were huge challenges. The conference was very white, largely ignoring race and the many places where racism and ableism intersect, overlap, and connect. These oversights, absences, and manifestations of white privilege were powerfully articulated by the people of color and mixed race caucus. Chris Bell, one of the participants of that caucus, has characterized the gathering as an example of White Disability Studies. Additionally, the conference re-created a hierarchy of disability that has existed within the Disability Rights Movement for several decades: people with physical disabilities privileged, and those with psych disabilities, cognitive disabilities, and non-apparent disabilities marginalized. You can find the important and powerful statements from the psych disability caucus and the people of color and mixed race caucus at the Queer Disability Conference website.

I was scheduled, along with activist and writer Diana Courvant, to speak at the

Eli Clare, "Sex, Celebration, and Justice: The Queerness and Disability Conference." Edited by the author from a version first developed for a keynote for the 2002 Queerness and Disability Conference. Reprinted by kind permission of the author.

closing plenary, which never happened. Instead it turned into a town hall meeting where people of color and people with psych disabilities challenged the gathering in fundamental and necessary ways. Diana and I facilitated the meeting but didn't keynote. What follows is the text of the speech I didn't give.

Imagine: The room is jammed, full of people using wheelchairs, crutches, ventilators, canes, service dogs, full of queer crips and our friends, allies, and partners. One team of people types out real-time captioning for the proceedings. Another team translates spoken English into American Sign Language. Whatever our differences, most of us bring a shared sense of queerness as familiar and good; a shared understanding of disability as neither tragic nor pitiful, but rather as an integral part of who we are, the social conditions of ableism as important as the bodily, cognitive, sensory, and/or emotional impairments we face. This is the roomful of people for whom I wrote the following speech.

Speech

What a wild, intense ride this has been. For months I've been pondering what I would say here this afternoon. So much has been talked about in the last two jam-packed days: sex and relationships, physician assisted suicide and Not Dead Yet,[1] the pathologizing of bodies and the connections between intersex and disability organizing, getting the care we need and coming out, street activism and legal strategy, theory and performance, stories and painting. We've laughed, cried, danced, raged. We've asked questions, listened hard, faced necessary challenges.

Yet I sit here knowing how much we've missed. We could start again right here, right now, talk for another two days, never repeat a single idea, question, or connection, and still be going strong. Such an exciting plenty exists among us. At the same time, what has been left out is profound and needs acknowledgement.

This gathering has been very white and for the most part has neglected issues of race and racism. All of us here in this room today need to listen to queer disabled people of color and their experiences. We need to fit race and racism into the matrix of queerness and disability. I need to ask myself not only "What does it mean to be a pansexual genderqueer with a long butch dyke history, a walkie with a disability that I acquired at birth," but also, "What does it mean to be a *white* crip?"

We haven't asked enough questions about class, about the experiences of being poor and disabled, of struggling with hunger, homelessness, and a lack of the most basic healthcare, of institutionalization—whether it be in nursing homes, group homes, or psych wards. I want to hear from working-class folks who learned about disability from bone-breaking work in the factory, mine, or sweatshop. We need more exploration of gender identity and disability. How do the two inform each other? I can feel the sparks fly as disabled trans people are just beginning to find each other. We need to listen more to Deaf culture, to people with psych disabilities, cognitive disability, to young people and old people. We need not to re-create here in this space, in this budding community, the hierarchies that exist in other disability communities, other queer communities. Naming these absences isn't meant to accuse or undercut the strength and power of the past two days, but rather to suggest the complexity and breadth of work we have to do as we begin to come together as queer crips, friends, lovers, partners, and allies.

With all that has been said and all that hasn't, all the connection and all the challenge, what am I going to leave you with? It's an awesome thing to sit up here in front of this room, look out at all your shining faces, and know that soon we'll each be going home, taking this experience with us into our daily worlds. Being up here on stage right now gives me the magnificent and overwhelming opportunity to tell you what I'd like you to take home.

First, a challenge about sex. And when I say sex, I don't mean a code for queerness. When those straight, well-meaning disability studies profs ask me ever so politely to come to their school and talk about disability and sexuality, they aren't requesting a presentation about heterosexuality, much less the whole universe of sexual possibility. Rather they mean that other sexuality, that exotic sexuality, that queer sexuality. Or I get asked by nondisabled queer activists to be part of panels about sexuality and disability. I never know if they're really serious about doing anti-ableism education or if truly they just want another believe-it-or-not freak show, a tell-all about what crips do in bed. And guess what: this butch top, used-to-be-stone, still-dealing-with-the-aftershocks-of-incest crip isn't interested in being part of a freak show. I have no desire to tell them how I can reach, thrust, tease with my shaky right hand, if only my arm and shoulder don't lock with tension. No desire to tell them what my lover asks for and what I might do.

But here in this room when I say sex, I'm not talking code. Rather, I mean the steamy, complex, erotic, sometimes pleasure-filled, sometimes mundane, sometimes mystical, sometimes painful, sometimes confusing behaviors, activities, and fantasies we call sex. It's a radical act, a daring act, a brand new act for queer crips to talk about sex.

On one hand, as queers, we are perverse and depraved, shaped either as oversexed child molesters or invisible creatures, legislated out of existence. On the other, as crips, we are entirely desexualized, fetishized or viewed as incapable of sexual responsibility. We navigate through such a confounding maze of lies and stereotypes: the wheelchair-using gay man who's a quad and can't find a date; the bi woman amputee sought after, pursued, even sometimes stalked, by devotees—those mostly straight men who fetishize amputations; the cognitively disabled dyke who is told in so many ways that she's simply a sexual risk to herself and the world. Never are we seen, heard, believed to be the creators of our own desires, passions, and sexual selves. Inside this maze, the lives of queer crips truly disappear. I say it's time for us to reappear. Time for us to talk sex, be sex, wear sex, relish sex, both the sex we do have and the sex we want to be having.

I say it's time for some queer disability erotica, time for an anthology of crip smut, queer style. Time for us to write, film, perform, read, talk porn. I'm serious. It's time. I want to get hot and bothered: I want to read about wheelchairs and limps, hands that bend at odd angles and bodies that negotiate unchosen pain, about orgasms that aren't necessarily about our genitals, about sex and pleasure stolen in nursing homes and back rooms where we've been abandoned, about bodily—and I mean to include the mind as part of the body—differences so plentiful they can't be counted, about sex that embraces all those differences. It's time. I want to watch smut made by and for queer disabled people and our lovers, friends, allies, our experiences told from the inside out. I want plain old rutting, delicious one night affairs, but please don't leave out the chivalrous romance. Let's face it: I want it all. It's time. I want us to turn the freak show on its head, to turn away from the folks who gawk and pity us, who study and patronize us, who ignore us or fetishize us. I want us to forget the rubes and remember each other as we declare and create our sexualities. It's time. In the past several years, there's been an outpouring of identity-based erotica anthologies. On my bookshelves, you can find *Best Transgender Erotica*, *Bearotica*, and *Zaftig: Well Rounded Erotica*, all fiercely asserting the sexuality of people whose sexualities have been marginalized. Now it's time for queer crips to join this line up, time for tantalizing tales about queer crip sex. And if we don't write them, then who?

But that's not all. Here's a second thing I want us to take home, a thing bigger than queer crip sex, a thing about celebrating our queerness, our differences in all their complexity. I want us to tell stories, to talk about our bodies, to be real about our shame and our pride. We're good at talking about oppression and how disability is truly about the material and social conditions of ableism—not about our paralysis but rather about the stairs without an accompanying ramp, not about our blindness but rather about the lack of Braille, not about our depression or anxiety but rather about a whole host of stereotypes—as if our bodily experiences of bone and muscle, tendon and ligament, are somehow irrelevant.

We're good at carving out our space as queer by naming ourselves and then defining and defending those identities, as if single words could ever name the entirety of our queer bodily desires. We're good at saying the word *pride*, as if shame has nothing to do with it. I'm glad we've become good at those things, but let's not stop talking about our bodies, about the messiness and contradictions.

It's risky work, particularly in a world that gawks and taunts, moralizes and pities, medicalizes and condemns, in a world that demands an explanation at every turn, in a world where complete strangers feel free to ask, "What's your defect?" But I want us to take that risk, not to feed the pity machine, the super-crip machine, the you're-so-perverted machine, but to celebrate our bodies and create them as ordinary and familiar. So let me start by telling you three stories to bring my right arm, my skin, my buzzed hair and broad stance into this room.

My crip body. I spent years hating my right arm, hating the tremors that start behind my shoulder blade, race down that track of muscles from shoulder to bicep, forearm to fingertip, hating the tension that follows behind to clamp the shaking, hating that I couldn't will either away. I never talked about the red hot pain that wraps around the tension. Never talked about how being touched can make the tremors worse. Never talked about my yearning to play the piano or fiddle, hammer a nail, fling my body into the powerful grace of a gymnast, rock climber, dancer. I wanted to cut my right arm off, ream the tremors out of me, my shame that vivid.

Still today I have to work not to hide my right hand, tuck it beneath my body, pull the tremors into me, let no one else feel them. Work to remember that my lover means it when he says, "I can't get enough of your shaky touch." Work to love my right arm, my trembling. My body, not pitiful but ordinary.

My white body. The only person of color in my childhood home—a backwoods logging town in Oregon—was an African-American kid, adopted into a white family. I grew up to persistent rumors of a lynching tree way back in the hills, of the county sheriff running people of color and gay men out of town. I grew up among working-class white men who made their livings by clearcutting the steep slopes, not so long ago stolen from the Tunis, the Umpquas, the Coquille peoples. Grew up among white men disabled by the body breaking work of logging—missing limbs, hearing loss, nerve damage, broken bones knitted back together crooked. Grew up surrounded by disability and whiteness never spoken.

For a long time after moving to the city, college scholarship in hand, all I could do was gawk at the multitude of humans: Black people, Chinese people, Chicanos, drag queens and punks, vets down on Burnside Avenue, white men in their wool suits, limos shined to sparkle. I watched them all, sucking in the thick weave of Spanish, Cantonese, street talk, English. This is how I became aware of being white. My body threaded with unspoken privilege.

My trans body. Not so long ago, a woman stopped me on the street. She wanted to know, "You a boy?" I said, "Nope." Who knows why I answered that way; it would have been simpler to say, "Yup," and closer to the truth. She responded, "You a girl?" looking truly puzzled. I left quickly. There is no short answer.

I learned about my gendered body flying kites in the hayfields and sheep pastures, digging fencepost holes and hauling fire-wood with my father. He raised me, his eldest daughter, as an almost son. I had no desire to be a girl but knew I wasn't a boy. My body never learned to walk in high heels—what a joke my few attempts were, trying to fit my broad stance and shaky-heeled gait into those shoes. Never learned to feel strong and comfortable, much less sexy, in a skirt. Never stopped feeling at home in my work boots and flannel shirts, my butchness shaped by those white loggers I grew up among, overlaid by a queer urban sensibility.

Not man, not woman: I don't have one-word answers for my gendered body, just stories. Learning to knob a tie and look in the mirror at age 32. Being cruised by bears on the Castro, feeling my skin flush warm. Finding pleasure and trouble as my boyfriend and I hold hands on the subway, harassed as gay men, even though later that night I'll be called ma'am at the restaurant. Using the men's room often enough to know the etiquette, often choosing to brave a full bladder, rather than risk the women's room. I can only tell my gender in stories. My body, not perverse, but familiar.

Stories about our bodies tangle sexuality, race, gender, class, and disability together. Some theorists and activists seem to like the notion of double (or triple or quadruple) identity, suggesting that all of who we are could stack up in some quantifiable way. Do they mean I might peel off my queerness, leaving my CP, or peel off the disability, leaving my whiteness, or peel off my white privilege, leaving my rural, working-class roots? Or they talk about double oppression, often creating a hierarchy among different kinds of discrimination. Can any of us tell what the gawkers are gawking at? Are they trying to figure out whether I'm a woman or a man, dyke or fag, why I walk with a shake, talk with a slur, or are they just admiring my polished boots and denim jacket? I'll never know.

The idea of our bodies as ordinary and familiar flies in the face of the gawkers and bashers who try to shape us as inspirational and heroic, tragic and pitiful, perverse and unnatural. We don't get to simply be ordinary and familiar very often. And when it does happen, it's such a relief. Don't mistake me: I don't mean that we need to find normal—that mythical center against which everyone is compared—and make it our own. In truth, I want us to smash it to smithereens and in its place celebrate our irrevocably different bodies, our queerness, our crip lives, creating for ourselves an abiding sense of the ordinary and familiar.

And finally there's a third thing I want us to take home, bigger than queer crip sex, bigger than resisting normal and celebrating our bodies, a thing about living in this world as we build community. When 9/11 happened, I was already immersed in the work of organizing this conference. In the days and weeks following the hijackings as I processed waves of grief, shock, fear, and outrage at U.S. imperialism, as U.S. bombs started to rain on Afghanistan, I asked myself repeatedly, "Why am I choosing to do this queer disability work rather than peace work?" Why, I asked as the bombs continued to fall, as civil liberties here in the U.S. tightened, as Arabs, Arab Americans, and Muslims were—and still today are being—harassed and detained.

Why, I asked, and friends reminded me about the phrase "peace and justice." Why, I asked and remembered how war and disability are tangled together, how veterans helped create disability rights activism. Why, I asked and every day heard spiritual leaders and political leaders, war mongers and peace activists alike refer to disability. They said, "An eye for an eye will make the world blind," disability becoming a metaphor for the consequences of revenge. They said, "These attacks crippled Wall Street," assuming without question that crippled equals broken. They said, "The leader of the Taliban, that one-eyed Mullah," using disability as a marker of evil. Not once did I hear about the real lived experience of disability as a marker of evil. Not once did I hear about the real lived experience of disability as the World Trade Center collapsed, bombs fell, and landmines exploded. I wanted to go to a peace rally with a placard that said, "Another cripple for peace," or "Imperialist revenge is corrupt, not blind." I stopped asking why, started to understand yet again how, even at a time of escalating military violence, queer disability work is in truth justice work.

Justice is a big word. It means food and houses and jobs and health care and education. It means art that tells untold stories bald-faced and art that turns an image, a metaphor, into pure revelatory magic. It means coming to fill our bodies to the very edges of our skin. It means theory that teases new thinking out of our brains and theory that helps refigure the world. It means hate won't reign like bombs and hunger, house fires and baseball bats, Jerry Lewis's telethon and the locked doors of nursing homes and psych wards. It means liberation, challenge, compassion. *Justice* is a big word.

I want us to cruise justice, flirt with it, take it home with us, nurture and feed it, even though sometimes it will be demanding and ask uncomfortable questions. Clearly I'm not talking about a simple one night stand but a commitment for the long haul.

Sex, celebration of our queer crip bodies, and a commitment to justice: that's all I'm asking for as we head back to our homes. In the end, let us turn the world into a place where, to quote the poet Mary Oliver:

> . . . *each life [is] a flower, as common as a field daisy, and as singular,*
>
> *and each name a comfortable music in the mouth,*
> *tending, as all music does, toward silence,*
>
> *and each body a lion of courage and something precious to the earth. (10)*

Notes

1. Not Dead Yet is a disability rights organization opposing assisted suicide and euthanasia from a secular, disability-based perspective. For more information, see http://www.notdeadyet.org.

Works Cited

Bell, Chris, "Introducing White Disability Studies: A Modest Proposal." *The Disability Studies Reader: Second Edition.* Ed. Lennard J. Davis. Routledge: New York, 2006.

Blank, Hanne, ed. *Zaftig: Well Rounded Erotica.* Cleis Press: San Francisco, 2001.

Blank, Hanne, and Raven Kaldera, eds. *Best Transgender Erotica.* Circlet Press: Cambridge, MA, 2002.

Oliver, Mary. *New and Selected Poems.* Beacon Press: Boston, 1992.

Queer Disability Conference: Closing Plenary. 3 January 2009 http://www.disabilityhistory.org/dwa/queer/panel_closing.html.

Suresha, Ron, ed. *Bearotica.* Alyson Publications: Los Angeles, 2002.

48 Belisa González

Can't We All Just Move Beyond?

Everyday Manifestations of the Black/White Binary

Introduction

Like the question mimicked in the title to this paper "Can't we all just get along?", moving beyond this black/white binary has proved far more easily said than done. Many sociologists have expressed the need to move beyond the black/white binary (Darder and Torres 2004, Davis 1993, Manning 1994, Martinez 1998, Omi and Winant 1994, Waldinger 1996). However, these discussions tend to focus on how this binary affects the identities of those people who "do not fit" within the categories of black or white and fall just short of making suggestions for example *how* to move beyond. Findings presented here suggest that the encompassing strength of the binary creates many challenges for organizers that are particularly difficult to articulate at the moments they occur. This paper explores how the black/white binary manifests in organizing with particular attention paid to how the binary structures the way African American women and Latina respondents think about themselves and others. The black/white binary is presented here as an obstacle to cross-racial organizing, particularly in reference to the challenges they present in obtaining collective understanding of cognitive liberation. More specifically, I

contend that this framework flattens and simplifies the way organizers understand each others' identity in such a way that prevents them from recognizing each others' cultural and experiential nuances that are so important in cross-racial organizing.

Black/White Binary

Many scholars have written about the need to move beyond the black/white binary, so prevalent in discussions of race and ethnic relations. Of relevance here is not only the presence of the binary, but its dominance in organizing the way scholars and activists frame discussions of race relations between communities of color. In his 1984 essay "On being 'White' . . . and Other Lies," James Baldwin illustrates the artificial foundation of the black/white binary arguing that it is a white supremacist creation that has been used to organize power in America (Baldwin 1998: 178). Darder and Torres build on this essay and suggest that the black/white binary (they use the word paradigm) is in fact predicated on capitalism, not white supremacy.[1] The intention here is to introduce the encompassing nature of the paradigm, whether constructed and perpetuated by white supremacy, capitalism or both. What is useful is

Belisa González, "Can't We All Just Move Beyond? Everyday Manifestations of the Black/White Binary." Edited from a version first presented at the American Sociological Association Annual Meeting, August 2007. Reprinted by permission of the author.

Darder and Torres' discussion of the limitations of the black/white paradigm. They argue that to limit understanding of race relations to a black/white framework "fails to recognize the pre-colonial origins of racism" (2004:112). Quoting Anthias and Yuval-Davis they continue, "The dichotomous categories of Black as victims, and Whites as perpetrators of racism, tend to homogenize the objects of racism, without paying attention to the different experiences of men and women, of different social classes and ethnicities" (1992:15). Thus, the black/white binary literally cannot acknowledge the nuanced and complex identities experienced by my respondents.

Moreover, Darder and Torres (2004) explain, "there is little room to link, with equal legitimacy and analytical specificity the continuing struggles against racism by . . . other racialized populations of the world (including Africans racialized by Africans) to the struggles of African Americans" (2004:112). They go on to suggest that the discussion of race relations and the black/white paradigm should be reframed in terms of its relation to capitalism, however, of importance here is how our current understanding of the binary limits the framing of race relations to that of black and white, making it impossible, according to Darder and Torres, to link the experiences of those who fall outside this paradigm with that of African Americans. Being able to link one's experiences, particularly with oppression to those of African Americans, is key to cross-racial organizing. In addition to these limitations, I suggest that the black/white binary also limits the ability to see African Americans as complex heterogeneous people and communities that encompass more than their history with racial

oppression. This critique of the binary is in no way meant to downplay the significance of historical or contemporary racial oppression, but rather to ague that the binary reinforces a one-dimensional understanding of African Americans that is dependent solely on their relationship to oppression. The following discussion of what I call the *traditional* and *race relations* hierarchies created by the binary will further explain how the limited identity of African Americans as victims is continually reinforced.

The hierarchy of the *traditional* black/white binary is relegated by one's real/perceived access to power. The two ends of the continuum black and white represent the least and most access to power respectively. Within this binary everyone is defined as either white, black, or in some cases, somewhere in between, literally in terms of skin color and figuratively in terms of access to power. Within this hierarchy, one's place in the binary is inextricably linked to access to power, meaning the greater one's access to power, the closer that person or group is to white. However, when we consider this binary from the perspective of intergroup relations between communities of color or what I will call the *race relations binary*, the relationship of the hierarchy shifts to one that is predicated on one's legitimacy as measured by relationship to racial oppression. To understand one's place in this version of the binary a group must consider its relationship not to power, but oppression. That is, the more oppressed a group is or historically has been, the closer that group/individual is to the black end of the spectrum. This version of the hierarchy reverses the hierarchical order of the traditional binary so that being closer to the black end of the continuum is the desirable position because it brings with it a type of legitimacy. Legitimacy in this case is measured by a person's or group's experience with oppression. The legitimacy stems from a sense that the more a person has been oppressed by a system, the more equipped that person is to understand and combat it. In some ways this idea of legitimacy is tied to Collins's (2000) standpoint theory which states that because black women occupy a marginalized position in society, they are in a better position to recognize the larger social processes at work within that society. Building on this idea, there is a hierarchy of oppression which is a proxy for how well a person can recognize the systems of oppression (i.e., how legitimate one is). Elizabeth Martinez has written about the competition for this position as racial/ethnic groups competing in the "Oppression Olympics" (1997). The binary is arranged in such a way that African Americans gain legitimacy from their ties to racial oppression and thus other racial/ethnic groups try to position themselves within the hierarchy by emphasizing this same relationship. As we will see in this paper, the inability of the binary to accommodate multiple identities creates both inter- and intragroup conflict and distrust between organizers. At first glance, it might seem odd to be vying for a position of most oppressed or that this position would be desirable and at the top of a hierarchy. However, if we consider that in the post–civil rights era this position has been linked to tangible resources via programs like affirmative action,[2] competing for the position of "most oppressed" makes more sense.

Intertwined with both hierarchies is the notion that one's position is determined by how much a person or group possesses of a finite amount of resources, both tangible and intangible (e.g., money, jobs, subsidies, etc.) and intangible (e.g., power, privilege, legitimacy, etc.). Everything within the binary is determined by this framework, meaning that a person or group cannot gain resources (however measured) without another person or group losing those resources. The most often cited example of this is a new immigrant group moving into a region and "taking" jobs away from residents. Two of the many problems with this argument are that it does not take into account the jobs that immigrant groups create or the vacant status of those jobs when the population arrived (Olzak 1993). The critiques of this argument are in essence a critique of the zero sum frame as they point out the context within which, in this case jobs, become filled predominantly by new immigrants. Through a discussion of quotations extracted from field notes and interviews I will illustrate how these frames manifest in day-to-day operations of cross-racial organizing.

Methods

Data were collected through formal and informal in-depth interviews with women currently involved in or with recent experience with cross-racial organizing in Georgia, and six years of participant observation in relevant public arenas such as protests, town hall meetings, marches, rallies, retreats, conferences, caucuses, etc., as well as appropriate private venues, such as meetings, workshops, and discussion groups. I used multiple snowball sampling to identify 20 women from each racial/ethnic group (n=40). Initial interviews were conducted with women I knew through my own organizing. To identify potential respondents, I attended meetings, political rallies, marches, town halls, and gatherings at the capital and conferences that I thought would appeal to activists/organizers in Georgia. These included "Undoing and Dismantling Racism" trainings, diversity trainings, sisters talking across race about race conversations, political conversations, the Latino Summit sponsored by the Latin American Association (LAA), GALEO (Georgia Association for Latino Elected Officials) and LAA social events, LULAC (League of United Latin American Citizens) meetings, Students of Color receptions sponsored by the Emory University Black Student Association, Latino section meetings at the American Sociological Association, Latina Leadership committee meetings, a sub-group of the Feminist Women's Health Center, Dia De La Mujer Latina events, holiday celebrations, election return gatherings, health fairs, work fairs, panel discussions, key note addresses, political receptions, and fund raisers. Some of these events were also used as opportunities for participant observation.

Participant observation began in the fall of 2000 and continued through the fall of 2005, during which I attended on average one organizing event per week. Interviews were conducted between May of 2004 and December of 2005. All interviews were transcribed and each along with field notes from participant observation was uploaded into Atlas-ti, a Visual Data Management Software package. Each transcript was coded using codes and categories created from the literature cited previously and from themes that emerged from the data. Once coded, I used the tools in Atlas to identify patterns in the data and make links to past literature.

My African American population includes women of African descent who were born and raised in the United States. These women self-identified as one of the following: African American, black, Afro-American, or of African descent living in America. Three of these respondents mentioned that they were bi-racial during interviews but identified as black on an everyday basis. Thirteen of the 20 women had at least a year of post-secondary education with the remaining 6 completing high school. Black respondents tended to be slightly older than Latinas. Specifically, only one black respondent was between the ages of 20–29, while 5 were between 30–39, 7 between 40–49, 5 between 50–59 and 2 between 60–69 years of age. Incomes ranged from under $10,000 to 69,000 and organizing experience ranged from 3 years to "longer than I have been alive."

While 73% of foreign-born immigrants in the new settlement South are of Mexican descent, this is not reflected in my sample. Seven of my respondents identify as Puerto Rican, 8 as Mexican American, and the remaining were Brazilian, Chilean, Columbian, Cuban, Peruvian or Venezuelan-American. It should also be noted that within the Puerto Rican sample 3 women identified as black Puerto Rican. Twelve of the 20 Latinas I spoke with had at least a year of post-secondary education and only one had not completed high school. On average Latinas had been involved in organizing for almost 9 (8.55) years, with a minimum of 1 and a maximum of 20 years of organizing experience. Three of the women were between the ages of 20–29, seven between 30–39, four between 40–49 and six between 50–59. Latina income levels ranged from under $10,000 to 49,000.

The Power of Binary

It is logically possible to be racially essentialist without imposing a hierarchy on those racial categories. What is more likely to happen is that an undeniable characteristic, like phonotype, becomes connected with the idea that "we" are superior to "them" and that "we" need to be protected from what would happen if "they" were to gain access to resources and rights (Appiah 1990). The following are examples of how respondents talked about "we" and "them," and explanations of how those categories are framed within the black/white binary.

One of the most common themes of data collected during participant observation was that racialized conversations or conversations that incorporated a racial analysis inevitably turned into, if not began as, conversations restricted to the experiences of blacks and whites. So prevalent was this framing in participant observation episodes that it became routine to count only those incidents when it did not occur. Indicators that a black/white frame was being utilized include participants making statements like, "everyone, both black and white," or the more progressive form of the black/white binary frame, "black, white and everyone in between." The intention of all these phrases was to be inclusive of all races and ethnicities. On all but two occasions the speaker either self-identified as black or white. However, on these two separate public occasions, the speaker of the phrase "we are all here for the same reason, every one of us coming together, black, white and everyone in between," was Mexican American (field notes May 2005). It was unclear if the speaker of this final phrase considered herself white, black or something in between. The use of these phrases and the like are indicators that even in attempts to be inclusive, organizers/activists frame inclusion in terms of black and white. It is important to note that in-clusion was extended by naming racial and ethnic categories such as black, white, Hispanic, etc. American Indian and Asian were the categories most often omitted from this type of inclusion. Even with this alternative attempt at inclusion, the predominant word choice was "everyone, black *and* white."

At a retreat held in the Fall of 2003 for a multi-racial committee of organizers, Mary, an elder black woman and veteran organizer in Georgia and other southern states, reflected on the weekend's events and conversations by reporting that she thought the purpose of the weekend had come into balance after "struggling through" many "real" conversations. She said that she had been feeling very anxious about the weekend because of all the problems that the multi-racial organizing committee had been experiencing prior to the weekend, but that as she sat there on the close of the second day she felt a sense of balance. She added that she wasn't going to say anything but as she looked around the room she noticed that there was a balance of people in the room, 8 black and 8 white. She said she took the balance as a sign that everything was going to be alright. The following are field notes from that weekend:

It happened again, this time after 2 days of talking about the changing demographics of Atlanta and how to have a more inclusive conversation about race relations in Georgia. Mary was reflecting on how much she had struggled with the conversation over the last 2 days and what she had learned from the stories of other people . . . when she finished, everyone was silent and looking around as if to count and categorize the people in the room. Those who were counting stopped with the only non-black person of color in the room a Mexican American woman involved in the same organizing committee as Mary. (field notes Fall 2003)

The above section illustrates the power of the black/white binary as Mary includes a Mexican American woman with whom she had been organizing for three years as a white woman in her count and racial categorization of people in the room. This incident occurred after two days of conversations about cross-racial organizing and the need to expand the anti-racist discussion beyond the scope of black and white. Additionally, Mary understood the "balance" of black and white people in the room to be a sign of harmony, further indicating her reliance on the black/white binary. Further discussion of this event appears at the end of this paper, but for now its purpose is to illustrate how deeply engrained the black/white binary is in racialized discourse among respondents involved in cross-racial organizing.

Situations that arose during people of color caucuses[3] serve as another example of the strength of the black/white binary. Participants of all of the people of color caucuses and women of color caucuses I attended were predominantly African American and women.[4] The number of Latino participants and other non-black people of color ranged from one to ten at any given caucus. The caucuses were hosted by four separate organizations and attended from two to twenty times each. All the caucuses had been in existence for at least a year prior to my arrival and in the case of one had been meeting annually for twenty years. They were all founded as attempts to include other non-black people of color in the organizing of the respective host organi-

zations. Of the four caucuses attended three had separate black caucuses and all but the one annual caucus has stopped meeting. Findings presented here are from data collected at caucuses named "people of color" or "women of color."

Despite the intentional attempt at inclusion with the name people of color and open invitation to those who so identified, caucuses were often referred to as "the black caucus" at meetings and in casual conversation. The replacement of people of color with black was perceived by non-black participants of color as a subtle message of where they fell in the binary of black and white. Some non-black participants took this as an indication that the black participants thought they were white, while others, reported feeling "invisible," or like they "didn't have anything to add to the conversation" because their experience did not "fit" with that of African Americans. This sentiment was also reported by many Latina respondents during formal interviews. Here we find evidence of the difficulty Darder and Torres refer to as linking the experiences of racialized people with that of African Americans (2004). Because generational divides proved to be a key variable in cross-racial organizing, it is important to note that these comments were almost exclusively made by non-black women of color under the age of thirty. Equally as important were the challenges to the exclusive language and lack of inclusion of other people of color made by younger black women ranging in age from 18–39. The following is a section from field notes taken after a "People of Color" caucus in November of 2003.

I just returned from a People of Color caucus. It took about 5 minutes for the conversation to shift from people of color to black and white. It's hard to know what to say, if anything. The main issue for the meeting was to write a letter to the [host organization] asking that steps be taken to include people of color in the anti-racist workshops they organize. There were problems with the wording. How to balance showing respect for the content of the workshop as it is now *and* firmly suggest that trainers should adjust it to meet the needs of different regions [of the country]. Everyone agreed that the workshop should use local examples and reflect the communities they are located in. Someone made a comment about most of the participants in Atlanta being black and so the regional workshop in Atlanta did not need to be adjusted. To which someone else replied that the fact that most participants are African American in Atlanta doesn't mean that it necessarily reflects the community, that it could mean that the committee was not reaching other communities. The conversation quickly turned to the changing demographics of Atlanta and the downfall of black owned businesses on Auburn Avenue . . . this is popular topic of conversation. One that has come up many times before. (field notes November 2003)

This selection describes a typical scenario of being inclusive in name but not content. In this case, the point of the meeting was to write a letter of support for a more inclusive anti-racist workshop of which the participants were all a part. While everyone agreed that the workshop needed to reflect the host communities, the sentiment of many participants was that the training held in Atlanta did not need to include examples from other communities of color because

the participants were majority black. Reflecting the generational divide noted above, Leslie, a black woman in her early thirties, raised the question of reaching other non-black communities of color to an elderly black woman's comment that the trainings were representative of the area. As the field notes report, the discussion quickly digressed to one concerning the black community in Atlanta, a legitimate concern that reflected the experiences of the majority of participants in the caucus, but not the purpose for which the meeting was scheduled. Similar shifts in conversations occurred when Latinos were the majority of participants, however, always with a black/white binary.

How Latino participants maintain the binary is less clear primarily due to the fewer participant observation opportunities where Latino/as outnumbered African Americans. Preliminary findings suggest that Latina organizers situate the experiences of Latino/as or respective nationalities within the black/white binary as a way of legitimating those experiences as suggested by the race relations hierarchy. Data collected from interviews shed more light on this process; however, a brief description of typical public organizing within predominantly Latino/a spaces provides a helpful context for that discussion.

Despite the limited number of occasions for participant observation, findings show that the black/white binary is never questioned in public spaces. Instead it is legitimated by Latino/as situating themselves within it. This was most often done in reaction to a statement claiming that experiences of African Americans were "worse" than those of Latino/as. Public discourse about the similarities of oppression is that the two groups have much in common. As we see in the following summary, however, of a two-hour coalition meeting in the Spring of 2004, those similarities were argued within the black/white binary.

In a meeting of predominantly Latinas the question of the rights of undocumented day laborers was raised. While everyone present agreed that they did have rights, the question led to a discussion about job competition between day laborers and black men. The consensus of the 3 black women present was that while the day laborers might be discriminated against in terms of wages, they were still preferred by employers over black men. To this the Latina co-leading the meeting began comparing the experiences of undocumented Latino laborers to the slave labor used to build the U.S. Although she never made a direct comparison to African American slavery in the South, the comparison was clear to all present. At one point she put up her hands one on top of the other to indicate a hierarchy where whites were on top, holding one hand up and blacks were on the bottom, holding the other hand under it and undocumented Latinos were "right there" with African Americans bringing her other hand down side by side with the one she was using to indicate the bottom of the hierarchy.

The situation of Latinos within the binary is used as a way of legitimating their experiences with discrimination/oppression. It should be noted that the above discussion did not end with this statement, but rather digressed into a detailed comparison of the historical realities of African Americans and Latino/as, particularly Mexicans, in the U.S. The summary of this meeting also serves as an illustration of how the binary

limits our understanding of African Americans as almost solely limited to their experiences with racial oppression. Instead of trying to relay the conditions of day laborers on their own merits, the experiences were compared to those of black men, a strategy observed only in discussions of racial discrimination/oppression. The strict boundaries of the binary structure thinking about African American such that the Latinas I spoke with primarily relate to them in terms of racial oppression. These findings support the writings of Anthias and Yuval-Davis (1992) who propose that the structure of the black/white binary does not allow for "equal legitimacy" in terms of struggles with or against racism. In order to be seen as legitimate, Latino/as attempt to position themselves within the binary, simultaneously reinforcing it.

Finally, both groups illustrated an allegiance to the binary by continually steering conversations away from African Americans and Latinos to relations, coalitions, organizing between blacks and whites. This occurred not only during participant observation, but also during the majority of interviews. During interviews, conversations constantly had to be steered back to experiences between African Americans and Latinas and away from African Americans and whites. In many cases respondents were asked to clarify the race/ethnicity of the person(s) to whom they were referring.

Data in this next section are taken primarily from interviews and presented to further illustrate the dominance of the black/white binary. In particular, the selected quotes highlight respondents' awareness of the binary and its consequences, an aspect of organizing that did not occur in participant observation conducted in public spaces.

In general, both black and Latina respondents were aware of the dominance of the black/white binary and the difficulty it creates for organizing between Latino/as and African Americans. According to them, much of the challenge stems from trying to incorporate Latino/as into a structure, analysis, organization or strategy that assumes a black/white binary. One of the challenges this process creates is having to convince participants that there are non-white, non-black racial/ethnic groups present in a given area. In the following quote, Lisa, an African American woman whose current organizing centers on tenant rights, describes her frustration with trying to get fellow black organizers to include Latino/as in their racial analysis of oppression and organizing efforts.

It's like growing, obvious and then like nobody [is] talking about [it], I mean just not nobody but that there's still this notion of black and whiteness is so deeply ingrained that I think in some ways it could, with no effort on our part, it could be true that there were a majority of Latinos here and we would think it's a black and white thing. (Lisa)

According to Lisa, the black/white binary is so prevalent in organizing that even if Latinos were the majority-minority, the conversation would continue to be framed in terms of black and white. This quote is representative of many respondents who expressed frustration over trying to situate the experiences of Latinos within a binary that did not include them or included them as part of the white racial category. The next quote illustrates the latter situation. Describing her experience in a local organization's effort to bring community leaders together Adriana, a thirty-five-year-old black organizer, states:

Trying to deal with two groups of people of color who make up the majority of the people of color in the organization and don't want to have shit to do with each other. It's a mess! You know. . . . The black folks talk about the Latinos like they're white. White folks talk about the Latinos like they're white. . . . We're so clear on the way that we talk about race that it becomes, it seems clear to everybody else in the world that we're only talking about black and white you know. And so people come here thinking that it's black and white. Um, which is brilliant in the sense that it keeps us really divided . . . (Adriana)

This quote is a prime example of two important issues. The first is the tendency of those in the organization to discuss race relations in terms of black and white to the extent that Latinos are talked about "as if they are white" by black and white participants. This illustrates a more extreme version of the binary than previous quotes, which simply left Latinos out altogether. Here Latinos are included, but lumped in with whites, a phenomenon which is not conducive to cross-racial relations in the organizations. The term white is being used as a socio-political construction defined primarily by one's access to privilege and power. In this case, the inclusion of Latino/as in the white category is reinforcing the idea that they have not experienced oppression and therefore should not be considered in an analysis of racial oppression. The second important illustration is the awareness on the part of Adriana that the binary is creating divisions, a strategy she describes as "brilliant." In the selected quote and throughout her interview, she implies that as long as organizers continue to see only black and white, communities of color will remain divided. Essentially there are only two choices and Latinos as people of color do not fit either.

Further evidence of the strength of the black/white binary can be found in the resistance expressed to challenging it. The following is an illustration of the resistance that can occur when organizers try to challenge the absolute nature of the binary. In this next quote Helen, a black woman involved primarily with an ideologically based coalition of organizers, describes a situation where a historically black and white host organization attempted to incorporate Latinos into its efforts.

It's been around for a really long time and has historically been a black and white organization. It has all the challenges of the you know historical white leadership and black folks sort of playing secondary roles to that leadership, but now has a number of like fierce Latinos with analysis about race that includes them. You know. And there's a politeness about it, but I think I was surprised at how resistant the black folks in that organization were because they have the same [experience]. . . . This is not fresh. This is not the first time they've had the conversation and I watched it totally dissolve into a screaming match. Where at one point, even with the other Latinos in the room, we [black participants] just screamed at each other. When the Latinos left the room, we screamed at each other. Just about, they were pissed at me for thinking it was an important thing to keep fighting about. They were pissed at themselves I think because they knew they

weren't as close to really thinking that. It was intense. (Helen)

The "screaming match" that ensued over Helen's challenge of the binary is typical of the experiences reported by other respondents. Here Helen is describing an organization that has all the makings of a traditional black/white organization, "historical white leadership and black folks sort of playing secondary roles to that leadership." It is only when "a number of . . . fierce Latinos" disrupts that binary that it becomes apparent how invested the black members of the organization are in it. Moreover, the scene to which Helen is referring is not the first time a challenge to the binary has occurred. This quote both illustrates the strength of the black/white binary, by describing the emotional response elicited by its challenge, and the conflict (obstacle) associated with exposing it to people who have structured their understanding of race relations within it. Although not the focus of this paper, it is important to recognize that the white participants are colluding and "benefiting"[5] from the reinforcement of this binary.

While the overwhelming majority of respondents recognized the binary as creating challenges, a few women continued to work within it even as they admitted to the multiracial nature of race relations.

It's just that the landscape has become more complex. It used to be really clear, us and them (laughing) now it's almost like little us and big us and little them and big them. (Emma)

Clearly Emma, an African American organizer whose organizing spans many issues, recognizes that the demographics or "landscape" is becoming more diverse, yet she continues to frame the participants of this shift within a binary of us and them. She accommodates the changes within the preexisting hierarchy of us and them. After some additional questioning about to whom she was referring, Emma replaced us and them with black and white, categorizing non-black people of color as either little white or little black.

Another example of the binary's inability to accommodate complex identities is shown through a conversation with Sabrina, a self-identified black Latina who occupies multiple positions within and outside of the binary. The following quote highlights a few of the issues associated with being a black Latino/a in a black/white world.

And it's a really huge statement because most of those kids are black kids who are also Latino and some of them have one parent who's whatever racial type of Latino and an African-American parent, but many of them are truly black Latinos meaning of African descent from some country in Latin American, which is great. And this kind of says that black Latinos are settling in Georgia in African-American areas and those kids are flying under the radar as Latinos since it's easier to just pass for African-American. (Sabrina)

Black Latinos are a part of the complicated landscape discussed in Emma's quote above. Sabrina makes an interesting observation about her own experience and that of her students when she says that her black Latino students are "passing" as African American. She also states that it is easier for them to pass as African American than be Latino, a subject she discusses at great length throughout the interview. Important here is that the respondent and her students, who are both black and Latino/a, are perceived within a black/white binary that cannot comprehend an identity that encompasses both black and Latino. In contrast to the way "passing" is usually referenced, the ease of passing as African American is not grounded in the idea that being African American is "easier" than being Latino in terms of privilege or access to resources, but rather that having a definitive place in the binary is easier than occupying an ambiguous one. Sabrina described many of the issues that arose for her once people realized that she was Latina. "I didn't quite fit what they thought and that just causes all kinds of problems." For her and her students being Latino/a and black means that they do not quite fit into the racial binary used to understand people's identity. According to her and other black Latinas I spoke with, it was a choice between the façade of fitting the binary by denying their Latino identity and not fitting the binary by maintaining their Latino identities. It is important to note that all of my respondents who identified as black Latina grew up with this identity.

As the above quotes illustrate the black/white binary is used by many respondents and other organizers to frame race relations in such a way that limits their analysis and action to that of black and white. In particular, the binary makes it difficult to recognize other communities of color, creates conflict when challenged, leaves no room for other communities of color or includes them in one of the binary extremes. In essence all of these obstacles manifest when the binary is challenged. Underlying many of the ensuing conflicts is a related concept called zero sum framing. Together these two processes create a situation where resources, broadly defined, are finite and linked to one's position in the traditional and race relations hierarchy. That is, where one falls in the hierarchy of whiteness and blackness, whether within the traditional or race relations, is linked to the amount of resources (i.e., traditional—access to power, race relations—legitimacy) a person is allotted.

Conclusion

This paper addressed one of the most persistent challenges to cross-racial organizing, the black/white binary. As illustrated with data gathered through participant observation and interviews, this framework limits the understanding of race relations and creates challenges of exclusion and competition in cross-racial organizing. In particular, the black/white binary makes it difficult for organizers and organizations to even acknowledge, let alone take into consideration, non-black communities of color because this framework literally does not provide the tools to conceptualize what that would mean. This is further evidenced by the attempts at inclusion of other non-black people of color which, merely include, in this case Latino/as, in one of the binary extremes. This inability to accommodate the complex experiences and realities of coalition membership (both black and Latino) is a major stumbling block in trying to develop a common vision of political opportunity because it literally structures and thus limits the possibilities of that vision to one that is dependent upon binaries and hierarchy.

One of the everyday manifestations of this is the simplification of both extremes black and white to one dimensional static categories of people and experiences. Of concern here was the reduction of black identity as defined solely by experience with racial oppression a pattern found throughout the data. This oversimplification of black identity to one based solely on one's relationship to oppression often meant that black identity was not questioned, taken as a static given and the yardstick against which Latino/as, experiences and identity were measured. This simplification also meant that there was again literally no room for a variety of experiences or even for black organizers to challenge the binary and their place within it. This is significant given that the binary "theoretically" includes them and yet still limits our understanding of the nuances of black identity which, as I write about elsewhere, is imperative to building successful cross-racial coalitions. Findings reveal that African American and Latino/a organizers both actively reinforce the binary through everyday action. Any challenge to the binary either by an influx of a community that does not fit within it or by a fellow organizers is met with much resistance.

Is There Hope for Another World?

In short, I contend that there is hope for another world, if that world can be envisioned. While this paper has focused on the manifestations particular to cross-racial organizing between African Americans and Latinos in Georgia, similar and unique observations could be made in a variety of settings. Once we begin to recognize how dominant frameworks of binaries and hierarchies structure and more importantly limit our ability to envision another world, we become better equipped to move beyond those frameworks. As an illustration of that movement I return to a story presented previously. If the reader will recall, during a discussion of the strength of the black/white binary I described a situation where Mary, an elder black woman referred to a Mexican American woman, whom she had organized with for several years, as a white woman. Her public categorization of this woman as white came after two days of discussions about expanding her organizing committee's racial analysis to include other people of color. Later that year I asked her to recall that weekend's event and describe what happened next. What follows is a paraphrase of her recollection:

I really believed what I was saying when I said it. I mean the spirit moved me and I knew I had to say something about what I was seeing. But something happened when I did. Something changed in the room and then when I walked outside there was something on the wind that told me I had hurt somebody I loved. That I had done something to someone I cared about. That stayed with me all night. And she didn't say anything to me, even when I saw her the next morning, she was just as kind to me as she always was, even though I had hurt her in a way that we've talked so much about. Something just told me what I said was not right. So I revised my count, in front of the whole group. It had to be in front of everyone. I revised my count, I said "there are eight black folks, *seven* white folks and one Mexican in the room [long pause] and we are working toward the balance for all people [emphasis hers].

I end with this story because, like so much of the research on cross-racial organizing, mine focuses primarily on conflict and challenges, and this discussion of the limitations of the black/white binary is no exception. However, behind all of the quotations, field notes, memos and conversations are stories like Mary's. Self revelations, movement, changed minds, openness, alliances from the most unlikely sources, transcendence of binaries black/white and otherwise, "ah ha" moments, relationships, love, family, stories, momentum and vision. I thought this story captured all of those components as Mary's self-reflection, which grew out of a deep and honest relationship, challenged not only her but everyone in the room. Moments like that described above should not be underestimated, nor should the hope that they inspire.

Notes

1. I use the word binary to discuss what is sometimes referred to in the literature as a paradigm because it is the term preferred by my respondents.

2. There is a debate as to whether programs like affirmative action actually helped improve the lives of the under-class or middle-class. My point here is not to weigh in on this debate but to suggest that the position of most oppressed is thought to be tied to resources by those within it.

3. People of color caucuses are meetings or social events restricted for organizers who identify as people of color on a daily basis. Caucusing by racial and other identity categories (gender, sexuality, nationality, class, religious affiliations or intersections of the aforementioned) was a common occurrence in the groups in which I participated.

4. I make the distinction between women of color and people of color caucuses because people of color caucuses were open to all genders. However, participation was always predominately female.

5. I place quotations around the word benefiting because I argue that the binary doesn't actually benefit anyone, but rather limits everyone's understanding. A more accurate way to put it might be to say that the white participants are comfortable with the black/white binary.

Bibliography

Aldridge, Delores. 2000. "One Race and Culture: Beyond Afrocentrism and Eurocentrism to Cultural Democracy." *Sociological Forces* 33:1.

Allport, Gordon W. 1958. *The Nature of Prejudice.* New York: Anchor.

Anzaldúa, Gloria. 1990. *Making Face, Making Soul/Haciendo Caras: Creative and Critical Perspectives by Feminists of Color.* San Francisco: Aunt Lute Books.

Barrera, Mario. 1979. *Race and Class in the Southwest: A Theory of Racial Inequality.* Notre Dame: University of Notre Dame Press.

Barth, Fredrick, ed. 1969. *Ethnic Groups and Boundaries.* Boston: Little Brown.

Bean, Frank, and Marta Tienda. 1987. "The Structuring of Hispanic Ethnicity: Theoretical and Historical Considerations." In *The Hispanic Population of the United States.* New York: Russell Sage Foundation.

Bergesen, Albert, and Max Herman. 1998. "Immigration, Race, and Riot: The 1992 Los Angeles Uprising. *American Sociological Review* 63:39–54.

Blalock, Herbert M. 1967. *Toward a Theory of Minority-Group Relations.* New York: John Wiley and Sons.

Blauner, Bob. 1969. "Internal Colonialism and Ghetto Revolt." *Social Problems* 16:393–408.

———. 1972. *Racial Oppression in America.* New York: Harper Row.

Bobo, Lawrence, and Vincent Hutchings. 1996. "Perceptions of Racial Group Competition: Extending Blumer's Theory of Group Position to a Multiracial Social Context." *American Sociological Review* 61:6.

Bonilla-Silva, Eduardo. 1996. "Rethinking Racism: Towards Structural Interpretation." *American Sociological Review.* 62:465–80.

Borjas, George J. 1990. *Friends or Strangers: The Impact of Immigrants on the U.S. Economy.* New York: Basic Books.

Campell, Angus. *White Attitudes Toward Black People.* Ann Arbor, MI: Institute for Social Research, University of Michigan.

Carmichael, Stokely, and Charles V. Hamilton. 1967. *Black Power: The Politics of Liberation in America.* New York: Random House.

Clark, William A. V. 1991. "Residential Preferences and Neighborhood Racial Segregation: A Test of the Schelling Segregation Model." *Demography* 28(1):1–19.

Cox, Oliver. 1942. "The Modern Caste School of Race Relations." *Social Forces* 21:218–226.

Davis, Mike. 1993. "Who Killed Los Angeles? Part Two: The Verdict Is Given." *New Left Review* 199:29–54.

DeSipio, Louis. 1996. "The Engine of Latino Growth: Latin American Immigration and Settlement in the United States." In *Pursuing Power: Latinos and the Political System.* Chris Garcia, ed. Notre Dame: University of Notre Dame Press.

Deutsch, Morton, and Mary Evens Collins. 1951. *Interracial Housing: A Psychological Evaluation of a Social Experiment.* Minneapolis: University of Minnesota Press.

Dolbeare, Kenneth M. 1986. *Democracy at Risk: The Politics of Economic Renewal.* New York: Chatham House Publishers.

DuBois, W. E. B. 1989[1903]. *The Souls of Black Folk.* New York: Bantam Books.

Eisinger, Peter K. 1976. *Patterns of Interracial Politics: Conflict and Cooperation in the City.* New York: Academic Press.

Espiritu, Yen Le. 1999. "Asian American Panethnicity: Bridging Institutions and Identities." In *Rethinking the Color Line.* Charles A. Gallagher, ed. Mountain View: Mayfield.

Farley, Reynolds, Charlotte Steech, Maria Krysan, Tara Jackson, and Keith Reeves. 1994. "Stereotypes and Segregation: Neighborhoods in the Detroit Area." *American Journal of Sociology* 100(3):750–780.

Fix, Michael, and Jeffrey S. Passel. 1994. *Immigration and Immigrants: Setting the Record Straight.* Washington, DC: Urban Institute.

Gamson, William. 1997. "Social Psychology of Collective Action." In *Social Movements: Perspectives and Issues.* Mountain View: Mayfield.

Hardy-Fanta, Carol. 1997. "Latina Women and Politics in Boston: *Somos La Vida, La Fuerza, La Mujer.*" In *Pursuing Power: Latinos and the Political System.* Notre Dame: University of Notre Dame Press.

Heer, David. 1996. *Immigration in America's Future*. Boulder, CO: Westview.

Hero, R. E., and C. J. Tolbert. 1996. "Race/Ethnicity and Direct Democracy: An Analysis of California's Illegal Immigration Initiative." *The Journal of Politics* 58(3): 806–818.

Hondagneu-Sotelo, Pierrette. 1994. *Gendered Transitions: Mexican Experience of Immigration*. Berkeley: University of California Press.

Hurtado, Ada. 1997. *The Color of Privilege: Three Blasphemies on Race and Feminism*. Ann Arbor: University of Michigan Press.

Jackson, B., E. R. Gerber, and B. E. Cain. 1994. "Coalitional Prospects in a Multi-Racial Society: African-American Attitudes Toward Other Minority Groups." *Political Research Quarterly* 47(2):277–294.

Jackson, Mary R. and Marie Crane. 1986. "'Some of My Best Friends Are Black . . .': Interracial Friendship and Whites' Racial Attitudes." *Public Opinion Quarterly* 50:459–486.

Jenkins, J. Craig, and Craig M. Eckert. 1986. "Channeling Black Insurgency: Elite Patronage and Professional Social Movement Organizations in the Development of the Black Movement." *American Sociological Review* 51:812–829.

Jennings, James. 1994. "Changing Urban Policy Paradigms: Impact of Black and Latino Coalitions." In *Blacks, Latinos, and Asians in Urban America: Status and Prospects for Politics and Activism*. James Jennings, ed. Westport, CT: Praeger.

———. 1997. "Blacks and Latinos in the American City in the 1990s: Toward Political Alliances of Social Conflict." In *Pursuing Power: Latinos and the Political System*. Notre Dame: University of Notre Dame Press.

Kallish, Susan. 1995. "Multiracial Births Increase as U.S. Ponders Racial Definitions." *Population Today* 24 (April): 1–2.

Kochhar, Rakesh, Roberto Suro, and Sonya Tafoya. 2005. *The New Latino South: The Context and Consequences of Rapid Population Growth*. Washington, DC: Pew Hispanic Center.

Lewis, Staughton Y. 1994. "Impacts of U.S. Natives' Employment and Earnings: A Summary of the Evidence." In *A Stone's Throw from Ellis Island: Economic Implications of Immigration to New Jersey*. T. J. Espenshade, ed. Lanham: University Press of America.

Lofland, John, and Lyn H. Lofland. 1995. *Analyzing Social Settings: A Guide to Qualitative Observation and Analysis*. Belmont: Wadsworth Publishing.

Macionis, John J. 2002. *Social Problems*. New Jersey: Prentice Hall.

Martinez, Elizabeth. 1998. "Seeing More Than Black and White: Latinos, Racism, and the Cultural Divides." In *Race, Class, and Gender: An Anthology*. Margaret L. Andersen and Patricia Hill Collins, eds. New York: Wadsworth.

Massey, Doug, and Nancy Denton. 1988. *American Apartheid: Segregation and the Making of the Underclass*. Cambridge, MA: Harvard University Press.

McClain, Paula. 1996. "Coalition and Competition: Patterns of Black-Latino Relations in Urban Politics." In *The Politics of Minority Coalitions: Race, Ethnicity, and Shared Uncertainties*. Wilbur Rich, ed. Westport, CT: Praeger.

Melucci, Alberto. 1985. "The Symbolic Challenge of Contemporary Movements." *Social Research* 52:4.

Montejano, David. 1987. *Anglos and Mexicans in the Making of Texas 1836–1986*. Austin: University of Texas Press.

Mooney, Patrick H., and Theo J. Majka. 1995. *Farmers' and Farm Workers' Movements: Social Protest in American Agriculture*. New York: Twayne Publishers.

Moraga, Cherríe, and Gloria Anzaldúa, eds. 1981. *This Bridge Called My Back: Writings by Radical Women of Color*. New York: Kitchen Table Women of Color Press.

Myrdal, Gunnar. 1944. *An American Dilemma*. New York: Harper and Row.

Nagel, Joane. 1994. "Constructing Ethnicity: Creating and Recreating Ethnic Identity and Culture." *Social Problems* 41(1):152–176.

Olzak, Susan. 1993. *The Dynamics of Ethnic Competition and Conflict*. Palo Alto, CA: Stanford University Press.

Olzak, Susan, Suzanne Shanhan, and Elizabeth H. McEneaney. 1996. "Poverty, Segregation, and Race Riot, 1960–1993." *American Sociological Review* 61:590–613.

Omi, Michael, and Howard Winant. 1994. *Racial Formations in the United States from the 1960s to the 1990s.* 2nd ed. New York: Routledge.

Pardo, Mary. 1997. "Mexican American Women Grassroots Community Activists: 'Mothers of East Los Angeles.'" In *Pursuing Power: Latinos and the Political System.* Notre Dame: University of Notre Dame Press.

Park, Robert. 1950. *Race and Culture.* Glencoe: Free Press.

Portes, Alejandro. 1984. "The Rise of Ethnicity: Determinants of Ethnic Perception Among Cuban Exiles in Miami." *American Sociological Review* 49:383–397.

Rich, Wilbur C. 1996. *The Politics of Minority Coalitions: Race, Ethnicity, and Shared Uncertainties.* Westport, CT: Praeger.

Rodriguez, Nester. 1996. "U.S. Immigration and Intergroup Relations in the Late Twentieth Century: African Americans and Latinos." *Social Justice* 23:3(655):111–124.

Schaefer, Richard T. 1998. *Race and Ethnic Groups.* 7th ed. New York: Addison Wesley.

Schwartz, Mildred A. 1967. *Trends in White Attitudes Toward the Negro.* Chicago: National Opinion Research Center, University of Chicago.

Simon, Julian. 1989. *The Economic Consequences of Immigration.* Cambridge: Basil Blackwell.

Skerry, Peter. 1997. "E Pluribus Hispanic?" In *Pursuing Power: Latinos and the Political System.* Notre Dame: University of Notre Dame Press.

Smith, Wade. 1981. "Racial Tolerance as a Function of Group Position." *American Sociological Review* 46:559–73.

Sonenshein, Raphael J. 1990. *Politics Is Black and White: Race and Power in Los Angeles.* Princeton: Princeton University Press.

Southern Regional Council. 2001. "The October Report: Issues Facing New Immigrants and Long-Standing Residents in Georgia."

Spigelman, Lee, Timothy Bledsoe, Susan Welch, and Michael W. Combs. 1996. "Making Contact? Black-White Social Interaction in an Urban Setting." *American Journal of Sociology* 101:1306–1332.

Spillman, Lyn. 1994. "Imaging Community and Hoping for Recognition: Bicentennial Celebrations in 1976 and 1988." *Qualitative Sociology* 17:3–28.

Strauss, Anselm, and Juliet Corbin. 2000. "Grounded Theory Methodology: An Overview." In *Handbook of Qualitative Research.* Norman K. Denzin and Yvonna S. Lincoln, eds. Thousand Oaks: Sage.

Tixier y Vigil, Yvonne, and Nan Elsasser. 1976. "The Effects of the Ethnicity of the Interviewer on Conversation: A Study of Chicana Women." In *Sociology of the Language of American Women.* Betty L. DuBois and Isabel Crouch, eds. 161–169. San Antonio, TX: Trinity University Press.

Tuan, M. Chapter 3 in *Forever Foreigners or Honorary Whites? The Asian Ethnic Experience Today.*

U.S. Bureau of the Census. 2000. Populations Projections Program, Population Division. Washington, DC: U.S. Government Printing Office.

Waldinger, Roger. 1996. *Still the Promised City? African Americans and New Immigrants in Postindustrial New York.* Cambridge: Harvard University Press.

Warren, Amrk. 2001. *Dry Bones Rattling: Community Building to Revitalize American Democracy.* Princeton: Princeton University Press.

Weiss, Robert S. 1994. *Learning from Strangers: The Art and Method of Qualitative Interview Studies.* New York: Free Press.

Zavella, Patricia. 1992. "Reflections on Diversity Among Chicanas." In *Women of Color in U.S. Society.* Philadelphia: Temple University Press.

Zinn, Maxine Baca, and Bonnie Thornton Dill. 1994. "Difference and Domination." In *Women of Color in U.S. Society.* Philadelphia: Temple University Press.

Zuckerman, Phil. 2004. *The Social Theory of W. E. B. DuBois.* Thousand Oaks: Pine Forge Press.

CHAPTER 7 STUDY QUESTIONS

1. Challenge your friends to read the Web article on gender-normative privilege. Can you think of other things to add to the list?

2. How do you feel about Robert Heasley's article (Reading 44) on "queer" straight guys? Is it hard or easy to relate to? Can you see yourself or your friends in any of his examples? Why or why not?

3. Some of the articles in this chapter may seem to be fairly specific to the issues they present and discuss (e.g., Verta Taylor and Leila J. Rupp [Reading 46], Eli Clare [Reading 47], Belisa González [Reading 48]). What are the bigger, underlying social structures? Can you see gender and intersectionality in all these articles?

4. What kinds of calls to action are all the authors making? Who are they trying to inspire, and what are they hoping to inspire readers to do?

5. Now that you've read the entire book (we presume!), how would you describe the gender and social change efforts described in this chapter? Can you see gender performances as a foundational aspect of each of these calls for change?

ACKNOWLEDGMENTS

Every book is the result of labor, love, and ideas that are mostly invisible; the finished product is always more than the sum of its parts. I need to start by thanking Lis Maurer, who has been a colleague, ally, buddy, and kindred soul for many years—there really are not enough words to acknowledge my gratitude. Some work and thinking on this project was accomplished during two periods of funding provided by Ithaca College. The initial idea for this book was germinated way too long ago, while I was stressfully completing my first book with Westview. Steve Catalano was my editor then, a voice of reason who suggested that I give it a minute, take a rest, and *then* work on this. Thanks to him for handing it off to Alex Masulis and everyone else at Westview—it really was a dream of mine to publish with the press, and to do it twice is just bonus gravy. (Maybe now I need a new dream!?)

At work, I am indebted to the students and alumni who have made this endeavor so worthwhile, including Philip DuBois (research assistance) and a core group (A, A, B, N, T) who have encouraged me to think deeply, regularly, and profoundly. Several colleagues have provided the occasional diversion in the form of coffee, lunch, and good humor.

Brody Burroughs has my back. He keeps me going when I get stuck and reminds me of what the point of all of this really is.

Rebecca F. Plante

First and foremost, to Rebecca Plante, my coconspirator and fellow thinker, my ally, colleague, and friend.

Thanks also to:

Susanne Morgan, who wisely put us together in the same room at the same time, a happenstance from which this initial project percolated.

My professional colleagues of the American Association of Sexuality Educators, Counselors, and Therapists, the Advanced Sexuality Educators and Trainers group, and other groups and organizations for creating an atmosphere in which ideas, creativity, and camaraderie can flourish.

All those who have shepherded me in my academic, professional, and personal journeys, especially my brother, Bill, and my friends and mentors Roey Thorpe, Maggi Boyer, Joan Garrity, Ann Thompson Cook, Mara Keisling, and Paisley Currah, who challenge me with critique, encouragement, additional assigned readings, support, pizza, or poker at all the appropriate moments.

My fifth grade teacher Mrs. K., whose attempts to force me into a gender box instead helped foster an intense gender curiosity that I've successfully cultivated from then until now . . . and to a new teacher just discovered this fall, who taught me that "an attack is a gift of energy." Mrs. K., it took quite awhile, but I have successfully transformed your gifts into energy that I hope lives on in all who encounter this work.

Special thanks to Maureen Kelly for her thoughtful and important presence in my life, and for truly loving all that I am and all I can be.

To the wonderful folks of Westview Press.

Lis M. Maurer

ABOUT THE EDITORS

Rebecca F. Plante is Associate Professor of Sociology at Ithaca College in Ithaca, New York. Plante has written *Sexualities in Context: A Social Perspective* (Westview, 2006) and coedited (with Michael S. Kimmel) *Sexualities: Identities, Behaviors, and Society* (Oxford, 2004). Plante's work has also appeared in diverse sources, including the *Journal of Homosexuality, Advances in Gender Research*, and in a monthly column in the *University Reporter*, a national college/university newspaper. Schools including Cornell University, the University of Ottawa, LeMoyne College, and Nazareth College have hosted Plante's presentation on "hooking up" and sex on campus (based on mixed-method research). The New York Sociological Association also hosted Plante as a keynote speaker on media and sexualities.

Also affiliated with the Women's Studies Program at Ithaca College, Plante teaches about and studies gender and sexualities, with special interests in masculinities, pop culture, the body, and the construction of the sexual self. Plante has extensive training and certification as a sexuality educator and has worked in diverse communities providing sexuality education to adolescents, teens, and adults. Having done program evaluations of HIV/AIDS services in Georgia and Kentucky, Plante also works to apply academic sexuality scholarship to issues affecting teens and young adults. "Latex & Vinyl," a college radio call-in show about sex, featured Plante (as Dr. "Victoria Monk") answering questions about everything from best sexual positions to having better orgasms.

Lis M. Maurer is the founding coordinator of the Center for Lesbian, Gay, Bisexual, and Transgender (LGBT) Education, Outreach, and Services at Ithaca College in Ithaca, New York. A sexuality educator, consultant, and trainer for more than twenty years, Maurer provides training for national and international audiences on a variety of issues including sexual orientation, gender identity, developmental disabilities, curriculum development and design, and diversity and multiculturalism. Diverse audiences such as college and university classes, state correctional facilities, Head Start classrooms, religious education groups, programs for individuals with developmental disabilities, retirement communities, Girl Scout troops, and international conferences have all hosted Maurer's lectures and presentations. Maurer also teaches graduate and undergraduate courses in human sexuality and gender studies at the State University of New York at Cortland and Ithaca College. In addition, Maurer serves on the Editorial Advisory Board of the *American Journal of Sexuality Education*. Designated a Certified Family Life Educator by the National Council on Family Relations and a Certified Sexuality Educator and Counselor by the American Association of Sex Educators, Counselors, and Therapists, Maurer's written work has appeared in a variety of publications.

INDEX

Abortion, 64
Accountability, 337
Activism, gender as social structure and, 496–498. *See also* Social change
Adolescents
  fag discourse and, 85–98
  gender identity and, 126–128
  See also African American adolescents; Children
African American adolescents
  effect of hip hop images of African American women on, 153–170
  fag discourse and, 94, 95
African American men
  cool pose of, 456
  definitions of manhood and, 103
  occupations with highest concentrations of, 60
  stereotypes of, 68–69
African Americans
  black/white binary and, 522–534
  doing gender in families, 346–366
  homosexuality and, 356, 360–361
  sexualization of, 265
African American women
  with bachelor's degree or higher, 60
  black/white binary and, 522–534
  domestic violence and, 66
  drive to marry, 318
  images in hip hop, 153–170
  occupations with highest concentrations of, 60
  stereotypes of, 58, 154–155
  See also Women of color
Ageism, 204–206
Aging
  avoiding stigma of, 207

heterosexual and gay men and, 204–212
  race-ethnicity and, 62
Alcohol consumption, masculinity and, 402–403, 445
All-gender bathroom, 416
Ambiguous genitalia, 38, 42
American Beauty (film), 81
American Journal of Human Biology (journal), 33
Americans with Disabilities Act, 417, 423
American University, 423
Analytic cross-case analysis, 217
Androgyny, 286, 296
Anorexia nervosa, ethnicity and, 201–203
ANOVA, 313–314
Anzaldúa, Gloria, 255
Arab American femininities, 245–262
  class and, 250–253
  lesbianism and, 253–257, 260–261
  Orientalism and, 257–260
Arab Americans, Muslim *vs.* Christian, 251–252, 253, 254–260
Archives of Pediatrics and Adolescent Medicine (journal), 34
Arrest, bathroom access and, 422
Asian American masculinities, 263–279
  attitudes toward women and, 273–274
  attractiveness, power, and caring and, 272–273
  heterosexual, 265–268
  model minority maleness, 268–269
  negotiating, 273, 274–276
  women's attitudes toward Asian-American men, 271–272
  women's construction of, 276

543